The History
of Christianity

The History of Christianity

An Introduction

Bradley P. Nystrom

California State University, Sacramento

David P. Nystrom

North Park University, Chicago

Boston   Burr Ridge, IL   Dubuque, IA   Madison, WI   New York   San Francisco   St. Louis
Bangkok   Bogotá   Caracas   Kuala Lumpur   Lisbon   London   Madrid   Mexico City
Milan   Montreal   New Delhi   Santiago   Seoul   Singapore   Sydney   Taipei   Toronto

THE HISTORY OF CHRISTIANITY: AN INTRODUCTION
Published by McGraw-Hill, a business unit of The McGraw-Hill Companies, Inc., 1221 Avenue
of the Americas, New York, NY 10020. Copyright © 2004 by The McGraw-Hill Companies, Inc.
All rights reserved. No part of this publication may be reproduced or distributed in any form or by
any means, or stored in a database or retrieval system, without the prior written consent of The
McGraw-Hill Companies, Inc., including, but not limited to, in any network or other electronic
storage or transmission, or broadcast for distance learning.

Some ancillaries, including electronic and print components, may not be available to customers
outside the United States.

This book is printed on acid-free paper.

1 2 3 4 5 6 7 8 9 0 DOC/DOC 0 9 8 7 6 5 4 3

ISBN 0-7674-1436-5

Vice president and editor-in-chief: *Thalia Dorwick*
Publisher: *Ken King*
Sponsoring editor: *Jon-David Hague*
Field Publisher: *Greg Brueck*
Project manager: *Christine Walker*
Production supervisor: *Enboge Chong*
Senior designer: *Jean Mailander*
Cover designer: *Laurie Anderson*
Interior designer: *Claire Seng-Niemoeller*
Art manager: *Robin Mouat*
Manager, Photo research: *Brian J. Pecko*
Compositor: *G & S Typesetters*
Typeface: *10/12 Caslon*
Printer: *R. R. Donnelley/Crawfordsville, IN*

Translations from the Bible are from *New Revised Standard Version Bible,* copyright 1989,
Division of Christian Education of the National Council of the Churches of Christ in the United
States of America. Used by permission. All rights reserved.

The credits section for this book begins on page 397 and is considered an extension of the copyright
page.

Library of Congress Cataloging-in-Publication Data

Nystrom, Bradley P.
   The history of Christianity / Bradley Paul Nystrom, David Paul
Nystrom.— 1st ed.
      p. cm.
Includes index.
   ISBN 0-7674-1436-5 (pbk. : alk. paper)
1. Church history.   I. Nystrom, David P., 1959-   II. Title.
BR145.3 .N97 2003
270—dc21

                  2002010357

www.mhhe.com

For our parents

Contents

Preface   *xvii*

Chapter 1   ***Backgrounds to Christianity***   *1*

Overview   1

Judaism and the Context of Christian Origins   1

    The History and Thought of Ancient Judaism   2

The Greeks   5

    Greek History   5

    The Legacy of Alexander   5

    Greek Thought   8

Rome and Roman Expansion   11

The Beliefs and Practices of First-Century Jews   13

    Judaism in the Greco-Roman World   13

    Judaism in Palestine   14

    Jewish Political Parties   16

    Apocalyptic and Jewish Messianic Expectation   17

Summary   19

Questions for Review and Reflection   19

Notes   19

Chapter 2   ***The Birth of Christianity***   *22*

Overview   22

John the Baptist and Christian Origins   22

The Life and Teachings of Jesus   25

    The Sources   25

    Childhood, Baptism, and Temptations   28

Miracles   28
Teaching: The Kingdom of God and the Son of Man   29
Jesus the Radical   32
The Passion   33
The Resurrection and the Early Church   33

Paul   34
Paul's Theology   35
Christology   36
Judaism   37
Salvation   37
An Apocalyptic Preacher   38
Transformation, Freedom, and Responsibility   38
Christian Community   39

The Gospel of John   41
The Context of the Gospel   41
John's Theology   42

Summary   43
Questions for Review and Reflection   44
Notes   44

Chapter 3   *Christianity in the Roman World*   48

Overview   48
Zenith and Decline of the Empire   48
The First Century   49
The "Five Good Emperors"   49
The Crisis of the Third Century   50
Diocletian and Constantine   51
The End of the Empire   54

The Growth of the Church   55
Converts and Conversion   55
Persecution   58
Martyrs and Martyrdom   61
The Question of the Lapsed: Cyprian, Novatian, and Donatus   64

Early Christian Writers   66
Justin Martyr   67
Clement of Alexandria   68
Origen   69
Tertullian   72

The Beginnings of Monasticism   73
Egypt: Anthony and Pachomius   74
Syria, Palestine, and Asia Minor   76
The West: Benedict and the Benedictine Rule   76

Summary   78

Questions for Review and Reflection   78

Notes   78

Chapter 4   *Councils and Creeds: Defining Orthodoxy in Late Antiquity*   **80**

Overview   80

Establishing Ecclesiastical Authority   81

    Challenges: Gnosticism, Marcionism, and Montanism   81

    Bishops and Apostolic Succession   82

    The Creation of the Canon   86

    Rules of Faith and the Apostles' Creed   87

Controversies, Councils, and Creeds   88

    Monarchianism   89

    The Arian Controversy and the Council of Nicaea (325)   89

    The Cappadocian Fathers and the Doctrine of the Trinity   91

    The Christological Controversy and the Council of Chalcedon (451)   92

Theologians of the Fourth and Fifth Centuries   96

    The Cappadocian Fathers   96

    John Chrysostom   97

    Jerome   98

    Ambrose   98

    Augustine   100

The Practice of Christianity   106

    Holy Days   106

    Baptism and the Eucharist   106

    Worship   108

    The Cult of Saints   109

Summary   110

Questions for Review and Reflection   110

Notes   111

Chapter 5   *The Rise of the Church in the Early Middle Ages*   **113**

Overview   113

The Western Church, the Franks, and Feudalism   114

    The Merovingians and the Church   114

    Charlemagne   117

    The Carolingian Renaissance   119

    The Conversion of Spain, England, and Ireland   119

    The Rise of Feudalism   123

    The Church in the Feudal World   124

The Eastern Church and the Byzantine Empire   125

Justinian   125
Byzantium after Justinian   126
The Church in the Byzantine World   128
The Conversion of the Goths and Slavs   130
The Islamic Challenge   131
Muhammad and Islam   131
The Growth of Islamic Civilization   132
Developments in the Eastern Church   133
The Seven Ecumenical Councils   133
The Iconoclastic Controversy   134
John of Damascus   136
Monasticism and Mysticism   136
Developments in the Western Church   139
Early Theories of Papal Authority   140
Gregory the Great   140
John Scotus Eriugena   142
Predestination   142
The Sacraments   143
The Saints and the Virgin Mary   145
The Filioque   146
Summary   147
Questions for Review and Reflection   147
Notes   147

Chapter 6   The Church and Christian Culture in the High Middle Ages   151

Overview   151
The West in the High Middle Ages   151
Economic, Social, and Political Change   152
The Holy Roman Empire   153
Reform and Revival in the Church   154
Monastic Reform   154
Papal Reform under Leo IX and Nicholas II   156
The Reform Ideology of Gregory VII   157
Gregory VII, Henry IV, and the Investiture Controversy   158
The Papal Monarchy   160
Alexander III   160
Innocent III   161
The Papacy in the Thirteenth Century   163
The Crusades   163
Background   163
The Course of the Crusades   164
Consequences of the Crusades   167

Scholasticism   167
    The Rise of the Universities   167
    Aristotle   169
    Anselm of Canterbury   170
    Peter Abelard   172
    Hugh of St. Victor and Peter Lombard   174
    Thomas Aquinas   175
Women and the Virgin Mary   179
Cathedrals: Praise in Stone and Glass   180
    Romanesque Style   181
    Gothic Style   182
Summary   185
Questions for Review and Reflection   186
Notes   186

Chapter 7

Dissent, Division, and Reform in the High and Late Middle Ages
189

Overview   189
The West in the Late Middle Ages   190
    Decline of the Holy Roman Empire   190
    Political Developments in France, England, and Spain   191
    Social Unrest   191
    The Black Death   192
Decline in the Western Church   192
    The Babylonian Captivity   193
    The Great Schism and the Conciliar Movement   193
    Decline in Monasticism and among the Secular Clergy   195
    Pilgrimage, the Cult of Saints, and Indulgences   197
Heretics and Reformers   200
    The Cathari and Waldenses   200
    The Dominicans and the Inquisition   202
    The Franciscans   203
    John Wycliffe and Jan Hus   205
Mystics and Mysticism   206
Theology in the West   209
    John Duns Scotus   209
    William of Ockham   210
    Theology and Political Theory   211
The Church and the Renaissance   212
    The Renaissance in Italy   213
    Humanism in Northern Europe   214
    The Renaissance Popes   214

The Eastern Orthodox Church   216
    The Break with Rome   217
    The Fall of Byzantium   218
    The Orthodox Church and the Ottoman State   218
    The Russian Orthodox Church   219

The Smaller Churches of Africa and Asia   220
    The Coptic and Ethiopian Churches   221
    Monophysitism in Syria and Armenia   221
    Nestorian Christianity   222

Summary   222

Questions for Review and Reflection   223

Notes   223

Chapter 8   *The Protestant Reformation*   225

Overview   225

Europe on the Eve of the Reformation   226

Martin Luther   228
    The Complexity of Martin Luther   228
    The Young Luther   229
    Professor and Reformer   230

Luther's Theology   234
    Scripture   236
    Knowledge of God   236
    The Human Condition and Salvation   236
    The Church   237

Why the Reformation Succeeded   238

The Early Progress of the Lutheran Movement   239

The Urban Reformation   242
    The Late Medieval City   242

The Peasant Revolts of 1525   245

Zwingli and the Swiss Reformation   247

The Radical Reformation   250
    The Anabaptists   250
    The Spiritualists and the Evangelical Humanists   253

Summary   253

Questions for Review and Reflection   253

Notes   254

Chapter 9   *Protestant Expansion and Catholic Response*   *256*

Overview   256

The European Scene   256
    Royal Absolutism   258

Calvin   259
    Calvin's Theology   264

The Spread of Protestantism   267
    The Reformation in England and Scotland   269
    The Reformation in England   269
    The Reformation in Scotland   273
    The Puritans   275
    Cromwell and Puritan Political Power   278
    The Glorious Revolution   279

The Catholic Reformation   279
    Reforming Voices   279
    The Council of Trent   283

Eastern Orthodoxy   284

Summary   285

Questions for Review and Reflection   286

Notes   286

Chapter 10   *The Church in an Age of Division and Expansion*   *288*

Overview   288

The Scene in Europe: Politics, Religion, and Strife   289
    Germany, Sweden, and the Thirty Years' War   289
    France and the Huguenot Struggle   291
    The Netherlands   293
    Prussia, Russia, and the Empire   294

Catholic Orthodoxy   295
    Popes and Kings   295
    Divergence within Catholicism   296

Lutheran Orthodoxy and Protestant Scholasticism   298

Currents in Intellectual Life: The Enlightenment, Rationalism, and the Scientific Revolution   300
    The Scientific Revolution   301
    Rationalism in Philosophy and Religion   302
    Descartes and Continental Rationalism   303

Empiricism   303
The Kantian Synthesis   304
The Philosophes of France   305
Religions of the Head, Religions of the Heart   306
Deism   306
Religions of the Heart   307
Pietism   309
The Great Awakening   313
The Orthodox Church in an Embattled Era   313
The Church in Russia   313
Summary   315
Questions for Review and Reflection   315
Notes   315

Chapter 11   *Christianity in the Modern World:*
The Nineteenth and Early Twentieth Centuries   *318*

Overview   318
The Modern World: Social, Political, and Economic Change   319
Romanticism and Liberalism   319
Imperialism and Industrialization   320
World Wars and Communist Revolutions   321
The Modern World: Intellectual Change   321
The Natural Sciences   322
The Social Sciences   322
Philosophy   323
History and Biblical Criticism   325
The Roman Catholic Church in the Modern World   326
Napoleon and the Church   326
The Nineteenth Century   327
The Early Twentieth Century   329
Catholic Theology in the Early Twentieth Century   330
John XXIII and the Second Vatican Council (1962–65)   331
Protestantism in the Modern World   332
Nineteenth-Century Liberal Theology   332
Critics of Liberal Christianity   334
Revivalism   335
Protestant Theology in the Early Twentieth Century   336
New Churches   338
The Church of Jesus Christ of Latter-Day Saints   338
Christian Science and New Thought   339
Seventh-Day Adventists   340
Jehovah's Witnesses   341

The Eastern Orthodox Church in the Modern World   342
  Orthodoxy and the Autocephalous Churches   342
  The Russian Orthodox Church   343
The Expansion of Christianity   345
  North America   345
  South America   346
  Africa   348
  India   349
  China   351
  Japan   352
Summary   353
Questions for Review and Reflection   354
Notes   354

Chapter 12   *The Church and the Challenge of the New Century*   *356*

Overview   356
Theologies Old and New   356
  Biblical Criticism   356
  Biblical Theology   359
  Theologies of Hope   359
  Liberation Theologies   360
  Secular Theology   363
Currents in Church Life and Practice   364
  Fundamentalism   364
  Evangelicalism   367
  The Pentecostal and Charismatic Movements   369
  Success and "Signs and Wonders" Christianity   370
  The Ecumenical Movement   370
  The Roman Catholic Church after Vatican II   372
  Hans Küng   373
  John Paul II   373
World Christianity: Trends and Prospects   374
Summary   378
Questions for Review and Reflection   378
Notes   378

Glossary   383

Suggested Readings   393

Credits   397

Index   399

Preface

For two millennia, Christianity has had an incalculable influence on individual lives and entire civilizations—offering answers to some of the most basic problems of human existence, shaping political and social institutions, contributing to the formation of cultural values and ideals, and inspiring masterpieces of art and literature. Accordingly, scholars have explored its historical development and significance from every conceivable perspective and in innumerable texts, each with its own aims and audience.

This book is intended for those seeking an introduction to the great themes, events, movements, and personalities in the history of Christianity. It assumes no familiarity with the subject on the part of the reader, nor does it adopt any particular doctrinal or denominational point of view. Overall, our purpose has been to offer a comprehensive and balanced treatment of the development of theology and doctrine, the growth of Christian institutions, popular piety, sects and heterodox groups, and the relationship between Christianity and culture. Our focus is primarily western, but readers will find extensive discussion of the eastern churches, and especially the Eastern Orthodox tradition, as well as the growth of Christianity in Asia, Africa, and North and South America in addition to Europe.

Beyond this, we have sought to provide more substantial descriptions of social, political, and intellectual trends than are generally found elsewhere. Our hope is that these will enable readers to grasp more easily the connections between religious belief and practice and their wider historical and cultural contexts. Greater attention has also been given to concepts and ideologies (e.g., Platonism, sacrament, predestination, nominalism) that many students might find new or difficult. Whenever possible, we have included sufficient biographical detail to reveal important figures as flesh-and-blood realities, each with his or her own personal circumstances, flaws, ideals, and aspirations, rather than as mere names associated with particular ideas or events. Extensive quotations from primary sources allow such personalities to speak for themselves. Finally, in addition to the major traditions within Christianity, most chapters include discussion of variant forms of the faith — including churches that are highly visible features of modern society, such as the Church of Jesus Christ of Latter-Day Saints, Christian Science, Seventh-Day Adventism, and the Jehovah's Witnesses.

To promote understanding, each chapter begins with an overview of major themes to be covered and concludes with a brief summary. Notes gathered at the end of each chapter elaborate on discussions in the text and direct interested readers to primary and secondary sources. The reader will find a short bibliography of good texts covering each chapter's topics in the "Suggested Readings," found at the end of the book. The glossary defines important terms and identifies important people discussed in the chapters.

Acknowledgments

We owe a debt of gratitude to good friends and colleagues who made valuable contributions to this book. Professor Phyllis Jestice of the University of Southern Mississippi and Professors Sonia Bodi and Scot McKnight of North Park University devoted many hours to reading the manuscript and offered helpful suggestions for its improvement. Professor James Straukamp of California State University, Sacramento, allowed us to include some of his fine photographs. We would also like to acknowledge the invaluable advice and commentary of the following reviewers: Timothy M. Renick, Georgia State University; Dell deChant, University of South Florida; Rebecca Moore, San Diego State University; Richard Layton, University of Illinois at Urbana-Champaign; Rosalie Beck, Baylor University; Thomas Davis, Indiana University-Purdue University Indianapolis; Thomas Smith, Loyola University New Orleans; Special thanks must also go to Jon-David Hague, Ph.D., our sponsoring editor; to Ms. Christine Walker, our project manager at McGraw-Hill, who transformed a manuscript into a book; and to Ms. Wendy Nelson, who made a valuable contribution with her expert copyediting.

Our families demonstrated more patience and understanding than we had a right to expect during the course of this project. We are grateful for their forbearance and encouragement. Finally, we dedicate this book with love and gratitude to our parents, Paul and Aileen Nystrom, our first and best teachers.

CHAPTER 1

Backgrounds to Christianity

Overview

The story of Christianity begins in ancient Palestine. Sometime around the year 30 CE[1] a young Palestinian Jew from the northern region of **Galilee** was executed outside Jerusalem. His name was Yeshua, or Joshua, but most people know him by the Greek form of the name, Jesus. The execution was particularly brutal — crucifixion — and it took place under the Roman provincial governor Pontius Pilate.[2] That the Romans crucified Jesus for a crime against Rome is perhaps the one incontestable fact in the story of his life.[3] The Romans reserved crucifixion for those they considered a threat to political stability. It was intended to be a warning to any who might think of challenging Roman authority. Hundreds of Jews were executed during this period on charges similar to those made against Jesus.

Jesus lived in a time of great tension and political passion, and apparently was caught up in forces and expectations that spiraled out of control. It was in this turbulent context that primitive Christianity developed. To understand the origins of Christianity we should become familiar with the forces that shaped this world. The first of these was the history of Israel and the nature of Judaism, for whatever else we say about him, Jesus was a Jew who lived, taught, and died within the world of first-

century Judaism. But first-century Judaism was itself influenced by contact with the cultures of Greece and Rome. This chapter explores these three cultures with an eye to constructing a picture of the social, political, and intellectual terrain of Jesus' world.

Judaism and the Context of Christian Origins

Christianity and first-century Palestinian Judaism share a great deal of history and theology. Scholars sometimes describe Judaism as an historical religion. More specifically, ancient Judaism[4] was based on the belief that God had acted in history for the benefit of humanity. For this reason the stories of God's activity were remembered and studied. These stories are represented in a collection of thirty-nine documents known in Judaism as the Tanakh. The Tanakh is divided into three sections — *Torah* (**"law"**), *Neviim* ("prophets"), and *Kethuvim* ("writings")[5] — and is also known as the Hebrew Bible or Jewish Scriptures. Christians have traditionally referred to it as the Old Testament. Both Judaism and Christianity hold the Hebrew Bible to be sacred scripture. This means that both consider these documents especially able to convey central theological concepts, such as the character of God and God's revelation. Both religions consider it authoritative; that is, Jews and Christians believe that the Hebrew Bible contains truths that ought to be believed and acted upon.

Among the many documents produced in antiquity by Jews and Christians, only a select few came to be considered scripture. These documents constitute the **canon** (from the Greek word for "measuring stick"). The documents collected in the Bible were written over a span of hundreds of years. While there is theological diversity within the canon, the Bible as a whole affirms a belief in **monotheism**. For both Jews and Christians there is only one God,[6] the Creator of the universe:

> So acknowledge today and take to heart
> that the Lord is God in heaven above
> and on the earth beneath; there is no
> other. (Deuteronomy 4:39)

THE HISTORY AND THOUGHT OF ANCIENT JUDAISM

The earliest stage of biblical history is known as the ancestral period, or the period of the founders. Setting a time frame for this period is difficult, but the years from 2000 BCE to about 1400 BCE are a good estimate. The Book of Genesis tells the story of Abraham and Sarah, the first of the ancestors, who lived in Mesopotamia (the area roughly equivalent to present-day Iraq). Abraham was a nomad who crossed back and forth between Egypt and Mesopotamia, and for this reason Genesis 14:13 refers to him with the Hebrew word *hibri*, meaning "crosser." Some scholars believe this is the origin of the term *Hebrew.*

According to the biblical account, the story of God's interaction with the Hebrews began when God spoke to Abraham:

> Go from your country and your kindred
> and your father's house to the land I
> will show you. I will make of you a
> great nation, and I will bless you, and
> make your name great, so that you will
> be a blessing. I will bless those who

> bless you, and the one who curses you I
> will curse; and in you all the families
> of the earth shall be blessed. (Genesis 12:1–3)

According to the story, God did not identify the land in question or tell Abraham how to get there. God simply asked for Abraham's trust. In return, Abraham would receive divine blessing and the promise that all of humanity would be blessed through him. Abraham was asked to "walk before" God and "be blameless" (Genesis 17:1), as well as to commit to a life of righteousness and justice (Genesis 18:19). He was also asked to be circumcised, and to ensure that male children born to his descendants would be circumcised as well (Genesis 17:9–11, 23–27). Abraham accepted, and this agreement the Bible calls a **covenant**. In some ways this agreement was *the* covenant, for all later covenants would be based on it. According to the stories found in the Hebrew Bible, God continued to intervene in history to bring about his purpose.

The covenant was to become a central symbol within Judaism. According to Genesis, God also made covenants with the descendants of Abraham. Genesis claims that Jacob, the grandson of Abraham, once wrestled with an angel sent by God, and for this reason he received a new name, *Israel*, which means "the one who strives with God" (Genesis 32:28). In time the descendants of Jacob would go by the name *Israelites*. Genesis asserts that the Israelites settled in Egypt during a famine and that they later became enslaved there.

The Book of Exodus tells how Moses led the Israelites out of Egypt. According to the story, God sent several plagues to convince the Pharaoh to allow them to leave. The last plague was the death of the firstborn of all except the Israelites; God passed over the homes of those who followed Moses' instructions to place the blood of a sacrificed lamb on the doorposts of their homes (Exodus 12:21–32). This is the origin of the feast of Passover, which celebrates God's delivering the Israelites from the bitterness of slavery. The Exodus became the defining story for the Israelites. Some among them concluded that no matter how difficult the situation, God would always rescue them by sending a deliverer. According to the story, those who fled Egypt in the Exodus eventually settled in Canaan, an area that roughly corresponds to present-day Israel. The Book of Exodus claims that God gave this land to the Israelites.

The Exodus event was significant not only for the miraculous escape from Egypt, but also because it expanded the covenant. Up to this point the covenant had been made between God and individuals. At Mount Sinai the Israelites as a whole entered into a covenant with God. According to the Book of Exodus, Moses ascended Mount Sinai and received from God the Ten Commandments. The people promised to obey God, and God promised to be with them.

At this juncture the style and subject of the Book of Exodus change markedly, from the stories of God dealing with the Israelites to a highly detailed set of laws. It is likely that these laws come from a much later period, long after the people settled in Canaan, but were attributed to the time of Moses. These laws were intended not only to govern the nature of worship and the temple ritual, but also to regulate social behavior. Central to worship was the idea that a sacrifice was needed in order to atone for, or "cover," human **sin**— to reconcile erring human beings with God. Further, the Israelites were commanded to care for the poor and oppressed in their midst, and not to covet the possessions of their neighbors. Other laws concerned agricultural practices, commerce, and religious and moral standards. In Leviticus 19:18[7] God enjoins the Israelites to love others as they wish to be loved; and in Exodus 22:22–23[8] God claims to be the defender of the defenseless. These passages reflect the moral sensibilities of early Judaism. Unlike modern western systems of jurisprudence, the Israelites combined civil, criminal, and religious law.

According to the biblical narrative, when Moses died, leadership passed to Joshua, whose task it was to take the people into the land of Canaan. This period of "conquest" was most likely a combination of military action and peaceful assimilation.[9] After all, the Bible claims that Jerusalem remained a Canaanite city for another two centuries until king David conquered it.[10]

After Joshua died, the Bible says, judges, including some female judges such as Deborah, governed the individual tribes of Israel.[11] During the period of the judges (1200–1020 BCE) there was a recurrent pattern of what scholars call cyclical apostasy— a cycle of rejecting and then embracing religious convictions. Early in the Book of Judges we read that after a generation true to God had died, the next generation worshiped the gods of the other peoples living in the land.[12] According to Judges, "going after other gods" meant a repudiation not simply of God but also of the social ideals the laws given to Moses were meant to nurture. Judges claims that God sent enemies to threaten the Israelites so that they would remember and turn back to God. God then would send a deliverer.

The period of the judges ended when a new people, the Philistines, appeared on the scene. Israel was no match for the Philistines militarily. To many Israelites the logical response to this crisis was to select a great warrior chieftain who could unite the tribes; that is, they decided to have a king. This decision caused something of a theological crisis, as Israel was supposed to be a theocracy (a form of government in which God is king). The first king, Saul, was little more than a warlord, as he had no standing army and very little bureaucracy to support him. Although some scholars dispute the accuracy of the story, the Bible asserts that David, the second king, created a standing army, defeated the Philistines, captured Jerusalem and made it his capital city, and managed to secure the borders of the large state he created. According to 2 Samuel 7:16, God promised to establish the throne of David "forever." This promise was later linked to messianic expectation.

David's successor was his son Solomon, the builder of the temple in Jerusalem. During Solomon's reign Israel became wealthy, or at least the aristocracy became wealthy. The Bible records that Solomon had seven hundred wives and three hundred concubines.[13] The unmistakable message was that a great gulf existed between the few who had power and wealth and the many who did not. Solomon apparently nurtured the conditions of social and economic stratification that the laws of Moses were designed to prevent.

When Solomon died, unhappiness over excessive taxation erupted in a brief civil war. The result was that Israel, which had been a united kingdom under Saul, David, and Solomon, split into two states. The northern kingdom, which took the name Israel, was composed of ten tribes ruled initially by Jeroboam, the leader of the revolt (1 Kings 12:1–19). Rehoboam, the son of Solomon, ruled the southern kingdom, which took the name Judah. Israel and its capital, Samaria, suffered conquest by the Assyrians in 722–721 BCE. Judah survived until 586 BCE and the Exile in Babylon: Jerusalem was overrun and the temple destroyed by the neo-Babylonians, who took many Jews to Babylon as captives.

According to the Hebrew Bible it fell to the prophets to "speak for God" and to point out the waywardness of Hebrew society. The Hebrew word for prophet, nev'i, means "one who has been called," reflecting the prophets' role as spokespersons for God. Contrary to popular opinion, prediction of the future was a relatively minor task of the prophets. Far more important was their responsibility for serving as the moral conscience of the nation. The prophets proclaimed that God stood for social justice and compassion, and that God would not long tolerate the oppression of one group by another.

The prophets employed a variety of images to make their point. Hosea (fl. 720 BCE) said that Israel was like an unfaithful wife to God, the faithful husband. Isaiah (fl. 700 BCE) compared God to a caring vintner and Israel to the vineyard; the vineyard produced poor fruit, causing the vintner to tear out the vineyard and begin again (Isaiah 5:1–7). Jeremiah (fl. 600 BCE) compared God to a shepherd and the people to a flock of wayward sheep.

Beyond this the prophets argued several specific points. They claimed that the ritual associated with the temple service was useless if it did not result in moral behavior (Amos 5:21–24); that God was concerned with all peoples, not just the Israelites (Jonah, Isaiah 2:2–4; 42:6–7); and that God wanted the people to repent (Amos 5:14–15).

Beginning with the Exile in Babylon three significant developments took place. The first was a growing recognition that the prophets were correct. The Book of Lamentations observes that before the Exile the people had chosen to listen to false prophets who assured them that all was well:

Your prophets have seen for you false
and deceptive visions; they have not
exposed your iniquity to restore your
fortunes, but have seen oracles for you
that are false and misleading. (Lamentations 2:14)

A second development concerned new patterns in worship. Beginning about 500 BCE, Jews began to disperse throughout the Near East and Mediterranean basin. Many lived far from Jerusalem and were faced with the dilemma of worshiping God without easy access to the temple. The solution to this problem was the synagogue. The origins of the synagogue remain a mystery. Some scholars claim it developed during the Exile in Babylon, others point out that the term synagogue is of Greek origin and argue for a much later date. The synagogue was not only a place of worship; during the week it was also a place of instruction in the lessons of Jewish history. The teachers and leaders of the synagogues were called rabbis. By the time of the New Testament a synagogue service consisted of prayers, the reading of scripture, and a short sermon or homily on a scriptural text. The aim of the sermon was to consider how to apply the lessons taught by the text to the practical matters of everyday life.

The third development was what some have called the creation of community. As the Jews looked back on their history, they realized that they had run afoul of God when they interacted with other cultures. It appears that the Jews in exile decided that the way to remain true to God was to create a sense of community through limited contact with other peoples. In 538 BCE Cyrus, the ruler of the Persian Empire, allowed Jews to return to their homeland. The Book of Ezra tells the story of the return to Palestine of one group of Jews. Their leader, Ezra, discovered that Jews had intermarried with other peoples living in the area, and ordered a mass divorce (Ezra 9–10).

The experience in Babylon seems to have cemented in the minds of many Jews the importance of strict observance of their tradition. For some two hundred years they enjoyed religious autonomy under the rule of the Persians. But by 330 BCE the western portion of the Persian Empire had fallen to Alexander the Great, and the Jews were absorbed into Alexander's empire. After Alexander's death,

Palestine was ruled by the Greek Ptolemaic dynasty in Egypt, and then after 198 BCE by the Greek Seleucid dynasty in Syria.

Although the Jews enjoyed relative religious autonomy under Greek rule, the attraction of **Hellenism** (Greek culture) to the wealthy elites among them proved powerful. The deuterocanonical[14] Book of 1 Maccabees bemoans this development as evidence of a lack of commitment to God:

> In those days certain renegades came
> out from Israel and misled many,
> saying, "Let us go and make a covenant
> with the Gentiles around us, ..." So
> they built a gymnasium in Jerusalem,
> according to the Gentile custom, and
> removed the marks of circumcision, and
> abandoned the holy covenant. They
> joined with the Gentiles, and sold
> themselves to do evil. (1 Maccabees 1:11–15)

In 167 BCE Antiochus Epiphanes, the ruler of the Seleucid Empire, invaded Jerusalem. He plundered the temple of its riches, sacrificed a pig on the altar, and declared that the temple had become a shrine to Zeus. According to 1 Maccabees 1:20–64, Antiochus made it illegal to study Jewish law and tried to coerce the Jews to abandon the worship of their God. This sparked a rebellion led by Judas Maccabee (Judas "the hammerer") that resulted in the recapture of Jerusalem in 164 BCE. Chanukkah is the festival that celebrates the success of the Maccabean rebellion and the cleansing of the temple. This story, like that of the Exodus, taught that God will always deliver his people from their oppressors.

The Jews enjoyed relative political and religious freedom from 164 BCE until the Roman general Pompey entered Palestine in 63 BCE. From that point on, the Jews of Palestine were ruled by the Romans.

The Greeks

The political, intellectual, and cultural accomplishments of the ancient Greeks are often referred to as Hellenism. Hellenism had far-reaching consequences for Judaism, Christian origins, and later Christian history. The term *catholic* in *catholic Church,* for instance, means "universal." The idea of the Church as a worldwide organization is derived not only from the command of Jesus,[15] but also from the world empires of Alexander and of Rome. The Greek philosophical tradition dominated the intellectual climate of the Mediterranean world beginning about 300 BCE, and both Judaism and Christianity had to come to terms with it. Furthermore, Greek patterns of thought and logical discourse became standard and served as vehicles for much of later Christian theology.

GREEK HISTORY

Beginning about 600 BCE, several city-states in Greece began to distinguish themselves. Sparta developed a regimented and conservative system served by a small but highly effective military. Athens developed a democratic form of government and an open society. From about 500 to 350 BCE, Athens was a center of artistic and intellectual creativity—home to playwrights like Aeschylus, Sophocles, and Aristophanes; historians like Thucydides; and philosophers like Socrates and Plato. But by about 350 BCE the Greek city-states, exhausted by years of civil war, came under the domination of the kingdom of Macedon just to the north. The Greeks had traditionally viewed the Macedonians as backward and uncouth. But to at least one Greek thinker, the rhetorician and philosopher Isocrates, the rise of Macedonia had an appealing aspect. The Greek city-states had never been unified, and to Isocrates this unification was a philosophical necessity. After all, he said, the universe was ordered and intelligible, but the political situation in Greece was chaotic. Finally, unification was forced on the Greeks by king Philip of Macedonia, the father of Alexander the Great.

THE LEGACY OF ALEXANDER

Alexander ascended to the Macedonian throne at the age of twenty following the assassination of his father in 336 BCE. He was a young man of enormous energy and a gift for accomplishing by reckless daring and force of will what others only

Figure 1.1   Alexander the Great In the late fourth century, this Macedonian king brought Greek civilization to much of the eastern Mediterranean region and Near East, thereby inaugurating the Hellenistic age.

dreamed of achieving. In the span of eleven years he created an empire that stretched from Greece and Egypt in the west to India, Afghanistan, and southern Russia in the east. It was the largest empire then known. Alexander died at the age of thirty-three, and with him died any chance of a unified political empire, for none of his generals proved able to hold his empire together.

Though Alexander's dream of a unified political empire did not survive him, his career did result in a lasting cultural unity. This extraordinary development was due to three cardinal factors. The first is the religious and philosophical syncretism that marked Alexander's foreign policy. When Alexander conquered a people, he did not assert that his gods had defeated those of his enemies. Instead, he

argued that all peoples worshiped the same gods but knew them by different names. Politically, this policy tended to pacify the conquered. The Greek philosophers had already argued that the mythological stories of the Olympian deities must be taken not literally, but rather as allegories that point to a deeper truth.[16] Alexander applied this idea to all religious systems he encountered. He allowed each culture to retain its traditions while inviting conquered peoples to perceive a deeper unity in which all religions shared.

The second major source of cultural unity was the city. Everywhere Alexander went, he founded cities. He populated them with veterans of his army, merchants, and traders as well as officials responsible for managing the affairs of these new urban communities. The effect of this policy was the widespread dissemination of Greek culture and the Greek language — not classical Greek, but the everyday Greek of the marketplace, called *koine.* Within two centuries *koine* was known from Italy and Egypt to India. It was especially this popularity of *koine* that accounted for the wide acquaintance with Hellenism in the areas Alexander had conquered, and why today we refer to the period after Alexander as the "Hellenistic" (Greek-like) age, from *Hellas,* "Greece."

A final factor that contributed to cultural unity was the creation of an elite culture that remained somehow Greek. For the next several centuries Egypt and Syria were ruled by Greek dynasties, and wherever Greek rulers were in place, Greek patterns of education and refinement were fostered. One of these institutions was the *gymnasium.* In Greek life the *gymnasia* served several functions. They were an integral part of the education of the young as a setting for physical, intellectual, and aesthetic training; and they served adults as places for leisurely reflection on philosophy, politics, literature, and music. Other important features of Greek culture that were transplanted east were the library and the theater. These were established for the training of new generations of Greek rulers, but were also available to native elites. Even Greek dress played a role in the "hellenization" of peoples whose lands had been conquered by Alexander. The deuterocanonical book 2 Maccabees, for instance, notes that young

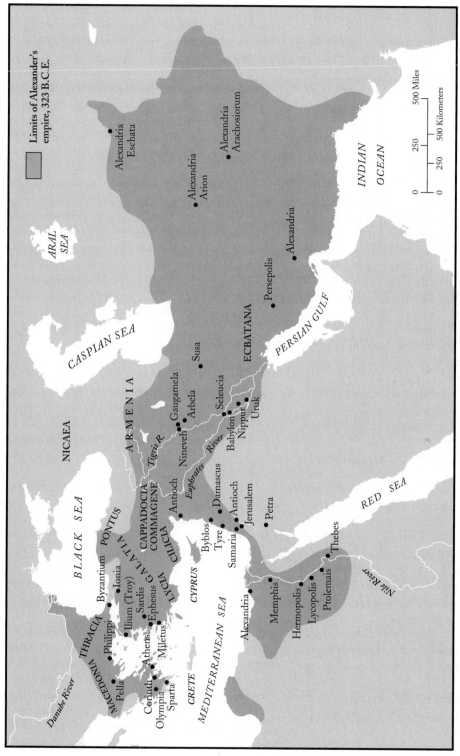

Figure 1.2 **Alexander's empire** Extending from Macedonia and Greece in the West to India in the East, Alexander's conquests included such great cultural centers as Athens, Jerusalem, Babylon, and Persepolis.

Jewish men took to wearing the apparel of Greek youths.[17]

By encouraging recognition of the common features of religions, building Greek cities, and filling them with Greek institutions, Alexander began a process of hellenization that was to give the culture of the eastern Mediterranean region a distinctively Greek flavor.

GREEK THOUGHT

Perhaps the single greatest achievement of the ancient Greeks was their intellectual legacy. This manifested itself in an astonishing array of fields, including mathematics (Archimedes), history (Herodotus, Thucydides), and medicine (Hippocrates). But at the pinnacle stands Greek philosophy.

The earliest Greek philosophers lived mostly in Ionia in western Asia Minor. They are sometimes called "natural philosophers" because they were primarily interested in drawing conclusions from the observation of nature. The Ionian philosophers believed that the universe was an orderly, rational system, and that certain universal laws could be deduced from the observation of nature. This orderliness renders the universe intelligible and therefore a cosmos (*kosmos,* "order") and not chaos. The Ionian commitment to observation and reason allowed a reinterpretation of the Homeric picture of the gods. The Olympian gods described by the poet Homer[18] were not rational at all; instead they were vain and temperamental, just like human beings. For this reason Xenophanes (ca. 550 BCE) said that people always construct images of the gods that mirror how they see themselves.[19] Xenophanes wanted to create a more accurate image of divinity. He argued that however churlish the portrait of the gods in Homer, the reality is that God, if God exists, must be worthy of human worship. God must be one and perfect. Anything else would be less than God. The Roman writer Cicero noted that when the Greek philosopher Thales (ca. 585 BCE) said "god" what he meant was "the mind which forms all things."[20] For the Greek philosophers "god" was the principle of order and truth in the universe.

The next great phase in Greek philosophy took place in Athens, where philosophers also noted the orderliness of the universe and concluded that the gods must be deities of order and intelligence. They believed that absolute truth exists and is enshrined in the laws of the universe. Some of these laws are expressed in mathematics and logic. Others govern human life and inform human virtue.

The Athenian philosopher Socrates (469–399 BCE) believed that the proper topic of study for a human being was humanity itself, and that human beings had an obligation to ask questions about all things, including themselves. "The unexamined life is not worth living," he said. Socrates believed in the existence of absolute truth and claimed that it was knowable. Whereas his contemporary Protagoras[21] understood human beings as creatures shaped by sense perceptions, Socrates saw them as thinkers of universal concepts. These concepts, Socrates held, lie within the soul of every human being. The goal of human thought is to draw them to the surface through the process of inductive questioning.

Socrates was most concerned with virtue, with how human beings could come to live the good or virtuous life. For him there were absolute standards of courage, piety, and good citizenship. He believed that coming to know these truths led to a more fulfilling life, the "good" life. Socrates left no writings and is known principally through the dialogues of his brilliant pupil, Plato (427–347 BCE).

Like Socrates, Plato believed that truth is something that can be known. He also recognized that in the arena of human interaction there is little agreement about truth.

Plato arrived at a solution to this dilemma. He believed that the ideas and objects encountered in this world—such as beauty, justice, tables, cities, people—are merely imperfect and particular examples of the perfect and unchanging realities of Beauty, Justice, Table, City, and Humanity. These realities are the spiritual essences of their particular expressions here on earth. Plato also taught that the essences of things—he called them "forms" or "ideas"—exist in a spritual realm that he depicted in his famous "Parable of the Cave."[22] Plato describes a dark cave in which prisoners are bound in

Figure 1.3   Bronze statue of Zeus (ca. 460 BCE) A sky god believed to be the power behind clouds, lightning, and other phenomena associated with storms, Zeus also came to represent the forces of order and justice in the cosmos.

such a way that they cannot see each other, nor have they ever been outside. Behind them is a fire. Behind the prisoners and in front of the fire walk people carrying figures of animals and other objects whose shadows are thrown on the far wall of the cave. The prisoners see only these shadows. Plato says the prisoners represent the vast majority of humankind, people who see shadowy representations of things and mistake them for the things themselves. It is a distorted view of the world. If one of the prisoners were to escape from the cave, the true nature of reality would become apparent and he would know the shadows in the cave for what they really are.

Plato thus posited a dualistic view of the universe. The material world, symbolized by the shadows cast on the cave wall, is the world of particulars. It is characterized by change, decay, and disagreement. Here there are different and imperfect understandings of truths such as "justice" and "humanity," as well as matter, which is also imperfect. The world of the forms, on the other hand, is entirely spiritual, perfect, and true.

Plato also believed that buried deep within the soul of every human being is knowledge of absolute truth. This led him to conclude that the human soul is eternal and belongs to the world of the forms. Souls, however, become trapped in the imperfect flesh of human existence. When the body dies, the soul is temporarily transported to the spiritual realm, where it beholds the forms and therefore gains absolute knowledge. When the soul is reborn in the flesh, much of this knowledge is forgotten. Differences in character among human beings can be attributed to the varying degrees to which souls remember the ideal of "humanity." Those with the greatest integrity remember more truly the absolute standard for human existence. Further, human beings can train themselves to recall absolute truth through the process of rational inquiry.

Plato's greatest student was Aristotle (384–322 BCE), whose interests ranged from philosophy to rhetoric, biology, and botany. Aristotle believed that the acquisition of knowledge must begin with observation of the physical world rather than recognition of spiritual truths. In this he differed from his great teacher. Moreover, while Plato wrote dialogues, Aristotle wrote treatises, many of them on the patterns or categories of human thought. For example, in his *Posterior Analytics* he distinguished between the logic of science, which aims at truth; dialectic, which deals with probable premises; and eristic, which deals with success in debate.

Aristotle, then, was a systematic organizer who laid stress on the material world. He is sometimes described as an empiricist or materialist because he claimed that the "real" is what can be observed in the physical world, as opposed to Plato, who is considered an idealist because he held to the primacy of ideas over things encountered in the material world. Aristotle's writings are orderly and logical, reflecting this orientation. In contrast, Plato's dialogues are charged with drama, irony, and humor. Plato was more the philosopher of metaphysics and stressed the "divine" world. For Plato, "truth" was something not only to be known with the mind, but also to be explored and felt with the heart.

The philosophical culture of the Hellenistic age was dominated by two schools of thought, Stoicism and Platonism. Like earlier Greek philosophers, the Stoics believed that the universe is characterized by order and harmony. They argued that these qualities were created through the action of the *logos*

spermatikos ("seminal reason"), an aspect of the divine *logos* ("word" or "reason") that maintained the essential rationality of the universe through natural law (*nomos*). The Stoics went on to note that human society often lacked the orderliness found elsewhere in nature. What was needed, then, was for human beings to conform themselves to the *logos*. This would allow them to live virtuous and happy lives.[23] Some Stoics developed a doctrine of "universal brotherhood" according to which all people are related by their common humanity and all human relations should be based on reason and mutual respect. Only an inability or unwillingness to conform to the *logos* prevented the realization of this ideal.

Like Plato, the Platonists of the Hellenistic age saw the universe as composed of two very different kinds of reality—matter and spirit. Unlike the Stoics who held that the divine realm interpenetrated the material realm, they believed there could be no direct contact between matter and spiritual reality. A divine force, the Platonists held, could not have created the physical world. Rather, as Plato relates in his *Timaeus*, the *demiurge*, a less than divine "craftsperson," was responsible for the creation of the material universe.

Platonists also believed that the human soul is actually part of the eternal spiritual world, but is trapped within a material body. As a result, the soul and body are at odds with one another. Somehow the soul must be liberated from the physical prison of the body. Like the Stoics, Platonists acknowledged that evil eixts in the world, but the soul by an exercise of will can resist the baser passions of the body and train itself in virtue.

The philosophical traditions of Platonism, Aristotelianism, and Stoicism exercised great influence on the development of Christian thought. Theologians such as Augustine stood in the tradition of Plato. Others, such as Thomas Aquinas, would tend to favor Aristotle. The Stoic concept of *logos* influenced the ways in which early Christians thought about Christ. There remains one more important factor to discuss in exploring the forces that shaped first-century Judaism and therefore early Christianity: Rome.

Rome and Roman Expansion

By the final decades of the first century BCE, Rome had become the dominant military and political force in the Mediterranean basin. It had begun the process of conquest while it was still a republic ruled by its people through assemblies and the senate. During a series of wars of expansion the military gained enormous influence, and powerful Roman generals such as Sulla, Pompey, and Julius Caesar vied with each other for control of the state. Rome became an imperial power when one of these leaders, Octavian, defeated Mark Antony and Cleopatra at Actium in 31 BCE. He was the last of the great military figures left alive, and after Actium he inaugurated a long period of relative peace. In gratitude, the Roman senate granted Octavian extraordinary power along with the titles *imperator* ("commander" or "leader") and *Augustus.* Augustus was the first emperor of Rome.

Augustus's administrative plan included dividing the empire into senatorial and imperial provinces. Areas that had long been peacefully under Roman control were left to the senate to manage, usually by appointed *proconsuls.* Provinces that were new to the empire or where military action was a possibility were assigned governors responsible directly to the emperor. Depending on circumstances, these individuals were known as *legates, procurators,* or *prefects.* Some provinces were particularly difficult for the Romans to govern directly. Here the Romans often selected a person with local influence that they installed with an impressive title like *ethnarch* ("ruler of a nation") or king.[24] These titles appear to indicate political independence, but the rulers who held them were clearly a part of the Roman system and beholden to the Roman government.

The Roman state had two chief aims in the administration of a province: collecting taxes and maintaining law, order, and stability.[25] The provincial administrative system was relatively simple because the Romans used whatever patterns of taxation and administration happened to be in place.[26] Part of their genius was to allow the wealthy among those they conquered to serve as their agents.

Figure 1.4   The emperor Augustus After defeating his rivals, Augustus ruled (27 BCE–14 CE) as Rome's first emperor and laid the foundations for two centuries of relative peace and stability known as the *Pax Romana,* or "Roman peace."

When Pompey annexed Palestine to the Roman state in 63 BCE, he did not make it a province: instead, he relied on prominent local figures to administer the region for Rome. One of these was a wealthy non-Jew familiar with Judaism named Antipater. In 40 BCE Antipater's son, Herod "the Great," was declared "king of the Jews" by the Roman senate. Herod was shrewd and loyal enough to survive the uncertainties of Roman politics. When he died, the Romans allowed his three sons to rule. Archelaus was given half of Herod's kingdom and was granted the title *ethnarch.* Herod Philip and Herod Antipas were each given one-quarter of their father's territory and ruled as *tetrarchs* ("rulers of a fourth"). When Archelaus proved incompetent, the Romans

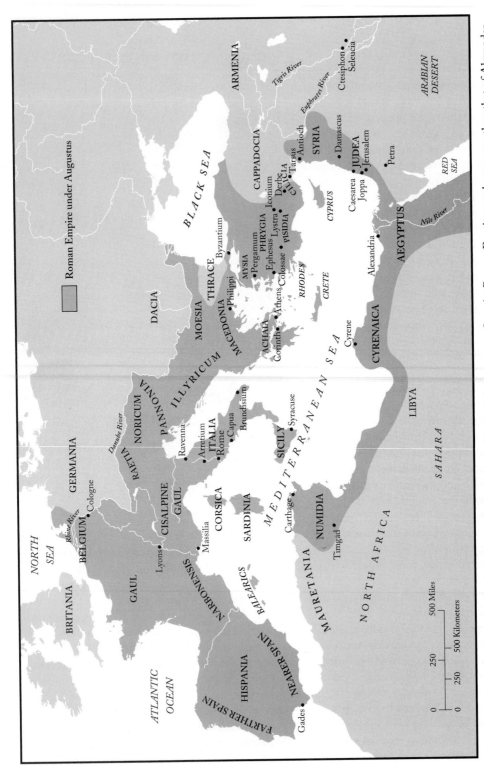

Figure 1.5   The Roman Empire under Augustus Nearly encircling the Mediterranean Sea, the Roman Empire was larger even than that of Alexander and included much of the territory Alexander had conquered.

removed him, made his kingdom the province of Judea, and installed a prefect (6 CE). Herod Philip and Herod Antipas continued to rule, Philip in regions of northern Palestine and Antipas in Galilee.

The Jewish historian Josephus wrote that soon after the Roman occupation began, additional taxes were levied, villages were burned, and people were slaughtered by Roman armies.[27] The Romans also demanded the performance of religious and civil ceremonies that most Jews regarded as forms of pagan worship. When observant Jews refused to participate in them, the Romans granted a special dispensation. Jews were allowed to offer sacrifices on behalf of, rather than to, the *genius* ("spirit") of the emperor.[28] Despite this, Roman rule inspired strong resentment among the Jews. To many, Roman occupation must have seemed a catastrophe similar to the time of slavery in Egypt. The combination of economic stress and religious fervor that resulted from the Roman presence and policies in Palestine helps explain the many revolutionary movements that flared up during the period of Roman rule.

A major theme in Roman culture was the balance of authority with service. The Romans believed that their conquests were laid upon them by fate, that they had a mission to civilize the rest of the world.[29] Virgil wrote in his *Aeneid* that it was the task of the Romans to "submit the whole world to the rule of law."[30] The Romans believed that it was for the good of other peoples that they conquered. By some measures they were accurate. At times and in some places Rome could be a beneficent and generous master.[31] But the vast majority of those living under Roman rule undoubtedly saw the matter differently. Jewish farmers whose families were murdered by the Romans for failure to pay their taxes often turned to banditry and open rebellion.[32] Such persons were likely to become committed to the violent overthrow of Roman rule in Palestine.[33] These insurrectionists were known to attack Romans and wealthy Jews as they traveled the roads of Palestine.[34]

This was the world into which Jesus was born and in which Christianity first developed. It was a world of tension between Romans, Greeks, and Jews, between the few who were wealthy and the many who were poor and oppressed. It was also a world in which hope, however feeble, was still present in the minds and hearts of the Jewish people. For many Jews of the period, their history taught them two important lessons: God would intervene, and God would send a deliverer. They waited for both.

The Beliefs and Practices of First-Century Jews

By the first century CE, Judaism was a religion of extraordinary diversity. Jews lived in virtually every area of the Mediterranean region, and local customs inevitably colored their lives. The religious beliefs and practices of Jews varied, but a central core existed that most were aware of, even if not all embraced it completely.

JUDAISM IN THE GRECO-ROMAN WORLD

By the time of the birth of Jesus there were more Jews living outside of Palestine than within its borders. The city of Alexandria in Egypt, for instance, was home to a very large Jewish population, and there were important Jewish communities in cities throughout Asia Minor and Greece. By the third century CE these communities were culturally distant enough from Palestine that familiarity with the Hebrew language could no longer be assumed. This inspired Jewish translators to create a Greek version of the Hebrew Bible called the Septuagint.

The fact that Jews living in the **Diaspora** (or "Dispersion," because they were dispersed from Palestine) spoke Greek as their first language had a significant effect on Judaism. For example, in the Hebrew Bible the idea of "the word of God" is prominent. It can mean communication with human beings in a given situation or God's actions as expressions of the divine purpose. In Genesis 1, God creates the universe simply by speaking. Where the Hebrew text of the Bible has *dabar* for the "word" of God, the Greek text of the Septuagint uses *logos*. For a Greek-speaking Jew raised in the

Diaspora it would be natural for Greek ideas associated with *logos* to become intermingled with the ideas the Old Testament associated with *dabar*.

Judaism survived in part because many of its traditions were starkly different from those of the peoples the Jews encountered. With Hellenism, however, Judaism encountered a threat more serious than any previously experienced. Hellenism was widespread and had become an important part of the intellectual life of millions of Jews, especially those in the Diaspora. As we have just seen, even rendering the Old Testament into Greek could have a profound "hellenizing" effect on the understanding of the text. Further, Hellenism was capable of absorbing contradictory and critical religious traditions within itself, so that their distinctive characteristics were lost. Finally, many Jews were eager to become "Greek." How could Judaism survive in this climate?

Philo of Alexandria (ca. 20 BCE – 40 CE) came up with one answer. Philo was a devout Jew living in Alexandria and an older contemporary of Jesus. He saw it as his task to harmonize Judaism with Greek philosophy, which he did by appropriating some of the categories of Greek thought and arguing that the content of Judaism fit within them. Philo, who knew that Greek culture prized the older over the newer, pointed out that Moses lived long before Socrates, Plato, or Aristotle, and claimed that the Greeks learned philosophy from Moses. He said that the *logos* or divine law was, in fact, the Torah. He noted that Proverbs 8 speaks of the wisdom of God as an independent entity, "lady wisdom" (in both Hebrew and Greek "wisdom" is a feminine noun), who participated in creation. This certainly looked much like the Stoic *logos*. Greek philosophy was also concerned with virtue and right action. Socrates held that right knowledge guaranteed right action. Many of Plato's dialogues are concerned with the cultivation of human virtue. Philo argued that Jewish law was likewise concerned with human virtue and its cultivation. Judaism also had an explanation for the existence of evil. Within each human being, the rabbis said, are two impulses, one evil, the other good. Individuals choose which one to nurture. The cultivation of the good impulse results in moral development. In this way Philo and

other representatives of Hellenistic Judaism were able to claim that Judaism represented the true form and nature of the religious impulse within all peoples.

JUDAISM IN PALESTINE

In the middle of the twentieth century an extensive collection of documents from antiquity was discovered near the Dead Sea. Until then it was common for scholars to speak of "first-century Palestinian Judaism" as if it were a monolithic religion set in contrast to "Hellenistic Judaism." But the Dead Sea Scrolls have made it clear that there is no easy distinction between Judaism in Palestine and Judaism in the Diaspora. The scrolls have further demonstrated that Jewish religious expression in Palestine was marked by tremendous diversity, so much so that scholars now routinely speak of "Judaisms." This diversity makes any attempt to summarize first-century Judaism problematic. Nevertheless, it is clear that most Jews did share certain fundamental beliefs.

What was the nature of first-century Judaism, particularly within Palestine? A saying the Mishnah[35] attributed to a high priest named Simeon (ca. 200 BCE) can serve as a good starting place. Simeon reportedly said, "By three things is the world sustained: the law, the [Temple-] service, and by deeds of lovingkindness."[36] First-century Jews believed that God is revealed in the Torah, and that human beings should study, obey, and safeguard it. They also believed that this was not only a duty, it was also wise.[37] In the Torah God revealed to humanity how best to live. The Jews understood the Torah as their special heritage from God. The temple service was important because it provided an appropriate way to seek the forgiveness of God after error. They believed lovingkindness to be one of the chief features of God's character. To perform deeds of lovingkindness was to be like God. We can expand Simeon's observation by discussing Torah, temple, and synagogue. Beyond these we may also note a number of practices and political parties.

The Jews were a people of the Torah.[38] The Torah contained the story of God's self-revelation

Figure 1.6   Torah scroll Consisting of the first five books of the Bible, the Torah contains commandments that are the foundations of Jewish Law.

in history. Jews read the Torah, studied it, and discussed it with one another. It contained the law codes that shaped their lives and set them apart as a distinct people. It was instrumental in creating an ethnic and cultural identity through the telling of the story of God acting in history with and for them. The New Testament suggests that study and discussion of the Torah with an eye to its implications for daily life were prominent features of Palestinian Jewish experience in the first century CE.

The Jews were a people of the temple. They believed that an inclination to sin is within every human being, that everyone sins and that sin alienates the individual from God. In the temple service God provided a way to be forgiven. The temple of Solomon was destroyed by the neo-Babylonians, but a second temple was built after Cyrus allowed the Jews to return to Palestine. This temple, the one that Jesus knew, stood on the eastern edge of Jerusalem, commanding the attention of the entire city. Jews called it "the house of God," although they were not so simple as to believe that God actually lived there. It was often said that the temple was the place where God's name dwelt; that is, it was a place

that served as a powerful symbol of God's presence among them. It reminded them that they were God's chosen people, that God had acted in history to bring about a purpose for them, and that God was with them. It was also a visible and tangible reminder of God's accessibility to them.

The temple was divided into concentric areas of increasing levels of exclusion. The outer area was called "the court of the Gentiles."[39] The other areas were called "the court of the women," "the court of the men," and finally "the court of the priests," each area named for the group which could go no further. The innermost area of the temple was called "the holy of holies," where God's presence was symbolized. This area was sacred and could be entered only by one person, the High Priest, and only on one day a year, the Day of Atonement. On the Day of Atonement a special sacrifice took place intended to cover, or "atone" for, the sins of the people for an entire year. A goat was sacrificed and its blood sprinkled on the ark of the covenant, a symbol of the sins of the people being "covered over." The temple, then, was a sign of God's presence and holiness[40] and his desire to forgive sin.

Figure 1.7   Model of Herod's Temple in Jerusalem A half-century after the destruction of Solomon's Temple by the neo-Babylonians, Jews returning from exile in Babylon began work on the Second Temple. It was completed in 515 BCE. Herod the Great rebuilt and improved this structure, in the first century BCE making it one of the most famous buildings in the ancient world.

The Jews were a people of the synagogue. Because synagogues were places of daily instruction in the practice of Judaism as well as places of weekly worship, synagogue Judaism might have appeared both a religion and a philosophy.[41] There was only one temple, and it was in Jerusalem. Synagogues were found wherever there were enough Jews. The availability of the synagogue made it a powerful force in the religious life of the Jewish people. Even Gentiles were known to attend. Especially in the synagogues of the Diaspora, one could often see semi-converts known as "God-fearers" who were attracted to the high moral standards and monotheism of Judaism.

JEWISH POLITICAL PARTIES

First-century Palestinian Jews were a people of many religious and political parties. These groups had different political aspirations for the Jewish people as well as their own ideas concerning the Torah, temple, and synagogue.

One of these groups was the Sadducees. The Sadducees were a religious and political party that traced its heritage at least to the period of the Maccabean rebellion. Although the temple was rededicated in 164 BCE, the last vestige of Syrian Greek political influence was not removed from Palestine until 142 BCE. By this time Simon, the brother of Judas Maccabee, was the leader of the rebellion. After the final defeat of the Syrian Greeks he declared himself High Priest and became the founder of the Hasmonean dynasty. In effect, the Hasmoneans were the rulers of the Jewish state. The Sadducees are usually identified with the priestly aristocracy centered in Jerusalem who allied themselves with the policies of the Hasmoneans. Not all priests, however, were Sadducees, nor were all Sadducees priests. The Sadducees were politically conservative; any disturbance would be a threat to their social and economic interests. When the Romans arrived, the Sadducees became their allies. Both desired political stability. The Sadducees considered only the written Torah or the first five books of Tanakh (Genesis, Exodus, Leviticus, Numbers, Deuteronomy) authoritative. Because of this, they did not share with other Jews a belief in the resurrection of the dead to the afterlife.

A second group was the Pharisees. The term *Pharisee* seems to be derived from the Hebrew word *paras,* meaning "separated." It is unclear, however, from what or which group the Pharisees sought to be separate. Josephus, himself a Pharisee, says that they were scrupulous about their obedience to the commandments found in the Torah. Their own set of legal traditions, which circulated orally until about 200 CE and came to be known as the Mishnah, indicates that the Pharisees were devoted to the Torah and committed to applying its principles to every aspect of daily life.[42] The Pharisees appear to have been especially concerned with ritual purity, which required the avoidance of "unclean" things such as certain foods, blood, dead bodies, and leprosy. The Pharisees also discouraged contact between Jews and non-Jews, who did not share their religious beliefs.

The Pharisees were not priests, but they were religious leaders. The synagogues were their base of power and support. They believed in the authority not only of the whole of Tanakh, but also of their oral tradition — the "tradition of the elders," as the New Testament puts it.[43]

A third important group was the Essenes. Until the discovery of the Dead Sea Scrolls, which they are thought to have written, in 1947, evidence for the Essenes was limited to a few references in ancient texts. Josephus describes them as a monastic community that had withdrawn from society to live in the wilderness, but the scrolls reveal far more.[44] The Essenes were apparently a priestly sect that had split with the Sadducees. They withdrew because they saw the rest of Jewish society, including the Pharisees, as corrupt. They believed that they were living on the verge of some great cataclysm that God would inaugurate, and that they were the only

"true" Jews, the remnant through whom God would bring about his divine purpose. They saw themselves as the "sons of light" fighting a battle against the "sons of darkness." They anticipated at least one messiah and perhaps two,[45] who would arise from within their own group.

A fourth group was the Zealots. A revolt that brought together disparate groups in a unified anti-Roman front occurred 66–70 CE, and from this date scholars speak of "the Zealots." These people desired the violent overthrow of Roman rule in Palestine. Their theology told them that God was king, yet the political reality was that the Romans were in charge. Their targets were Roman officials and members of the Jewish elite who supported Roman interests in Palestine. The New Testament refers to some of these insurrectionists as *lestai* ("bandits," "robbers"). The Zealots were ardent anti-Roman nationalists in the tradition of the Maccabees.

Perhaps no more than 10 percent of Palestinian Jews were associated with any of these four groups. Economic hardship and family responsibilities left most with little opportunity for political involvement or religious expression beyond observance of the Sabbath and other holy days and occasional pilgrimages to Jerusalem. Still, it appears that the Jewish people as a whole were deeply affected by the centuries of oppression they had suffered under the series of foreign conquerors that had ended with the Romans. The expectation that God would soon deliver them, as they had been delivered from Egypt and Babylon, found expression in apocalyptic literature and hope for the coming of a messiah.

APOCALYPTIC AND JEWISH MESSIANIC EXPECTATION

The term *apocalyptic* derives from the Greek word *apokalypsis,* meaning "revelation" or "unveiling." In English it has a wide range of meanings, one of which points to a particular branch of **eschatology**. Eschatology (*eschaton,* "end") refers to any teaching or speculation about the end of the world. Apocalyptic literature makes extensive use of symbols (e.g., "666" in Revelation 13:18 in the New Testament) and vivid imagery (such as savage beasts emerging from a churning sea in Daniel 7:2–3), and is known for its imaginative conceptions of the supernatural world. In general, apocalyptic literature is concerned with revealing the course of future events, describes the interaction of the supernatural and natural worlds, looks forward to a violent and cataclysmic clash between the forces of good and the forces of evil, expects that the forces of good will win in the end, and assumes that the end is very near.

The writing of apocalyptic literature began in the middle of the third century BCE, when it seemed to many Jews that the forces of evil were about to overwhelm and destroy good in the world. There followed a period of speculation about the cause, shape, and end of evil and the development of apocalyptic themes such as conflict, judgment, and the restoration of God's rule on earth.

A good example of apocalyptic literature is the Book of Daniel. Most scholars believe it was written in the middle of the second century BCE, making it the latest of all the books in the Hebrew Bible. According to this text, the prophet Daniel experienced visions in which he saw beasts representing the Babylonian, Median, Persian, and Greek empires emerging from a churning sea, a symbol of evil. Daniel's visions also revealed that the beasts would be judged by God, the "Ancient of Days," and stripped of their power. Finally, authority over the earth would be given to a righteous ruler chosen by God:

> As I looked, thrones were placed and one that was ancient of days took his seat . . . the court sat in judgment, and the books were opened. . . . I saw in the night visions, and behold, with the clouds of heaven came one like a son of man, and he came to the Ancient of Days and was presented before him. And to him was given dominion and glory and kingdom, that all peoples, nations and languages should serve him; his dominion is an everlasting dominion, which shall not pass away, and his kingdom one that shall not be destroyed. (Daniel 7:9–14)

Here the prediction is that God will intervene in history and take back from humankind the "dominion and glory" that was given to Adam in Genesis 1 in order to bestow it upon a representative, "one like a son of man." The phrase *son of man* is in Hebrew an elliptical way of saying "human being."[47] In later apocalyptic literature it sometimes carries divine connotations. In Daniel 7 the term refers to an individual who will reestablish God's kingdom on earth.

Related to apocalypticism was messianism. *Messiah* ("anointed") is a term with a wide range of meanings. Originally it denoted someone who had been anointed with oil and thereby set apart by God for a special purpose. Kings, for example, were anointed. Still later the term came to refer to agents of God who would, like the kings of Israel, establish and safeguard God's standards on earth. Finally it came to refer to a deliverer who would overthrow evil rulers and institutions and restore righteousness.

In the years from 100 BCE to 100 CE, conditions in Palestine were such that many Jews expected God to intervene and replace the rule of the Romans with divine rule. It would be a mistake to say that the Judaism of this period was a messianic religion. Most Jews did not shape their religious lives around the notion of a messiah, nor did all Jews expect one. But there certainly were many who did. Nor would it be accurate to say that there was one expectation of the messiah. In fact, there was an astonishing variety. Some Jews expected a heavenly or angelic figure. Others expected a priestly messiah who would purify the religious practices of Judaism. Still others expected a return of the Davidic monarchy with a descendant of David on the throne. Finally, many hoped for a military messiah who would crush the Romans, just as Judas Maccabee had defeated the Syrian Greeks and Joshua had defeated the Canaanites.

First-century Jews were a people of expectation. Their faith taught them that God was their king and that they were a chosen people. But they could not ignore the hard reality that they were a conquered people ruled by the Romans. Theirs was a world of conflict between Romans and Jews, rich and poor, pacifists and insurrectionists, urbanites and people of the countryside, collaborators and nationalists, Jews and **Gentiles**. Within this world of conflict was the expectation, based on their religious story, that God would intervene to save them. There was no general agreement as to *when* and *how* God would act, but few doubted that he would. For this the Jewish people watched and waited in confident expectation.

Summary

Christianity first developed in Roman Palestine. The Palestine Jesus knew and in which Christianity was born was shaped by three primary cultural traditions. The most important was Judaism, which taught the existence of a single, universal God and stressed the importance of religious texts and traditions that revealed God's nature and will for human beings. Another cultural tradition that influenced the world of early Christianity was that of Greece. Even before Alexander, Greek language and patterns of thought had penetrated Palestine. Later, the Jews had lived under the rule of Greek empires. At times this rule was beneficent. At other times it was politically and culturally aggressive. Finally, Rome brought oppressive taxation, an unwanted military presence, and offenses against Jewish religious sensibilities. The interplay of these three cultures created an explosive mix of religious and political passions.

QUESTIONS FOR REVIEW AND REFLECTION

1. What were the most important religious beliefs shared by the majority of Jews in the first century?

2. What kind of social, political, and intellectual climate was created in first-century Palestine by the influence of Greece and Rome?

3. How would you describe the religious mood of Palestine in the early first century?

NOTES

1. CE means "common era," and is replacing the older designation of AD or *anno Domini*, which is Latin for "in the year of (our) Lord." BCE, which means "before the common era," is likewise becoming standard in place of BC or "before Christ."

2. Christian sources, such as the Gospels and the Nicene Creed, record this event and name Pilate. So does the Roman historian Tacitus.

3. See G. B. Caird and L. D. Hurst, *New Testament Theology* (Oxford: Clarendon Press, 1994), 353; and A. E. Harvey, *Jesus and the Constraints of History* (London: Duckworth, 1982), 11.

4. The term *ancient Judaism* here refers to Judaism up to the second century CE. Judaism is a living religion, and has developed and changed in various ways since the ancient period.

5. See *Tanakh: A New Translation of the Holy Scriptures* (Philadelphia, New York and Jerusalem: Jewish Publication Society, 1985).

6. Some judge Christianity to be a tritheistic religion, as Christians worship God in three persons: Father, Son, and Holy Spirit.

7. "You shall love your neighbor as yourself. . . ."

8. "You shall not abuse any widow or orphan. If you do abuse them, when they cry out to me, I will surely hear their cry."

9. See Norman K. Gottwald, *The Hebrew Bible: A Socio-Literary Introduction* (Philadelphia: Fortress Press, 1985), 261–88.

10. 2 Samuel 5:6–15.

11. Although the Hebrew Bible reflects the prejudice of a patriarchal society, there are passages where women stand out. Miriam, the sister of Moses, plays a significant role. In Proverbs 31 the wise woman/good wife is discussed. She is described in terms that make it clear she acts as an agent independent from her husband.

12. Judges 2:6–19.

13. 1 Kings 11:3.

14. "Deuterocanonical" books (sometimes called the Apocrypha) are a collection of ancient Jewish writings from the post-exilic period.

15. In Matthew 28:19 Jesus says to his disciples, "Go therefore and make disciples of all nations."

16. Years later Cicero wrote that the Greek philosophers identified the gods with "the mighty law everlasting and eternal" and that the Greek philosopher Zeno did away "with the customary and received ideas of the gods altogether . . . [teaching that their] names have been assigned allegorically." See Cicero, *On the Nature of the Gods*, 1.40 and 1.36.

17. 2 Maccabees 4:12.

18. According to tradition, the two great epic poems of ancient Greece, the *Iliad* and the *Odyssey*, were composed

by Homer. The *Iliad* tells the story of Helen, who was kidnapped from Greece and taken to Troy, and of the Greek army led by Agammemnon and Achilles sent to Troy to bring her back. The *Odyssey* tells the story of the Greek hero Odysseus. After the fall of Troy, Odysseus made claims that angered the gods, and he wandered the Mediterranean for many years before he arrived home.

19. "If oxen or lions had hands to be able to . . . make images as men do, the horses as horses and the oxen as oxen they would portray their gods." Xenophanes, fragment 15.

20. Cicero, *On the Nature of the Gods*, 1.25.

21. Protagoras was a sophist. The sophists did not believe in the existence of absolute truth.

22. Plato, *Republic*, 514a–518d.

23. The Old Testament Book of Proverbs is based on similar assumptions. For instance, there are certain "rules" that govern human existence ("Lazy hands make someone poor, but diligent hands bring wealth," 10:4) and these laws can be discerned by observing nature ("Ants are a small creature, yet they store up food in summer," 30:25). The superficial parallel between Proverbs and Greek philosophy helps to explain how even Judaism could be made to harmonize with the new Hellenistic culture.

24. See Martin Goodman, *The Roman World: 44 BC–AD 180*, (London and New York: Routledge, 1997), 110.

25. Peter Garnsey and Richard Saller, *The Roman Empire: Economy, Society and Culture*, (Berkeley and Los Angeles: University of California Press, 1987), 20.

26. See Garnsey and Saller, *The Roman Empire*, 20; and Goodman, *The Roman World*, 107. Goodman writes, "The management of the empire did not require a great many officials, because so much was done semi-willingly by the provincials themselves, or at least by the provincial aristocracy."

27. Josephus, *Antiquities* 14.120.

28. See Goodman, *The Roman World*, 256.

29. The Romans used the Greek word *oecumene* to refer to the world, or more properly the inhabited world. This word, derived from *oikos*, the Greek word for "house," indicates the degree to which the Romans understood their "right" of patronage. The Emperor Hadrian even constructed a sprawling palace complex at Tibur (modern Tivoli) in which were displayed flora, fauna, and replicas of buildings from around the world. The point, obviously, is that the entire world was the proper home of the Romans.

30. Virgil, *Aeneid*, IV. 231.

31. Three examples will suffice. Under the emperor Trajan a policy was established whereby Trajan lent money from his imperial treasury to Italian landowners, under the condition that they pay a 5 percent tax into a municipal chest, the revenue to be used to care for the children of needy families in that area. Historians refer to this practice with the term *alimentary institutions*. A second example can be seen in the correspondence between Trajan and Pliny, his legate. In it we read of the concern of Trajan for mundane matters such as a proper water supplies for provincial municipalities. Finally, there is the case of the second emperor, Tiberius. When he was advised to raise taxes in the provinces, Tiberius replied that it is the part of a shepherd to shear the flock, not skin it (Suetonius, *Tiberius*, XXXII).

32. Josephus tells us that the combination of Roman taxes and the temple tax "bled the country dry" (see Josephus, *Antiquities*, 17.304–308). On banditry as a peasant movement in Palestine under Roman rule, see Gerd Theissen, *The Shadow of the Galilean* (Philadelphia: Fortress Press, 1989); and S. Applebaum, "Judaea as a Roman Province: The Countryside as a Political and Economic Factor," *Aufstieg und Niedergang der römischen Welt*, 2nd series, vol. 8, ed. H. Temporini and W. Haase (Berlin: de Gruyter, 1977), 355–99.

33. Such persons are commonly called "Zealots," although many scholars have pointed out that the term *zealot* was not used to describe all of these various groups until the war beginning in 66 CE.

34. See Theissen, *The Shadow of the Galilean*, 75–82.

35. The Mishnah is the written form of the oral law of the rabbis. It is the product of several centuries of reflection by Palestinian rabbis on the application to life of the Torah. Most scholars think this written form appeared about 200 CE. See H. Danby, *The Mishnah Translated from the Hebrew with Introduction and Brief Explanatory Notes* (Oxford: Oxford University Press, 1933).

36. *Aboth* 1.2. *Aboth* is one of the tractates in the Mishnah.

37. This idea of the law may seem strange to us, because we generally see "law" as an impediment. Stephen Carter, professor of law at Yale University, has said, "Law has only two functions. Law says that you must do what you don't want to do, or that you cannot do what you do want to do." See Michael Cromartie, "How We Muddle Our Morals: Stephen Carter's Three-Step Program for Achieving Integrity," *Books and Culture* (May/June 1996), 14. The Hebrew understanding of law was different. For them law was an ally, like a guide through uncharted territory. The Torah was more than a set of laws; it elucidated obligations that nurtured a healthy relationship with God and with others.

38. Earlier we defined the Torah as the first five books of Tanakh, and this is true. But the word *Torah* can also stand for the entire Tanakh.

39. *Gentile* refers to anything or anyone not Jewish. This designation was probably in recognition of the promise to Abraham that through his descendants would all the peoples of the earth be blessed (Genesis 12:3), but perhaps also of Isaiah 42:6, where Israel is called to be a "light" to the Gentiles (Isaiah 42:6). See Scot McKnight, *A Light among the Gentiles: Jewish Missionary Activity in the Second Temple Period* (Minneapolis:

Fortress Press, 1991). No Gentile was allowed to progress farther into the temple complex than the court of the Gentiles. Josephus tells us that warnings in Greek and Latin were inscribed in the stone wall separating the court of the Gentiles from the rest of the temple complex (Josephus, *Jewish War,* 5, 193–94). In 1871 one of these warning notices was discovered. It reads, "No man of another nation to enter within the fence and enclosure round the temple. And whoever is caught will have himself to blame that his death ensues." See C. K. Barrett, *The New Testament Background: Selected Documents.* (San Francisco: Harper and Row, 1987), 53.

40. The implication here, of course, is that separation from impurity is tied up with holiness, just as for Ezra the people needed to be separate from the other peoples living around them.

41. See Samuel Sandmel, *Judaism and Christian Beginnings* (New York: Oxford University Press, 1978), 230.

42. The connection of the Pharisees of the first century to the Mishnah of the second is not completely clear. The rabbis of the Mishnaic period never refer to the earlier sages as "Pharisees," and the only one of these early sages described as a Pharisee is Gamaliel in Acts 5:34. Nevertheless, most scholars see the Pharisees as the forebears of the rabbis of the Mishnah.

43. See Matthew 15:1–2.

44. The vast majority of scholars believe that the scrolls discovered near Qumran on the northwestern shore of the Dead Sea were produced by the group Josephus identifies as the Essenes. The identification, however, is not completely certain.

45. The notion of two messiahs at Qumran has become almost an article of faith among scholars. It has been challenged by L. D. Hurst, "Did Qumran Expect Two Messiahs?" *Bulletin for Biblical Research* 9 (1999): 157–80.

46. See George W. E. Nickelsburg, "Son of Man," *The Anchor Bible Dictionary,* vol. 6, ed. David Noel Freedman (New York: Doubleday, 1992), 137.

CHAPTER 2

The Birth of Christianity

Overview

The story of Christian origins is in some ways an account of different interpretations of the lives and teachings of three figures; John the Baptist, Jesus, and Paul. John the Baptist called his fellow Jews to a new way of thinking about God's Kingdom. Jesus inspired a little noticed, nonviolent renewal movement within Judaism, and was executed by the Romans for sedition. Paul believed that his life had been transformed through an encounter with the risen Christ and focused the energies of the early Christian movement in such a way that it could spread throughout the empire. This chapter begins by considering the meaning of the activity of John the Baptist. It then reviews the life and teachings of Jesus. The chapter concludes with a discussion of the early Church, especially the teaching of Paul and the Gospel of John, representing two different but important early understandings of the legacy of Jesus.

John the Baptist and Christian Origins

From the outset, Jewish resentment over Roman rule in Palestine was obvious. When the Roman general Pompey entered Jerusalem in 63 BCE, he offended Jewish sensibilities by entering the holiest part of the temple where he "saw all that which it is unlawful for any other men to see, but only for the high priests."[1] A few years later the Roman general Crassus looted the temple[2] and made slaves of thirty thousand Jews.[3] Cassius conquered several towns in Galilee in 43 BCE and enslaved the inhabitants.[4] Like other Roman conquerors, he imposed heavy taxes.[5] In 4 BCE a Roman officer plundered treasuries in Jerusalem. A revolt followed when thousands came to the city for a festival and camped around the Roman garrison. The Roman commander panicked and fighting broke out. Varus, the legate of Syria, marched to Jerusalem to quell the revolt. He destroyed several villages and towns in his path and sold the inhabitants into slavery. Varus rounded up the leaders of the revolt and, to make an example of them, crucified two thousand.[6]

Many revolts were relatively minor. But in the years after Jesus there were several that were serious. About 45 CE a self-proclaimed Messiah named Theudas persuaded the masses to follow him to the Jordan River, which he expected to part for him as it had once parted for Joshua. He was captured and beheaded by the governor Fadus.[7] After him came someone known as "the Egyptian" who led thirty thousand people into the wilderness in preparation for a triumphant return to the Mount of Olives outside of Jerusalem modeled on Joshua's campaign against Jericho. From the Mount of Olives, he said, he would order the walls of Jerusalem to fall down. He was captured before he could complete his mission.[8] A violent revolt against the Romans shook Palestine a generation after Jesus, and the ensuing war (66–70 CE, although the last of the revolutionaries held out at the fortress of Masada until 73 CE) resulted in a Roman victory, the destruction of the temple, and the sack of Jerusalem. After a second revolt (132–135 CE) the Romans took the unusual action of banning Jews from Jerusalem. They renamed the city Aelia Capitolina, and built a shrine to Jupiter on the site of the temple.[9]

Jesus was born into this turbulent context about 4 BCE.[10] As was the case wherever the might of Rome had come, traditional life in Palestine was colored by Roman influence. The Romans were proud of their culture. In their eyes it conveyed to the conquered a wealth of benefits including justice, good government, and finally peace after more than two centuries of warfare around the Mediterranean. If the Romans felt any pangs of conscience concerning their aggression, they were mollified by the concrete achievements of their self-appointed "civilizing" mission.

Those conquered by the Romans often had a different view, for the empire both created and exploited conflict to suit its own needs. Highly class-conscious, the Romans appealed to the same snobbery among the elite classes of those they conquered. Most effective was a policy by which the Romans recruited to their service minions from among their subjects. Their countrymen generally viewed these collaborators with contempt. Jewish tax collectors fit this pattern. Though these tensions were found throughout the empire, in Palestine they reached flood tide due to a particularly deep sense of ethnic loyalty and the passion with which the Jews clung to their religious beliefs and practices. The Jewish historian Josephus,[11] who was perhaps thirty years younger than Jesus, left a valuable record of these conflicts in Palestine in the first century.

Pontius Pilate arrived as the new Roman governor of Palestine in 26 CE. He was apparently unaware of the unique character of Judaism and the seriousness with which the Jews took their faith. Pilate appropriated funds from the sacred temple treasury, intending to secure an improved water supply for Jerusalem. This was typical Roman policy, and he meant to benefit the Jews, yet they complained bitterly.[12] They also protested when a Roman procession through Jerusalem included standards with images the Jews considered idolatrous.[13] In their eyes the standards violated Jewish traditions and laws against the making of images and the worship of other gods. Pilate tried to bully the Jews into submission by declaring that if they did not disperse he would have them executed. To his surprise the protesters were not cowed, but offered him their necks rather than surrender the issue. Pilate was forced to capitulate.[14] During Pilate's tenure as governor, some Jews began to believe that conflict had reached such a fever pitch that God's action was imminent. To these Jews the appearance of a strange man in the wilderness might have seemed like the signal of divine intervention:

> In the fifteenth year of the reign of
> Emperor Tiberias, when Pontius Pilate
> was governor of Judea . . . the word of God
> came to John son of Zechariah in the
> wilderness. He went into all the region
> around the Jordan, proclaiming a
> baptism of repentance for the
> forgiveness of sins. . . . "Even now the ax
> is lying at the root of the trees;

Figure 2.1   The Jordan River Pictured here is the site where tradition says Jesus was baptized by John.

every tree therefore that does not bear good fruit is cut down." . . . And the crowds asked him, "What then shall we do?" In reply he said to them, "Whoever has two coats must share with anyone who has none; and whoever has food must do likewise." Even tax collectors came to be baptized, and they asked him, "Teacher, what should we do?" He said to them, "Collect no more than the amount prescribed for you." Soldiers also asked him, "And we, what should we do?" He said to them, "Do not extort money from anyone by threats or false accusation, and be satisfied with your wages." (Luke 3:1–14)

The New Testament claims that in the early decades of the first century John the Baptist appeared in the wilderness near the Jordan River baptizing Jews with a baptism of repentance. He adopted the behavior patterns of an Old Testament prophet, wearing clothing made of camel hair and eating wild honey. These identified him as a man of protest. Like the prophets, John brought a message of impending doom that could be avoided only if swift action were taken. The ax is already at the root

of the trees, he said, and someone is coming whose job it is to swing that ax. So repent and be baptized. The gospel portrait of John is theologically charged, and most scholars think that to a substantial degree it reflects the thought of the gospel writers.

Baptize means "to dip" or "to immerse." The word can refer to ordinary washing or to a ritual cleansing symbolic of spiritual or moral purification. There were many types of baptism in Judaism, but several features of John's baptism mark it as distinct from the others.

The Gospels of Mark (1:5) and Luke (3:7) indicate that great crowds went out to John in the wilderness. Josephus mentions this also, and adds that Herod became fearful of John's influence over the crowds, perhaps sensing the potential for popular revolt.[15] For the Jews the wilderness had long been a symbol for preparation. The Hebrews had wandered in the wilderness of Sinai before entering the land of Israel, and the Book of Hosea has God speak of leading the people out into the wilderness for the purpose of renewing their covenant relationship (Hosea 2:14–15).

The Gospels of Luke (3:3) and Matthew (3:11) refer to John's baptism as a baptism of repentance.

The Hebrew Bible indicates that the sacrificial system in the temple was the vehicle by which sins were forgiven and the people purified before God. According to Matthew and Luke, John was offering an alternative to the temple system. It is possible he meant to declare the sacrificial system of the temple unable to fulfill its function as a vehicle of repentance and forgiveness. Some of the prophets had made the same charge years before.[16] John also had much in common with the Essenes. They also withdrew to the wilderness, apparently protesting the lack of commitment to God on the part of other Jews.

Matthew and Luke (3:10–14) add an important moral component to this baptism. Tax collectors, who were notorious for their dishonesty, should stop overcharging. The rich should share their wealth with the poor. Soldiers should stop bullying the people. Both Matthew and Luke assert that John combined a message of impending judgment with the idea that the way of the Lord must be prepared. Many scholars regard this as a way of saying, "God is about to act."

Even more startling is the implication of baptizing Jews with a baptism of repentance. The Jews of Jesus' day considered themselves the children of Abraham, and viewed keeping the law not as a way to earn God's favor, but as a way of maintaining that favor granted them as Abraham's descendants and members of the covenant.[17] Proselyte baptism (baptism of non-Jews who wished to convert) was known in Judaism[18] and some scholars think John's baptism of repentance was a type of proselyte baptism.[19] If these scholars are right, then John was saying that the Jewish people needed a new commitment beyond ethnic heritage.[20] This fits rather well with the material in the Gospels. In both Matthew 3:9 and Luke 3:8, John the Baptist argues that God can make Israelites out of stone; that is, having Abraham as an ancestor was not enough.

The Gospels allege that John's activity electrified disparate forces of unease and protest with his message of crisis and imminent divine action. Josephus agrees with the Gospels on this point. John's activity also alerted the authorities to this mood of heightened expectation.

The Life and Teachings of Jesus

It has been said that the problem of the historical Jesus is among the most difficult issues confronting historians.[21] We would not be too far off the mark to say that Jesus is the most studied figure within ancient history. Yet there is little agreement concerning what he actually said and did. At bare minimum, historians claim to know that Jesus grew up in Nazareth and that at about the age of thirty he began a public career as a kind of traveling teacher. He spoke of God's Kingdom or God's Reign in short, memorable sayings and attracted a considerable following. He had a reputation as a healer and a worker of miracles. He was known to deviate from social norms and expectations. He ran afoul of the authorities after somehow challenging the temple system. The Romans executed him as a political troublemaker.[22] This slim portrait is far more sparing than the one found in the Gospels. The chief difficulty in constructing a more complete portrait of Jesus, of course, involves our sources.[23] What are the sources? How trustworthy are they?

THE SOURCES

The written accounts of Jesus and his teachings are called "Gospels," a word that means "good news." The canonical Gospels in the New Testament (Matthew, Mark, Luke, and John) were all written in Greek and have traditionally been the chief sources used by scholars for information about Jesus. But they are not our only sources. References to Jesus can be found in non-Christian sources and in early Christian texts that did not become part of the canon.[24]

The Gospels are an unusual type of literature. They are not works of history in the modern sense, but proclaim Jesus as Lord and messiah.[25] They do so by presenting their cases as based on historical events, but it is clear that the writers considered themselves free to adapt and change material for theological purposes. For instance, Mark has Jesus tell a story about unfaithful renters who kill the son of the owner of a vineyard and then throw his body outside the vineyard (12:8). Both Matthew (21:39) and Luke (20:15) alter the story slightly, claiming that the renters first took the son out of the vineyard and then killed him. Scholars see in this an attempt by Matthew and Luke to make the story fit what the Gospels later claim happened to Jesus; he was taken outside of Jerusalem and then executed.

The Gospels contain a great deal of biographical information about Jesus, but they are not biographies in the modern sense. A good deal of recent scholarship sees them as consistent with an ancient form of biography[26] although even here they defy easy characterization. Each is mostly concerned with only the last week or so of the life of Jesus. Only two record any information about his life before he reached the age of about thirty. Nor do the writers agree about the chronology of his life. Matthew, for instance, gathers several parables (stories Jesus told to illustrate his teaching) together in one long section (Matthew 13); Luke leaves them dispersed. John seems to indicate that Jesus went to Jerusalem four times over the course of at least two years. The other Gospels record one trip to Jerusalem and mention a single Passover festival, leaving the impression that Jesus' career lasted only one year.

The Gospels are partly devotional literature, written with an eye to informing the spiritual lives of believers. They are also part apology (*apologia,* "a defense"). The writers had committed their lives to the belief that Jesus was Lord and wanted others to believe this as well.

The reliability of the Gospels also involves the problem of Jesus' words. The New Testament was written in *koine* Greek, and although it is quite possible that Jesus could speak Greek,[27] the Gospels describe him of speaking Aramaic, the common language of Jews in Palestine (Mark 5:41; 7:34; and 15:34).

If anyone thought to write down accounts of Jesus and his activity while he was alive, these records are lost. Almost all scholars believe that stories about Jesus circulated only in oral tradition for many years, and were not written down until at least forty years after his death. The authors of the Gospels used these oral stories and perhaps shorter written materials to compose their works. Even the final composition of the Gospels is disputed. The majority of scholars believe the canonical Gospels are the products of different hands sifting and editing the material. Whatever their composition, each Gospel tells the story of Jesus, but from its own viewpoint.

Scholars think that the Gospel of Mark reached final form about 70 CE, Matthew and Luke about 80–90 CE, and John between 90 and 100 CE.[28] Matthew, Mark, and Luke contain a great deal of shared material, and for this reason are often called the Synoptic Gospels (*synopsis,* "to view together") because their presentations of Jesus are so similar. John's Gospel is very different in character and tone. For instance, John's Jesus tells no parables, nor does John's Gospel make any mention of lepers or demon possession, which are features of the Synoptic Gospels. These differences, along with the theological complexity of John, have led most scholars to believe that the Synoptic Gospels are more trustworthy than John when attempting to reconstruct what Jesus actually said and did. On the other hand, it must be remembered that all of the Gospel writers present their cases for a particular purpose, and therefore their accounts of Jesus' life are overlaid with interpretation. They were evangelists, but they wanted to present their cases historically.

The striking similarity of the Gospels of Matthew, Mark, and Luke has long been noted. Mark is mainly narrative material describing Jesus' actions. More than 90 percent of Mark is to be found in Matthew, who adds a number of "sayings" (teachings of Jesus) to the material he inherited from Mark. Luke also preserves a good deal of Mark, about 60 percent. Further, Matthew and Luke share a broad range of material. For instance, the specific temptations Jesus suffered are found in Matthew 4:1–11 and Luke 4:1–13; Mark 1:12–13 mentions that Jesus was tempted but does not provide the specifics.[29] Each Gospel contains material not found in the others. For instance, only Luke claims that John the Baptist and Jesus were related (Luke 1:36).

Each Gospel emphasizes certain features of the story of Jesus. Mark's Gospel is known for its vivid action. For instance, it describes a wealthy man who "ran up and knelt before" Jesus in order to ask him a question (Mark 10:17). Matthew 19:16 and Luke 18:18 tell us simply that the man asked his question. Matthew's gospel portrays Jesus as the fulfillment of prophecies found in the Hebrew Bible and one who recapitulates in his own life important events in the history of ancient Israel. The birth of Jesus, the slaughter of innocent children in Bethlehem, and many other events in Matthew are presented in this way. Matthew also depicts Jesus as a rabbi who has authority to reinterpret the Jewish law. Luke's Gospel emphasizes Jesus' concern for the outcast and oppressed peoples of the world and the mercy and respect he shows for women, the poor, and those pushed to the margins of society. It also includes a detailed narrative Jesus' birth. John's Gospel is the most thoroughly theological. It has no birth narrative, but instead begins with a philosophical prologue in which the author identifies Jesus with the divine *logos*. Its purpose is to portray Jesus as one who is in perfect communion with the Father and who reveals God and God's will to humankind.

In addition to the Gospels there are other sources for the life of Jesus. The Jewish historian Josephus, writing near the end of the first century CE, mentions Jesus. In one passage he recounts the actions of the high priest Ananus. It reads: "he convened the Sanhedrin and brought before them James, the brother of Jesus who is called the Christ, and certain others."[30] Remarkably, apart from Josephus there is virtually no mention of Jesus in Jewish sources in the first century.

There is no reference to Jesus in Roman sources until the second century. About 113 CE, Pliny the Younger noted the presence of Christians in Asia Minor[31] and wrote that they sang praises to Christ "as if to a God." Tacitus, writing about 115 CE,[32] mentions that Nero persecuted Christians and makes specific reference to Jesus: "The founder of this group, one Christus, had been put to death during the reign of Tiberius by the procurator Pontius Pilate."[33] Other writers, such as Suetonius, mention Christians but, unlike Josephus, Tacitus, and (apparently) Pliny, do not mention Jesus himself. The unavoidable conclusion is that Christianity left very little imprint on the empire in its first century.

Early Christianity included many groups that were later deemed heretical (promoting teaching or beliefs opposed to established **doctrine**), and in recent decades some scholars have asserted that lodged within their writings is material that might be helpful for understanding the historical Jesus. The noncanonical or apocryphal Gospels vary widely in trustworthiness. Many, especially the so-called infancy Gospels, are a mix of stories from the canonical Gospels and the fanciful speculation of early Christians. The Infancy Gospel of Thomas, written in the middle of the second century,[34] for instance, claims that "a child ran and dashed against his shoulder. And Jesus was provoked and said unto him: You shall not go all the way. And immediately he fell down dead."[35] The infancy Gospels are of limited benefit for understanding Jesus, but they do illumine the great variety of expression within early Christianity, a variety that goes far beyond the narrower boundaries of what later came to be called "orthodoxy" (correct belief or doctrine).

Other noncanonical Gospels, however, are seen by many scholars as holding far more promise. John Dominic Crossan, for instance, has reconstructed a hypothetical "Cross Gospel" from the second-century apocryphal Gospel of Peter.[36] Although there is no other evidence for the existence of this text, Crossan argues that it must have existed before the canonical Gospels and was the source for the passion narrative—the account of the suffering and death of Jesus found in all four canonical Gospels. He follows a similar line in his *The Historical Jesus: The Life of a Mediterranean Jewish Peasant*.[37] Crossan's argument has failed to convince most scholars, but he is surely correct in supposing that there is valuable material to be found in the apocryphal gospels.

Another noncanonical Gospel is the Gospel of Thomas. Discovered near the Egyptian village of Nag Hammadi in 1945, *Thomas* is a collection of 114 sayings of Jesus without connective narrative material. Many of these sayings are similar to those found in the canonical Gospels.[38] Many scholars argue that some of the material in *Thomas* is earlier than the canonical Gospels. If this is so, the Gospel of Thomas must be considered an important source for the life of Jesus. Other scholars are highly skeptical of the value of Thomas. They point out that there is insufficient evidence for its early date. They also note that the few sayings contained in Thomas that may be authentic offer no new insight into Jesus. Several have pointed out that the sayings in Thomas seem more likely to depend on the canonical Gospels and not the other way around.[39] Debate over the value of the *Gospel of Thomas* continues, but most scholars now agree that non-canonical sources may have much to offer in reconstructing the life of Jesus.

CHILDHOOD, BAPTISM, AND TEMPTATION

The New Testament asserts that Jesus was born in the village of Bethlehem near Jerusalem during the reign of Herod the Great. Only Matthew and Luke include birth narratives. Both relate that Jesus' mother, Mary, was a virgin and that he was conceived by the power of the **Holy Spirit**. Although the claim of a virgin birth became important in later Christian teaching, it is almost completely ignored by Paul and the Gospels of Mark and John.

Little is known of Jesus' childhood and youth. Among the Gospels only Luke provides even a glimpse, and he relates a single story, an account of how Jesus debated the Jewish law with teachers in the temple when he was only twelve (2:41–51). The Gospels claim that Jesus was raised in the Galilean village of Nazareth, and that Joseph, his father, was a carpenter. Jesus was probably educated no differently than other children. He attended synagogue (Luke 4:16) and learned the scriptures.

The Gospels relate that when he was about thirty Jesus withdrew into the wilderness to be baptized by John the Baptist. They also claim that there was something extraordinary about his baptism, for as he emerged from the water a "voice from heaven" spoke, saying: "This is my Son, the Beloved, with whom I am well pleased" (Matthew 3:17; cf. Mark 1:11; Luke 3:22). Some scholars see here a combination of two passages from the Hebrew Bible. "This is my Son" recalls Psalm 2:7 which speaks of

David: "He said to me, 'You are my son; today I have begotten you.'" The point of Psalm 2 is that God "adopts" the king and expects him to carry out the divine will. The words spoken from heaven also recall Isaiah 42:1: "Here is my servant, whom I uphold, my chosen, in whom my soul delights; I have put my spirit upon him; he will bring forth justice to the nations."

If this is the correct way to interpret the account of Jesus' baptism, then the Gospels argue that God chose him to be the agent of the divine purpose; that this purpose was to bring justice and righteousness to the nations; that Jesus as God's agent would have the Spirit of God; and that the attainment of God's purpose depended entirely on the servant of the Lord who would suffer humiliation and apparent defeat (Isaiah 53:4–9). What Jesus actually believed about himself is, of course, an open question.

The Synoptic Gospels claim that after his baptism Jesus went into the wilderness to be tempted by Satan. Satan, whose name might derive from a word meaning "to accuse" or "to oppose," is a shadowy figure in the Bible. He is rarely mentioned in the Tanakh, and when he does appear (Job 1 and 2; Zechariah 3) takes the role of prosecuting attorney. Satan has a somewhat more prominent role in the New Testament. In the wilderness he offers Jesus three temptations. According to Matthew, the first is to turn stones to bread in order to satisfy his own hunger. The second is to leap from the high point of the temple in order for the angels of God to save him. The third is to bow down and worship Satan and thereby be given the kingdoms of the earth to rule. Jesus rejects all three.

MIRACLES

The Synoptic Gospels assert that after his temptation Jesus embarked upon his ministry. During this period he won recognition as a teacher and worker of miracles. The stories of his miracles have theological implications. The nature miracles, for example, often portray Jesus acting as God did in the Hebrew Bible. Thus, in John 6:16–21 Jesus walks on water in a fashion that seems to parallel Psalm

77:19 and 107:28–30. Jesus' exorcisms suggest that the Kingdom of God was breaking into the world and undoing the forces of evil that had long held sway over it (Matthew 9:32–33; Mark 5:1–15). Stories about Jesus' miraculous healings and occasions on which he raised the dead (Matthew 9:18–25; Luke 8:40–56) were meant to show that Jesus acted in concert with the power of God.

The Gospels indicate that some witnesses to Jesus' miracles took him for a wonder-worker and nothing more. They even depict Jesus' occasional frustration with such an attitude: "If they do not listen to Moses and the prophets, neither will they be convinced even if someone rises from the dead" (Luke 16:31). According to the Bible, Jesus was not alone in being able to perform miracles. The prophets (2 Kings 5:1–19), some of Jesus' own followers (Acts 19:11–12), and even those allied with Satan are said to work them (2 Thessalonians 2:9–10). Thus, the ability to perform miracles indicates only that one is in touch with some sort of spiritual force. The Gospels make it clear that the power at work in Jesus' miracles comes from God.

TEACHING: THE KINGDOM OF GOD AND THE SON OF MAN

The Gospels claim that after his temptation Jesus gathered his disciples and began to travel to different towns and villages teaching. Nearly 90 percent of what Jesus taught was connected with two themes: the Kingdom of God and the Son of Man.

Few issues in New Testament scholarship have elicited as much study as the question of what Jesus meant by the Kingdom of God. Typically scholars begin by investigating the meaning of the term in the Hebrew Bible and in first-century Judaism, with the assumption that what Jesus' contemporaries understood the phrase to mean is what Jesus himself meant when he used it. But as one prominent New Testament scholar has wisely noted, "if the Synoptic Gospels are right to insist that Jesus spent much of his time explaining what *he* meant by the Kingdom, would it not follow that he did not mean what everybody else meant by it?"[40] In short,

there is little scholarly consensus on what the Gospel writers want to claim that Jesus taught concerning the Kingdom or Reign of God.

According to the Gospels, Jesus did not understand the Kingdom of God as an earthly or political entity. In this he offered a radically different view than that embraced by his contemporaries, many of whom dreamed of a revived Davidic kingdom. Rather, Jesus' notion of the Kingdom seemed to revolve around his ideas about God as parent and the ethics of the Kingdom.

Many of the parables, or stories Jesus used to illustrate his teaching, concern the Kingdom of God. He pictured God as a parental figure, frequently using the term *abba* or father.[41] "What is the Kingdom of God like?" Jesus asked. God is like a shepherd who searches for the one lost sheep (Luke 15:4–7); God is like a woman who rejoices when she has found a coin that has been lost (Luke 15:8–10); God is like a loving father who rejoices when his dissolute and disrespectful son returns home (Luke 15:11–32). The point of many of the Kingdom parables is that God is primarily a God of compassion. Unlike John the Baptist, whom the Gospels represent as expecting repentance before acceptance by God, the Gospels generally depict Jesus asserting that acceptance by God comes first, followed by inner moral development for those who respond. As a number of prominent scholars have noted, Jesus' practice of eating with "sinners and tax collectors" (Mark 2:16) demonstrates this distinctive break from accepted social and theological patterns.[42]

This flows directly into the way the Gospels present Jesus' teaching on ethics. According to the Gospels, Jesus' view was that ethics are less a matter of right behavior than of a right heart. If the heart is right, then mercy and justice will follow:

> Either make the tree good, and its
> fruit good; or make the tree bad, and
> its fruit bad; for the tree is known by
> its fruit. You brood of vipers! How can
> you speak good things, when you are
> evil? For out of the abundance of the
> heart the mouth speaks. The good person
> brings good things out of good

treasure; and the evil person brings
evil things out of an evil treasure.
(Matthew 12:33–35)

According to the Gospels, Jesus insisted on a particular view of Torah. He apparently stressed what he viewed as the intention of Torah. This intention was to nurture justice and righteousness, and to encourage an attitude of openness to God and a willingness to be shaped by God. Jesus stressed the compassion of God, not only as a model for human behavior, but also as the essence of God's attitude to humankind:

> But love your enemies, do good, and
> lend, expecting nothing in return. Your
> reward will be great, and you will be
> children of the Most High; for he is
> kind to the ungrateful and the wicked.
> Be merciful, just as your Father is
> merciful. (Luke 6:35–36)

The Gospels present a Jesus with little patience for an attitude toward the law at variance with his own emphasis on mercy and justice. There is little doubt that Jesus had compassion for sinners. At the same time, however, the Gospels picture him as against sin. He forgave sins (Mark 2:5–10), but he also called sinners to repentance (Luke 5:32).

The question of the Kingdom also involves the question of Jesus' expectation of the end. It is often argued that Jesus expected an imminent end of the world and the judgment of God. Perhaps the best-known exponent of this view was Albert Schweitzer. In 1906 he published *The Quest of the Historical Jesus*.[43] In this influential study Schweitzer argued that Jesus was an **apocalyptic** figure who believed in the imminent end of the world; that is, Jesus understood the Kingdom of God to be an otherworldly, supernatural realm that would be established on earth once God brought an end to history and judged the nations. At some point in his ministry, said Schweitzer, Jesus became impatient and took it upon himself to prompt God to act. He went to Jerusalem and provoked the authorities, thinking he could set in motion a series of events in which God would intervene. When he was crucified, Jesus realized that he was mistaken, and so the words of anguish and disappointment on his lips—"My God, my God, why have you forsaken me?" (Mark 15:34)—were meant literally.

The British New Testament scholar C. H. Dodd challenged Schweitzer's view.[44] Dodd noted that the Gospels contain several clues that the Kingdom of God is in some sense present now, not awaiting the aftermath of a great cataclysm.[45] Dodd argued that with Jesus the Kingdom of God has begun to break into this world, but it is a long process. That is, the Kingdom is slowly overlaying itself on the present world system. It is present now, in the hearts of the followers of Jesus, but it is not always obvious to the world at large. The portraits of both Schweitzer and Dodd are persuasive enough to have endured. But if we cannot be certain what the Gospels teach concerning the Kingdom of God, it stands to reason that we can be even less certain what Jesus meant by the phrase.

Did Jesus expect an imminent end of the world? This is a difficult question, and many scholars argue that Schweitzer's basic analysis was correct; that is, Jesus did expect an imminent end of the world.[46] Certainly many early Christians did.[47]

According to the Gospels, Jesus also issued apocalyptic warnings concerning judgment (Matthew 25:31–46). The Gospels therefore depict Jesus employing a dual definition of the Kingdom—often as a present reality, but also as the final vindication of God's purposes and the material realization of a supernatural reality of justice and peace:

> There will be weeping and gnashing of
> teeth when you see Abraham and Isaac
> and Jacob and all the prophets in the
> kingdom of God, and you yourselves
> thrown out. Then people will come from
> east and west, from north and south,
> and will eat in the kingdom of God.
> (Luke 13:28–29)

This points to the theme of reversal in the teaching of Jesus. Those who have power will lose it. Those who oppress will be punished. The lowly will be raised, and the high brought low.

The most famous example of Jesus' teaching is the "Sermon on the Mount" found in Matthew 5–7. Here Matthew has Jesus say, "Everyone who hears these words of mine and acts on them will be like a wise man who built his house on rock" (Matthew

Figure 2.2   According to tradition, this site, overlooking the Sea of Galilee, is where Jesus preached his famous Sermon on the Mount (Matthew 5-7).

7:24). Matthew's point, it appears, is that Jesus' teaching is the true route to security and to pleasing God.

This understanding is supported by Jesus' prophetic action in the temple, reported in all four Gospels (Matthew 21:12–13; Mark 11:15–17; Luke 19:45–46; John 2:13–23). In the outer courts of the temple were arrayed those who sold animals for sacrifice and exchanged secular money for temple money. Roman money often bore the image of the emperor, and was therefore unacceptable in the temple. According to Luke, Jesus entered the temple precincts and overturned the tables of the money-changers with the words, "It is written, 'My house shall be a house of prayer'; but you have made it a den of robbers" (Luke 19:46), based on quotations of Isaiah 56:7 and Jeremiah 7:11. The Greek word here translated "robber" is a form

of *lestes*, which is the word the New Testament uses to refer not to common bandits, but to the revolutionaries who sought to expel the Romans by force. It appears that Luke at least wants to claim that the Kingdom of God is not a nationalist's vision. It is not a kingdom of "God for us" and against everyone else. If this is true, then Jesus saw the temple as a symbol of a false view of what it meant to be Israel.[48] The Gospel writers apparently thought of Israel's temple as a symbol not only of Israel's devotion to God, but also of Israel's responsibility to the world as a "light to the nations" (Isaiah 42:6), announcing to the world that Israel's God was about to bring his Kingdom to earth by stripping human authorities of their dominion and installing a Kingdom of justice and righteousness.[49]

Early in the Sermon on the Mount, Jesus claimed to be bringing forth the meaning of the law: "Do not think that I have come to abolish the law or the prophets; I have come not to abolish but to fulfill" (Matthew 5:17). He went on to offer forgiveness of sins to people on his own authority. Forgiveness was the province of the temple ritual and could be offered only by God (see Luke 5:21). According to the Gospels, Jesus was claiming to have both the ability and the authority to forgive sins. It is possible he understood his teaching and his person to be the temple, the point of contact between humans and God, and that he believed he was ushering in the Kingdom of God.

Perhaps the most disputed issue in New Testament studies is the question of the "Son of Man." The Gospels present this phrase as Jesus' favorite description of himself, on his lips more than eighty times. By contrast, Jesus refers to himself as "messiah" only once or twice (see Matthew 26:63–64; John 4:25–26). New Testament scholars disagree sharply over what Jesus meant by the phrase *Son of Man,* and many think he never used it.[50] However, the Gospels present Jesus as using it, and this use is a prominent feature of the theological enterprise of the Gospel writers.

The phrase has its origins in the Tanakh, and in Hebrew can mean merely "human being," as it often does in Ezekiel. But it later came to have apocalyptic connotations, as in the perplexing vision found in Daniel 7. As we saw in the previous chapter, Daniel has a vision of a churning sea at night. Out of the sea come four monstrous beasts that terrorize and devour humankind. The scene then turns to heaven, where a divine figure identified as "the Ancient of Days" (7:9) sits in judgment over the beasts. "The Ancient of Days" strips from the beasts their dominion, and turns over "dominions and glory and kingship" (7:14) to a figure described as "one like a human being" or literally "one like a son of man." The vision also reveals that "all peoples, nations and languages" should serve this son of man (7:14), and that this son of man will share "kingship and dominion" with "the holy ones of the Most High" (7:27). It is possible that the Gospel writers place the phrase on Jesus' lips for theological reasons. The figure in Daniel's vision is the agent of God who ushers in God's Kingdom on earth, who helps overturn the power structures of society, who

is served by humankind, and who shares rule in the Kingdom with the "holy ones of the Most High."

According to Mark, Jesus began his career by proclaiming "The time is fulfilled, and the kingdom of God has come near; repent, therefore, and believe in the good news" (Mark 1:15). In short, his announcement in Mark seems to echo the son of man image in Daniel. In Mark, Jesus points out that something is dreadfully wrong with human society and repentance is necessary. Like the son of man in Daniel 7, Jesus acts to overturn the power structures of society. Unlike the son of man in Daniel 7, however, the Gospels present Jesus as "the Son of Man" who rejects the right to be served. Instead, he preached an ethic of service to others: "the Son of Man came not to be served but to serve, and to give his life a ransom for many" (Mark 10:45). This redefinition of the son of man vision is odd. The Gospels explicitly point to Jesus, not with the indefinite "a son of man," but with the definite article, "*the* Son of Man."[51] Many scholars see here a combination of Daniel 7 with Isaiah 53, where the "Servant of the Lord" suffers in the place of others:

> But he was wounded for our
> transgressions, crushed for our
> iniquities; upon him was the punishment
> that made us whole, and by his bruises
> we are healed. (Isaiah 53:5)

If the Gospels are making a connection between Daniel 7 and Isaiah 53, it is a connection made for the first time.[52]

JESUS THE RADICAL

According to the Gospels, Jesus taught nonresistance and was an articulate advocate for justice and righteousness. An earlier scholarly consensus, following Schweitzer, held that Jesus should be understood within the framework of apocalyptic eschatology. The majority of scholars continue to hold this view, but it can no longer be regarded as the broad consensus. A second approach sees Jesus as a type of prophet announcing a renewal movement within Judaism. Some see this renewal as social; other scholars consider it a blend of heightened spiritual awareness and a concern for justice. A considerable amount of modern scholarship has focused on this newer picture of Jesus,[53] and it certainly appears to have a good deal to commend it. According to this view, Jesus was convinced that the existing order was malignant, that it needed to be changed, and that he knew what needed to be done.

Jesus was apparently successful in attracting to himself a following representing the entire social spectrum in Palestine. The Gospels represent this startling variety even within the cadre of his disciples, among whom were two whose paths in life would normally have made them mortal enemies: Matthew the tax collector and Simon the "Zealot" (Luke 5:27–32, 6:15). The bulk of his followers most likely were drawn from the impoverished lower classes. The Gospels also record that some prominent and wealthy women were attracted by his ministry and message.[54] Finally, some religious authorities apparently embraced his message of reform, in spite of the fact that many of his actions called into question the legitimacy of the central features of first-century Judaism.

One way to look at Jesus' message is as an ethic of overturning the established order. The policies of the Roman Empire fortified lines of social stratification and demarcation. In Palestine these were overlaid with religious ideas that heightened social and economic separation. According to the Gospels the message of Jesus was that the wealthy were to be brought low and the poor raised up, that the central features of God's character, holiness, purity, and righteousness, were manifested in mercy and compassion.

THE PASSION

According to the New Testament, near the end of his life Jesus journeyed to Jerusalem for the Passover celebration. This final week of his life is often referred to as his passion, or "suffering." According to the Gospels large crowds surrounded Jesus as he entered Jerusalem. References to the palm branches that were laid before him (Matthew 21:8; Mark 11:8; John 12:13) were probably meant to recall the palm branches laid before the victorious Maccabees (1 Maccabees 13:51; 2 Maccabees 10:7). The Gospels report that Jesus shared a meal with his disciples in which he announced a new covenant in his own person.

According to the Gospels, later that night Jesus was arrested and brought before the Sanhedrin (a gathering of the Jewish authorities), where he implied that he considered himself the agent of God. A decision was reached to seek Jesus' execution. The Gospels therefore lay the blame for the death of Jesus at the feet of the Jewish authorities despite the fact that it was the Romans who executed him. Many perceive here more than a hint of anti-Semitism.[55] Jesus might not have been a political revolutionary, but he died like one. The Gospels describe his crucifixion and say that his body was taken by some of his followers and buried in a tomb.

According to the Gospels, Jesus rarely used the term *messiah*. Yet it is very likely that the Gospel account of a placard affixed to his cross bearing the words "King of the Jews" (Matthew 27:37; Mark 15:26; Luke 23:38; John 19:19) is historically accurate.[56] The Romans were certainly aware of his popularity and had good reason to regard him as a threat of political upheaval and revolution. It is possible that the title on the placard was intended ironically, to say this man was not king of the Jews.

When Jesus died, it must have seemed to his disciples that his mission was a failure. The Gospels relate that they were disheartened and contemplating a return to their former lives.

THE RESURRECTION AND
THE EARLY CHURCH

But the Gospels also say that something extraordinary happened after the crucifixion. They relate that on the Sunday morning following Jesus' death, his disciples discovered that his tomb was empty. The followers of Jesus then came to believe that he had risen from the dead. The New Testament records several occasions when the risen Jesus encountered his followers. On one of these he instructed his disciples to go into the entire world with the good news of his life, teachings, and resurrection, making disciples of all peoples (Matthew 28:18–20). Belief in the resurrection became foundational to early Christianity.

When we encounter the stories of the resurrection of Jesus, we are in contact with one of the great enigmas of history. It seems certain that something of importance happened to the disciples. When other first-century "messiahs" were killed, their followers found someone new to follow. But the disciples of Jesus continued to follow him, even after his death. For this there is no explanation, other than to say that they believed in Jesus' resurrection, and ancient tradition holds that some went to their deaths rather than deny that belief.

The Gospels and the Book of Acts tell us that after his resurrection Jesus appeared several times to his followers and then ascended to heaven. After the ascension of Jesus the community of his followers met regularly in Jerusalem. Virtually everything we know about the early Church (*ekklesia,* "assembly") in Jerusalem is found in the Book of Acts, which scholars think was written between 80 and 95 CE.

According to Acts, the early Church was led by Peter, the disciple of Jesus, and by James, Jesus' brother. These early Jewish Christians saw themselves as both believers in Jesus the Christ (*christos,* "anointed," "messiah") and observant Jews, as a group within Judaism. Acts provides a brief description of the life of the early Church in Jerusalem:

> They devoted themselves to the apostles' teaching and fellowship, to the breaking of bread and the prayers. Awe overcame everyone, because many wonders and signs were being done by the apostles. All who believed were together and had all things in common; they would sell their possessions and goods and distribute the proceeds to all, as any had need. Day by day, as they spent much time together in the temple, they broke bread at home and ate their food with glad and generous hearts, praising God and having the goodwill of all the people. And day by day the Lord added to their number those who were being saved. (Acts 2:42–47)

Acts reports that some fifty days after Passover, when travelers from all over the empire were in Jerusalem for the feast of **Pentecost,** the Holy Spirit came upon the believers in Jerusalem. On that occasion Peter preached a sermon that resulted in the conversion of some three thousand persons to the Christian movement (2:41). Many were only visitors in Jerusalem, and they carried their newfound faith back home with them. The early Christians were apparently convinced that the same Spirit that had directed Jesus now was at work in their own lives. According to the New Testament, it was this belief in the guidance of the Spirit that eventually led Peter and the others to conclude that Jesus' message was intended for the entire world, and not just for Jews.

According to Acts the success of Peter's sermon at Pentecost contributed to growing uneasiness about the early Christian movement on the part of the Jewish authorities in Jerusalem. The Church in Jerusalem began to suffer persecution, which forced some Christians to spread out from Jerusalem to the rest of the empire. But according to the New Testament the most significant force in the spread of the Christian message was not this persecution, but rather the conviction of a single person. He was an unlikely advocate for the faith, yet he became perhaps its ablest exponent. His name was Paul.

Paul

The legacy of the teaching and ministry of Jesus was initially in the hands of his closest disciples. According to Acts, these early Christians seemed to possess little idea that Christianity should be anything other than a theologically revolutionary sect within Judaism. It was the lasting achievement of Paul to focus the legacy of Jesus in such a way that Christianity penetrated the social and intellectual world of the Roman Empire. Paul not only attempted to grant to early Christianity the theological and intellectual resources for this endeavor; he also imbued it with the mark of his personal story. His message was of the dawning of a new age, and with it the possibility of a radical inward transformation he described as producing a "renewed mind" (Romans 12:2) and making the individual a "new creation" (2 Corinthians 5:17). Paul believed that this transformation carried with it a heightened commitment to social responsibility and morality.[57]

Virtually everything we know about Paul (he was also called "Saul" when in Jewish circles) is derived from his letters in the New Testament. Paul was born to Jewish parents in the city of Tarsus in present-day Turkey. At some point he moved to Jerusalem and became a Pharisee. There is speculation that he was a member of the Sanhedrin,[58] but Paul never makes this claim. In his letter to the Galatians he wrote, "I advanced in Judaism beyond many among my people of the same age, for I was far more zealous for the traditions of my ancestors" (Galatians 1:14). Even after he had been a Christian for some thirty years Paul claimed that he "gloried" in the Jewish law.[59]

Acts relates that when the Jewish authorities became aware that the movement associated with Jesus had not died out, they grew concerned. To them it was a heretical and scandalous sect. It was also dangerous, as it had the potential to inflame messianic expectations. Paul perceived the threat, and he became a persecutor of the early Church. Acts claims that on the way to the city of Damascus to arrest Jewish Christians, he encountered the risen Christ (see Acts 9:1–22, 22:4–16, 26:9–18). Paul does not mention the Damascus road story in his letters, but it is clear he believed that he had a powerful mystical experience of the risen Christ. The event changed his life, and Paul became an advocate of the movement he had once intended to destroy.

After some time in seclusion Paul became a missionary for the Christian movement and made three journeys in which he brought the gospel to Asia Minor, Macedonia, and Greece. These are described in Acts, a source that some scholars believe is not entirely trustworthy for reconstructing Paul's life. It appears that he founded churches in cities such as Ephesus and Corinth and that many Gentiles joined the Christian movement. It is also evident that the conversion of Gentiles was problematic, for they did not follow the Jewish law, but a decision was eventually reached whereby Gentiles were allowed to join without first becoming Jews.

According to his letters, Paul believed that the work of Christ set human beings free from bondage to sin. He believed that nothing was more im-

Figure 2.3   Paul This ancient mosaic conveys the same intensity and commitment to his missionary work that are evident in Paul's letters.

portant than to spread this news and to introduce people to the risen Christ (1 Corinthians 9:19–23). He believed that the freedom of believers was tempered by their responsibility to care for one another. For this reason, Christians should be prepared to give up their rights at times, just as Jesus had given up his rights for the benefit of others (Philippians 2:1–11). Paul's vision was of a community without distinctions of race, class, or gender.[60] Paul was also an apocalypticist. He apparently believed that God would intervene in history and destroy the world in his own lifetime. At the least he counseled Christians that they should live according to this expectation (1 Corinthians 7:25–31; 1 Thessalonians 4:13–18).

Paul's Theology

Paul is not easy to comprehend. The New Testament itself acknowledges this in 2 Peter 3:15–16, where we read concerning Paul's letters, "there are some things in them hard to understand." For centuries theologians saw the key to Paul's thought in his doctrine of justification by grace through faith.

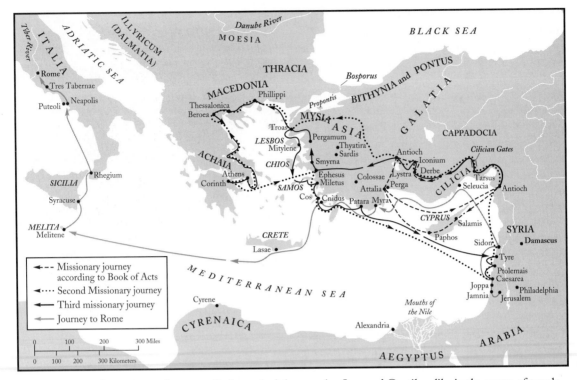

Figure 2.4   Paul's missionary journeys Paul preached the gospel to Jews and Gentiles alike in the course of travels that took him to Syria, Asia Minor, Macedonia, Greece, Cyprus, Crete, and Italy.

That idea is clearly an important feature of Paul's thought, but it is not at all certain that there is *one* key to Paul's thought. Rather, there seem to be a number of central ideas. Another difficulty is the nature of the evidence. Representatives from various Christian communities wrote to Paul informing him of problems they were experiencing and asked him for advice (1 Corinthians 1:11, 7:1). Unfortunately, these letters did not survive. What has survived are some of the letters Paul wrote in response. Paul's letters, therefore, are occasional in nature and not intended as a systematic theology. This makes any reconstruction of Paul's thought somewhat problematic.

CHRISTOLOGY

Paramount in Paul's thought is his understanding of Jesus Christ. He believed that Jesus suffered, died, and then rose again, all according to the scriptures (1 Corinthians 15:1–7). In addition, this death and resurrection somehow had the power to bridge the gap between human beings and God. Paul came to the conclusion that God was somehow especially present in Jesus. This allowed Paul to refer to Jesus as "Lord" (Romans 1:4). As a Jew, Paul believed in God the Father and also in the Spirit of God. For Jews, belief in the Spirit of God did not threaten monotheism, for the Hebrew Bible spoke of God's Spirit. Although Paul did not work out a comprehensive theology of God as three persons along the lines of later Christian thinking, he seems to have considered Jesus Christ worthy of worship, without compromising the monotheism that Christianity inherited from Judaism (Colossians 1:15–19). Paul believed that after his resurrection Jesus ascended to heaven to occupy a place at the right hand of God the Father, and that all will ultimately confess Jesus as Lord (Philippians 2:5–11).

JUDAISM

Paul wrote extensively on Judaism and its relation to Christianity. He claimed to regard his entire previous life in Judaism "as loss because of Christ. More than that, I regard everything as loss because of the surpassing value of knowing Christ Jesus my Lord" (Philippians 3:7–8). Yet he did not feel that he had left Judaism.

Paul came to the conclusion that Jesus was the agent of God. Therefore, to follow him was truly to follow Judaism. He also came to think that Gentiles could share in the covenant relationship even without obeying the specific commandments in the law, such as those concerning circumcision and clean and unclean foods. He pointed out that Abraham, the founder of the Jewish nation, had faith in God long before there was a Torah, and "the Lord reckoned it to him as righteousness" (Romans 4:3). Paul therefore argued that it has always been God's will to grant salvation to those who believe (Romans 3:21–26; Galatians 3:6–9). This allowed him to write, "a person is not a Jew who is one outwardly, nor is true circumcision something external and physical. Rather, a person is a Jew who is one inwardly, and real circumcision is a matter of the heart" (Romans 2:28–29).

Figure 2.5   Identification collars and tags like these were meant to prevent Roman slaves from escaping their masters. Paul might well have had such devices in mind when he described human beings as enslaved by sin.

SALVATION

A third pivotal point for Paul is salvation. In Romans 1–3 Paul argued that all human beings, Jews and Gentiles alike, are guilty of sin and therefore separated from God. He related that it is impossible for human beings to save themselves. God desires to be in relationship with human beings, Paul said, and has supplied the solution. In his grace, God determined to bridge the gap between himself and humanity by sending Jesus to suffer and die in the place of human beings. Under the traditional sacrificial system, the sacrifice atoned for sin and reconciled the sinner to God. Here the sacrifice was made by a human being. Paul believed that by his resurrection Christ proved himself victorious over death, and that the results of this act can be appropriated vicariously by human beings. Human beings can be justified (reconciled to God); all that is

required is that they accept in faith what God has done in Christ:

> All have sinned and fall short of the glory of God; they are now justified by his grace as a gift, through the redemption that is in Christ Jesus, whom God put forward as a sacrifice of atonement by his blood, effective through faith. (Romans 3:23–25)

Paul's understanding of salvation calls upon the image of the slave market. Human beings are enslaved to sin, he argued, and through the death and resurrection of Jesus, God has allowed them to be set free. Paul related that this new freedom can lead to a mystical union with Christ. Galatians provides an apt summary:

> We know that a person is justified not by the works of the law but through faith in Jesus Christ. And we have come to believe in Christ Jesus, so that we might be justified by faith in Christ, and not by doing the works of the law, because no one will be justified by the works of the law. . . . I have been crucified with Christ, and it is no

Figure 2.6   Corinth One of the largest and most prosperous cities in Greece, Corinth was home to one of the churches founded by Paul. Paul must have been familiar with the street shown here and with the Acrocorinth, the city's citadel, which rises above it.

longer I who live, but it is Christ who lives in me. And the life I now live in the flesh I live by faith in the Son of God, who loved me and gave himself for me. (Galatians 2:16, 19–20)

AN APOCALYPTIC PREACHER

Paul's thought also had an apocalyptic strain. He believed that ultimately all creation would be judged and would acknowledge the lordship of Jesus Christ. He put it this way:

And being found in human form, he humbled himself and became obedient to the point of death — even death on a cross. Therefore God also highly exalted him and gave him the name that is above every name, so that at the name of Jesus every knee should bend, in heaven and on earth and under the earth, and every tongue confess that Jesus Christ is Lord, to the glory of God the Father. (Philippians 2:7–11)

For Paul, a result of the death and resurrection of Jesus Christ is that the powers of evil have been disarmed and are awaiting final judgment. Paul's vision included the idea that it is Christ's task to bring God's Reign to earth. "Then comes the end, when he hands over the kingdom to God the Father, after he has destroyed every ruler and every authority and power. For he must reign until he has put all his enemies under his feet" (1 Corinthians 15:24–25). This passage anticipates an end of the world marked by conflict. Concerning the exact nature of that conflict Paul is silent. He only claimed that Christ will be victorious and then the end will come.

There is further evidence that Paul expected an imminent return of Christ and the end of the world. In 1 Thessalonians, he responded to questions concerning the return of Christ and told the church there that when "the Lord" comes again, both the living and the dead will be brought to God through Jesus (4:15–16) following the sound of the trumpet and the call of the archangel. Paul further said that this "day of the Lord" will come "like a thief in the night," so be ready. Those who are not ready will think they are safe, but "suddenly destruction will come upon them" (5:2–3).

TRANSFORMATION, FREEDOM, AND RESPONSIBILITY

Another idea central to Paul's thought is his notion of the transforming power of Christ both for the person and for society. "Do not be conformed to this world, but be transformed by the renewing of your minds, so that you may discern what is the will of God" (Romans 12:2).

Paul said that without Christ human beings are held in bondage by sin and their own sinful desires. He also said that all are slaves to the spiritual and material forces of evil. In the work of Christ, Paul maintained, human beings are liberated from all of these forms of bondage. He employed legal imagery to explicate his point. "But now that you have been freed from sin, and enslaved to God," he wrote, "the advantage you get is sanctification. The end is eternal life. For the wages of sin is death, but the free gift of God is eternal life" (Romans 6:22–23).

In a passage that is remarkable for its simplicity Paul declared, "For freedom Christ has set us free. Stand firm, therefore, and do not submit again to a yoke of slavery" (Galatians 5:1). But he goes on to argue that with complete freedom comes responsibility. "For you were called to freedom, brothers and sisters; only do not use your freedom as an opportunity for self-indulgence, but through love become slaves to one another" (Galatians 5:13). Elsewhere Paul wrote, "'All things are lawful for me' but not all things are beneficial" (1 Corinthians 6:12). Paul believed that commitment to Christ brought the possibility of heightened spiritual awareness of the will of God through the Holy Spirit and responsibility for living according to the Sprit. "Live by the Spirit, I say, and do not gratify the desires of the flesh" (Galatians 6:16).

Paul's vision is more than personal. He believed that the effects of human sin had infected all of society—society had become dominated by institutionalized greed and selfishness. For Paul the political order, while morally neutral, is weak and easily co-opted by the structural forces of selfishness and sin. Paul considered some of the concrete manifestations of these forces to be the rigid divisions of race, class, and gender that characterized his age.

The transforming power of Christ is strong enough, in Paul's view, to overcome these differences. "There is no longer Jew or Greek, there is no longer slave or free, there is no longer male and female; for all of you are one in Christ Jesus" (Galatians 3:28). Paul remained a Jew, but he believed

that Gentiles had a place within the covenant. Paul ate with Gentiles and strongly rebuked Peter when he refused to share table fellowship with Gentiles. To Paul, Peter's attitude represented a fundamental misunderstanding of the gospel. In Galatians he said that Peter and his asscoiates "were not acting consistently with the truth of the gospel" (Galatians 2:14). For Paul, the power of the gospel overcame even traditional sexual roles. "The wife does not have authority over her own body, but the husband does;" Paul wrote, echoing the sentiment generally accepted throughout the Mediterranean. But then Paul went on to write something remarkably progressive for its time, "likewise the husband does not have authority over his own body, but the wife does" (1 Corinthians 7:4).

In closing his letter to the Galatians, Paul wrote, "Grace to you and peace from God our Father and the Lord Jesus Christ, who gave himself for our sins to set us free from the present evil age, according to the will of our God and Father" (Galatians 1:3–4). In Paul's view "this present evil age" was passing away, but it was not exhausted yet. Its lingering effects, he claimed, could be displaced only under the influence of the Spirit of God, and through this influence people gradually would begin to embrace the compelling vision of equal membership in the family of God.

CHRISTIAN COMMUNITY

In 1 Corinthians 12, Paul outlined his notion of the individual Christian community as a body. He likened the members of the local church to the parts of the body, and said that although the various parts have different functions, all them are necessary. "The eye cannot say to the hand, 'I have no need of you', nor again the head to the feet, 'I have no need of you'" (1 Corinthians 12:21). Each member is the servant of and dependent upon each of the others. Gifts and abilities are given by God to individuals in order to benefit the community, not the individual who happens to possess them.

Paul pressed this point home by using the image of the family to describe how members of the Church should relate to one another. Christians should accept others, he said, because each of

Figure 2.7 Ancient Christian codex The codex, a form of manuscript consisting of separate pages bound together, is the ancestor of the modern book. The page shown here is from the Gospel of John.

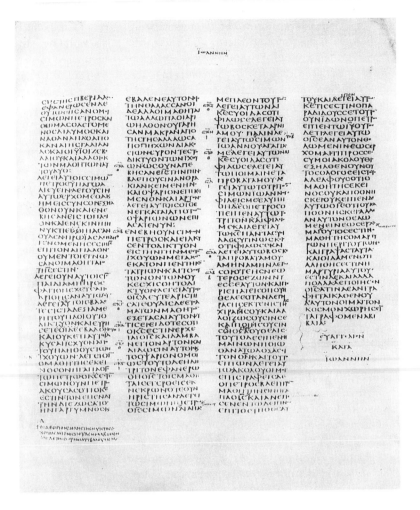

them had been adopted by God (Romans 15:7; Galatians 4:4–5). Paul made liberal use of terms of great affection. "I long for you all with the compassion of Christ" he wrote (Philippians 1:8). He asked Christians to love each other (1 Thessalonians 3:12) and "to bear one another's burdens, and in this way you will fulfill the law of Christ" (Galatians 6:12).

Paul's attitude toward women is difficult to discern. 1 Corinthians 14:33–36 seems to exclude women from leadership roles, but some scholars argue this passage intends only a prohibition against disturbing a worship service. 1 Timothy 2:11–15 asserts that women should not teach or have authority within the Christian community. Some point out that Paul probably did not write this letter. Others note that the Greek word for "exercise authority" used here probably means "to domineer." Nonetheless, the text does appear to argue that women should be silent in church and that they are to have no leadership role. Yet in 1 Corinthians 11:5 Paul assumed that women will "prophesy" or "speak the word of the Lord" in public; the only question is how they are to be dressed. In Romans 16 Paul mentioned the names of women who were teaching men in matters of the faith (16:1,3) and described a certain Junia as "prominent among the apostles" (16:7). Current scholarship tends to see Paul as generally supportive of women in leadership roles and objecting to their involvement only in cases where some special problem was evident.[61]

An instructive case study in Paul's thought concerns the church in Corinth.[62] Paul visited Corinth and founded the church there on his second missionary journey, staying eighteen months. Corinth had been destroyed by the Romans in 146 BCE, but repopulated with Roman citizens by Julius Caesar in 44 BCE.[63] Paul's first letter to the Corinthian church deals with the contrast between what he calls "the wisdom of the world" and "the wisdom of God." Many in the church were, apparently, committed to the pursuit of the wisdom of the world; that is, they were using the church as an opportunity to display wealth and status. Paul felt constrained to chastise the church regarding its practice of the Lord's Supper, a ceremonial meal that Christians believe Jesus inaugurated on his last night with his disciples. In 1 Corinthians Paul is angry because the church had used this meal in order to enforce social distinctions: the wealthy ate first and apart from the rest of the church (1 Corinthians 11:20–22).

This practice mirrored a feature of civic life within the empire, the *sportula* feast. As a means of displaying wealth and superior social station, wealthy individuals sometimes hosted a meal for an entire city. They made certain, however, that members of the higher classes enjoyed better food and in the company of their peers. It seems that wealthy members of the church at Corinth had applied this pattern in their own congregation. They had used the church for purposes related to pride and social status.

In castigating the Corinthians Paul said, "you show contempt for the church of God and humiliate those who have nothing" (1 Corinthians 11:22).[64] Paul contrasted the wisdom of the world, which prizes wealth, status, and power, with the wisdom of God, which prizes love and the interests of others. Paul wrote:

> For the message about the Cross is
> foolishness to those who are perishing,
> but to those of us who are being saved it
> is the power of God. . . . Has not God made
> foolish the wisdom of the world? . . . For

God's foolishness is wiser than human wisdom. (1 Corinthians 1:18–19, 25)

Paul's own experience convinced him that the selfish human nature within him was still present and active, but he was committed to spiritual renewal. He understood that the Church existed for the sake of sinners, but he expected Christians to open their lives to the Spirit and wisdom of God and to commit themselves to spiritual growth.

The Gospel of John

The Gospel of John has enjoyed a long and wide popularity and is often considered the most theologically complex document in the entire Bible.[65] This opinion has an ancient pedigree. The fourth-century Christian historian Eusebius quotes Clement of Alexandria, who lived a century earlier, as having written, "Last of all, John, aware that the physical facts had been clearly set forth in the other gospels . . . composed a spiritual gospel."[66] In other words, John got to the heart of the matter instead of focusing on the "physical facts" concerning the life of Jesus. In 1966 Ernst Käsemann noted that John's Jesus is not at all the Jesus of history, but he also asked, "Does he [John] not also show us the one final testament of the earthly Jesus and his glory?"[67]

THE CONTEXT OF THE GOSPEL

According to tradition, John the son of Zebedee, one of the original disciples of Jesus, wrote the Gospel that bears his name. Few modern scholars believe this. Instead, scholarly opinion is that the Gospel of John went through several stages of development, each layer representing different theologcal positions, before the final contribution and editing was done by the "Johannine community," a term used to describe the church of John's followers.[68] If they are right, the Gospel refects the Johannine church of the second century more than the historical Jesus, even though the characters in John are the same as in the Synoptic Gospels.

In contrast, a small group of scholars think John's Gospel is largely the product of a single author [69] and that at least some of the material can be attributed to John the disciple of Jesus. Whatever its origin, the Gospel of John proved to be an influential force in shaping Christian attitudes about Jesus.

The Gospel of John has also been described as a source of Christian anti-Semitism, particularly because it tends to make "the Jews" responsible for Jesus' suffering and death and distances itself from Judaism. But it seems that the author did not intend to convey the idea that all Jews were the enemies of Jesus. John has a Samaritan woman identify Jesus as a Jew (4:20), has Jesus say "salvation is from the Jews" (4:22), refers to Jews who believe in Jesus (8:31), and leaves no doubt that Jesus and the disciples were all Jews. Nevertheless, John presents a sharper polemic between Jesus and the Jewish authorities than do the other Gospels. At times, John's Jesus separates himself from Judaism. He refers to "your law" (8:17, 10:34), tells the Jewish authorities that Satan is their father (8:44), and uses his own suffering as an example of the persecution the disciples will face (15:18–20).[70] The Gospel of John claims that "the Jews" engineered the process that ended in Jesus' crucifixion, describing the Jewish authorities as pleading with and then threatening a reluctant Pilate, who finally agrees to have Jesus crucified.[71] Whatever the intentions of its author, the Gospel of John supplies ample raw material for later anti-Jewish feeling.

JOHN'S THEOLOGY

The Gospel of John begins with a theologically dense and philosophically potent prologue (1:1–18). It asserts that the *logos,* or "Word" of God was present with God in the beginning, was the force that created the universe, and was God. The *logos* then became flesh and revealed the glory, grace, and truth of God. This becoming flesh is called the **incarnation**.

John's Gospel presents intricate theological concepts through the use of startling imagery, unexpected discourse, and a collection of word themes (among them "light," "life," "truth," "to be in," and

"to send"). In John, Jesus claims to be "the light of the world" (9:5), "the bread of life" (6:35), and "the way, the truth and the life" (14:6). John's Jesus not only works miracles, he is life and light and truth personified. He is the revealer of heaven: "If I have told you about earthly things and you do not believe, how can you believe if I tell you about heavenly things? No one has ascended into heaven except the one who descended from heaven, the Son of Man" (3:13–14). He is the very revelation of God: "Whoever has seen me has seen the Father" (14:9). Another feature of John's Gospel is its strong **dualism**. There are contrasts, for example, between light and dark (in 8:12 Jesus says, "I am the light of the world. Whoever follows me will never walk in darkness but will have the light of life"); and between above and below (in 3:31 Jesus says, "The one who is from above is above all; the one who is of the earth belongs to the earth").

The focus of John's Gospel is the author's understanding of the person and work of Jesus Christ. It is a measure of John's achievement and complexity that in later **Christological** controversies (debates concerning the person and work of Jesus Christ) this Gospel was the chief source of evidence for all parties. Theologians whose views were later condemned relied upon John as much as those whose views were later judged orthodox.

John's Gospel claims that Jesus was perfectly at one with the will of the Father, that Father and Son share purpose and mutual love, and that Jesus was the agent of God the Father, accomplishing the purpose of the Father on earth. John expresses this by having Jesus say, "The Father and I are one" (10:30), "the Father is greater than I" (14:28), and "The Father is in me and I am in the Father" (10:39). There is ample material here for controversy. Later Christians sometimes emphasized either the "human" side of Jesus ("the Father is greater than I") or the "divine" side ("I and the Father are one") at the expense of the other, and this propelled many of the theological controversies of the next few centuries. Modern scholarly opinion on this matter is similarly varied.[72]

The Gospel can be divided into three parts: the opening prologue (1:1–18); the "Book of Signs," named after several miracles or "signs" that Jesus performed (1:19–12); and the passion narrative (13–21).

The prologue begins with the assertion, "In the beginning was the *logos*" (1:1). As many scholars have noted, this is language that immediately calls to mind not only the opening words of the Hebrew Bible, but also one of the chief ideas of Greek philosophy. The Gospel continues to describe the *logos* as with God and as God, as the creative force responsible for the universe, and as having "become flesh" (1:14). At the very least it seems that the author wants to appeal to both a Jewish and an educated Gentile audience.

The use of vocabulary and imagery that recall Greek philosophy led earlier generations of scholars to argue that the intellectual home of John's Gospel was Greek philosophy, as so many of the thought forms seemed alien to Judaism.[73] Since the discovery of the Dead Sea Scrolls, however, scholars now argue that the intellectual home of John's Gospel is Palestinian Judaism, but that the author writes with an eye to a Greek audience.

In chapters 1–12 of John the focus is all on Jesus: What sort of person is this who claims special insight from God, who breaks the Sabbath in order to heal people of disease and physical affliction, who walks on water? The answer is that Jesus is the one who abides in the will of the Father (1:18, 5:19–20, 30). In chapters 1–12 only Jesus abides there, but the disciples are invited to watch and see what it looks like to abide in the will of the Father. Throughout the first eleven chapters of the Gospel, Jesus declares, "My hour has not yet come." But in 12:23–24 Jesus says, "The hour has come for the Son of Man to be glorified. Very truly I tell you, unless a grain of wheat falls into the earth and dies, it remains just a single grain; but if it dies it bears much fruit." In John's Gospel, *glorified* is a word that points to the crucifixion. The crucifixion of Jesus opens the way for others to live "in the will of the Father." It is left to chapters 13–21 to develop this point.

According to the last section of John's Gospel, Jesus' death and resurrection (his "glorification") will usher in a new era in which all believers can experience the clarity of vision that union with the Spirit imparts. John includes a short speech by Jesus concerning the coming of the Spirit: "You will know him, because he abides with you, and will be in you" (John 14:17). That is, the same Spirit they know to abide in and with Jesus will come to be in them. Jesus goes on to say that God the Father and the Son will come and "make our home" (literally "abide") with believers (14:23).

John's Gospel offers a vision of sharing the love relationship and unity of purpose that marked the relationship of God and Jesus. Like Paul, John presents God as acting to bridge the gap between himself and human beings. John's unique vocabulary and style contrast with Paul's, but the message of mystical union is remarkably similar.

Summary

Beginning in the turbulent environment of the obscure Roman province of Judea, Christianity developed from a sectarian expression of Judaism to become a separate faith and to establish itself in many parts of the Roman Empire. The inspiration for Christianity was the life and teachings of a Jewish peasant named Jesus. This prophet-like figure was baptized by John the Baptist and then embarked on a career of teaching and performing miracles. He offered a different view of God's Reign than was current, and he also appears to have believed that he had a central role to play in the coming of this Kingdom. Like John, Jesus challenged the temple system. He also appears to have attracted great crowds, and this may have caused the Romans alarm. He was executed by the Romans on the charge of sedition. His followers came to believe that he had been raised from the dead.

Besides Jesus himself, two figures who contributed to the New Testament greatly influenced Christian thought and practice. The first was Paul, a Jewish contemporary of Jesus who preached the gospel throughout the eastern Mediterranean region and founded churches there. His letters to these churches reveal his conviction that God had acted in Christ for the salvation of all of sinful humanity—Jews and Gentiles alike. The second was the author of the Gospel of John, who believed that Jesus Christ was a revelation of God on earth and made use of Greek philosophical thought and language in communicating his message. Combined with the teaching of Jesus, the works of these two early Christian writers formed much of the foundation on which Christianity would develop during the twenty centuries that separate their time from our own.

QUESTIONS FOR REVIEW AND REFLECTION

1. What do we know about Jesus, and how do we know it?

2. How do John the Baptist and Jesus relate to the larger picture of Jewish life and thought in the first century?

3. It is sometimes claimed that Paul fundamentally altered the message of Jesus. What is the evidence for and against this assertion?

4. How Jewish was the message and ministry of Jesus? How Jewish is the thought of Paul and of John?

NOTES

1. Josephus, *Antiquities* 14.72.
2. Josephus, *Antiquities* 14.105.
3. Josephus, *Antiquities* 14.120.
4. Josephus, *Antiquities* 14.275.
5. Josephus, *Antiquities* 14.272.
6. Josephus, *Antiquities* 17.289, 295.
7. Josephus, *Antiquities* 20.97.
8. Josephus, *Antiquities* 20.170. Although captured, "the Egyptian" escaped. When Paul was arrested in Jerusalem, some suspected that he was "the Egyptian." See Acts 21:38.
9. See Martin Goodman, *The Roman World: 44 BC–AD 180* (London and New York: Routledge, 1997), 258.
10. For a discussion of the date of Jesus' birth, see John P. Meier, *A Marginal Jew: Rethinking the Historical Jesus*, vol. 1 (New York: Doubleday, 1991), 205–230.
11. Josephus was an unwilling general for the rebellion during the Jewish war of 66–70 CE, and after he was captured by the Romans he collaborated with his captors. He also wrote extensively of the war, of Palestine as he knew it, and concerning the history of the Jews. See David P. Nystrom, "Josephus," *Dictionary of the Later New Testament and its Developments* (Downers Grove, Ill.: InterVarsity Press, 1997), 599–600.
12. Josephus, *Antiquities* 18.60–62.
13. Josephus, *Jewish War* 2.169–174, *Antiquities* 18.55–59.
14. Josephus, *Antiquities* 18.55–59.
15. Josephus, *Antiquities* 18.118.
16. See, for example, Hosea 6:6: "I desire steadfast love and not sacrifice." Or Jeremiah 7:4–7: "Do not trust in these deceptive words: 'This is the temple of the Lord, the temple of the Lord, the temple of the Lord.' For if you truly amend your ways and your doings . . . if you do not oppress the alien, the orphan, and the widow . . . then I will dwell with you in this place, in the land that I gave of old to your ancestors for ever and ever."
17. This was one of the seminal contributions of E. P. Sanders's book *Paul and Palestinian Judaism* (Philadelphia: Fortress Press, 1977).
18. See Samuel Sandmel, *Judaism and Christian Beginnings* (New York: Oxford University Press, 1978), 231.
19. Morna Hooker, *The Gospel According to Saint Mark* (London: Black, 1991), 39, writes, "No real parallel to John's baptism has been discovered in contemporary Jewish practice." Hooker claims that John's was a proselyte (convert) baptism offered by John to Jews. Josephus (*Antiquities* 18.116–117) did not, apparently, understand John as practicing a proselyte baptism.
20. Bruce M. Metzger, *The New Testament: Its Background, Growth and Content* (Nashville: Abingdon, 1987), 110, argues for this understanding of John's baptism.
21. The eminent American papyrologist and ancient historian C. B. Welles once compared the problem of the historical Jesus to the historical Alexander, to the effect that these are the two most difficult cases in ancient history. "In both cases the evidence is a generation or two later than the events in question . . . and in both cases the evidence is contradictory and tendentious. One's difficulty is to know what to believe." See his review of F. Schachermeyr's *Alexander der Grosse, Ingenium und Macht*, in *American Journal of Archaeology*, 55 (1951): 433–36.
22. The portrait of Jesus that emerges from the Jesus Seminar (a group of scholars researching the historical Jesus) is not much more detailed than this. See Robert W. Funk and the Jesus Seminar, *The Acts of Jesus* (San Francisco: HarperSanFrancisco, 1998), 527.
23. Early Christianity produced an astonishing number of documents that have survived. A very few were judged by later church councils to be important enough to be considered scripture, and these constitute the New Testament. But this decision-making process took place more than two hundred years after the events described in the New Testament. During that time expressions of Christian faith became more varied. Excluded from the list of New Testament books were some (like 1 and 2 Clement) that the Church considered worthwhile and orthodox. There were other documents the Church considered heretical, but the teachings and faith expressed in them were embraced by some of the early Christians,

and they are a part of the story of the early Christian movement.

To the best of our knowledge Jesus himself left no written documents. Those we do have represent what early Christians believed he said and did. For most of the years between the first century and today, people have assumed that the New Testament documents could be trusted. In the last two centuries, however, scholars have begun to question the historical accuracy of the New Testament. In his 1934 book *Jesus,* which was published in English as *Jesus and the Word,* trans. L. P. Smith and E. H. Lantero (New York: Scribner's, 1958), Rudolf Bultmann wrote, "I now believe that we can know almost nothing concerning the life and personality of Jesus" (p. 8). Bultmann's point was that the New Testament and especially the Gospels are religious literature and are, therefore, biased. Because this is true, reasoned Bultmann, we cannot simply assume that they accurately represent what Jesus actually said and did.

24. The story of the early church is broader and more varied than the account we have in the New Testament. For instance, Acts tells us about Paul's missionary journeys, but not too much about the missionary activity of others whom it does mention (Apollos, Philip), let alone those it does not. Within the New Testament there is ample evidence of contrary views held by early Christians, even of violent theological disputes. In Galatians, Paul is incensed that some Christians from the church in Jerusalem had traveled to Galatia and taught the Christians in Galatia a "different gospel" than he had preached (Galatians 1:6). This angered Paul enough to write, "if anyone proclaims to you a gospel contrary to what you received, let that one be accursed!" (Galatians 1:9). Paul may have wanted them cursed, but the ones preaching this different gospel were nonetheless a part of the early Christian movement.

The "orthodox" position was fashioned largely on the foundation of Paul and John. That there were other estimates of the life and death of Jesus within early Christianity is a certainty. Of course, it is the New Testament material that came most to influence later history. What is called "orthodoxy" is just one tradition, marked by internal variations, that the later church endorsed.

25. In Greek the word for "lord" could refer to an authority figure or it could be used as a sign of respect. In Jewish and Christian literature, however, it is also used to refer to God.

26. See Richard A. Burridge, *What Are the Gospels? A Comparison with Graeco-Roman Biography* (Cambridge: Cambridge University Press, 1992). But see also Willem S. Vorster, "Gospels, Genre of," *The Anchor Bible Dictionary,* ed. David Noel Freedman, vol. 2 (New York: Doubleday, 1992), 1079, who concludes that the Gospels are largely ancient biography but still a distinct genre.

27. See Martin Hengel, *Judaism and Hellenism: Studies in Their Encounter in Palestine during the Early Hellenistic Period,* trans. John Bowden (Philadelphia: Fortress, 1974), 58–65.

28. Dating the Gospels is notoriously dangerous. In an effort to point out the infirm foundation upon which many of the claims for dating the New Testament rest, J. A. T. Robinson in his *Redating the New Testament* (Philadelphia: Westminster Press, 1977) argued that every book in the New Testament could be dated before 70 CE.

29. The question of and explanation for the similarities among the Synoptic Gospels are called "the synoptic problem." Most scholars agree with the solution worked out first by Holtzmann in 1863 and refined by B. H. Streeter in 1924. According to this theory, Mark is the earliest of the gospels and served as a blueprint for both Matthew and Luke. But there is material that Matthew and Luke share that is not found in Mark. This, scholars say, came from a hypothetical source that has been lost. Scholars call this source "Q," probably from the German word *Quelle,* which means "source." Scholars believe that "Q" was a written collection of the sayings of Jesus and not simply an oral collection, primarily because Matthew and Luke generally relate "Q" material in the same order. Material that is unique to Matthew scholars call "M," and material that is unique to Luke scholars call "L."

30. Josephus, *Antiquities* 20.200. Josephus mentions Jesus once more, this time calling Jesus "the Messiah" (Josephus, *Antiquities* 18.6364). Virtually all regard this last passage as an alteration of the original text by later Christian copyists.

31. Pliny, *Letters* 10.96.

32. See A. Lintott, "Roman Historians," in *The Roman World,* ed. John Boardman, Jasper Griffin, and Oswyn Murray (Oxford and New York: Oxford University Press, 1988), 236.

33. Tacitus, *Annals* 15.44.

34. Paul Allen Mirecki, "Thomas, The Infancy Gospel of," *The Anchor Bible Dictionary,* ed. David Noel Freedman, vol. 6 (New York: Doubleday, 1992), 540.

35. The Infancy Gospel of Thomas 4.1. See *The Apocryphal New Testament,* trans. M. R. James (Oxford: Clarendon Press, 1924).

36. John Dominic Crossan, *The Cross That Spoke: The Origins of the Passion Narrative* (San Francisco: Harper & Row, 1988).

37. Crossan, *The Historical Jesus.* Here Crossan reconstructs a hypothetical version of the second-century Secret Gospel of Mark and claims that along with his reconstructed "Cross Gospel" he has isolated two sources that predate the canonical Gospels. Crossan's arguments concerning these hypothetical reconstructions have been challenged, with several scholars demonstrating that both are based on the canonical Gospels and not the

other way around (Joel B. Green, "The Gospel of Peter: Source for a Pre-Canonical Passion Narrative?" *Zeitschrift für die neutestamentliche Wissenschaft* (1987), 293–301).

38. Bentley Layton, *The Gnostic Scriptures* (Garden City, N.J.: Doubleday, 1987), 376–79.

39. The arguments for and against are summarized by John P. Meier, *A Marginal Jew: Rethinking the Historical Jesus*, vol. 1 (New York: Doubleday, 1991), 128–39. For example, Thomas sometimes agrees with Matthean and Lukan editing of the material. See C. A. Evans, "Jesus in the Agrapha and Apocryphal Gospels," *Studying the Historical Jesus: Evaluations of the State of Current Research*, ed. B. Chilton and C. A. Evans (Leiden: E. J. Brill, 1994), 479–533.

40. G. B. Caird and L. D. Hurst, *New Testament Theology* (Oxford: Clarendon Press, 1994), 367.

41. James Barr has shown that, contrary to popular belief, "Abba" did not mean "Daddy." See his article "'Abba' Isn't 'Daddy,'" *Journal of Theological Studies* 39 (1988): 28–47.

42. Among a host of scholars are Marcus Borg, E. P. Sanders, John Dominic Crossan, and N. T. Wright.

43. Albert Schweitzer, *The Quest of the Historical Jesus* (London: Black, 1954).

44. This Dodd did first in his *The Parables of the Kingdom* (London: Nisbet, 1941). In this work Dodd did not fully recognize the importance of the future sayings of Jesus. He later corrected this oversight.

45. For example, in Luke 7:28 Jesus declares that John the Baptist was the greatest of the prophets, but "the least in the kingdom of God is greater than he." Jesus' parables of the Kingdom presuppose that the Kingdom could be entered even while Jesus was alive.

46. Marcus J. Borg, "An Orthodoxy Reconsidered: The 'End-of-the-World Jesus'," in *The Glory of Christ in the New Testament: Studies in Christology in Memory of George Bradford Caird*, ed. L. D. Hurst and N. T. Wright (Oxford: Clarendon Press, 1987), pointed (pp. 207–17) out that the scholarly "orthodoxy" of an "end of the world Jesus" is based almost wholly on a group of texts that involve Jesus' sayings concerning "the Son of Man," whether he meant himself or someone else. Yet many of the same scholars who argue for an "end of the world Jesus" also, noted Borg, claim that these "Son of Man" sayings were never uttered by Jesus. In short, the evidence scholars use to support the "end of the world" Jesus is the very evidence that scholars say is untrustworthy. G. B. Caird in *The Language and Imagery of the Bible* (London: Duckworth, 1980) pointed out that the Biblical writers often used "end of the world" imagery to describe events that they well knew were not the end, but that were of sufficient gravity to prefigure the end they believed would come one day. This means that an accurate interpretation of what the Gospels intend by placing apocalyptic language on the lips of Jesus is difficult to decipher.

47. The two letters to the Thessalonians in the New Testament demonstrate this.

48. The Gospels present Jesus questioning the temple in other ways. In John's Gospel, Jesus refers to his body as the temple (John 2:19), and in Mark's Gospel we read that at his trial witnesses against him said, "We heard him say, 'I will destroy this temple that is made with hands, and in three days I will build another, not made with hands'" (Mark 14:58). According to both Mark and John, whatever else Jesus intended by the obscure reference to himself as the temple, it is clear he wished to put forward his teaching as an alternative way to understand Israel.

49. The significance of the temple in this regard has been noted especially by N. T. Wright, *Jesus and the Victory of God* (Minneapolis: Fortress Press, 1996). Marcus Borg has declared that he has come to see the temple system even more central to Jesus' aims. Marcus J. Borg, *Conflict, Holiness and Politics in the Teaching of Jesus*, 2nd ed. (Harrisburg, Pa: Trinity Press International, 1998), 10.

50. Yet the phrase meets the most common standard for determining the authenticity of the sayings of Jesus: It is extremely rare in early Christian literature, so there seems no reason for the Church to invent Jesus' use of it; and the phrase had no clear meaning in contemporary Judaism except "human being." An older perspective saw the phrase as an apocalyptic title within first-century Judaism, but in the last several decades a flood of scholarship has overturned this view. The current appraisal is that in first-century Judaism the phrase meant "a person" or "this person"; or perhaps it functioned as an oblique self-reference. See George W. E. Nickelsburg, "Son of Man," *The Anchor Bible Dictionary*, vol. 6, ed. David Noel Freedman (New York: Doubleday, 1992), 137–50, and I. H. Marshall, "Son of Man," *The Dictionary of Jesus and the Gospels*, ed. Joel B. Green, Scot McKnight, I. Howard Marshall (Downer's Grove, Ill: InterVarsity Press, 1992), 775–81. For an opposing view, see Bart Ehrman, *The New Testament: A Historical Introduction to the Early Christian Writings* Oxford: Oxford University Press, 1997. 225–28.

51. C. F. D. Moule noted that the use of the definite article here is striking. See C. F. D. Moule, *The Origin of Christology* (Cambridge: Cambridge University Press, 1977), 11–22.

52. C. H. Dodd pointed this out years ago in his slender volume *According to the Scriptures* (London: Nisbet, 1952). He noted that Paul's message already presupposes this reading, and that Paul claimed to have received this teaching. Dodd concluded that someone before Paul came up with this idea, and that that person must have been Jesus.

53. One of the seminal works in this area is Marcus J. Borg, *Conflict, Holiness and Politics in the Teaching of Jesus* (London: Mellen, 1984). The updated second edition was published by Trinity Press International in 1998. Borg argued that the heart of Jesus' teaching was the compassion of God, and that this teaching was meant to overturn political and social forces of oppression. For a more recent treatment of Jesus as a social revolutionary who sought to overturn lines of social stratification, see Crossan, *The Historical Jesus.*

54. See the insightful treatment by Gerd Theissen, *The Sociology of Early Palestinian Christianity,* trans. John Bowden (Philadelphia: Fortress Press, 1978).

55. See Samuel Sandmel, *Anti-Semitism in the New Testament* (Philadelphia: Fortress Press, 1978).

56. N. A. Dahl, *The Crucified Messiah and Other Essays* (Minneapolis: Augsburg, 1974) pointed out that the early church would not wish to invent a title so clearly ethnic in orientation, and further it is not a charge that any Jew collaborating with the Romans for the demise of Jesus would have invented.

57. See Daniel Boyarin, *A Radical Jew: Paul and the Politics of Identity* (Berkeley: University of California Press, 1994). Recent decades have seen a growing interest in Paul on the part of Jewish scholars. Boyarin's book, which sees Galatians and Paul's experience of transformation and freedom as key, is just one example. Another is Alan Segal, *Paul the Convert: The Apostolate and Apostasy of Saul the Pharisee* (New Haven: Yale University Press, 1990). Segal points out that Paul provides important information concerning first-century Jewish mystical traditions.

58. Acts records several speeches by Paul defending his actions, and in 26:10 he relates his career persecuting Christians: "I also cast my vote against them when they were being condemned to death." This statement has caused scholars to speculate that Paul was a member of the Sanhedrin, as there does not appear to be any other forum in which Paul would have "cast" such a vote.

59. C. H. Dodd, "The Mind of Paul I," in *New Testament Studies* (Manchester: The University Press, 1953), 77.

60. This view is tempered by the household codes reflecting social stratification, but these are present in letters that are considered "deutero-Pauline," that is, letters that Paul did not write. See P. H. Towner, "Household Codes," *The Dictionary of the Later New Testament and Its Developments,* ed. Ralph P. Martin and Peter H. Davids (Downer's Grove, Ill.: InterVarsity Press, 1997), 513–20.

61. On this matter see Ben Witherington III, "Women (NT)," *The Anchor Bible Dictionary,* vol. 6, ed. David Noel Freedman (New York: Doubleday, 1992), 957–61.

62. See Gerd Theissen, *The Social Setting of Pauline Christianity: Essays on Corinth,* ed. and trans. John H. Schütz (Philadelphia: Fortress Press, 1982).

63. See Donald Engels, *Roman Corinth: An Alternative Model for the Classical City* (Chicago and London: University of Chicago Press, 1990).

64. This radical social ethic is not unique to Paul. The New Testament Book of James (2:1–4) contains a similar warning against showing favoritism to the wealthy.

65. C. H. Dodd in *The Interpretation of the Fourth Gospel* (Cambridge: Cambridge University Press, 1953), writes (p. 6), "There is no book, either in the New Testament or outside of it, which is really like the Fourth Gospel." E. Hirsch in *Das vierte Evangelium in seirner ursprünglichen Gestalt verdeutscht und erklärt* (Tübingen: Mohr, 1936), writes that John is the book that has most firmly "sealed itself against superficiality" (p. 145). Ernst Käsemann, one of the most accomplished scholars of the twentieth century, wrote about John's gospel: "Much of what he says is quite understandable and frequently we are deeply moved by it. But his voice retains a strange otherworldly quality" and that when writing on John "I must begin . . . with the unusual confession that I shall be discussing a subject which, in the last analysis, I do not understand." See Ernst Käsemann, *The Testament of Jesus,* trans. Gerhard Krodel (London: SCM Press Ltd., 1968), 1–2.

66. Eusebius, *History of the Church,* 6.14.7.

67. Käsemann, *The Testament of Jesus,* 78.

68. This view is supported by the fact that there are obvious gaps in the narrative; for example, between chapters 14 and 15.

69. See John A. T. Robinson, who against the stream of scholarly opinion argued that John's Gospel is the work of a single author who worked on the material for a lifetime, and then died before the final editing could be completed. See his *The Priority of John* (London: SCM Press Ltd. 1985). His argument has been described as brilliant but unconvincing.

70. See Claudia Setzer, *Jewish Responses to Early Christians: History and Polemics 30–150 CE* (Minneapolis: Fortress, 1994), 83.

71. See Frederiksen, *From Jesus to Christ,* 119.

72. Ernst Käsemann, in his *Testament of Jesus,* argues that John's Jesus is a thoroughly docetic figure, "Jesus as God walking on the face of the earth" (75). Marianne Meye-Thompson in her *The Humanity of Jesus in the Fourth Gospel* (Philadelphia: Fortress Press, 1988) emphasizes the various ways John's Gospel portrays Jesus as human.

73. The most significant example is Dodd, *Interpretation of the Fourth Gospel.*

CHAPTER 3

Christianity in the Roman World

Overview

The Roman Empire was at the height of its power when Christianity first appeared in one of its most distant provinces. Rome's gradual decline, leading to a final collapse in 476, occurred during the same centuries that saw the rise of the new religion.

Relations between Christians and Rome were generally troubled, due to persistent suspicions that Christians were disloyal to the state, its rulers, and its gods. As a result, there were sporadic persecutions. In addition, rumor and misunderstanding of Christian practices encouraged agitation against Christians at the popular level. Christians responded in two important ways: Martyrs rejected the state by giving their lives for the sake of the faith and their own salvation, and **apologists** produced literary defenses of Christianity. Some apologists underscored the differences between Christian and pagan beliefs and values. Others sought to minimize them by emphasizing points of agreement.

Because many Christians capitulated in the face of persecution, questions about the nature and function of the Church arose during this time. Should it be a society of saints or sinners? Should those guilty of serious sin, even apostasy, be excluded in order to maintain high standards of faith and morals, or should the Church be open to every-

one in order to make salvation available to those who were most in need?

Finally, although the legalization of Christianity early in the fourth century encouraged most Christians to participate fully and comfortably in society, there were some whose ardent faith led them to withdraw from society altogether. These were the founders of the monastic movement, which established itself as an important feature of Christian culture in both the East and the West by the end of antiquity.

Zenith and Decline of the Empire

The growth of Christianity in its first five centuries was influenced by the government of Rome and conditions in the Roman Empire, which provided the setting for its early development. Official persecutions, for example, forced Christians underground, discouraging growth in their numbers but encouraging thought about the nature of the Church and its place in the world. Social, political, and economic conditions helped determine the extent to which Christians and their religion were accepted by their neighbors. Various features of the Roman political and administrative systems were adopted by the Church. Because of this interrelationship, it is important that we briefly survey the history of Rome in the imperial period (31 BCE–476 CE).

In chapter 1 we noted the rise to power of Augustus, Rome's first emperor (31 BCE–14 CE), who brought an end to a century of bloody civil war and inaugurated an era of stability and prosperity known as the *pax Romana*. During the two centuries of "Roman peace" that followed, Rome's armies guarded the empire's far-flung frontiers against envious outsiders while Roman citizens and soldiers introduced their way of life throughout the Mediterranean world. From Britain in the far West to Mesopotamia in the distant East and from the Danube to the African Sahara, the elements of Roman civilization were so firmly established that many became permanent features of western civilization. Municipal governments were modeled on that of Rome itself; legal disputes were adjudicated in Roman courts and in accordance with Roman law; Roman roads connected the capital city with every corner of the empire; and everywhere its inhabitants acknowledged Rome's authority by paying taxes and obeying its laws. Additionally, the order and affluence afforded by Roman rule encouraged a flowering of art, architecture, literature, and science. Few who lived during this apogee of Roman power and cultural achievement would have denied the magnificence of what Rome had achieved; and to some, at least, it must have seemed that the empire would endure forever.

Yet the forces that would bring its collapse half a millennium later were already being set in motion. Incompetent rulers, inadequate resources, inflation, the strain of ruling a highly diverse population within Rome's borders, and the difficulty of defending the empire against hostile peoples beyond them — these and other factors contributed to a progressive decay that brought an end to the *pax Romana* by the third century and the fall of the western half of the empire at the end of the fifth.

THE FIRST CENTURY

The Roman historian Tacitus discerned the beginnings of this process as early as the reign of Augustus — who, as Tacitus put it, "won over the entire population with the sweetness of peace."[1] Indeed,

Augustus's skill in exploiting the gratitude of the senate and people of Rome for his restoration of peace gave him unprecedented power that signaled the end of government by citizens and its replacement by the rule of emperors. The senate, assemblies, and other republican institutions continued to function, but they had little power, for Rome's emperors came to rely on the support of the army rather than on the people. Under men of integrity and ability the new imperial system worked well, but in the hands of lesser rulers absolute power proved to be dangerous and destructive.

This was the case in Augustus's own Julio-Claudian dynasty, which produced two emperors, Caligula (37–41) and Nero (54–68), whose gross immorality, cruelty, and megalomania threatened stability in government and ultimately brought them down. As we will see, Nero was also the first emperor to persecute Christians. In a year of political chaos following Nero's forced suicide in 68, four men followed him on the throne — a sure sign that Rome lacked the means for ensuring orderly succession. Finally Vespasian, a general who had been besieging Jerusalem, secured the support of the East, left his command to his son Titus, and marched on Rome. Making himself emperor (69–79), he restored order and founded the Flavian dynasty. Its two other members, Titus (79–81) and his brother Domitian (81–96), also showed a talent for administration. But Domitian was arrogant and vindictive. He proclaimed himself *dominus et deus* ("lord and god"), executed his political enemies, and was so hated by the senate that it formally condemned his memory after his assassination in 96. By this time the problems associated with autocracy were becoming painfully evident, but after more than a century it had become too well established to be undone. There would be no return to the days of the republic.

THE "FIVE GOOD EMPERORS"

Happily, Domitian was succeeded by a series of competent and enlightened rulers who have come to be known as the "Five Good Emperors": Nerva (96–98), Trajan (98–117), Hadrian (117–38), Antoninus Pius (138–61), and Marcus Aurelius (161–80), whose *Meditations* qualifies him as one of the great Roman Stoic philosophers. Setting the interests of good government above the temptation to found imperial dynasties, all but Marcus Aurelius looked outside their own families for qualified successors and designated them as heirs by adopting them as sons. This wise practice contributed to making the second century the greatest period in Rome's history. So did the high ideals of these emperors, who minted coins proclaiming their aims of justice, security, and well-being for all inhabitants of the empire. These rulers generally disapproved of Christianity, which they regarded as a disruptive superstition, though none made a serious attempt to eradicate it. On the whole, their policies suggest imperial uncertainty about how to deal with Christians. Trajan ordered that the government should not seek them out but insisted that they be punished if identified in court. Although Hadrian attempted to protect the rights of Christians in court and to discourage informers, his reign saw more than a few martyrdoms. Marcus Aurelius took no official actions against Christians but allowed violent local persecutions. The most likely explanation for this inconsistency is that Christianity was not yet important enough to demand the full attention of the Roman government. In any case, it is clear that the Five Good Emperors had other issues to deal with and that they handled them well. Their rule brought good government, widespread prosperity, internal peace, and impressive cultural achievements.

But in the reign of Marcus Aurelius there were clear signs of troubles to come in the next century. Soldiers returning from Mesopotamia brought with them a devastating and persistent plague that seriously damaged the social and economic health of the empire. Wars against northern tribes, inadequate troops, poor harvests, and economic failure all marred the reign of the last of the Five Good Emperors, who was reportedly forced to auction off his palace furnishings to raise cash. The situation was further complicated by his designation of his son Commodus as his co-emperor and successor in 177. Three years later Marcus Aurelius fell victim to the plague while fighting along the lonely Danube frontier.

Commodus (180–92), whose name ironically suggests an amiable and obliging nature, turned out to be a monster. Unfit for the demands of imperial office and psychologically troubled, he committed Rome to unfavorable treaties with its northern neighbors, massacred his opposition in the senate, drained the treasury, and devoted his energies to self-indulgence. Having proclaimed that he was both Hercules and the greatest of gladiators, he was poisoned and strangled to death on the day before he was to make his first appearance in the arena.

THE CRISIS OF THE THIRD CENTURY

Remarkably, the government continued to function despite Commodus's excesses, thanks primarily to a highly developed and efficient imperial bureaucracy. But threats to the security of the empire continued to grow. Germanic tribes exerted greater and greater pressure along the Rhine and Danube, Rome's northern frontiers. The East was similarly threatened, in this case by an aggressive Sasanid dynasty in Persia. Devaluation of the currency, a strategy initially employed to meet the financial demands of the army, had led to a staggering rate of inflation that was ruining the middle class, and disruptions in trade and agricultural production made life difficult for all segments of the population. As conditions worsened, the decline of Rome was hastened by thousands who abandoned its gods in favor of new religions, many of them from the East, which promised greater security. Even more dangerous was the growing power of the army, without whose support it was no longer possible to govern. Nearly all of the emperors of the third century were generals whose reliance on the support of the legions meant that Rome's government was, in effect, a military dictatorship.

The first of these were the rulers of the Severan dynasty (193–235). Its founder, a North African general named Septimius Severus (193–211), ruled much like an oriental potentate and lost the loyalty of many citizens by confiscating private property and levying new taxes on urban centers. His immediate successors — Caracalla, Geta, and Macrinus — lacked even his minimal abilities as an administrator. The last two Severan emperors were too young and inexperienced to command either respect or loyalty. The dynasty died with Severus Alexander (222–35), a teenage ruler whose mother was the real power in Rome during much of his reign. Ignoring the enfeebled imperial government, the army and the provinces now began to go their own ways. The result was chaos.

Between 235 and 285, imperial authority nearly vanished. Rebellions, civil wars, and assassinations were so common that it is difficult to trace the political history of this half-century, though by most accounts at least twenty commanders were recognized as emperor only to be murdered shortly thereafter — some by their own troops. These "barracks emperors" were the product of a disintegration of government ranging from the highest levels to the lowest ranks of provincial administrations. In view of its many other difficulties — impending economic collapse, unstable borders, civil revolts, and a decline in population at a time when additional manpower was needed to save the state — Rome's situation was clearly desperate. Swift and effective action was necessary to save the empire.

DIOCLETIAN AND CONSTANTINE

It came in the reforms of Diocletian (285–304), a soldier-emperor whose tough administrative policies led to a thorough reorganization of the government. As we will see later in this chapter, he was also a ruthless persecutor of Christians. Recognizing that the empire was too large to be ruled by a single individual and that it lacked a means for ensuring peaceful succession, he devised a government of four, or "tetrarchy." Under this system the empire was divided into western and eastern halves, each ruled by an Augustus. To assist him, each of the Augusti appointed a junior emperor or Caesar who would succeed to the office of Augustus on the death or retirement of his senior partner. Diocletian intended that an Augustus and his Caesar would divide their administrative responsibilities. Thus, the West was partitioned into Italy-Africa-Spain and Gaul-England and the East into Asia and the Balkans. These four regions were further divided into units called **dioceses** controlled by lesser officials. Both the division of the empire into eastern and

western halves and the diocese, which the Church would adopt as an administrative unit headed by a bishop, contributed to the shaping of Christianity in the following centuries.

Diocletian's reforms, which included giving the central government greater control over the economy, worked well for as long as he remained in power. But the tetrarchy began to fail soon after his retirement in 305. Bitter rivalries among the tetrarchs broke out into violence that rocked the empire until one of the tetrarchs, Constantine, finally overcame his colleagues and managed to make himself sole emperor in 324. His success, which he attributed to the favor of the Christian God, would have immeasurable consequences for the future of the western world.

According to Eusebius (ca. 260–ca. 340), a bishop of Caesarea whose *Church History* covers Christianity's first three centuries, the emperor's attraction to Christianity began with a vision he had on the eve of an important battle against his rival Maxentius in the year 312. A cross appeared above the sun and on it the words, *By this conquer.* Lactantius, another early Christian writer, adds that Constantine had a dream in which Christ commanded him to draw the Chi Rho (☧), a monogram consisting of the first two letters of the word *Christ* in Greek, on the shields of his soldiers in order to gain a victory. His success in the Battle of the Milvian Bridge outside Rome the following day convinced Constantine that he had found favor in the eyes of the God of the Christians. The following year, he and his colleague Licinius jointly issued the Edict of Milan, which ended the persecution of Christians by declaring freedom of religion. It was a first step toward making Christianity the official religion of the empire.

Gradually, Constantine withdrew his support from traditional cults and began to favor Christianity by extending special privileges and imperial patronage to its hierarchy and their churches. In addition to exempting ecclesiastical property from taxation, the emperor embarked on an ambitious program of church-building throughout the empire. Impressive churches were constructed in Italy, North Africa, Gaul, and Syria, many of them provided with lavish endowments. With his mother,

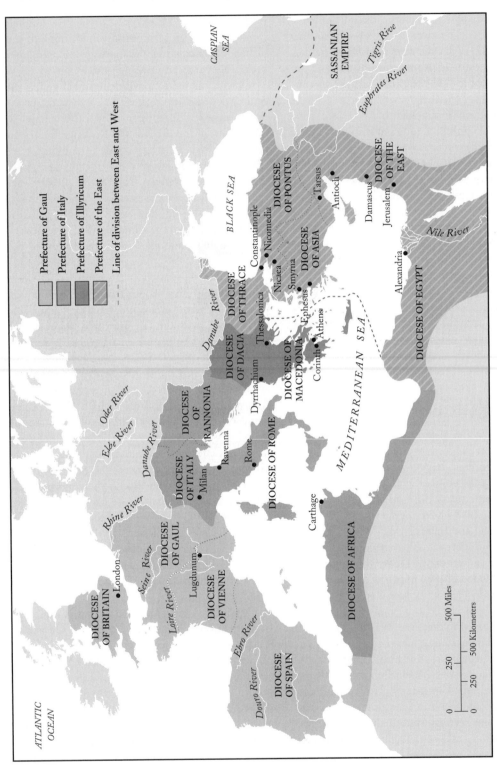

Figure 3.1 The Roman empire in the fourth century This map shows the administrative dioceses into which Diocletian divided the empire.

Helena, he also built churches in the holy places of Palestine, such as the Church of the Holy Nativity in Bethlehem and the Church of the Holy Sepulcher near Jerusalem. Some of Constantine's efforts to promote the Church tended to bring it under state control. By giving bishops judicial authority within their dioceses and employing them as political aides and advisors, for example, he made them responsible to the state as well as to the Church. In addition, Constantine saw himself as a bishop at large who had the right, which he freely exercised, to express his opinions on theological matters and even to preside over "other" bishops. He is famous for having done both at the Council of Nicaea (325), which produced the Nicene Creed, an early statement of Christian belief. By conferring civil authority on church leaders and assuming ecclesiastical authority for himself, the emperor ensured that he had authority over the Church as well as the state.

One of the most important of Constantine's reforms was his dedication of a new capital in 330. This was Constantinople (modern Istanbul) on the Bosporus, a *Nova Roma* ("new Rome") he envisioned as the Christian capital of a Christian empire. The move made good sense strategically, for the city of Rome in western Italy was far removed from the urban centers and cultural activity of the eastern Mediterranean. But by shifting power eastward the creation of the new capital contributed to the decline and ultimate fall of the western half of the empire and, as we shall see, heightened tensions between western (Latin) and eastern (Greek) Christianity.

Was Constantine sincere in his profession of the Christian faith, or did he merely exploit it, hoping that by encouraging the growth of a common religion he might bring unity to the Roman world? Unfortunately, we cannot be certain of his personal convictions. Cynics point out that he continued to worship the Invincible Sun until his rivals had been eliminated, that he presided over pagan rites as high priest of the Roman state religion (*pontifex maximus*), and that he delayed his **baptism** until just before his death. Those who believe that his faith was genuine point out that a sudden break with paganism would have been extremely risky at a time when

Figure 3.2   The Tetrarchs This sculpture, now found on the corner of the Church of St. Mark in Venice, portrays Diocletian and his fellow Tetrarchs. Dressed for battle and clinging to each other in a display of solidarity, they seem aware of the dangers facing the Roman Empire.

most of the population was not Christian. Under the circumstances, they say, Constantine's policy of detaching himself and the empire slowly from the pagan past was much more sensible. As for deathbed baptism, it was a strategy sometimes employed by those who feared they might jeopardize their salvation by committing serious sins after receiving the **sacrament** and so does not necessarily argue for Constantine's insincerity. There is no question, however, that Constantine understood

Figure 3.3 Constantine These pieces of sculpture are among the few that survive of a great statue of Constantine. Almost forty feet in height, Constantine had the image placed in the Roman Forum.

the potential of Christianity as a unifying force and sought to use it as such.

THE END OF THE EMPIRE

Roman order and culture continued to deteriorate following Constantine's death in 337. For a brief period in the middle of the fourth century, the emperor Julian ("the Apostate"; 361–63), who despised Christians and Christianity, sought to restore Rome's fortunes by returning to its traditional religion, but his effort was cut short by his premature death. Meanwhile, the number of Christians continued to grow.

With the accession of Theodosius I ("the Great"; 379–95) the triumph of Christianity was made certain. Content at first merely to discourage paganism, in 391 Theodosius issued a law that forbade it in any form. He was no less opposed to forms of Christianity he considered unorthodox. In 380 he declared that the true faith was that based on the Nicene Creed and taught by the bishop of Rome. A year later he ordered the surrender of all churches to bishops who supported the Nicene Creed and arranged for the condemnation of Arianism, Nicene Christianity's most serious competitor, at the Council of Constantinople (381). The effect of these measures was to make Nicene Christianity the official and only legitimate religion in the Roman Empire. In addition, by asserting his right to appoint and depose bishops and to make theological judgments on the distinction between orthodoxy and **heresy**, Theodosius brought the Church even more completely under his control than had Constantine. In the East, the domination of the Church by the state would continue for a millennium. Only in the West, where imperial authority was fading, would ecclesiastical rulers exercise a measure of independence.

Though successful in his dealings with the Church, Theodosius could not prevent the further degeneration of the empire. By this time it had become impossible to defend its frontiers. To ease the pressure, a group of Visigoths had been allowed to migrate into the empire. But they had revolted, dealing the emperor Valens a crushing defeat at the Battle of Adrianople in 378, a year before the beginning of Theodosius's reign, and then moving freely and destructively throughout the Balkans. Unable to defeat them, Theodosius had no choice but to buy peace by granting them lands on which to settle, an arrangement that clearly illustrates Rome's weakness. His death in 395 made a bad situation worse. By bequeathing the western and eastern halves of the empire to his sons Honorius (393–423) and Arcadius (393–408) respectively, he brought about its formal division into two separate realms.

The eastern portion of the empire would become the Byzantine Empire (from **Byzantium**, the original name of the site of Constantinople) and would survive into the fifteenth century. The empire in the West was not as fortunate. Unable to resist any longer the advance of Germanic and other tribes, it was overrun by Angles, Saxons, Jutes, Burgundians, Lombards, Franks, Alemanni, and other peoples who established themselves on whatever lands they were able to seize and defend. With the emperor in Constantinople too weak to offer protection, Rome itself was left vulnerable. The city was sacked by the Visigoths in 410 and by the Vandals in 455.

In 472 a Pannonian general named Orestes captured the city and made his young son emperor under the name Romulus Augustulus. This "little Augustus" was deposed in 476 by Odoacer, a Germanic chieftain who chose not to take the title of emperor. The event had little immediate impact on the Romans themselves, but historians have argued that, in light of the loss of its territory and imperial office, it makes little sense to speak of an empire ruled by Rome after 476. The West had fallen.

The Growth of the Church

As we turn now to examine the growth of Christianity in its early centuries, we must ask several important questions. Why did Christianity prove so attractive to converts? What were the specific complaints of its critics? What were the reasons behind the persecutions of Christians sponsored by the Roman state and what form did these take? Finally, what impact did persecution have on Christian thought regarding the nature of the Church and its place in the world?

CONVERTS AND CONVERSION

At the end of the second century, Tertullian, a Christian writer from North Africa, wrote:

> We are but of yesterday, and we have filled every place among you — cities, islands, fortresses, towns, marketplaces, the very camp, tribes, companies, palace, senate, forum — we have left nothing to you but the temples of your gods.[2]

His claim may have been an exaggeration, but Tertullian was correct in noting that Christianity was indeed spreading rapidly throughout the Roman world. How can we account for its appeal and consequent expansion? The promotion of the new religion by emperors beginning with Constantine certainly had much to do with its ultimate success, but this came late. How can we explain the growth of Christianity even in its first three centuries, when it met with both competition from other religions and persecution by the Roman state? There are several important factors to consider.

First, Christianity recognized and responded to basic human needs. To the oppressed it offered the encouraging reminder that Christ, too, had suffered. To those burdened by guilt it gave assurances of divine forgiveness. To those who despaired of a world in which nothing endured it preached the existence of an eternal and unchanging realm of the spirit. To those who feared death it promised eternal life.

Second, many features of Christian teaching were similar to those already popularized by other religions and philosophies. From Judaism, for example, Christianity inherited monotheism and a high ethical standard, both of which were highly respected even among non-Jews. Like Platonism, it taught both a cosmological dualism (reality is divided into material and spiritual dimensions) and anthropological dualism (human beings are constituted of both physical and spiritual components). And, just as the Stoic philosophers preached a doctrine of universal brotherhood, Christianity proclaimed the equality of all men and women before God.

Third, Christianity, which began as a Jewish sect in western Asia, quickly adapted to Greco-Roman culture. Greek and then Latin became its primary languages. Christian theologians explained its teachings and worked out doctrinal difficulties with reference to concepts from Greek philosophy and Roman law. When Christian art began to emerge in the fourth century it introduced new themes but generally conformed to the norms of Greek and Roman art.

Fourth, like other successful religions of the time, Christianity offered visible signs and symbols

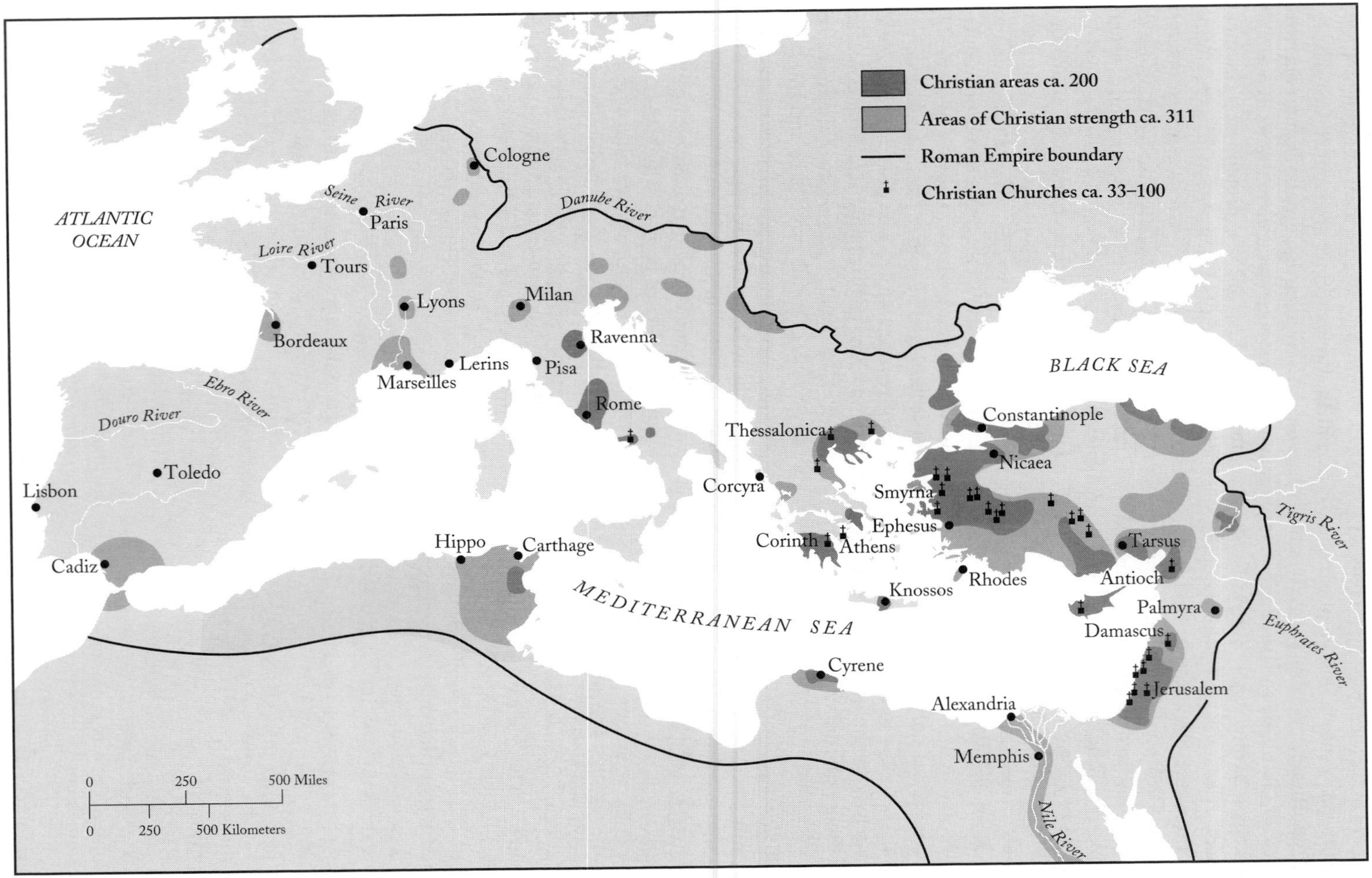

Christian areas ca. 200
Areas of Christian strength ca. 311
Roman Empire boundary
Christian Churches ca. 33–100
ATLANTIC OCEAN
BLACK SEA
MEDITERRANEAN SEA
Seine River
Loire River
Danube River
Ebro River
Douro River
Tigris River
Euphrates River
Nile River
Cologne
Paris
Tours
Lyons
Milan
Bordeaux
Ravenna
Lerins
Pisa
Marseilles
Rome
Toledo
Lisbon
Cadiz
Hippo
Carthage
Thessalonica
Corcyra
Corinth
Athens
Constantinople
Nicaea
Smyrna
Ephesus
Knossos
Rhodes
Tarsus
Antioch
Palmyra
Damascus
Jerusalem
Cyrene
Alexandria
Memphis
0
250
500 Miles
0
250
500 Kilometers

Figure 3.4 Growth of Christianity to the early fourth century By 311, Christianity had established itself in regions throughout the Roman Empire, with particular strength in the East.

of the truths it taught. Immersion in the waters of baptism, for example, was an effective way of representing the inner cleansing of the believer's sins. Similarly, celebrations of the **eucharist** were a vivid reminder that the spiritual communion of Christians with Christ was as intimate as the fellowship Christ shared with his disciples at the **Last Supper**.

Fifth, the hierarchical structure of authority in the early Church enabled bishops to supervise priests, who in turn oversaw **deacons** and the laity. This organizational system encouraged effective leadership, communication between the **clergy** and the laity, and uniformity of belief and practice.

Finally, in recent years social scientists have shown that the social and private habits of the early Christians might help explain the increase in their numbers. For example, Christian avoidance of birth control and abortion, both of which were widely practiced by non-Christians, was probably an important factor, as was the tendency of Christian women to bring their unbaptized husbands and children into the Church.[3] New converts were also attracted by Christian charity, so much so that the emperor Julian urged pagans to compete with Christians, who had "devoted themselves to philanthropy" and who supported "not only their own poor, but ours as well."[4] Social-scientific methods of investigation and analysis have offered other insights into the rise of Christianity and are likely to improve our understanding of it in coming years.

Although these are only a few of the reasons for the success of Christianity, their variety suggests the complexity of a phenomenon that had psychological, philosophical, social, and even aesthetic aspects as well as religious ones. An equally important question concerns the identity of converts. What kind of people were they? Where did they live? To what social classes did they belong?

Some of our earliest reports on the social identities of Christians come from their opponents, who tended to describe them in unflattering terms. In his scathing *True Doctrine,* **Celsus**, a particularly harsh second-century critic, claimed that Christians deliberately discouraged intelligent people from joining their ranks and sought out instead "the foolish, dishonorable and stupid, and only slaves, women and little children."[5] To many anti-Christian writers like Celsus, Christianity was a religion for the ignorant, the disenfranchised, and the poor.

Until recently, most historians assumed that early Christianity was, in fact, a lower-class phenomenon. In the 1930s, for example, a well-known scholar characterized the majority of early Christians as "the servants and slaves of society."[6] But in the last third of the twentieth century a reassessment of the evidence brought a change in scholarly opinion. This new outlook takes into account factors such as New Testament references to wealthy and influential Christians and the obvious sophistication of Christian intellectuals in the second and later centuries. Today, most scholars believe that the constituency of early Christianity represented a cross-section of the general population.[7]

Having asked why people converted to Christianity and who these converts were, we have only to consider the extent of conversion. Where did Christianity take root? How many inhabitants of the empire embraced the new faith? Our literary and archaeological sources suggest that Christianity began as an urban phenomenon and moved gradually into the countryside. This may well have been the case, though it is important to remember that ancient literature tends to reflect urban situations and that the smaller populations in rural areas would have been less likely to build large and lasting monuments to the presence of Christians there. In any case, by the end of the first century there were churches in forty to fifty cities in the Roman Empire — nearly all of them in Syria, Asia Minor, Greece, Macedonia, North Africa, and Italy — and perhaps fifty thousand Christians. The second century saw a proliferation of churches in these same areas. The progress of Christianity in the third century was especially impressive as the Church became a powerful force in central North Africa and the labors of missionaries began to bear fruit in Spain, Gaul, and Germany. By the middle of the fourth century, Christians were beginning to claim that they constituted a majority in the empire. Despite the impressive number involved — more than thirty million Christians out of a total population of roughly sixty million — some scholars believe that such an assertion made fifty to a hundred years later would not have been far off the mark.[8] It is likely that 60 percent of the population was Christian by the end of antiquity at the close of the fifth century.

PERSECUTION

The transition to Christianity did not occur without reaction from the Roman government and traditional pagan culture. For the most part, Christians led ordinary lives much like those of other citizens. Except for their religious beliefs and avoidance of pagan religious rites, there seemed to be little that set them apart from their neighbors. Yet, from the beginning Christians attracted suspicion and hostility that led to nearly three centuries of intermittent persecution.

There was no shortage of charges made against them by their antagonists. In some cases their religious practices were misrepresented or misunderstood to the point of making them appear criminal. References to the body and blood of Christ in the eucharist, for example, resulted in accusations of cannibalism. Some critics claimed that celebrations of the eucharist were actually orgies in religious disguise. A more extreme allegation was ritual murder. The third-century Christian writer Minucius Felix recorded the charge that Christians beat babies to death, drank their blood, and then engaged in drunkenness and copulation "in random unions."[9] More common were complaints of Christian superstition and aggressive proselytizing. It is not difficult to imagine how rumors and suspicions could combine with social and economic tensions to produce hostility and, in extreme situations, mob actions against Christians.

From the point of view of the Roman state, the primary difficulties presented by Christians were their obstinacy and apparent disloyalty. We can see the former issue illustrated in the correspondence of the emperor Trajan and Pliny the Younger, his legate to Bithynia (111–13) in what is now northern Turkey. Unsure of how to handle proceedings against persons accused of being Christians, Pliny asked if he was acting reasonably in executing those who refused the three opportunities he gave them to deny the charge (obstinacy in judicial proceedings being a punishable offense under Roman law).

Trajan assured him that he was. A little more than half a century later, Marcus Aurelius pointed to what he saw as the same unreasonable stubbornness among Christian martyrs, arguing in his *Meditations*[10] that it is a good thing to be willing to die, though not, like the Christians, out of mere obstinacy.

The much more serious question of Christian disloyalty to Rome can be traced to the New Testament itself. Paul, for example, had urged Christians to obey civil authorities, but he had also stated unambiguously that "our citizenship is in heaven" (Philippians 3:20). The issue here is dual citizenship. As citizens of a worldly kingdom *and* a spiritual one, to whom did Christians owe their highest loyalty: to Caesar or Christ? Some observers wondered if the devotion of Christians to their God and Church implied a lack of concern for the welfare of the state and their fellow citizens. According to one critic disturbed by their failure to participate in public activities, Christians had "no understanding of civic responsibility."[11] This complaint was based on the idea, central to classical culture, that every citizen had a duty to uphold society by taking part in its affairs. The person who remained aloof was a burden at best and, at worst, an enemy.

It is no wonder, then, that Christian disinterest in military service, festivals, public banquets, dramatic presentations, athletic contests, and the like led to the view that Christians were subversive and dangerous. Their unwillingness to join other citizens in sacrificing to the gods of Rome and to the *genius* or "guardian spirit" of the emperor was particularly disturbing and at times led to charges of atheism. The point of such accusations was not that Christians did not believe in a deity, but that they did not believe in and serve the gods who were most deserving of worship—the traditional gods of Rome, who had for centuries guided the Roman people and made their empire great. When asked why they refused to participate in rites that others regarded as little more than patriotic recognition of the state's gods, Christians explained that they could acknowledge no god but their own. Their critics were not satisfied. "This is the language of sedition," said Celsus, "and is only used by those

Figure 3.5   Nero As emperor (54–68), Nero made scapegoats of the city's Christians when he blamed them for a fire that burned much of downtown Rome. According to the Roman historian Tacitus, many were burned to death as punishment.

Figure 3.6   This excavated chamber beneath the Vatican is thought by some to be the tomb of St. Peter. Ancient tradition says that Peter died as a martyr in Rome after serving as leader of the church there.

who separate themselves and stand aloof from all human society."[12] Rome agreed, and argued that it persecuted Christians for the sake of preserving the empire.

The first known persecution occurred in 64 when the emperor Nero, widely suspected of ordering a fire that destroyed entire districts of Rome, defended himself by blaming the city's Christians instead. According to Tacitus, the Roman Christians were already "a class despised for their abominable crimes."[13] Tacitus does not specify what these crimes were, though he suggests that the arrest, conviction, and "exquisite tortures" inflicted on Nero's victims had more to do with popular disapproval of their "hatred of humanity" than with the charge of arson. He tells us that some Christians were covered with the skins of wild beasts and torn to pieces by dogs. Others were crucified. Still others were burned alive, illuminating the nighttime spectacle of their own deaths as the emperor, dressed as a charioteer, chatted with onlookers. Although the Neronian persecution lasted only until the end of Nero's reign and appears to have been limited to Rome itself, it foreshadowed troubles to come. According to ancient tradition, both Peter and Paul died as martyrs in Rome during this period.

Christians encountered no further serious difficulties until the reign of Domitian. Eusebius says that the emperor executed great numbers of Christians without trial and banished others. He adds that it was under Domitian that John, said to be the author of the Book of Revelation, was exiled to the island of Patmos where he received his apocalyptic visions and wrote of Christian suffering in the cities of Asia Minor.[14]

Persecution intensified in the second century. To judge by the correspondence of Trajan and Pliny, by this time it was a punishable offense merely to be a Christian. Thus, second-century actions against Christians were seen as legitimate and necessary measures taken against criminal enemies of the state. Though frequent, most were short-lived and localized. The most significant took place under Marcus Aurelius and Septimius Severus. The second century also saw repeated instances of mob violence against Christians. In Greece and Asia, Christans were held responsible for natural disasters that occurred under Antoninus Pius, and there was a mass persecution in Vienne and Lyons in Gaul in 177.

Anti-Christian sentiments also began to appear in literature at this time. The satirist Lucian of Samosata (fl. 165) targeted Christians as well as adherents of other religions and schools of philosophy. His *The Passing of Peregrinus* describes the life of a convert to Christianity who subsequently becomes a Cynic philosopher and then arranges for his own death by burning in Athens. For Lucian, such characters — decent, but ignorant and easily duped — were the sort of people who were attracted to Christianity. A much more severe critic was Celsus (fl. 178), some of whose comments we have already noted. His sole work, *True Doctrine,* has survived only in quotations and paraphrases found in *Against Celsus* by Origen, a Christian theologian of the third century. Celsus attacked the Jewish background of Christianity, Jesus, the early leaders of the Church, and Christian beliefs and practices in a comprehensive polemic whose tone is one of unmistakable contempt. The fact that Origen felt compelled to respond to *True Doctrine* half a century after its publication indicates how seriously Celsus's arguments were taken.

Persecution of Christians eased in the first half of the third century, but this respite came to an abrupt end in the short reign of Decius (249–51). Convinced that Rome must return to the traditions of the past, in 250 Decius issued an edict requiring all citizens of the empire to demonstrate their loyalty to Rome's gods by sacrificing to them. It is not likely that this measure was meant to target only Christians, but its practical effect was to force upon them a choice between martyrdom and apostasy. Many chose the former. Others offered sacrifice and received *libelli,* certificates that verified their compliance. Still others found a way between martyrdom and capitulation by purchasing forged *libelli.* All, no doubt, experienced something of the terror and confusion described in Eusebius's account of the edict's impact in Alexandria:

> Terror was universal, and of many public figures some at once came forward through fear, others who were in state employment were induced by professional reasons, others were dragged forward by the mob. Summoned by name, they approached the unclean, unholy sacrifices. Some came white-faced and trembling, as if they were not going to sacrifice but to be sacrificed themselves as victims to the idols, so that the large crowd of spectators heaped scorn upon them and it was obvious that they were utter cowards, afraid to die and afraid to sacrifice. Others ran more readily towards the altars, trying to prove by their fearlessness that they had never been Christians.[15]

Persecution abated during the three decades following the reign of Decius. These were the worst years of the crisis of the third century, a time when there was little consistency in Roman government, including its policies toward Christians. But the situation changed suddenly under Diocletian, who inaugurated the Great Persecution after completing his reorganization of Rome's government. After expelling Christians from the army (ca. 295) and ordering all palace and military personnel to sacrifice to the gods of Rome, Diocletian mounted an all-out assault on Christianity with a series of four increasingly severe edicts beginning in February 303. This was no haphazard action; the emperor had given careful consideration to his objectives and the steps necessary to attain them. His purpose was not to kill Christians, for there were too many by this time to make eradicating them a possibility. Instead, he hoped to destroy their religion. Accordingly, he ordered the burning of churches and books of scripture, the removal of Christians from public office, the forfeiture of their honors and special privileges, and an end to the practice of purchasing the freedom of Christian slaves.

In some regions the Christian response was dramatic. On two occasions Diocletian's palace in Nicomedia in northwestern Asia Minor was set on fire. There was also a rebellion in Syria. In turn, the emperor called for the imprisonment of all higher clergy. Galerius, Diocletian's Caesar, further intensified the persecution in 304 by requiring all people to sacrifice to Rome's gods or suffer death or forced labor as punishment. This demand, which seems inconsistent with Diocletian's original intention of avoiding the creation of martyrs, resulted in large-scale arrests and executions.

Both the cruelty of the persecutors and the fortitude, even enthusiasm, of the martyrs were recorded by early Christian writers. Eusebius, who was an eyewitness, offers this account of the cruelties suffered by Egyptian Christians during the Great Persecution:

> Words cannot describe the outrageous agonies endured by the martyrs in the Thebais. They were torn to bits from head to foot with potsherds like claws till death released them. Women were tied by one foot and hoisted high in the air, head downwards, their bodies completely naked without a morsel of clothing, presenting thus the most shameful, brutal and inhuman of all spectacles to everyone watching. Others again were tied to trees and stumps and died horribly; for with the aid of machinery they drew together the very stoutest boughs, fastened one of the martyr's legs to each, and then let the boughs fly back to their normal position; thus they managed to tear apart the limbs of their victims in a moment. In this way they carried on, not for a few days or weeks, but year after year. . . .
>
> I was in these places, and saw many of the executions for myself. Some of the victims suffered death by beheading, others punishment by fire. So many were killed on a single day that the axe, blunted and worn out by the slaughter, was broken in pieces, while the exhausted executioners had to be periodically relieved. All the time I observed a most wonderful eagerness and a truly divine power and enthusiasm in those who had put their trust in the Christ of God. No sooner had

the first batch been sentenced, than others from every side would jump on the platform in front of the judge and proclaim themselves Christians. They paid no heed to torture in all its terrifying forms, but undaunted spoke boldly of their devotion to the God of the universe and with joy, laughter and gaiety received the final sentence of death; they sang and sent up hymns of thanksgiving to the God of the universe till their very last breath.[16]

The Great Persecution continued until Galerius, who had succeeded Diocletian as Augustus in the East, issued an Edict of Toleration in 311. This decree did not win the full support of the tetrarchs (Maximin Daia, ruler of Egypt and Syria, continued his persecution) and, unlike Constantine's Edict of Milan (313), it offered no restitution to Christians for damages done to them. Still, it did allow them to practice their religion and rebuild their churches. The text of the Edict leaves no doubt that the primary complaint against the Christians had been their abandonment of the religious traditions of their ancestors. Its issuance was an acknowledgment that their numbers, organization, and determination to resist their persecutors had put the future of their religion beyond the power of the Roman state.

MARTYRS AND MARTYRDOM

Inevitably, the persecution of Christians produced heroes whose courage inspired others to resist Rome's efforts to extirpate their religion. Chief among them were the **martyrs** ("witnesses"), who testified to their devotion to Christ by giving up their lives rather than deny him. There were also **confessors** who boldly proclaimed their faith before the Roman authorities and somehow survived.

In an age when faith was tested by terror, it was natural for Christians to venerate such men and women and to treasure the stories of their heroism. Many have come down to us in the various *Acts of the Martyrs*, which focus on their trials and the judgments leading to their execution, and *Martyrdoms*, which describe their last days and the details surrounding their deaths. We also have numerous legends of the martyrs as well as accounts of their deaths in the works of writers such as Eusebius and Lactantius. These stories did more than simply inspire the faithful. Recent scholarship has shown that they also underscored the differences between the Christianity of the martyrs, which regarded their suffering as a noble imitation of Christ's passion, and that of other Christian groups. The gnostic Christians we will describe in chapter 4, for example, held that Christ had not been truly human and therefore had not suffered on the cross. To them, the suffering of the martyrs was foolishness and a waste of human life.[17]

Among the earliest martyrs was Ignatius of Antioch. The elderly bishop of that city, he was arrested and taken to Rome (ca. 107) to stand trial. On the way, Ignatius wrote seven letters of encouragement and instruction to the churches at Ephesus, Magnesia, Tralles, Rome, Philadelphia, and Smyrna as well as a personal letter to Polycarp, the bishop of Smyrna. These tell us a great deal about his thoughts on his impending martyrdom. We have no record of how Ignatius actually met his death, but his letters reveal that he looked forward to it. Fearing that the Christians in Rome might attempt to save him, he urged them not to intervene and told them of his hope that he would prove himself to be "the pure bread of Christ" while being "ground by the teeth of the wild beasts."[18] Believing that his suffering would make him a true disciple of Christ, who had also suffered, Ignatius expected his death to bring him into unity with God and to promote unity in the Church.[19]

We have a more detailed account of the martyrdom of Polycarp, the bishop of Smyrna, thanks to the *Martyrdom of Polycarp*. Written by members of his church shortly after his death in the middle of the second century, it is the oldest of the *Martyrdoms*. The text relates how Polycarp was arrested by Roman soldiers and brought to the amphitheater in Smyrna. The spectators, who had already witnessed eleven executions of Christians that day, shouted that they would not be satisfied until they had seen Polycarp die as well. When the presiding official told the bishop that he could go free if he would only curse Christ, Polycarp replied, "For eighty-six years I have been his servant, and he has never done me wrong. How can I blaspheme my king who

saved me?"[20] Outraged by his seeming insolence, and no doubt convinced that death was a reasonable punishment for persons guilty of subversion, the crowd demanded that Polycarp be burned alive. A fire was prepared, but the flames miraculously refused to touch him. Instead of the expected odor of burning flesh, there was "a wonderful fragrance, like a breath of frankincense or some other costly spice." Death did not come until the impatient authorities ordered a *confector,* whose job was to dispatch victims who were slow to expire, to kill Polycarp with his sword. He did so, but such a great quantity of blood flowed from the wound that the fire was quenched. According to the *Martyrdom,* these miraculous signs of divine favor made a powerful impression on the pagans who witnessed them. Most had earlier reviled the saintly bishop, but now the crowd was "astonished at the difference between the unbelievers and the elect."

The stories of lesser-known martyrs are no less spectacular. Potamiaena, a young woman from Alexandria, was covered, drop by drop, with boiling pitch. Attalus, a leader of the church in Lyons, was roasted to death when he was made to sit on an iron chair heated to the point that it glowed red. Blandina, a slave girl from the same city, was subjected to a variety of tortures and then bound up in a bag and thrown into the arena, where a bull gored her to death. Others suffered hours of agony as fire was applied to the soles of their feet or bits of flesh were cut from their bodies and fed to hungry dogs. Again and again, we are told how the martyrs accepted death with quiet dignity, grateful to Christ for strengthening them and believing that in their suffering they had already entered into his presence. Even when condemned to death, said Tertullian, the Christians gave thanks.[21]

According to ancient Christian writers, the courage of the martyrs had a powerful effect on nonbelievers. There were, of course, convinced pagans who regarded them scornfully as prime examples of Christian obstinacy and irrationality. Yet early Christian literature includes numerous stories of individuals, some of them spectators and even executioners, who were inspired by the example of the martyrs. "The blood of the martyrs," said Tertullian, "is seed." What some saw as obstinacy, he continued, was actually a heroic resolve that led others to conversion and even to the glory of their own martyrdom:

> That very obstinacy which you rebuke is the teacher. For who is not stirred by the contemplation of it to inquire what is really beneath the surface? And who, when he has inquired, does not approach us? Who, when he has approached, does not desire to suffer so that he may procure the full grace of God? [22]

Among the Christians themselves, the example of the martyrs inspired an ethic and even an incipient theology of martyrdom. Those faced with the possibility of arrest and execution were encouraged to remain faithful by works such as Cyprian's *To Fortunatus,* Tertullian's *To the Martyrs,* and Origen's *Exhortation to Martyrdom.* But Christians were urged not to seek out martyrdom, for there was a growing sense that it was a kind of special grace or gift conferred by God—and only on a chosen few. The suffering of the martyrs came to be thought of as an imitation of, and even a participation in, the suffering of Christ, who was believed to be with them as they died. United with him in this way, and filled with the Holy Spirit, they were somehow raised above the level of ordinary human existence in the final moments of their lives and at death were said to be taken immediately into heaven and the presence of God rather than having to await the general resurrection. This belief in the union of the martyr with Christ and the Holy Spirit was no mere sentiment but a conviction that had practical consequences for the life of the Church. As we will see, considerable confusion was caused by the view that even martyrs-to-be and confessors were sufficiently spirit-filled to have the power to forgive sins and reconcile penitents to the Church—an authority otherwise limited to clergy.

Alongside the beginnings of a theology of martyrdom there also developed a cult of the martyrs, "cult" meaning here a reverential "tending" of the memory of the martyr. This practice became a highly visible feature of public life once the persecution of Christianity came to an end in the beginning of the fourth century. The tombs of the martyrs had long been considered sacred places where the faithful would go to pray, but now impressive memorial buildings known as *martyria* were built over them. Believing that martyrs would have special power at the time of the resurrection, many Christians sought to be buried near these holy places. Others made pilgrimages to them and left inscriptions asking for intercession, a practice that seemed reasonable in light of the martyrs' union with Christ in heaven and ancient beliefs concerning the communication of the living with the dead. And, just as the Greeks and Romans honored deceased family members by holding annual banquets on their birthdays, Christians feasted in the *martyria* on the spiritual birthdays of the martyrs—the anniversaries of their deaths. Originally these banquets had a thoroughly religious character and included prayer vigils, readings from scripture, hymns, and a panegyric, or eulogy, on the martyr. In time, however, they lost much of their solemnity and took on the character of more ordinary public festivals.

An especially interesting aspect of the cult of the martyrs was the veneration of their **relics.** Most of these were bodily remains, usually bones, thought to be suffused with the holiness of the martyr. This meant that they possessed the power to bring physical and spiritual benefits to those who approached and regarded them prayerfully. Relics were thought to be especially effective in combating the power of demons and effecting healings. In some regions enthusiasm for the veneration of martyrs and their relics reached such a pitch that it became necessary to caution the faithful against idolatry. It was not until early in the eighth century, however, that the Byzantine monk and theologian **John of Damascus** finally articulated the classic distinction on this issue. It was appropriate to venerate holy men and women, he said, but only God is worthy of true worship.

As persecution subsided and the age of martyrs came to an end, popular piety was redirected toward men and women who sacrificed themselves in other ways for the sake of the faith. These included monks and nuns who withdrew from society in search of holiness and priests who remained in the world to work for the salvation of others. The self-denial of such individuals was seen as a kind of interior martyrdom, a "dying" to the world. The veneration of the most admired among them, along with the veneration of martyrs, would ultimately be transformed into the cult of saints, an important feature of medieval Christianity.

THE QUESTION OF THE LAPSED:
CYPRIAN, NOVATIAN, AND DONATUS

Not all Christians had the courage of the martyrs. Many apostasized, whether by cursing Christ, by sacrificing to the gods, or in some other fashion. The question of how to deal with lapsed Christians took on particular importance in the years following the widespread Decian persecution of 250–51, when many whose faith had proved weak sought forgiveness and reinstatement from their congregations. Tensions generated by the debate over their status ran especially high in North Africa, where the persecution had been severe and the Church insisted on a high standard of morality.

The issue did not allow for a simple solution. Many believed that apostasy was a sin for which there could be no forgiveness. For them, readmission to the Church was unthinkable. To those who were inclined to restore the lapsed to fellowship, it seemed reasonable that distinctions should be made among the offenders. Some, after all, had agreed to sacrifice only under torture. Were they to be judged as harshly as the *sacrificati,* who had willingly sacrificed, or the *libellatici,* whose resolve had never been tested because they had purchased forged *libelli?* And who would render judgment? As we have seen, confessors claimed the right to reconcile sinners to the Church by virtue of their demonstrated faithfulness and special status, but they were challenged by local bishops who claimed to have greater authority.

Few of the principals involved in this issue were more passionate than **Cyprian**, one of the most influential Christian thinkers in the West. A rhetorician who converted to Christianity in his mid-forties, he had risen quickly to become the bishop of Carthage (249–58). When the Decian persecution broke out, Cyprian fled the city but continued to direct the affairs of the Church through letters carried by emissaries. Upon his return, he was alarmed by the leniency shown by the confessors in pardoning those who had yielded to the Roman authorities. This was an issue of immense importance, for vast numbers of North African Christians had lapsed. Cyprian's opposition to the confessors and their "laxist" policies was based on his fears for the unity and moral purity of the Church. He argued that these were the responsibility of the bishops, who had inherited their authority from the **Apostles** themselves. Cyprian left little doubt as to his estimation of the importance of bishops. "The Church is the bishop," he wrote in one of his letters, "and the bishop is the Church."[23] This view was approved by Cyprian's fellow bishops at a council held at Carthage in 251. It was an important step in establishing the authority of the ecclesiastical hierarchy.

Though he remained adamant in defending the role of bishops, Cyprian eventually softened his position on the lapsed. In a move that was to have lasting significance for the Church, he agreed to a compromise that contributed to the development of a system of **penance** that gave sinners an opportunity to demonstrate their contrition and make reparation for sin in ways prescribed by their spiritual leaders. Once a penance had been satisfactorily completed, the penitent would be eligible for absolution, a formal remission of sin. Some justification for this practice could be found in scripture. Paul, for example, had implied that the Church had the authority to judge and even excommunicate sinners when he instructed the Christians of Corinth to expel a man found sleeping with his father's wife (1 Corinthians 5:1–5). In addition, the Gospel of Matthew (18:18) represents Jesus as conferring on the Church the right to make binding decisions concerning the status of sinners.

Until a generation or so before Cyprian there was no general agreement concerning the remission of serious sins committed after baptism. Many believed that forgiveness for such offenses was impossible because baptism, which was thought to wash away only sins committed before it was performed, could occur only once. They, too, quoted scripture; for example, Hebrews 6:4–6, according to which "it is impossible to restore again to repentance those who have once been enlightened, and have tasted the heavenly gift . . . and then have fallen away." In time, however, there was increasing acceptance of the idea that a single opportunity for secondary remission of sin might take place under certain circumstances. We first see this view in *The Shepherd of Hermas,* a text from the middle of the second century. It was later advocated by Tertullian and others who considered lesser or "venial" sins forgivable after contrite confession and prayer but demanded greater discipline for more serious offenses. According to Tertullian, this consisted of extended periods of fasting, wearing of mourning clothes, prayer, weeping, kneeling before members of the church, and asking for their prayers. These acts of contrition were preceded by a confession of sin before the whole church and followed by a rite of absolution, also public, in which the reconciliation of sinner and church was symbolized by the laying on of the hands of the bishop.

The compromise worked out for the North African churches by Cyprian and his fellow bishops allowed for the restoration of the *libellatici* to their congregations after they performed penances whose severity depended on individual circumstances. Forgiveness was extended even to the *sacrificati,* whose sin was far greater, though it was to be delayed until death was imminent. To many, this middle course between the demand of the moral rigorists that the lapsed be left outside the Church and the leniency of the confessors seemed an ideal solution to a difficult problem. The church in Rome, for example, based its own policy on the North African compromise. Still, there were troublesome repercussions in both Italy and Africa.

At their center was **Novatian**, a leader in the church at Rome whose theological works, and in particular his *On the Trinity,* had earned him the admiration even of his enemies. His position on the lapsed, however, posed a serious threat to the unity of the Church. During the Decian persecution, Novatian had been the leader of a rigorist faction that feared the Church would be made impure by readmitting apostates. When the moderate Cornelius became bishop of Rome, Novatian allowed himself to be made counterbishop and began installing rival bishops in other cities as well. He was eventually expelled from the church at Rome, thanks in part to the efforts of Cyprian, but not before Novatianist

churches had been established in many parts of the empire. Many survived him, persisting until the fifth century in Rome and even longer in Constantinople.

Although Rome and Carthage agreed on a more moderate policy on the lapsed than that advocated by Novatian, they came into conflict over the question of how to deal with former Novatianist Christians who sought admission to their own churches. Were Novatianist baptisms valid despite the fact that they had been performed by priests who were, in their view, outside the Church? Cyprian and other North African bishops maintained that they were not valid. By leaving the true Church, they said, Novatianist priests had, in effect, renounced God and become ritually impure. No longer having the Holy Spirit within themselves, they could not possibly convey the Spirit in baptism.[24] There was only one Church, Cyprian insisted, and "no salvation outside the Church." Thus, those who had received baptism outside the Church, even if the rite itself had been performed correctly, would have to be rebaptized. The church in Rome did not agree. Stephen, a successor of Cornelius as the city's bishop (254–57), maintained that it was the performance of the rite that mattered, not the moral character of the priest. Therefore, any baptism performed in the name of the **Trinity** was legitimate. In support of his position, he added what was one of the earliest claims of the primacy of the Roman bishop based on Matthew 16:18–19, where Jesus appears to designate Peter his successor as leader of the Church.[25] In essence, Stephen argued that other bishops and their churches should follow the example of the bishop of Rome, whose authority could be traced back to Peter. Stephen died before the conflict was resolved, but the African churches eventually adopted the Roman position on both the matter of Novatianist baptism and the primacy of the bishop of Rome.

Half a century after the furor over the lapsed first erupted it broke out again. As before, the scene was North Africa, where the Great Persecution launched by Diocletian early in the fourth century had been centered. Trouble began in 311 when rigorist elements in the church at Carthage refused to recognize a certain Caecilian as their new bishop because his consecration that same year had been performed by a bishop who had been accused of capitulating during the persecution. Claiming that Caecilian's consecration was invalid, the rigorist party chose a counterbishop. He was succeeded in 316 by Donatus, who gave his name to what has come to be known as the Donatist controversy. During the next three decades, Donatus led African Christians in building a new church in which there was no room for clergy who had committed serious sins.

Boasting 270 bishops at one point, the Donatist churches threatened to eclipse the influence of the Roman church in Africa. The reasons for its success were ethnic and cultural as well as theological. On the one hand, the Donatists saw themselves as members of the true Church, zealously defending the ideal of a morally pure society of God's elect. At the same time, they also expressed popular resentment of Rome and the Latin immigrants who represented Roman power on African soil. For its part, the Roman church saw Donatism as a dangerous threat to Christian unity. Rulings against Donatus's claims by the bishop of Rome, a synod of western bishops, and Constantine himself did nothing to discourage the Donatists. Neither did Donatus's arrest and exile to Gaul in 346 after radical followers known as Circumcellions attacked an imperial commission sent to investigate the situation. A generation later the great theologian **Augustine** of Hippo urged the Roman state to force the Donatists back into the Roman church for the sake of their salvation and in order to preserve public order. The Donatist churches survived, however, and continued to divide North African Christians for the next three centuries.

These conflicts illustrate some of the most important issues faced by Christians in late antiquity and point to later developments as well. One issue was the nature of the Church itself. Was it a society of saints whose holiness and moral purity set them apart from all others? If so, great care would have to be taken to ensure that its standards were high and that its members, and especially its leaders, lived up to them. Or was the Church a society of sinners who differed from those outside only in their devo-

tion to Christ? In this case a more relaxed attitude could be adopted; God's grace was sure to make its way to believers through the preaching of the gospel and the sacraments even though their priests and bishops might not be morally pure. The decisions to readmit lapsed Christians to the Church and to recognize the validity of baptisms performed by Novatianist priests argued for the latter view, which ultimately triumphed.

A second issue was the unity of the Church. Could there be more than one Church? Who was responsible for unity, however it might be conceived? Although he was not the first to do so, Cyprian argued forcefully that there can be only one Church and that its bishops are ultimately responsible for the unity of their congregations. Stephen's claim as bishop of Rome to primacy among his fellow bishops can be seen both as an attempt to unify the Church and as a step toward establishing the papacy as an institution destined to play an important role in western Christianity and culture.

Finally, the issue of how to deal with sinners without expelling or excluding them from the Church altogether was solved by a compromise that combined discipline with compassion. This was the system of penance, which was destined to become one of the most prominent features in western Christianity during the Middle Ages.

Early Christian Writers

In addition to the persecutors who threatened their lives, early Christians came under attack by others who challenged their beliefs and questioned their morals. We have already noted that the most powerful literary assault on Christianity was Celsus's *True Doctrine,* but Christians and Christianity were also criticized by some of the great names of antiquity, among them Galen, Lucian of Samosata, Epictetus, Porphyry, Apuleius, and Marcus Aurelius. For the most part, critics focused on apparent inconsistencies and embarrassing features of Christian belief and scripture. Why didn't the risen Christ put the fact of his resurrection beyond doubt by appearing to great crowds instead of to just a few disciples? How could Christians be foolish enough to believe that God, who is perfect, eternal, and unchanging spirit, was transformed into a mortal human being existing in the material world? If God is omnipotent, couldn't he have saved humanity by divine fiat rather than going to the trouble of coming to earth and suffering crucifixion? Why are there differences in the Gospels' accounts of the life of Jesus? To questions like these were added the charges of atheism, disloyalty, and immorality that lay behind the persecutions.

They were answered by the apologists, literary defenders of the Christian faith. Most apologies ("defenses") were written in the second and third centuries, though some came considerably later. The most famous, Augustine's *City of God,* belongs to the fifth. No less energetic than their opponents, the apologists went beyond merely refuting specific allegations. They also offered positive reasons for embracing Christianity, pointed to contradictions in the teachings of the philosophers, and ridiculed pagan religions for the crude **anthropomorphism** and immorality of their gods. Some of the apologists saw Christianity as largely incompatible with the values of traditional society and urged an outright rejection of Greco-Roman culture. Others understood their faith as the full realization of all that pagan culture had striven for, however imperfectly. They encouraged dialogue between believers, who had seen the truth fully revealed in Christ, and those who had only glimpsed it in the philosophy, poetry, drama, and mythology of the Greeks and Romans.

The earliest known apologist was Quadratus, a Christian from Asia Minor who wrote a defense of the faith to the emperor Hadrian sometime between 120 and 130. According to Eusebius, who possessed a copy of this "pamphlet," Quadratus argued for the truth of Christianity by pointing to the many people who had been healed or raised from the dead by Jesus. Aristides of Athens, Quadratus's contemporary, addressed his *Apology* to Hadrian as well, contending that the superior morality of Christians was proof that they worshiped the true God. Tatian, a second-century Christian from

Syria, wrote a *Discourse to the Greeks* that was apologetic in its reasoned defense of Christianity but polemical in its violent attack on the evils of Greek civilization. He also composed a *Diatessaron* that harmonized the four Gospel accounts of the life of Jesus in a single version meant to demonstrate their essential agreement. Athenagoras, who lived late in the second century, wrote a *Plea on Behalf of the Christians* to the emperor Marcus Aurelius in order to rebut charges of atheism, cannibalism, and incest. We can see in writers like these the beginnings of the effort to explain Christian beliefs and practices to a non-Christian world. Other writers continued the defense of the faith and, in doing so, gave it intellectual respectability and made important contributions to its developing theology. We will discuss four of them here: **Justin Martyr** and **Tertullian**, who rank among the most famous apologists, and **Clement** and **Origen**, two Alexandrian theologians who composed works that both defended and explained the faith.

JUSTIN MARTYR

Born in Palestine to pagan parents, Justin Martyr (ca. 100–ca. 165) studied Stoicism, Aristotelianism, Pythagoreanism, and Platonism before becoming a Christian. After his conversion he came to Rome, where he presided over a school of Christian philosophy and wrote two eloquent *Apologies* addressed to Antoninus Pius.[26] In these he appealed to the emperor for justice for Christians, whom he described as moral and socially responsible citizens. He also composed the *Dialogue with Trypho,* in which he explained that the fulfillment of Old Testament prophecies in Christ was a clear indication that the Church had displaced Israel as God's covenant people. According to the *Acts of Justin,* an account written some years after his death, the apologist's life was cut short when he was arrested during the reign of Marcus Aurelius. After cheerfully confessing his faith and refusing to sacrifice to the gods, he was beaten and then beheaded.

The essence of Justin's thought can be seen in his description of his conversion: A mysterious old man approached him and explained how God had spoken through Moses, the prophets, and, finally, Christ. "My spirit was immediately set on fire," he said. "While pondering on his words, I discovered that his was the only sure and useful philosophy. Thus it is that I am now a philosopher."[27]

For Justin, then, Christianity was the best of all philosophies. Accordingly, he represented himself as a philosopher in both his writings and his dress—he was in the habit of wearing the *pallium,* or cloak, of a philosopher—though he left no doubt that the controlling factor in his thought was not human reason, as it was for other philosophers, but the revelation of divine truth in the Bible. This, he said, is the source of all genuine wisdom, including that of the Greeks. In his *First Apology* he wrote, "Everything the philosophers and poets said in speaking about the immortality of the soul, or retribution after death, or speculation on celestial matters . . . they took from the Prophets."[28]

Justin was the first Christian writer to use Greek philosophical terminology in attempting to demonstrate the essential agreement of the Christian faith and Greek reason. The most striking example of this effort is his elaboration of the identification of Christ with the divine Logos found in the Gospel of John. We have already seen that *logos,* which means "word" in Greek, has the additional sense of "reason" or "divine reason" in philosophical contexts. Building on the Stoic teaching that human reasoning is a participation in the Logos and John's claim that the Logos, or "Word," became flesh in Christ, Justin concluded that Christ is present wherever and whenever people engage in rational thought. This was the case even before the incarnation. In the *First Apology* he wrote, "Those who lived by reason are Christians, even though they have been considered atheists."[29] Such reasoning allowed Justin to make the remarkable claim that Greek philosophers such as Socrates and Heraclitus had been "Christians before Christ."

Justin was not unaware of basic differences between Christianity and classical culture. He was sometimes critical of philosophy, which he regarded as inaccessible to most people, and he condemned mythology as the work of the same demons who had been behind the deaths of Socrates and Christ.

Despite this, some scholars argue that he oversimplified both philosophy and Christianity in his effort to demonstrate their agreement. Though such criticism may have merit, we cannot doubt Justin's importance for the history of Christianity. He represents the beginnings of Christian dialogue with pagan culture and what William Placher has aptly called "an alliance with philosophy"[30] that enabled Christian thinkers to proclaim their faith clearly and powerfully using the Greek language and the concepts and categories of Greek thought.

CLEMENT OF ALEXANDRIA

Another writer who defended Christianity by demonstrating its affinities with Greek thought was Clement of Alexandria (ca. 150–ca. 215). We know very little about his life. Thanks to the few autobiographical details he included in his writings, we can at least be certain that in his early years Clement traveled throughout the eastern Mediterranean searching for a complete understanding of the gospel. After studying in Italy and Palestine, he finally "found rest" in Alexandria with a teacher he does not name. Eusebius says his mentor was Pantaenus, a scholarly convert from Stoicism who was the master of a prestigious catechetical school in Alexandria. According to Eusebius, Clement regarded Pantaenus as one who had received and passed on the original teaching of the Apostles.[31] He eventually succeeded his teacher as head of his school, which attracted intellectually sophisticated converts interested in understanding Christianity in relation to Greek philosophy.

Clement produced three texts that are especially important for the study of early Christianity. The first is the *Protrepticus,* or *Exhortation to the Greeks,* an appeal to unbaptized persons to turn to the study of Christianity.[32] A second work, the *Paidagogus (Instructor),* seeks to instruct new Christians in the ethical principles underlying Christian life. Finally, the *Stromata,* or *Miscellanies,* presents Clement's thought on a variety of issues ranging from marriage to the life of Moses to the relation of Greek reason to Hebrew revelation. Although there is no unifying theme running through the *Stromata,*

Clement's discussion of the various issues raised there is considered by many to represent his most penetrating thought. Some believe he intended it for advanced Christians who had already passed through stages of instruction represented by his first two works.

Clement was highly cultured and thoroughly familiar with Greek literature; in his own works he quotes nearly five hundred other writers. Like Justin, he understood himself as a Christian philosopher whose aim was to demonstrate that Christianity was the true and final philosophy. Central to his thought is the Logos, through whom God expresses his love for humanity, educating them in higher truths in order to raise them to himself. For Clement, as for Justin, the Logos was the source of all true wisdom and the teacher, in one way or another, of all peoples everywhere. "Our instructor," he wrote, "is the holy God, Jesus, the Logos who is the guide of all humanity."[33] In the *Stromata* he speculates that, in the case of the Greeks, divine guidance was given through philosophy, a gift transmitted through the Logos to prepare them for the ultimate revelation of the truth in Christ. "For this [i.e., philosophy] was a schoolmaster [meant] to bring the Hellenic mind, as the Law the Hebrews, to Christ."[34] Despite its achievements, however, Clement left no doubt that philosophy had been superseded by Christianity:

> Wherefore, since the Word [Logos] Himself has come to us from heaven, we need not . . . go any more in search of human learning to Athens and the rest of Greece, and to Ionia. For if we have as our teacher Him that filled the universe with His holy energies in creation, salvation, beneficence, legislation, prophecy, teaching, we have the Teacher from whom all instruction comes; and the whole world, with Athens and Greece, has already become the domain of the Word. . . .
> We who have become the disciples of Christ have received the only true wisdom; and that which the chiefs of philosophy only guessed at, the disciples of Christ have both apprehended and proclaimed.[35]

According to Clement, the Logos refines and informs the souls of men and women. Through its loving influence they receive true education and come to understand more of the nature and will of God. As they do, they become more like Christ. Just as the Logos is the image and likeness of the Father, they are in the image of the Logos and have the potential to grow into its likeness if they are committed to spiritual advancement.

In formulating and presenting his own ideas, Clement made extensive use of other systems of thought, including Judaism, Stoicism, and Platonism. His belief that scripture must be interpreted allegorically, for example, he inherited from Stoicism and, perhaps, from Philo, the Alexandrian Jewish philosopher who had used this technique to demonstrate the fundamental agreement of the Hebrew Bible and Greek philosophy. Another interesting feature of Clement's thought is his use of feminine imagery. Speaking of the Logos, he said that Christians "flee to the Word, 'the care-soothing breast' of the Father. And He alone, as is befitting, supplies us children with the milk of love."[36] This spiritual nourishment, said Clement, makes it possible to grow from unbelief to faith, from faith to knowledge, and from knowledge to love, until the believer attains "the condition of being equal to the angels."[37]

ORIGEN

Clement's successor as Alexandria's leading Christian intellectual was Origen (ca. 185–ca. 254), one of the greatest of all Christian thinkers. Origen was just seventeen when his Christian father was arrested and taken off to be executed during the persecution under Septimius Severus. Yearning to become a martyr himself, the boy tried to follow but was stopped by his mother, who hid his clothes. Thereafter, he turned to **asceticism**, surviving on a miminum of food and sleep and allowing himself few personal comforts. One of them was philosophy, which he studied under the famous Ammonius Saccas, who was also the teacher of Plotinus, the founder of **Neoplatonism**.

The power of Origen's intellect and the depth of his faith soon attracted the attention of the leaders of the Alexandrian church. When Clement fled the continuing persecution in Alexandria (ca. 202), Origen, still in his teens, was made a teacher in the city's Christian school and then its head. Inspired by his ascetic and spiritual ideals, he appears to have been ready to make any sacrifice for the sake of the gospel. According to Eusebius,[38] when Origen began to fear that his contact with female students might lead to scandal, he castrated himself in literal application of Matthew 19:12 ("There are eunuchs who have made themselves eunuchs for the sake of the kingdom of heaven. Let anyone accept this who can.") Although we cannot be certain of the truth of this story, there is little doubt that boldness in thought and action was one of Origen's most notable qualities. Though many considered him a sage, some Christians regarded his views as unusual and dangerous. His greatest critic was Demetrius, the bishop of Alexandria, whose enmity was made certain when Origen allowed himself to be ordained **presbyter** ("elder") by another bishop while visiting Caesarea in Palestine. Excommunicated by the Alexandrian church, he spent most of his last twenty years in Caesarea. He died about 254 after being imprisoned and tortured during the Decian persecution.

Origen's literary output was astonishing. He is said to have composed some two thousand works, including commentaries on nearly every book in the Bible and hundreds of sermons. Of those that have survived, the most important are his *On First Principles,* Christianity's first systematic theology, and the apologetic *Against Celsus,* a refutation of the many charges made against Christians in Celsus's *True Doctrine.* These reveal Origen as a Christian thinker who had a profound understanding of Greek philosophy and recognized, like Justin and Clement, its points of agreement with Christianity. But Origen was not so taken by philosophy as they were. Alexandrian **Middle Platonism** colored and informed much of his theology—more, perhaps, than he might have admitted—but his contention was always that scripture is what really matters. For Origen, only careful study and prayerful reflection on scripture led to genuine wisdom.

In order to work from the most accurate text of the Bible (here, the Old Testament), Origen spent years compiling his famous *Hexapla,* of which only fragments survive. This work presented six different texts in parallel columns: the original Hebrew, a transliteration of the Hebrew into Greek characters, the Septuagint, and three other Greek versions. Believing that there was more to scripture than its literal meaning, he made extensive use of the allegorical method of interpretation in order to get at its deeper, spiritual significance. In doing so, he joined Clement in borrowing from the Greek Stoics and Philo an exegetical method on which Christian theologians would rely for centuries to come. The reasonableness of allegorical interpretation seemed obvious to him, especially in cases where the literal meaning of a text could not be taken seriously. Concerning the story of creation in Genesis, he wrote:

> For who that has understanding will suppose that the first, and second, and third day, and the evening and the morning, existed without a sun, and moon, and stars? and that the first day was, as it were, also without a sky? And who is so foolish as to suppose that God, after the manner of a husbandman, planted a paradise in Eden, towards the east, and placed in it a tree of life, visible and palpable, so that one tasting of the fruit . . . obtained life? and again, that one was a partaker of good and evil by masticating what was taken from the tree? And if God is said to walk in the paradise in the evening, and Adam to hide himself under a tree, I do not suppose that anyone doubts that these things figuratively indicate certain mysteries, the history having taken place in appearance, and not literally.[39]

The broad outlines of Origen's thought on God, the world, and human nature and destiny are set out in his *On First Principles.* There is one God, the ultimate source of all spiritual and material being. Creation was originally immaterial, consisting of rational spirits made in the image of the Logos, the image of God. These spirits were equal and perfectly satisfied, for in their communion with God they possessed what they most desired: knowledge of him. Those who remained in this state are the angels. The rest, who chose to turn away from God, became the souls of human beings and, in some cases, demons. As a consequence of their sin, God gave them bodies and placed them in a new and inferior order of creation — the material realm.

In Origen's thought, the return of human souls to God is part of the much larger drama of the restoration of all things to their original unity with him. In the case of human beings, restoration is made possible by faith (which, for Origen, amounts to intellectual assent to the basic tenets of the apostolic faith) and the work of the Logos, God the Son. The incarnation of the Logos took place when it united with the sinless soul of Jesus, which was in turn united with a human body. God revealed himself in the material world through this union of the human with the divine, offering to human souls the knowledge of himself that was the glory of their original communion with him.

Like Clement, then, Origen saw the Logos as teacher and salvation as a process of education. He also described the action of the other persons of the Trinity upon the soul. Sustained by the Father, the soul is sanctified by the Holy Spirit as it moves through stages of purification in which imperfections resulting from sin are removed until it is restored to its original perfection and communion with God: "In this way, then, by the renewal of the ceaseless working of the Father, Son and Holy Spirit in us . . . shall we be able at some future time perhaps, although with difficulty, to behold the holy and the blessed life."[40]

Much of Origen's thought was worked out in response to the teachings of Platonists and gnostics, for both were highly influential in cosmopolitan Alexandria. Some of his ideas resemble theirs. His image of souls falling away from God, for example, is reminiscent of gnostic creation myths, and his disinterest in the material world in favor of the spiritual order fits well with the attitude of Platonists and other philosophers of the time. Elsewhere, however, he rejects gnostic and Platonist views. Thus, while gnostics personified evil in the form of a demonic god and his powers, Origen spoke of it as a condition of cosmic disorderliness arising from the misuse of freedom. He also opposed the gnostics in describing the material world as the work of God, rather than some lesser power. Although Pla-

tonists and other philosophers attached little significance to history, Origen saw it as the great story of the return of souls to God. Further, while philosophers generally spoke of God as impersonal and therefore indifferent to human affairs, Origen clung to the biblical view of a personal God who was intensely interested in humanity. Like us, he argued, God has passions; he suffers, he has compassion, and, above all, he loves.[41]

Despite the enthusiasm of some Christians for Origen's teachings, they were harshly criticized by others. His work was attacked for giving too little attention to the literal meaning of scripture. His belief that human souls existed before they were united with bodies seemed strange to many, and his doctrine that even the fallen spirits that became demons would ultimately be saved left no place for hell, which most Christians considered a necessary feature in the scheme of divine justice. Origen's view that the Logos was "eternally generated" by the Father was also problematic. Did it mean that the Logos is God's equal, since eternal generation would mean co-eternality with God? Or did generation by the Father mean that the Logos was subordinate to the Father, as Origen argued in some passages? Though Origen also made it clear that because Logos was not subject to time or change it was in no sense a creature — that is, an entity belonging to creation. When the issue of the nature of Christ (Was he truly God, or a creature of God?) came to a head during the Arian controversy of the fourth century, both sides would enlist Origen in their respective causes, one emphasizing his notion of the "eternal generation" of the Logos and the other his subordinationism.

The grand sweep and originality of his thought left Origen vulnerable to criticism that was not always deserved. The careful qualifications he included in speculative passages were not always noted, and later "Origenists" often made his views seem more extreme than they really were. The controversy over his thought was often bitter and continued from the third century until the sixth, when he was declared a heretic at the Second Council of Constantinople (553). Thus, Origen, who had lived a hundred years before the Council of Nicaea, was judged according to a standard of orthodoxy developed during the three centuries following his death. Despite this, his work was destined to have a powerful influence on Christian thought well into the Middle Ages.

TERTULLIAN

Justin Martyr, Clement, and Origen found much of value in pagan culture and sought to establish connections between it and Christianity. Tertullian (ca. 160–ca. 225), whom we met earlier, had a very different point of view. The son of a Roman centurion, he was middle-aged when he converted to Christianity. His writings indicate that he had received a good education in law, literature, philosophy, and history, and that he spent the greater part of his career in Carthage. Like other North African Christians, whose church suffered more than most in times of persecution, Tertullian was a moral rigorist. For him, the Church was an assembly of martyrs and spirit-filled believers whose survival depended on its rejection of pagan culture and commitment to the values found in the Bible and the apostolic faith. His apparent defection to the rigorist and **charismatic** Montanist sect late in life was in protest against what he saw as moral laxity in the church of Rome and even in that of Africa.

Tertullian was the first important Christian thinker to write in Latin and the greatest theologian in the West until Augustine. He wrote vividly and forcefully about questions of interest to individuals concerned about the practical aspects of sin, salvation, and Christian life. Why do we sin? On what does salvation depend? What should Christians think of pagan philosophy? How should they dress? Attention to questions like these distinguished Tertullian and western theologians in general from the more speculative thinkers of the Greek East, whose interests were focused on the mysteries of the incarnation and the Trinity.

Tertullian's belief that the Church must remain separate from society provided the basis for his views on the life of Christians in the world. Christians must not serve in government or the army, he said, because these institutions supported pagan values and practices. They were also to avoid public entertainments that glorified immorality and were held in honor of false gods. In his *Apology,* written (ca. 196) when Carthaginian Christians were being accused of disloyalty in Roman courts, Tertullian assured Rome's rulers that Christians were loyal citizens: "Without ceasing, for all our emperors we offer prayer. We pray for life prolonged; for security to the empire; for protection to the imperial house; for brave armies, a faithful senate, a virtuous people, a world at rest." [42] There is little reason to doubt his sincerity. After all, Rome maintained peace and order in Tertullian's world. Yet his vision of the eventual vindication of the Church included the destruction of the same earthly powers for whose safety he was willing, for the present, to pray. In his *On Shows,* a denunciation of the events held in Roman theaters, he wrote with a passion that was more polemical than apologetic of the scene that Christians would witness on the Day of Judgment:

> How vast a spectacle then bursts upon the eye! What there excites my admiration? . . . Which sight gives me joy? Which rouses me to exultation? . . . I see so many illustrious monarchs, whose reception into heaven was publicly announced, groaning now in the lowest darkness with great Jupiter himself . . . and governors of provinces, too, who persecuted the Christian name, in fires more fierce than those with which they in the days of their pride raged against the followers of Christ. [43]

A generation before the controversy over the treatment of lapsed Christians began in North Africa, Tertullian set forth his views on the consequences of serious sin committed after baptism. His treatise *On Penitence* left no doubt as to the dangers of backsliding: "He who, through repentance for sins, had begun to make satisfaction to the Lord will, through another repentance of his repentance, make satisfaction to the devil, and will be more hateful to God . . . and more acceptable to His rival." [44] In the same work he argued that a Christian could be forgiven only once for falling into serious sin. In later years he reconsidered this issue and adopted the harsher stance of the Montanists: there could be no forgiveness for lapsed Christians.

For Tertullian, the strictness of this position made sense in view of what was at stake — the purity of the Church. This purity, he believed, was also threatened in the area of doctrine. It was the responsibility of the churches to cling to the teachings that had been handed down through generations of bishops reaching back to the Apostles. Tertullian insisted that this apostolic faith required no supplementation or explication from outside. Even pagan philosophy, for all its supposed wisdom, had nothing to offer Christianity. This is a curious feature of Tertullian's thought, given that he was clearly influenced by Stoicism. On occasion, he even seemed to recognize some value in philosophy if it coincided with Christian truth (e.g., Plato's doctrine of the immortality of the soul). For the most part, however, he maintained that philosophy was useless. It seems likely that he had philosophy in general in mind when he wrote this derisive denunciation of Aristotle:

> Unhappy Aristotle! who invented . . . dialectics, the art of building up and pulling down; an art so evasive in its propositions, so far-fetched in its conjectures, so harsh in its arguments, so productive of contentions — embarrassing even to itself, retracting everything, and really treating of nothing!"[45]

Not surprisingly, Tertullian protested against those who emphasized the similarities between Christianity and philosophy. It was impossible, he said, to harmonize two traditions that, despite certain similarities, were fundamentally antithetical:

> What indeed has Athens to do with Jerusalem? What concord is there between the Academy and the Church? . . . Away with all attempts to produce a mottled Christianity of Stoic, Platonic, and dialectic composition!. . . With our faith, we desire no further belief."[46]

In defending the faith, Tertullian made important contributions to Christian thought. He was the first theologian to develop a clear doctrine of the Trinity, describing a divine "substance" expressed in three distinct but substantively undifferentiated "persons" — Father, Logos-Son, and Holy Spirit.[47] He also worked out a theory of the incarnation according to which the Logos (he used the Latin *verbum,* "word") "took humanity to himself" and "mingled God and humanity in himself." In developing these ideas, Tertullian coined many of the terms (e.g., *trinitas, personae*) on which Latin theology would thereafter depend, though his use of them was sometimes vague. Beyond this, he criticized forms of Christianity whose doctrines seemed dangerous to him. In his *Against Praxeas,* for example, he attacked Monarchianism, which stressed the unity of God to the point that it allowed for no real distinction between the Father and the Son. He also wrote the anti-gnostic treatise *Against the Valentinians.* We will examine these and other early forms of Christianity in chapter 4.

Tertullian saw the Church as the endangered society of believers in a hostile world controlled by demonic powers. For it to endure until the eventual vindication of the saints, it must maintain the purity of its membership and doctrine. For this reason Tertullian warned against compromising the faith in order to make it acceptable to non-Christians. If the world considered Christianity unreasonable, he claimed, this was but another indication of its divine origin. Referring to Paul's comments in 1 Corinthians 1:18–25 on the value of worldly wisdom, he declared, "You will not be 'wise' unless you become a 'fool' to the world."[48] With this in mind, we can perhaps grasp Tertullian's meaning in a famous passage from his treatise *On the Flesh of Christ:* "The Son of God was crucified; I am not ashamed because men should be ashamed of it. And the Son of God died; it is by all means to be believed, because it is absurd. And He was buried, and rose again; the fact is certain, because it is impossible."[49]

The Beginnings of Monasticism

One of the most remarkable features of ancient Christianity was monasticism, the practice of living in a state of separation from the world for the purpose of attaining spiritual perfection. The idea of separation is indicated by the word *monk* itself, which is based on the Greek *monos* ("alone") and means "one who lives alone." A "monastery" was originally the cell in which a monk or nun lived and only later the compound of buildings in which cells were clustered. The terms **anchorite**, **anchoress**, and *hermit* also suggest the solitary life. The former are based on the Greek word for "withdrawal" and the latter on that for "desert," the preferred destination of those who left the world.

Scholars have searched widely for the antecedents of Christian monasticism, hoping to find its pre-Christian roots in such possible points of origin as the Jewish Essene community at Qumran near the Dead Sea and among the recluses associated with the temples of the Egyptian god Sarapis. Thus far, no clear links have been established to these or any other groups. We can, however, point to certain factors that encouraged the appearance of monasticism. First, the increasing pessimism in Greco-Roman culture concerning both the material world and human society no doubt moved some Christians to flee the transitory in search of the eternal. Second, ascetically minded Christians could find more than a few passages in the Bible that appeared to recommend monastic practices such as **celibacy** (Exodus 19:14–15; 1 Corinthians 7:1–9) and fasting (Matthew 4:2, 6:16–18; Acts 13:2). Third, these and other austerities—such as frequent and extended prayer and abstinence from sleep, alcohol, cosmetics, expensive clothing, and jewelry—were already widely practiced by individuals who sought isolation in their homes or near their towns or villages.[50] Finally, the end of the era of persecution and martyrdom had created the need for a new kind of Christian hero. Christians were no longer forced into martyrdom by society, but they could reject society in favor of the solitary life, a new arena in which they might die to the world just as the martyrs before them had died. The reputed holiness of the men and women who withdrew from the world in search of God made them popular among ordinary people, who sought them out for spiritual counsel and healing, and in some cases gained them later recognition as saints. At the same time, these charismatic figures represented a subtle threat to the authority of the Church, for their attainment of sanctity often seemed to occur without benefit of the preaching and sacraments it offered.

EGYPT: ANTHONY AND PACHOMIUS

Discussions of early monasticism often begin with Anthony (ca. 251–356), an Egyptian Christian who lived in the desert lands along the Nile. We know him primarily from the *Life of Anthony* by Athanasius, his friend and the bishop of Alexandria. This glowing, even propagandistic portrait of the monk has encouraged an exaggerated view of his importance; he was not, as has been often suggested, the sole founder of monasticism in Egypt. Still, Athanasius's depiction of Anthony's habits and ideals gives us a valuable insight into the spirit of Egyptian monasticism.

According to Athanasius, Anthony was between eighteen and twenty when his parents died, leaving him to care for a younger sister. One day in church he heard a reading of Matthew 19:21: "If you wish to be perfect, go, sell your possessions, and give the money to the poor, and you will have treasure in heaven; then come, follow me." He immediately went out and sold the property he had inherited from his parents, gave the proceeds to the poor, and placed his sister in the care of some pious virgins. For a time he lived alone near the edge of his village, devoting himself to prayer and manual labor. There he was tempted by the devil, who hoped to distract him from his pursuit of holiness:

> He attacked the young man, disturbing him by night and harassing him by day, so that even the onlookers saw the struggle which was going on between them. The one would suggest foul thoughts and the other would counter them with prayers, the one fire him with lust, the other, as one who seemed to blush, fortify his body with faith, prayers and fasting. And the devil . . . one night even took upon him the shape of a woman and imitated all her acts simply to beguile Anthony. But he, his mind filled with Christ, . . . quenched the coal of the other's deceit.[51]

Seeking greater solitude, Anthony moved to a cemetery away from his village and then to an abandoned fort, where he spent the next two decades. During this time he struggled continually with demons. On one occasion they filled his cell in the form of menacing lions, serpents, scorpions, and leopards. At other times they beat him or tempted him by setting gold on the path before him. Once the devil himself appeared to him in the form of a monk who came to his cell with loaves of bread and urged him to give up his fasting. In each case, however, Anthony triumphed over his tormentors, growing in spiritual strength with every victory.

After twenty years of struggle, his seclusion was interrupted by the intrusion of the faithful and curious who had heard reports of his holiness. When they tore away the door from his cell, he emerged "initiated in the mysteries and filled with the Spirit of God."[52] This was a charismatic Anthony, a monk who healed the sick, cast out demons, and moved great crowds to turn from bitterness and sorrow to love of God. His example so inspired others, says Athanasius, that soon the desert was filled with monks who had left their homes seeking "citizenship in the heavens."

He moved again, this time to a desolate spot near the Red Sea, but soon found himself surrounded by admiring monks who persuaded him to become their spiritual advisor. In this loosely organized society of independent hermits each monk lived alone in his cell at some distance from his neighbors. Each was free to practice his own form of asceticism, although for most Anthony's way of life provided the model. Athanasius tells us that Anthony prayed unceasingly, often through the night, and devoted himself to contemplation of the Bible. He ate only once each day, sometimes only once in four, and limited himself for months at a time to a diet of bread and water.

In all of this, Anthony had little contact with the organized Church, which was by now a real force in the cities and villages of Egypt. Far from the nearest priest, he and his monks could not have received the eucharist or participated in the spiritual fellowship enjoyed by town dwellers. That they earned a reputation for holiness despite their separation implied a challenge to the view that salvation depended upon the established Church and its clergy.

But their isolation was not complete. Anthony was willingly enlisted by Athanasius in the Church's struggle against Arianism, a form of Christianity we will discuss in chapter 4. Athanasius also noted Anthony's respect for ordained clergy, insisting that he honored them above himself.[53] In making this claim, as in drawing Anthony into the Arian controversy, Athanasius was no doubt attempting to bring about a closer alignment of the secular clergy with their monastic brothers, who tended to regard them as their spiritual inferiors.

Other figures joined Anthony in leading the monastic movement in the Egyptian desert. Ammun, one of his contemporaries, lived as a celibate with his wife for eighteen years before founding a community of nearly five thousand monks at Nitria in the Nile delta. Macarius the Great (fl. 360) was a village anchorite before beginning nearly six decades as leader of a large group of monks at Scete. In these and other settlements there was no formal rule to moderate the asceticism of the monks, and so we hear unbelievable tales of spiritual competition among them. Eager to outdo all other ascetics, Macarius of Alexandria went without sleep for twenty days and nights. On another occasion he remained standing through an entire Lenten season, subsisting solely on cabbage leaves, which he ate only on Sundays. Heron of Alexandria allowed himself a meal only once every three months, otherwise eating only a bit of wild lettuce now and then. The monk Ammonius gained control over his passions by burning his flesh repeatedly with a hot iron. He was said to have memorized all of scripture and no less than six million lines from the writings of Egyptian theologians such as Origen and Didymus the Blind.[54]

Stories from the desert also describe the austerities of women ascetics. A certain Alexandra, for example, immured herself in a tomb where she lived in darkness for ten years, never seeing another human face. Such rigorous asceticism could bring women recognition as the spiritual superiors of men. Struck by the holiness of an anonymous nun at Tabennisi, a saintly anchorite named Piteroum fell down before her, begging for her blessing and calling her his "spiritual mother."[55]

The founding of the first monastery in which monks lived together under a formal rule is usually credited to **Pachomius** (ca. 290–346). This was communal, or cenobitic, monasticism. His original monastery at Tabennesi grew so quickly that Pachomius soon had to build others. By the time of his death, he was in charge of nearly three thousand monks in nine monasteries and the nuns who filled two convents. The level of organization in these institutions went far beyond any found in the communities we have already mentioned. Each was ruled by an abbot who carefully supervised the monks' activities. These were divided among communal meals, worship, and shared work, all in accordance with a detailed monastic rule worked out by Pachomius himself.

The Pachomian model of monasticism quickly took hold in Egypt, with similar monasteries soon appearing in the desert all along the Nile. According to the reports of travelers at the end of the fourth century, there were so many monasteries in cities such as Oxyrhynchus that their walls reverberated with the voices of monks.[56] The monastic impulse was so great that the desert wastes of Egypt may have been home to as many as a hundred thousand monks in the last years of antiquity.[57]

SYRIA, PALESTINE, AND ASIA MINOR

Monasticism in Syria seems to have originated independently of events in Egypt. From the beginning, Syrian monks favored uniquely Syrian forms of asceticism. The most famous was Simeon the Elder (ca. 390–459), also known as Simeon "Stylites" ("pole dweller") because he separated himself from the world by living above it. For thirty years he remained on a small platform atop a sixty-foot column. From this height he preached to crowds of pilgrims who came to see him, performed miraculous cures, involved himself in church politics, and is said to have persuaded moneylenders to reduce their rates of interest. He had countless imitators in a tradition of pole dwelling that lasted for centuries.

The beginning of monasticism in Palestine has generally been traced to Hilarion (ca. 291–371), whose *Life* by **Jerome** seems to mingle legend with history. According to this account, Hilarion was moved to take up the solitary life by his contact with Anthony and lived alone for more than twenty years in the wilderness of Gaza before beginning to establish monasteries. Additional communities were founded by Euthymius (377–473), his disciple Sabas (439–532), and others, so that by the end of the sixth century both Gaza and the Judean wilderness were dotted with monastic settlements.

Farther north, Eustathius (ca. 300–ca. 377) established a monastic tradition in Asia Minor in the middle of the fourth century. But it was his student and disciple, **Basil of Caesarea** ("the Great"; ca. 330–79), who organized it and gave it its most distinctive features. After completing his education at Constantinople and Athens, Basil traveled for a year among the ascetics of Egypt and Palestine. Returning home, he founded a monastic community on his family's lands in Pontus. Although he was to make a name for himself as a theologian rather than as a monk, Basil's interest in monastic life was so great that he supervised its development in Asia Minor throughout his lifetime. Like Pachomius, he sought to moderate asceticism by requiring monks to live communally, regulating their daily activities, and making them obedient to the abbot. He urged that monasteries be built near cities and towns so that, instead of focusing on self-denial, monks might engage in service to others, whether by caring for travelers or ministering to the poor and the sick. His instructions for monastic life were compiled and circulated as the *Longer Rules* and *Shorter Rules*, which later became the model for both Greek and Russian monasticism.

THE WEST: BENEDICT AND THE BENEDICTINE RULE

Monasticism first came to the West through Athanasius, who lived for a time in exile at Trier and Rome, and his *Life of Anthony*. Initially, its appeal was most evident among members of the upper classes. Roman women in particular were attracted to the cause. Melania the Elder built a convent near Jerusalem where for nearly thirty years she presided over a community of fifty ascetic women. Paula, a disciple of Jerome, co-founded with him a double monastery of men and women at Bethlehem.

The earliest known monastic institution in the West itself was that of Martin of Tours (ca. 335–97), a hermit who led a community of fellow anchorites at Ligugé near Poitiers before becoming bishop of Tours. At almost the same time, Eusebius of Vercelli founded a community of ascetic priests. This innovative combination of the monastic and clerical ways of life would later be adopted by both Ambrose and Augustine. Another impetus to western monasticism was John Cassian, who founded two monasteries at Marseilles about 415. He wrote his *Institutes* and *Conferences* in order to acquaint western monks with the practices of their Egyptian brothers, among whom he had traveled in his youth. From Gaul, the monastic tradition made its way to Britain, where it became one of the most visible features of Christian culture. This was particularly true of Ireland, where the exceptional rigor of monastic life was reflected in the *Rule for Monks* written by Columbanus (543–615).

But it was the *Rule* of **Benedict of Nursia** (ca. 480–ca. 550) that became the foundation of western monasticism. In his late teens Benedict had taken up the solitary life in a cave near Subiaco in Italy. In time he found himself surrounded by disciples who persuaded him to become their abbot. About 529 he brought some of them to Monte Cassino, about forty miles from Capua, where they founded the monastery for which he wrote his *Rule*.

Benedict's ideal was a self-sufficient monastery whose members practiced a moderate and communal asceticism. After serving a novitiate, a candidate for the monastery was required to make formal vows in which he committed himself to remain forever within its walls, strive for spiritual perfection, and be obedient to the abbot. The abbot was to be chosen by the monks and was expected to consult with them, but his decisions were final and his authority unquestioned. The goal of the *Rule* was to create a communal environment in which monks found happiness through the imitation of Christ rather than in severe asceticism and detachment from the world. Accordingly, it allowed them two good meals each day, including a small amount of wine, and a mattress, pillow, and blanket for sleeping. At the same time, however, monks were to speak only when necessary and to avoid frivolous behavior, which might distract them from their true purpose. Within the monastery, distinctions relating to wealth and social class were ignored, and no monk was allowed to have possessions of his own. For Benedict, as for Basil the Great, the monastery was to be of service to the surrounding population. Whether they came for rest, a meal, or healing, guests were to be welcomed with humility and love: "All shall adore Christ in them, Who, indeed, is received in their persons."[58]

Under the Benedictine *Rule*, the daily lives of monks were divided into three kinds of activity: work, communal worship, and *lectio divina*, or private reading and meditation. The first might involve labor in the fields, kitchen, library, or scriptorium, where copies of scripture and other texts were made. Work performed with the proper attitude was an opportunity for spiritual growth; idleness was considered "an enemy of the soul." Worship was organized around the **canonical hours**, when the monks would gather in their chapel to recite the chants, readings, and prayers that made up the Divine Office. The *Rule* prescribed eight hours, which were typically observed at the following times: nocturns (2 A.M.), matins/lauds (before dawn), prime (6 A.M.), terce (9 A.M.), sext (noon), none (3 P.M.), vespers (at sunset), and compline (before bed). *Lectio divina* usually involved reading of the Bible, the **church fathers**, or some other religious text as well as prayer. Thus, the monk's life was one of endless devotion to God, whether in labor, praise, or study and introspection.

The Benedictine form of monasticism spread quickly throughout the West, eclipsing others and discouraging by its emphasis on regulation and moderation the ascetic extremes of the East. As we will see, the monastic movement in general was destined to become a powerful force in the Christian world, both East and West, making major contributions to theology, playing an important role in ecclesiastical politics, and producing some of the Church's most influential leaders.

Summary

The reasons for the rise of Christianity within the Roman Empire are complex, ranging from anxiety over the decline of Roman civilization to the wide appeal of Christian beliefs and even the social and private habits of Christians. In a world in which religious diversity and toleration were the norm, Christians often found themselves misunderstood and persecuted even as their numbers grew. Both non-Christians and the state questioned their loyalty to the empire, pointing to Christians' unwillingness to recognize Rome's traditional gods and their refusal to participate in various social activities. Meanwhile, Christian apologists sought to defend the faith, usually by emphasizing its similarities to Greek philosophy and the social responsibility of Christians themselves, but in some instances by denouncing Greco-Roman culture in general. Inevitably, persecution produced martyrs, spiritual heroes whose sacrifice of their own lives for the sake of the gospel helped inspire the courage of others until Christianity was legalized early in the fourth century. By then a new class of heroes — monks and nuns — had begun a movement that would play a major role in the development of both eastern and western Christianity in the coming centuries.

QUESTIONS FOR REVIEW AND REFLECTION

1. How would you explain the reactions of the Roman state and the people of the Roman Empire to Christian teaching and practice?

2. What were the views of early Christian writers concerning the nature of the Church and its relationship to classical culture and the Roman state?

3. What contributions did early monasticism make to the developing Christian tradition?

NOTES

1. Tacitus, *Annals* 1.2.1.
2. Tertullian, *Apology* 37.4, trans. S. Thelwall, in *Ante-Nicene Fathers,* ed. Alexander Roberts and James Donaldson, vol. 3, 45.
3. See especially Rodney Stark, *The Rise of Christianity* (San Francisco: Harper San Francisco, 1996), 95–128.
4. Julian, "Fragment from a Letter to a Priest," in *The Works of the Emperor Julian,* trans. W. C. Wright, vol. 2, Loeb Classical Library (Cambridge, Mass.: Harvard Univ. Press, 1923), 337. See also Julian's Letter 22 (to Arsacius, high priest of Galatia) in vol. 3, 71.
5. R. Joseph Hoffmann, *Celsus on the True Doctrine: A Discourse Against the Christians* (New York: Oxford University Press, 1987), 72–73. Our only source for Celsus's *True Doctrine* is a rebuttal by Origen, a Christian writer, in his *Against Celsus.*
6. Erwin R. Goodenough, *The Church in the Roman Empire* (New York: Henry Holt, 1931), 37.
7. For a brief discussion of this shift in scholarly opinion, see Wayne Meeks, *The First Urban Christians* (New Haven, Conn.: Yale University Press, 1983), 51–73.
8. See Stark, *Rise of Christianity,* 3–27, for a survey of scholarly estimates of the growth of the number of Christians.
9. Minucius Felix, *Octavius* 9.
10. Marcus Aurelius, *Meditations* 11.3.
11. Minucius Felix, *Octavius* 12.
12. Origen, *Against Celsus* 8.2, trans. Frederick Crombie, in Roberts and Donaldson, *Ante-Nicene Fathers,* vol. 4, 640.
13. Tacitus, *Annals* 15.44.
14. Eusebius, *Church History* 3.17–18.
15. Eusebius, *History of the Church* 6.41, trans. G. A. Williamson (New York: Dorset Press, 1984), 277.
16. Eusebius, *Church History* 8.9, in Williamson, *History of the Church,* 337–38.
17. For a good discussion of this issue, see Elaine Pagels, *The Gnostic Gospels* (New York: Random House, 1979), 70–101. See also Irenaeus (*Against Heresies* 3.18), who condemned gnostic Christians as "false brothers" who had little sympathy for those who suffered as Christ had suffered.
18. Ignatius, *To the Romans* 4.1.
19. Ignatius, *To the Romans* 6.3, 4.2.
20. Eusebius, *Church History* 4.15, in Williamson, *History of the Church,* 171.
21. Tertullian, *Apology* 50.
22. Tertullian, *Apology* 50, in *The Fathers of the Church,* vol. 10, trans. Rudolph Arbesmann, Emily Daly, and Edwin Quain (Washington, D.C.: Catholic University Press of America, 1950), 126.
23. Cyprian, *Epistle* 68(66), 8.
24. Cyprian found a scriptural basis for his position in passages such as Exodus 19:22, 28:43 and Leviticus 21:17.
25. A slightly earlier claim is that of Irenaeus, who regarded Rome as the greatest of the apostolic sees and urged all others to follow it (*Against Heresies* 3.3.2.).
26. The *Second Apology* was originally an appendix or supplement to the first.
27. Justin Martyr, *Dialogue with Trypho* 8, in *Saint Justin Martyr,* trans. T. B. Falls (New York: Christian Heritage, 1948), 160.
28. Justin Martyr, *First Apology* 44, in Falls, *Saint Justin Martyr,* 81.

29. Justin Martyr, *First Apology* 46, in Falls, *Saint Justin Martyr*, 83.

30. William Placher, *A History of Christian Theology* (Philadelphia: Westminster Press, 1983), 55–67.

31. Eusebius, *Church History* 5.10–11.

32. There were precedents for such a work. Among the lost works of Aristotle, for example, was a *Protrepticus* that exhorted educated persons to undertake the study of philosophy.

33. Clement of Alexandria, *Paidagogos* 1.7.55, in Roberts and Donaldson, *Ante-Nicene Fathers*, vol. 2, 223.

34. Clement of Alexandria, *Stromata* 1.5.28, in Roberts and Donaldson, *Ante-Nicene Fathers*, vol. 2, 305.

35. Clement of Alexandria, *Protrepticus* 11, in Roberts and Donaldson, *Ante-Nicene Fathers*, vol. 2, 203.

36. Clement of Alexandria, *Paidagogos* 1.6., p. 220.

37. Clement of Alexandria, *Stromata* 7.10., p. 539.

38. Eusebius, *Church History* 6.8.

39. Origen, *On First Principles* 4.16, trans. F. Crombie, in Roberts and Donaldson, *Ante-Nicene Fathers*, vol. 4, 365 (Greek text).

40. Origen, *On First Principles* 1.3.8, p. 255.

41. Origen, *Homilies on Ezekiel* 6.6.

42. Tertullian, *Apology* 30.4, in Roberts and Donaldson, *Ante-Nicene Fathers*, vol. 3, 42.

43. Tertullian, *On the Shows* 30, trans. S. Thelwall, in Roberts and Donaldson, *Ante-Nicene Fathers*, vol. 3, 91.

44. Tertullian, *On Penitence* 6, trans. S. Thelwall, in Roberts and Donaldson, *Ante-Nicene Fathers*, vol. 3, 660.

45. Tertullian, *Prescription against Heretics* 7, trans. Peter Holmes, in Roberts and Donaldson, *Ante-Nicene Fathers*, vol. 3, 246.

46. Tertullian, *Prescription against Heretics* 7, 246.

47. But Tertullian's theology was not entirely in agreement with that worked out in the church councils of later centuries. For example, there is more than a hint of subordinationism in his view that the divine Logos did not become a distinct divine person until the creation of the world. The manifestation of the Holy Spirit as a divine person came later. Thus, neither the Son nor the Spirit was co-eternal with the Father.

48. Tertullian, *On the Flesh of Christ* 5, trans. Peter Holmes, in Roberts and Donaldson, *Ante-Nicene Fathers*, vol. 3, 525.

49. Tertullian, *On the Flesh of Christ* 5, 525.

50. See, for example, Athanasius's *Life of Anthony*, 3.

51. Athanasius, *Life of Anthony* 5, trans. A. Robertson, in *Nicene and Post-Nicene Fathers*, 2nd series, ed. Philip Schaff and Henry Wace, vol. 4 (Peabody, Mass.: Hendrickson, 1994), 197.

52. Athanasius, *Life of Anthony* 14, in Schaff and Wace, *Nicene and Post-Nicene Fathers*, 200.

53. Athanasius, *Life of Anthony* 67, 214.

54. Palladius, *Lausiac History* 18 (Macarius), 26 (Heron), and 11 (Ammonius).

55. Palladius, *Lausiac History* 5 (Alexandra) and 34 (the nun at Tabennisi).

56. *Enyclopedia of Early Christianity*, ed. Everett Ferguson (New York: Garland, 1990), s.v. "monasticism."

57. Jacob Burckhardt, *The Age of Constantine the Great*, trans. Moses Hadas (Berkeley: University of California Press, 1949), 330.

58. Benedict of Nursia, *Rule* 53, in *Christianity through the Thirteenth Century*, ed. Marshall Baldwin (New York: Walker, 1970), 92.

CHAPTER 4

Councils and Creeds

Defining Orthodoxy in Late Antiquity

Overview

We have seen how the growth of Christianity was influenced by its interaction with the government and people of the Roman Empire. The early martyrs and apologists, Christian thought about the nature of the Church, the rise of monasticism — these can be understood, at least in part, as responses to the Roman world. In this chapter we will continue our investigation of the rise of Christianity, focusing now on how Christianity defined itself in terms of organization and belief at a time when the Christian movement included different and competing forms of the faith. As the process of self-definition progressed, a "mainstream" Christianity began to emerge that gradually claimed recognition as orthodox, or doctrinally correct.

Three developments were of particular importance. First, to govern the Church an ecclesiastical hierarchy was established in which bishops had the greatest share of authority and were responsible for maintaining Christian unity. By claiming that their authority and teachings were the same as those

Christ had given to the Apostles, the Church was able to enhance the prestige of bishops, represent the faith they taught as orthodox, and condemn divergent views as heretical. Second, agreement on a canon of scripture also served to define mainstream Christianity, for once the canon had been established the Church considered no theology orthodox unless it agreed with this body of texts. Finally, the development of creeds was also important, for these succinct and formal statements of Christian belief clearly distinguished between what was held to be the true apostolic faith and **heterodox** ("different in opinion or belief") teachings. The influence of the Greek language and elements of Greek philosophy in the formulation of the creeds was an indication that by the fourth century Christianity had become a product of Hellenism as well as Judaism.

During this period Christian thinkers such as the Cappadocian Fathers, John Chrysostom, Jerome, Ambrose, and Augustine played important roles in shaping the structure and beliefs of the Church. In addition, important aspects of Christian life and worship such as the **liturgy**, sacraments, religious holidays, and the cult of saints were taking shape as features of a developing Christian culture that was displacing the older pagan culture of the Mediterranean world.

Establishing Ecclesiastical Authority

By the second century, Christianity was beginning to establish an effective organizational structure and system of authority. Some of its leaders were already speaking hopefully of a united and universal Church,[1] but the rapid growth in the number of Christians and the proliferation of Christian communities meant that unity among them would be difficult to achieve without an ecclesiastical government capable of ensuring common beliefs, loyalties, and traditions from above the local level. A Church governed in this way would also be more likely to succeed in promoting its understanding of the apostolic faith and defending it against alternative views.

CHALLENGES: GNOSTICISM, MARCIONISM, AND MONTANISM

Early Christian theology was fluid and diverse. Most Christians shared certain basic beliefs — that Christ had somehow been both human and divine, for example, and that his death and resurrection had made salvation from sin possible — but even these ideas were sometimes disputed, and there were considerable differences of opinion on many other issues. A substantial body of Christian doctrine would be formulated by the end of the fifth century, but in the interim the ideas that would ultimately become doctrine were challenged by differing views on issues as fundamental as the nature of God, the humanity of Christ, salvation, the material world, and ecclesiastical authority. This aspect of early Christianity is easily seen in the thought of three important groups: the Gnostics, Marcionites, and Montanists.

Gnosticism was a philosophical religion that reached the height of its popularity in the second and third centuries. Because it took a great variety of forms, scholars have found it difficult to define Gnosticism with any precision, and some prefer not to use the term at all. The question of its origins is equally complex, for some Gnostic teachings can be traced to Judaism, others to Greek philosophy, and others still to Egyptian religion and Persian Zoroastrianism. Another source of Gnostic teaching was Christianity. Although some scholars believe that Gnosticism had its origins in pagan thought and later adopted elements of Christian belief and imagery, others are convinced that it was a form of Christianity from the beginning. This view was shared by the majority of second- and third-century Christian writers who were critical of Gnosticism.

However we might explain their origins, by the second century there were groups of Christians who were sufficiently Gnostic in their beliefs that we can speak of Gnostic Christianity as a distinct movement. For many years it was known primarily through the writings of authorities who were hostile to it, most notably **Irenaeus** (ca. 130 – ca. 200), a bishop of Lyons in southern France who described and denounced various Gnostic Christian sects and their teachings in his *Against Heresies*. Then, in 1945, a cache of Gnostic Christian texts was discovered at **Nag Hammadi** in southern Egypt. Written in Coptic, the language spoken by most Egyptians in late antiquity, they were translations of works originally written in Greek, in some cases perhaps as early as the second half of the first century. The find included Gnostic Gospels, such as the Gospel of Thomas,[2] the Gospel of Philip, the Gospel of Truth, and the Gospel of the Egyptians, as well as other texts whose titles attributed them to Jesus' followers, such as The Apocalypse of Peter, the Secret Book of James, and the Letter of Peter to Philip. Although the Nag Hammadi texts show that there were considerable differences among Gnostic Christians, it is also clear that they agreed with each other and with other Christians on certain fundamental ideas. For example, they imagined a cosmos divided by conflict between forces of good and evil, lamented their separation from God, and looked forward to eventual union with him. They recognized Christ as savior and made a place for biblical ideas, events, and personalities in their systems of thought.

From the point of view of more mainstream Christians, however, such similarities were dangerous because of their potential to seduce the unsuspecting into embracing other beliefs that were incompatible with their own understanding of the faith. In contrast to the biblical view of the world as something beautiful created and sustained by God, for example, Gnostic Christians believed that matter was evil and the work of a lesser being, the Demiurge. Moreover, they argued that God's perfect goodness meant that he could never be directly involved with the material realm, though he might wish to save humanity from it. Most Christians believed in the resurrection of the body, which they regarded as an essential component of human nature, but Gnostics claimed that the human body was evil and the enemy of the spiritual self. Gnostic Christians also differed from others in their belief that salvation was made possible by secret knowledge (*gnosis*) revealed by the savior rather than by the atoning death of Christ. Although Christians generally believed that the humanity of Christ was a necessary part of God's plan for salvation, the Gnostic Christians' views on matter led most to reject the humanity of Christ and, consequently, the reality of his suffering and death. Finally, by insisting that they possessed a higher wisdom revealed secretly to their predecessors by Christ, Gnostic Christians suggested that the gospel as it was preached publicly in the churches was incomplete. Thus, Gnostic Christianity challenged beliefs that were central to emerging mainstream Christianity and also questioned the authority of the churches founded by the Apostles. For this reason, much of the phrasing of the creeds produced by church councils in the fourth and fifth centuries was anti-Gnostic in intent.

The teachings of **Marcion** posed similar challenges. A native of the city of Sinope in Asia Minor, Marcion was the originator of one of the most popular and widespread heresies of antiquity. After making a fortune as a shipowner, he came to Rome about 140 and joined the church there. He made an extravagant gift of money to the congregation, apparently expecting that he would be rewarded with an audience for his ideas, but these turned out to be so unorthodox from the Romans' point of view that he was **excommunicated** and his money returned. Thereafter, Marcion founded churches of his own. They multiplied rapidly, so that his influence was felt in virtually every part of the Roman Empire by 160.

The basis of Marcion's thought was his rejection of the God of the Jewish Scriptures, who, he said, had created an imperfect world plagued by evil. His literal reading of scripture allowed Marcion to conclude that this was a deity who could be arbitrary, unjust, angry, and even barbaric. The loving, merciful God of whom Jesus and Paul had spoken seemed so radically different to him that Marcion reasoned there must be two gods — the evil, or at least uncaring and incompetent, god of the Jewish Scriptures, and the supremely good and loving God revealed by Christ. In this respect, Marcion's thought was much like that of the Gnostics, who distinguished between a higher, good God and the Demiurge. Like them, he also favored a docetic Christology, according to which Christ had only appeared to have a physical body. An entirely spiritual Christ, he said, had suddenly appeared in Galilee in the year 29 without benefit of human birth. But Marcion differed from the Gnostics in maintaining that human beings are a part of the material world rather than spiritual strangers who have found themselves imprisoned in it. For him, salvation from the realm of matter was not a restoration to an original union with the divine, as the Gnostics believed, but an undeserved gift from a God who, though not responsible for our existence or miserable condition, chose to love humanity. This emphasis on God's love, or **grace**, is a quality Marcion shared with Paul, whose letters and the Gospel of Luke, when carefully edited, constituted the Marcionite canon.[3] On the whole, however, Marcion's Christianity was not at all Pauline. Moreover, his views on such basic issues as divinity, the material world, and the nature of Christ were at odds with the assumptions of most other Christians; and his rejection of the Jewish Scriptures called into question the authority of sacred texts on which they had relied since the first days of the Jerusalem Church.

Another challenge was presented by charismatic prophets. According to the New Testament, prophecy was an important part of the life of the early Church, but by the beginning of the second century the influence of prophets was becoming disruptive, especially when they contradicted church leaders. Good evidence of this is provided by the *Didache* ("Teaching"), a Syrian text from the late first or early second century that warns churches against allowing itinerant prophets to remain too long with them.

One movement to arise from the teachings of such figures was Montanism. Known to its adherents as "the New Prophecy," it originated about 170 with the appearance in Asia Minor of **Montanus**, a self-proclaimed prophet. Claiming that the Holy Spirit spoke through him, Montanus was joined by two women, Maximilla and Priscilla, in prophesying in an excited and unrestrained manner that offended many Christians. The fourth-century historian **Eusebius** quotes one of their critics:

> There is, it appears, a village near the Phrygian border of Mysia called Ardabau. There it is said that a recent convert named Montanus . . . in his unbridled ambition to reach the top laid himself open to the adversary, was filled with spiritual excitement and suddenly fell into a kind of trance and unnatural ecstasy. He raved, and began to chatter and talk nonsense, prophesying in a way that conflicted with the practice of the Church handed down generation by generation from the beginning. Of those who listened at that time to his sham utterances some were annoyed, regarding him as possessed, a demoniac in the grip of a spirit of error, a disturber of the masses. They rebuked him and tried to stop his chatter, remembering the distinction drawn by the Lord, and His warning to guard vigilantly against the coming of false prophets. Others were elated as if by the Holy Spirit or a prophetic gift, were filled with conceit, and forgot the Lord's distinction.[4]

Apart from the deviation of their flamboyant prophetic style (which they attributed to being completely overcome by the Spirit) from "the practice of the Church handed down generation by generation," the Montanists were criticized for their eschatology, according to which Christ was about to return to a new Jerusalem that would soon appear near the town of Pepuza in Phrygia. The movement's sudden popularity was also a cause for concern, for it spread rapidly throughout Asia Minor and to Syria, North Africa, and Rome before eventually losing its momentum in the fourth century. Converts like Tertullian saw the moral rigorism and eagerness of Montanists for separation from the world as evidence that the Holy Spirit had greater influence among them than with other Christians. But these issues were insignificant compared to the Montanists' claim that they preached just what their name indicated — a new prophecy. The newness of the Montanist message forced the Church to consider the meaning and consequences of continuing prophecy. Would the teachings and practices of the Church need to be revised to accommodate every new revelation? If new truths could be added to Christianity, wouldn't that imply that Christianity was incomplete and changeable? Did their inspiration give charismatic prophets and teachers an authority greater than that of other church leaders?

Taken together, then, the Gnostic, Marcionite, and Montanist movements raised serious questions about ecclesiastical authority, scripture, and Christian belief. The Church responded by claiming for its leaders an authority greater than the inspiration of charismatics, creating a **canon of scripture** on which all teaching and doctrine were to be based, and clearly defining and expressing its beliefs in councils and creeds.

BISHOPS AND APOSTOLIC SUCCESSION

The earliest Christians looked to the Holy Spirit for guidance, believing that the divine will was sometimes revealed in visions, **glossolalia**, and prophecies. The Spirit might speak through anyone, whether man or woman, slave or free, and any Christian under its inspiration could expect to be regarded as having a certain authority in her or his congregation. As a result, much of the leadership in the first-century Church was charismatic — that is, dependent upon the *charismata*, or "gifts," granted to certain individuals by the Spirit.

Ongoing revelation must have encouraged the first Christians in their faith and enlivened their worship, but charismatic leadership was not conducive to the growth of the Church as a unified institution. Instead, the cohesion of the Christian congregations that were spreading throughout the Roman world by the beginning of the second century was made possible by an organizational structure in which bishops governed individual churches and, later, the churches in a given region. It was the responsibility of bishops to maintain unity among themselves and their churches and to promote uniform beliefs and practices within and among their congregations. With certain modifications, the system of church organization and authority that began to take shape in the second century has survived until our own time in the Eastern Orthodox and Roman Catholic churches.

The early history of this system is difficult to trace, for the structure of the early churches varied and allowed for different forms of leadership. This variety is evident even in the New Testament. According to Acts, the members of the Jerusalem Church looked to the Apostles for guidance and recognized three of them—James, Peter, and John—as having special authority. Paul calls these three "pillars" of the Church in Galatians 2:9. The political structure of Paul's own churches was rather different. In 1 Corinthians 12:28 he lists prophets and teachers among the leaders found there. The New Testament texts also speak of more familiar figures, such as deacons ("servants" or "ministers"), presbyters ("elders"), and bishops (from Greek *episkopos*, "overseer"), though it is only in the pastoral epistles (1 and 2 Timothy and Titus), which may not have been written until the middle of the second century, that these are used as technical terms to denote clearly defined church offices.[5]

Bishops and deacons are clearly the most important church officials in *1 Clement*, a letter written ca. 96 to the Church in Corinth and traditionally assigned to Clement, the third bishop of Rome (88–97). The author addresses himself to the problem of factionalism in the church at Corinth, where younger members had deposed some of their older leaders. Warning the Corinthians that they had no right to remove these men from their ministry, he reminds them that bishops and deacons receive their authority through a line of predecessors reaching back to the Apostles themselves.[6] These offices were sanctioned by God even before the founding of the Church, he argues, citing in support of this claim the Septuagint version of Isaiah 60:17: "I will give your rulers in peace and your overseers [*episkopoi*] in righteousness."[7] He also notes that bishops and deacons have the approval of those to whom they minister, for they are appointed only with "the consent of the entire Church."[8] To challenge them, then, would be to risk violating offices ordained by God and approved by the Church. *1 Clement* also speaks of *presbyters* but seems to consider this title the equivalent of *bishop*. Thus, the letter assumes a dual leadership of the Church, with bishop-presbyters assuming greater authority than the deacons who assisted in their ministry.

The seven letters written by **Ignatius of Antioch** on his way to martyrdom in Rome (ca. 107) reflect the situation in the churches there and in Asia Minor roughly two decades after *1 Clement*. Ignatius distinguishes between bishops, who presided over individual congregations, and presbyters, who appear to have constituted a kind of council or advisory body around them.[9] In later years individual presbyters (i.e., priests) would have their own congregations, but in Ignatius's time the presbytery was a council of elders who related to the bishop "as the strings to a harp."[10] Bishops and presbyters were assisted by deacons, who formed a third tier of church leadership. Their responsibilities included ministering to the poor and sick, maintaining order in the Church, and assisting the bishop in the eucharist. This threefold structure would become standard by the end of the second century. For Ignatius, it was absolutely dependent upon the bishop, without whom the Church could not function, or even exist. The bishop was appointed by Christ—Ignatius even said he "represents the mind of Jesus Christ"[11]—and was to be accorded the same respect that Christ himself deserved.[12] Without the bishop there could be no baptisms, nor could the eucharist be celebrated.[13] In all things, said Ignatius, Christians were to follow the example and acknowledge the authority of their bishop. They were also to respect the presbyters and deacons who shared in his ministry:

> Follow your bishop, every one of you, as obediently as Jesus Christ followed the Father. Obey your clergy [i.e., *presbyters*] too, as you would the Apostles; give your deacons the same reverence that you would to a command from God. Make sure that no step affecting the church is ever taken by anyone without the bishop's sanction. The sole eucharist you should consider valid is one that is celebrated by the bishop himself, or by some person authorized by him. Where the bishop is to be seen, there let all his people be; just as wherever Jesus Christ is present, we have the worldwide Church.[14]

Alongside the office of bishop developed the concept of **apostolic succession**, according to which the authority and teaching of bishops could be traced back through their **episcopal** predecessors to the Apostles themselves. We have already seen its beginnings in *1 Clement,*[15] where it served as a basis for the author's argument that bishops and deacons cannot be removed from office by their congregations. About 185 the idea was stated more explicitly by Irenaeus in his *Against Heresies.* According to Irenaeus, Christ chose the Apostles to carry on his ministry, they chose the first bishops as their successors, those bishops chose others to succeed them, and so forth.[16] For Irenaeus, apostolic succession guaranteed that the true and complete teaching of the Apostles was available in the churches of the bishops, who had received it from them. Thus, when Gnostics claimed that they possessed secret teachings of Christ that had been passed down to them, Irenaeus countered that no secret tradition had ever existed. Christ would have given such teachings to the Apostles, he argued, and they in turn would have taught them to their successors, who would have made them a part of the gospel they preached in their churches.[17] That this had not happened was proof that the doctrines of the Gnostics were false. As far as Irenaeus was concerned, no teaching that went beyond or was contrary to that proclaimed publicly by the bishops could possibly be true, for they were the custodians of the complete and genuine apostolic faith.

The authority of the bishops, then, was undergirded by the doctrine of apostolic succession, leaving no doubt that each was the true leader of his congregation. But there was more to a church than its bishop. It would have been incomplete without its presbyters, deacons, and the laity they served. Taken together, these constituted a complete and properly organized *ekklesia* ("assembly" or "church") capable of functioning independently of others.

In fact, however, churches communicated and cooperated regularly in matters of mutual concern. The many interchurch letters that have survived, such as *1 Clement* and the letters of Ignatius, illustrate how congregations corresponded in order to encourage, admonish, and instruct each other. Cooperation was taken to a higher level when bishops met to resolve some important issue. The council of North African bishops convened by Cyprian at Carthage in 251 to consider the status of lapsed Christians is a good example. So is the series of **synods** called by Victor I, bishop of Rome (189–98), to end disagreement between the eastern and western churches on the matter of when to celebrate Easter.[18]

This sort of collaboration among bishops provided the basis for the growth of ecclesiastical organization above the local level in the third century. The churches that took the lead in these efforts were most often those located in the larger cities or provincial capitals of the empire. Thus, the church in Carthage was preeminent in Africa and its bishop was regarded as first among the African bishops. The bishop and church of Alexandria represented the highest level of authority in Egypt. The churches of Italy, of course, looked to Rome for leadership.

Beginning in the fourth century, the bishops of provincial capitals came to be known as **metropolitan** bishops (from *metropolis,* "mother city") in recognition of the authority they held over entire provinces.[19] A handful of five metropolitan bishops were eventually given even greater distinction. In the fifth century, the emperor Theodosius II referred to two of them, the bishops of Rome and Constantinople, as **patriarchs**. Before long they were joined by the bishops of Alexandria, Antioch, and Jerusalem in a "Pentarchy" of five patriarchs whose influence extended far beyond provincial boundaries. In theory, these five sees, or episcopal "seats," had roughly equal authority. It was clear, however, that the bishops of Rome and Constantinople had greater prestige. They would soon emerge as the unchallenged leaders of the western (Latin) and eastern (Greek) traditions in Christianity.

THE CREATION OF THE CANON

The creation of the New Testament canon was another important development. Once it had been established, the orthodoxy of any new teaching or practice could be judged by the extent of its agreement with this body of scripture.

The word *canon* originally meant "measuring stick," but later it was used more broadly to refer to almost any kind of standard. Thus, the New Testament canon is a collection of texts considered to have special authority because they met certain standards established by the early Church. The canon had an important precedent in the Jewish Scriptures, the collection of sacred writings that the first Christians had in mind when they referred to "scripture." The earliest Christian writer to use the terms *Old Testament* and *New Testament* to distinguish between Jewish and uniquely Christian bodies of scripture was Irenaeus,[20] though at the time when he was writing, in the late second century, there was no general agreement on what a "New Testament" might contain beyond the four Gospels[21] and the thirteen letters ascribed to Paul. The remaining New Testament texts already existed, and most were widely known, but it would be some time before they acquired the status that would make them worthy of inclusion in the canon. In addition, Christians treasured many texts that would never achieve canonical status. Some of these, such as the Didache, The Shepherd of Hermas, the Epistle of Barnabas, 1 Clement, and the Epistles of Ignatius, belong to a collection of very early texts composed by writers known as the **Apostolic Fathers**.

The concept of a Christian canon antedates Irenaeus by about half a century. The first to suggest a collection of specific texts appears to have been Marcion, whose hostility toward Judaism and conviction that only Paul truly understood the teaching of Jesus limited the number of works he found acceptable. As we have seen, he approved only the letters of Paul (excluding the pastoral epistles) and an expurgated version of the Gospel of Luke for use in his churches. Thus, Marcion's canon was not suitable for most Christians, but his *idea* of recognizing the special authority of a limited number of texts helped set into motion the process that would ultimately lead to the creation of the canonical New Testament.

In subsequent years various lists of books favored for inclusion were drawn up and circulated. Most of these have been lost, although we do have the so-called *Muratorian Canon*.[22] Thought to have been written in Rome at the end of the second century, it includes the four Gospels, Acts, and the letters of Paul but omits Hebrews, James, and 1 and 2 Peter and adds the Apocalypse of Peter and the Wisdom of Solomon. We can also see evidence of interest in defining a canon in Irenaeus's *Against Heresies*[23] and in a passage from Eusebius's *Church History* that preserves Origen's views on scripture.[24] Progress was slow, however; even in the fourth century the authority of some works was still disputed, most notably Hebrews, 2 Peter, 2 and 3 John, Jude, and Revelation. It was not until 367 that a list containing all twenty-seven books of the canonical New Testament was composed. It came in the form of an Easter Epistle by Athanasius, bishop of Alexandria. Owing to his influence and judicious selections, Athanasius's canon rapidly gained acceptance in both the East and West. By the early fifth century it had become standard.

The actual process of defining the canon was guided by several criteria.[25] The first was apostolicity. Apostolic authorship meant that a text's reliability in transmitting the teaching of Christ was beyond question. Apostolicity was not a necessary precondition for inclusion in the canon (no such claim could be made for the Gospels of Mark and Luke, Acts, Hebrews, or 2 and 3 John), but no work generally believed to have come from the hand of one of the Apostles was excluded. A second criterion was conformity with the gospel as it had been transmitted through generations of bishops. Popular belief that the gospel had always been preached in the same way may not have been justified, for there were differences among the churches, but conformity was an important standard nonetheless. A third criterion was consensus. Texts that were generally recognized as authoritative and widely used in worship were more likely to be included in the canon, especially if they were approved by the churches of Rome, Alexandria, and Antioch, whose lead was usually followed by others. A fourth and final criterion was antiquity. The prestige of a text was enhanced by its age, particularly if it could be traced back to the time of the Apostles. The author of the *Muratorian Canon,* for example, rejected The Shepherd of Hermas because he believed it had been written too close to his own time.

Of course, the process by which the New Testament canon was determined was far more complicated than described here. Even the statement that it concluded with Athanasius in 367 can be misleading, for there were some churches that did not accept the twenty-seven books he recommended. The Nestorian Christians of eastern Syria settled on a canon of only twenty-two books, rejecting 2 Peter, 2 and 3 John, Jude, and Revelation. In Africa, the Ethiopian Church created a canon of thirty-eight books, including The Shepherd of Hermas and the Apostolic Constitutions.[26] In the West, the process of determining the contents of the canon was not finalized until the sixteenth century. The Roman Catholic canon was fixed by the Council of Trent (1545–63), which accepted the Septuagint version of the Old Testament and the twenty-seven books of the New Testament. The Protestant canon was set by Martin Luther, who accepted the same New Testament but rejected Septuagint books not found in the original Jewish Scriptures.[27]

RULES OF FAITH AND THE APOSTLES' CREED

The effort to distinguish between orthodoxy and heterodoxy also led to the formulation of "rules of faith" that began to appear late in the second century. Each rule of faith was an attempt to state the

essence of Christianity with an accuracy and concision that would make it a useful standard in preaching, instructing **catechumens**, and interpreting scripture. Unlike creeds, rules of faith differed in phrasing and in the order in which articles of belief were stated, but they agreed on the fundamental tenets of the faith and in tracing its transmission back to the Apostles. Thus, the rule of faith found in Irenaeus's *Against Heresies* begins: "The Church, though dispersed throughout the whole world, even to the ends of the earth, has received from the Apostles and their disciples this faith."[28] In some cases concern for the threat represented by other forms of Christianity was expressed explicitly, as in the rule of faith found in Tertullian's treatise *Against Praxeas:*

> [We] believe . . . in one only God, . . . that the one only God also has a Son, his Word who has proceeded from himself, by whom all things were made and without whom nothing has been made: that this [Son] was sent by the Father into the virgin and was born of her both man and God, Son of man and Son of God, and was named Jesus Christ: that he suffered, died and was buried, according to the scriptures, and, having been raised up by the Father and taken back into heaven, sits at the right hand of the Father and will come to judge the quick and the dead: and that thereafter he, according to his promise, sent from the Holy Spirit the Paraclete, the sanctifier of the faith of those who believe in the Father and the Son and the Holy Spirit. That this Rule has come down from the beginning of the Gospel, even before all former heretics, not to speak of Praxeas of yesterday, will be proved as well by the comparative lateness of all heretics as by the very novelty of Praxeas of yesterday.[29]

In addition to rules of faith, early Christians formulated creeds. These were formal confessions of faith meant to be recited on occasions such as baptisms when a concise statement of belief was required. Their function is indicated by the word *creed* itself, which is derived from the Latin *credo* ("I believe"). In the West, the most famous example is the Apostles' Creed, which grew out of Jesus' command that the Apostles baptize new believers "in the name of the Father and of the Son and of the Holy Spirit."[30] According to Hippolytus, a Roman theologian, third-century candidates for baptism in the church at Rome were asked if they believed in the three persons of the Trinity: "Do you believe in God the Father, All Governing? Do you believe in Christ Jesus, the Son of God who was begotten? Do you believe in the Holy Spirit?"[31] Put into declarative form, augmented by additional articles of belief, and attributed to the Apostles, this "interrogatory creed" ultimately developed into the Apostles' Creed. The version familiar to Christians today is based on a manuscript dating to about 700, but its essential features are found in earlier creeds that represent its earlier stages of development. A good example is the Creed of Marcellus, a bishop of Ancyra (modern Ankara) in Asia Minor. It dates from the middle of the fourth century:

> I believe in God, All Governing; and in Christ Jesus His only begotten Son, our Lord, who was begotten of the Holy Spirit and the Virgin Mary, who was crucified under Pontius Pilate and buried, who rose from the dead on the third day, ascending to the heavens and taking his seat at the Father's right hand, whence he shall come to judge both living and dead; and I believe in the Holy Spirit, the holy Church, the forgiveness of sins, the resurrection of the body, [and] life everlasting.[32]

These lines not only set forth the basic features of the apostolic faith, they were also meant to defend it against heresy. Thus, the affirmation of belief in "God, All Governing" rejects the Gnostic and Marcionite claim that God had nothing to do with the creation and management of the material realm. The subsequent lines on the incarnation, suffering, death, and resurrection of Christ were also intended to counter Gnostic and Marcionite views, for they leave no doubt that he was both the son of the Creator and truly human. The assertion that the risen Christ is seated at the right hand of the Father suggests the oneness of God, a unity that was threatened by the notion of a higher, good God and a lesser God responsible for the creation of the material world.

The Apostles' Creed became the standard baptismal creed in the West; the eastern churches favored the Nicene Creed, which was adopted early in the fourth century, as we shall soon see. The two differ, but both proclaim what mattered most—the incarnation, suffering, and death of Christ, his resurrection and ascension into heaven, and his expected return as judge.

Controversies, Councils, and Creeds

The ecclesiastical hierarchy, canon of scripture, rules of faith, and early creeds were all important contributions to the development of a Church that would eventually claim to be both catholic ("universal") and orthodox.[33] But orthodoxy, or "right belief," was defined only over time and with great effort.

This is not surprising, for the theological claims of Christianity were bound to invite a wide range of interpretation in a Mediterranean world conditioned for centuries by the speculative spirit of Greek philosophy. Attention was focused primarily on the idea of the Trinity, according to which God, though one, was also three, and on the nature of Christ, who most Christians believed was both human and divine. But how could God be one and yet three? How did the Father, Son, and Holy Spirit relate to each other? Were all three equally divine? In what sense was Christ the Son of God? Had he always been the Son of God? What was the relationship of the human and the divine in Christ? Did God, who is pure spirit, really involve himself in the material world, even to the point of suffering and dying on a cross?

These and similar questions were addressed in church councils in which bishops assembled for the purpose of defining Christian belief. The issues of the nature of Christ and his relationship to the Father were addressed by the Council of Nicaea (325), the Council of Constantinople (381), and in the later formulation of the doctrine of the Trinity. The relationship of the human and divine in Christ was taken up in the fifth century by the Council of Chalcedon (451).

MONARCHIANISM

One early attempt to deal with the issue of the Trinity was **Monarchianism,** a theological movement that emphasized the unity of God but only by leaving little room for the discrete identities of the Father, Son, and Holy Spirit. Flourishing in the second and third centuries, Monarchianism took two basic forms. Dynamic Monarchians believed that Jesus was in no sense an incarnation of God but a man to whom God had given divine power (*dynamis*). Because of their view that Jesus had been chosen by God, Dynamic Monarchians are also called Adoptionists. Far more prominent were the Modalist Monarchians, who taught that the one God had expressed himself at various times as "Father," "Son," and "Holy Spirit," but that these were only names for modes in which he had temporarily operated and not distinct and eternal personalities of a triune God.

This doctrine was apparently brought to Rome about 190 by a certain Noetus, who had been forced out of the church in Smyrna in Asia Minor for teaching it there. In Rome its most famous defenders were Praxeas and **Sabellius.** They believed that they were defending the unity of God against the **ditheism** of other Christians who, in speaking of the Father and the Son as separate entities, seemed to be describing two different Gods. When Noetus was criticized for making a simple identification of God and Christ, he defended his views by arguing that the many scriptural references to the oneness of God gave him no choice but to conclude that Christ and the Father were one and the same.[34] "If therefore I acknowledge Christ to be God," he said, "He is the Father Himself, if He is indeed God."[35] For Modalist Monarchians, to recognize Christ as the Father was to glorify him, but their opponents did not agree. Writers like Hippolytus, Tertullian, and Epiphanius saw Monarchianism as an assault on the idea of the Trinity and therefore on the very nature of God. They accused the Monarchians of devaluing Christ by making him a mere mode of divine action and of thereby calling into question whether it was the Father or the Son who suffered on the cross.[36] In their view, the divine personalities of the Trinity were distinguished by real and permanent differences that were illustrated in scripture. Writing a century and a half after the beginning of the controversy, Hilary of Poitiers put it this way:

> Let Sabellius, if he dare, confound Father and Son as two names with one meaning, making of them not Unity but One Person. He shall have a prompt answer from the Gospels, not once or twice, but often repeated, *This is my beloved Son in whom I am well pleased* [Matthew 17:5]. He shall hear the words, *The Father is greater than I* [John 14:28], and *I go to the Father* [John 14:12], and *Father, I thank thee* [John 11:41], and *Glorify Me, Father* [John 17:5], and *Thou art the Son of the living God* [Matthew 16:17].[37]

According to scripture, then, Christ was the Son *of* the Father, had been beloved and glorified *by* the Father, and had gone *to* the Father. Clearly, said Hilary, the Son was *other* than the Father.

THE ARIAN CONTROVERSY AND THE COUNCIL OF NICAEA (325)

And yet most Christians also believed that Christ was divine. Did this mean that there were two Gods? The Monarchian controversy had raised a question of fundamental importance: How can the oneness of God be reconciled with the belief that the Father, Son, and Holy Spirit are both divine and distinct? Those who attempted to answer it focused their attention at first on the Father and the Son, often offering explanations that made the Son seem subordinate to the Father. Tertullian, for example, suggested that their relationship resembled that of the sun and a ray of light it sends forth into the world.[38] Like others, this metaphor succeeded in showing how two entities might be distinct and yet the same in substance and undivided; but it also gave the impression that one was inferior to the other, for the ray derives from the sun and represents only a part of its totality. Tertullian tried to explain this feature of his metaphor by pointing out that Christ had said, "The Father is greater than I" (John 14:28), but in doing so he only anticipated theological difficulties that would soon arise over claims of the inferiority of Christ, God the Son, to God the Father.

These were expressed nowhere better than in the teachings of **Arius**, a popular presbyter in the Church at Alexandria, where the Gospel of John's declaration that the Word (Logos) had become flesh (1:1–18) was always the starting point for discussions about the nature of Christ. About 318 Arius clashed with Alexander, the city's bishop, over their conflicting interpretations of the divinity of Christ. Arius claimed that the Logos-Son, though divine, was less so than the Father because he was created by the Father and therefore a creature rather than the Creator. Moreover, because the Logos had been created "in time," he did not share in the eternality of the Father but was temporal — that is, belonging in time. In a letter to his fellow bishops, Alexander described the heresy of Arius and his followers this way:

> The dogmas they have invented and assert, contrary to the scriptures, are these: . . . That the Word [i.e., *logos*] of God was not from eternity, but was made out of nothing . . . wherefore there was a time when he did not exist, inasmuch as the Son is a creature and a work. . . . He is neither like the Father as it regards his essence, nor is by nature either the Father's true Word, or true Wisdom, but indeed one of his works and creatures.[39]

These views raised serious concerns. First, if the Son was not of the same divine "essence" or substance as the Father, then he was necessarily less than the Father — that is, less than God. But Arius also insisted that the Son was divine, making it difficult to avoid the conclusion that there were two Gods. Second, as a temporal creature the Son would be capable of change, at least in theory, for nothing that belongs to time can be expected to last. This possibility seemed to threaten salvation, for how could anyone be confident in a salvation dependent on one who, having once changed by passing from nonexistence into existence, might change again?

Arius's critics protested that the Son was equal in divinity with the Father, that he was not created (and was therefore not a creature), and that he was eternal, having always existed with the Father. Despite this, there were many who were attracted to Arius's views. Soon the controversy had attracted such attention that the Arian aphorism "There was a time when the Son was not" was set to a popular tune and sung by thousands in the shops and streets of Alexandria. When Arius ignored Alexander's order to cease teaching his doctrines, Alexander had him deposed and excommunicated by a council of Egyptian bishops. By that time, however, Arius had fled to Palestine. While in exile, he managed to win the backing of powerful figures such as Eusebius, a bishop of Nicomedia who had great influence with the imperial court, and other eastern bishops. Before long the Arian movement had become powerful enough to threaten permanent division among Christians. For the sake of Christian unity and the unity of his empire, the emperor Constantine intervened and called for the matter to be settled at a council to be held in Nicaea, near Constantinople. The **Council of Nicaea** (325) was attended by more than three hundred bishops representing the entire Roman world, though the vast majority were from the East.

Although his activity was mostly behind the scenes, the true architect of the anti-Arian strategy at Nicaea was Athanasius, Alexander's assistant and eventual successor.[40] As bishop (328–73), Athanasius dominated Alexandrian theology for half a century. Against the Arians he argued that they could not have it both ways: Christ could not be created *and* divine. Athanasius found the Arian term *created* problematical, not only because created things are secondary to their creators but because they are never of the same substance. He advocated instead the word *begotten* (as in "only-begotten" Son[41]) because it was scriptural and suggested sameness of substance. Children, after all, get their substance from that of their parents. Of course, a child comes after its parents in time, but Athanasius insisted that this was not the case with the Son; being divine, the Son exists eternally with the Father and is eternally begotten by him.

In the end, Athanasius and the anti-Arian party prevailed at Nicaea. Both Arianism, which saw too great a difference between the Father and the Son, and Modalist Monarchianism, which allowed for no real distinction between them, were condemned. The Council affirmed that the Father and the Son were the same in substance (*homoousios*), that the

Son was begotten and not created, and that there had never been a time when he had not existed. The bishops included these points in a creed that was later revised by the councils of Constantinople (381) and Chalcedon (451), the result being the Nicene Creed familiar to Christians today. The original version, known as the Creed of Nicaea, appears below. Note the phrasing adopted to counter Arian theology:

> We believe in one God, the Father almighty, maker of all things, visible and invisible;
>
> And in one Lord Jesus Christ, the Son of God, begotten from the Father, only-begotten, that is, from the substance of the Father, God from God, light from light, true God from true God, begotten not made, of one substance with the Father, through Whom all things came into being, things in heaven and things on earth, Who because of us men and because of our salvation came down and became incarnate, becoming man, suffered and rose again on the third day, ascended to the heavens, and will come to judge the living and the dead;
>
> And in the Holy Spirit;
>
> But as for those who say, There was [a time] when He was not, and, Before being born He was not, and that He came into existence out of nothing, or who assert that the Son of God is from a different hypostasis or substance, or is created, or is subject to alteration or change — these the Catholic Church anathematizes.[42]

THE CAPPADOCIAN FATHERS AND THE DOCTRINE OF THE TRINITY

The history of Christian doctrine would be less confusing had the Council and Creed of Nicaea brought an end to debate about the relationship of the Father and the Son, but they did not. Despite the victory of *homoousios* theology, some of the eastern bishops began to fear that its emphasis on the consubstantiality or "sameness of substance" of the Father or the Son allowed for too little distinction between them. Consequently, they began to favor *homoiousios* ("of *similar* substance") over *homoousios* ("of the same substance"). As is often pointed out, the two terms were distinguished by only a single iota, but they were worlds apart theo-

logically because similarity of substance implied the existence of two separate divine beings.

Those bishops who favored *homoiousios* were backed by an Arian movement that still had much popular support. Arian influence reached even to the highest levels of power. The emperor Constantius II (337–61), for example, was an Arian Christian. As for the Nicene party, it was led by Athanasius from his succession as bishop of Alexandria until his death in 373. Thereafter, the champions of Nicene Christianity were three great theologians from **Cappadocia** in what is now northern Turkey. These **Cappadocian Fathers—Basil ("the Great")** of Caesarea, his brother **Gregory of Nyssa**, and **Gregory of Nazianzus**— saw clearly the necessity of preserving the "sameness of substance" that made the Father, Son, and Holy Spirit equal in divinity while at the same time demonstrating that they were discrete entities.

Writing in Greek, the Cappadocians explained that there is one divine *ousia* ("substance") but three *hypostaseis* (also, *hypostases*). The word *hypostasis*, which literally means something that stands beneath or provides a foundation for something else, can also mean "substance" or "essence." Despite the potential synonymy of *ousia* and *hypostasis*, the Cappadocians made a distinction between the two by using *hypostaseis* to refer specifically to the three ways in which the single *ousia* or substance of divinity is expressed. In his short treatise *On "Not Three Gods,"*[43] Gregory of Nyssa used the analogy of "humanity" and three particular people— Peter, James, and John — to illustrate this relationship. These three individuals are made of the *ousia* or "stuff" ("humanity") common to all human beings, so that we might accurately identify any one of them as "humanity." But they are also distinct, so that they might also be identified individually as Peter, James, and John — that is, as particular *hypostaseis* or expressions of "humanity."

Like all analogies, this one is imperfect, in this case because although the number of people in the world may change, the number of divine *hypostaseis* is eternally three. According to the Cappadocian Fathers, it is simply in the perfect and unchanging nature of divinity to express itself in a threefold way as Father, Son, and Holy Spirit. Another weakness in the analogy is that, despite their shared humanity, Peter, James, and John *act* differently from and independently of each other. Is this also true of the Father, Son, and Spirit? If so, it would seem that they are three different Gods. The Cappadocians anticipated this objection by saying that there is complete unity in divine action, for all three *hypostaseis* are fully involved whenever God acts.[44] Thus, God is one not only in what God *is* but also in what God *does*.

The Cappadocian view of the Trinity appears to have been formulated by about 375.[45] Before long, it was the most common (though certainly not the only) way of understanding the triune nature of God in both the Greek-speaking East and the Latin West. Latin writers used the word *substantia* ("substance") to translate *ousia* and *persona* ("person") to denote each of the three *hypostaseis* (*personae*) of the Trinity: one God in three persons. Confusion was occasionally caused by the fact that *substantia*, like *hypostasis*, has the literal meaning of "something that stands beneath." As a consequence, Latin-speaking Christians sometimes made the mistake of taking Greek references to the three *hypostaseis* to mean that there were three divine substances, but this difficulty was eventually eliminated by general agreement that Latin and Greek Christians meant the same thing though they had different ways of talking about it. The peculiarities of language could also create uncertainty in another way, for *persona* means "mask" as well as "person." Understood in this way, it could stress the unity of God by making the Father, Son, and Holy Spirit look more like guises in which God appears outwardly rather than distinct persons integral to the divine nature. This possibility no doubt appealed to Latin Christians, who tended to emphasize God's oneness. Greek Christians, on the other hand, viewed divinity primarily in terms of its individual *hypostaseis*, even addressing their prayers to the Father, Son, or Holy Spirit in particular.

Commenting a generation or so after the Cappadocian Fathers on the idiosyncrasies of the Greek and Latin ways of speaking about the Trinity, Augustine noted that the triune nature of God is ultimately beyond the grasp of human reason and language.[46] Most Christian thinkers have

agreed. Perhaps the most remarkable thing about the Cappadocian explanation of the unexplainable, then, is that it managed to gain such widespread and enduring acceptance. For more than sixteen centuries the Cappadocian formula of one God in three consubstantial yet distinct persons has been foundational to the Christian understanding of God.

THE CHRISTOLOGICAL CONTROVERSY AND THE COUNCIL OF CHALCEDON (451)

Along with questions about the Trinity, Christian thinkers addressed issues relating to Christology, the branch of Christian theology concerned with the nature of Christ and his role in salvation. By far, the most important of these was the relationship of the human and the divine in Christ. This problem, no less difficult than that of the Trinity, was complicated by the rivalry of two great schools of Christological thought, one associated with Antioch in Syria and the other with Alexandria in Egypt. Making sense of the Christological controversy is easier if we remember that the Antiochene theologians emphasized the two natures in Christ, stressing the importance for salvation of his humanity as well as his divinity and taking care that these were not confused. Alexandrian theologians, on the other hand, emphasized Christ's divinity. In seeking to compensate for the perceived errors of the other side, the tendencies of each school were sometimes greatly exaggerated. Thus, some Antiochene theologians suggested that the human and divine natures in Christ were completely separate and independent. For their part, Alexandrian theologians sometimes emphasized the divinity of Christ to the point of seeming to deny his humanity altogether. Just as the Council of Nicaea had been called to settle the Arian controversy and clarify the idea of the Trinity, the **Council of Chalcedon** (451) was convened to define the nature of Christ.

The history of the Christological controversy prior to Chalcedon was long and sometimes bitter. For modern observers with no background in theology, the issues involved might seem inconsequential; but for the theologians who sought to resolve them, nothing less than the salvation of humanity was at stake. This is because what Christ was able to *do* in the drama of salvation depended on who he *was*. Christians emphasized different aspects of what Christ had done, but they generally agreed that both his humanity and his divinity were critical to his work as savior. This view can be traced back to the New Testament itself. The author of the Gospel of John, for example, began his work with the assertion that the divine Logos had been made flesh (1:1–18).

Theories of salvation current in later years also stressed the importance of Christ's two natures. Most were elaborations on the theme of recapitulation found in Paul, for whom Christ was a second Adam.[47] By living a life of perfect obedience to God — a successful second attempt at the kind of human existence God had always intended — Christ had undone the damage sin had done to human beings and their relationship with God ever since the disobedience of the first Adam.

Some theologians (e.g., Clement of Alexandria, Irenaeus, Origen, and Gregory of Nazianzus) argued that salvation amounts to a kind of "divinization" resulting from the individual's assimilation to Christ, who, as the incarnate Logos, had united with humanity in order to elevate human beings to the level of divinity. In the words of Irenaeus, Christ was "the only true and steadfast teacher . . . who did, through his transcendent love, become what we are, that he might bring us to be even what he is himself."[48] Similarly, Origen wrote that "With Jesus human and divine nature began to be woven together, so that by fellowship with divinity human nature might become divine."[49] According to another, very different version of recapitulation described by Gregory of Nyssa, Augustine, and others, Christ made salvation possible by tricking Satan just as Satan had once deceived Adam in Eden. By choosing to sin, Adam had put himself and all subsequent humanity under the power of Satan. Constrained by his own perfect justice to respect Adam's choice, God could do nothing until Satan, seeing only the humanity in Christ, mistakenly tried to bring him down into death as he had all other human beings. This assault on one who was divine (as well as human) was an offense against God, who could now retaliate by destroying Satan's

tyranny over humanity. Other theories of salvation offered their own explanations of the significance of Christ's humanity and divinity. As we will see, the real problem lay in giving just the right amount of emphasis to each of these natures.

The consequences of failing to do so first became apparent in the late fourth century with the teachings of **Apollinaris** (also Apollinarius; ca. 310–ca. 390), a Syrian bishop with strong ties to the Alexandrian school. Like many people of his time, Apollinaris believed that human beings consist of a body and a soul, the latter consisting of a lower part, where emotions and basic urges are centered, and a higher part consisting of the intellect or mind. Reasoning that if there were two complete natures in Christ they would be *competing* natures, one of them even capable of sin, Apollinaris proposed instead that Christ had the body and lower soul of an ordinary human being but that in him the divine Logos took the place of a human mind. Thus, Christ had a single composite nature. In Apollinaris's view, this solution neatly explained how humanity and divinity could exist in Christ without a conflict of wills or the involvement of the sinful thoughts that would inevitably be present in a human mind. We may regard it as an example of the Alexandrian tendency to emphasize the divinity of Christ at the expense of his humanity, in this case by not taking into account that part of the human being usually identified as the essential self — the mind.

The reaction against Apollinaris came from two directions. The Cappadocians Gregory of Nyssa and Gregory of Nazianzus objected that his Christology threatened salvation. In Christ, they said, the Logos had assumed human nature so that human beings might take on the divine nature and thus be saved. But Apollinaris's claim that there was no human mind in Christ implied that salvation was incomplete, because, as Gregory of Nazianzus put it, "that which he [i.e., the Logos] has not assumed he has not healed."[50] Protests also came from Antiochene theologians such as **Theodore of Mopsuestia** (ca. 350–428), who argued that Christ's experiences of emotion and intellectual growth, described in the New Testament, could not have occurred in the divine Logos but only in a complete and truly human mind.

Although Apollinarianism was condemned at the Council of Constantinople in 381, its influence continued to be felt. In Antioch, it spurred the development of a rival Christology whose first great exponent was Theodore of Mopsuestia. According to him, Christ was one person in whom there were two complete natures. This union occurred when the Logos came to "dwell" in the man Jesus, joining with him in a "perfect conjunction of natures."[51] But this did not mean that the two natures were in any way mixed or confused. Just the opposite, for Theodore distinguished clearly between them, insisting that the qualities of one could not be attributed to the other. Thus, New Testament references to Christ weeping, hungering, or being tempted applied only to his human nature, whereas only his divine nature was at work when he performed miracles and taught higher truths. This arrangement allowed Theodore to argue, against Apollinaris, that humanity was fully present in Christ. It also enabled him to focus attention on the reality of Christ's human suffering, a part of salvation that Antiochene theologians thought was too often ignored by the Alexandrian school. But Theodore's emphasis on the differences between the human and divine natures in Christ also disturbed other Christians who feared that it undermined the unity of Christ or whose beliefs and practices were threatened by its implications.

Such fears soon erupted into a stormy controversy over the popular custom of referring to the Virgin Mary as **Theotokos** ("God-bearer" or "Mother of God"). The principal figure on the Antiochene side was **Nestorius** (ca. 381–ca. 451), a Syrian monk who became bishop of Constantinople in 428. Following the lines of Theodore's thought to their logical conclusion, Nestorius argued that human birth was not a quality that could be attributed to divinity. Mary could not have been the mother of the divine nature in Christ, he said, so it was not appropriate to call her *Theotokos*. Recognizing the depth of popular devotion to Mary, however, he suggested an alternative title, *Christotokos* ("Christ-bearer" or "Mother of Christ"), which acknowledged Mary as the mother of the man in whom the Logos chose to dwell, though not of divinity itself.

Nestorius's views offended many Christians who took his position against the *Theotokos* as a defamation of the Virgin Mary. They also alarmed theologians such as Cyril of Alexandria, the city's bishop (412–44), who feared (or at least claimed to fear) that Nestorius was arguing not merely for two distinct natures in Christ, but for two separate *persons* or *beings*.[52] It is likely that Cyril exaggerated his suspicions in order to encourage anti-Nestorian sentiment, but Nestorius himself may have added to the confusion by explaining the union of the two natures in Christ in terms that were either unclear or too subtle for his critics. The precise nature of his teachings is still disputed. Until recently, scholars tended to view Nestorius from Cyril's point of view, but his *Bazaar of Heracleides,* discovered at the end of the nineteenth century, has convinced many that he was actually an orthodox theologian whose Christology was a skillful attempt to strike a compromise between Antioch and Alexandria. For Cyril, in any case, Nestorius's Christology raised issues ranging from salvation (If only the humanity in Christ suffered and died, does salvation depend only on the man Jesus and not on God?) to the sacraments (Does the separateness of Christ's humanity and divinity mean that only the body and blood of Christ, and not his divinity, are present in the eucharist?). Seeking to preserve the unity of Christ, Cyril argued that Christ had *one* nature, that of the divine Logos, and that his humanity was a way of existing the Logos had assumed upon being born to the Virgin Mary (who therefore deserved the title *Theotokos*). To express this view he used a phrase borrowed unknowingly, but perhaps tellingly, from Apollinaris: "One incarnate nature of the divine Logos."[53]

Nestorius was a persuasive speaker who held a powerful office, but he was no match for Cyril, who had a reputation for both brilliance and ruthlessness. The latter was certainly in evidence in 431 when he and his supporters arrived in Ephesus for a council called to settle the Nestorian question. Without waiting for the Antiochene bishops to arrive, and with Nestorius in town but terrorized by a mob incited against him by the city's bishop, Cyril convened the Council of Ephesus. Under his direction, and in the absence of his opponents, it took just one day to condemn Nestorius as "the new Judas,"[54] strip him of his authority, and vindicate the *Theotokos*. Forced into exile in southern Egypt, Nestorius died in obscurity years later, still protesting that he had been misunderstood. Nestorianism itself managed to survive by moving eastward into Mesopotamia, Persia, and, ultimately, China. Small Nestorian communities can still be found today, most of them in Syria, Iraq, and Iran.

It seemed that Cyril had won, but the issue was still far from settled. Under imperial and ecclesiastical pressure to restore good relations with Antioch, he soon agreed to soften his earlier stance. According to the terms of the *Formula of Reunion* (433), a compromise confessional formula written by Bishop John of Antioch (428–41) and embraced by Cyril, Nestorius was once again condemned and the title *Theotokos* once again approved. In addition, Christ was described as "complete God and complete human being," which pleased the Antiochene faction, *and* as a "union of two natures . . . as a consequence of which we confess . . . one Son," which was meant to satisfy the Alexandrians.[55] Cyril himself found compromise with Antioch possible by coming to understand Christ as having *one* nature (*hypostasis*) arising *out of* two natures. The distinct identities of his humanity and divinity were retained, Cyril said, though their unity was assured by the fact that what was true of one nature might be attributed to the other. According to this doctrine, known as the *communicatio idiomatum* (a "sharing" or "imparting of peculiar qualities"), the miracles performed by the divinity in Christ had also been worked by the humanity in him. Similarly, although Mary had given birth to a human being, it was also true that she had borne his divinity.

For as long as Cyril and John of Antioch were alive their willingness to compromise preserved the peace, but upon their deaths conflict between Alexandria and Antioch broke out once again. This time trouble was instigated by Eutyches, a monk from Constantinople who allowed that there had been two natures *before* the incarnation but claimed that they were so well blended in their union that afterward there was only one divine (i.e., deified human) nature. Eutyches' Monophysite ("one nature") Christology won the support of Cyril's suc-

cessor, Dioscorus, who regretted that Cyril had abandoned his early views. Hoping to reestablish an Alexandrian Christology closer to that of Apollinaris and the early Cyril, he presided over another council at Ephesus (449) that affirmed Eutyches' views and forbade any mention of "two natures" after the incarnation. But this "Robber Council," as it was later called by Pope Leo I (440–61), was a farce. Dioscorus had taken full advantage of an imperial order giving him the right to silence his opponents and had also brought with him a troop of fanatical Egyptian monks to intimidate them. In addition, he had refused to allow a reading of a papal letter, the so-called *Tome* of Leo, which endorsed the *communicatio idiomatum*.

There were few apart from Monophysite Christians who could accept the decisions of the Robber Council. To reach a more legitimate outcome, another council was called at Chalcedon, not far from Constantinople, in 451. The bishops who attended this historic meeting produced the Definition of Chalcedon, a statement of faith that rejected Monophysitism and embraced a Christology essentially like that of the later Cyril: Christ was one person in whom there were two natures, human and divine, each sharing attributes of the other (the *communicatio idiomatum*). The Definition reads:

> Therefore, following the holy Fathers, we all with one accord teach men to acknowledge one and the same Son, our Lord Jesus Christ, at once complete in Godhead and complete in manhood, truly God and truly man, consisting also of a reasonable soul and body; of one substance (*homoousios*) with the Father as regards his Godhead, and at the same time of one substance with us as regards his manhood; like us in all respects, apart from sin; as regards his Godhead, begotten of the Father before the ages, but yet as regards his manhood begotten, for us men and for our salvation, of Mary the Virgin, the God-bearer (*Theotokos*); one and the same Christ, Son, Lord, Only-begotten, recognized in two natures, without confusion, without change, without division, without separation; the distinction of natures being in no way annulled by the union, but rather the characteristics of each nature being preserved and coming together to form one person and subsistence (*hypostasis*), not as parted or separated into two

persons, but one and the same Son and Only-begotten God the Word, Lord Jesus Christ; even as the prophets from earliest times spoke of him, and our Lord Jesus Christ himself taught us, and the creed of the Fathers has handed down to us.[56]

Clearly, the framers of the Definition intended to steer a middle course between the extreme forms of the Alexandrian and Antiochene Christologies. The assertion that in Christ there were two complete natures existing without confusion or change was a rejection of Eutyches and Monophysitism, just as the references to their coexistence "without division, without separation" and to Mary as *Theotokos* were a repudiation of Nestorius. By insisting on Christ's "reasonable soul" and his being "of one substance with the Father," the Definition also dealt with the teachings of Apollinaris and the Arians respectively.

It may be said that, all in all, the Council of Chalcedon was a success because it laid down Christological principles that have been recognized as orthodox by most Christians until our own time. Still, no compromise pleases everyone. Some saw it as a victory for Nestorius, who had died just a year earlier, and registered their protest by joining the Monophysite churches, which continued to grow despite their condemnation. Monophysitism still exists in the Coptic Christianity of modern Egypt and among the Amharic Christians of Ethiopia.

Theologians of the Fourth and Fifth Centuries

The stormy centuries that saw the great debates over Christ and the Trinity also produced important personalities whose influence in shaping Christian belief and practice can still be felt today. We have already had occasion to mention some of them, though without commenting on the full range of their work. In the East, the Cappadocian Fathers were among the most influential Christian thinkers, as was John Chrysostom. In the West,

Jerome, Ambrose and, above all, Augustine played major roles in shaping Christianity.

THE CAPPADOCIAN FATHERS

We have already encountered the Cappadocian Fathers — Basil of Caesarea (ca. 330–79), Gregory of Nazianzus (ca. 329–ca. 390), and Basil's younger brother, Gregory of Nyssa (ca. 331–ca. 395)—in noting the role of Basil ("the Great") as a founder of monasticism in Asia Minor and in describing their involvement in the Trinitarian controversy. The accomplishments of the Cappadocians go so far beyond this, however, that it is difficult to exaggerate their overall significance.

Their influence was felt especially in the East, where Basil and Gregory of Nazianzus have been venerated for centuries with John Chrysostom as founders of the Eastern Orthodox tradition. Both men were ascetics whose abilities drew them into the political and intellectual life of the Church. Basil eagerly sought consecration as bishop of Cappadocian Caesarea and then used his influence to secure a bishopric for Gregory, with whom he had formed a close friendship while they were students in Caesarea and Athens. But the more retiring Gregory did not have Basil's flair for politics. Having already been forced into the priesthood by his father as a young man, he felt betrayed when Basil, seeking to fill the hierarchy with anti-Arians, tried to thrust him into public life by making him bishop of Smasia, a backwater postal station. Gregory never so much as visited the town. Later, he narrowly escaped being made bishop of Nazianzus, the office his father had held, by fleeing to a monastery. Toward the end of his life he reluctantly agreed to serve as bishop of Constantinople, but he resigned after serving less than a year in order to spend the rest of his life writing in seclusion.

Their friendship and shared love of Origen led Basil and Gregory to collaborate in producing the *Philocalia* ("Love of What Is Beautiful"), a collection of what they considered to be the most important passages from the writings of the Alexandrian sage. Basil's own theological writings, such as his treatise *On the Holy Spirit* and his three "Books against Eunomius," testify to his brilliance as a theologian and defender of Nicene orthodoxy. Gregory, who earned the epithet "the Theologian," distinguished himself as such by his "Five Theological Orations," which include a persuasive appeal for recognition of the divinity and the consubstantiality of the Holy Spirit. He also wrote forty-five *Orations,* most of them preached in church services, and numerous letters and poems on religious and theological topics.

The third of the Cappadocians, Gregory of Nyssa, composed polemical treatises against Apollinaris and the Arian extremist Eunomius, but it was as a mystical theologian that he truly excelled. Powerfully influenced by Origen and Neoplatonism, he saw in the natural world reflections of higher, spiritual realities. These, he said, offer glimpses of higher truths, and even of God, the union of whose *hypostaseis* is mirrored in the union of the mind, reason, and soul in every human being. At times Gregory's imagery can be breathtaking, as in this description of the love of the soul for God:

> When she has torn herself from her attachment to sin, and by that mystic kiss she yearns to bring herself close to the fountain of light, then does she become beautiful, radiant with the light of truth. . . . Like a steed she races through all she perceives by sense or by reason; and she soars like a dove until she comes to rest with longing under the shade of the apple tree. . . . Then she is encompassed by a divine night during which the spouse approaches but does not reveal Himself.[57]

The idea that the soul's attraction to God is analogous to the erotic attraction of lovers is a major theme in Gregory's work. In the passage below he uses the analogy of a bride and her new husband to illustrate his conception of the soul being raised to ever higher levels of illumination by the Logos-Christ:

> We see the Word, then, leading the bride up a rising staircase, as it were, up to the heights by the ascent of perfection. . . . He bids the bride draw near to the light and then to become beautiful by being changed, in the light, into the form of a Dove. And then, even though she has enjoyed her share of good things as far as was in her power,

He nonetheless continues to draw her on to a participation in transcendent Beauty as though she had not yet tasted of it. In this way her desire grows in proportion with her progress to each new stage of development; and because of the transcendence of the graces which she finds ever beyond her, she always seems to be beginning anew. For this reason the Word says once again to His awakened bride: *Arise;* and, when she has come, *Come.* For he who is rising can always rise further; and for him who runs to the Lord the open field of the divine course is never exhausted. We must therefore constantly arouse ourselves and never stop drawing closer and closer in our course. For as often as He says *Arise* and *Come,* He gives us the power to rise and make progress.[58]

The beauty and insight of passages like these help to explain why Gregory of Nyssa is considered one the the the greatest of Christian mystics.

JOHN CHRYSOSTOM

Another towering figure in the ancient Church was **John Chrysostom** (ca. 347–407), whose astonishing skill as a preacher earned him the epithet "golden-mouthed" (*chrysostomos*). Like the Cappadocians, he had a thorough training in Greek rhetoric and literature as well as in scripture and theology, ideal preparation for a pastoral career. Like them, too, he was drawn to asceticism. In his youth he had withdrawn from society to live as a hermit, and throughout his career he praised the solitary life as the highest to which a Christian could aspire.

Born in Syrian Antioch, where he studied under the famous pagan rhetorician Libanius, John remained in the city until 398 when he became patriarch of Constantinople. Rising through the ranks of lector (reader), deacon and priest, he dealt with all the issues, civic as well as theological, affecting the Christians of Antioch. He did so primarily in his sermons, many of which are extant. When Antiochene mobs destroyed statues of the emperor and his family in anger over oppressive taxes, John delivered a series of *Homilies on the Statues.* When the agitation of radical Arians in Antioch appeared to threaten the stability of the Church, he preached another series *On the Incomprehensibility of God.* When the attraction of Christians to Jewish observances led to their participation in them, John responded with eight discourses *Against Judaizing Christians,* whose ugly language (he goes so far as to call Jews "God's enemies") was later made to serve the interests of medieval anti-Judaism. Alongside these were hundreds of orations in praise of martyrs, sermons on books of the Bible, and discourses on various aspects of Christian life. The Liturgy of St. John Chrysostom, standard in the Eastern Orthodox churches, probably does not go back to him.

We can see in these works an impatience with moral laxity and corruption that created difficulties for John as patriarch. He did not seek the patriarchate, but his fame left him little opportunity to refuse it after the death of Nectarius, his predecessor. He soon became enmeshed in ecclesiatical conflicts and imperial intrigues from which his honesty, high standards, and direct speech (some would say tactlessness) would not allow him to emerge unscathed. He made a dangerous enemy of his rival, Theophilus, patriarch of Alexandria, by defending Origenism at a time when it had been outlawed in Egypt. He also angered the empress Eudoxia by criticizing her for her greed and injustice and even comparing her to Jezebel, a biblical queen known for her wickedness. He was deposed, reinstated, and then deposed once again. He died in 407 while en route to a distant exile on the Black Sea, but not before setting high standards in preaching and the interpretation of scripture.

JEROME

Jerome (ca. 345–420) was a Bible scholar translator, polemicist, and ascetic. Born in Dalmatia, a Roman province on the eastern coast of the Adriatic, he studied at Rome and traveled in Gaul before joining friends who had taken up the ascetic life in the city of Aquileia near the head of the Adriatic Sea. He later spent nearly five years living as a hermit and learning Hebrew in the Syrian desert before moving on to Antioch, where he was ordained a priest. After visiting Constantinople he returned to Rome, where he became secretary to Pope Damasus I (366–84). Upon Damasus's death, Jerome

journeyed to Egypt and then to Palestine. About 386 he settled in Bethlehem, where he spent the rest of his life presiding over a monastery and devoting himself to study.

Jerome is famous primarily for his work in translating the Bible from the original Hebrew and Greek into a Latin version known as the **Vulgate** (from *vulgatus,* the "common" language). This project began as a revision of the Old Latin version of the Bible suggested by Damasus but soon evolved into an entirely new translation that served as the standard Latin text of scripture from the early Middle Ages until our own time. Jerome also composed influential commentaries on books of the Bible and polemical works against such figures as Helvidius, who taught that Mary gave birth to children after Jesus, Jovinian, who claimed that virginity was not superior to marriage, and Pelagius, who emphasized freedom of will and good works over the power of sin. He also helped to lay the foundations of medieval Christianity by advocating celibacy, monasticism, and the veneration of saints.

AMBROSE

Another bridge-builder between ancient and medieval Christianity was **Ambrose** (ca. 339–97), bishop of Milan and one of the original Latin **Doctors of the Church**, theologians noted for their exceptional merit and saintliness, along with Jerome, Augustine, and Gregory the Great.[59] Educated at Rome, he practiced law and served as a provincial governor in northern Italy until his intervention in a disputed election to the see of Milan in 374 led to his being appointed bishop himself.

Ambrose excelled as a preacher, theologian, and administrator responsible for representing the interests of the Church before civil authorities. There is little doubt that he was a major force behind the emperor Gratian's decision to remove a pagan altar from the Roman senate in 382 and the edicts issued by Theodosius I after 391 forbidding the worship of pagan gods. He also defended Nicene Christianity against a powerful Arian movement that was well represented in the imperial court in the person of Justina, the mother of Valentinian II. When she persuaded her son to issue an edict giving control of

Figure 4.1 **Christ as the Good Shepherd** This painting from a ceiling in the cata-
combs in Rome depicts Christ as the shepherd who lays down his life for the sake of his
sheep (John 10:1–18; compare Matthew 18:12–14 and Luke 15:4–7).

church buildings to Arian Christians, Ambrose
managed to force its cancellation, claiming that "the
emperor is within the Church, not above it."[60] He
invoked the same principle some years later when
Theodosius I permitted his troops to massacre seven
thousand citizens of Thessalonica in their hippo-
drome as punishment for the murder of a government official. Ambrose excommunicated the emperor, barring him from the eucharist until he
presented himself in the cathedral of Milan to beg
forgiveness and do penance. It was the first time
that a Christian ruler had publicly bowed to the authority of the Church. In conceiving of two separate

spheres of authority, spiritual and secular, with the
former having priority over the latter, Ambrose anticipated the medieval Church's conception of the
relationship between church and state.

Although he was not an especially innovative
theologian, Ambrose's knowledge of Greek and
Greek Christian thinkers such as Origen, Athanasius, Basil, and Cyril of Jerusalem made him unusual among western Christians and enabled him to
promote awareness of Greek ideas in the western
Church. He was even more familiar with Latin
writers. His most important theological work, *On
the Duties of the Clergy*, is a collection of ethical

teachings inspired by the Roman statesman Cicero's *On Duties.* Ambrose also deserves credit for making singing a part of Christian worship in the West. Christian hymns were certainly known before his time, but Ambrose popularized congregational singing by encouraging the composition of works that were poetic and yet simple enough to be within the ability of most people. Scholars agree that at least four extant Latin hymns can be attributed to him.[61] One of them, *God, Creator of All,* a beautiful evening hymn, evinces Ambrose's faith in a God on whom humanity is completely dependent and gives us a feeling for pious sentiment in Rome in the late fourth century:

> Maker of all things, God most high,
> Great ruler of the starry sky,
> Who, robing day with beauteous light,
> Hast clothed in soft repose the night.
>
> That sleep may wearied limbs restore,
> And fit for toil and use once more,
> May gently soothe the careworn breast,
> And lull our anxious griefs to rest.
>
> We thank thee for the day that's gone;
> We pray thee for the night come on;
> O help us sinners as we raise
> To thee our hymn of votive praise.
>
> From every carnal passion free
> O may our hearts repose in thee!
> Nor envious fiend, with harmful stare,
> Our rest with sinful terrors share.
>
> Christ with the Father ever one,
> Spirit! the Father and the Son,
> God over all, the mighty sway,
> Shield us, great Trinity, we pray.[62]

Despite Ambrose's contributions as a defender of the Church, theologian, and hymnographer, his greatest gift may well have been his influence on a young man who was destined to play a far greater role in shaping western Christianity than any other figure since Paul. His name was Augustine.

AUGUSTINE

Augustine was born in Thagaste in the Roman province of Numidia (modern Algeria) in 354. The son of a pagan father, he had a Christian mother, Monica, who wanted nothing more than for her son to join her in the faith. Testing her patience, he delayed his baptism until the age of thirty-two. By that time he had spent years in worldly pursuits and investigations of religious and philosophical alternatives to the Christianity she had taught him as a child. Fortunately, he has left us a wonderful account of this spiritual journey in his autobiographical *Confessions,* which offers a richly detailed description of the spiritual and intellectual culture of late antiquity as well as valuable insights into his own thought and experience.

In the *Confessions* we discover an Augustine whose character was complex even in adolescence. Brilliant and sensitive, he was also capable of vandalism. His parents, who were ambitious for him, sent him at sixteen to school in nearby Madaura, where he studied grammar and Latin literature. He later went to Carthage, where he completed his academic training and found a post teaching rhetoric. By this time Augustine had also begun a fifteen-year relationship with a woman he never names but with whom he lived and had a son, Adeodatus ("Given by God"). It was against this background that at the age of nineteen he read Cicero's *Hortensius,* a call to the study of philosophy, and committed himself to a lifelong search for truth.

It led him at first to **Manichaeism**, a religion based on the teachings of Mani, a third-century Babylonian prophet. Combining belief in Christ as savior with Persian dualism and elements of other religions, Manichaeism had become fashionable among North African intellectuals. Augustine was intrigued by its cosmic dualism, which seemed at first to offer a sound explanation of the problem of evil. This issue is always problematical for monotheistic religions because a single, universal God may reasonably be held accountable for the evil in the world as well as the good. But Mani had followed the Gnostics in speaking of two gods—a good one who had created the spiritual realm and an evil one who ruled over matter. The goal of human life, he said, was to escape evil by withdrawing from the world, largely through abstinence from such things as meat and sex, and moving toward the "realm of light." Augustine was also attracted by the Manichaeans' claim that their teachings were demonstrably rational. Even their careful charting of the stars, which they believed determined the destiny of every human being, was said to be scientific.

But Augustine soon found inconsistencies in their doctrines that even the most learned Manichaeans could not explain. He was troubled, too, by the Manichaean tendency to blame sin on the stars and on the inherent evil of the body, within which the spiritual self was entrapped. Much later in life he would write that, when he had first embraced Manichaeism, "It flattered my pride to think that I incurred no guilt. . . . I preferred to excuse myself and blame this unknown thing which was in me but was not part of me. The truth, of course, is that it was all my own self."[63] This conviction, that he was morally flawed and that there was something fundamentally wrong with human nature generally, would become central to the thought of Augustine the Christian.

As his interest in Manichaeism waned, Augustine found himself drawn to Platonism. In later years he would compare Plato to a demigod[64] and make Plato's philosophy part of the foundation of his theology, but the form of Platonism in which he now dabbled was little more than skepticism. Soon, though, he would find a more satisfying interpretation of Plato.

At twenty-nine Augustine left Carthage for Rome and then Milan, where he had been offered a prestigious post as professor of rhetoric. There he read the works of Plotinus and other Neoplatonist philosophers, who spoke of God as the ultimate reality and of the mystical and spiritual nature of higher truth. He was fascinated by these ideas, as well as by the Neoplatonist conception of evil as the absence of good rather than as an entity having its own objective reality, as the Manichaeans claimed. In Neoplatonism he found a system of thought more compelling than any he had yet encountered, but not the end of his search. Instead, it led him back to Christianity, for in its teachings he found convincing philosophical expression of biblical truths he had heard from Monica as a child. He had drunk Christ with his mother's milk,[65] he once said. After years of searching, he was about to turn to him again.

Monica, who had followed Augustine to Milan, now persuaded him to attend the sermons of Ambrose, whose typological and allegorical interpreta-

tion of the Bible revealed to him new depths of meaning in scripture. He was moved, too, by the beauty of the hymns sung in the city's cathedral. Gradually, Augustine allowed himself to be pulled into the orbit of the Church, thanks in part to his discovery of intellectual circles that blended Neoplatonism and Christianity. Sensing that her son was at last prepared to give up the sins of his youth, Monica arranged a marriage for him. Adeodatus's mother was sent back to Africa, and Augustine, now thirty-two, agreed to wait for his bride to reach the marriageable age of twelve. But he could not keep his promise. Within weeks he had found another companion. Ironically, even as he took this new lover he was considering with friends how they might retire from the world in order to devote themselves to study and contemplation.

This conflict between his simultaneous attractions to sensual gratification and spiritual understanding was suddenly resolved one afternoon in 386 when, in a garden in Milan, a mysterious voice told him to "Take and read, take and read." There was a Bible nearby, which Augustine opened randomly to a passage in Paul's Letter to the Romans (13:13–14) and read: "Let us live honorably as in the day, not in reveling and drunkenness, not in debauchery and licentiousness, not in quarreling and jealousy. Instead, put on the Lord Jesus Christ, and make no provision for the flesh, to gratify its desires." His life was changed. The following Easter he was baptized by Ambrose along with Adeodatus and his old friend Alypius who, like Monica, had followed him to Italy. Resolved to take up the ascetic life, the four set out for Africa. Sadly, Monica fell ill and died at Ostia, Rome's port, but Augustine, Adeodatus, and Alypius returned to Thagaste and in 388 founded there a community of seekers devoted to poverty, celibacy, study, and prayer. It was the beginning of the Augustinian order of monks. Augustine apparently intended to spend the rest of his life as a monk, but it was not to be. On a visit to the North African city of Hippo in 391 he was seized by a crowd of admirers who, ignoring his protests, made him presbyter. Shortly thereafter he was made the city's bishop, a position he held until his death in 430.

It was as bishop, then, that Augustine worked out his monumental theology. Many of its most important features were forged in the midst of two great conflicts — one with the Donatists and another with Pelagius and the Pelagians — and as he created a Christian philosophy of history.

By Augustine's time, Donatism had flourished in North Africa for nearly a century. In chapter 3 we saw its origins in the persecutions of the third and fourth centuries, when the African Church was divided over the status of Christians who lapsed in the face of persecution. Believing that the sanctity of the Church depended on the morality of its members, the Donatists had withdrawn from the traditional Church because of its leniency towards those who were guilty of serious sin. Among the worst offenders were the *traditores* ("those who hand over"), priests and bishops who had surrendered copies of scripture to their persecutors. The Donatists contended that by their actions these **clerics** had forsaken not only their faith but their priestly authority as well. Abandoned by the Holy Spirit, they were no longer priests, and without legitimate leaders their congregations were no longer churches.

The Donatist crisis was the first great challenge Augustine faced as bishop. Thousands had rushed to join an alternative Christian movement that denied the legitimacy of his own. In nearly every city and town rival congregations coexisted uneasily in mutual suspicion and hostility. Standing outside his cathedral in Hippo, the new bishop must have been unnerved by the sight of the Donatist basilica that stood nearby. But he understood what was at stake. If the Donatists were correct in claiming that the validity of sacraments performed by clergy depended on the clergy's moral purity — something about which no one could ever be certain — then the status of countless baptisms, eucharists, confirmations, marriages, **ordinations**, confessions, and acts of penance would be in doubt. Aside from this practical consideration, Augustine objected that the moral expectations of the Donatists were unreasonable. Like other Christians, he said, priests and bishops are imperfect human beings, yet God works through them despite their imperfection, making them effective leaders of their congregations and ensuring the validity of the sacraments they perform. It is not the moral character of a priest that determines his ability to administer a sacrament effectively, he argued, but his ordination and the proper performance of the action itself. As medieval theologians would put it centuries later, the actual accomplishment of baptisms, marriages, ordinations, and other sacraments is not *ex opere operantis* (by virtue of the person acting) but *ex opere operato* (by virtue of the action performed).

Despite his conviction that the Donatists were in error, Augustine believed that God was present among them and that the proper course of action was to seek their reconciliation to the Church. He gave public lectures and published pamphlets meant to win them back, but these had little effect. As religious violence increased, most of it perpetrated by Donatists, he concluded that only the intervention of the Roman state would bring an end to the schism. Rome, for its part, was eager to see the matter settled. In 405 the emperor Honorius issued edicts outlawing Donatist churches and calling for the confiscation of their property. In 411 more sweeping measures reduced Donatism to an almost insignificant movement that managed to survive in isolated spots until the advance of Islam in the seventh and eighth centuries all but eradicated North African Christianity altogether.

Augustine justified the Church's request that Rome take action against the Donatists by pointing to individuals whose minds had been changed by the imposition of penalties. He also appealed to a parable in the Gospel of Luke (14:15–24) in which Jesus compares the Kingdom of God to a great banquet. When the invited guests do not show up, the host orders his servants to go out into the streets and bring people in by force if necessary. To Augustine, the application of this principle — that sometimes people must be compelled to do what is in their best interests — must have seemed both reasonable and necessary in the case of the Donatists. After all, human souls and the integrity of the Church were in danger. But it would prove to be an unfortunate precedent. In later years the words "Compel people to come in" (Luke 14:23) would often be cited by ecclesiastical and secular authorities whose aims were not always spiritual. Augustine's theory that war may be justified when fought for the sake of peace and the good of society would also be repeatedly abused.

The second great conflict in which Augustine became involved was the Pelagian controversy. **Pelagius** was a British ascetic who arrived in Rome about 390. Disgusted by the immorality he witnessed among the Christians there and disturbed by their tendency to excuse their behavior by claiming that baptism alone was enough to guarantee salvation, Pelagius argued that God holds sinners responsible for their sins and that Christians should therefore strive earnestly for moral perfection. When some objected that perfection was unattainable, he responded that God would not have given the commandments found in the Bible if human beings did not have the ability to obey them. Through scripture and in Christ, he said, God had given humanity knowledge of the difference between right and wrong. Moreover, he had given every human being freedom of choice. It was the responsibility of every Christian, who had been freed from the power of sin at baptism, to make appropriate use of this gift. Fleeing the Visigothic sack of Rome in 410, Pelagius and his disciple Coelestius appeared shortly thereafter in North Africa, eager to take up the issues of human nature, sin, and salvation with Augustine.

Of course, Pelagius was not the first to call for moral reform in the Church, and he was certainly not alone in his own day. In Rome and throughout southern Italy and Sicily, like-minded Christians were making the same demand. What brought Pelagius into conflict with Augustine was his optimistic view of human nature and, more specifically, his assertion that perfection lies within the grasp of every human being.

In his younger days Augustine might have been more sympathetic toward Pelagius's claims about human freedom and potential; after all, one of his reasons for leaving the Manichaeans had been that their belief in the controlling influence of the stars left little room for freedom of choice. But time and reflection had led him to the conclusion that human nature, far from being what Pelagius imagined, was so thoroughly corrupt that human beings were incapable of doing anything truly good unless they were inspired and assisted by God's grace. In a famous passage from his *Confessions,* published when he was nearly fifty, Augustine illustrated the depravity of human nature by recalling how he and some other teenagers had once stolen pears from a neighbor's tree. What shocked him about this incident was not the severity of his sin, which was little more than adolescent mischief, but the fact that he had been so powerfully attracted to evil and had found such great pleasure in doing it:

> We took away an enormous quantity of pears, not to eat them ourselves, but simply to throw them to the pigs. Perhaps we ate some of them, but our real pleasure consisted in doing something that was forbidden. . . . The evil in me was foul, but I loved it. I loved my own perdition and my own faults, not the things for which I committed wrong, but the wrong itself.[66]

Augustine saw the will to sin as characteristic of human beings in general. More than mere disobedience, it seemed to him a fundamental flaw in human nature that clouds moral vision and perverts the will by directing it toward what is evil rather than to that which is good. Given such assumptions about the moral condition of humanity and the powerful grip sin has on human lives, it is no wonder that Augustine could not agree with Pelagius that perfection can be attained through human effort. Instead, he could only conclude that human beings are morally and spiritually helpless and therefore absolutely dependent upon God and divine grace if they are to be saved from the consequences of their sin.

Reasoning still further along these lines, Augustine formulated a theory of **predestination** that more firmly established his position against Pelagius. Despite their sin, he said, God does save some people by extending to them a grace that enables them to respond to him in faith and love. Divine grace is irresistible, he said, for a love that could be resisted would be imperfect and therefore incompatible with God's perfection. But this does not mean that grace opposes or limits the freedom of the individual. Rather, it strengthens and purifies the will so that it gladly turns away from evil and begins to desire its original and only proper object — God. Thus, those to whom God extends his grace are destined to be saved. Augustine argued that it is impossible to know why God chooses to save some people and not others. At the same time, however, he insisted that God is not unjust, for although God allows some people a destiny better than they deserve, he does not add to the suffering the rest have brought on themselves. Nor is God arbitrary. Instead, he is perfectly rational and has good reasons for his decisions, though they may be difficult for human beings to discern.

Augustine's doctrine of predestination must have been shocking to Pelagius, who never abandoned his position that God gave human beings the ability to live righteously and therefore to determine their own destinies. But it was not the first time he had been distressed by his antagonist's ideas. Years earlier his reading of the *Confessions* had convinced Pelagius that Augustine's emphasis on the moral helplessness of human beings amounted to an easy excuse for sin. Of course, this had not been Augustine's intention. He had stressed the corruption of human nature in order to underscore humanity's dependence on divine grace for salvation. His very negative evaluation of human nature turns up everywhere in Augustine's works. In fact, it is fair to say that much of his theology rests on it. But what led him to such pessimism?

Scripture, of course, left no doubt about human imperfection. Neither did Augustine's own observations of human behavior and society. Sin and the inclination to sin, he concluded, are present everywhere, even in the supposed innocence of infancy. "I have myself seen jealousy in a baby," he wrote. "He was not old enough to talk, but whenever he saw his foster-brother at the breast, he would grow pale with envy."[67] For Augustine, the presence of sin even in new human life contradicted the belief held by some, such as Pelagius, that sin was an acquired habit. If we are not born into a state of sin, he asked, why does the Church baptize infants? The condition of sinfulness, he reasoned, must be part of human nature at birth. But why should this be so? And how does it happen?

Augustine gave his answer in his famous doctrine of **original sin**, according to which all of humanity somehow participated in Adam's sin (Genesis 3:1–24) and inherited the guilt and punishment for it. As a scriptural basis for this view, he cited Paul, who had written that "sin came into the world

through one man, and death came through sin, and so death spread to all because all have sinned" (Romans 5:12). The idea of original sin had been adopted by Latin theologians even before Augustine. Tertullian had suggested that ever since Adam a predisposition to sin had been given to each new soul by its parents,[68] and Ambrose had described the involvement of all of humanity in Adam's sin and the guilt inherited by all generations of his descendants.[69]

But it was Augustine who gave the doctrine of original sin its classic form. All of humanity, he said, sinned with Adam "as in a lump," for at the time of their sin Adam and Eve *were* humanity, with all future generations present in them. Thus, when Adam made himself sinful by choosing to disobey God, this original sin was bound to affect all of his descendants. It was, said Augustine, "the one sin, in and by which all human beings have sinned . . . since all were that one man [i.e., Adam]."[70] Adam's sin had disastrous consequences, for through Adam's prideful disobedience the human will, which ought to be guided by reason toward a love of God and a desire to obey him, was corrupted, as was human reason itself. As a result, said Augustine, we have been left at the mercy of the physical and psychological passions that reason was meant to control. Subject to their irrational influences, we no longer have (as Adam once had) the ability not to sin. Sin, in fact, is inevitable. Only God's grace, given in baptism, can free us from its power and restore to the will its original desire to draw closer to God.

As for the mechanism by which the effects of original sin have been transmitted, Augustine reasoned that, because the only sinless person to have lived was born to a virgin, they must be passed from generation to generation by sexual intercourse. By sinning, he said, Adam and Eve had corrupted their bodies as well as their souls, so that sex, which God had intended to be something truly sublime under the influence of reason, had devolved into mere lust and the means by which sin could infect all humanity.

It appears that Augustine was never entirely comfortable with some of the harsher features of his thought on original sin and predestination. To his friend Jerome he confided his uneasiness about the sinfulness of babies.[71] One senses, too, that he wanted desperately to understand why God granted salvation to some people but not to others. In the end, though, Augustine always argued that God's ways are often hidden and that, when they are, Christians have no choice but to believe that he is just and merciful, even though he might not seem to be. This view, that belief must take priority over understanding, would become one of the distinctive features of the Augustinian tradition.

A final feature of Augustine's thought is his theology of history, which seeks to explain history's great themes and overall significance. To understand his thinking here, we must remember that Augustine lived at a time when the imminence of Rome's fall was taken for granted. In the years that followed the Visigothic sack of Rome in 410, thousands of terrified Romans and other Italians had fled to North Africa with tales of death and destruction. In 428 Africa itself was invaded by the Vandals, who, having crossed over from Spain, paused long enough to establish a kingdom with its capital at Carthage before invading Italy and plundering Rome in 455. Augustine, who died in 430, spent the last two decades of his life watching the collapse of Roman civilization in North Africa.

In those dark days many pagans complained that Christianity was to blame for Rome's woes. The Romans had abandoned their ancestral gods in order to worship Christ, they said. As a result, the old gods had withdrawn their favor and protection from Rome and its empire. To refute this view, Augustine wrote his *City of God,* which he began in 413 and completed in 428, as the Vandals were besieging Hippo. His basic premise was that humanity has always been divided into two "cities"—an earthly city and the city of God—each defined by its greatest love:

> Accordingly, two cities have been formed by two loves: the earthly by the love of self, even to the contempt of God; the heavenly by the love of God, even to the contempt of self. The former . . . glories in itself, the latter in the Lord. For the one seeks glory from men; but the greatest glory of the other is God. . . . The one lifts up its head in its own glory; the other says to its God, "Thou art my

glory, and the lifter up of mine head." In the one, the princes and the nations it subdues are ruled by the love of ruling; in the other, the princes and the subjects serve one another in love. . . . The one delights in its own strength, represented in the persons of its rulers; the other says to its God, "I will love thee, O Lord, my strength."[72]

These cities cannot be identified with particular peoples, nations, or civilizations, for their constituents have been found everywhere and in all times. Ultimately, in fact, the innumerable forms that human society has taken through the ages have no real meaning. According to Augustine, "There are no more than two kinds of human society. . . . The one consists of those who wish to live after the flesh, the other of those who wish to live after the spirit."[73] Thus, Augustine's "cities" are actually types or sets of people — those whose primary impulse is love of self and those whose greatest attraction is to God. The error of the earthly city does not lie in loving things other than God, for it is right to love the good things that God has created, but in not loving God more than anything else. History, which reaches from the fall of humanity in Genesis to the final judgment, is the process by which these two "cities" take shape as men and women choose one or the other. In the end, all will experience the consequences of their respective loves.

Augustine recognized that many of his fellow Christians had looked upon the newly Christianized Roman Empire as proof of God's power over evil and as the basis for a Christian society that would be perfected with the second coming of Christ. For them, Rome's decline and fall were tragic. He was willing to admit that Rome's achievements were admirable and even to recognize the virtue of the early Romans. But he also noted that once they had built their empire the Romans gave themselves over to love of wealth, glory, and power. "There is no reason why they should complain against the justice of the supreme and true God," he said, "for they have had their reward."[74] For Augustine, the lesson of history is clear: sin brings destruction, while love of God leads to perfection.

Augustine's thought ranged far beyond the little we have covered here, and his literary output was phenomenal. The sixth-century theologian Isidore of Seville said that anyone who claimed to have read all of Augustine was a liar. His doctrinal works, and especially *On Christian Doctrine* and *On the Trinity,* provided the foundation for much of medieval theology. They were complemented by dialogues, moral treatises, a rule for monks, sermons, and letters. His use and defense of the allegorical interpretation of scripture established the acceptability of this method in the West. Augustine's influence, at its peak in the Middle Ages, nevertheless extended well beyond them. In the sixteenth century both Protestant and Catholic reformers enlisted him in support of their causes, Protestants citing his insistence that it is grace that justifies sinners before God and Catholics appealing to his teachings on the sacraments and the unity of the Church. Even today, serious Christian dialogue on subjects such as the Trinity, human nature, sin, and salvation can scarcely take place without taking Augustine into account.

The Practice of Christianity

Having surveyed the establishment of authority in the Church, the effort to define orthodoxy, and the work of some important theologians, we may turn our attention now to the actual practice of Christianity. What kinds of things did the Christians of late antiquity *do* to give expression to their faith? What holy days did they observe? In what special rites and rituals did they participate? How did they worship? And in what ways did they honor and relate to the saints who, though in heaven, remained part of the Church?

HOLY DAYS

By the fourth century, Christian life had taken on a calendrical rhythm based on the regular observance of holy days. In addition to the weekly observance of Sunday, which Constantine established as an official holiday in 321, there was an annual cycle of celebrations in which the most sacred time was the fifty-day period between **Easter** and Pentecost. These two celebrations were closely linked, with Pentecost, which commemorates the outpouring

of the Holy Spirit after Christ's resurrection and ascension, being considered the conclusion of Easter. Gradually, the custom arose of observing Lent, a forty-day season of fasting prior to Easter that culminated in Holy Week and special ceremonies on **Palm Sunday**, **Maundy Thursday**, and **Good Friday**. In addition, the fortieth day after Easter came to be observed as a holy day commemorating the ascension of Christ into heaven.

Two holy days associated with the incarnation, Epiphany and **Christmas**, were celebrated in midwinter. Epiphany ("manifestation") was the earliest. Originating in the East, most likely in Alexandria, it commemorated the birth of Christ as well as his baptism and the manifestation of his glory in his first miracle at Cana (John 2:11). By the middle of the fourth century, Epiphany had made its way to the West, where the church in Rome made its principal theme the manifestation of Christ to the gentiles, represented by the Magi who came to adore the infant Jesus.

Christmas, a celebration of the nativity, had its beginnings in the West but was widely observed in the East by the middle of the fifth century. Because no date for the birth of Jesus is given in scripture, various suggestions were made; Clement of Alexandria mentions April 19, April 20, and May 20. The eventual decision to observe the anniversary of Jesus' birth on December 25 was made by the church in Rome early in the fourth century and with the express purpose of competing with and Christianizing a popular pagan holiday. Since 274, when the emperor Aurelian built a temple in honor of the *Sol Invictus,* or "Invincible Sun," the solstitial "birthday" of the sun and its promise of the coming spring and rebirth in nature had been celebrated on December 25. Christians celebrating the birth of the savior on that day could also look forward to spring, with its assurances at Easter of the resurrection of Christ and the rebirth into eternal life of those who loved him.

BAPTISM AND THE EUCHARIST

The sacraments have been traditionally understood as rites instituted by Christ as special means by which grace is made available to human beings. The word *sacrament* itself is based on the Latin *sacramentum*, a sacred oath that bound two parties together — such as the oath by which a soldier bound himself in allegiance to the Roman Emperor.[75] For Christians, *sacramentum* denoted a means by which the sacred bond between a Christian and Christ was created or strengthened, giving the believer a deeper experience of Christ. This was thought to occur through the operation of grace conveyed through the sacrament. By the fourth century, Christians made use of a variety of rites, but only two, baptism and the eucharist, were universally recognized as sacraments.

Baptism, of course, is the sacrament by which one is formally inducted into the Church. Although the practice of baptizing infants and older children was widely known and accepted in the second and third centuries, by the fourth century adult baptism seems to have been more common. In most cases, persons seeking baptism spent a considerable time as catechumens ("hearers" or "students") before receiving the sacrament. Many remained catechumens for years, sometimes even until death was imminent, whether out of unwillingness to embrace sooner than necessary the moral demands of Christian life or out of a sincere commitment to preparing adequately for it. Catechumens had a secondary status in the Church; they did not share in all the privileges enjoyed by baptized members. At Sunday worship, for example, they were allowed to participate in the liturgy up to and including the reading and expounding of scripture but were not permitted to witness the eucharist.

Catechumens ready for baptism usually made a formal announcement of their intention at the beginning of Lent. If their candidacy was approved, they embarked on a course of formal instruction in which they were taught the true meaning of the faith and its symbols. The sacrament itself was administered in the dark hours of Easter morning as the Church prepared to celebrate Christ's resurrection. This is because baptism was understood both as a participation in the death and resurrection of Christ, who rose from the dead early on a Sunday morning, as well as a washing away of sin. Stripped of their clothing, the candidates entered the baptismal waters and were immersed three times as they confessed their belief in each of the three

Figure 4.2   Ancient Christian baptistery from the Basilica of St. John in Ephesus

persons of the Trinity. They were then reclothed and invited to participate for the first time in the eucharist.

Although details varied from church to church, the basic order of the baptismal ceremony was the same in both East and West. The following excerpt from the *Mystagogic Cathecheses* of Cyril of Jerusalem (ca. 348) describes a typical ceremony as well as the belief that baptism involved a vicarious participation in the death and resurrection of Christ:

> As soon as you entered, you took off your clothes; this was a symbol of stripping off the old man with his behavior. And after undressing, you were naked, thus imitating the naked Christ on the cross. . . . And you bore the likeness of the first-formed Adam, who was naked in the garden without feeling shame [Genesis 2:8].

Then, after stripping, you were anointed with exorcized oil from the hairs on top of your head to your feet, and were thus connected with the good olive tree, Jesus Christ. You were cut off from the wild olive and grafted on the good one [Romans 11:4]. . . . The oil symbolized participation in the richness of Christ, a remedy to drive away all trace of hostile power. . . .

After this you were led by the hand to the holy pool of divine baptism, as Christ was taken from the cross to the appointed sepulchre. And each of you was asked if he believed in the Name of the Father, and of the Son, and of the Holy Ghost. And you made that saving confession; you descended into the water and came up again three times, thus alluding symbolically to the three days burial of Christ. . . . In the very same moment you died and were born; and that water of salvation became both your grave and your mother.[76]

For Cyril, as for most theologians of his and later times, the ritual of baptism involved a *symbolic* sharing in Christ's death and resurrection that brought about *real* changes: "Christ," said Cyril, "was actually crucified, and actually buried, and truly rose again; and all these things he has freely bestowed upon us, that we, sharing his sufferings by imitation, might gain salvation in reality."[77]

Unlike baptism, which was the sacrament of initiation into the Church and therefore was administered only once, the eucharist ("thanksgiving") was celebrated as the central act of worship on nearly every occasion when Christians assembled. It originated in the last supper shared by Jesus and his disciples before his arrest and crucifixion. On that occasion he identified the bread and wine with his body and blood (Mark 14:22–25). This connection remained central to eucharistic thought, so that from the beginning there was general agreement concerning the "real presence" of Christ on the altar. Thus, the eucharist was a ritual meal in which Christ was made truly present and available to all baptized persons who wished to receive him. To do so was to be drawn into deeper union with him, even to be caught up in the divine life. As Cyril of Jerusalem put it:

> In the symbol of bread his body is given to you, and in the symbol of wine his blood; so that by partaking of the body and blood of Christ you

may be made of the same body and blood with him. For in this way we become Christ-bearers, since his body and blood is distributed in the parts of our body. Thus, as blessed Peter says [in 2 Peter 1:4], we "become partakers of the divine nature."[78]

In a very real sense, then, the eucharist was understood as spiritual nourishment. Ancient Christians sometimes referred to it as the "food" or "medicine of immortality." In the words of Cyril of Alexandria:

> We approach the consecrated gifts of the sacrament, and are sanctified by partaking of the holy flesh and the precious blood of Christ. . . . We do not receive it as common flesh (God forbid) . . . [but] as the flesh that belongs to the Word himself. For as being God he is in his own nature Life, and when he became one with the flesh which is his own, he rendered it life-giving.[79]

WORSHIP

The primary features of Sunday worship were the preaching of the gospel and the celebration of the eucharist. The actual order of worship was prescribed by the liturgy ("public service" in honor of God). At any given time there were a number of liturgies in use, all of them evolving, but their many shared features make it possible to describe the basic sequence of events that one would be likely to witness in a Sunday service in the fourth or fifth century.

Upon entering the church, the worshiper's attention was drawn to the altar at its eastern end, beneath which were kept the relics of a martyr. Behind the altar the presiding bishop or presbyter sat with other clergy arranged on either side of him. The floor of the church was often covered by mosaics, many of them donated by wealthy members of the congregation, and the walls hung with scenes from Bible stories. To the side stood a baptismal font, though some larger churches had a separate structure or even an outdoor pool for this purpose. There was also a raised pulpit from which scripture was read.

After an entrance rite accompanied by the singing of psalms, the service moved to a reading of

Figure 4.3 This mosaic from the fifth century depicts a Christian church. The structure is built in a style that later came to be known as Romanesque because it incorporates elements of Roman architecture (e.g., round arches, apse).

lessons from scripture — one from the Old Testament, another from the epistles, and a third from the Gospels. More psalms were sung between the readings. The bishop or presbyter then preached on the passages from scripture that had just been read, sometimes delivering a sermon but more often a homily, a less formal and shorter form of address (some of Augustine's homilies could not have taken more than ten minutes). The congregation's attention was then turned to the celebration of the eucharist, which began with the people's presentation of their gifts of bread and wine. Once these had been arranged on the altar by the deacons, the celebrant began an elaborate eucharistic prayer. This included an introductory dialogue between the celebrant and the congregation known in the West as the *Sursum corda* ("Lift up your hearts"), a recitation of Christ's words of institution, an affirmation that the sacrament was being celebrated in remembrance of Christ's death and resurrection, a prayer of offering, and a **doxology**, or hymn of praise. In the East another prayer would then be recited in which the Holy Spirit was called down upon the elements to transform them into the body and blood of Christ (in the West the elements were thought to be transformed with the recitation of Christ's words of institution). At this point the people would have the opportunity to receive the consecrated elements from the celebrant and his as-

sisting clergy. Once they had done so they were dismissed with a benediction.

THE CULT OF SAINTS

One of the most visible expressions of Christian piety in late antiquity was the cult of saints. Although in the first century the term *saint* ("holy person") was applied to all Christians, it was soon reserved for a spiritual elite whose holiness was recognized posthumously. To this group belonged the martyrs who perished at the hands of the Romans and whose relics and tombs were honored along with their memory. Thought to be charged with spiritual power, the bones of holy men and women were said to work wonders for those who approached them with reverence and respect. This possibility, combined with the special memorials and other events held in the presence of relics, was often enough to turn the tomb of a saint into a shrine.

But the cult of saints had more to offer than miracles worked by their relics. Although they had already entered into eternal life with God in heaven, the saints were thought to remain in communion with the Church on earth; as Paul had said, all believers constitute one body in Christ (Romans 12:4–8). Living Christians prayed for others, so it seemed reasonable that those in heaven would do the same. Evidence of this belief is not difficult to find in early Christian literature. Eusebius, for example, tells how moments before her death the Alexandrian martyr Potamiaena promised the soldier Basilides that she would pray for him as soon as she was with God.[80]

From belief that the saints prayed for the living, it was just a small step to the practice of invoking them through prayer and making specific requests for their intercession. Of course, the most effective heavenly advocates were those whose reputation for holiness left little doubt that they were in God's presence, but appeals were made to lesser (or, at least, less famous) souls as well. Christians sometimes inscribed petitions for intercession on the stones marking the graves of friends and family members, a practice that appears to have been well established by the end of the sixth century. Inscriptions discovered in Rome offer numerous examples. "Augendus," reads one, "live in the Lord and pray for us!" "Pray for us," says another, "that we may be saved." The children of a deceased parent wrote simply, "Pray for thy children," while the bereaved mother and father who had once watched after their little boy now asked for his prayers on their behalf: "To [our] son Philemon, who lived happily for two years with his parents. Pray for us, together with the saints!"[81]

Recent scholarship has compared the saints to the aristocratic Roman patrons who protected their less privileged clients.[82] Just as a patron would offer a client material benefits in return for his loyalty, a patron saint offered spiritual guidance and protection in the face of life's dangers and trials. A saint, in fact, might even share his or her own spiritual merit with those in need of it. Thus, the epitaph of Felix, a priest and physician buried in Rome in the cemetery of St. Valentinus, a martyr, asks that Valentinus's merits might be added to his own.[83] Given the variety of ways in which saints were believed to benefit the living, it is not surprising that they were greatly loved, that pilgrims flocked to their tombs, and that their feast days soon filled the Christian calendar. Popular devotion to them would continue to grow, especially as the figure of Christ became exalted and remote, so that the veneration of saints would become one of the most important features of medieval Christianity.

Summary

The theology and organizational structure of the Church developed slowly over the course of its first five centuries. Although most Christians agreed on the central tenets of the faith and accepted the roles of ecclesiastical officials such as bishops, presbyters, and deacons, there was much disagreement and diversity within the Christian movement. The differences among competing forms of Christianity — Gnostics, Monarchians, Montanists, Marcionites, Arians, Nestorians, Monophysites, and others — made the definition of orthodoxy, or "correct belief," an extremely difficult business. Three developments were crucial in promoting unity among Christians: the organization of a hierarchical form of church government, the creation of a canon of scripture, and a series of church councils that addressed questions concerning the nature of Christ and the Trinity and produced statements of belief in the form of creeds. The development of the Church during this period was also encouraged by the work of figures such as the Cappadocian Fathers and John Chrysostom in the East and, in the West, Jerome, Ambrose, and Augustine. During this time the basic patterns of Christian worship also were established.

QUESTIONS FOR REVIEW AND REFLECTION

1. What dangers did some early Christians see in the teachings of Marcion, Montanus, and Gnostic Christianity?

2. In what specific ways did the creation of a canon of scripture, the establishment of an ecclesiastical hierarchy, the doctrine of apostolic succession, and creeds produced by church councils work to encourage Christian unity?

3. What issues contributed to the theological controversies that were addressed by the church councils of the fourth and fifth centuries? How were these controversies resolved?

4. What contributions to Christian thought and practice were made by Ambrose, Augustine, Jerome, John Chrysostom, and the Cappadocian Fathers?

NOTES

1. For example, Ignatius of Antioch (ca. 35–107) in his *Letter to the Smyrnaeans* 8.
2. Fragments of this gospel, written in Greek, were first discovered in the 1890s at Oxyrhynchus, another site in Egypt.
3. Marcion did not include the pastoral epistles in his canon. The reason for this is unclear; either he did not know them or, more likely, he did not approve of their content. He ignored or expurgated passages in Paul and Luke that contradicted his own teachings.
4. Eusebius, *History of the Church* 5.16, trans. G. A. Williamson (New York: Dorset, 1984), 218–19. For "the Lord's distinction" see Matthew 7:15–20, where Jesus tells his disciples that false prophets can be recognized by the fruits of their prophecies.
5. And yet the relationship of bishops and presbyters varies from text to text. 1 Timothy 3 appears to distinguish the bishop from the body of presbyters, while Titus 1 describes presbyters as though they were bishops.
6. Clement of Rome, *1 Clement* 44.
7. Clement of Rome, *1 Clement* 42.
8. Clement of Rome, *1 Clement* 44.
9. Ignatius, *Letter to the Trallians* 3.
10. Ignatius, *Letter to the Ephesians* 4.
11. Ignatius, *Letter to the Ephesians* 3.
12. Ignatius, *Letter to the Ephesians* 3 and 6.
13. Ignatius, *Letter to the Smyrnaeans* 8; *Letter to Polycarp* 5.
14. Ignatius, *Letter to the Smyrnaeans* 8, in *Early Christian Writings: The Apostolic Fathers,* trans. M. Staniforth (New York: Dorset Press, 1986), 121.
15. Clement of Rome, *1 Clement* 44.
16. Irenaeus, *Against Heresies* 3.3.1.
17. Of course, Gnostic Christians had their own ideas about who was or wasn't an apostle. The Gnostic *Gospel of Mary* describes Mary Magdalene as a disciple to whom Christ gave secret knowledge, and she is called an apostle in at least one other Gnostic text (*Dialogue of the Savior* 139.12–13).
18. The controversy was largely over the question of whether Easter should be celebrated at the same time as the Jewish Passover or on the following Sunday. The churches of Asia Minor thought that it should coincide with Passover, which begins at the end of the fourteenth day (*die quarto decima;* hence "Quartodeciman controversy") after the full moon that falls on or after the spring equinox (the fourteenth day of the lunar month of Nisan).
19. The first instance of the use of this term is Canon 4 of the Council of Nicaea (325).
20. Irenaeus, *Against Heresies* 4.28.
21. The Gospel of John did not gain acceptance as readily as the Synoptic Gospels. Writing ca. 150, Justin Martyr was unclear as to his estimation of the Fourth Gospel. A generation later, Irenaeus accepted all four of the canonical gospels as scripture (*Against Heresies* 3.11.8–9).
22. A fragment of 85 lines in Latin, it is named for L. A. Muratori, who discovered it in the Ambrosian Library in Milan and published it in 1740.
23. Irenaeus, *Against Heresies* 3.11.
24. Eusebius, *Church History* 6.25.
25. *Encyclopedia of Early Christianity,* ed. Everett Ferguson (New York: Garland, 1990), s.v. "canon."
26. A collection of eight texts from the end of the fourth century on subjects such as the treatment of widows and orphans, martyrs, the gifts of the Holy Spirit, Church discipline, etc.
27. These "deuterocanonical" or "apocryphal" ("hidden") works are 1 and 2 Esdras, Tobit, Judith, additional chapters of the Book of Esther, The Wisdom of Solomon, Ecclesiasticus, Baruch, A Letter of Jeremiah, The Song of the Three, Daniel and Susanna, Daniel, Bel and the Dragon, The Prayer of Manasseh, and 1 and 2 Maccabees.
28. Irenaeus, *Against Heresies* 1.10, trans. A. C. Coxe, in *Ante-Nicene Fathers,* ed. Alexander Roberts and James Donaldson, vol. 1 (Peabody, Mass.: Hendrickson, 1994), 330–31.
29. Tertullian, *Against Praxeas* 2, trans. Ernest Evans, in *Creeds of the Churches,* ed. John Leith, 3rd ed. (Louisville, Ky.: John Knox Press, 1982), 21–22.
30. Matthew 28:19.
31. Hippolytus, *Apostolic Tradition* 21.
32. John Leith, *Creeds of the Churches,* 23. Marcellus left this creed with Julius, bishop of Rome, before leaving the city ca. 340 after a stay of two years. He had been forced into exile by the influence of Arians in Ancyra.
33. The first writer to describe the Church as "catholic" was Ignatius (*Letter to the Smyrnaeans* 8).
34. Hippolytus, *Against the Heresy of One Noetus* 2.
35. Hippolytus, *Against the Heresy of One Noetus* 2, trans. S. D. F. Salmond, in Roberts and Donaldson, *Ante-Nicene Fathers,* vol. 5, 224.
36. For this reason they were sometimes called "Patripassians," a term that suggests the Father suffered as well as the Son.
37. Hilary of Poitiers, *On the Trinity* 2.23, trans. E. W. Watson, in *Nicene and Post-Nicene Fathers,* 2nd series, ed. Philip Schaff and Henry Wace, vol. 9 (Peabody, Mass.: Hendrickson, 1994), 58.
38. Tertullian, *Against Praxeas* 8.
39. Quoted in Socrates, *Ecclesiastical History* 1.6, trans. A. C. Zenos, in Schaff and Wace, *Nicene and Post-Nicene Fathers,* 2nd series, vol. 2, 4.

40. This is the same Athanasius who wrote the *Life of Anthony* (the desert monk) described in chapter 3.

41. John 1:14, 18; 3:16, 18; 1 John 4:9.

42. J. N. D. Kelly, *Early Christian Doctrines,* rev. ed. (San Francisco: Harper, 1978), 232. *Hypostasis* is here synonymous with *substance. Catholic* means "universal" and should not be understood as a reference to the Roman Catholic Church. To "anathematize" means to curse or detest.

43. Gregory of Nyssa, *On "Not Three Gods",* trans. H. A. Wilson, in *Nicene and Post-Nicene Fathers,* 2nd series, ed. Schaff and Wace, vol. 5, 331–32.

44. Divine action originates with the Father, proceeds through the Son, and is perfected by the the Holy Spirit.

45. The date of composition for Gregory of Nyssa's *On "Not Three Gods".*

46. Augustine, *On the Trinity* 7.4.

47. Romans 5:12–21.

48. Irenaeus, *Against Heresies* 5 (prefact), trans. A. C. Coxe, in Roberts and Donaldson, *Ante-Nicene Fathers,* vol. 1, 525.

49. Origen, *Contra Celsum* 3.28, trans. H. Chadwick (Cambridge, England: Cambridge University Press, 1965), 146.

50. Gregory of Nazianzus, *Letter* 101, trans. C. Browne and J. Swallow, in Roberts and Donaldson, *Ante-Nicene Fathers,* vol. 7, 440.

51. Kelly, *Early Christian Doctrines,* 306.

52. See the discussion of this issue in Kelly, *Early Christian Doctrines,* 311.

53. Williston Walker et al., *A History of the Christian Church,* 4th ed. (New York: Scribners, 1985), 167.

54. Kelly, *Early Christian Doctrines,* 327.

55. Richard Norris and William Rusch, eds., *The Christological Controversy* (Philadelphia: Fortress, 1980), 142.

56. Henry Bettenson, *Documents of the Christian Church,* 2nd ed. (New York: Oxford University Press, 1967), 51–52.

57. Gregory of Nyssa, *Commentary on the Canticle 1001,* in Herbert Musurillo, ed., *From Glory to Glory: Texts from Gregory of Nyssa's Mystical Writings* (London: John Murray, 1962), 247–48.

58. Gregory of Nyssa, *Commentary on the Canticle 876,* in Musurillo, *From Glory to Glory,* 67–68.

59. The title *Doctor of the Church* was given in the Middle Ages to those theologians whose personal virtue and achievements set them above all others. The number of those so honored eventually grew to more than thirty.

60. Ambrose, *Sermon against Auxentius* 36.

61. *Aeterne rerum conditor, Deus creator omnium, Iam surgit hora tertia,* and *Intende qui regis Israel.*

62. Translated by John D. Chambers (1864). Cited in Tim Dowley, ed., *Eerdman's Handbook to the History of Christianity* (Grand Rapids, Mich.: Wm. B. Eerdmans, 1977), 139.

63. Augustine, *Confessions* 5.10, trans. R. S. Pine-Coffin (New York: Penguin, 1980), 103.

64. Augustine, *City of God* 2.14.

65. Augustine, *Confessions* 3.4.

66. Augustine, *Confessions* 2.4, 48.

67. Augustine, *Confessions* 1.7, 28.

68. Tertullian, *On the Soul* 16; *Testimony of the Soul* 3.

69. Ambrose, *Explanations of Twelve Psalms* 38.29; *On the Death of Satyrus* 2.6.

70. Augustine, *On the Merits and Forgiveness of Sins* 1.10.

71. See the discussion of this in William Placher, *A History of Christian Theology* (Philadelphia: Westminster Press, 1983), 117.

72. Augustine, *City of God* 14.28, trans. M. Dodds, in Schaff and Wace, *Nicene and Post-Nicene Fathers,* vol. 2, 282–83.

73. Augustine, *City of God* 14.1, 262.

74. Augustine, *City of God* 5.15, 97.

75. *Sacramentum* usually renders the Greek *mysterion,* which means "mystery" or "secret rite."

76. Cyril of Jerusalem, *Cathecheses* 4.1–6, in Henry Bettenson, ed., *The Later Christian Fathers* (New York: Oxford, 1970), 43.

77. Cyril of Jerusalem, *Catecheses* 20.5, trans. E. Hamilton, in Schaff and Wace, *Nicene and Post-Nicene Fathers,* 2nd series, vol. 7, 148.

78. Cyril of Jerusalem, *Catecheses* 22.3, in Bettenson, *Later Christian Fathers,* 45.

79. Cyril of Alexandria, *Letters* 17, in Bettenson, *Later Christian Fathers,* 267–68.

80. Eusebius, *Church History* 6.5.

81. Orazio Marucchi, *Christian Epigraphy,* trans. J. Willis (Chicago: Ares, 1974), 153–55.

82. For example, J. H. Corbett, "The Saint As Patron in the Work of Gregory of Tours," *Journal of Medieval History* 7 (1981): 1–13.

83. Orazio Marucchi, *Christian Epigraphy,* 165.

CHAPTER 5

The Rise of the Church in the Early Middle Ages

Overview

In this chapter we will investigate the growth of Christianity in the early Middle Ages, the period covering roughly the fifth through tenth centuries. In western Europe, this was a time of sudden change, uncertainty, and violence occasioned by the collapse of the old Roman order. Gradually a new society was built by combining elements of Roman civilization with ideas and institutions of the Germanic peoples who had overrun the western half of the empire in its final years. Conditions in the East were far better, for there the empire had remained intact despite the intrusion of Germanic tribes. This surviving portion of the Roman world would endure until 1453 as the Byzantine Empire, which took its name from Byzantium, the site on which Constantine had built his capital of Constantinople. Although the Byzantine state continued for centuries to understand itself as being somehow Roman, its culture was essentially Greek.

The changing political situation in the early Middle Ages was complicated by the rise of Islam, which first appeared in the Arabian peninsula early in the seventh century. Within less than a century of the death of the prophet Muhammad in 632, Is-

lam had brought powerful new religious, military, and political influences to virtually all of the Middle East, North Africa, and parts of Europe. Islam and Islamic civilization were destined to have an immense impact on Europe and Christianity.

During the early medieval centuries a variety of factors encouraged the development of distinctively western (Latin) and eastern (Greek) traditions in Christianity. Aside from their linguistic differences, the West and East were divided by differing theological inclinations. For the most part, the Latin West continued in the pragmatic tradition of the Romans by focusing on practical issues relating to sin and salvation. The Greek East, on the other hand, remained true to the inquisitive spirit of the classical Greeks in showing greater interest in **mysticism** and speculative theology. Political and ethnic problems, conflicts over specific theological issues, and disputes over jurisdiction by their leaders also separated the eastern and western churches. Gradually they grew apart, each developing in increasing isolation from the other. And yet the Church as a whole made important advances. Missionaries brought Christianity to the unconverted regions of northern and eastern Europe, monasticism became a highly visible institution with real power in matters of ecclesiastical leadership, and theologians tackled issues ranging from the use of images in worship to predestination.

This chapter begins with a discussion of how the Church established itself in relation to the dominant powers of the early Middle Ages — the Frankish kingdom in the West and the Byzantine Empire in the East. Then, after a brief description of the rise of Islam, it turns to the geographical expansion and theological development of Christianity in both the East and West and the unique expressions of monastic and popular piety in each region.

The Western Church, the Franks, and Feudalism

In the year 500 the western half of the empire once ruled by Rome was in the hands of invading Huns, Alemanni, Visigoths, Ostrogoths, **Franks**, Angles, Saxons, Lombards, and Vandals, all of whom were carving out kingdoms for themselves and striving to defend their fragile borders. By 750 the situation was simpler and more stable, for much of western Europe was controlled by just three Germanic peoples: the Lombards in Italy, the Anglo-Saxons in England, and the Franks in **Gaul** (roughly, modern France and Belgium). Of these three, the Franks were destined to create the largest state and have the greatest impact on the Church.

THE MEROVINGIANS AND THE CHURCH

As the Roman Empire crumbled, thousands of Franks migrated from their homeland along the lower Rhine and settled in northern Gaul, where they were soon united under the firm hand of Clovis (466–511), their first great king. An early ruler of the Merovingian dynasty, Clovis built a vast kingdom stretching from the Pyrenees to the English Channel and eastward into what is now Germany. He was a powerful monarch, but not an entirely independent one. To enforce his will he relied on the loyalty and military support of his nobles. In return, he recognized their right to control great

tracts of land. Most of Clovis's early successors were capable rulers, but the incompetence of later Merovingian kings led to the fall of their dynasty in 751 and its replacement by another, that of the **Carolingians**, which would surpass it both in power and cultural achievement.

The explosive rise of the Franks under Clovis ensured the victory of Nicene Christianity in the West. As we will see later in this chapter, most German Christians were Arians, having been converted by Arian missionaries who began working among them in the fourth century. But Clovis's wife, a Burgundian princess, had insisted that her unbaptized husband become a Catholic. At first he put her off, promising to accept her faith only if her God would give him a victory against the powerful Alemanni; when he did defeat them, Clovis kept his word. Legend says that he and three thousand of his warriors were baptized at Reims on Christmas Day in the year 496. From that time forward, Clovis and his armies saw themselves as defenders of the faith against Arians and pagans. Eager to assist him, the Church provided priests and missionaries to baptize and instruct the thousands of converts persuaded to accept Catholicism by the power of Frankish arms. In this way a natural alliance was formed between the Church, which feared both Arianism and the Germanic tribes that had embraced it, and the Franks, who hoped to make their rule over subject peoples more secure by promoting a common religion.

In addition to their work in Frankish lands, missionaries ventured deep into unconquered territory, where they preached fearlessly among pagan Frisians, Bavarians, Thuringians, and Saxons. The most famous is Wynfrith (ca. 675–754), a monk whose courage and accomplishments earned him sainthood and the nickname **Boniface** ("doer of good"). An Anglo-Saxon from Wessex in southern England, Boniface is legendary for his zealous and direct approach to missionary work. When this "Apostle of Germany" found that thousands worshiped a sacred Oak of Thor at Geismar in Hesse, he took an axe and began to cut it down. It was said that a great wind came to his aid, toppling the tree and breaking it into four beams of equal length.

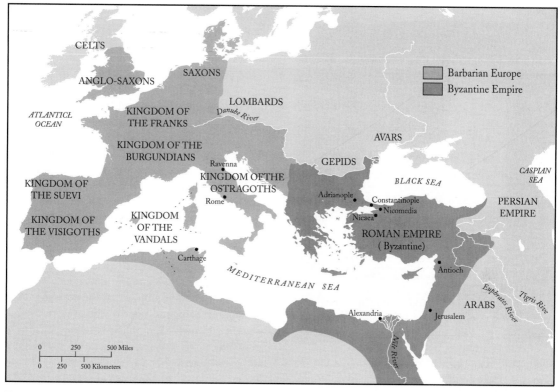

Figure 5.1   Europe and the Byzantine Empire ca. 500 The decline of Roman rule in the West opened the way for Germanic tribes such as the Franks, Vandals, Visigoths, and Ostrogoths to establish their own kingdoms there.

Awed by this display of divine power, the Germans who had been ready to kill him moments earlier helped him instead to build a chapel out of the wood. Boniface's fame eventually elevated him to the office of archbishop of Mainz, but he soon resigned in order to take the gospel into Frisia, where he died as a martyr.

Much of Boniface's success was due to the assistance he received from his cousin, Leoba, one of the remarkable women who, like St. Brigid in Ireland and St. Hilda of Whitby in England, worked to convert the peoples of northern Europe. As abbess of a women's monastery at Bischofsheim, Leoba trained German nuns who became abbesses in a growing network of women's monastic communities. In this way, and through the influence she exercised at the Frankish court, she had a significant impact on the growth of Christianity among the Germanic peoples.[1]

In addition to the work of missionaries, the growing presence of the Church among the Franks and neighboring peoples was evident in the appearance of monasteries. Often established with royal support, they brought Christianity to surrounding populations through their teaching, service, and example of the Christian life. Monasteries were also important components of local economies, because monks supported themselves by producing goods for sale. The Church was involved in government as well. Many members of the higher clergy were employed by the monarchy to work alongside secular officials in collecting taxes, rendering justice, and keeping the peace. In some cases Frankish kings gave bishops additional appointments as secular

Figure 5.2 This cancel of St. Paul's Church in Jarrow, England, was first constructed in the late seventh century and in the Saxon style.

lords, making them wealthy landowners with obligations to the state as well as spiritual leaders who owed their obedience to the Church.

Perhaps the most dramatic example of the Church's involvement with the Franks was its role in bringing the Carolingian dynasty to power. In 751, Pope Zacharias (741–52) approved the plan of Pepin the Short, the leading official in the Merovingian court, to take for himself the throne of the reigning king, Childeric III. Later that year Pepin was proclaimed king of the Franks, the first of the Carolingian rulers, with the public blessing of the pope.

The papacy had rendered a great favor, and it soon asked for one in return. In 753 the Lombards drove Zacharias's successor, Stephen II (752–57), from Rome and threatened lands in central Italy claimed by both the papacy and the Byzantine Empire. The pope appealed to Pepin to drive the Lombards out of Italy and to defend his rights to the contested territories. Pepin agreed and in 754 formed an alliance with the papacy against both the Lombards and the Byzantine Emperor. As a result, the Carolingian kings became the official protectors of the popes, who approved their rule by acknowledging them as "kings by the grace of God" and anointing them with holy oil, just as ancient kings of Israel such as David and Solomon had been anointed. In addition, Pepin took the title *patricius Romanorum*, "father-protector of the Romans." A year later the Franks defeated the Lombards, and the Frankish king, in what is often called the Donation of Pepin, delivered to the pope the lands he claimed in central Italy. In later years these came to be known as the Papal States.[2]

The Frankish victory over the Lombards might have saved the papacy, but it also called attention to the papacy's vulnerability and dependence upon a secular power. Some argued that the pope should be the supreme temporal ruler of the West as well as its spiritual leader. The most audacious attempt to make this papal dream a reality was based on a forged document that appeared at just about this time — the so-called **Donation of Constantine**. Allegedly Constantine's own account of his conversion, the document also lists extraordinary gifts he supposedly lavished on Pope Sylvester I (314–35) and his successors in gratitude for being cured by the pope of leprosy.[3] In addition to giving the bishops of Rome jurisdiction over all other bishops and their dioceses, it granted them the entire western half of the empire. As if this were not enough, the rule of the pope in the West was to be absolute and unhindered, for the *Donation* asserted that "it is not right that an earthly emperor should have authority there, where the rule of priests and the head of the Christian religion has been established by the Emperor of heaven."[4]

Contemporary accounts of Pepin's eagerness to support the pope suggest that he may well have been aware of the *Donation of Constantine*. Like others, he might have doubted its authenticity,[5] but he could not have failed to see the advantages it offered to the Frankish monarchy. As defenders of the Church, which would see to the spiritual needs of western **Christendom**, the Franks would be responsible for defending the Church against hostile powers outside its borders and maintaining order within them. As Pepin knew, such responsibilities bring wealth and power.

Of course, the aims of the *Donation of Constantine* were never realized, though the document was cited for centuries as one of the bases of papal claims to authority in the West and was not proven to be a forgery until 1431. Still, to Stephen II it must have seemed that his alliance with the Franks *had* elevated the papacy to a level approximating its rightful position in the world. In the next half-century Rome and the Frankish monarchy would be drawn even more closely together, cooperating to their mutual benefit but at the same time setting the stage for later power struggles between the Church and secular rulers in the West.

CHARLEMAGNE

The Carolingian kings who ruled at the height of Frankish power took their name from their greatest representative, **Charlemagne** (Carolus Magnus, or Charles the Great; ca. 742–814). Like all Frankish kings, Charlemagne was first and foremost a warlord. Endlessly campaigning, he pacified his northern frontier by conquering the pagan Frisians and Saxons. In the East, his armies advanced along the Danube and added Slavic and Avar lands to his realm. In Italy he delivered a final, crushing blow to the Lombards and made himself lord of the entire peninsula except the Papal States, Byzantine Sardinia, and some Byzantine territories in the south. Driving southward across the Pyrenees, he attacked Spanish Muslims who had invaded France sixty years earlier and annexed much of northeastern Spain to his kingdom. By the time of his death in 814, Charlemagne ruled an empire covering all of modern France, Belgium, Holland, and Switzerland, most of Italy and western Germany, and parts of eastern Europe and Spain.

Although Charlemagne's military successes gave him great power, he insisted that his objectives were spiritual as well as temporal. Like Clovis, he saw himself as the defender of a Church threatened by barbarians, pagans, and heretics. Inspired by Augustine's *City of God,* he envisioned a realm unified by the Catholic faith and committed to making God's will a reality on earth. To this end, he promoted Christianity by supporting missionaries; remembering Augustine's policy concerning the Donatists, he used force when necessary to produce conversions. On several occasions he gave defeated Saxons, the archenemies of the Franks, a choice between baptism and death. In addition, Charlemagne supported the foundation of monasteries, enforced their strict observance of the Benedictine Rule, asserted the authority of bishops, protected ecclesiastical property, and collected an income tax from all Christians to ensure the financial health of the Church. In all of this Charlemagne sought the guidance and counsel of the papacy, especially Hadrian I (772–95).

The mutual benefits of the papacy's alliance with the Franks became especially evident at the end of the eighth century. In 799, Pope Leo III (795–816) was forced to flee to Charlemagne after Roman nobles who had opposed his election had him kidnapped and beaten and then attempted to force him from office with accusations of immorality.[6] As defender of the papacy, Charlemagne returned with Leo to Rome the following year and arranged for him to be safely reestablished in office. Charlemagne remained in Rome for a time and on Christmas Day in the year 800 attended **mass** in St. Peter's Basilica. According to one account:

> When Christmas Day came, all once more assembled in this church of the blessed apostle Peter. And then the venerable and bountiful bishop with his own hands crowned Charles with a most precious crown. Then all the loyal Romans . . . cried with one high-sounding voice, by the will of God and the blessed Peter, the keeper of the keys of the kingdom of heaven: "Long life and victory to Charles the most pious Augustus, the great and peace-making Emperor, crowned by God!" Before the sacred tomb of the blessed apostle Peter they declared this three times, calling upon the various saints: and he was made Emperor of the Romans by them all.[7]

And so the Romans, and the whole of the West, once again had an emperor—the first since 476. Einhard, Charlemagne's confidant and biographer, says that the king would not have entered the church that day if he had known what the pope had

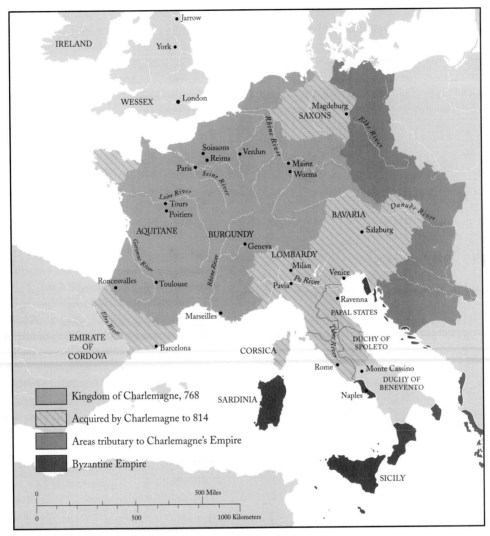

Figure 5.3 The empire of the Franks under Charlemagne (ca. 800) Charlemagne's many military campaigns vastly expanded Frankish territory and influence and resulted in thousands of conversions to Christianity.

planned, though it seems just as likely that he and Leo III had carefully orchestrated his coronation from the beginning.[8] Either way, Charlemagne was no longer merely a king but an emperor who ruled over what was, at least in theory, a revived Roman Empire. This **Holy Roman Empire**, as it would later be called, would be an important force in the West for centuries. The papacy also benefited from the coronation of Charlemagne. The coronation solidified the relationship between the papacy and its Frankish defenders, and it had even managed to suggest, because the ceremony had been performed by the pope and in Rome, that the Church had the right (perhaps even the exclusive right) to confer temporal authority on secular rulers, even including emperors.

THE CAROLINGIAN RENAISSANCE

Another important feature of Charlemagne's reign was a revival of learning known as the Carolingian renaissance. This was a more limited phenomenon than the Italian Renaissance of the fifteenth and sixteenth centuries, but at a time when literacy was rare it had a refreshing effect, reawakening an appreciation of the past and anticipating the flowering of literature and the arts that would give later medieval culture its distinctive flavor.

Charlemagne was convinced that a cultural revival must be a religious revival as well. Accordingly, he imposed higher educational and moral standards on the clergy, who shouldered most of the responsibility in this effort, calling upon them to "adorn their ministry by good behavior" and to establish schools in which boys of all classes would learn to read.[9] At his capital at Aachen, near modern Cologne, he established a "palace school" to which he invited learned individuals from Spain, England, Ireland, and Italy. Of these, the most notable was **Alcuin of York** (ca. 740–804), an English scholar who directed many developments in cultural life from the royal court and, later, as abbot of the monastery of St. Martin at Tours. Although Charlemagne himself could barely write — Einhard says he could form letters only with great difficulty — he labored to set a good example by energetically devoting himself to the study of subjects he would never master, including rhetoric, dialectic, and astronomy.

Under the leadership of Alcuin and other scholars at the palace school, a uniquely Christian understanding of education emerged. Its purpose was now seen as preparing the individual to understand the Bible, the writings of the church fathers, and other religious literature. The first step toward this goal was gaining an understanding of Latin, the language of religion and scholarship in the West throughout the Middle Ages. The second was the acquisition of critical and oratorical skills as well as a general education through the study of the seven liberal arts. These were organized into two groups of disciplines: the elementary *trivium*, which consisted of grammar, rhetoric, and dialectic (logic), and the more advanced *quadrivium*, which included arithmetic, geometry, music, and astronomy. A student who had mastered the liberal arts was ready to move beyond them to what really mattered — the Bible and theology. Because all study was dependent upon the availability of books, scholars were engaged to establish the authentic texts of the books of the Bible, the writings of early theologians, and numerous examples of classical Latin literature. The tedious but important work of producing countless copies of these was performed by monks laboring in special monastic workshops called *scriptoria*. It was here that the elegant Carolingian handwriting known as *minuscule* was invented and the production of exquisitely beautiful manuscripts became an art form.

Scholars have argued that the Carolingian renaissance influenced popular morality by promoting an awareness of sin and ethical responsibility.[10] On the other hand, it had very little impact on the intellectual lives of most people. The great majority remained illiterate. Still, there were now glimmerings of renewed interest in literature and scholarship. Biography made a comeback in Einhard's *Life of Charlemagne* and the many lives of saints composed at this time. Paul the Deacon (ca. 720–ca. 800), a monk of Monte Cassino who spent more than four years among the Franks, wrote a *History of the Lombards*. The ancient art of literary correspondence was revived in the lively letters of figures like Alcuin and Hincmar of Reims. Rabanus Maurus (ca. 780–856) wrote poetry, a textbook on grammar, commentaries on the books of the Bible, and a handbook for priests *(De institutione clericorum)*. With few exceptions, the achievements of Carolingian learning and scholarship were the work of priests and monks whose subjects were directly related to the interests of the Church.

THE CONVERSION OF SPAIN, ENGLAND, AND IRELAND

According to tradition, Spain was first evangelized by St. Paul and St. James. Although there is little evidence to support this claim,[11] St. James in particular has always been a favorite of the Spanish, who know him as Santiago and have honored him for centuries at Compostela, where his relics are said to have been preserved. The earliest undisputed reference to Christianity in Spain comes in a letter by Cyprian of Carthage (254), which describes the organization of the Church there. A half-century later the persecution of Christians under Diocletian produced accounts of the deaths of Spanish martyrs[12] and of the Council of Elvira, which was convened (ca. 306) to determine how Spanish apostates should be treated.

In the fourth century the problem of persecution was eclipsed by that of Arianism. Despite the energetic opposition of bishops such as Hosius of Cordoba and Gregory of Elvira, the heresy managed to establish itself in some segments of the population and then became the accepted form of Christianity when the Visigoths overran most of Spain in the fifth century. For a time, Arian Christianity flourished; a Gothic liturgy was composed and a form of ecclesiastical government was worked out in which bishops were dependent upon the monarchy. But Spanish Arianism was eventually brought to an end by Catholic resistance and religious differences among the Visigoths themselves. Horrified by the execution of his Catholic brother by his Arian father shortly before his accession to the throne, King Recared I (586–601) resolved to promote peace through religious unity. He recalled exiled Catholic bishops and convened a council at Toledo (589), which formally renounced Arianism. This reversal of Visigothic religious policy allowed the Catholic culture of Spain to begin to take shape. A collection of **canon law** known as the *Hispana* was developed, monasticism flourished, and Spanish thinkers such as Isidore of Seville (ca. 560–636) and Julian of Toledo (ca. 644–90) began to make important contributions to theology. The conquest of most of Spain in the eighth century by Muslim armies from North Africa slowed this process, but the Islamic principle of toleration allowed for its continuation until the end of the thirteenth century. By that time the *Reconquista* or "reconquest" of the country had restored nearly all of it to Christian rule.

Christianity appears to have made its way quite early to Roman Britain, where by the fourth century the form of ecclesiastical organization resembled that found in other parts of the Roman Empire. Our sources mention bishops, priests, deacons, and lay elders and refer to three Latin-speaking British bishops who participated in the Council of Arles in 314. They also suggest that the Catholic faith was first established in towns and villas, where Roman influence was greatest, and only later moved into the countryside. In western England, and especially in Wales, there was also a Celtic Christianity much like that practiced by the Celtic peoples of Roman Gaul.

This situation was complicated by the invasions of pagan Saxons, Angles, and Jutes that began early in the fifth century. Taking advantage of the withdrawal of Roman troops recalled to protect Rome's interests on the continent, these Germanic peoples settled in eastern and southern England. As a result, some of the British were forced to the west and north, taking with them what remained of the Christian religion and Latin language they had learned from the Romans, while the rest were absorbed by the Germanic newcomers. For a time the survival of the faith in Britain was in doubt, but even in that dark hour monks and missionaries were working to transform the whole of the British Isles into a bastion of medieval Christianity.

Among the earliest of these missionaries was Patrick, the "Apostle of the Irish," who was active in the middle of the fifth century. A native of Britain and the son of a deacon, he was captured by Irish pirates at the age of sixteen and spent the next six years as a slave in Ireland. After escaping, he made his way back to Britain, where he was persuaded by a vision that God wanted him to work for the conversion of the Irish. "I hear the voices of children, as yet unborn, calling me from Ireland," he used to say.[13] Returning as a priest and later becoming a bishop, Patrick spent the rest of his life among those to whom he had once been enslaved, preaching the gospel, converting local rulers, and establishing bishoprics and monasteries. Patrick's achievements are impressive even if we do not accept the legends of his driving the snakes from Ireland and performing miracles that put competing druids to shame.

Monasticism in particular was to become a dominant feature of Irish Christianity. In a land whose population was almost entirely rural, it was natural that the monasteries scattered across the country-side should become pastoral centers and their abbots, who were nearly always sons of ruling families, the leading figures in the Church. In other lands leadership was more often in the hands of bishops who ruled their sees from cities. Some Irish monastic communities eventually grew into towns, such as Bangor ("monastery"), Armagh, Cork, and Kildare. Most were centers of learning where the study of scripture and theology flourished, classical literature was preserved, and Latin thrived as the language of scholarship in a land never conquered by Rome.

Irish spirituality, which emphasized the virtue of leaving home and family for the sake of the gospel, led many monks far afield. In the sixth century Columba established a monastery on Iona, an island off the coast of Scotland, from which he converted the Picts of Caledonia and organized the Church there along Irish lines. His contemporary, Columbanus, a monk from Bangor, evangelized Burgundy, what is now Switzerland, and northern Italy, establishing new monasteries wherever he went. A century later Kilian was preaching in German Franconia and Thuringia. In the early medieval centuries these and hundreds of other missionaries from tiny, faraway Ireland brought a stabilizing and civilizing influence to a Europe still disorganized after the collapse of the old Roman order and disrupted by the invasions of Slavs, Magyars, and Muslims.

Irish monks also came to England, where they had great success in Northumbria, Mercia, and other kingdoms. The most famous is Aidan (d. 651), a monk of Iona who set out on numerous missionary journeys from his headquarters on the island of Lindisfarne. Another effort to convert the Angles and Saxons was directed primarily by Rome. In 597 a mission sent by Pope Gregory I and headed by the monk Augustine landed at Kent in the south. Gregory had hoped for the conversion of Ethelbert, the king of Kent and nominal overlord of the neighboring Anglo-Saxon kingdoms of Essex and East Anglia. Accounts of Augustine's arrival say that the king insisted they meet on an open field, for he feared that the monk was also a powerful magician. But Ethelbert was soon persuaded of the truth of Christianity and was baptized at Easter in 601 along

with thousands of his warriors. Augustine then established a metropolitan see for himself at Canterbury, whose archbishops have ever since been the leaders of the Church in England, and bishoprics in Rochester and London.

These were the original centers from which Christianity was to be taken to the rest of England. A second metropolitan see was founded later at York along with additional bishoprics. A letter written by Gregory in 601 to Mellitus, the leader of a Roman mission from Gaul, demonstrates the pope's keen interest in the conversion of England and his conviction that it would be most easily accomplished if pagan traditions were gradually transformed into Christian ones rather than simply rejected.

> Let blessed water be prepared and sprinkled in [their] temples, and altars constructed, and relics deposited, since if these same temples are well built . . . they should be transferred from the worship of idols to the service of the true God. . . . And since [the people] kill many oxen in sacrifice to demons, they should have also some solemnity of this kind in a changed form, so that on the day of dedication, or on the anniversaries of the holy martyrs whose relics are deposited there, they may make for themselves tents of the branches of trees around these temples that have been changed into churches, and celebrate the solemnity with religious feasts. . . . For it is undoubtedly impossible to cut away everything at once from hard hearts, since one who strives to ascend to the highest place must . . . rise by steps or paces, and not by leaps.[14]

The successes of the Roman mission soon brought it into conflict with Celtic Christianity, much of which had been introduced by the Irish. It was still favored by the native British, many of whom resented the presence on their soil of foreign intruders, whether Roman or Germanic. Augustine's arrogance in dealing with the Celtic bishops and their consequent rejection of his authority as archbishop only heightened tensions. According to Bede the Venerable (ca. 673–735), a monk whose *Ecclesiastical History of the English People* is one of our most important sources for this period, Augustine's failure to unify the Celtic and Roman

Figure 5.4   Lindisfarne Gospels (ca. 698) This page from the beginning of the Gospel of Matthew illustrates the skill of Celtic artists in creating beautiful manuscript illuminations.

churches, part of the mission entrusted to him by Gregory, was due to his demands that the British accept the Roman date for Easter and participate in the mission to the Angles and Saxons.

The way toward the union of the two traditions was gradually smoothed as the Celtic Church began to cooperate in the Anglo-Saxon mission. Additional impetus was provided by the Synod of Whitby (664), which placed Northumbria under the authority of Rome, setting an example that was quickly followed in other regions. The papal appointment four years later of Theodore of Tarsus (the birthplace of St. Paul in Asia Minor) as archbishop of Canterbury also encouraged the unification of English Christians. A Greek who had once studied in Athens, Theodore had organizational ability, sensitivity to ethnic concerns, and a willingness to adopt features of Celtic-Irish Christianity such as private confession. These qualities enabled him to create a truly national church at a time when political unity in England still lay far in the future, all but guaranteed the complete conversion of England, and encouraged a flowering of Anglo-Saxon culture. Cathedral and monastic schools such as those at York, Wearmouth, and Jarrow in Northumbria, where Bede wrote on grammar, scripture, and history, became cultural and intellectual centers. The artistic genius of the Celts also expressed itself, particularly in vividly illuminated copies of scripture such as the Lindisfarne Gospels. This was the culture that produced learned monks like Boniface, who took the gospel to distant parts of Europe, and scholars such as Alcuin of York, who brought English art and learning to the kingdom of the Franks.

THE RISE OF FEUDALISM

The ninth century saw the decline of the Carolingian Empire. For years the ancient Frankish custom of dividing a king's realm among his sons had rarely come into play, but in 843 three of Charlemagne's grandsons split the lands of the Franks into three kingdoms. Carolingian power continued to wane during subsequent generations, so that by the early tenth century the Carolingians were only petty rulers and the empire of their ancestors a mere memory. Pressures from outside also contributed to the breakdown of the Carolingian order. Pagan Vikings sailed out of Scandinavia to plunder towns and monasteries along the Atlantic, Baltic, and North Sea coasts. Magyars from central Asia, the ancestors of the Hungarians, burst into eastern Europe on horseback and disrupted ordered society. In the south, Muslim raiders known as Saracens launched attacks from North Africa and Sicily on the coasts of Italy and southern France. The inability of Carolingian rulers to manage the defense of their lands made their position even more precarious, for they were forced to make local officials and nobles responsible for raising and leading armies and to reward them with grants of land. These lords became increasingly powerful and independent of the Carolingians as the number and size of their lands grew and as they gained the loyalty of those they protected.

Figure 5.5   Lothar Cross (1000) The seal of Lothar II, great-grandson of Charlemagne, appears below a cameo of the Roman emperor Augustus. The wreath upon Augustus' head symbolizes the imperial authority claimed by the Carolingians.

The medieval practice of exchanging land for service—**feudalism**—was based on a ceremony in which a lesser lord declared in an act of *homage* his desire to be the man (*homo*) of a greater lord, swore an oath of *fealty* or allegiance to him, and received in the rite of **investiture** a symbol of the land (**fief**) granted to him in return for his loyalty and military support. Within this arrangement the lesser lord was the **vassal** of the one he served, but he could have vassals of his own by granting portions of his own land as fiefs to still lesser lords. In this way a hierarchy was formed in which the king stood at the apex of the feudal pyramid above many levels of lords. Despite the appearance this picture gives of unity among feudal lords and a common allegiance to their king, a lord could go to war against anyone to whom he was not formally bound by ties of feudal loyalty. In addition, there was often tension between kings, who wanted to concentrate power in their own hands, and their vassals, whose independence was threatened by a strong royal government. Thus, the feudal system was capable of generating considerable conflict and is partly to blame for the incessant warfare that ravaged Europe in the central Middle Ages.

THE CHURCH IN THE FEUDAL WORLD

The Church was fully involved in the feudal organization of western society. While ecclesiastical participation in the feudal system promoted the Church's influence in the secular sphere, it also gave secular authorities influence over the Church, thus creating the potential for future conflicts.

Difficulties began to arise in the eighth and ninth centuries, when the Church found itself in possession of vast amounts of land. Some had been given as gifts by pious individuals, but most had been granted by secular lords as fiefs to bishoprics (i.e., to bishops or their dioceses), monasteries, and individual churches. Such grants made vassals of the bishops, abbots, and priests who received them and obligated them to render services to the benefactors who had become their feudal lords. To meet their obligations and protect and exploit their lands, ecclesiastical lords embraced the feudal system and adopted the proven methods of their secular counterparts: they imposed serfdom on the peasantry, granted parcels of church land as fiefs to secular lords in return for promises of military protection, collected feudal dues, and presided at feudal courts. Of course, the immense weight of these responsibilities necessarily drew them away from pastoral concerns and into the world of the secular aristocracy, whose values and loyalties often became their own. In many cases no such transformation was necessary, because secular lords frequently used their influence to secure the appointment of family members and trusted associates to ecclesiastical office. Such persons were often eager to accept positions in the Church in order to enjoy the material blessings they conferred.

It is fair to say, then, that the majority of bishops and abbots with feudal holdings belonged as much to the secular world as to the Church. Their divided loyalties compromised not only their dedication to the Church's mission but also their ability to provide leadership to the thousands of lower clergy who depended upon them for direction. As we have seen, reforms enacted by Charlemagne had improved standards and conditions among the clergy early in the ninth century, but the decline of the Carolingian dynasty allowed for a deterioration in clerical education, morals, and discipline. This in turn affected the religious lives of ordinary people, who were often left without adequate guidance from competent and committed priests and other spiritual leaders.

At the same time, the Church's involvement in secular affairs and institutions had the benefit of giving church leaders considerable influence in the shaping of medieval society. It was the Church, after all, that formulated the medieval conception of the properly ordered society as consisting of three classes, each with its own responsibilities — those who prayed (monks and the clergy), those who fought (the feudal aristocracy), and those who worked (serfs and free peasants). The oaths that bound lord to vassal and undergirded the entire feudal system were sacred oaths sanctioned by the Church. The values of Germanic and Roman warriors were replaced by Christian values in the code of chivalry, which began to emerge in the eleventh century as the behavioral standard for aristocratic warriors. The themes and subjects of medieval art, which was just beginning to come into its own in the tenth century, were biblical and Christian. Education, when it was available at all, was almost always offered by the Church. Finally, the Church was present at all the critical junctures and phases of individual lives: baptizing the newborn, instructing the young, consecrating marriages, praying and caring for the sick, burying the dead, and explaining as best it could through its teachings and sacraments the mysteries of human existence.

Despite its many faults, the Church played a major role in rescuing western society from the chaos of the early medieval centuries by preserving literacy and learning and contributing to the establishment of the feudal system. In doing so it also helped to prepare the way for cultural developments and improvements in human life generally that would follow in the later Middle Ages.

The Eastern Church and the Byzantine Empire

The division of the Roman Empire begun by Diocletian at the end of the third century and completed by Theodosius I at the end of the fourth left the East and West to defend themselves more or less independently against the onslaught of Huns and Germans. When Rome fell, the eastern emperors claimed authority over the entire Roman world. As it turned out, the West would never be regained, but in Constantinople and its eastern realm a dynamic new Byzantine civilization was taking shape.

JUSTINIAN

Just when the Greek East became distinctively Byzantine is hard to say, but most scholars agree that the reign of the emperor **Justinian** (527–65) was an important turning point. With the help of his wife, the empress Theodora, a woman of astonishing intelligence and political skill, Justinian became the first truly great figure in the East since Constantine.

Justinian's greatest desire was to recapture the West. Thanks largely to the ability of his brilliant generals Belisarius and Narses, he managed a partial success by driving the Vandals out of North Africa, retaking Italy from the Ostrogoths, and capturing a small amount of territory in southeastern Spain from the Visigoths. But these gains came at the expense of losses in the East to the Sasanid Persians and eventually proved impossible to preserve. A more lasting achievement was Justinian's codification of Roman law, a massive collection of statutes, rulings, decrees, and judicial opinions that had accumulated over the course of a thousand years. His commission of legal experts eventually produced the *Corpus juris civilis,* which both summarized Roman law and identified its underlying principles. This great work of legal scholarship was to become one of the bases of later European law.

Justinian's law code established the principle that both the material and the spiritual welfare of the empire depended upon the orthodoxy of the emperor and his subjects. In addition, it made the emperor responsible for defending the Church and guaranteeing the purity of its teaching. Justinian described this mutual dependency of church and state in his *Sixth Novella* (535), an early statement of Byzantine political theory:

> There are two main gifts bestowed by God upon men: the priesthood and the Imperial authority. . . . Of these, the former is concerned with things divine, the latter with human affairs. . . . Nothing is of greater importance to the Emperors than to support the dignity of the priesthood, so that the priests may in their turn pray to God for them. We, therefore, are highly concerned to maintain the true doctrines, inspired by God, and to honour the priests. The prosperity of the realm will be secured if the Holy Canons of the Apostles, preserved and explained by the Holy Fathers, are universally obeyed.[15]

For Justinian, then, as for Constantine two centuries earlier, the imperial office carried with it the responsibility to oversee the affairs of the Church and take any action necessary to ensure its unity and orthodoxy. On the basis of this principle he persecuted pagans, Montanists, and Arians, closed the famous Academy of Plato in Athens, and restricted the religious and civil rights of Jews. When disputes over theological issues threatened ecclesiastical and social order, he was quick to call upon bishops and theologians to explain themselves. Justinian's conception of a Church dependent upon and guided by the emperor would become one of the essential features of Byzantine civilization.

One of the ways in which Justinian sought to support the Church was through an ambitious building program. Throughout the empire he raised asylums, hospitals, orphanages, schools, and monasteries. In Constantinople alone he built or rebuilt thirty-four churches, far exceeding even the efforts of Constantine.

The most impressive testimony to Justinian's devotion to Christianity is also his most enduring

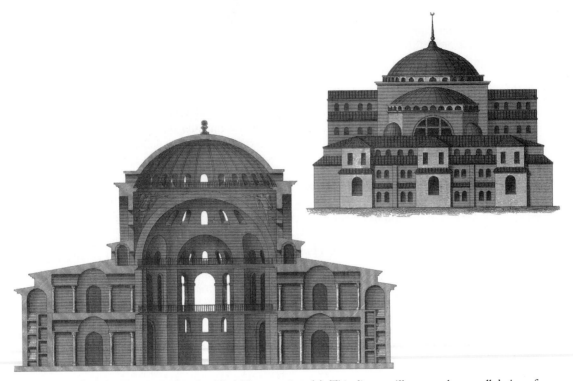

Figure 5.6 Church of Hagia Sophia, Istanbul (Constantinople) This diagram illustrates the overall design of Justinian's magnificient church. Its most famous feature is the great dome.

achievement — the Church of Hagia Sophia ("Holy Wisdom"; also St. Sophia) built in honor of the divine wisdom embodied by Christ. Taking the form of a Greek cross (i.e., a cross with four arms of equal length), Hagia Sophia is enormous. Justinian's architects filled its interior with gold mosaics and costly stone from all over the empire: white and polychrome marble, porphyry, emeralds, onyx, and "an abundance of crystals, like milk poured upon a surface of glittering black [marble]."[16] The altar, fashioned of gold, was surrounded by embroideries of silk, silver, and gold depicting scenes from the life of Christ. Above the center of the church, the dome rises to a height of 180 feet, about eighteen stories, and seems to float above its supports, suspended under heaven. Light pours in from the windows surrounding its base, symbolizing divine wisdom emanating from heaven and filling the church with a sense of the holy. "Whenever anyone enters this church to pray," said the sixth-century historian Procopius, "he understands at once that it is not

by any human power or skill, but by the influence of God, that this work has been so finely turned. And so his mind is lifted up toward God and exalted, feeling that He cannot be far away."[17] The magnificence of his creation was not lost on Justinian, who compared himself to the biblical king who built the temple in Jerusalem. As he stood inside Hagia Sophia for the first time, marveling, he was overheard to whisper, "Solomon, I have surpassed thee!"

BYZANTIUM AFTER JUSTINIAN

But the glories of Justinian's Byzantium were soon threatened and would remain so throughout the rest of its history. In 568, just three years after Justinian's death, the Germanic Lombards captured much of Italy, leaving in Byzantine hands only Venice, a strip of land connecting Ravenna and Rome, and southern Italy. Far more dangerous was the continuing conflict with the Persians, who mounted a ma-

Figure 5.7   The walls of Constantinople

jor offensive in the last years of the sixth century. After seizing Byzantine territories in Egypt, Palestine, and Syria, they advanced through Asia Minor, intending to make Constantinople theirs as well. At the same time the Avars, aggressive warriors from central Asia, joined forces with migrating Slavs along the Danube and began ravaging Byzantine lands on their way south through the Balkans. By the seventh century it seemed certain that the Byzantine state would be crushed between these powerful peoples. Fortunately, salvation came in the person of the emperor Heraclius (610–41), who spent more than a decade reorganizing the military and rebuilding his treasury as his enemies closed in around him. Just as their armies began menacing the outskirts of the capital he unleashed his own forces, driving the Persians far back into Asia and scattering the Avars and Slavs northward. Catastrophe had been narrowly averted.

But in Heraclius's final years a new and greater power appeared as armies of Muslim Arabs poured out of the Arabian peninsula, capturing territories in Egypt, Syria, and Palestine that had only recently been won back from the Persians. By the early eighth century they had established themselves in North Africa and part of Byzantine Asia Minor as well. In 717–18 a Muslim army besieged Constantinople. This time the city and its empire were saved by Leo III ("the Isaurian"; 717–41). Although Leo succeeded in driving the enemy away from Constantinople and even out of Asia Minor, the eastern provinces were never regained. What was left (a modest empire confined to the Balkans, Asia Minor, and a bit of southern Italy) was not powerful enough to prevent the rise of the rival Frankish empire in the West or to arrest the growing influence of Muslim peoples to the east and south.

Despite his success in defending his Christian empire against the Muslims, Leo III was an extremely unpopular ruler thanks to his efforts to eliminate what he regarded as excesses of popular piety, and especially the veneration of **icons**. His successors in the Isaurian dynasty[18] (717–867) also suffered the backlash from his policies, which some of them continued. To complicate matters, during their reigns Byzantine possessions in Italy were seized by the Franks and, closer to home, the Slavic Bulgars became increasingly aggressive.

This threat was met by the new Macedonian dynasty (867-1057), which destroyed the Bulgar state and then pushed northward far beyond it up into central Europe and Russia. The Macedonians also recaptured control of the seas around the empire and drove the Muslims from eastern lands they had taken earlier. At the same time, an economic boom brought renewed prosperity to the empire. Trade relations were established with western Europe, which was eager for eastern goods such as silk and metalwork, and reestablished with markets in Asia. Orthodox Christianity followed Byzantine soldiers and traders and spread among the Bulgars, Russians, Croats, and Serbs. But dynastic infighting in the first half of the eleventh century weakened the Byzantine state and left it vulnerable once again.

When the Macedonian dynasty fell in 1057, the empire was confronted with yet another threat — the Seljuk Turks, who had by this time made themselves the masters of much of the western part of the Muslim world. Alarmed by the strength of the Turks, who would ultimately destroy Byzantium, the emperors appealed to the Christian states of the West for help. As we will see in chapter 6, "help" came in the form of the **Crusades**, which did the empire of the East far more harm than good.

THE CHURCH IN THE BYZANTINE WORLD

At the center of the Byzantine system was the emperor, whose rule over his subjects was supposed to reflect God's rule over the celestial society of heaven. As God's representative on earth, the emperor was the guarantor of the spiritual well-being and physical security of his people. As such, he played an important role in the life of the Church.

He convened church councils, influenced appointments to high ecclesiastical office, sponsored the conversion of pagan peoples, supervised the ecclesiastical bureaucracy, and oversaw its finances. Though not a priest, he sometimes seemed to be one, for he was entitled to wear special vestments during worship and on certain occasions even to preach sermons or cense the altar.[19]

One indication of the emperor's importance in the Church is the imperial epithet *isapostolos* ("equal to the Apostles"), which was first adopted by Constantine, who took it seriously. Contemplating his death and how future generations might regard him, the first Christian emperor had built the magnificent Church of the Holy Apostles and then scoured the empire for their relics so that they might be preserved there along with his own remains. According to Eusebius:

> He had in fact chosen this spot in the prospect of his own death, anticipating with extraordinary fervor of faith that his body would share their title with the Apostles themselves and that he should thus even after death become the subject, with them, of the devotions which should be performed in their honour in this place. He accordingly caused twelve sarcophagi to be set up in this church, like sacred pillars in honor and memory of the number of the Apostles, in the center of which his own was placed, having six of theirs on either side of it.[20]

With such a precedent, it is not difficult to understand later Byzantine assumptions about the nature and extent of imperial authority. The view that the emperor's leadership was as important in matters of religion as in affairs of state was no less firmly established in the last years of the empire than in the time of Justinian. About 1395, a half-century before the fall of Constantinople to the Turks, Patriarch Antony of Constantinople wrote:

> The holy emperor has a great place in the church. He is not as other rulers and the governors of other regions are; and this is because the emperors, from the beginning, established and confirmed true religion in all the inhabited earth. . . . It is not possible for Christians to have a church and not to have an empire. Church and empire have a great unity and community; nor can they be separated from each other.[21]

Thus, Byzantium not only recognized the importance of the emperor in spiritual affairs, it also saw church and state as complementary parts of a single whole. Each had its own sphere of authority, though it was not always easy to determine just where one sphere ended and the other began. In the West a distinction between the two would be continually reinforced by conflicts over their rival claims to power. In the East, however, the coexistence of church and state was a symbiosis elevated under ideal circumstances to the level of a *symphonia* ("harmony") in which they worked together in the pursuit of shared aims and ideals.

Historians have sometimes described this relationship as **caesaropapism**, suggesting that the emperor was also the supreme authority in the Church.[22] But this label has been criticized as inappropriate by scholars who point out that the emperor was not the ruler of the Church in theory and did not always dominate it in practice.[23] They also note that the Church was capable of opposing the emperor when circumstances demanded. It maintained, for example, that a heretical emperor should not be obeyed and formally condemned the memory of more than a few.[24] Eastern saints such as Athanasius of Alexandria, John Chrysostom, Maximus the Confessor, and John of Damascus were venerated partly because they had been willing to take a stand against emperors whose beliefs and policies did not accord with those of the Church.

The highest-ranking ecclesiatical figure in the Byzantine Empire was the bishop of Constantinople. As we saw in chapter 4, Constantinople was one of five episcopal sees that had assumed far greater authority than all others by the fourth and fifth centuries and whose bishops came to be called patriarchs. Three of these great sees, or patriarchates—Rome, Alexandria, and Antioch—were recognized by the Council of Nicaea (325). Constantinople and Jerusalem were acknowledged more than a century later by the Council of Chalcedon (451). Unlike the other four patriarchates, Constantinople could not claim any special association with the Apostles. Instead, its elevation resulted from its status as an imperial capital, the "New Rome." Noting that the earlier Council of Constantinople (381) had already recognized an "honorary precedence" that set the bishops of Rome and

Constantinople above all others, the bishops at Chalcedon wrote:

> The fathers rightly granted privileges to the throne of Old Rome, because it was the imperial city. And one hundred and fifty most religious bishops [at Constantinople], actuated by the same considerations, gave equal privileges to the most holy throne of New Rome, justly judging that the city which is honored with the presence of the emperor and the senate and enjoys equal [civil] privileges with the old imperial Rome should, in ecclesiastical matters also, be magnified as she is and rank next after her.[25]

Because such a noble city and its patriarch deserved a suitably impressive patriarchate, the bishops granted Constantinople jurisdiction over more than four hundred episcopal sees in Europe and Asia. These were augmented in the eighth century by the addition of Illyricum, on the eastern shore of the Adriatic, and parts of southern Italy. New missionary dioceses in the Caucasus, the Crimea, and the lands of the Slavs gave Constantinople even greater influence in eastern Christendom.[26]

At the end of the sixth century, the patriarchs of Constantinople adopted the title *ecumenical patriarch*.[27] This was meant not as a challenge to papal primacy (*ecumenical* means "universal" or "worldwide"), as it seemed to the bishops of Rome, but as an assertion that the patriarch had a place just behind the emperor in the *oikoumene*, the Christian empire ruled from Constantinople. Just as the emperor had religious responsibilities, the patriarch was obligated to involve himself in the secular sphere in order to promote the material welfare of Byzantine society. Patriarchs could even substitute for emperors under certain circumstances and serve as regents when they were not yet old enough to rule.[28] In the ninth century a complete description of the rights and responsibilities of emperors and patriarchs was published in the form of a legal compendium known as the *Epanagoge*.

Although Justinian had prescribed that patriarchs should be chosen by an electoral college of ordained clergy and distinguished citizens, the latter were soon excluded from the process. By the tenth century the selection of a new patriarch was left to a special group of metropolitan bishops, who devised a list of three candidates, and the emperor, who made the final decision.[29] Once he had been selected, the patriarch ruled the Byzantine Church with the assistance of the "holy synod," an assembly of bishops whose sees were close to Constantinople. Almost always in session (so that it is sometimes called the "permanent synod"), its members, their staffs, and the patriarch himself constituted the highest levels of ecclesiastical government.

Despite the often negative influences of politics and personalities, the great majority of patriarchs proved worthy of their office. Most were distinguished by their great learning, saintliness, or both. Such qualities no doubt added much to the richness of Byzantine Christianity. They must also have contributed to the longevity of the Byzantine Empire, though in a state notorious for its endless palace intrigues and political instability (two-thirds of all Byzantine Emperors were killed or otehwise forced from the throne[30]) such influence would be difficult to measure.

THE CONVERSION OF THE GOTHS AND SLAVS

We have already seen how in the West the papacy and the Franks encouraged the work of missionaries such as Boniface among the Germanic tribes of northern Europe. Eastern missionaries were also active in German lands. In the fourth and fifth centuries, though, most were Arian Christians who, from the point of view of Nicene orthodoxy, did little more than make heretics out of pagans. But they were extremely successful. Their efforts made Arian Christianity a powerful force in Germanic territories such as Vandal Africa, Visigothic Spain, and the Ostrogothic lands of northern Italy through the sixth century. Arianism might have endured for centuries longer, dramatically changing the course of European history, had it not been for the conversion of Clovis and the Franks to Catholic Christianity.

The greatest of the Arian missionaries was Ulfilas (ca. 311–83), often called "the Apostle of the Goths." The **Goths** were a Germanic people who later divided into Visigoths (western Goths) and Ostrogoths (eastern Goths). The grandson of Cappadocian Christians taken captive during a Gothic invasion of Asia Minor, Ulfilas was born and raised among the Goths in their lands north of the Danube. Much of his early adult life was spent in Constantinople, then a center of Arianism under Constantius II. About 341 Ulfilas was consecrated bishop of the Goths by Eusebius of Nicomedia, the capital's bishop and an Arian Christian. Not long afterward he returned to his native land, intent on its conversion. Recognizing that the Goths would find the gospel most attractive if presented in their own language, Ulfilas translated the Bible from Greek into Gothic (except for the Books of Kings, which he feared might encourage their warlike spirit). In the process he created a Gothic alphabet and produced the first literary work in any Germanic language. It was largely through Ulfilas's influence, won by his obvious devotion to their culture as well as their salvation, that the Goths embraced Arian Christianity and transmitted it to other Germanic peoples.

The invasion of eastern Europe by the Slavs at the beginning of the sixth century left Byzantium exposed to powerful pagan peoples across its northern borders. By the middle of the ninth century, however, the Slavs were being drawn into the western Church by German missionaries, who insisted that Latin, Greek, and Hebrew might have a place in Christian worship, but not Slavonic.[31] They were also under pressure from the Frankish kingdom of Louis the German, the grandson of Charlemagne, who had designs on their lands as well as their souls. Willing to cooperate in the Christianization of his people, but not to submit to western domination, Prince Ratislav of Moravia, the largest Slavic state in the region, wrote to the Byzantine Emperor asking for missionaries who could preach and pray in the Slavonic language.

Michael III recognized the potential in this invitation. Eager to bring the Slavs into the eastern Church and under the influence of the Byzantine state, in 863 he dispatched two remarkable brothers, Cyril (826–69) and Methodius (815–85), as missionaries to Moravia. These two "Apostles of the Slavs" were highly educated and well-prepared to explain every nuance of the faith. More important, they spoke Slavonic as well as the Greek of their native Thessalonica. There was not yet a satisfactory way of writing the language of the Slavs, so they devised a Slavonic alphabet[32] and began the translation into Slavonic of the Bible and various Greek liturgical texts. Armed with these and speaking the language of the people, Cyril and Methodius were welcomed in Moravia and neighboring Slavic lands and soon won thousands of converts from all levels of society. When German bishops and missionaries protested against their use of Slavonic instead of Latin, which few Slavs could understand, the brothers appealed to scripture, citing the account in Acts 3 of the Holy Spirit inspiring the Apostles to praise God in many languages at Pentecost. They also traveled to Rome and won a papal blessing for their work.[33] Cyril died there, but Methodius returned to Moravia to continue their work.

Despite their dramatic successes, Cyril and Methodius were to have no lasting influence in the lands where they had labored so hard. Methodius had been dead only a few years when Pope Stephen V (885–91) forbade the use of the Slavonic liturgy, and the invasion of the pagan Magyars completely disrupted the order of religious life that the brothers had established. By the end of the tenth century the Slavs of Moravia, Bohemia, and Slovakia had been won over to Latin Christianity. The kingdoms of Poland and Hungary were soon to follow. But the Cyrillic alphabet (a modified version of that developed by Cyril and Methodius) and the Slavonic Bible and liturgy did find permanent acceptance in the Balkans, most notably in Bulgaria and Serbia, where they ensured a lasting commitment to the Orthodox Church.

A century later Russia converted to Orthodox Christianity. Slavic tribes had begun migrating to Russia in the sixth century and constituted the bulk of the population by the tenth. The greatest of Russian cities at that time was Kiev, which controlled vast lands directly and through trade. According to legend, Kiev embraced Christianity after its Grand Duke Vladimir (979–1015) determined that it should abandon paganism and sent envoys to foreign lands in search of the best religion. Their reports on Judaism, Islam, and Latin Christianity left him unimpressed, but what he heard of the faith of the Greeks persuaded him that theirs was the religion for Russia. It was said that Vladimir was especially moved when the agents he had sent to Constantinople claimed that they had been so overcome

by the splendor of the Byzantine liturgy in the cathedral of Hagia Sophia that they could not tell whether they were still on earth or had been caught up into heaven. How much history is preserved in this story is uncertain, but we do know that by 989 Vladimir was energetically establishing the Orthodox faith in Kiev by encouraging mass baptisms and building churches and monasteries. The priests he sent out to convert the rest of his lands did their work well, so that by 991 even Novgorod, far to the north, was a Christian city. Here, as among the southern Slavs, the language of worship was Slavonic. Although Vladimir was unwilling to recognize any ecclesiastical authority outside of Russia, his son Iaroslav the Wise (1019–54) acknowledged the patriarch of Constantinople as the supreme authority over the Russian Church. By formally uniting Russian Christianity with the eastern Church, he inaugurated a millennium of Russian Orthodoxy.

The Islamic Challenge

The few hints we have given thus far of the influence of Islamic civilization on Christendom do not begin to describe its actual extent. Islam was a powerful military threat to the Christian world. Within a century of the death of Muhammad in 632, Arab armies had brought the new religion and Islamic forms of social and political organization to formerly Christian lands reaching from Spain in the West to the gates of Constantinople in the East. The conflict between the Christian and Islamic worlds was intensified and complicated by the competing claims of their religions, which are related both historically and theologically. Given all of this, it makes sense to pause briefly in our survey of Christianity to consider the beliefs and early history of Islam.

MUHAMMAD AND ISLAM

The prophet Muhammad was born about 570 in Mecca, a city in what is now Saudi Arabia. At the age of forty he received the first of a series of revelations that would continue for the rest of his life.

It took the form of a "recitation" (*qur'an*) of the word of God (Allah) revealed through the angel Gabriel. In earlier times Allah had spoken to other peoples through other prophets, among them Adam, Noah, Abraham, Moses, John the Baptist, and Jesus. Now Muhammad learned that he was to be Allah's final prophet and that the revelations he received were the perfect expression of the divine will for all humanity.

Commanded to preach what had been revealed to him, Muhammad boldly proclaimed to the polytheistic Arabs that there was no God but Allah and that the Qur'an, the collected texts of his revelations, was God's word. He warned them against idolatry, dishonesty, and mistreatment of the weak and less fortunate. At the end of time, he said, there would be a bodily resurrection of the dead and a final judgment. Nonbelievers and the disobedient would be consigned to eternal punishment, but those who acknowledged and obeyed God, sought his guidance, and asked for his forgiveness would be rewarded with paradise.

The Qur'an calls those who obey God *Muslims* ("those who submit" to God). Their religion is *Islam*, which means "submission" to the will of God. Islam, says the Qur'an, is true religion, which God also gave to Jews, Christians, and all other peoples through prophets who preceded Muhammad. This attitude toward non-Muslims explains the interest the Qur'an takes in biblical personalities and events. The Qur'an describes the creation of Adam, includes narratives about Noah and the flood, knows of Cain and Abel, and speaks with great reverence of Abraham, Jacob, Joseph, David, and Solomon. It regards Jesus as an authentic prophet of God, accepts his virgin birth, and includes narratives on Mary and John the Baptist. At the same time, however, the Qur'an regards Judaism and Christianity as corruptions of true religion: although Jews and Christians may be above the level of pagans (the Qur'an calls them "people of the book" whose religions must be tolerated[34]), many of their beliefs are false and a grave danger both to themselves and to others who might be misled by them.

THE GROWTH OF ISLAMIC CIVILIZATION

From the very beginning, Islam displayed a missionary zeal that sprang from the conviction that Allah's message in the Qur'an must be taken to all the world. Although at first there were few converts, by the time of Muhammad's death in 632 virtually all of Arabia had been won over to Islam. The next century brought vast lands and other peoples under the banner of Islam. Persia was defeated; Syria, Palestine, and Egypt were wrested from the Byzantine Empire; and armies of Arabs and native Berbers raced across North Africa, bringing what had once been Christian lands under Muslim rule. In 711 a Muslim army crossed the Strait of Gibraltar and conquered much of Spain. The defenders of Christendom were helpless before the advance of Islam until Leo III drove back a Muslim army after an unsuccessful siege of Constantinople (717–18) and the Franks defeated an invading army at Tours (732) in France and forced it back across the Pyrenees into Spain.

The new Islamic empire was ruled at first from Damascus, then from Baghdad. By the tenth century, however, it was breaking apart into independent states studded with culturally vibrant cities such as Fez, Cairo, Palermo, and Cordoba, where there was an eagerness to discover and exploit all the achievements of the earlier civilizations. The great value set on learning and scholarship brought dramatic advances in mathematics, medicine, astronomy, pharmacology, and architecture. At a time when literacy was rare in Christian Europe, nearly every mosque boasted a library and great universities flourished in Cairo, Baghdad, and Cordoba.

Christian reaction to the rise of Islam was largely negative. Christians saw Muslims as *infidels*, or "unbelievers," and Islam as a false religion. In addition, they regarded the loss of so much territory to Islam, and especially the capture of the sites of Jesus' birth and burial in the Holy Land, as a enormous tragedy. Much of the vitality of medieval Christian civilization was spent on largely unsuccessful efforts to recover what had been lost. And yet Christendom also benefited in many ways from its contact with the Islamic world, which offered exotic spices, medicines, music, poetry, and an abundance of books. Western scholars made their way to the Spanish

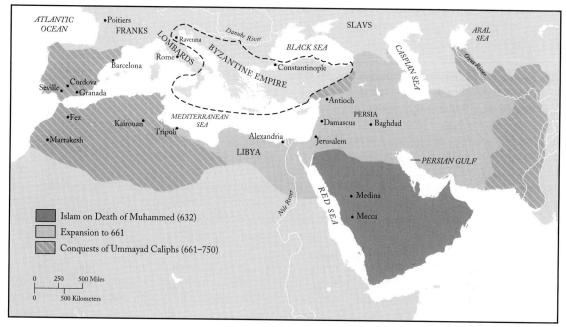

Figure 5.8   The expansion of Islam Beginning in Arabia, Islam had spread across North Africa, into Spain, and deep into Asia within a century after the Prophet's death in 632.

cities of Cordoba and Toledo in search of the works of Plato, Aristotle, and other classical authors. The Latin translations they found there were often based on Arabic versions of the Greek originals. It was in this indirect way that much of classical Greek literature made its way into medieval Europe. As we will see, both Greek philosophy and its interpretation by Muslim scholars would be important forces in western intellectual life during the later Middle Ages.

Developments in the Eastern Church

The eastern Church's alliance with the Byzantine Empire and its expansion into the lands of the Goths and Slavs were only two features of its success in the early medieval centuries. The same period saw other important developments. In a series of church councils, theologians completed the work of defining orthodoxy begun centuries earlier at Nicaea. In addition, in the monasteries of the Byzantine world a mystical tradition began to take shape that would have an enduring influence on eastern piety.

THE SEVEN ECUMENICAL COUNCILS

Late in the eleventh century John II, metropolitan of Russia (1080–89), expressed as clearly as any other eastern **prelate** the Orthodox view of the seven **ecumenical councils** that began at Nicaea in 325: "All profess that there are seven holy and Ecumenical Councils, and these are the seven pillars of the faith of the Divine Word on which he erected his holy mansion, the Catholic and Ecumenical Church."[35]

For Orthodox Christians these seven ecumenical councils—the only ones recognized by the Orthodox Church[36]—defined the true faith and the proper form of ecclesiastical organization. We have already discussed four of them: Nicaea (325), which condemned Arianism, and recognized the special significance of the episcopal sees of Rome, Alexandria, Antioch, and Jerusalem;[37] Constantinople (381), at which the bishops revised the Nicene Creed in order to affirm the equality of the Holy Spirit with the Father and the Son and assigned a place of honor to the new capital of Constantinople just behind that of Rome; Ephesus (431), which condemned Nestorianism; and Chalcedon (451), which repudiated the errors of Monophysitism and Nestorianism.

Arianism eventually faded from the scene; Nestorianism and Monophysitism did not. Nestorianism, for the most part, withdrew beyond the eastern frontiers of the Byzantine Empire, but large populations of Monophysites remained in Egypt and Syria, steadfastly refusing to accept the Council of Chalcedon. Culture as well as theology separated them from the rest of the Church, for many of these speakers of Coptic and Syriac resented the extent of Greek-speaking Constantinople's political and ecclesiastical influence. Hoping to restore unity, the emperor Justinian convened a fifth ecumenical council, the Second Council of Constantinople (553), and urged it to appeal to the Monophysites by taking a more favorable attitude than Chalcedon to Alexandrian Christology. The bishops did so by condemning sixty of the propositions of Theodore of Mopsuestia, the primary architect of Antiochene two-natures Christology.[38] Despite this gesture, however, the Monophysites remained unreconciled to Chalcedonian Christianity.

Efforts at reunification continued. One proposal for emphasizing the unity and divinity in Christ while remaining true to Chalcedonian Christology was **Monothelitism**, which held that although Christ had two natures he possessed only one will (*thelema*). The nature of this single will was generally understood to have been divine, with the result that the opponents of Monothelitism argued, as others had earlier against Apollinaris, that incomplete humanity in Christ would mean incomplete salvation. To reinforce this point, the great Byzantine theologian John of Damascus quoted the words Gregory of Nazianzus had once directed against Apollinaris: "What has not been assumed [by Christ] cannot be healed."[39] Critics also claimed that the New Testament contradicted Monothelitism, for Christ appeared to have distinguished

clearly between his human and divine wills when he prayed to the Father at Gethsemane, "My Father, if it is possible, let this cup pass from me; yet not what I want but what you want" (Matthew 26:39).

Although Monothelitism was rejected by the sixth ecumenical council, the Third Council of Constantinople (680–81), it continued to be troublesome in Syria and Egypt, where it was most popular, until the Arab conquest of these lands eliminated Christian heresy in the process of converting them to Islam. The Third Council of Constantinople is also significant for its decision to brand Pope Honorius I (625–38) a heretic. In correspondence with the Monothelite Patriarch Sergius of Constantinople a half-century earlier, the pope had appeared to support the idea of one will in Christ. In doing so he became the first pope to take the losing side in a controversy decided by one of the ecumenical councils. Although there is some ambiguity surrounding the matter (Was the pope deliberate or only careless in referring to the "one will" of Christ?), Honorius's error has been one of the most powerful arguments made by Protestant and Eastern Orthodox Christians against the Roman Catholic **dogma** of **papal infallibility** (not formally declared until the First Vatican Council in 1870).

THE ICONOCLASTIC CONTROVERSY

The seventh and final ecumenical council, the Second Council of Nicaea (787), was occasioned by a lengthy and often violent conflict over the use of icons ("images") of Christ, the Virgin Mary, and the saints. This controversy rocked eastern Christendom from the lowest classes of society to the highest levels of ecclesiastical and imperial government. Keeping in mind Deuteronomy 4:16, in which God had warned ancient Israel against the making of idols, the early Church had made little use of images. In time, however, icons became common throughout the Christian world. In the East, the Greek passion for giving material expression to the sublime was irrepressible. Byzantine Christians considered icons "windows into heaven" and honored them accordingly — kissing them, burning candles and incense before them, and pointing to them as the causes of miracles. The iconoclastic controversy, in which **iconoclasts** ("icon-smashers") attempted to put an end to what they regarded as the superstitious and idolatrous practices of **iconodules** ("icon-venerators"), involved more than the place of icons in the Church. It also called into question the attitude of Christianity toward Christ's humanity and the material world in general.

Conflict broke out in 726 when the emperor Leo III informed ecclesiastical leaders of a new imperial policy of removing images from churches and other public places. To illustrate his intentions, Leo ordered the destruction of one of Constantinople's most famous icons, an immense golden image of Christ positioned above the gate to the emperor's palace. His motives are unclear. He may have been moved by the conviction that spiritual realities could not possibly be represented in material form, or perhaps he was reacting to Muslim charges of Christian idolatry. Whatever Leo's reasons might have been, there is no doubt that iconoclasm began as an imperial rather than as an ecclesiastical initiative.

Popular reaction was immediate. The crowd that witnessed the destruction of the great icon of Christ killed the officer in charge on the spot. Angry demonstrations quickly erupted throughout Constantinople as word of the new policy spread, and within days there were mutinies in the army and navy. For the masses of Byzantine Christians, iconoclasm was an outrage against both God and popular piety that could never be tolerated. But the emperor and his supporters, many of whom belonged to the higher clergy, were undeterred. When Patriarch Germanus (715–30) stood in defense of icons, Leo deposed him and appointed a new patriarch more sympathetic to his views. When monks assumed leadership of the iconodules, Leo and his iconoclastic successors made them targets of intimidation and violence. Leo's son, Constantine V (741–75), was particularly vicious. He executed hundreds of monks and maimed countless others by having their eyes gouged out, their tongues and noses cut off, and their beards set on fire.

Iconodules defended themselves by arguing that their devotion was not directed to mere images made of material elements but to the higher spiritual realities they symbolized. This point was made

a century before the beginning of the controversy by Leontius of Neapolis:

> We do not make obeisance to the nature of wood, but we revere and do obeisance to Him who was crucified on the Cross. . . . When the two beams of the Cross are joined together I adore the figure because of Christ who on the Cross was crucified, but if the beams are separated, I throw them away and burn them.[40]

In addition to denying that they worshiped wood, paint, and the other elements of which images were made, iconodules explained that icons were a necessary reminder that the salvation of humanity depended on Christ's assumption of a material nature. They protested that to deny the involvement of the divine in the material, as the iconoclasts seemed to do, was to fall once again into old and dangerous heresies concerning the person of Christ. As for the Old Testament prohibition of images, they argued that it had lost its validity the moment God took human form. John of Damascus wrote:

> In former times God, who is without form or body, could never be depicted. But now when God is seen in the flesh conversing with men, I make an image of the God whom I see. I do not worship matter; I worship the Creator of matter who became matter for my sake, who willed to take His abode in matter; who worked out my salvation through matter. Never will I cease honoring the matter which wrought my salvation![41]

The assault on icons begun by Leo III did not come to an end until 787. In that year the empress Irene (797–802), then acting as regent for her son, Constantine VI, convened the Second Council of Nicaea. In attendance were representatives of Pope Hadrian I (772–95), whose interest in the matter was great—not so much because iconoclasm had disrupted religious life in the West (it had not),[42] but because it seemed to the West as well as to the East a denial of the humanity of Christ and the role of matter in God's plan for salvation. It did not take the bishops at Nicaea long to proclaim the restoration of icons to their former places of honor in "the holy churches of God, on holy vessels and vestments, on walls and in pictures, in houses and by the roadsides."[43] Once again, the Byzantine world was filled with images offering glimpses of the divine.

But the Second Council of Nicaea was careful to distinguish between the proper and improper use of images. Adopting the distinction made by John of Damascus in his treatise *On the Divine Images*, it urged Christians to offer veneration to images of Christ, the Virgin, and the saints, but to reserve actual worship for God alone. Despite this settlement, iconoclasm flared up once again in 815 when the emperor Leo V (813–20) revived the policies of Leo III and Constantine V. This time the attack on icons was ended permanently by the empress Theodora, whose final restoration of images in 843 is known among Orthodox Christians as "the Triumph of Orthodoxy" and is celebrated annually on the first Sunday of Lent. Along with the Second Council of Nicaea, this event marks the end of the period in which the essential features of Orthodox doctrine and practice were defined and implemented both at the popular level and within the overall structure of the Byzantine state. From Nicaea II until our own time, Orthodox theology has devoted itself largely to the analysis and elaboration of what was proclaimed by the bishops in the seven ecumenical councils.

JOHN OF DAMASCUS

His prominent role in the iconoclastic controversy was only one aspect of the life and work of John of Damascus, who is generally regarded as the last and one of the greatest of the fathers of the Orthodox Church. Born in Damascus about 650 into a prosperous Christian family, he received an excellent education in both Greek and Arabic before following in the footsteps of his father, who had served as a high-level official in the court of the Ummayad caliph, the most powerful of Muslim rulers. John was one of the caliph's chief advisors when, about 725, he resigned his position in order to withdraw to the monastery of St. Sabas near Jerusalem. There he was ordained a priest and spent the rest of his life as a virtual recluse. Deep in Muslim territory, this learned Christian found the freedom to write theology and preach in the churches of Jerusalem without fearing the reactions of iconoclastic emperors and other critics.

John's most famous work is *The Fountain of Knowledge*. Divided into three parts, the first is an introduction to philosophy — especially to Aristotelianism and Neoplatonism — and the second a history of heresies ending with Islam. The most important part, however, is the third, generally known as *The Orthodox Faith*. Consisting of one hundred chapters divided into four books, it is a systematic account of the faith that draws upon and synthesizes the teachings of Nicene and post-Nicene theologians so extensively that it has been considered the basic statement and standard of Orthodox theology ever since its composition. Its pages include masterful descriptions of every essential idea and doctrine. John demonstrates the existence and unity of God, explains the incarnation and relationship of the two natures and wills in Christ, develops a Mariology that includes Mary's exemption from the stain of sin and her assumption into heaven, presents predestination in a way that comes as close as any other to doing justice both to divine omniscience and human freedom, and insists that in the eucharist the bread and wine truly become the body and blood of Christ.

The authority, depth, and clarity of *The Fountain of Knowledge* led eventually to its translation into Latin and consequent popularity in certain circles in the West. Thomas Aquinas, who attempted his own summation of the Christian faith in the thirteenth century, knew it well. John also wrote the *Sacred Parallels* (which has been preserved only in fragments), a vast collection of material on Christian morality in which virtues and vices are treated in pairs, and composed hymns that were later included in the Greek liturgy. Given his many contributions, it is no wonder that he is widely considered one of the most important representatives of Orthodox Christianity.

MONASTICISM AND MYSTICISM

Eastern monasticism flourished during the Middle Ages. It differed from western monasticism in that Byzantine monks were never divided into different orders, though almost from the beginning there was a distinction between those who lived as hermits and others who preferred the communal environment of a monastery. In addition, no single monastic rule ever assumed the authority carried by the Benedictine Rule in the West. Instead, the well-known practices of the Desert Fathers and Basil the Great provided guidance and a normalizing influence.

One of the most prominent features of Byzantine monasticism was a mystical tradition that emphasized the themes of **deification** through the action of divine grace and the otherness and unknowability of God. The first was based on New Testament passages such as 2 Peter 1:4 ("Thus he has given us . . . his precious and very great promises, so that through them you . . . may become participants of the divine nature") and supported by the doctrine that the Holy Spirit is at work in every believer, transforming the old sinful nature into a spiritual one (Romans 8; John 14–17). The second seemed an obvious consequence of God's infinite and transcendent majesty and found support in the Neoplatonist idea of the unknowable One, the ultimate source of all things. Both themes can be traced back to the works of early theologians such as Irenaeus, Clement of Alexandria, Athanasius, and Cyril of Alexandria, who emphasized God's transcendence and spoke of deification as something made possible by the union of humanity and divinity in Christ. Athanasius, for example, is famous for his assertion that "God became man that we might become divine."[44] But it was through the influence of later thinkers like Pseudo-Dionysius, Maximus the Confessor, Simeon the New Theologian, and Gregory Palamas that these ideas became central to Orthodox theology.

Pseudo-Dionysius is the name commonly assigned to the author of four treatises on mystical theology. Two have been especially influential in both the East and West since late antiquity: *On the Divine Names,* which deals with the essence and attributes of God, and *Mystical Theology,* which describes the ascent of the soul and its ecstatic experience of union with God, the ultimate goal and purpose of human existence.[45] Although these works were long thought to have been composed by the Athenian Dionysius whose conversion by Paul is described in Acts 17:34, modern sholars believe that Pseudo-Dionysius was probably an anonymous Syrian monk writing sometime around 500.

Whoever he was, Pseudo-Dionysius was a devout Christian whose faith was deeply influenced by Neoplatonism. This is especially evident in his conception of God as One who is utterly beyond ordinary knowing because he is completely unlike anything that can be experienced in ordinary reality. Because God transcends all other realities and their attributes, even concepts as basic as "being" and "nonbeing" are useless in describing the divine nature. The mystic must put all labels aside and pass through the successive stages of purification, illumination, and perfection, a threefold process that became almost universal in later Christian mysticism. When this is done, it becomes possible to behold God and even to be transformed through *theosis* ("deification") into that which is beyond all else. Much of this is described in the opening lines of *Mystical Theology:*

> O Trinity, beyond essence and beyond divinity and beyond goodness, guide of Christians in divine wisdom, direct us toward mysticism's heights, beyond unknowing, beyond light, beyond limit, there where the unmixed and unfettered and unchangeable mysteries of theology in the dazzling dark of the welcoming silence lie hidden, in the intensity of their darkness all brilliance outshining, our intellects, blinded — overwhelming with the intangible and with the invisible and with the illimitable. Such is my prayer. And you, beloved Timothy, in the earnest exercise of mystical contemplation abandon all sensation and all intellection and all objects sensed or seen and all being and all nonbeing and in unknowing as much as may be, be one with the beyond being and knowing. By the ceaseless and limitless going out of yourself and out of all things else you will be led in utter pureness rejecting all and released from all, aloft to the flashing forth, beyond all being, of the divine dark.[46]

This description of God as completely *beyond*— "beyond essence and beyond divinity and beyond goodness"— is characteristic of the *via negativa,* the "negative way," which assumes the best way to talk about a God who is completely unlike anything we know is to focus on what God is not. Pseudo-Dionysius called this "apophatic" ("denying") or "negative theology," coining a phrase that is commonly used to describe any theology that emphasizes God's otherness.

The unknowability of God was also emphasized by Maximus the Confessor (ca. 580–662), a monk and theologian who was one of the most outspoken critics of Monothelitism and wrote a commentary on Pseudo-Dionysius. But Maximus is best known for his theory of *theosis*, according to which the supernatural union of the Christian with Christ makes possible the fulfillment of the natural desire to achieve identification with God. The force that shapes and perfects the individual united to Christ is grace. "Love, the divine gift," said Maximus, "perfects human nature until it makes it appear in unity and identity with the divine nature."[47] But this can occur only with an assent of the human will, so that deification is an essentially collaborative effort.

The view that the individual contributes to deification had become a feature of eastern monasticism even before Maximus. Tradition attributes to the fourth-century monk Macarius of Egypt the saying, "The will of man is an essential condition, for without it God does nothing."[48] Writing more than half a century after Maximus, John of Damascus observed that "it depends upon ourselves whether we are to persevere in virtue and be guided by God who invites us to practice it."[49] This emphasis on the human contribution to salvation distinguished eastern thought from that of the West, which generally followed Augustine in claiming that salvation depends on grace alone. Eastern Christianity also differed in its tendency to regard deification as a lifelong *process* in which *theosis* would be fully realized in the age to come. Western theologians, on the other hand, generally spoke of salvation as a *transition* from a state of sin to a state of grace that would ultimately result in union with God, though not in outright identification with him.

The character of eastern mysticism and mystical theology underwent further development in the eleventh century with the emergence of **Hesychasm**, a form of mystical prayer and contemplation that came to be associated primarily with the monks of Mt. Athos in northern Greece. Although Hesychasm's roots can be traced back to early figures such as Gregory of Nyssa and Evagrius Ponticus, a fourth-century spiritual writer from Asia Minor, credit for its origination is usually given to Simeon the New Theologian[50] (949-1022), abbot

of the monastery of St. Mamas in Constantinople. The Hesychasts, whose practice took its name from the Greek word for "quietude" (*hesychia*), employed special contemplative techniques. These included controlled breathing, placing the chin on the chest in order to fix the eyes on the place of the heart, and repetition of the Jesus Prayer: "Lord Jesus Christ, Son of God, have mercy on me." Under the influence of grace, these practices were said to produce an inner quiet and harmony in which the prayer filled and unified one's being and expressed itself spontaneously and without effort. Ideally, the practice of Hesychasm led to a vision of the same divine and uncreated light that Peter, James, and John had seen enveloping Christ during his transfiguration on Mt. Tabor. Simeon described his own experience of the light in his *Discourses*:

> One day, as he stood and recited, "God, have mercy upon me, a sinner" . . . a flood of divine radiance appeared from above and filled all the room. As this happened the young man lost all awareness [of his surroundings] and forgot that he was in a house or that he was under a roof. He saw nothing but light all around him and did not know if he was standing on the ground. He was not afraid of falling . . . nor did anything pertaining to men and corporeal beings enter his mind. Instead, he was wholly in the presence of immaterial light and seemed to himself to have turned into light. Oblivious of all the world he was filled with tears and with ineffable joy and gladness.[51]

Accounts like this of the power and beauty of the divine light encouraged the growth of the Hesychast movement. But they also raised an obvious question: How could such experiences of God be reconciled with the apophatic idea that God is unknowable? After all, by insisting that they had seen *uncreated* light, and not merely the light that God had created in Genesis 1:3, the Hesychasts seemed to be saying that they had had immediate experiences and knowledge of God, who alone is uncreated.

This apparent contradiction was only one of the reasons the Hesychasts were denounced in the fourteenth century by their most bitter critic, Barlaam of Calabria. A monk who had been educated in that Italian city, Barlaam preferred philosophy to mystical theology. He advocated a radical matter/spirit dualism and an extreme form of the doctrine of God's "otherness." Arguing that God can be known only indirectly, Barlaam claimed that what the Hesychasts had seen was not God but merely created light. He also criticized them for their conviction that the body could contribute to spiritual knowledge. How, he asked, could human eyes behold the unknowable God? Finally, Barlaam ridiculed the Hesychasts' use of bodily postures, and especially the technique of directing their gaze downward, calling them *omphalopsychoi,* or "men with bellybutton souls."

The great defender of the Hesychasts was Gregory of Palamas (1296–1359), a monk who had embraced Hesychasm in his twenties while at Mt. Athos and eventually became archbishop of Thessalonica. In 1337 he entered into debate with Barlaam and a year later published his famous *Triads in Defense of the Holy Hesychasts.* Gregory met Barlaam's objections relating to the place of the body in prayer by affirming the traditional Christian view that it is an essential component of the whole person. If prayer is to be performed with one's entire being, he said, then the body has an important part to play:

> Although God makes those who pray sincerely go out of themselves, rendering them transcendent to their natures and mysteriously ravished away to heaven, yet even in such cases . . . it is through the mediation of the soul and body that God effects things supernatural, mysterious and incomprehensible to the wise of this world.[52]

Concerning the more important question of how an unknowable God can be known, Gregory agreed that the divine essence (*ousia*) is beyond knowledge. "The essence of God," he wrote, "is inaccessible and incommunicable."[53] The light experienced by the Hesychasts, he explained, was one of the divine *energies,* God's actions and revelations of himself in the world. Because these are uncreated, and because God is completely present in them, they *are* God, and not parts of creation, though they are not God in his unknowable essence. In this way, said Gregory, it *is* possible to know the unknowable God — a God who is transcendent yet immanent in the world and eager to enter into a relationship with those who live in it.

In making his arguments against Hesychasm, Barlaam had urged that the standards of logic and philosophy be rigorously applied to theology. Gregory appealed to other authorities: tradition and mystical experience. Both these and his views on the otherness of God and the human experience of the divine were upheld when the debate was brought before councils of eastern bishops held at Constantinople in 1341, 1347, and 1351.[54] In formally endorsing Hesychasm, which has remained a feature of eastern Christianity ever since, the Orthodox Church affirmed its identity as a Christian tradition committed to the ideals of mysticism and its inseparability from theology. Gregory expressed the essentially mystical nature of Orthodox Christianity in inviting others to experience divinity for themselves: "Come, let us ascend the holy and heavenly mountain, let us contemplate the immaterial divinity of the Father and the Spirit, which shines forth in the only Son."[55]

Developments in the Western Church

In addition to its progress in converting the peoples of Gaul, Spain, Ireland, England, and Germany, the western Church made other important advances during the early Middle Ages. The theoretical groundwork was laid for the later rise of the papacy, theologians turned their attention to questions such as predestination and the nature and purpose of the sacraments, and popular devotion to the saints was more firmly established as a form of popular piety. During this era growing conflict between the eastern and western churches also became increasingly evident.

EARLY THEORIES OF PAPAL AUTHORITY

The papacy of the early Middle Ages was nothing like the powerful institution that would arise in the eleventh and twelfth centuries, yet claims of papal primacy were already being made. In fact, the idea that the bishop of Rome held a place of honor above all other bishops was widespread as early as the fourth century and accepted by significant numbers of eastern as well as western bishops.[56] Pope Damasus (366–84), in seeking to underscore the pre-eminence of Rome among the other patriarchates, described it as "*the* apostolic see." His successor, Siricius (384–99), apparently assumed that the decisions he announced in papal letters known as **decretals** were universally binding.[57]

By the middle of the fifth century an explicit argument for papal primacy had been worked out. Known as the Petrine Doctrine, it was based in part on Rome's status as imperial capital and its association with the Apostle Peter, who was said to have been the leader of the Christians of Rome before being martyred there. It also depended upon the scriptural account of Jesus' response to Peter's confession of faith in Matthew 16:18–19, which was interpreted as describing how Peter, traditionally seen as Rome's first bishop, was given a unique authority that was claimed in turn by each of his successors: "And I tell you, you are Peter, and on this rock I will build my church, and the gates of Hades will not prevail against it. I will give you the keys to the kingdom of heaven, and whatever you bind on earth will be bound in heaven, and whatever you loose on earth will be loosed in heaven."

The eastern Church was ambivalent on the question of papal primacy. On the one hand, eastern bishops at the councils of Constantinople (381) and Chalcedon (451) had recognized Rome's "honorary precedence" even as they were seeking to elevate the patriarchate of Constantinople to substantially the same status. But in the Orthodox view, precedence has never been taken to mean that the bishops of Rome have supreme authority in the Church. Instead, they have generally been regarded as the first among episcopal equals.

In addition to claiming primacy over all other bishops, the bishops of Rome made increasingly bold assertions of their authority in the secular sphere. One of the first popes to take a leading role in secular affairs was Leo I ("the Great"; 440–61). At a time when the city of Rome lay defenseless before its enemies, it was Leo, and not some civil official, who negotiated with Attila the Hun (452) and Gaiseric the Vandal (455) for the safety of its inhabitants. Relying on the popular support such actions brought him, Leo aggressively promoted his doctrinal views,[58] intervened in the affairs of churches from Gaul to North Africa, and prevailed upon the western emperor Valentinian III to issue an edict commanding obedience to the bishop of Rome in recognition of the "primacy of St. Peter."[59]

Gelasius I (492–96) went a step further than Leo by advancing a theory of church-state relations according to which the primacy of the Church must always be recognized. According to Gelasius, there are two forms of power, secular and spiritual; both derive from Christ, who is both king and priest of the universe. Each has its own proper sphere, so that only when when these appear to intersect does the question of precedence arise. This must always be resolved in favor of priests, whose responsibility for preparing souls for eternity is much weightier than the concerns of kings. The greatest of priests is the pope, said Gelasius, for he is a successor of Peter, upon whom Christ founded the Church. Moreover, the association of Rome with Peter and Paul, who had been martyred there, had raised the Roman Church "over all the others in the whole world."[60] By such reasoning Gelasius set the bishop of Rome above all other rulers, both secular and spiritual.

GREGORY THE GREAT

Gelasius's vision of the papacy's rightful place in the world had little to do with the realities of the late fifth century. In 490, just two years before Gelasius became pope, Italy had been occupied by the Ostrogoths under their king Theodoric. For the next thirty-five years the papacy was caught between two great powers, the Arian Ostrogoths and the Byzantine Empire, neither of which showed much interest in theories of papal supremacy. The Byzantine reconquest of Italy begun by Justinian a decade after Theodoric's death in 526 also limited opportunities for the papacy to assert itself.

This situation changed in 568 with the invasion of the Lombards. As we have seen, they soon established a kingdom in northern Italy that lasted until it was conquered by the Franks in the eighth century. Surrounded by these pagan intruders, who later converted to Arian Christianity, Rome found itself isolated from the rest of the orthodox Christian world. It was a dangerous time, and in the absence of capable secular leaders it was left to the bishops of Rome to save the city by taking control of political as well as religious affairs.

None met the challenge more effectively than Gregory I ("the Great"; 590–604). Born into an aristocratic Roman family, Gregory had already begun a career in civil service when, in his early thirties, he felt himself called to religious life. After giving part of his inheritance to the poor and using the rest for the foundation of monasteries, he became a monk himself. Shortly afterward he was pressed into more active service on behalf of the Church as one of the seven deacons of Rome and later as papal ambassador to the imperial court at Constantinople. In 590 he reluctantly agreed to succeed Pelagius II as pope—the first pope to have been a monk.

The problems before him were enormous. The decay into which Rome had fallen centuries earlier had by now progressed to the point that the city's walls and buildings were collapsing and its aqueducts no longer functioned properly. To make matters worse, the Ostrogothic occupation had impoverished much of the population, food shortages threatened many with starvation, floods had ravaged the city, a plague had recently broken out, and the Lombards were becoming more and more threatening.

Gregory took immediate action. Under his direction armies were raised, parts of the city were rebuilt, the food supply was augmented, and care was given to those stricken by poverty and disease. Many of the resources necessary to meet these needs were provided by church lands in Italy, Sicily, Gaul, and North Africa, which Gregory defended and managed so effectively that their productivity increased even despite difficult circumstances and his insistence on the humane treatment of laborers. Negotiating on his own authority with both the Lombards and the Byzantine Empire, Gregory established a peace that kept Rome safe throughout his pontificate. He also supervised the Roman mission to England, began the enforcement of clerical celibacy, and ably defended the idea of papal primacy, particularly against the patriarchs of Constantinople.[61] All in all, Gregory not only saved the "rotten old vessel," as he had once called the Roman see,[62] but greatly increased its prestige. In doing so, he became the most influential of early medieval popes and, in effect, the ruler of central Italy. As such, he may well have deserved the title of *consul dei* ("God's consul") attributed to him after his death, for like the consuls of ancient Rome he exercised great power for the public good. His favorite title, however, was *servus servorum Dei* ("servant of the servants of God").

More than an ecclesiastical statesman and administrator, Gregory also helped shape medieval Christian thought on a number of practical issues. He defined the essential features of the sacrament of penance (contrition, confession, and satisfaction) and contributed to its growing importance by arguing that satisfaction must be made for sins committed after baptism and can be accomplished through good works performed in love.[63] Recognizing that satisfaction for sin is not always made in life, he also contributed to the development of the doctrine of **purgatory**, an intermediate state between this life and the next, by claiming that lesser, or "venial," sins can be purged there before the final judgment.[64] Gregory's belief that there is expiatory power in the eucharist led him to recommend that masses be celebrated on behalf of the dead, so that they might be delivered from purgatory, as well as for the living, so that they might better perform penances.[65] He also encouraged the veneration of saints and their relics. His fabulous tales of the miracles and extraordinary powers of saints, recorded in his *Dialogues,* and his writings on dreams, visions, prophecies, demons, and the hierarchical orders of angels in heaven show how easily Gregory combined theological sophistication with the folk piety of his time.

A final area in which Gregory had great influence was public worship. He preached frequently and left behind numerous homilies. These tend to be simple and straightforward and give us a good idea of how the Church sought to reach the great mass (masses) of ordinary Christians. He also made important contributions to the early Latin liturgy and, like Ambrose two centuries before him, encouraged the use of music in worship. Most scholars agree that he had an influence on the development of the form of **plainsong** that came to be known as Gregorian chant.

Gregory's stature as one of the great figures in the history of the medieval Church is widely acknowledged. His achievements were recognized in his canonization, which took place by popular acclamation almost immediately after his death, and by his later acknowledgment as one of the four original Latin Doctors of the Church, along with Ambrose, Augustine, and Jerome.[66]

JOHN SCOTUS ERIUGENA

The early Middle Ages was not a time of great theological productivity in the West. The exigencies arising from social and political instability and economic deterioration demanded attention that might otherwise have been devoted to study and reflection. In addition, only in monasteries and among some segments of the clergy and secular aristocracy was it possible to find centers of literacy and learning. Still, intellectual activity in the monastic communities of Ireland, England, and the Frankish Empire did spark significant controversies relating to predestination, the sacraments, and the Holy Spirit.

The greatest theologian of the time was John Scotus Eriugena. His name identifies him twice as a native of Ireland, for at the time of his birth (ca. 810) it was known both as Scotia and Erin.[67] A wanderer like so many other Irish, Eriugena left his homeland for the kingdom of the Franks, where his brilliance earned him a position as head of the palace school in the court of Charles the Bald. He was unusual among western theologians for his knowledge of Greek and his appreciation of Greek philosophy and theology. It was Eriugena who introduced the works of Pseudo-Dionysius to the West by translating them into Latin, but he was equally famous for his treatise *On the Division of Nature,* a synthesis of Neoplatonism and Christianity that displayed his erudition but raised questions about his orthodoxy. Starting with the Neoplatonist doctrine that the universe emanates from God in diminishing levels of being and will ultimately be drawn back into its source, Eriugena went on to as-

sert that God, who in his own essence is unknowable, is at the same time "everything that truly exists, for he makes all things and is made in all things." This suggestion of pantheism was not the only unorthodox feature of Eriugena's thought. He also taught that creation is eternal, that all beings are immortal, and that heaven and hell are not actual places but conditions of the soul.

Respect for his great learning drew Eriugena briefly into debates on predestination and the eucharist, but for the most part he was isolated by his unusual views and use of Greek sources that few others could understand. *On the Division of Nature* was eventually condemned as heretical in the early thirteenth century, when Pope Honorius III ordered that all copies be sent to Rome for burning. We are not certain what happened to Eriugena himself. The twelfth-century historian William of Malmesbury says that he returned to England, where angry students stabbed him to death with iron pens — an apocryphal story, perhaps, but one that appeals to some. However he died, his passing foreshadowed the end of that period in which Plato was the greatest external influence on Christian thought. As we will see in chapter 6, the West's rediscovery of Aristotle would soon bring a revolution in theology.

PREDESTINATION

The early medieval debate on predestination was occasioned by an extreme interpretation of Augustine's views on the subject by the monk Gottschalk (ca. 804–ca. 869) and the responses of the abbot Rabanus Maurus and Archbishop Hincmar of Reims. The controversy had a very personal dimension, for as a child Gottschalk had been placed against his will in Rabanus's monastery at Fulda in Germany. When Gottschalk later asked for permission to leave, Rabanus refused, allowing him only to move first to the monastery at Corbie and then to Orbais, both in France. The enmity between the two men was exacerbated years later when Rabanus learned that his former monk had gone beyond Augustine in advocating a theory of "double predestination" according to which God had not only predestined the elect to salvation but all others to damnation as well. It was foolish, said Gottschalk, to pretend that God's decision to extend saving grace to some people did not also imply his decision to withhold it from everyone else. Gottschalk also argued that Christ had not died for all human beings but only for the elect. Hoping to silence him, Rabanus engineered the condemnation of his teachings at two synods at Quiercy (849 and 853), where Gottschalk was beaten and condemned to life imprisonment under the authority of Hincmar, whose cruelty led the unfortunate monk to declare his certainty that the archbishop was among the damned.

Gottschalk's critics could not accept his conception of a God who did not seek the salvation of all human beings and who predestined the condemned as well as the elect. Some feared that his emphasis on Augustine's ideas concerning the corruption of human nature and the absolute importance of grace left little, if any, room for human effort in the process of salvation. Others asked how the Church and its role in making grace available through the sacraments could have any value if salvation depended solely upon grace working through predestination.

Hincmar, not Rabanus Maurus, was Gottschalk's most bitter opponent. After writing a brief treatise of his own on predestination, the archbishop called on a number of the greatest scholars of his time to help him demolish Gottschalk, only to be shocked when some defended him instead or offered support that did more harm than good. Eriugena, for example, argued that double predestination is impossible, but only because the sin and evil to which the damned would be consigned do not actually exist. A temporary truce between Gottschalk's critics and supporters was achieved at the Synod of Douzy in 860, but it resulted more from frustration than from a satisfactory explanation of how the perfection of God, and especially his perfect grace and knowledge of what will be, can be reconciled with the freedom of human beings to make meaningful decisions about their lives and destinies. It is a puzzle that has never been solved.

THE SACRAMENTS

Augustine's definition of a sacrament as an outward and visible sign of invisible grace captures as well as any other the essence of the Church's teaching about the special rites through which grace is said to bring Christians into closer communion with Christ. It also allowed him to consider as sacraments such acts as baptismal exorcisms, the presentation of blessed salt to catechumens, and recitation of the Lord's Prayer, leaving him with a total far exceeding the number recognized today.[68]

Uncertainty about the number of the sacraments continued throughout much of the Middle Ages. At the beginning of the sixth century, Pseudo-Dionysius identified six (baptism, the eucharist, unction, the ordination of priests, the consecration of monks, and the funeral service), and as late as the twelfth century Hugh of St. Victor listed no fewer than thirty. Gradually, however, medieval theologians came to the conclusion that there were seven: baptism, the rite of initiation into the Church; the eucharist, in which bread and wine are consecrated and consumed in remembrance of Jesus' suffering and death; confirmation, a rite that recognizes spiritual maturity and brings one into full membership in the Church; penance, in which an individual recognizes and confesses sin, accepts a punishment, and receives **absolution**; unction, an anointing with oil for the benefit of the sick and dying; holy orders, or the ordination of priests; and holy matrimony, or marriage. These were formally and exclusively affirmed as sacraments in the West by the Council of Florence in 1439.

For medieval theologians the sacramental status of the eucharist was never in doubt, for its institution by Christ is made clear by the New Testament.[69] The *nature* of the eucharist, on the other hand, became the focus of a debate initiated in 831 when Paschasius Radbertus, abbot of the monastery at Corbie, published his treatise *On the Body and Blood of the Lord.* Ever since the first century most Christians had agreed that the body and blood of Christ were somehow truly present in the eucharist, for Christ's words of institution ("This is my body" and "This is my blood"; Mark 14:22–25) seemed unambiguous. Moreover, the doctrine of the "real presence" of Christ had been approved by the Second Council of Nicaea in 787. But Radbertus argued, in a way that struck many as crudely literal, that in the eucharist the bread and wine ceased to exist and became instead the very same body and blood that were present on the cross. He added, however, that this change took place only for believers who accepted it in faith; the elements remained bread and wine for nonbelievers, and the appearance of bread and wine remained for believers and nonbelievers alike.

Radbertus's critics followed Augustine in saying that Christ is truly present in the eucharistic bread and wine, though in a spiritual way that can be discerned by faith but not by the senses. The most notable was Ratramnus, also a monk of Corbie, who wrote in his *On the Body and Blood of Christ* that it is a mistake to think that "something heavenly and divine" can be smelled, touched, or tasted. Although they are called the body and blood of Christ, he said, the bread and wine on the altar *are* bread and wine, though Christ is spiritually present within them:

> How then can they be called the body and blood
> of Christ when no change can be seen to have
> taken place? . . . As far as the physical appearances
> of both are concerned, they seem to be things
> which have been physically created. However, as
> far as their power is concerned, in that they have
> been created spiritually, they are the mysteries of
> the body and blood of Christ.[70]

The reaction against Radbertus continued long after his own lifetime. In the eleventh century, Berengar of Tours (ca. 1010–88) reiterated Ratramnus's argument for Christ's spiritual presence in the eucharist. To him the idea that the earthly body of Christ was in the eucharist seemed ludicrous. How could a bit of bread become Christ's body, he asked, when that body had been taken up into heaven a thousand years earlier?

But to many Christians the spiritual presence of Christ was not enough. Popular piety demanded something much closer to the literal body of Christ advocated by Radbertus. Still, the question remained: How could Christ be physically as well as spiritually present in the eucharist without being perceived as such by the senses? The answer was supplied in the eleventh century by Lanfranc of Bec, a monk from Normandy who said that bread and wine become the body and blood of Christ through a transformation of their essential substances that leaves secondary qualities like taste, texture, and smell unchanged. This argument was made possible by Aristotle, who had distinguished between the unchanging *substances* of things and their variable "accidental" *qualities* perceived by the senses. By saying that a miraculous reversal of this situation occurs in the eucharist, theologians could claim that the substances of the bread and wine become the divine substance of Christ even while their accidental properties remain the same. This doctrine of **transubstantiation** was widely accepted in the twelfth century and formally approved in the thirteenth by the Fourth Lateran Council (1215), though it would be another half-century before its details would be worked out by Thomas Aquinas.

Early medieval theologians also devoted considerable thought to the sacrament of penance. We have already seen how in the third century Cyprian and other leaders of the North African Church had found in penance a way of allowing sinners to remain in the Church. At that time, individuals who had committed serious sins were required to make a public confession, after which they were for a time denied the eucharist and required to accept a penance. This typically involved the wearing of coarse clothing, fasting, intensive prayer, and abstinence from sex and certain kinds of food and drink. The satisfactory completion of penance brought reconciliation with the Church, signified by an act of absolution in which the bishop placed his hands on the penitent and declared the forgiveness of his sin. Procedures varied somewhat from region to region, but penance was always public and never administered more than once. For this reason it was common to delay it. The sixth-century archbishop Caesarius of Arles complained that he often heard people say, "When I reach old age or am hopelessly ill with some great infirmity, then I will do penance."[71]

The impractical custom of limiting Christians to a single penance was soon remedied by the adoption of the Celtic-Irish monastic custom of making frequent private confessions followed by repeated penances. This made it possible for sinners to confess their sins in confidence to a priest, perform the required penance, and negate the effects of later sins by a repetition of this process. In the words of Boniface, the "medicine" of penance was a "second form of cleansing after the sacrament of baptism, so that the evils we do after the washing of baptism may be healed."[72]

The penances assigned for particular sins were sometimes prescribed in special manuals for priests called "penitentials." They were often harsh even for lesser sins. The sixth-century *Penitential of Finnian* from Ireland, for example, required a person who had thought about illicit sex but not actually engaged in it to abstain from wine and meat for a year. Similarly, in 923 Frankish bishops ordered a group of soldiers who had misbehaved to limit their consumption of food and drink to bread, salt, and water for three periods of forty days.[73] In time a system of substitution made it possible to avoid such hardships by making a payment of money (technically, by giving **alms**) to the Church. This practice was described in the eleventh century by the theologian Peter Damian:

> When priests impose a penance of many years on certain sinners, they sometimes indicate the sum of money necessary for remission of the annual stint, so that those who dread long fasts may redeem their misdeeds by alms. This money payment is not found in the ancient canons of the Fathers, but is not therefore to be judged absurd or frivolous.[74]

However penance was accomplished, its successful completion was extremely important. In the early Middle Ages it was widely believed that to die without having paid the debt for sins committed after baptism meant exclusion from heaven. This danger was eased by the gradual development of the doctrine of purgatory, the state between earthly life and heaven in which it was possible to suffer whatever punishment was still required for sins for which penance had not been made. Still, purgatory was a place of great pain, and although it was clearly preferable to hell, penance performed while one was still alive seemed a more appealing way to atone for sin.

Early medieval thought about penance represented a softening of former attitudes, not only by allowing repeated penances, but in acknowledging them as human contributions to the struggle against sin. The belief that salvation depends entirely on God's grace remained unchallenged, but

penance made a place for human effort in atoning for sins committed after baptism. Similarly, the doctrine of purgatory made the human condition seem less difficult by providing for the completion of atonement for sin after death. The same tendency toward making the path to God a bit easier is also evident in early medieval eucharistic theology, which proclaimed that Christ is truly present and available to Christians in the eucharist and even attempted to explain how divinity can take the forms of bread and wine.

THE SAINTS AND THE VIRGIN MARY

As we saw in chapter 3, the first Christian saints were martyrs who died under Roman persecution. When persecution ended, the custom of venerating martyrs was expanded to include a wider variety of spiritual heroes. By the early Middle Ages any person whose holiness was widely recognized might gain recognition after death as a saint. Although saints had already entered into heavenly glory, it was believed that they remained in communion with the Church on earth and could be invoked by those seeking their intercession. Moreover, the Church could draw on the merits of their good works to reduce the punishments imposed upon penitents.

Saints were first and foremost models of virtue, but they were also venerated for the spiritual power associated with their holiness. The *Dialogues* of Gregory the Great are filled with stories of holy men who could make themselves invisible, move boulders through prayer alone, and raise the dead. Even the relics saints left behind were said to heal the sick, make the blind see, and work endless other wonders. The official teaching of the Church was that the saints and their relics had no power other than that of God, who worked *through* them. But this distinction was rarely noted by most people, who saw saints as heavenly patrons able to work miracles on their own. A typical example is St. Swithun, who had been bishop of Winchester in England in the ninth century. A century after his death, he commanded that his bones be moved from his grave to a place of honor within the cathedral. According to a contemporary account:

Then the bishop Aethelwold with abbots and monks raised the saint with chanting. And they bore him into the church, St. Peter's house, where he stands in honoured memory, and worketh wonders. There were healed, by the holy man, four sick men within three days. And during five months few days were there, that there were not healed at least three sick persons. . . . Within ten days two hundred men were healed, and so many within twelve months that no man could count them. The burial ground lay filled with crippled folk, so that one could not easily visit the minster.[75]

Given the widespread belief in their extraordinary virtue and the miracle-working power of their relics, it is not difficult to understand the popularity of the cult of saints. But who determined who was a saint? At first this decision was local and public; an individual's saintliness was established by popular acclamation in the region where he or she had lived and died. We have already seen this, for example, in the case of Pope Gregory the Great. But this process was unregulated and subject to abuse. Gradually, it was brought under the control of the papacy. In 1170, Pope Alexander III declared that no one should be venerated as a saint without the approval of the Roman Church.[76] Since then canonization has occurred only after an exhaustive investigation of the candidate conducted under the supervision of Rome.

By the eleventh century the Virgin Mary had been elevated to a position that brought her greater honor and devotion than any other saint. Her unique status as the Mother of God, affirmed at the Council of Ephesus (431), had always made her much beloved in the East. In the West, however, her popularity had grown very slowly, though the importance of her special virtues had not gone unnoticed. For example, Augustine's theory that the effects of original sin are transmitted through sexual intercourse made her virginity crucial to the sinlessness of Christ and, consequently, to the salvation of humanity. Though not divine herself, Mary increasingly came to represent Christ in his gentler and more loving aspect at a time when greater emphasis was given to his roles as ruler and judge of the universe. For those who stood in fear before God's majesty, Mary's loving and maternal intercessions made him seem more approachable and the burden of human sin easier to bear.

As Mary's importance grew, so did theological speculation about her unique character and qualities. The doctrine of her perpetual virginity, which can be traced back to Ambrose, Augustine, and Jerome, was approved by a Lateran synod in 649.[77] The beliefs that she had been conceived without being tainted by original sin and that she had been taken up bodily into heaven at the time of her death were also widespread in the early Middle Ages, although they did not officially become the doctrines of the **Immaculate Conception** and Assumption until 1854 and 1950 respectively.

Just as early medieval theology emphasized the availability of grace in the sacraments, the Church's teachings about Mary and the saints also underscored the fact that sinners were not left to struggle alone against sin and human imperfection. They had powerful examples of the way to holiness in the lives of those who had already trod that path and intermediaries in heaven prepared to intercede with God on their behalf, not only for the sake of their salvation but for the mitigation of life's trials and tragedies as well.

THE FILIOQUE

A final theological debate concerned the relationship between the Holy Spirit and the other persons of the Trinity and generated a controversy that aggravated political and theological tensions between the East and West. In the East, theologians had never departed from the language of the Nicene Creed,[78] according to which the Spirit "proceeded" from the Father just as the Son was "begotten" of the Father. Beginning with Augustine, however, the West had increasingly thought of the Spirit as divine love that unifies the Father and Son and, because it is mutual, necessarily proceeds from the Father *and* from the Son. By the beginning of the Middle Ages, western Christians were beginning to add the phrase **filioque** ("and from the Son") whenever they recited the Creed,[79] thereby describing the Spirit as the third person of the Trinity "who proceeds from the Father and from the Son." The custom spread throughout the West without official sanction until it was finally endorsed by the papacy in the eleventh century.

By then, however, the *filioque* had long been an outrage to eastern Christians. Though willing to allow that the Spirit might proceed from the Father "through the Son," they believed that "double procession" threatened the unity of God by making it dependent upon two bases, Father and Son, rather than on the Father alone. They also rejected as heretical the implication that the Spirit was subordinate to the Son. Finally, Orthodox Christians considered the addition of the *filioque* to the Creed a unilateral and unjustifiable innovation on the part of the West. Only an ecumenical council, the East argued, could change what had been done at Nicaea. When Byzantine monks in Jerusalem confronted western monks in the city with these accusations, a synod of Frankish bishops at Aachen (809) responded with a declaration, supported by Charlemagne, that it was the Greeks who were heretics. A half-century later, Patriarch Photius (858–67; 878–86) vigorously denounced the *filioque* in the midst of an ugly struggle with Pope Nicholas I (858–67). Subsequent papal efforts to avoid further antagonizing the East included use of the Apostles' Creed (which did not include the *filioque*) but did not bring a resolution of the problem itself. As we will see in chapter 7, in 1054 the lingering issue of the *filioque* contributed to a schism between the churches of the East and West that still separates them today.

Summary

By the close of the tenth century, Christianity was firmly established as a central feature of civilization in both the East and the West. In the East, the centrality of the Church in public as well as religious life was made certain by a system of government based on the cooperation and shared ideals of spiritual and civil authorities. In the West, local bishops and abbots participated in the creation of a new feudal society and in the rise of the Frankish kingdom. The coronation of Charlemagne in 800 as the Christian emperor of a revived empire in the West was a triumph for the western Church as well as the Frankish state. In both East and West, the monastic movement sponsored missions, promoting literacy and learning, and encouraged the growth of theology.

At the same time, however, disruptive forces threatened some of the gains that had been made. The Byzantine East was divided by controversy over the use of icons and endangered by the expansion of Islam. The West was destablilized by the decline of the Carolingian Empire after Charlemagne and the invasions of Vikings, Magyars, and Muslim Saracens. Despite its claims to authority, the papacy was not yet in a position to effectively rule the Church in the West.

And yet there were good reasons for optimism as the Church completed its first millennium. In the East, the seven ecumenical councils had completed the process of defining doctrine, the controversy over iconoclasm had been resolved, and a distinctively Byzantine mystical theology was flourishing in the monasteries. In the West, uniform patterns of Christian belief and worship had become widely accepted and, as we will see in chapter 6, a monastic reform movement was taking shape whose values and ideals would soon have an immense impact on the Church and society in general.

QUESTIONS FOR REVIEW AND REFLECTION

1. In what ways did Islam and Islamic civilization represent a challenge to Christianity and the Christian world in the early Middle Ages?

2. In what ways did the Franks contribute to the creation of a Christian culture in Europe in the early Middle Ages?

3. How did the relationship of church and state in the Byzantine East differ from the situation in the West?

4. What were the essential features of Byzantine Christianity in the early Middle Ages?

NOTES

1. J. A. McNamara, *Sisters in Arms: Catholic Nuns through Two Millennia* (Cambridge, Mass.: Harvard University Press, 1996), 125, 139.

2. These endured in one form or another until 1870, after which only the state of Vatican City remained.

3. The story of this cure had long been the stuff of popular legend. In the sixth century Gregory of Tours alluded to it in his *History of the Franks* (2.31).

4. *Donation of Constantine,* in *Documents of the Christian Church,* 2nd ed., ed. Henry Bettenson (New York: Oxford University Press, 1967), 101.

5. Suspicions about the authenticity of the *Donation of Constantine* arose soon after it appeared. By ca. 850 it had already been included in the *False Decretals,* also known as the *Decretals of Isidore,* collected and published under uncertain circumstances in France. It was not until the fifteenth century, however, that Lorenzo Valla proved conclusively that the *Donation of Constantine* was a forgery.

6. They were led by ambitious relatives of Leo's predecessor, Hadrian I.

7. *Liber Pontificalis,* ed. L. Duchesne, II (1892), 7, in *Sources for the History of Medieval Europe,* trans. Brian Pullan (Oxford: Basil Blackwell, 1971), 13.

8. Most historians believe that Charlemagne did not approve of the form of the coronation ceremony, though he welcomed its result. It is noteworthy that he, and not the pope, crowned his son Louis the Pious in the ceremony that made Louis co-emperor in 813.

9. *Admonitio generalis* (cap. 72), in Bettenson, *Documents of the Christian Church,* 99–98.

10. This is discussed extensively, for example, in Heinrich Fichtenau, *The Carolingian Empire* (Toronto: University of Toronto Press, 1978).

11. This tradition dates back to the seventh century but is now given little credence. Paul is generally thought to have died as a martyr in Rome without having traveled farther west. Acts 12:2, which describes the martyrdom of St. James under Herod Agrippa I, argues against his presence in Spain.

12. Prudentius, a fourth-century Christian poet and hymnographer from Spain, describes the deaths of many of these in Latin verse in his *Peristephanon* ("On the Crowns of Martyrs").

13. H. Daniel-Rops, *The Church in the Dark Ages* (New York: Dutton, 1959), 210.

14. Gregory the Great, *Letter* 76, trans. J. Barmby, in *Nicene and Post-Nicene Fathers,* vol. 13, 2nd series, ed. Philip Schaff and Henry Wace (Peabody, Mass.: Hendrickson, 1994), 85.

15. In Nicolas Zernov, *Eastern Christendom* (London: Weidenfeld & Nicolson, 1961), 66.

16. Paulus Silentiarius, *Description of St. Sophia* 617.

17. Procopius, *Buildings* 1.1., trans. H. B. Dewing, Loeb Classical Library (Cambridge, Mass.: Harvard University Press, 1961), 27.

18. Isauria was a region of Asia Minor located in the Taurus mountains between Pisidia, Lycaonia, and Cilicia.

19. Timothy (Kallistos) Ware, *The Orthodox Church* (Baltimore: Penguin, 1964), 48.

20. Eusebius, *Life of Constantine* 4.60, trans. E. Richardson, in Philip Schaff and Henry Wace, *Nicene and Post-Nicene Fathers,* 2nd series, vol. 1, 555. Translation revised.

21. Cited in Kallistos Ware, "Eastern Christendom," in *The Oxford History of Christianity,* ed. John McManners (New York: Oxford University Press, 1993), 133–34.

22. In ancient times the title *pope* was given to bishops generally. A number of bishops are still called pope, including the patriarch of Alexandria in the Eastern Orthodox Church.

23. See Ware, "Eastern Christendom," 135; Ware, *The Orthodox Church,* 49; and John Meyendorff, *The Byzantine Legacy in the Orthodox Church* (Crestwood, N.Y.: St. Vladimir's Seminary Press, 1982), 14.

24. For example, Constantius I (337–61), Leo III (717–41), Constantine V (741–75), and Michael VIII (1250–82). See Meyendorff, *Byzantine Legacy,* 14.

25. Canon 28 of the Council of Chalcedon, in Meyendorff, *Byzantine Legacy,* 17.

26. Meyendorff, *Byzantine Legacy,* 20–21.

27. The first to use the title was John the Faster (582–95).

28. See Meyendorff, *Byzantine Legacy,* 20.

29. Meyendorff, *Byzantine Legacy,* 20.

30. Meyendorff, *Byzantine Legacy,* 15.

31. See Zernov, *Eastern Christendom,* 92. These were the three languages that appeared on the placard Pilate ordered posted on the cross of Jesus.

32. It is known as Glagolitic. The Cyrillic alphabet still used in Russia, Bulgaria, and other Slavic countries is similar and has traditionally been attributed to Cyril, though his connection with it is uncertain.

33. The appeal of these Greek priests to Hadrian II (867–72) must have been a welcome, if unexpected, acknowledgment of his authority, because at that time the bishops of Rome and Constantinople were involved in an ongoing dispute over jurisdiction. In addition, by giving his blessing to the efforts of their Greek competitors, Hadrian was able to check the power of the German bishops.

34. Sura 29:46.

35. Cited in Ware, *The Orthodox Church,* 26.

36. Most Christian communions outside the Roman Catholic Church agree that the seventh and last ecumenical council was the Second Council of Nicaea (787). The Roman Catholic Church recognizes fourteen additional councils as ecumenical, the last being Vatican II (1962–65).

37. Constantinople was not mentioned because its inauguration as a imperial capital was still five years away. Despite the fact that Jerusalem was said to hold a place of honor just behind Rome, Alexandria, and

Antioch, it remained subject to the metropolitan of Caesarea.

38. The works of two other extreme Antiochene theologians, Theodoret of Cyrrhus (ca. 393–460) and Ibas, bishop of Edessa (435–49 and 451–57), were also condemned.

39. John of Damascus, *The Orthodox Faith* 3.6 (quoting Gregory's *Letter* 101).

40. Cited in Ware, *The Orthodox Church*, 40.

41. John of Damascus, *On the Divine Images* 16.1, trans. David Anderson (Crestwood, N.Y.: St. Vladimir's Seminary Press, 1980), 23.

42. This is not to suggest that the controversy was without effect in the West. Cities in parts of Italy controlled by the Byzantine emperor rebelled, and Pope Gregory II (715–31) condemned Leo III for overreaching his authority.

43. Definition of the Second Council of Nicaea, in Bettenson, *Documents of the Christian Church*, 93–94.

44. Athanasius, *On the Incarnation of the Word* 54.

45. The other two texts by Pseudo-Dionysius are *The Celestial Hierarchy*, according to which knowledge of God is mediated to humanity by three orders of angelic beings, and *The Ecclesiastical Hierarchy*, which focuses on the ways divine truths are made evident in the world of sense and matter.

46. Pseudo-Dionysius, *The Mystical Theology* 1, in *An Anthology of Christian Mysticism*, ed. Harvey Egan (Collegeville, Minn.: Liturgical Press, 1991), 96–97.

47. Maximus the Confessor, *Book of Ambiguities* 41, quoted in Vladimir Lossky, *The Mystical Theology of the Eastern Church* (London: James Clarke, 1957), 214.

48. Quoted in Lossky, *Mystical Theology*, 199. The saying comes from the *Spiritual Homilies*, traditionally ascribed to Macarius but considered by modern scholars to be the work of an anonymous writer of the late fourth or early fifth centuries.

49. John of Damascus, *The Orthodox Faith* 2.30, trans. F. Chase, in *The Fathers of the Church*, ed. B. Peebles et al., vol. 37 (Washington, D.C.: Catholic University of America Press, 1958), 264.

50. Simeon earned this title in recognition of his teachings on Hesychasm. It gave him a place of honor just behind that of the theologian par excellence, Gregory the Theologian (i.e., Gregory of Nazianzus).

51. Simeon the New Theologian, *Discourses* 22, in *Symeon the New Theologian: The Discourses*, trans. C. J. de Catanzaro (New York: Paulist Press, 1980), 245–46.

52. Gregory Palamas, *Triads* 2.2.14, in *Gregory Palamas: The Triads*, trans. N. Gendle (New York: Paulist Press, 1983), 53.

53. Gregory of Palamas, *Triads* 2.3.8, in Gendle, *Gregory Palamas*, 57.

54. The pronouncements of these councils were never accepted in the West.

55. Gregory of Palamas, *Triads* 3.1.16, in Gendle, *Gregory Palamas*, 76.

56. For example, the eastern bishops who appealed to Julius I (337–52) for approval of the depositions of Athanasius and Marcellus of Ancyra.

57. Thomas Bokenkotter, *A Concise History of the Catholic Church* (New York: Doubleday, 1990), 78.

58. As expressed, for example, in his *Tome*, which was approved by the Council of Chalcedon as a standard of orthodox Christology.

59. Kenneth Latourette, *A History of Christianity*, rev. ed., vol. 1 (San Francisco: Harper, 1975), 187.

60. Latourette, *A History of Christianity*, 187.

61. At this time the patriarchs of Constantinople, beginning with John the Faster (582–95), began using the title *ecumenical patriarch*, which was taken in the West as threat to papal primacy.

62. Latourette, *A History of Christianity*, 338.

63. Good works were made possible by God's prevenient grace and the cooperation of the human will with grace. Original sin and sins committed prior to baptism were covered by that sacrament.

64. Gregory the Great, *Dialogues* 4.41.

65. Gregory the Great, *Dialogues* 4.57.

66. The title *Doctor of the Church* was given in the Middle Ages to those theologians whose personal virtue and achievements set them apart from all others. The number of those so honored eventually grew to more than thirty.

67. *Eriugena*, which means "Irish-born," is sometimes (though less correctly) spelled Erigena. *Scotus* derives from the Scotti, a Celtic tribe from Ireland that invaded England and Scotland in the sixth century and eventually gave its name to the latter. As early as the third century, Latin speakers referred to the Irish as *Scotti* rather than *Hiberni* or *Iverni* and to Ireland as Scotia rather than Hibernia. See *Encyclopedia of the Early Church*, vol. 2, ed. A. Di Berardino (New York: Oxford University Press, 1992), s.v. "Ireland.".

68. J. N. D. Kelly, *Early Christian Doctrines*, rev. ed. (San Francisco: Harper, 1978), 423–24.

69. The New Testament contains four accounts of the institution of the eucharist, one by Paul (1 Corinthians 11:23–25) and three in the Synoptic Gospels (Matthew 26:26–28; Mark 14:22–24; Luke 22:17–20).

70. Ratramnus, *On the Body and Blood of Christ* 2.16, quoted in *The Christian Theology Reader*, ed. A. E. McGrath (Cambridge, Mass.: Blackwell, 1995), 297.

71. Caesarius of Arles, *Sermon* 64.3, trans. M. Mueller, in *The Fathers of the Church*, ed. R. J. Deferrari et al., vol. 31 (New York: Fathers of the Church, 1956), 309.

72. Boniface, *Sermon* 8.1, in J. Pelikan, *The Growth of Medieval Theology* (Chicago: University of Chicago Press, 1978), 32.

73. R. W. Southern, *Western Society and the Church in the Middle Ages* (New York: Penguin, 1978), 226.

74. Cited in Southern, *Western Society*, 227.

75. R. Brooke and C. Brooke, *Popular Religion in the Middle Ages* (London: Thames & Hudson, 1984), 37.

76. The first documented instance of canonization by papal authority occurred in 993, when Pope John XV declared Ulrich of Augsburg a saint.

77. However, the synod failed to explain how Mary's perpetual virginity was possible in gynecological terms. This resulted in a debate on the manner of Christ's birth. Did he pass through Mary's body in the normal manner or in some miraculous way? The latter view was upheld by the ninth-century theologian Paschasius Radbertus in his *On the Parturition of St. Mary*.

78. This term was first proposed by Gregory of Nazianzus, *Oration on the Holy Lights*, 12.

79. That is, the Creed formulated by the Council of Constantinople in 381. Based on the earlier Nicene Creed, which contained only one reference to the Holy Spirit ("And [we believe] in the Holy Spirit"), the Constantinopolitan Creed was more descriptive: "And [we believe] in the Holy Spirit, the Lord and life-giver, who proceeds from the Father, who is worshiped and glorified together with the Father and the Son, who spoke through the prophets."

CHAPTER 6

The Church and Christian Culture in the High Middle Ages

Overview

By the beginning of the eleventh century, great changes were beginning to take place in both eastern and western Christendom. In this chapter we will focus on developments in the West, though to explain them we will make frequent reference to events in the East. There the Byzantine Church had by the year 1000 extended its influence northward throughout much of eastern Europe and deep into Russia. Despite the Church's successes to the north, however, to the east and south the Byzantine Empire was gradually losing its territory to Islamic peoples. To protect Christian pilgrims and shrines in the Holy Land and, ostensibly, to help defend Byzantium against Muslim armies, the West launched a series of Crusades lasting nearly two centuries.

The social, political, and economic decline that had become prevalent in the West in the ninth century was reversed by new forces that combined to inaugurate an era of greater stability, prosperity, and creativity known as the high Middle Ages (roughly 1000–1300). For the Church, this was a time of consolidation and reform that reinvigorated the monastic movement and brought the papacy to the zenith of its power and prestige. Great cathedrals —

symbols of popular devotion to the Church and visible expressions of its teachings — rose above the skylines of growing cities. Here the first western universities appeared, where the most distinguished faculty were theologians and the premier intellectual enterprise was scholasticism, which sought to demonstrate the essential harmony of faith and reason. This was an era when churches and monasteries filled the towns and countryside, when popes struggled with emperors for temporal power in the West, and when Christian values and ideals inspired and informed art, architecture, literature, intellectual life, and popular sentiment. It was a time when no institution was more central to western civilization than the Church.

The West in the High Middle Ages

The factors that contributed to the revival of the West included advances in agriculture, population growth, urbanization, greater availability of labor and material resources, and an increased demand for consumer goods. These reshaped medieval society and profoundly influenced the Church as well.

For example, theological activity moved from isolated monasteries to universities that arose in growing cities. Similarly, the crusaders' persistent efforts to establish a foothold for the West in the Holy Land can be explained in part by the lure of new markets and profits in the East. Given the impact of social, economic, and political changes on the Church in the high Middle Ages, it makes sense to give them our attention here, if only briefly.

ECONOMIC, SOCIAL, AND POLITICAL CHANGE

One of the most dramatic developments in the high Middle Ages was a population explosion that doubled the number of Europeans (from about thirty-five million to about seventy million) between 900 and 1350. This dramatically increased the demand for food and consumer goods. Fortunately, this was also a time of agricultural innovation in which new farming techniques and technologies combined to produce surpluses — raising the overall standard of living and leaving a greater portion of the population free to pursue occupations other than agriculture. Growing numbers of rural serfs and peasants moved to towns, initiating a process of urbanization that has continued until our own time.

Population growth and urbanization encouraged trade and manufacturing. In the tenth century, most economic activity had been limited to the production of the food, clothing, and supplies needed on self-sufficient manors. New products were rare, and there was little demand for them. The small amount of trade usually involved barter rather than an exchange of money. But such economic stagnation became a thing of the past in the eleventh century as the labor, materials, and markets necessary for healthy commerce became more readily available. Manufacturers and merchants took their goods to great fairs and then to more permanent markets in cities and towns.

At first trade involved mostly the exchange of foodstuffs and simple manufactured goods between the manors and urban areas, but soon aggressive merchants began to participate in the lucrative trade centered in the Byzantine and Islamic East. They sold cargoes of western timber, metals, and cloth in Constantinople, Acre, Antioch, and Alexandria. Their ships returned loaded with new products, including luxuries (spices, glassware, ceramics, and silks) which they sold in western commercial cities like Venice, Pisa, and Genoa. Acting as financial and distribution centers, these and other Italian cities grew rich. Trade also brought wealth to the north, transforming cities like Bruges, Antwerp, Paris, Lyons, London, Lübeck, Bremen, and Augsburg.

Economic change brought social change. During the twelfth and thirteenth centuries, serfs frequently bought their freedom from the lands to which they had formerly been bound. Many made their way to the cities and towns, where a new middle class of merchants and artisans known as the *bourgeoisie* established itself and demanded recognition and rights. The feudal nobility remained the dominant class, though the rising economic and political power of the townspeople increasingly threatened their position. In addition to being holders of fiefs, nobles retained their identity as mounted warriors, though a new code of conduct known as chivalry (from *chevalier*, "knight") now refined their morals and manners. Originating in southern France and then spreading throughout western Europe, chivalry emphasized the importance of virtues such as bravery, courtesy, honor, and gallantry. These were held to be fundamental to the character of a good knight, whose professional obligations included the defense of the Church and all those less powerful than himself, especially women.

The most important political trend in the high Middle Ages was the creation of larger states with centralized royal governments capable of controlling their populations, managing the nobility, and supporting themselves through the collection of taxes. The smaller feudal principalities that had dominated western Europe in the tenth century began to diminish in size, number, and influence as increasingly powerful kings reclaimed many of the lands, rights, and privileges they had once extended to lesser nobles in exchange for military support.

The larger states that were beginning to emerge by 1300 were feudal monarchies that continued to rely on feudal practices. In this sense they were very different from modern states. But they possessed a level of political organization and authority that western Europe had not seen since the twilight years of Roman civilization nearly a millennium before. In some, such as England and France, we can easily detect the origins of their modern counterparts. In others, the process of state-building was longer and more complicated, so that it is difficult to discern in 1300 anything that resembles present reality. One such case was Germany, where individual states combined to form a restored western empire, later known as the Holy Roman Empire, which presented one of the greatest challenges faced by the medieval Church.

THE HOLY ROMAN EMPIRE

When, in 800, he set the imperial crown on the head of Charlemagne and proclaimed him emperor of the Romans, Pope Leo III lent inestimable prestige and considerable power to the Frankish monarchy. But the division of Frankish lands among Charlemagne's successors soon left the empire in fragments and no Carolingian ruler in a position to claim the title of emperor. In Germany, the powerful dukes of Saxony, Lorraine, Swabia, Franconia, and Bavaria joined forces in 911 to bring Carolingian rule to an end with the election of one of their own, Duke Conrad of Franconia, as king. He was succeeded by Henry I, duke of Saxony. It was Henry's son and successor, Otto I (936–73), who laid the groundwork for the restoration of Charlemagne's western empire, whose center would now be in Germany. After winning acceptance of his overlordship from his nobles, Otto further enhanced his position by invading Italy and proclaiming himself its king. A still more dramatic moment came in his stunning victory over the invading Magyars at the Battle of Lechfeld in 955. These achievements gave him real control of Germany, though its shape was rather different from than that of the modern German state.

A critical feature of Otto's state-building strategy was his extensive use of local bishops and abbots, who seemed to him more reliable partners than the German nobles because of their education and childlessness. The latter was an especially important consideration in feudal society because one of the greatest threats to monarchy was posed by noble families who gained hereditary control of fiefs, which they often considered their private and independent domains. Bishops, who had no legitimate heirs, could not pass property on to a new generation. Thus, a king could intervene upon the death of a bishop and appoint whatever individual he preferred for the job. It was largely for this reason that Otto created ecclesiastical fiefs throughout Germany. To be certain of the loyalty and ability of the men who received them, he assumed the authority to appoint them himself. In this practice, called "lay investiture," the king, and not the Church, conferred upon new bishops the ring and staff that were the symbols of their office. Despite this secular appropriation of its prerogatives, the Church waited another century to challenge lay investiture.

Having established himself as king, Otto set his sights on an even greater prize — the imperial office. His opportunity to claim it came in 961, when Pope John XII's appeal for rescue from political difficulties and personal danger gave Otto an excuse to seize Rome. The price Otto demanded for coming to the pope's aid was his coronation as emperor of the Romans. The ceremony took place on 2 February 962 in deliberate emulation of the coronation of Charlemagne. The western empire of the Romans — the Holy Roman Empire, as it would later be called[1] — had been revived.

Otto's intention to create an empire that would rival Charlemagne's was now unmistakable. His next step was to recognize the existence of the Papal States and make himself their official protector. Realizing too late that the Church he was supposed to rule was now firmly in the grip of the German emperor, John XII made a weak attempt to resist him. But Otto's response was swift and sure. He quickly called for an ecclesiastical synod to depose John on a charge of treason and replaced him with a new pope of his own choosing. To further cement his position, Otto proclaimed that henceforth no pope would be allowed to assume office without first taking an oath of loyalty to the emperor. Thus, Otto returned to Germany not only as emperor but as master of the Church.

It is important to note that secular control of the Church was not limited to its treatment at the hands of Otto and his imperial successors. The same practices they used so effectively were routinely employed elsewhere, making secular involvement in ecclesiastical affairs common throughout the whole of Europe in the tenth and eleventh centuries. This system would soon be challenged, however, by new forces of reform and revitalization that were about to be set loose in a French monastery at Cluny, hidden in the hills of Burgundy.

Reform and Revival in the Church

Ever since the fourth century, when monks began to replace martyrs as Christianity's spiritual heroes, much of the popular support enjoyed by the Church had been inspired by their example. To those who labored in fields and shops, cared for families, and attended to all the other responsibilities of ordinary life, the monks and nuns who devoted themselves to prayer and the pursuit of holiness in nearby monasteries and convents offered a reminder of the higher aims of human existence and a standard against which the judge their own lives. While **parish** priests lived a more secular existence in the "world," often owning property and enjoying the comforts of marriage or concubinage,[2] monastics followed the ancient tradition of withdrawing from worldly comforts and relationships. There were, of course, abundant instances of misbehavior and immorality in monasteries. On the whole, however, the men and women who lived in them were widely and reasonably regarded as the spiritual elite of the Church.

The phenomenal growth in new monastic communities in the tenth and eleventh centuries testifies to their great popular appeal. Yet by this time many monasteries, like the episcopate, had fallen under the influence of secular lords who chose their abbots, used their lands, and appropriated their revenues. The need for change was obvious. To be effective, it would have to go beyond merely minimizing secular interference in monastic life. Many believed it would have to be eliminated altogether.

MONASTIC REFORM

This was exactly what Duke William the Pious of Aquitaine had in mind when in 909–10 he made a gift of land to a group of twelve monks at Cluny in central France. According to the charter he drafted for the new monastery, it was to be self-governing, with the monks themselves choosing their abbots, and in all other respects completely independent of both secular lords and bishops, whom it warned to stay away in the name of God "and all his saints, and by the awful day of judgment."[3]

By the time of Odo (927–42), Cluny's first great abbot, a Cluniac tradition of strict morality in accordance with the Benedictine principles of stability, commitment to spiritual perfection, and obedience to superiors had been well established. The daily lives of the monks were carefully regulated and spent almost entirely in the company of other members of the community. Like other western monks, they gathered eight times each day to pray and read scripture in observance of the canonical hours. Another portion of the day was set aside for manual labor, and there was limited time as well for private meditation and reading of the Bible and other religious literature.

Aside from its independence, what made Cluny different from many other monasteries was that within its walls the Benedictine Rule was rigorously observed. In addition, much more time was devoted to communal prayer and worship. Word that here was a monastic community truly dedicated to purity and prayer brought a rush of enthusiasm for Cluny and its ideals. Recognized for their wisdom and vision, Cluny's abbots were sought out by kings and popes. As a result, they gained immense influence far beyond the walls of their own cloister. Odo, for example, was invited to reform countless monasteries, including all those in Rome and even Monte Cassino, which Benedict himself had founded in the sixth century. Other Cluniac monks joined in this work, bringing existing communities into the movement and founding new ones as well. By 1100, Cluny had more than a thousand "daughter" houses championing the cause of reform throughout France, England, Germany, Poland, Italy, and Hungary. These were not ruled by their own abbots, as was customary elsewhere, but by "priors" appointed by the abbot of Cluny, to whom all Cluniac monks professed obedience. Thus, the Benedictine ideal of the independent monastery was abandoned in recognition of the fact that local autonomy meant vulnerability to local authorities. In its place there appeared a monastic movement whose many member houses were united by their common rule and commitment to Cluny itself.[4]

Its efficient organization and popularity made the Cluniac movement a powerful force for change whose influence was felt outside as well as within its monasteries. Its commitment to the cultivation of personal sanctity encouraged genuine piety among both clergy and laity, and its ideal of ecclesiastical independence from secular influences contributed to reforms affecting clergy from ordinary parish priests to the popes themselves in the eleventh and twelfth centuries.

But Cluny was not the only center of monastic renewal. The Benedictine monastery of Gorze near Metz, founded in 933, had an impact similar to Cluny's, especially in Lorraine and Germany. More open to secular involvement than Cluniac monasteries, Gorzian communities were equally rigorous in their commitment to disciplined spiritual life. They also had great influence on life outside their walls, thanks to the promotion of bishops in feudal society by Otto I and his successors, for many bishops called upon the abbots of Gorze to assist them in reforming monasteries, offering education, and working in other ways to improve moral and spiritual life in their dioceses. Many of the missionaries sent to convert the Slavs and Magyars were Gorzian monks. All in all, Gorze had a great impact on German piety, though by the end of the eleventh century its influence was beginning to wane.

The eleventh century brought charges that Cluny itself was in need of reform. Although it had managed to protect its freedom from outside interference, critics complained that the movement had lost much of its former spirit and discipline. Clu-

niac monasteries had acquired large tracts of land on which they built extravagant churches. Monks now spent little or no time performing manual labor, as the Benedictine Rule required.

Hoping to revive the monastic ideal, Robert of Molesmes, the former prior of the abbey at Moutier-la-Celle, established a new monastery at Cîteaux in Burgundy in 1098. In doing so he also laid the foundations for a new monastic order, that of the Cistercians, or "White Monks," dedicated to a more ascetic and primitive interpretation of the Benedictine Rule. This return to basics inspired notable Cistercians like Stephen Harding (d. 1134), the English saint and mystic who was Cîteaux's third abbot, and **Bernard of Clairvaux** (1090–1153), who founded a daughter abbey at Clairvaux. Bernard was a famous mystic and theologian as well as a vigorous critic of Cluny. The Cistercian movement spread throughout France and then to most other parts of Europe, so that by 1300 there were more than seven hundred Cistercian communities, including convents of Cistercian nuns. The rigors and rewards of Cistercian life were described by Ailred of Rievaulx, a twelfth-century monk who wrote:

> Our food is scanty, our garments rough; our drink is from the stream and our sleep often upon our book. Under our tired limbs there is but a hard mat; when sleep is sweetest we must rise at a bell's bidding. . . . Self-will has no scope; there is no moment for idleness or dissipation. . . . Everywhere peace, everywhere serenity, and a marvelous freedom from the tumult of the world. Such unity and concord is there among the brethren, that each thing seems to belong to all, and all to each. . . . To put all in brief, no perfection expressed in the words of the gospel or of the Apostles, or in the writings of the Fathers, or in the sayings of the monks of old, is lacking to our order and our way of life.[5]

Though not as centralized as the Cluniac movement, the Cistercian order was able to safeguard its independence by placing every monastery directly under the authority of the one that founded it. In doing so, it created lines of filiation that reached back through generations of houses and converged at Cîteaux itself, the site of annual meetings, or "chapters," at which Cistercian abbots set policy under the supervision of the abbot of Cîteaux.

Other monastic orders proliferated, some of them even more ascetic than the Cistercians. A good example is the Carthusian order, which began in 1084 at La Grande Chartreuse in the French Alps. Falling somewhere between the moderation of the Benedictine Rule and the extremes of the ancient desert monks, the Carthusians preferred rugged and isolated sites for their communities, took vows of silence, lived in private cells, endured long fasts, and otherwise subsisted on an extremely spare diet that reflected their commitment to poverty. Other groups included the Gilbertines, a double order of monks and nuns founded in England and based on the Augustinian rule, and the Camaldolese, who began as an Italian order dedicated to silent prayer and extreme poverty. Despite such diversity, the monasticism of the eleventh and twelfth centuries was characterized by two fundamental impulses — a commitment to independence from secular control and a desire to return to the monastic ideals established in antiquity.

PAPAL REFORM UNDER LEO IX AND NICHOLAS II

The influence of the monastic reform movement began to make itself felt in Rome in the middle of the eleventh century. Ironically, it was brought there by one of the strongest of the German emperors, Henry III (1039–56), whose piety did not keep him from dominating the Church, though he clearly wished to see it free of corruption. Thus, when he found himself faced with an ugly quarrel between three unworthy claimants to the papal throne, Henry dismissed all of them. After first appointing the short-lived Clement II and Damasus II, he made a fateful choice in a German bishop who became Leo IX (1049–54).

Leo arrived in Rome accompanied by two brilliant associates: Hildebrand (ca. 1015–1085), a monk who was also a superb administrator and politician, and Humbert (d. 1061), a bishop and scholar who would soon publish his *Against the Simoniacs,* a scathing denunciation of lay investiture and the controlling influence of secular rulers over the Church. A third figure, Peter Damian (1007–72), served Leo from a distance. An ascetic and theologian who was then prior of a Camaldolese monastery, he wrote angry denunciations of **simony** (the sale and purchase of ecclesiastical offices), clerical marriage, and servile clergy who, seeking material honors and rewards, sold themselves into "the service of rulers with disgusting subservience like captive slaves."[6] To these three Leo added scores of the most capable clergy he could find, appointing them to key positions and introducing them into the ranks of cardinals, a select group of deacons, priests, and bishops who served as high-level administrators and papal advisors. Then, having brought the whole machinery of papal government in line with his own thinking, Leo went to work.

In April 1049 he organized a synod at Rome that condemned simony, threatened simoniacs with severe penances or deposition, and forbade clergy to accept money from anyone in return for their services. Having made his intentions clear, Leo embarked on an extensive tour of France and Germany to see for himself the state of the Church outside of Italy. In October 1049 he convened a synod at Reims, where it was decreed that bishops and abbots would henceforth be chosen by the clergy and the people rather than by secular lords. Leo also conducted an inquiry into the lay use of church property, the sale of ecclesiastical offices, and the condition of monasteries. Bishops were made to account for their behavior; some offenders were forgiven, others were given severe penances, still others were excommunicated. From Reims, Leo traveled to Mainz, where another synod with Henry III in attendance took similar actions, including an explicit condemnation of clerical marriage.[7] By the time he returned to Rome in 1050, Leo had made it clear to the clergy of France and Germany that they owed their loyalty to him alone and given them good reason to respect his authority. When his short pontificate ended in 1054, it was obvious that Leo had made real progress in expanding the presence and influence of his office through most of Europe.

The death of Henry III two years later left the empire temporarily weakened, for it was now ruled by a regent on behalf of his six-year-old son, Henry

IV (1056–1106). Taking advantage of this opportunity, Stephen IX (1057–58) reigned without the imperial approval Otto I had required a century earlier. Much more significant were the reforms of Nicholas II (1059–61), who in 1059 condemned lay investiture and clerical marriage and issued a startling decree on papal elections.[8] Recognizing that his demand that bishops be elected by the clergy and people would be empty if this practice were not followed in Rome itself, he announced that the selection of popes would thereafter be left to the college of cardinals. The people would participate, though only through public acclamation of the individual the cardinals had chosen. In this way the unwelcome lobbying, bullying, and public disorder that noble families and political factions brought to the process would be eliminated.

Although the decree acknowledged that the emperor was somehow deserving of "honor and reverence"[9] in connection with the selection of a new pope, its language was vague and made no specific provision for his involvement. It was, in effect, a declaration of papal independence. To enforce it, Nicholas created an alliance with Robert Guiscard, a Norman ruler who was anxious for papal recognition of the kingdom he had carved out for himself in southern Italy. He received it, though only after accepting feudal status as a vassal of the pope. Thus, the Norman army that now prepared to defend the integrity of the papacy was not, strictly speaking, that of some foreign power, like the Frankish armies on which popes Zacharias, Stephen II, and Leo III had depended in the eighth century, but one under the pope's own authority as the feudal overlord of its commander.[10] This arrangement would allow Nicholas's reforms to survive his death in 1061. As he had hoped, the college of cardinals did indeed elect his successor, Alexander II (1061–73), but the real test did not come until twelve years later with the election of Hildebrand, his trusted advisor, as Pope Gregory VII in 1073.

THE REFORM IDEOLOGY OF GREGORY VII

There is no doubting the ferocity of Gregory VII's commitment to reform. The fiery Peter Damian, who referred to himself as Gregory's "thunderbolt,"[11] is said to have described Gregory with admiration and awe as a "holy Satan."[12] Indeed, it is difficult to think of anyone who was more aggressive in championing the cause of the Church or bolder in envisioning its place in the world. Gregory had three great objectives: to reform the clergy, to eliminate lay investiture, and to unify the West under the spiritual leadership of the papacy. Much of this program was derived from the writings of Humbert, but historians have shown that Gregory was also deeply influenced by the three hundred-year-old *Donation of Constantine,* according to which the whole of the West was to be subject to the pope.[13]

Apart from lay investiture itself, which by this time was widely considered a kind of simony, the greatest problem in reforming the clergy was clerical marriage. In the tenth and eleventh centuries it was not uncommon for priests to marry or to keep concubines. The latter was always scandalous, but the immorality of clerical marriage was not always taken for granted. In some regions, in fact, the marriage of priests was so common as to be expected, for economic security was nearly impossible without the help of a wife and children. In the East, of course, priests had always been encouraged to marry, but the western Church had taken the opposite position ever since the Council of Elvira in 306. Its rationale was that a priest's loyalty to his wife and children would necessarily compromise his commitment to the Church. Moreover, his desire to accumulate wealth for the sake of their security might lead him to bequeath his office or ecclesiastical property to his sons, thereby bringing them under hereditary control and alienating them from the Church. And so in 1074 Gregory renewed Nicholas II's ban on clerical marriage (1059).

Resistance was strong. Some priests threatened to leave the Church rather than their wives. Many bishops simply ignored the pope, allowing and even encouraging their clergy to marry.[14] Gregory responded with excommunications and commanded secular lords to bar recalcitrant priests from entering churches in their lands. In the end he failed to stop this old and widespread practice, but Urban II (1088–99), Paschal II (1099–1118), and Calixtus II (1119–24) reaffirmed his decrees, and in 1139 the Second Lateran Council made clerical marriage both illegal and invalid. Under such pressure it slowly disappeared.

To Gregory, the rationale for ending lay investiture seemed obvious and irrefutable. The Church was the body of Christ, ruled on earth by bishops whose authority came from God. It was a violation of the Church and the proper order of society, he argued, for persons without spiritual authority to appoint bishops and invest them with its symbols. Yet secular rulers also had a case to make. Didn't the lands controlled by bishops and abbots give them temporal power that fell under secular jurisdiction? Didn't secular lords then have the right to determine, in the interests of good government and social order, who should hold these important offices? And didn't bishops and abbots owe their overlords the same dues, services, and loyalty in temporal matters expected of other vassals? These were important questions, for in many regions a weakening or elimination of the ties that bound bishops and their lands to secular overlords would have severely disrupted social and political order.

The issue of lay investiture was also part of the much larger and more complex question: Who should rule the West, the emperor or the pope? The German emperors claimed that their authority was no less divine in origin than that of bishops and a necessary precondition for social order. They also argued that, as successors to the emperors of ancient Rome, they had the right and responsibility to rule Christendom, defending and sustaining it while offering the Church the paternal protection that allowed it to pursue its sole mission of saving souls.

For his part, Gregory followed in the tradition of Gelasius I, maintaining that the authority of emperors was indeed divine in origin but that this hardly implied their right to dominion over the Church. The emperor may be responsible for doing the will of God in the secular sphere, he said, but it is the Church that teaches him what God's will *is*. In this, as in all other respects, he insisted, the mission and authority of the Church and its ruler, the pope, are greater than those of any secular figure, including the emperor.[15] Gregory found the basis for these views in scripture. Thus, when Bishop

Hermann of Metz asked him for a summation of his thought concerning the relation of papal and imperial power, Gregory began by citing Matthew 16:18–19, where Jesus promises Peter that "whatever you bind on earth will be bound in heaven, and that whatever you loose on earth will be loosed in heaven." "Are kings excepted here?" he asked. "Are they not among the sheep which the son of God entrusted to St. Peter?"[16]

GREGORY VII, HENRY IV, AND THE INVESTITURE CONTROVERSY

The German monarchy was not Gregory's only target, for secular rulers everywhere dominated the Church to the extent that circumstances allowed, each of them inviting the pope's wrath. Soon after taking office, for example, Gregory complained to the bishop of Châlons that France's King Philip I was selling bishoprics and suggested the possibility of his excommunication. The following year he demanded that the French bishops confront Philip, but they were so cautious in approaching the king that little changed. Had the abuses of the French king been more egregious, subsequent events might have been played out in France. But the German empire was far more threatening, in part because its territory extended into northern Italy, the pope's "front yard." Thus, Germany would be the arena in which church and state would come to blows over lay investiture.

By the time Hildebrand became Pope Gregory VII in 1073, young Henry IV had reached his early twenties and was prepared, or so he must have thought, to take on the veteran reformer and strategist. The king was probably not surprised when, in February 1075, Gregory reaffirmed his predecessors' decrees against simony, clerical marriage, and lay investiture. Yet he must have been shaken a month later by the blunt assertions of papal prerogative in Gregory's famous *Dictatus Papae* ("The Dictates of the Pope"). Among its twenty-seven provisions were the following:

> the pope can be judged by no one;
> the Roman church has never erred and never will err till the end of time; . . .

the pope alone can depose and restore bishops;

he alone can make new laws, set up new bishoprics, and divide old ones;

he can depose emperors;

he can absolve subjects from their allegiance [to wicked lords];

all princes should kiss his feet.[17]

The confrontation that the *Dictatus Papae* seemed to demand broke out after Henry apparently ignored an earlier agreement with the pope concerning an appointment to the archbishopric of Milan and installed his own candidate.[18] In a letter of rebuke written in December 1075, Gregory warned that such actions in the future would bring dire consequences. Unfazed, Henry organized a council at Worms in January 1076 where the German bishops, fearing that Gregory wanted to subject them to Rome, joined the king in denouncing and deposing him. Henry clearly relished advising the pope of this action in a letter he addressed "to Hildebrand, now not Pope, but false monk."[19] In a second letter written to the German bishops, the emperor condemned Gregory for attempting to eliminate the divinely ordained duality of secular and spiritual authority by claiming for himself royal as well as priestly authority.[20]

Pulling no punches, Gregory excommunicated the bishops who had sided with Henry at Worms and then both excommunicated the king himself and released all of his subjects from their oaths of loyalty to him. This double assault had a devastating effect, for in one stroke it set Henry outside the Church, making him unfit to rule in the eyes of his Christian subjects, and also freed his vassals from their obligations to him. The German nobles, who had much to gain from a weakened monarchy, were quick to see the advantage for them in this development. In October 1076 they met at Tribur and announced that, unless the king repented and obtained absolution by 22 February 1077, they would replace him with another, more suitable ruler. To underscore their resolve, they also arranged for a diet, or assembly, to be convened at Augsburg on 2 February 1077, just weeks before this deadline. There, with Gregory himself presiding, Henry's future would be decided.

Faced with the eager opposition of his nobles and increasing desertions of bishops convinced that his cause was lost, the king realized that he had no choice but to submit. He sent word to Rome that he was prepared to go there and ask the pope's forgiveness, only to be told that Gregory would soon be leaving for Augsburg. Henry now settled on the desperate strategy of attempting to intercept the pope before he could meet with the German nobles. Making his way south across the Alps in the dead of winter, he found Gregory on 25 January 1077 at Canossa, where he had paused briefly at the castle of Countess Matilda of Tuscany. In a spectacular moment of papal triumph, Henry appeared for three days in succession before the castle gates, dressed in the rags of a penitent and begging for forgiveness as he stood barefoot in the snow. Urged by Abbot Hugh of Cluny and his other companions to forgive the king, Gregory granted him absolution. Henry had been humiliated, but he had managed to save his crown. His release from excommunication and reinstatement as king restored his identity as a worthy Christian ruler. More important, they precluded the rebellious actions his nobles were contemplating against him.

Or so it seemed. The German nobles had lost their religious grounds for deposing Henry, but their desire to be rid of him remained. They revolted anyway and elected Rudolf of Swabia as their new king. Gregory found himself drawn into the resulting civil war, during which he again excommunicated and deposed Henry, forbade Christians to support him, and promised absolution for all their sins to all who joined Rudolf (1080). As before, Henry retaliated by deposing Gregory. He then invaded Italy and occupied Rome. The pope, who had earlier looked down upon his enemy from the walls of one castle, now hid from him within the walls of another, the Castle of Sant' Angelo, as in March 1084 Henry installed the antipope Clement III (1084–1100) in his place and was in turn crowned emperor by him. A year later both Rome and Gregory were liberated by Robert Guiscard and his Norman soldiers, but the destruction they caused left Gregory no longer welcome in the city. "I have loved righteousness and hated iniquity." he said. "Therefore I die in exile." He did, utterly exhausted, at Salerno in 1085.

The investiture controversy continued under Gregory's successors, who found themselves in conflict with Henry IV's reckless and ambitious son, Henry V (1106–1125). The key to its eventual resolution was supplied when a distinction between royal and ecclesiastical rights of investiture allowed for the settlement of a similar conflict in England between Archbishop **Anselm of Canterbury**, whom we shall meet later in this chapter, and King Henry I (1100–35). In the **Concordat of Worms** in 1122, Henry V renounced the practice of investing bishops and abbots with the symbols of their spiritual authority. In return, Calixtus II recognized the emperor's right to be present at elections of German bishops, which were to be supervised by the Church and untainted by simony, to invest them with fiefs, and to impose on them certain feudal obligations, including loyalty to himself in temporal matters. This agreement, known as the Concordat of Worms, made German bishops and abbots more independent of the emperor, thereby weakening his position, but did nothing to diminish their interest in worldly wealth and affairs. Because their loyalties remained divided between the spiritual and temporal spheres, the Concordat of Worms was only a partial victory for the papacy; yet it did play a part in elevating that office to near-dominion over the West between the end of the eleventh century and the last years of the thirteenth.

The Papal Monarchy

The popes who ruled the medieval Church at the peak of its power shared Gregory VII's vision of a Europe unified under the spiritual and temporal rule of Rome. Building on the foundation that Gregory, Leo IX, and Nicholas II had established, their efforts to make it a reality often brought them into conflict with emperors and kings, but more often than not they emerged victorious. Much of their success was due to their willingness to use the weapons available to them — on occasion the armies of their defenders, but more often excommunication, deposition, and **interdict** (the exclusion of a person, district, or country from participation in the sacraments or Christian burial).

ALEXANDER III

The pontificate of Alexander III (1159–81) provides two good examples of papal power. The first concerns Frederick Barbarossa (1152–90), the first German emperor of the Hohenstaufen dynasty and the first to speak of the revived western empire as a "holy" empire, thereby reinforcing the claim that his imperial authority was no less sacred than that of his rival, the pope. When Alexander opposed his campaign against the free cities of northern Italy, Frederick angrily drove south and captured Rome, where he installed three successive antipopes.[21] Although Alexander was forced to spend much of his reign in France, in the end his statesmanship and alliance with the Lombard League, a confederation of northern Italian cities, resulted in a crushing defeat for Frederick. In a dramatic scene in Venice in 1177, the emperor fell to his knees and kissed the pope's feet, begging for reconciliation.

A second conflict broke out in England, where in 1164 King Henry II (1154–89) issued the *Constitutions of Clarendon*. By placing the election of bishops under control of the king and requiring that clergy be tried in civil rather than ecclesiastical courts, the *Constitutions* stood in the way of those who wanted to see greater autonomy for the Church in England. The most vocal among them was Thomas Becket, the archbishop of Canterbury, whose opposition resulted in his brutal murder by four of Henry's nobles in December 1170 as he stood before the altar in his cathedral. Reports of the incident hailed Thomas as a martyr and held the king responsible for his death. Alexander skillfully exploited the public outcry against Henry, forcing him to abrogate the *Constitutions of Clarendon* and do public penance at Becket's tomb, where the king submitted to the lash in full view of his subjects. Alexander had discovered the power of public opinion and demonstrated that even the most powerful of rulers could be made to bend to the will of the Church.

INNOCENT III

These lessons were not lost on Lotario di Segni, an Italian student of theology and philosophy at Paris who crossed the English Channel to see for himself the place where Thomas Becket had been cut down by the English king's men. Having also studied civil and canon law, and with influential connections in Rome, the dynamic young man was in a position to make his presence known there. By the age of thirty he was a cardinal deacon. At thirty-seven he became Innocent III (1198–1216) and was soon to make himself the most powerful pope in the entire history of the Church.

Innocent combined intellectual brilliance with diplomatic skill, incorruptibility, and determined devotion to the Gregorian ideal of papal supremacy. Believing that his office deserved a title more impressive than the customary "vicar of Peter," he was the first pope to call himself *vicarius Christi*, or "vicar of Christ." Innocent did not seek dominion in secular affairs outside the Papal States, but he insisted that secular rulers should always defer to the pope when they came into conflict with him — not merely because he considered spiritual matters weightier than worldly concerns, but because he believed that it was from the hand of the pope, and not directly from God, as some claimed, that the rulers of the world received their authority. He expressed this view in his famous analogy of "the Moon and the Sun":

> Just as the founder of the universe established two great lights in the firmament of heaven, a greater one to preside over the day and a lesser to preside over the night, so too . . . he instituted two great dignities, a greater one to rule over souls as if over day and a lesser one to rule over bodies as if over night. These are the pontifical authority and the royal power. Now just as the moon derives its light from the sun and is indeed lower than it in quantity and quality, in position and in power, so too the royal power derives the splendor of its dignity from the pontifical authority.[22]

For Innocent, the pope's position relative to all other rulers implied his right to approve their selection, enforce their morality, and demand their recognition of his overlordship. Ultimately, the legitimacy of the rule of any emperor or king depended upon papal sanction. This doctrine faced its first test the moment Innocent assumed the papal throne, for the death of Emperor Henry VI the previous year had thrown Germany into confusion with two rivals claiming the imperial crown. Using shrewd diplomatic maneuvers to play one against the other, he managed to throw Germany into such havoc that Frederick Barbarossa's accomplishments in rebuilding the Holy Roman Empire were almost completely undone. When Otto of Brunswick finally became king and then repaid papal support with broken promises and an invasion of Italy, Innocent excommunicated and deposed him. In his place he recognized Barbarossa's grandson, sixteen-year-old Frederick II of Sicily, first as king of Germany and then as Holy Roman Emperor. In return for these honors, Frederick acknowledged Innocent as his feudal overlord. He also agreed to give the pope greater control over the Church in Germany and never to encircle the Papal States by uniting Sicily and the Holy Roman Empire. He seemed to have forgotten these promises in later years, however, as he established himself solidly in southern Italy and gained such a reputation for sophistication and achievement that his admirers called him *stupor mundi*, the "wonder of the world." But he was no match for Innocent III's successors, Gregory IX (1227–41) and Innocent IV (1243–54), strong and uncompromising advocates of papal supremacy who prevented him from fully realizing his ambitions.

Innocent scored another victory, this time in England, during the reign of King John (1199–1216). Conflict began when John refused to allow the papal nominee for archbishop of Canterbury to set foot on English soil. To bend the king's will, Innocent imposed an interdict on England in 1208 and excommunicated John a year later, thus ending the formal practice of Christianity except for baptisms and burials and, in effect, leaving the English people without a Christian ruler. This endangerment of their salvation eroded their support for the king, who was already opposed by rebellious nobles. During the six years of the interdict, John vented his fury by seizing monasteries and churches and driving terrorized priests and bishops into exile. He was forced into submission only when Innocent created an alliance with the French king Philip Augustus (1180–1223) and threatened an invasion of England. Fearing that he would lose his crown, John managed to keep it only by placing it into the hands of a papal legate on 15 May 1213 and making the astonishing declaration that he was a vassal of the pope and that England was a papal fief.

Innocent had earlier used the weapon of interdict effectively against Philip Augustus himself. A day after marrying the Danish Princess Ingeborg in 1193, Philip suddenly refused to recognize his new wife as queen and married again without obtaining a divorce. Celestine III, Innocent's predecessor, had excommunicated Philip, though without the desired effect. Innocent's interdict was more difficult to ignore. No less incensed than King John in England, the angry Philip raged against the pope and deposed every bishop who suspended religious services, but his subjects' fear for the safety of their souls eventually forced him to yield to the papal will.

In addition to these conflicts, Innocent intervened successfully on behalf of the Church in countries ranging from Iceland to Armenia — including Poland, Hungary, Denmark, Bulgaria, Bohemia, Aragon, Leon, and Castile. Here and elsewhere he closely supervised its personnel and controlled its operations. He addressed the perennial problem of lax monastic discipline by ordering bishops and other ecclesiastical officials to regularly visit monasteries and convents. In disputed episcopal elections he reserved the right to make final decisions. After forbidding secular authorities to tax the clergy, he imposed his own taxes on them. The resulting revenues were immense, for much of Europe was under one form or another of ecclesiastical ownership. The laity were taxed as well, primarily through the tithe (one-tenth of all income produced on secular lands). Combined with the vast sums brought to Rome each year by pilgrims and litigants in papal courts, these sources produced for the Church an annual income far in excess of anything realized by secular states. It paid for a widening range of ecclesiastical interests and activities that were directed by the **curia**, the cardinals and other officials responsible for the administration of papal government. Innocent himself regulated many of the details of everyday life in the West by means of laws added to the corpus of canon law. Most took the form of decretals, written responses to specific questions on religious, moral, and social issues that were binding on all who lived under his apostolic authority.

Innocent's greatest triumph as a legislating pope came in 1215 at the Fourth Lateran Council. More than fifteen hundred bishops, archbishops, abbots, priors, and other dignitaries gathered in Rome in response to his command; it was the most imposing religious assembly in the entire history of the medieval West. Under Innocent's guidance the council officially affirmed the doctrine of transubstantiation and required that all Christians confess serious sin to a priest and receive the eucharist at least once each year. Relations between the laity and clergy were defined, as were those binding priests to bishops and bishops to the pope. Rules governing admission to the priesthood, the election of bishops, and acceptable forms of clerical dress and behavior were formulated. Guidelines were laid down concerning preaching in churches, and bishops were instructed that every cathedral should sponsor a school open to the poor. To eliminate a variety of abuses, the council called for monastic reforms, denounced and prescribed punishments for drunkenness, graft, and other forms of clerical immorality, and condemned the flourishing trade in fraudulent relics. Finally, it made bishops responsible for searching out and punishing members of unsanctioned and heretical religious groups, which were becoming increasingly common. This was the beginning of the infamous **Inquisition**, about which we will have more to say in chapter 7.

Like any powerful figure, Innocent had his critics. Emperors and kings resented his political ambitions. Many clergy accused him of worldliness. There is no denying that his aggressive leadership and manipulation of individuals, institutions, and states plunged him as deeply into worldly affairs as any secular ruler, but historians are generally agreed that his ambition was for the Church. By the time he died in 1216, shortly after the close of the Fourth Lateran Council, Innocent had brought it to unprecedented levels of organization, influence, and unity.

THE PAPACY IN THE THIRTEENTH CENTURY

The descent from this summit of papal supremacy occurred gradually throughout the remainder of the thirteenth century. On the whole, Innocent's successors, and in particular Gregory IX (1227–41), Innocent IV (1243–54), Clement IV (1265–68), and Gregory X (1271–76), rivaled him in their commitment to defending the Church and its interests, but most lacked his force of personality and their victories were mixed with significant defeats.

Ironically, the pontificate of Boniface VIII (1294–1303), the last of the thirteenth-century popes, marks both the height of papal claims to authority and the end of the papal monarchy established by his predecessors. Boniface had the misfortune to find himself locked in a lengthy battle with Philip IV (1285–1314) of France, whose views concerning royal authority did not include submission to the papacy. When Philip attempted to pay for his war with England by imposing taxes on the clergy, in violation of the immunity claimed by Innocent III, Boniface threatened to excommunicate anyone who demanded or paid them. In 1301 the pope issued the **bull** *Ausculta fili* ("Listen carefully, son"), in which he made a carefully worded appeal for Philip's obedience. When Philip burned this document before a great crowd in Paris, Boniface sent him another bull, **Unam Sanctam** (1302), the most potent statement of papal authority ever issued. There is one true Church, it said, and no possibility of salvation for those outside of it. The pope, who rules the Church as Christ's representative, entrusts kings with temporal power but reserves the right to instruct them in how it should be used. Whoever resists this exercise of papal power is in grave danger of damnation for, according to the bull's most famous line, "It is absolutely necessary for salvation that all men should be subject to the Roman pontiff." The most immediate results of *Unam Sanctam*, though, were signs of the changing times. Two French assemblies indicted Boniface for crimes ranging from murder to sorcery, and he was kidnapped by Philip's agents in Rome. The elderly pope was held in his palace at Anagni for three days, during which he refused repeated demands for his resignation. He died in October 1303, just days after his rescue by local nobles.

The reasons for this century of degeneration are complex. Two clear factors were the rise of powerful monarchies and the nascent nationalism that was beginning to direct loyalties toward the emerging national states. The continuing efforts of kings to dominate clergy and ecclesiastical property played an important role. So did increasing popular resentment of ecclesiastical taxes, the disproportionate influence of Italian clergy, clerical abuses that victimized the laity, and papal involvement in political affairs. However we may explain the decline, it became so dangerously precipitous that just six years after the death of Boniface the much weakened papacy fell into the hands of the French monarchy. We will return to this part of the story of the medieval papacy in chapter 7.

The Crusades

Between 1095 and 1270 the West launched a series of Crusades to free the Holy Land from the rule of Muslims. The crusaders came from a variety of social, economic, and national backgrounds. Although their objectives were said to be purely religious, there is little doubt that they were also driven by political and economic factors. Their ultimate aim of establishing permanent Christian control over the Holy Land was never realized, but the Crusades did have a unifying effect that promoted the position of the papacy in the West.

BACKGROUND

The immediate cause of the Crusades was the rise of the Seljuk Turks, a powerful Muslim people whose conquests in the Middle East included their seizure of Jerusalem from the Fatimid rulers of Egypt in 1070. A year later they inflicted a crushing defeat on the Byzantines at Manzikert. Reports of the persecution of Christian pilgrims and the desecration of holy places soon made their way to the West along with pleas for help directed to the pope.

The difficulty of the situation was aggravated by the weakness of the Byzantine Empire, which could not resist advancing Islamic armies.

Byzantium could not stand against the Turks, but some western powers were eager to try. Chief among them were the mercantile cities of Italy—Pisa, Amalfi, Genoa, Venice, and others—which expected to reap enormous profits if they could establish a secure foothold in Asia. Western knights saw opportunities to demonstrate valor and piety and to establish new kingdoms in foreign lands. A campaign to liberate the Holy Land offered even greater prospects to the papacy. Fought under the banner of the Church, it would enhance papal prestige, unify the warring feudal lords of Europe in an assault on a common enemy, and even provide the opportunity to bring the East and the eastern Church under the authority of Rome. The rank-and-file Christians who would do most of the fighting were attracted by papal assurances that participation in a Crusade would count as a great penance or be rewarded with an **indulgence**—a remission of the temporal punishment that must be suffered in atonement for sin before entering heaven.[23]

References to these motives were evident everywhere in the famous speech given by Pope Urban II in 1095 at the conclusion of the Council of Clermont in southern France. This address, perhaps the most influential in all of medieval history, set the First Crusade in motion. Appealing to the ethnic pride of his audience of thousands by describing them as Franks and recalling the greatness of their ancestors, Urban warned of the desperate situation in the East. The empire of the Greeks had been overrun, he said, by "a race completely alienated from God." He unfairly described Muslims as worshipers of demons who subjected their captives to cruel and bizarre tortures and forcibly circumcised the men among them, spreading their blood on altars and pouring it into baptismal fonts. These same infidels were destroying churches and desecrating holy places.

Having played in this way on the crowd's ethnic and religious sensibilities, Urban went on to describe the spiritual and material benefits that would accrue to those who heeded his call for a holy war.

The Crusade would be a "holy pilgrimage," he said, suggesting that it might serve as a penance for sin.[24] Those who vowed to join it and signified their intention by wearing the sign of the cross would be responding to the teaching of Christ, who had said, "Whoever does not take up the cross and follow me is not worthy of me" (Matthew 10:38). Some, of course, would die along the way or in battle, but they would be rewarded with an "immediate remission of sin." The pope also held out the prospect of rewards for those more eager for land than salvation, urging them to seize the Holy Land and make it their own.

THE COURSE OF THE CRUSADES

The cheer of *Deus vult!* ("God wills it!") raised by the crowd at Clermont soon echoed throughout Europe as word of the coming Crusade spread. Before the main body of crusaders led by trained knights could be organized, disorderly groups of peasants and townspeople set out for the East, pillaging homes and fields to feed themselves and sometimes attacking communities of Jews as they made their way along the Rhine and Danube. The Byzantine emperor Alexius Comnenus (1081–1118) welcomed them in Constantinople but feared what such a mob might do to his capital. He urged them to continue their journey across the Bosporus, where they were quickly annihilated by the Turks outside Nicaea.

This first wave was followed in the summer of 1096 by four separate armies led by knights rather than kings (Philip I of France, William II of England, and Henry IV of Germany were all under papal sentence of excommunication at the time of Urban II's speech). These armies met in Constantinople, where their leaders swore to recognize Byzantine rights to the lands they conquered in return for supplies and military support. After a dangerous march though Asia Minor and Syria, the crusaders succeeded in capturing Jerusalem in July 1099. They celebrated this victory with a frenzied slaughter of Muslim and Jewish men, women, and children. Forgetting their promise to the emperor Alexius, they established the Latin Kingdom of

Jerusalem and in 1100 chose one of their leaders, Baldwin of Flanders, as its king. Baldwin gave the neighboring territories of Edessa, Antioch, and Tripoli as fiefs to other crusading nobles who joined him in attempting to establish the feudal system in their new kingdom. Castles were built to defend strategic locations and new military monastic orders, such as the Knights Templar, the Knights Hospitaler, and, later, the Teutonic Knights, were founded and charged with the responsibility of defending Christians and Christianity in the East.

The Second Crusade (1147–49) was launched to recover Edessa after its capture by the Turks in 1144. Under the joint command of King Louis VII of France and Conrad III, the Holy Roman Emperor, the crusaders were almost completely destroyed by the Turks in Asia Minor. When Louis and Conrad finally arrived in the Holy Land with what was left of their forces, they were unable to contribute significantly to the defense of the Latin Kingdom. Four decades later the Muslim leader Saladin led the combined forces of Egypt and Syria against the crusaders, defeating the army of the Latin Kingdom of Jerusalem in 1187 and capturing all of its territory except for the coastal city of Tyre and a few castles. News of this tragedy resulted in the Third Crusade (1189–92), organized by the emperor Frederick Barbarossa, Philip II of France, and Richard I ("the Lionheart") of England. Barbarossa's death by drowning in Asia Minor on his way east and Philip's early departure left the English king in sole command for a year, during which he and Saladin exchanged a curious combination of chivalrous courtesies and violent attacks. In the end, Richard managed to recover some coastal territory, but Saladin remained in control of Jerusalem.

A Fourth Crusade (1202–04) was undertaken at the prompting of Innocent III, who had envisioned a march on Jerusalem via Egypt. But the commercial interests of the sponsoring Venetians and their involvement in Byzantine politics led instead to the capture and sacking of Constantinople in 1204. A Latin Empire of Constantinople was established with a Flemish noble as emperor and a Venetian priest as patriarch. In this way a forced political and religious reunification of East and West was

achieved, but it survived only until 1261 and left Greek Christians embittered toward the West for centuries.

The scandal of the Fourth Crusade persuaded many that only a return to the virtues and purer motives of the earlier Crusades would bring the liberation of the Holy Land. This was the conviction behind the so-called Children's Crusades of 1212. One was led by a certain Nicholas, a boy from Cologne who had been told in a vision that the young and innocent would succeed where adults had failed. Of the thousands who marched south with him to Italy, hundreds were lost to hunger and disease. The rest, who had been certain that God would part the sea so that they might walk to Jerusalem, were stranded when they could not arrange passage across the Mediterranean. In that same year Stephen of Cloyes, a twelve-year-old shepherd boy, appeared before King Philip Augustus of France and announced that he, too, had been told in a vision to lead a crusade of children. The king told him to go home, but Stephen and as many as twenty thousand followers instead made their way to Marseilles. There, say contemporary accounts, they were offered free passage to Palestine on ships that were in fact bound for Egypt and Tunisia, where those who weren't drowned on the way were sold as slaves.

The story of the Crusades beyond this point is essentially that of their collapse due to disorganization, incompetence, and flagging interest. Still convinced that the way to the Holy Land lay through Egypt, Innocent III organized a Fifth Crusade that captured the port of Damietta at the mouth of the Nile in 1219 but made no further progress until reinforcements arrived under the command of Frederick II. The Holy Roman Emperor had taken a crusader's vow in 1215 but did not leave for the East until 1228. He scored a major victory in 1229, however, when he negotiated a treaty with Sultan al-Kamil of Egypt that placed Jerusalem in Christian hands. It remained there until it was lost again in 1244. Determined to recover it, King Louis IX of France (1226–70), later recognized as St. Louis, led a campaign through Egypt in 1248–50. Unfortunately, his entire army was taken captive by

Figure 6.1   Portrait reliquary of St. Louis This reliquary, which dates to the early fourteenth century, was designed to hold the relics of Louis IX of France (1214–70). Renowned for his piety, Louis died in Tunis while on a crusade. He was canonized in 1297.

Muslims who kept him and his nobles alive but beheaded three hundred ordinary soldiers each evening because they were too difficult to guard. After being freed by the payment of a ransom raised by his wife and the Templars, Louis set out on a second disastrous crusade in 1270. He died later that year near Tunis with the words "Jerusalem, Jerusalem" on his lips. But the holy city was lost forever to Christendom. A few weak efforts to retake it accomplished nothing, for in 1250 a powerful new dynasty of Muslim rulers, the Mamelukes, had established itself in Egypt and virtually shut the door to invading armies. By 1291 the Crusaders had been forced from their last possessions in the Holy Land.

Only in Europe itself did the crusading spirit lead to significant victories against Islam. The Arab Muslims who had conquered Sicily in the ninth century were driven out in the eleventh by the Normans, and the expulsion of Muslims from Spain was completed in 1492. As we will see in chapter 7, the Church's actions against groups of dissenters and heretics were also seen by many as crusades.

CONSEQUENCES OF THE CRUSADES

On the whole, the Crusades were a failure. They won only intermittent control of the Holy Land, did little to slow the advance of Islam, and heightened enmity between Muslims and Christians. In former times Muslims had regarded Christians as "people of the book" whose faith, though a corruption of true religion, still gave them much in common. But the personal and military conduct of the crusaders encouraged the growth of a new and negative Muslim perception of western Christians as crude, land-hungry barbarians very different from themselves. The Crusades did encourage the expansion of western commercial activity in the East, but the extent to which they introduced Islamic culture and scholarship to the West is often overstated. For the most part, Muslims, not returning crusaders, brought Islamic culture to the West, especially through Spain and Sicily. Despite attempts to create kingdoms in the East, no western state gained any lasting benefit from the Crusades. Instead, the Crusades brought confusion to the Byzantine Empire and distracted western rulers from their responsibilities at home. Only the papacy profited, for the Crusades added much to its prestige. Urban II had been right in assuming that papal claims to supremacy would be advanced by the sight of kings and emperors fighting a common enemy in the service of the Church.

Scholasticism

The economic revival of Europe brought urbanization and a restructuring of society that made it increasingly complex. New interests and occupations emerged; with them came a demand for education. This led to the rise of the first great universities in the West. In these institutions the study of theology flourished, partly because the works of Aristotle and other classical authors had been recovered, largely through Muslim Spain and Sicily. The greatest intellectual movement of this period was **scholasticism**, which sought to demonstrate the harmony of faith and reason. Scholasticism had its beginnings in monastic learning but reached its peak at schools like the University of Paris, which was the center of medieval intellectual life in the high Middle Ages.

THE RISE OF THE UNIVERSITIES

By the time Paris had assumed such importance, however, the students and professors at the University of Bologna in Italy had already established many of the norms of medieval university life. Specializing in the study of civil and canon law, the university was a union of students who shared a common interest in study and recognized that there is strength in numbers. By organizing, they were able to defend themselves against exploitation by greedy and unscrupulous townspeople and to impose high standards on their professors.

While Bologna served as the model for southern universities, Paris set the standard in the north, where its organization of university life was imitated at Oxford, Cambridge, Toulouse, Heidelberg, and elsewhere. These institutions were run by professors rather than students. Their emphasis was on the liberal arts — divided as in earlier times into the *trivium* of grammar, rhetoric, and dialectic (logic) and the *quadrivium* of arithmetic, geometry, music, and astronomy — as well as advanced study in the disciplines of theology, medicine, and law. For those who specialized in the arts, the highest level of achievement was a master's degree; in theology, medicine, and law it was possible to earn a doctoral degree (from *doctus,* "learned"). Paris and other northern universities were essentially corporations of professors who decided what would be taught and imposed behavioral and academic standards on their students.

Before the rise of universities, education had been available only in monasteries and at cathedral schools such as those at Reims, Laon, Tournai, Chartres, and Notre Dame in Paris. In monasteries in particular, the acquisition of knowledge was quite unlike what we think of as education today. A monk learning theology would devote himself to the study

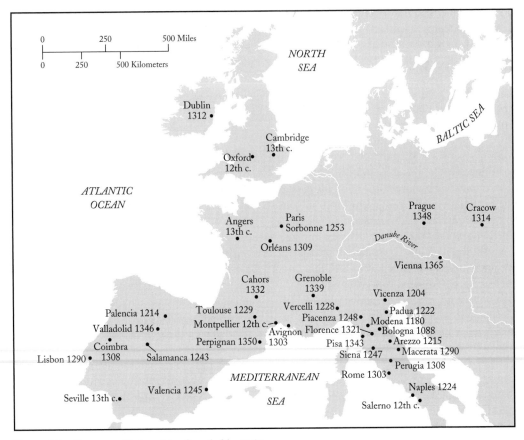

Figure 6.2   European Universities founded by 1350

of scripture and the church fathers. Typically, he would read a passage aloud and then reflect on its meaning. Reflection, which was contemplative as well as analytical, ideally led to a spiritual experience of the higher realities and truths described in the text as well as to their intellectual apprehension.

Learning took a new turn in the cathedral schools and universities, where teachers of theology and philosophy known as "schoolmen" (or scholastics) preferred a thoroughly analytical and speculative approach to knowledge. Here, the goal was not to discover some new truth but to bring together, consider, and harmonize what was known about a subject from existing sources — such as the Bible, the church fathers, and classical Greek and Roman writers — in order to clarify and deepen knowledge

of truths that were already accepted. The scholastic method, sometimes called the "questioning" or "dialectical method," consisted of three steps: asking a question, evaluating arguments for and against the answers suggested by earlier authorities, and coming to a conclusion (*sententia*) supported by logic. Its dependence on logic made the scholastic method rather different from the monastic approach to learning, which emphasized the role of faith and the expectation, common among contemplatives and mystics, that God would illuminate the mind of the seeker of truth. It also explains why Aristotle now became so important to western intellectual life, for in works such as the *Categories* and *On Interpretation* he had defined and elaborated the science of logic. Theologians were not the only ones to employ Aristotle and the scholastic method. Specialists in medicine and law used both to organize and understand the content of their own fields and would sometimes write a *summa,* or "summation," of all that was known about a particular topic. But it was in the field of theology, regarded in the medieval era as the "queen of the sciences," that the most important advances were made.

ARISTOTLE

There is some irony in the importance of Aristotle (384–322 BCE) for Christian thought in the high Middle Ages. Unlike Plato, in whom theologians had always found a fairly dependable ally, Aristotle often seemed to contradict Christianity. His teaching on the eternality of the world, for example, seemed to deny the biblical assertion that God had created it in time. Aristotle did not distinguish clearly, as Plato and traditional Christian thought did, between the body and the soul. Moreover, he had also rejected the immortality of the individual soul, a doctrine that was essential to the doctrine of a final judgment.

In addition to contradicting specific Christian doctrines, Aristotelianism included a theory of knowledge that challenged traditional assumptions in the Christian West. The monastic approach to learning, for example, had held that faith guides human reason and makes real knowledge possible. Aristotle had clearly not been a man of faith, but to the medieval mind his encyclopedic works on botany, zoology, astronomy, logic, epistemology, physics, metaphysics, political science, and ethics qualified him nonetheless as the greatest of polymaths. For most people he was simply "the Philosopher." Dante called him "the master of those who know." But how could such knowledge have been acquired apart from faith?

There was another way in which Aristotle raised questions—not only about knowledge, but about reality itself. In earlier times most theologians had followed Plato in asserting that we gain knowledge through the activity of the soul. Truth, Plato had said, belongs to the spiritual realm and can be fully known only by spiritual means—more specifically,

through reason, which belongs to the soul. Plato favored a deductive form of reasoning that worked from the top down; that is, from spirit to matter and from great truths to individual examples of them. Thus, a theologian working in the tradition of Plato would start with a spiritual truth known from the Bible or some other source and apply it to specific aspects of material reality in order to understand them better. For followers of Plato, it would be foolish to rely on the senses, because they are fallible and can tell us little about spiritual realities. Aristotle disagreed. Preferring empiricism to Plato's **idealism**, he argued that the search for knowledge must begin with the senses and their perceptions of the material world. He argued that Plato's ideal forms, the spiritual essences of things, have no independent existence in the world of spirit but can be found only in things themselves. Thus, if we want to discover universal or general truths, we must reason inductively—starting with particular instances of natural objects and processes and working our way from the bottom up. Whereas Plato had said that true reality is to be found in the realm of spirit, Aristotle gave an entirely new emphasis to the search for truth by insisting that truth is inseparable from the world of matter.

In the Middle Ages the view, associated with Plato, that there are spiritual essences or "universals" behind all that we perceive in the world of matter came to be called "realism." The opposite view, associated with Aristotle, was called "nominalism." It held that such "realities" are in fact only names (*nomina*) we use for the sake of convenience in identifying certain groups of things. Thus, while a realist would say, for example, that "tree" exists in the realm of spirit as the perfect essence and model of all trees in the material world, which are imperfect expressions of it, a nominalist would argue that "tree" is just a name (*nomen*), a label human beings have agreed to use when referring to leafy things with trunks and branches. For realists, there was an eternal and spiritual order of things, a way of classifying them that God himself had defined and that we therefore ought to follow. Nominalists countered that there was no such order and, consequently, no single "right way" in which to divide the world up into categories. As we will see, especially in chapter 7, nominalism was to have profound implications for Christian theology.

Islam encountered Aristotle long before he became a force in the Christian world. At a time when Latin translations of his works were rare, Aristotle was widely read throughout the Islamic world in Arabic and with the help of Arabic commentaries. Many of the latter were written in the tenth century by al-Farabi, a Turk who was so taken with Aristotle's *On the Soul* that he is said to have read it more than two hundred times. It was al-Farabi's commentary on the *Metaphysics* that made its meaning clear to the philosopher **Avicenna** (980-1037), whose own philosophy combined Aristotelianism with elements of Neoplatonism and exercised a great influence on early scholasticism as well as on later Muslim thinkers. The greatest of these was **Averroës** (Ibn Rushd; 1126–98), a philosopher, physician, and lawyer from Cordoba in Muslim Spain who considered Aristotle the supreme expositor of truth and whose extensive commentaries on Aristotle's works earned him universal recognition as "the Commentator."

Despite the Islamic world's fascination with Aristotle, however, his differences with Islam itself — the same differences, for the most part, that stood between him and Christianity — were too obvious to be ignored. Muslim thinkers went to considerable lengths to see if they might be reconciled or explained. The philosopher al-Ghazali (1058–1111) concluded that they could not and condemned Aristotle in his *The Destruction of Philosophy*. Averroës was more optimistic. He argued that points of conflict disappear when the Qur'an is interpreted allegorically and claimed that all religion, in fact, is simply an allegorical way of expressing philosophical ideas and truths.

The question of Aristotle's compatibility with religion also raised concerns among Christian thinkers in the West. By 1250, Latin translations of Aristotle's works had made their way north across the Pyrenees from Spain along with the commentaries of Averroës. Some Christians, such as Siger of Brabant (ca. 1240–ca. 1284), a popular professor at Paris, and other "Latin Averroists" accepted Aristotle and Averroës virtually without reservation,

even when they seemed to be in conflict with scripture. Others saw real danger not only in Aristotle, but also in Averroës's interpretation of him on issues such as the nature of the soul and human freedom. There were sporadic attempts to ban Aristotle from the universities, and he was frequently denounced by theologians of a Platonist and mystical bent, but his learning and logic were too formidable to be set aside. By the thirteenth century Aristotle's influence had surpassed that of his master Plato among western theologians.

ANSELM OF CANTERBURY

The antecedents of scholasticism can be found as early as Augustine and John Scotus Eriugena, both of whom acknowledged that reason can sometimes give a deeper understanding of truths accepted by faith. But with Anselm of Canterbury (ca. 1033–1109) discussions of the background of scholasticism usually begin in earnest. Born in Aosta in what is now northwestern Italy, Anselm entered the monastery at Bec in Normandy in 1059 and became its abbot in 1078. At Bec he wrote his great philosophical works, the *Monologion* and *Proslogion*. The proximity of Normandy to England and Anselm's reputation there led in 1093 to his appointment as archbishop of Canterbury, where he remained until his death sixteen years later. Much of his energy during his final years was spent defending the Church against the intrusive schemes of kings William II and Henry I, but in 1098 he managed to complete *Cur Deus homo* (*Why God Became Man*). All of Anselm's major works evince the priority he gave to faith over reason. Following Augustine, his motto was *"Credo ut intelligam"* ("I believe in order to understand"). But he was also convinced that reason could affirm and clarify truths known by faith, a view he expressed in the original title of his *Proslogion*, which included the explanatory phrase "faith seeking understanding."

In the *Proslogion* Anselm set out his famous **ontological argument** for the existence of God, according to which the very idea of God makes his existence certain. Everyone knows, he said, that *God* means something greater than which nothing can be imagined. This means that God cannot exist only in the imagination, for if he did it would still be possible to imagine something greater — a God who exists in reality as well. Therefore, there exists both in our minds and in reality one greater than which nothing exists, and that is God. This ingenious argument drew fierce and immediate criticism from theologians who objected to the very idea of making the content of a faith revealed by God (including the idea of God's existence) subject to question and debate. Others complained that there was something fallacious or tricky about Anselm's logic. One eleventh-century monk, Gaunilo of Marmoutiers, argued that a person could have the idea of a perfect island when in fact no such island existed, but Anselm pointed out that his argument applied only to God, who alone is "something greater than which nothing can be imagined."

Even today the ontological argument leaves many people with the feeling that they have been duped. On the other hand, it has been defended by some of the greatest names in philosophy.[25] Its significance for us, however, has less to do with its validity than with the fact that it illustrates a new approach to the acquisition of knowledge. Anselm believed in the existence of God long before he arrived at Bec, but he wanted to understand as well as to believe. To do so, he applied reason to theology by attempting to define what God is and determine whether the existence of such a being could be supported by logic.

Although Anselm's interest in what reason can do is evident everywhere in his works (which included an introduction to logic), it did not lead him further in the direction of Aristotle and nominalism. His position as an extreme realist was made clear when his contemporary, Jean Roscelin, one of the first nominalists, speculated that the Father, Son, and Holy Spirit must be three separate beings (because *God* is just an artificial category or label that does not unify them in any real way and because, if they were truly the same in substance, the Father and Holy Spirit would have become incarnate at the same time as the Son). Anselm replied that for one who denied the reality of universals — that is, categories such as "divinity" and "humanity" in the eternal order of things — it would be just as impossible to show that three people are united in

their humanity as it would be to demonstrate that the Father, Son, and Holy Spirit are one in their divinity.

Anselm's most important contribution to theology was the theory of salvation he presented in *Cur Deus homo*. For centuries, the most popular way of explaining the work of Christ was one we discussed in chapter 4 in connection with Gregory of Nyssa and Augustine. According to this theory, by sinning Adam had voluntarily placed humanity under the power of Satan. God had to respect Satan's rights over humanity until Satan, fooled by Christ's humanity into thinking he was *only* human, attempted to destroy him as well. Here he overreached his rights, for Christ was divine as well as human. God punished Satan by freeing humanity from his power, the first proof of this being the resurrection of Christ.

Anselm was uncomfortable with the element of divine deception in this theory as well as with the idea that Christ had been sent into the world as a ransom to be offered to Satan in exchange for fallen humanity. In *Cur Deus homo* he offered a new theory in which deception, ransom, and Satan had no place at all. By sinning, said Anselm, human beings had dishonored God and upset the divinely established order of things. To be set right with God, humanity either had to be punished or make satisfaction for its sin. God, who is merciful, sought reconciliation through satisfaction, but humanity had nothing to offer great enough to compensate for its infinite offense. Only God could make perfect restitution, hence the necessity of a God-man. As Anselm put it, "Only one who is truly divine *can* make satisfaction, and only one who is truly human *ought* to make it."[26] Christ's perfect obedience to God restored God's honor but did not make up for the damage done by the sins of the rest of humanity. This happened when Christ went far beyond the righteousness that could be expected of any human being by offering his life for the sake of all others. In doing so he earned infinite spiritual merit. This is made available to sinners through their faith and participation in the sacraments and ensures their salvation.

There are several important observations to make in connection with this "satisfaction theory" of atonement, which quickly displaced all others in the West. First, its dependence on the existence of universals, and in particular the "humanity" assumed by Christ, offers additional evidence of Anselm's conservative realism and the influence of Plato and Augustine on his thought. At the same time, however, there was something new in Anselm's argument, for he had attempted to demonstrate the logical necessity of the incarnation without appealing to the authority of scripture or faith. This effort to determine the relationship between faith and reason is precisely what all of later scholasticism would be about. Finally, Anselm's theory vividly reflects the values of the feudal world in which he lived, a world in which the virtues of trust and honor ensured good relations among lords and social order in general. Making this point, Friedrich Heer, one of the twentieth century's most eminent specialists in medieval history, wrote:

> God was fighting to redeem man who, because of his sin, had become the booty of another king, the devil. Christ, God's son, paid the penalty owed by man for his grave offences, by which he broke faith with God. "Felony," breaking faith, was the gravest crime known to this society. God the Son restored the damaged honour of the Lord of Heaven, his incarnation and his crucifixion reestablished "friendship" between God and man, and brought the kingdom of Heaven back to its just order.[27]

We might describe Anselm, then, as a Christian thinker who was thoroughly grounded in the traditions of early medieval thought and society. At the same time, however, we can see in his interest in reason and its potential for illuminating faith the beginnings of great changes that were to come in medieval theology.

PETER ABELARD

Just a year after Anselm became abbot at Bec, a second major figure in the history of scholasticism was born near Nantes in Brittany. This was **Peter Abelard** (1079–1142), who studied under some of the best minds of his time before outshining them all as the greatest theologian yet to teach at Paris. Like Anselm, Abelard was interested in the rela-

tionship between faith and reason. He seems never to have doubted that each would affirm the other; but whereas Anselm, like Augustine, had set faith before reason, Abelard placed them on more equal footing by arguing that the tenets of Christianity should be accepted on the basis of rational examination as well as faith. Moreover, instead of rejecting nominalism outright as Anselm did, Abelard found a middle ground between it and realism by arguing that although universals such as "humanity" and "tree" have no independent or objective reality of their own, they are not mere names. They are concepts, he said, formed by our minds from sense perceptions of features shared by entities belonging to categories of things. According to this view, often called "conceptualism" or "moderate realism," these concepts are real, though they are expressed only in particulars.

Abelard was brilliant, handsome, charismatic, and sincerely religious, but he was also vain, contentious, and worldly. By the time he reached his mid twenties, his virtues had attracted a large following of admirers, but his vices were already working against him. As a result, both tragedy and romance fill the pages of his autobiographical *Story of My Misfortunes*. There he tells how in his late thirties he arranged to become the tutor of Heloise, the seventeen-year-old niece of Fulbert, an influential canon at Notre Dame. As Abelard had planned, study soon led to seduction. "Under the pretext of work we made ourselves entirely free for love," he confessed. "There was more kissing than teaching; my hands found themselves at her breasts more often than on the book."[28] In time their relationship grew to involve mutual admiration as well as physical attraction, for Heloise had a keen intellect, spoke Latin as well as French, and had even studied Hebrew. Inspired, Abelard wrote love songs that his students sang in the streets of Paris, but when Heloise became pregnant their lives fell apart. The couple was secretly married, but it was not enough to satisfy Fulbert, who believed that Abelard had dishonored him. Bent on vengeance, he inflamed the anger of Heloise's kinsmen, who burst in upon the scholar as he slept and castrated him.

For a time it seemed to Abelard that his career was over. He recognized the poetic justice in the injury he had suffered but feared that his mutilation had damaged his reputation as well as his body. He had hoped to rise to prominence in the Church, but his marriage, which Heloise had resisted for his sake, now stood in his way. Seeing no alternative, he urged her to become a nun. She did, taking her vows at Argenteuil even as he took those of a monk at the abbey of St. Denis near Paris. For the rest of their lives they rarely saw each other, but they exchanged letters that testify to an enduring love they struggled to turn toward God. In the end they were buried side by side, two star-crossed lovers together at last, the perfect denouement to a medieval romance as tragic as any ever imagined by a poet or troubadour.

Whatever emotional pain Abelard felt in his early days at St. Denis was compounded by the hostility of his fellow monks, who bristled at his criticisms of their lack of discipline and twice tried to kill him. Undaunted, he devoted himself to a refutation of Roscelin's tritheism. The resulting treatise *On the Divine Unity and Trinity* came too close to Sabellianism, however, and was condemned at the Synod of Soissons in 1121.[29] Abelard was not allowed to speak in its defense, for his enemies claimed that his powers of persuasion were irresistible and forced a ruling that kept him silent. After being compelled to throw his book into the fire, he was sentenced to a year's confinement in the monastery at St. Medard.

A papal reprieve soon brought him back to St. Denis, but once again he angered the other monks, this time by questioning the legend of their abbey's founding by Dionysius (Denis) the Areopagite. With the blessing of his abbot, the great Suger, whom we will meet again later in this chapter, Abelard left St. Denis and established a hermitage in a desolate spot near Troyes. For three years he lectured to the students who joined him there, then he moved on to the monastery of St. Gildas in Brittany and, later, Reims. By 1136 he was back in Paris, where once again his teaching drew enthusiastic crowds. The next five years were the most productive of his life. His habit of constantly revising his works makes it difficult to assign exact dates, but we can be confident that it was in this period that Abelard completed his *Christian Theology*, *Sic et non*, and parts of his *Introduction to Theology*.

By now, however, he had also found a dangerous enemy in Bernard of Clairvaux, the famous mystic and Cistercian monk, who resented the intellectual pretensions of the new urban academics. Bernard considered Abelard's emphasis on reason misplaced and found further cause for concern in his teachings on the Trinity, atonement, original sin, and freedom of will. Largely through Bernard's influence, in 1141 the Council of Sens condemned sixteen major propositions from Abelard's writings. Broken by this second condemnation and a lifetime of tragedy, Abelard summoned the last of his strength and set out for Rome to appeal to the pope. He made it as far as Cluny, where he learned that Innocent II had already confirmed the council's decision. The pope had also commanded that Abelard should be forever silent and confined to a monastery. Bowing to the inevitable, Abelard withdrew within the walls of Cluny. He died a year later.

Of all his works, *Sic et non* is perhaps the most famous, for it illustrates so effectively Abelard's conviction that "by doubting we come to inquiry, and by inquiry we recognize truth." The work consists of 158 questions or propositions, many of them dogmas essential to Christianity, underneath which Abelard arranged in two columns, *sic* and *non* ("yes" and "no"), quotations from the Bible and the church fathers supporting both sides of each issue. He withheld his own judgments about these apparent contradictions, leaving it to readers to come to their own conclusions. Abelard insisted that his purpose was not, as some charged, to challenge the authority of scripture and the fathers. Instead, he said he hoped to stimulate independent thinking that would elucidate truths they sometimes left unclear. But this in itself seemed dangerous to many of his critics, who argued that doubting and inquiry are activities undertaken by fallible human minds and therefore do not necessarily lead to truth.

In opposition to Anselm's "satisfaction theory" of atonement, Abelard proposed what is often called the "moral influence theory." It was not necessary for Christ to make satisfaction for sin, he claimed, because God forgave the transgressions of human beings long before the coming of Christ.

Abelard was also disturbed by the legalism of Anselm's theory, and in particular by the idea that God would demand the innocent blood of his Son as the precondition for his reconciliation with humanity. God is love, he said, and in an act of infinite grace had assumed and disposed of the burden of sin without thought of any need to compensate for it. He also sent Christ, the God-man, whose perfect illustration of what divine love really is and what human beings should be awakens in men and women a desire to love God as he loves them:

> As a result, our hearts should be set on fire by such a gift of divine grace, and true love should not hold back from suffering anything for his sake. . . . Therefore, our redemption through the suffering of Christ is that deeper love within us which not only frees us from slavery to sin, but also secures for us the true liberty of the children of God, in order that we might do all things out of love rather than out of fear — love for him who has shown us such grace that no greater can be found.[30]

Abelard's critics complained that his theory of atonement made Christ a mere teacher whose voluntary death, the supreme lesson in the meaning of love, accomplished only part of the work of salvation and left the rest to be completed by human beings. Many of his contemporaries were also uncomfortable with his view of sin, according to which good and evil have more to do with the intentions behind human actions than with the actions themselves. More optimistic than Augustine in his estimation of human nature, Abelard held that we have within us the impulse to do what is good as well as what is evil. God gave us reason so that we might discover what the good is and, inspired by the example of Christ's love, will to do it.

Such views were not entirely consistent with the mood and outlook of medieval Christianity. Nor were Abelard's belief that the great philosophers of Greece and Rome were Christians before Christ, his interest in and tolerance of Judaism, his opposition to indulgences, and his argument that it is wrong to use force to compel correct religious belief. In these and other respects he ran counter to the currents of his time but also distinguished himself as one of the most interesting thinkers of the Middle Ages.

HUGH OF ST. VICTOR AND PETER LOMBARD

As we have seen, by Abelard's time it was becoming clear that the future of theology lay with universities rather than monasteries and that, in the universities at least, Christian thought would continue to move from an emphasis on the mystical approach to God toward greater reliance on reason.[31] Some regarded the intellectual and mystical paths to God as incompatible; others saw them as complementary. The latter view was adopted by the Victorines, an influential group of scholars, poets, and hymnographers from the Augustinian monastic community of St. Victor near Paris who combined a commitment to mysticism with an interest in reason and the dialectical method of the schoolmen.

The greatest of the Victorines was Hugh of St. Victor (1096–1142), who taught at the abbey's prestigious school and wrote on subjects ranging from grammar and geometry to theology. Hugh's realism is evident in his *On the Sacraments of the Christian Faith*, in which he contended that all material things are expressions of divine ideas and have a sacramental character because, like the sacraments themselves, they convey something of God to humanity. All knowledge is useful, he insisted, no matter how ordinary its object, for all things point to God. Hugh recognized philosophy and theology as two different branches of knowledge but saw no conflict between them. Some spiritual truths can be demonstrated by reason, he said, but as we move closer to God we encounter others that, though not contrary to reason, are too deep for it to grasp. These can be known only by the mystic who approaches them in faith aided by grace.

Peter Lombard (ca. 1100–60), whose name reflects his northern Italian origins, studied at Bologna and Reims before coming to Paris, where he was for a time the student of Hugh of St. Victor and, perhaps, of Peter Abelard. For a time he taught theology at the cathedral school at Notre Dame. In his later years he was bishop of Paris. Peter's *Four Books of Sentences* was, as the title suggests, divided into four books: the first dealing with God; the second with creation, sin, grace, freedom of will, and the need for salvation; the third with Christology; and the fourth with the sacraments and eschatology. Peter addressed these subjects by following the general plan of Abelard's *Sic et non,* formulating significant questions and theses and assembling quotations for and against each from the Bible, the church fathers, church councils, papal decrees, and other sources. However, unlike *Sic et non,* where Abelard had withheld his own opinions, the *Sentences* takes its name from the *sententiae* ("judgments" or "opinions") that Peter offered in the hope of demonstrating an underlying harmony of opinion. These were not especially innovative; whereas *Sic et non* had opened the door to questioning of the Church's teachings, the *Sentences* supported and defended them. But Peter's work was so well organized, thorough, and judicious in its treatment of the whole of theology that it quickly became the most widely read theological text in the West and earned for Peter himself the title *Master of the Sentences.*

THOMAS AQUINAS

Scholasticism reached its summit in **Thomas Aquinas** (ca. 1225–74), one of the greatest figures in the history of the western intellectual tradition. The son of the German count and countess of Aquino in southern Italy, he was also related to the emperor Frederick II. Thomas was only five when his father entrusted him to the Benedictine monks at Monte Cassino, with whom he remained for nine years before entering the University of Naples. Few cities could have offered more new perspectives on faith and belief—for Italy lay at the crossroads of East and West, and the cosmopolitan Frederick, the university's patron, encouraged interest in Greek philosophy, Islam, and Islamic arts and sciences. At Naples, Thomas, not yet twenty, joined the **Dominicans**, an order of **friars** dedicated to poverty and preaching. In doing so he seemed determined to cut himself off from any chance of ecclesiastical advancement. In the words of one modern commentator, "It is as if Napoleon had insisted on remaining a private soldier all his life."[32] Stunned by

his rejection of aristocratic privilege and a probable appointment as a Benedictine abbot, Thomas's family had him kidnapped and brought home to Roccasecca castle, where they begged him to reconsider. It was only after a year "imprisonment" left him unmoved that they finally relented and agreed to send him to Paris.

Thomas arrived there in 1245 and soon found a mentor in the famous Dominican scholar Albert the Great (ca. 1200–1280), from whom he learned to appreciate Aristotle as well as Plato and Augustine. Three years later he accompanied Albert to Cologne and lectured on theology. When his peers there dubbed Thomas "the dumb ox" in recognition of his great weight and quiet manner, Albert is said to have remarked that the lowing of this ox would soon be heard throughout the world. Returning to Paris, Thomas became *baccalaureus Sententiarum,* or lecturer on the *Sentences* of Peter Lombard, and began writing his lengthy commentary on that work as well as two treatises, *On Being and Essence* and *On Truth.* In 1259 he began a decade in Italy during which he taught as a member of the papal court and composed his second most important work, the *Summa contra gentiles,* intended to assist Dominican preachers in arguing against Islam, Judaism, and Christian heresies. 1268 saw Aquinas back in Paris, teaching and defending the moderate use of Aristotle in theology against those who sought to ban his works altogether on the one hand and the Latin Averroists on the other. By then he had also begun his masterpiece, the *Summa theologiae.*[33] In 1272 Thomas left Paris again, this time for good, to found a Dominican house of study in Naples. Pope Gregory X called him from Naples in 1274 to attend the Council of Lyons. Thomas had hardly begun the journey when he died at the Cistercian monastery of Fossanuova, south of Rome. He was only forty-nine, but he had written a hundred theological works whose clarity and insight won him recognition in the West as the "angelic doctor" and "universal teacher."

Aquinas's *Summa theologiae* is rivaled only by Dante's *The Divine Comedy* as a summation of medieval Christian thought. At twenty-one volumes, it may be the longest summary ever written, but its length reflects the vast scope of its subject. The *Summa* is divided into three basic parts, among which are arranged more than six hundred topic headings (Thomas called them "questions"). Under each of these come specific questions or "articles"— more than three thousand altogether. For example, under the "question" of "Sacred Doctrine" Thomas listed ten articles, including "Is sacred doctrine necessary?", "Is it a science?" and "Should it make use of metaphorical or symbolic language?" Each article includes a thorough investigation of the issue, employing the dialectical method found in Abelard (*Sic et non*) and Peter Lombard (*Sentences*), though in a more elaborate form. Thus, after posing each question Thomas stated arguments for the negative, gave arguments for the affirmative taken from scripture and the church fathers, offered a short essay on the subject in which he expressed his own views, and then concluded with responses to the arguments for the negative given at the beginning of the article. In this way he examined nearly every theological and philosophical issue of consequence to the medieval mind in a manner that was logically consistent, detailed in its analysis, and comprehensive in its assessment of the opinions of earlier authorities.

For Thomas, as for Aristotle, knowledge of the world comes to us through the senses. We cannot have direct knowledge of anything beyond what our senses describe for us, though it is possible to gain indirect knowledge of some things — another person's mind, for example, and certain aspects of God — by reasoning analogically with reference to what we know of the material world. We can also know something of the supernatural realm, though only what God has revealed through scripture and nature. Some things, however, such as the incarnation and the Trinity, will always be mysteries because they are suprarational (beyond the grasp of human reason). This does not mean that they are untrue or irrational, any more than a person's inability to understand calculus or astrophysics means that they are untrue or irrational. It is simply the case that suprarational things are incomprehensible without the assistance of divine grace. Ultimately, there is perfect agreement between reason and revelation, for both come from God.

For Thomas, both reason and revelation can lead us to knowledge of the one truth that matters more than any other — the existence of God.[34] Knowledge of God's existence is necessary for salvation, he said, but even an unsophisticated person who pauses to consider nature will see God revealed there. God's existence can also be demonstrated using reason. Thomas rejected Anselm's ontological argument because of its dependence on the unverifiable existence of a particular concept of God in people's minds. He also dismissed the Augustinian idea that we find God by probing the depths of our souls. In their place he offered five proofs for the existence of God known collectively as the "cosmological argument" because each is based on observation of the world, or cosmos. According to the first, every motion is caused by some previous motion, pointing back either to an infinite regression, which is impossible, or to a Prime Mover (God).[35] The second is similar, holding that because every cause must itself be caused by something prior to it, there must be a First Cause. The third argument is based on the observation that things pass in and out of existence, each being caused by those prior to it and being the cause of others still. Only the universe does not pass out of existence. Obviously, its existence does not depend on such "contingent" things. There must be something necessary and noncontingent on which it does depend. That something is God. These first three arguments are based on Aristotelian empiricism; for the fourth Thomas turned to the idealism of Plato and Augustine. We see in the world around us, he said, things that exhibit varying degrees of virtues such as goodness, truth, and beauty. Our ideas about perfection and degrees of imperfection (for example, "good" and "better") imply the existence of a best or perfect being who is the standard that gives meaning to such notions. That being is God. The fifth and final argument is based on the observation that there is order in nature, not only among living things but also among inanimate things, which are incapable of ordering themselves. There must be some intelligent being who is the cause of such order. That being is God.

Thomas went on to say that although reason can demonstrate *that* God is, it cannot give us certain knowledge of *what* God is. It would be foolish, he said, to suppose that our small minds might comprehend the Infinite. It is difficult for us even to grasp the fact that God is an immaterial spirit, because the human intellect, which is completely dependent upon the senses, has no direct knowledge or experience of things such as "immateriality" and "spirit." The best we can do is imagine that God is somehow like things we do know in the sensible world and consider carefully what he has revealed of himself in scripture.

Despite these limitations, Thomas confidently asserted that God's nature is expressed in the divine name he made known to Moses in Exodus 3:14: "He Who Is."[36] Taking this as an identification of God with Being itself, he found the same idea also in Aristotle. Like Aristotle, then, Thomas spoke of God as "pure activity" and as the one perfect being who has no potential because he is already everything that he can be. Although he had no need to do so (for divine perfection includes perfect self-sufficiency), God has expressed his perfect goodness by calling into being and sustaining creation. All things are arranged below him in descending order of their degrees of perfection, with the spiritual above the material, for "the more noble a form is, the higher it rises above corporeal matter."[37] All are subject to divine **providence**. All tell us something about the Creator. If, for example, we observe in ourselves and others qualities such as love, patience, and beauty, reason tells us that these must have their origins in God, who is the source of all good things and in whom they exist to an infinite degree. Similarly, the unity that is evident in the operation and appearance of the world suggests the oneness of God.

Just below God and at the highest level of creation are the angels, immortal and incorporeal beings who serve as God's agents in making his will known to the world. Angels guide the heavenly bodies on their courses and care for human beings, each of whom has a special guardian angel. Thomas wrote nearly a hundred pages on the intelligence, knowledge, habits, and emotions of angels and the organization of the angelic hierarchy in heaven. Like most medieval Christians, he also believed in demons who served Satan by leading souls astray. He warned that they have the power to fill human minds with lies and sometimes take human form to deceive the unwary. Rejoicing in the pain and confusion they cause, demons enable witches to harm children with the evil eye, make men impotent, seduce unsuspecting women, and stir up trouble in countless other ways.

Thomas's anthropological views were among the most provocative in his *Summa*, for here he boldly departed from Plato, Augustine, and twelve hundred years of Christian tradition in denying that human beings are composites of discrete bodies and souls, with the soul being the true self. Instead, he followed Aristotle in holding that body and soul are so thoroughly bound up with each other that it is impossible to distinguish neatly between them, let alone to say that one or the other is the "real" person. At the same time, he considered the rational soul an immaterial reality and in this sense entirely different from the body. When the body dies the soul survives, though only as an incomplete personality that will remain dysfunctional until it is made whole again with the resurrection of the body on the Last Day. Here we see one of the many ways Thomas demonstrated that he was no slavish follower of Aristotle, for Aristotle had denied the immortality of the body and held that only the "active intellect" (which is universal rather than personal) endures forever.

Of all the activities of the soul, said Thomas, rational thought is the highest, for this activity makes knowledge and understanding possible. "The proper activity of a human being is to understand,"[38] he wrote in the *Summa;* in his treatise *On Truth* he added that the greatest achievement of the soul in this life would be to know "the whole order of the universe" and the causes of all things.[39] Such knowledge would bring a happiness unsurpassed in the world. And yet it would still be imperfect, for the supreme goal of human existence is attained only after death, when in heaven the faithful attain to the Beatific Vision. This is a direct and overwhelming experience of God, the Lord of Being, in whom every perfection is realized and from whom all goodness and truth derive. To see God in this way, to know him as do the saints in heaven and find one's own being in him, is unending rapture, perfect and eternal bliss.[40]

Given this glorious possibility of heavenly union with God, Thomas reasonably defined moral goodness as behavior that leads to it. But goodness is difficult, for we are born with the stain of original sin. Originally, Adam possessed not only the four natural virtues of prudence, justice, courage, and self-control, but also an additional or "superadded gift" of the three Christian and supernatural virtues of faith, hope, and love. These enabled him to seek and love God and made him pleasing in God's eyes. But Adam lost the supernatural virtues when he turned away from God and chose to sin. As a result, he was left incomplete, no longer intent upon God and unable to please him. Worse, this condition was passed down through all later generations. Although the four natural virtues still allow for a limited happiness, our state of incompletion leaves us far short of the ultimate happiness God intended for us.

Like all Christian theologians, Thomas based his theory of salvation on the operation of divine grace, the free and unmerited love of God. According to him, Christ's self-sacrifice, offered in love on behalf of humanity, constitutes a satisfaction (as in Anselm's theory) that more than makes up for the sin of the world. A reward is due him, but he cannot receive it because nothing can add to God's perfection. Instead, the merits of Christ's sacrifice are offered to human beings through an "infusion" of grace, thanks to which sins are forgiven, the superadded gift is restored, and a new habit of love for God begins to grow within the redeemed that is nourished by the sacraments and inspired by the example of Christ (as in Abelard's view). In this state the human will can cooperate with divine grace in performing good works that merit eternal life. Good works can even bring spiritual benefit to others, Thomas argued, because merit that goes beyond what is required for eternal life is added to the superabundant merits of Christ and the saints. These constitute the **treasury of merit** on which the Church can draw to mitigate or remove the penalties sinners would otherwise be obliged to suffer on earth and in purgatory.

Interestingly, Thomas argued against Anselm's position that Christ's suffering and death were necessary for salvation. God might have chosen some other means of redemption, Thomas maintained, but the fact that he chose to accomplish his purpose through the incarnation tells us that this method was (like God himself) the most reasonable and efficient. Thomas's theology also included a theory of predestination made necessary by his view that no one receives eternal life apart from God's decision to save. For Thomas, predestination results from God's choice to extend to some individuals an unmerited gift of prevenient grace (i.e., a grace that "comes before") that encourages the will to respond to him in righteousness and love. Those who do not receive this gift he allows to sin and to suffer the consequences. There is nothing in predestination that contradicts freedom of will, he insisted, for God brings about what he intends through the operation of "secondary causes"[41] that somehow allow sufficient room for human freedom.[42] Predestination is also made necessary by God's desire to manifest his goodness in human beings; the elect illustrate his mercy, the reprobate his justice. All of creation, in fact, proclaims God's goodness, from the lower "grades" of being to the higher. Even the evils that God allows play their part, for they can give rise to good things, make them shine all the more brightly by comparison, and sometimes prevent greater evils.[43] As for evil itself, Thomas followed the Neoplatonists in asserting that it is simply nonexistence — the absence of something that ought to exist. That which God has created is always good, though some things are better than others.

Like this brief sketch of his thought, Thomas left much unsaid. On 6 December 1273, just months before his death, he had a powerful mystical experience while celebrating mass. The secrets revealed to him, he said later, made all that he had thought and written seem "like straw." He never wrote another word. The third and final part of the *Summa* was completed by his friend and secretary, Friar Reginald of Piperno.

Much of the initial reaction to the *Summa theologiae* was negative. Some feared that Thomas had elevated reason over revelation. Others wondered what place the coldly abstract and impersonal god of Aristotle could possibly have in Christianity, which emphasized the personal qualities of God and the humanity of Christ. Still others were of-fended by Thomas's failure to distinguish clearly between the body and the soul and his reliance on a pagan philosopher. In 1277 the bishop of Paris, act-ing on behalf of Pope John XXI, condemned 219 propositions found in Thomas's works. That same year the archbishop of Canterbury persuaded the professors of theology at Oxford to denounce many as well. Thomas was defended against such actions by his old teacher Albert the Great and others who pressed for a more sensitive and open-minded as-sessment of his thought. Their success is indicated nowhere better than in Thomas's canonization a half-century after his death (1323). Thereafter, "Thomism" became the dominant force in Roman Catholic thought, a fact formally recognized in 1879 when Pope Leo XIII pronounced it the offi-cial philosophy of the Church. Ironically, this dec-laration came just as dramatic changes in western culture were about to raise questions concerning the suitability of Thomas's medieval theology in the modern era.

Women and the Virgin Mary

The medieval Church inherited all of the biblical, Greco-Roman, and Germanic traditions that held women to be morally, intellectually, and physically inferior to men. Negative attitudes were no doubt reinforced by its male clergy, whose vows of chastity could not have encouraged an appreciation of women. One of the most famous of medieval monks, Bernard of Clairvaux, complained that merely to spend time in the company of a woman presented an irresistible temptation to sin. "To be always with a woman and not to have intercourse with her," he said, "is more difficult than to raise the dead."[44] The belief that women were a constant danger to men was expressed with particular brutal-ity by Abbot Conrad of Marchtal in explaining why his monastic order would no longer accept nuns:

> We and our whole community of canons, recog-nizing that the wickedness of women is greater than all the other wickedness of the world, and that there is no anger like that of women, and that

the poison of asps and dragons is more curable and less dangerous to men than the familiarity of women, have unanimously decreed for the safety of our souls, no less than for that of our bodies and goods, that we will on no account receive any more sisters to the increase of our perdition, but will avoid them like poisonous animals.[45]

Popular attitudes toward women were not gen-erally so extreme, but they did limit women's op-portunities in life. Modern scholarship has rejected the old assumption that a medieval woman could choose only between becoming a nun or a house-wife, for few were either. The vast majority of women worked outside the home and alongside men in shops and fields, because most families could not afford the luxury of allowing a capable la-borer to remain at home. Of those who desired to become nuns, only a few succeeded, for convents generally preferred an aristocratic membership and required a sizable dowry from postulants. Those fortunate enough to join a community of nuns found a welcome refuge from the harsh realities of secular life; some also found the chance to exercise leadership as abbesses and mothers superior. But these offices were the only positions of authority available to women in the Church, and those who held them were still under the authority of men.

In the twelfth century the shortage of religious communities for women led many to embrace less conventional forms of religious life. Thousands were attracted to movements led by charismatic leaders such as Robert of Arbrissel, a priest who preached the virtues of asceticism throughout the Loire Val-ley, and Norbert of Xanten, an evangelist renowned for the miracles he performed in northern France and Flanders. At first these charismatic leaders made little attempt to supervise the activities of their fol-lowers or even to enforce gender segregation among them. Within a generation, however, both move-ments yielded to pressure from the Church and set-tled into patterns of organization resembling those of monastic orders.

But the piety of medieval women was not always so easily managed or contained. Many simply de-vised their own ways of consecrating themselves to God. The most famous are the **Beguines** — unmar-ried and uncloistered women from the Rhineland,

Germany, and the Low Countries who rejected formal monastic vows and rules. Their male counterparts, far fewer in number, were known as **Beghards**. Sometimes living alone but more often forming themselves into irregular communities, the Beguines took no orders from the ecclesiastical hierarchy and sought holiness through poverty, prayer, chastity, and charity. By the end of the twelfth century, women in other parts of Europe, such as the *umiliate* ("humble women") of Italy, were also setting out on their own. In Lorraine, England, Italy, and Bavaria there were so many women living as religious solitaries that they outnumbered their male counterparts.[46] Both the Church and society regarded the presence of these women as dangerous and disturbing, for their numbers were large and they resisted efforts to make them fit into social positions that made them subservient to men or were otherwise inconsistent with their ideals.[47]

One of the paradoxes of medieval Christianity is that even as the Church excluded women from ecclesiastical office, perpetuated gynophobic attitudes, and even sanctioned wife-beating when necessary for the maintenance of domestic order, it also recognized marriage as a sacrament, made serious efforts to protect the rights of nuns, and acknowledged the dignity of women in general. Peter the Lombard upheld the spiritual and marital equality of women when he argued that Eve had been created from Adam's rib, rather than from his head or feet, because God intended her to be his partner rather than to rule him or be ruled by him. Peter Abelard went a step further, noting that the women who followed Christ were dearer to Christ than his male disciples and that it was to them that Christ first appeared after his resurrection. Abelard believed that women elevated humanity to a level of refinement and spirituality uncommon among men.[48] Such views were consistent with the ideals of chivalry and courtly love that became popular among the secular aristocracy in the twelfth and thirteenth centuries. These included the belief that women embodied the virtues to which all Christians should aspire and were therefore worthy of veneration by men, who would benefit from service and devotion to them.

It is no coincidence, then, that the number of women canonized as saints rose sharply during this period. To the medieval mind, of course, no saint was greater than the Virgin Mary. Through humble and obedient Mary, the very antithesis of proud and disobedient Eve, God had chosen to come into the world to save humanity from sin. Popular piety imagined Mary honored and glorified in the highest reaches of heaven, but every Christian knew how eager she was to help lowly sinners in need of her love and protection. Tales of her miraculous interventions described her as supporting with her unseen hands a thief about to be hanged, curing a sick monk by giving him her own milk, and saving the reputation of a wayward nun by taking her place until she repented of her sin and returned to her convent. At a time when many still regarded Christ fearfully as the stern judge of the Last Day, the Virgin Mary was seen as a benevolent intermediary whose intercessions her Son could not refuse. In gratitude for her favors and the inspiration of her example, monks, knights, peasants, and townspeople pledged themselves to her service, poets praised her virtues, images of her filled the cities and countryside, and hymns proclaiming her glory rose above cathedrals dedicated in her honor. Few features of popular Christianity in the Middle Ages were as visible or widespread as the veneration of the Virgin.

Cathedrals: Praise in Stone and Glass

Between 1000 and 1300, western Europe experienced an explosion of church-building. Great cathedrals (from *cathedra*, the "chair" from which a resident bishop preached) climbed steadily to dizzying heights in the capitals of dioceses. Lesser churches sprang up in surrounding towns and villages. The zeal of the cathedral builders was fired by their conviction that no work had a higher purpose — for the cathedral, or any church for that matter, was the most visible symbol of Christ on earth. In this sacred place, sinners were cleansed of original sin in baptism and received spiritual nourishment in the eucharist and other sacraments. In church the saving words of the gospel were heard and holy relics were displayed for the edification and healing of the faithful. Here men and women found the means by which to rise from the world's darkness into heavenly glory. Thus, the introit from the special mass celebrated at the consecration of new churches solemnly declared, "This is a place of awe. Here is the court of God and the gate of Heaven."[49]

In addition to being its spiritual center, a town's central church was also a kind of civic center where people gathered to socialize, conduct business, discuss local affairs, and enjoy morality plays and other entertainments. Cathedrals in particular were important sources of civic pride, for their size and beauty reflected the wealth, ability, and piety of the people who built them. Intercity competition was fierce, with each community striving to build a church longer, wider, and, most important, higher than all others.

ROMANESQUE STYLE

Until the middle of the twelfth century the standard style of church architecture was Romanesque, named for its dependence on ancient Roman architecture. Romanesque was especially reliant on the floorplan of the ancient basilica, a public hall built in the shape of an elongated rectangle. When adapted for use as a church, the basilica was bisected by a transept, giving it the form of a Latin cross. At one end was a semicircular apse, under whose half-dome stood the altar and around whose curved wall were arranged the seats of the priests and bishop. The church was divided along its length by a central nave flanked on either side by parallel rows of columns. At first the roof was low, flat, and wooden, but a dramatic improvement was made when the nave was spanned with a stone barrel vault—in effect, the underside of a round arch drawn horizontally through space. The vastly increased weight of these larger buildings was supported by massive walls, buttresses built directly against them, and three or more stories of round arches introduced between the columns along the nave. Windows were few and small, to minimize pressure on the walls, though a series of windows was incorporated along one story, typically the third, known as the clerestory ("clear-story") for its openness to light.

Although most of the essential features of Romanesque style existed as early as the fourth century,[50] it was not until the period ranging from the middle of the eleventh century to the end of the thirteenth that innovative builders brought it to the peak of its expression. In France, the solid wall of the apse was replaced by an ambulatory, or semicircular aisle, opening out into radiating chapels. This improvement not only added beauty where there had once been plain stone, but also allowed for the easy passage of pilgrims around the altars of churches like those at Vézelay, Cluny, and Conques, where famous relics were housed. German builders gave their attention to towers and massive western facades, as at Mainz, Speyer, and Worms. In Normandy and England the development of a distinctively Norman style was realized in Durham Cathedral, where rib vaulting, achieved by the diagonal intersection of arches, allowed for thinner, more graceful walls by supporting weight more efficiently. Italian Romanesque almost always featured bell towers, or campaniles, which stood apart from the main structure of the church, the most famous example being the Leaning Tower of Pisa.

The medieval woman or man who entered a Romanesque cathedral for the first time would have been astounded by its spectacular size. The largest Romanesque church, the third abbey church at Cluny, had a length of 555 feet and a vault that reached 96 feet—nearly ten stories. Insulated from the outer world and earthly cares by thick stone walls, the interior was illuminated only by the faint light that filtered through its clerestory windows and the gentle glow of candles and lamps around the altar. Once the mass began, the great structure resounded with the voices of the choir, who sang the service. Prayers, song, and the eyes of the priests and laypeople were drawn upward to the vast expanse of space above them, a powerful reminder of the heavenly heights for which they yearned. Altogether, the experience must have aroused a sense of awe appropriate to the mysteries celebrated there.

Figure 6.3 Romanesque architecture This view of a side aisle in the Church of La Madeleine at Vézelay in France illustrates some of the features of Romanesque architecture: round arches, barrel vaulting, and immense weight resting on thick columns.

GOTHIC STYLE

Even as the genius of Romanesque style was astonishing twelfth-century Europe, a new form of church architecture was taking shape in the abbey of St. Denis a few miles outside Paris. This was the Gothic style, named by early critics who considered it crude and barbaric. Unlike Romanesque, which evolved slowly, the creation of Gothic occurred in a brief span of eleven years (1133–44) during which St. Denis's Abbot Suger, who had counseled Peter Abelard during his unhappy stay there, directed the rebuilding of his monastery's church. The old church was too small to hold the hundreds of pilgrims who crowded inside hoping to glimpse the relics of St. Denis and a nail from the cross of Jesus,

Figure 6.4 Gothic cathedral architecture made extensive use of rib vaulting, screens of colored glass, and pointed arches, all of which can be seen here.

and Suger complained that women could approach the altar only by walking upon the heads of men. But the abbot wanted much more than a larger church. Suger envisioned a building less earthbound than the heavy Romanesque churches, a space in stone filled with light and grace, a sacred place in which the worshiper would feel caught up "in some strange region of the universe which neither exists in the slime of the earth nor entirely in the purity of Heaven."[51]

To achieve this effect, Suger combined three architectural forms that were already well known — the pointed arch, the rib vault, and the flying buttress. Pointed arches allowed him to raise the vaulting of his church to a height beyond what would have been allowed by round ones, which are less efficient in bearing weight. Rib vaults formed by intersecting pointed arches allowed for more complexity in the roof vaulting, for they could be built to cover a greater variety of rectangular shapes than vaults formed by round arches. By supporting the walls with graceful flying buttresses — thin stone arms reaching up to the building through empty space — Suger took much of the pressure off them. This allowed him to make the walls thin, even delicate, and to fill them with windows so expansive that in some places the church seemed to be made of glass rather than stone.

The effect was spectacular. We can imagine the amazement of King Louis VII, Queen Eleanor, the twenty bishops, and the hundreds of knights and nobles who attended the consecration of the new basilica of St. Denis in 1144. They found its interior bathed in glorious light, a symbol of divine

Figure 6.5 Reims Cathedral Dating from the thirteenth century, Reims Cathedral is considered one of the greatest examples of Gothic architecture. Its vertical lines and light-filled interior were intended to give worshipers a sense of being caught up in a spiritual realm unlike that of the everyday world outside.

grace. Transformed by stained glass into soft rays of exquisite, gemlike color, the light fell gently on the faithful—and on the altar, too, where all present knew that grace would soon produce the miracle of the eucharist. Soaring vertical lines in the church's windows, arches, and walls contributed to the impression that they had indeed been lifted into a wonderfully strange and ethereal region of the universe, just as Suger had intended.

Within a few years Gothic cathedrals were rising throughout France, first at Sens and Noyon, then at Senlis and Laon. But these were quickly eclipsed by the Cathedral of Notre Dame in Paris, begun in 1163 under the direction of Maurice de Sully. At four hundred feet in length and with a nave 114 feet high, its extraordinary dimensions covered 63,000 square feet and provided enough room for ten thousand people to gather inside. To make the outside of the building as magnificent as its interior, Maurice made exterior sculpture an important part of its design. This is especially true of the west facade, which he filled with detailed scenes featuring the Virgin Mary—Notre Dame de Paris ("Our Lady of Paris"), to whom the cathedral was dedicated. In these she is shown carrying the infant Christ in her arms, as the Queen of Heaven, as interceding with Christ on behalf of sinners at the Final Judgment, and being "assumed" bodily into heaven after her death.

The cathedral at Chartres, begun three decades after Notre Dame, is considered by many to be an even finer example of Gothic architecture. Chartres, too, was dedicated to the Virgin, and her tunic, its most prized relic, made it a major destination of pilgrims. Here, as at Notre Dame, sculpture became part of the building itself. In the portals alone there are nearly two thousand carved images. Everywhere, it seems, figures of men, women, children, demons, angels, and the persons of the Trinity describe the content of the faith. So do Chartres' famous stained glass windows, which tell the whole story of Christianity, beginning with Bible stories and concluding with depictions of the people of Chartres themselves. If the cathedral at Chartres sometimes seems alive, it is little wonder, for it speaks through nearly ten thousand figures in glass and stone.

The achievements of Notre Dame de Paris and Chartres prompted a competition in cathedral building that focused on the height of the vaulting. Chartres, begun in 1194, rose to a height of 123 feet, only to be outdone by a mere two feet by the cathedral at Reims, begun in 1211. Seven years later work began on a cathedral at Amiens that ascended to nearly 140 feet. Finally, Beauvais, begun in 1247, attained a height of 157 feet. Tragically, it collapsed soon after its completion. It was rebuilt, but fell again. Beauvais was never finished, for Gothic style and medieval engineering had reached their limits.

Figure 6.6   Cathedral of Notre Dame, Paris This view of the cathedral illustrates its great height (the interior vaulting reaches 115 feet), one of its famous rose windows, and the flying buttresses that support the weight of the building's walls.

Most of the Gothic cathedrals still stand as enduring monuments to the faith of the people who built them. They are impressive, not only because of their size and beauty, but also because they communicate so effectively in the language of architecture the same truths taught in homilies, music, and theology. One can easily see the cross, grace, and God's transcendence represented in their cruciform shape, light-filled interiors, and lofty heights, but each expressed the teachings of the Church in other, subtler ways. It has even been argued that their harmonious arrangement of contradictory motifs is an expression of the same impulse to reconcile the seemingly irreconcilable that moved the schoolmen to seek a harmony of faith and reason.[52] Like Aquinas's *Summa*, they have often been described as comprehensive statements of the content of a mature Catholic Christianity.

Summary

During the eleventh through thirteenth centuries, western Christianity benefited enormously from reforms that began in monasteries but ultimately strengthened the entire structure of the Church. The positive effects of reform were perhaps most evident in the papacy. The popes of the late twelfth and early thirteenth centuries enjoyed far greater prestige and control over the Church than their predecessors and were often more than a match for the kings and emperors with whom they came into

Figure 6.7   The Damned This sculpture is from the cathedral in Orvieto, Italy, begun in 1290. Its images of the terror experienced by souls about to enter hell were meant to illustrate the danger of sin and the importance of salvation.

conflict. The vigor of the Church was also demonstrated by the theologians of this era, who confidently attempted to show that the revealed truths of Christianity could be verified by human reason, and by the Crusades, which sought to restore Christian rule over the Holy Land. But success was accompanied by failure and disappointment. By the end of the thirteenth century the papacy was entering a period of decline. The Crusades failed to achieve their military objectives and, thanks to the sack of Constantinople in 1204, dramatically deepened the rift between the eastern and western churches. Finally, despite the many positive effects of reform, there were still abundant grounds for criticism of the clergy. As we will see in chapter 7, cries for reform and renewal in the Church would intensify in the fourteenth and fifteenth centuries.

QUESTIONS FOR REVIEW AND REFLECTION

1. What kinds of ecclesiastical reform movements were at work in the high Middle Ages? What were their consequences?

2. What were the causes and consequences of the Crusades?

3. What was scholasticism? How did it differ from earlier Christian theology? What were its goals and methods? In what ways did it find support in the philosophy of Aristotle?

4. What were the essential features of the thought of Thomas Aquinas?

NOTES

1. Beginning with Frederick I in 1157.
2. Clerical celibacy was not yet widely enforced.

3. "The Foundation Charter of Cluny (910)," trans. E. F. Henderson, in *The Crisis of Church and State: 1050–1300*, ed. B. Tierney (Englewood Cliffs, N.J.: Prentice Hall, 1964), 28–29.

4. T. Bokenkotter, *A Concise History of the Catholic Church*, rev. ed. (New York: Doubleday, 1990), 132.

5. Ailred of Rievaulx, *The Mirror of Love* 1.17, in *The Eerdman's Handbook to the History of Christianity*, ed. T. Dowley (Grand Rapids, Mich.: Eerdman's, 1977), 304.

6. Tierney, *Crisis*, 37.

7. Tierney, *Crisis*, 31–32.

8. Tierney, *Crisis*, 42–44.

9. Tierney, *Crisis*, 42.

10. W. Walker et al., *A History of the Christian Church*, 4th ed. (New York: Scribner's, 1985), 273.

11. W. Cannon, *History of Christianity in the Middle Ages* (New York: Abingdon Press, 1960), 157.

12. Walker et. al., *History*, 275.

13. R. W. Southern, *Western Society and the Church in the Middle Ages* (New York: Penguin, 1970), 100–102.

14. For example, Bishop Otto of Constance, to whom Gregory directed an angry letter of rebuke in December 1074. See Tierney, *Crisis*, 48–49.

15. J. Gonzalez, *A History of Christian Thought*, vol. 2, rev. ed. (Nashville: Abingdon Press, 1987), 140–41, 184–85. See also Gregory's references to Gelasius I in his letter to Bishop Hermann of Metz in B. Pullan, *Sources for the History of Medieval Europe* (London: Blackwell, 1966), 149, 151.

16. Pullan, *Sources*, 148.

17. Southern, *Western Society*, 102.

18. Gregory's letter of December 1075 to Henry refers to the latter's failure to observe the promises he made "in the Milan affair." See Tierney, *Crisis*, 57–59.

19. Tierney, *Crisis*, 59–60.

20. Tierney, *Crisis*, 61–62.

21. Victor VI (1159–64), Paschal III (1164–68), and Calixtus III (1168–78).

22. Tierney, *Crisis*, 132.

23. *Oxford Dictionary of the Christian Church*, 3rd ed., ed. E. A. Livingstone (New York: Oxford University Press, 1997), s.v. "indulgences."

24. Canon II of the Council of Clermont (1095) made this official: "If any man sets forth to liberate the church of God at Jerusalem out of devotion alone, and not for love of glory or of gain, the journey shall be accounted a complete penance on his part." See Pullan, *Sources*, 58.

25. The ontological argument was later criticized by Thomas Aquinas, who argued that human beings are incapable of constructing an adequate definition of God. Immanuel Kant objected for the same reason. In the early modern era it was defended by Descartes and Leibniz. It was championed by G. W. F. Hegel in the nineteenth century and C. Hartshorne and A. Plantinga in the twentieth.

26. Emphasis ours.

27. F. Heer, *The Medieval World: Europe, 1100–1350*, trans. J. Sondheimer (Cleveland and New York: World, 1962), 78.

28. Peter Abelard, *The Story of Abelard's Adversities*, trans. J. T. Muckle (Toronto: Pontifical Institute of Medieval Studies, 1964), 28.

29. Abelard constantly revised this treatise, whose Latin title is *De unitate et trinitate divina*, during the course of his lifetime, issuing it once as the *Theologia summi boni*, again as the *Theologia christiana*, and also as the first part of his greatest work, the *Theologia*.

30. Peter Abelard, *Exposition of the Letter to the Romans 2*, in *The Christian Theology Reader*, ed. A. McGrath (Cambridge, Mass.: Blackwell, 1995), 183–84.

31. Of course, these two approaches were not mutually exclusive. See, for example, Paul Tillich, *A History of Christian Thought* (New York: Simon & Schuster, 1967), 136–37.

32. G. K. Chesterton, *Saint Thomas Aquinas: "The Dumb Ox"* (Garden City, N.Y.: Image Books, 1956), 61.

33. Until recently, more popularly but less correctly known as the *Summa Theologica*.

34. Thomas Aquinas, *Summa Theologiae* 1a.1.1.

35. The Latin word *motus*, usually translated as "motion," can also mean "change." Some scholars prefer the latter translation.

36. This translates the Latin of the Vulgate: *Qui est*. The consonants *YHWH* constitute the name of God in Hebrew. In English, vowels are added to make *Yahweh*. This name is based on the Hebrew verb for "to be" and suggests that God is the source of all being and the one who sustains all existing things.

37. Aquinas, *Summa Theologiae* 1.76.1.

38. Aquinas, *Summa Theologiae* 1.76.1.

39. Aquinas, *On Truth* 2.2.

40. For Thomas, the blessed "see" the essence of God but never grasp it completely, for only a perfect and infinite being could fully comprehend the Infinite.

41. Aquinas, *Summa Theologiae* 1.22.3.

42. Aquinas, *Summa Theologiae* 1.23.5.

43. Aquinas, *Summa Theologiae* 1.23.5.

44. Bernard of Clairvaux, *Sermones in cantica* 65, cited in Southern, *Western Society*, 314.

45. From E. L. Hugo, *Annales Praemonstratenses* 2.147, quoted in Southern, *Western Society*, 314. Conrad belonged to the Premonstratensian Order.

46. J. K. McNamara, *Sisters in Arms: Catholic Nuns through Two Millennia* (Cambridge, Mass.: Harvard University Press, 1996), 239.

47. For excellent treatments of women and women's spirituality in the Middle Ages, see McNamara, *Sisters in Arms*, 99–383, and D. Herlihy, *Opera Muliebria:*

Women and Work in Medieval Europe (New York: McGraw-Hill, 1990). See also Southern, *Western Society,* 315–18, on the Cistercian nuns who gladly followed the rule of the order but refused to accept the authority and discipline of their male superiors.

48. Heer, *The Medieval World,* 85.
49. Heer, *The Medieval World,* 317.
50. For example, in the cathedral of Aquileia in Veneto, Italy.
51. E. Panofsky, *Abbot Suger on the Abbey Church of St. Denis and Its Art Treasures* (Princeton: Princeton University Press, 1946), 65.
52. E. Panofsky, *Gothic Architecture and Scholasticism* (Latrobe, Penn.: Archabbey Press, 1951), 67–88.

CHAPTER 7

Dissent, Division, and Reform in the High and Late Middle Ages

Overview

In chapter 6 we discussed the flowering of Christian culture in the eleventh through thirteenth centuries, a period that historians call the high Middle Ages. Although this was a time of great achievement in areas such as theology, church architecture, and monastic reform, it was also a time of growing dissatisfaction with the political intrigues and material interests of the Church. As we will see in this chapter, by the beginning of the thirteenth century a variety of movements calling for a return to spiritual values and concerns had taken shape. The Church sanctioned some of these groups and encouraged them to work for its revitalization; others it condemned as heretical.

Forces contributing to dissent and division increased during the late Middle Ages (roughly, the fourteenth and fifteenth centuries), a period of dramatic change for both the Church and society in general. In the West, the late Middle Ages saw the devastating effects of plague, the breakdown of traditional social institutions, and the beginning of the Renaissance — a revival of interest in Greek and

Roman culture that began in Italy and spread northward. In this age of transition the features of medieval civilization began to fade as society turned slowly toward modernity. Feudal monarchies gradually gave way to more centralized national governments with strong monarchs. The economic power of the growing middle class began to threaten the position of the old feudal nobility. Religion remained a dominant factor in nearly all aspects of life, but here and there signs of increasing secularism were beginning to show.

In many ways, this was a period of decline for the western Church. The papacy spent much of the fourteenth century in exile in France and then suffered through four decades of schism as rival popes claimed to be the legitimate successors of St. Peter. Ecclesiastical corruption increased. Standards fell in monasteries and convents as well as among the secular clergy. For growing numbers of Christians, the Church bore little resemblance to the spirit-filled community of believers described in the New Testament. But there were also positive developments. Groups committed to reform and renewal within the Church made progress. Mysticism flourished. There were also important advances in theology as

189

Christian thinkers investigated the implications of nominalism and reconsidered older issues, including the question of the Church's place in the world.

The eleventh through fifteenth centuries were also a time of great change in the East, which was powerfully affected by the decline and eventual collapse of the Byzantine Empire. As Orthodoxy in the Balkans struggled for survival, the Orthodox Church in Russia thrived with the support of rulers in Kiev, and later, Moscow. It was also during this period that cultural, political, and theological differences led to a separation of Roman Catholic and Eastern Orthodox Christianity.

Our primary focus in this chapter will be on the western Church in the fourteenth and fifteenth centuries, but we will have occasion to look as far back as the eleventh century when tracing the roots of the late medieval religious dissent and examining the events that led to the final break between Rome and Constantinople. A brief description of the later histories of some of the smaller churches of Africa and Asia, whose origins were described in chapters 4 and 5, will also take us outside the late medieval time frame.

The West in the Late Middle Ages

In the fourteenth and fifteenth centuries the political foundations of western Europe shifted as the Holy Roman Empire weakened and national monarchies grew more powerful. At the same time, the agricultural and economic systems that had brought stability and prosperity in earlier years proved unable to meet increasing demands. Their limitations combined with war, natural disasters, and the uncertainties that accompany political change to make the late Middle Ages a time of severe difficulties for the vast majority of Europeans.

DECLINE OF THE HOLY ROMAN EMPIRE

In chapters 5 and 6 we saw that Charlemagne and the Franks revived the western part of the Roman Empire in the ninth century and that both the idea of a Christian empire and the center of political power shifted eastward to Germany in the tenth. The German kings who claimed the title of emperor between 962 and 1250 expanded their influence far beyond their own borders, so that in addition to nearly all of what is now Germany, the Holy Roman Empire included northern Italy, eastern France, Belgium, the Netherlands, **Bohemia**, and western Austria. By the reign of Henry IV (1056–1106), however, the papacy and the German nobility were successfully challenging the power of the German emperors. The last of the great Holy Roman Emperors was Frederick II. After his death in 1250 both the empire and the ideal of a united western Christendom fell into gradual decline.[1] This worked to the advantage of the papacy, whose authority over the Church and sovereignty in the Papal States in central Italy had been threatened by the German emperors.

For a century after Frederick's death, powerful families fought to control the imperial office. Then, in 1356, Emperor Charles IV (1347–78) issued the *Golden Bull,* a decree requiring that future emperors be chosen by seven *electors*: the **archbishops** of Cologne, Trier, and Mainz, the secular princes of Saxony, Brandenburg, and the Palatinate, and the king of Bohemia. Under this arrangement the electors assumed such great importance that they had almost complete autonomy in their own territories. To protect their position, they generally chose weak and unthreatening emperors. As a result, the Holy Roman Empire rapidly became decentralized. The emperor had no imperial army with which to enforce his will, no reliable system for collecting taxes to finance his government, and no imperial courts through which to render justice. This enabled lesser nobles to follow the electors in ruling their lands almost as if they were independent states. By the time the Protestant Reformation began early in the sixteenth century, political disunity in Germany had created an ideal climate for religious dissent.

Decentralization also had important consequences in Italy. Economically robust northern city-states like Florence, Venice, and Milan gained independence from the emperor and established themselves as major regional powers. In central Italy the papacy struggled with local nobles over the Papal States in the fourteenth century and then gained control over them in the fifteenth. Divided after 1282 into the kingdoms of Sicily and Naples, southern Italy fell into a long period of decline.

POLITICAL DEVELOPMENTS IN FRANCE, ENGLAND, AND SPAIN

Like the Holy Roman Empire, the feudal monarchies of France and England also experienced important changes during this period. Serious economic and military demands were imposed on both as they fought the Hundred Years' War (1337–1453) over disputed territories in France. Although the English had won most of northern France by 1429, in that year the French were rallied by the peasant girl Joan of Arc, who turned the tide of events in their favor. Approaching Charles, the timid and disinherited son of the late king Charles VI, Joan told him that God had revealed to her his desire that Charles defeat the English and take the crown that rightfully belonged to him. After a resounding victory over the English at Orleans by a French army that included Joan dressed as a soldier, Charles found the courage to assume the throne. When the fighting ended twenty-four years later, the English had been driven from nearly all of France. In addition to fighting each other, both countries were torn by civil wars that pitted kings against their nobles and nobles against each other. Peasant revolts made this difficult situation even worse.[2]

The confusion brought on by these crises allowed for the transformation of the French and English monarchies into more centralized governments whose kings were much less dependent upon the support of the feudal nobility. By the end of the fifteenth century, French kings like Louis XI (1461–83) were strong enough to impose direct taxes on their kingdom and pay for a royal army. In England, Henry VII (1485–1509) took advantage of the weakened state of the English nobles at the end of the War of the Roses (1455–84) to bring them under his control. His reign ended with the English people forged into a single nation ruled by the king and Parliament.

Centralization of political power also occurred in Spain, where two formerly antagonistic kingdoms were brought together in the marriage of Ferdinand of Aragon and Isabella of Castile in 1469. Although at first the two realms remained constitutionally separate, each having its own army, finances, and laws, their combined power allowed Ferdinand and Isabella to gain much firmer control over their nobles and the internal affairs of their kingdoms. They were also able to complete the reconquest of Spain with the defeat of Granada, its last Muslim outpost, in 1492. Tragically, this victory was followed in that same year by the expulsion of Spain's Jews and (later) Moors, or Spanish Muslims, who refused to convert to Christianity. As a result of the policies of Ferdinand and Isabella, the united Spain ruled by their grandson, the emperor Charles V (1519–56; he was also Charles I of Spain), was one of the largest and most powerful kingdoms in Europe.[3] But Spain had also lost the remarkable ethnic diversity and tolerance that had made it one of the most culturally vibrant regions in medieval Europe.

SOCIAL UNREST

The steady economic growth enjoyed by western Europe between roughly 1000 and 1300 had been sustained in large part by a growing population and improvements in agriculture. In the late Middle Ages, however, plague and a succession of famines sharply reduced the population. At the same time, agricultural production decreased due to incessant war, the scarcity of labor, and poor climatic conditions. These and other factors resulted in a depression that lingered until the middle of the fifteenth century, producing widespread disruptions that affected all levels of society. Nobles struggled to maintain the profits from their fiefs as agricultural prices fell due to lower demand and the cost of labor rose. Peasants were forced to pay higher taxes to finance wars that ravaged the lands they farmed. Peasant uprisings, which were frequent, were savagely crushed by coalitions of kings and nobles supported by the Church. The urban population also suffered as decreased demand for manufactured goods left many without work. Riots against city governments and guilds controlled by wealthy entrepreneurs were no more successful than peasant rebellions in the countryside.

THE BLACK DEATH

This dismal state of affairs was exacerbated by the infamous Black Death, a plague that struck Europe with sudden ferocity in the middle of the fourteenth century. Carried by rats infected by fleas, it was brought from the East by merchant ships to Mediterranean ports from which it quickly spread northward. Within two years after its arrival in Venice in 1347, it had reached England and Scandinavia. By 1350 roughly one-third of the population of Europe had died of the disease. By the early fifteenth century, periodic recurrences of the plague had left the population of western Europe at little more than half of what it had been in 1300.

The symptoms of plague included dark discolorations of the skin as well as severe fever, vomiting, muscular pain, and delirium. Death usually came within days after infection. According to the Florentine writer Boccaccio, who described the plague in his *Decameron* (1353), the sight of dead bodies lying in streets became so common that people gave little more notice to them than to goats. Corpses were often carted away to mass graves and buried without benefit of customary funeral rites.

Naturally, people wondered what could have caused such a calamity. Many concluded that the plague was a sign of divine wrath and attempted to atone for the world's sin through extreme forms of public penance. The most striking was self-flagellation, which one fourteenth-century observer described as follows:

> People could not think what to make of the affliction or what remedy to offer for it, but many believed that this was . . . divine vengeance on the sins of the world. Hence it came about that some began thenceforward to do great penance. . . . Among others, the people of Germany began to go through the country on the main roads in companies, carrying crucifixes, standards and great banners, as in processions; they went through the streets, two by two, singing loudly hymns to God and our Lady, rhymed and with music; then they assembled together and stripped to their chemises twice a day and beat themselves as hard as they could with knotted lashes embedded with needles, so that the blood flowed down from their shoulders on all sides.[4]

These German **flagellants** were not alone. Wearing coarse penitential shirts and carrying candles, whips, and crucifixes, throngs of barefoot penitents crowded roads everywhere in processions that typically lasted thirty-three days, one for each year Christ had lived. The less fanatical filled churches and flocked to the shrines of saints seeking protection from the death around them. Some, despairing of salvation, gave themselves over to drink and promiscuity. Still others vented their anger and frustration in violent outbursts against Jews. In Germany, for example, Jews were accused of intentionally spreading the plague by poisoning wells. Many were arrested and forced under torture to confess. Thousands of others fled eastward to escape such Christian brutality.[5]

For the Church, the plague had devastating consequences. In some regions so many priests, monks, and nuns died that the Church was represented only barely or not at all. Undefended church lands were sometimes seized by unscrupulous opportunists. Convents and monasteries were sacked by thugs and freebooters. Many spiritual communities simply disintegrated, leaving their members to join the swelling ranks of the displaced and disorderly. To make matters worse, this social and religious ferment came at a time when the Church was already hard pressed to deal with internal problems that had called into question its moral and structural integrity.

Decline in the Western Church

We saw in chapter 6 that in the thirteenth century the Church attained levels of leadership, organization, and independence that made it the most powerful of all western institutions. Much of its success was attributable to the reforms of the eleventh and twelfth centuries. These culminated in the pontificate of Innocent III (1198–1216), in whom the papacy reached the peak of its influence and prestige.

By the beginning of the fourteenth century, however, the papal office had fallen into serious decline, thanks in part to the demands of the papacy's continuing struggle against the German emperors.

There were also conflicts with the kings of France. As we have seen, despite his assertions of papal authority in the bull *Unam Sanctam* (1302), Boniface VIII (1294–1303) had been bullied and kidnapped by France's Philip IV. Philip was enabled to do this not only by the weakness of the papacy but also by national sentiment that favored French interests over those of the papacy.

THE BABYLONIAN CAPTIVITY

After the death of Boniface's successor, Benedict XI (1303–04), Philip used his influence to ensure the election of a French archbishop, who reigned as Clement V (1305–14). Sickly and inexperienced, Clement was completely dominated by the aggressive Philip, who pressured him into modifying *Unam Sanctam* and making other concessions. For four years Clement wandered about southern France, afraid of straying too far from the French king and fearful that his nationality and the turbulent state of Italian politics would put his life in danger in Rome. In 1309 he settled at Avignon, which would remain the residence of the papal court until 1377. Thus began what the Italian poet Petrarch (1304–74) dubbed the **Babylonian Captivity** after the years spent by the ancient Jews as captives in Babylon.

Although Avignon lay on the east bank of the river Rhone, and therefore just outside of French territory, popular opinion charged Clement with delivering the papacy into the hands of the French monarchs and regarded the Avignon popes as their willing pawns. Critics scoffed that there was no danger in Italy and that it was in any case an outrage for bishops of Rome to shun the city of St. Peter. Although it is true that all seven of the popes at Avignon were French and that most cardinals in the curia had French sees, modern scholars tend to be more sympathetic. They note that civil unrest in Rome did present real dangers to the papacy. They also point out that what Clement had intended to be only a brief stay in Avignon was extended by unforeseen circumstances, in particular the coercive intrigues of the French kings, and that the Avignon popes were generally worthy individuals who did their best to gain administrative control over the Church in troubled times and under difficult circumstances.[6]

The most immediate concerns of the Avignon popes were financial, for they no longer controlled revenues from the Papal States that they would have received had they remained in Rome. This was a serious problem, for the cost of maintaining the papacy was extremely high. The increasing centralization of ecclesiastical authority required a large administrative bureaucracy. Defending the interests of the Church against external threats was also expensive. The Avignon popes quickly realized that they would have to rely on funds generated by benefices, or church offices, which had long been regarded as properties that might be bought, sold, or exchanged for favors. Large sums were raised by increasing the number of benefices reserved for papal appointments. Some offices were left vacant so that the income they produced might be channeled directly to Avignon. Additional revenues were procured through the sale of indulgences, fees charged for matters handled in papal courts, and taxes on papal documents.

Avignon's efficiency in raising money made its popes wealthy, but their preoccupation with finances inevitably encouraged corruption and institutional insensitivity. The imposition of new taxes was so common that Edward III of England once remarked that the pope was supposed "to lead the Lord's sheep to pasture, not to fleece them."[7] No one, it seemed, was safe from the financial demands of the papacy. On a single day in 1328, one patriarch, five archbishops, thirty bishops, and forty-six abbots were excommunicated for defaulting on payments of ecclesiastical taxes.[8] Laypeople suffered not only from the burden of taxes but also from a lack of spiritual guidance when church offices were sold to persons with no interest in pastoral responsibilities.

THE GREAT SCHISM AND THE CONCILIAR MOVEMENT

Tensions over Avignon eased when Gregory XI (1370–78) returned the papacy to Rome in January 1377. But an even more troublesome issue arose two months later when, following Gregory's death, the cardinals came under pressure to choose an Italian pope. Yielding, they elected Urban VI (1378–89). Although he had always been known as a judicious and even-tempered man, the new pope shocked the French cardinals with his frequent rages, during which he made wild accusations and threatened to replace them with Italians. The frightened cardinals soon withdrew from Rome, declared Urban's election invalid, and denounced him as a demon and Antichrist. A few days later they elected a cousin of the French king as Clement VII (1378–94).[9]

This was the beginning of the Great Schism, four decades during which the Church and the West in general were divided by the claims of rival popes. Urban VI was recognized by the Holy Roman Empire, England, the Netherlands, Poland, and Portugal. Clement VII, who took up residence at Avignon, was supported by France, Castile, Aragon, Scotland, Austria, and Luxembourg. With two papal courts to finance, ecclesiastical tax collectors now resorted to even harsher means of raising revenues than they had used before. In Rome, an increasingly unstable Urban suspected his cardinals of plotting against him; he had some of them tortured and others thrown into the sea from his warship. The prestige of the papacy plummeted, and as it did the rival popes and their successors became the objects of popular disgust and derision.

When political and military attempts to end the conflict failed, both ecclesiastical and secular leaders turned to a third possibility — the church council. Advocates pointed out that the ancient Church had resolved its greatest issues in general councils that had greater authority than any single bishop, including the bishop of Rome. A council, they argued, would provide the legitimate means for restoring the unity of the Church.[10] In spite of the challenge that these **conciliarists** represented to papal authority, popular demand for a settlement was so intense that they were able to force a series councils between 1409 and 1449.

The first was convened in Pisa in 1409. Neither of the two reigning popes chose to attend, and when both were deposed the townspeople outside the cathedral gleefully burned them in effigy. The bishops then elected a new pope, Alexander V

(1409–10), and drew up a list of complaints about past abuses. No reforms were enacted, however, and the bishops departed Pisa apparently unaware that they had succeeded only in making a bad situation even worse, for now there were three popes instead of two: Gregory XII in Rome, Benedict XIII in Avignon, and Alexander V in Pisa.

A second council was convened in Constance in 1414. Its most famous decree (the *Sacrosancta* of 1415) asserted the authority of councils of bishops over both Church and pope:

> This holy Council of Constance . . . declares . . . that it has its authority immediately from Christ, and that all men of every rank and condition, including the Pope himself, [are] bound to obey it in matters concerning the Faith, the abolition of the schism, and the reformation of the Church of God.[11]

To ensure the continuing rule of councils, the bishops at Constance also provided that future councils should be called after five, seven, and then every ten years, each one being announced before the conclusion of its predecessor. Then, after the resignation of Gregory XII of Rome and the depositions of Benedict XIII of Avignon and John XXIII of Pisa, they elected a new pope, Martin V (1417–31), who promised to uphold all that they had accomplished. After forty years, the western Church once again had a single pope.[12]

The Council of Constance had succeeded in ending the Great Schism. Aside from this, however, it was a disappointment, for it took no action to end the extortions of papal tax collectors, bribery and favoritism in papal courts, simony, absenteeism of bishops from their episcopal sees, the lack of education and discipline among the clergy, and corruption in the curia. The bishops had intended to address these problems, but their organization along national lines and the consequent interference of national interests had prevented significant action.

Five years after the Council of Constance, Martin V dutifully convened another council, which met at Pavia (1423) and then Siena (1424). Little was accomplished, however, because the plague prevented many bishops from attending. Seven years later he summoned the Council of Basel (1431–49), which began in July 1431 under his successor, Eugenius IV (1431–47). By this time the papacy was eager for an end to conciliarism. Eugenius attempted to adjourn the council in December 1431, but the bishops were determined to continue their work. As at Constance, they declared their superiority to the pope. They then restricted his ability to profit from ecclesiastical taxes and episcopal appointments so sharply that their actions, had they remained in force, would have left the papacy completely dependent upon the council for financial support. These were dark days for Eugenius, who found himself pressured by secular rulers to accept the dictates of the council and in such danger from his enemies in Italy that at one point he had to flee Rome in disguise. In 1433 he reluctantly agreed to accept all of the council's actions. For a moment it seemed that the conciliarists had so revolutionized ecclesiastical government that the Church would thereafter be ruled by an ongoing council.

But the bishops had gone too far. Eugenius might well have accepted less drastic reforms, but it seemed to him that the Council of Basel had left his office with little more than symbolic significance. His chance to undo the damage it had done soon came in the form of an appeal from the Byzantine emperor and patriarch of Constantinople.[13] As invading Turks tightened their noose around Constantinople, the Greeks suggested that in return for military aid they would be willing to discuss healing the breach between the eastern and western churches. They asked only that the Council of Basel be moved to a city closer to Constantinople. Seeing his opportunity, Eugenius moved it to Ferrera in Italy. His hunch that the bishops would find the restoration of Christian unity more important than business in Basel proved correct. Before long all but the most radical conciliarists had left to join the pope's council — which, because it was moved once again, became known as the Council of Florence (1438–45). By 1449 there was nothing left for the Council of Basel to do but declare itself dissolved.

The final blow against conciliarism was struck by Pope Pius II (1458–64). In 1460 he promulgated the bull *Execrabilis,* which forbade appeals above the pope to the authority of any future council. The papacy had triumphed, but its victory still left the Church riddled with corruption and falling into ever greater disfavor with the laity. Reforms were urgently needed, but neither the popes nor the councils attempted to enact them. In the end, the only real beneficiaries of the conciliar movement were western monarchs who won concessions from popes who sought their support. Charles VII of France, for example, won extensive rights to revenues from church lands and over the French clergy.[14] Similar gains were made by other rulers in agreements that limited papal power and encouraged the development of national churches whose ties to Rome were weakened by their obligations and loyalties to national governments. Aside from this, the most important consequence of conciliarism was its success in demonstrating that the power structure of the Church could be challenged.

DECLINE IN MONASTICISM AND AMONG THE SECULAR CLERGY

The deterioration of the papacy in the fourteenth and fifteenth centuries was accompanied by decline in other areas of religious life. Conditions in monasteries and convents were increasingly criticized. In some cases accusations verged on the sensational. The emperor Sigismund, for example, alleged that members of cloistered communities in Germany had abandoned their monastic rules, forced the poor into serfdom so that they might themselves avoid hard labor, and were "great drinkers and eaters, as if, in their evil way of life, they were in the world."[15] Similar charges were made by other critics, but it appears that the great problem of late medieval monasticism was not so much extravagant misbehavior as mediocrity. Most complaints about monastic communities focused on laxity, laziness, and financial mismanagement. Worldly influences in monasteries and convents were no doubt encouraged by monks and nuns who did not have true religious vocations. Many were children of the nobility — sons who had no better career prospects and daughters who had no husbands. Plague, social dislocation, and economic depression also took their toll, discouraging discipline in many communities and threatening the very existence of others.

Figure 7.1 Breviary (fourteenth century) Breviaries are liturgical books containing Psalms, hymns, prayers, and other texts used in reciting the Divine Office. They played an important part in the spiritual practices of monks.

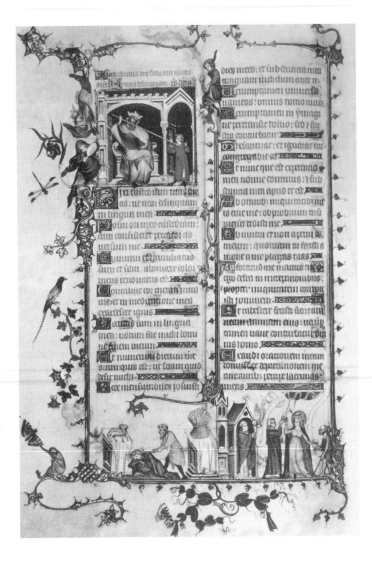

The secular clergy also came under criticism. The example set by members of the curia and other prelates is frequently cited as a major reason for clerical decline, for the wealth enjoyed by these "princes of the Church" and their cultivation of political power at Rome and Avignon suggested that worldly aims were as worthy as spiritual ones. The importance of money was also understood by the many bishops who paid for their offices and then recouped their investments by taxing the wealth of their dioceses. The absenteeism of bishops who rarely visited their sees was a frequent cause for complaint, as was **pluralism,** the practice of holding two or more benefices simultaneously.

As for the lower clergy, there is little reason to doubt that the great majority rendered valuable service in churches, hospitals, schools, almshouses, or other settings. But they, too, had their critics. The most commonly cited priestly faults were a lack of education, immorality, and a willingness to exploit the opportunities for personal gain that came with ecclesiastical office. A colorful example of shady practices is provided by the English poet Chaucer (1340–1400), whose *Canterbury Tales* describes a "pardoner"—not a priest, it seems, but one of those members of **minor orders** entrusted with some of the more routine responsibilities of the priesthood.[16] A shameless salesman, he makes a fortune preaching persuasive sermons against greed and by selling fake relics and indulgences. Traveling with a party of pilgrims to Canterbury, he boasts:

> By such hornswoggling I've won, year by year,
> A hundred marks since being a pardoner.
> I stand in the pulpit like a true divine,
> And when the people sit I preach my line
> To ignorant souls, as you have heard before,
> And tell skullduggeries by the hundred more.
> Then I take care to stretch my neck well out
> And over the people I nod and peer about
> Just like a pigeon perching on a shed.
> My hands fly and my tongue wags in my head
> So busily that to watch me is a joy.
> Avarice is the theme that I employ
> In all my sermons, to make the people free
> In giving pennies — especially to me.
> My mind is fixed on what I stand to win
> And not at all upon correcting sin.[17]

Probably few priests rivaled Chaucer's pardoner in villainy, but there was widespread feeling that priests should be held accountable for the proper performance of their duties. In some regions, such as Switzerland and the independent cities of Germany, limited attempts to make the clergy responsible to local governments met with varying degrees of success. Pressure for change would steadily grow, however, until reform of the clergy and the Church as a whole became an explosive issue in the West early in the sixteenth century.

PILGRIMAGE, THE CULT OF SAINTS, AND INDULGENCES

Despite the imperfections of the clergy, most Christians remained enthusiastically committed to the Church. Most accepted its doctrines, regarded its preaching as the primary source of all truth, and gratefully acknowledged its sacraments as the keys to salvation. But formal worship in church had come to involve more observation than participation. One of the most striking features of popular religion during this period of instability was an en-

thusiasm for practices that offered a more personal and satisfying religious experience and greater security in the face of spiritual and material uncertainties. Among the most important were pilgrimage, the veneration of saints, devotion to Mary and Jesus, and the purchase of indulgences.

Pilgrimage had grown steadily in popularity ever since Christians first began seeking out the tombs of martyrs in the third and fourth centuries. The most pious and adventurous of medieval pilgrims set out for the Holy Land, as did sinners obliged to perform serious penances. There, more than a thousand miles from home, they traced the steps of Christ from Galilee to Jerusalem and the **Holy Sepulcher**, experiencing vicariously his ministry, suffering, and death. Returning, they brought with them palm leaves as souvenirs and proof of their journey, earning in this way the name *palmers*. Others took the long road to Rome, where they visited the tombs of Peter and Paul. Besides these two great destinations, there were many others sanctioned by the Church. Each year countless pilgrims made their way to shrines like the cathedrals of Santiago de Compostela in Spain, where they saw the bones of St. James the Apostle, and Vézelay in France, where the relics of Mary Magdalene were on display. In England, the most popular site was Canterbury. Chaucer says that pilgrims flocked there from every part of the country seeking protection and healing at the shrine of the martyr St. Thomas Becket. "In England people ride to Canterbury from every countryside," he wrote, "to visit there the blessed martyred saint, who gave them strength when they were sick and faint."[18] Wherever they wandered, pilgrims believed there was spiritual merit in the hardships they faced and hoped for an experience of holiness at the end of their journey.

The fact that the roads they trod led so often to the shrines of saints points to the continuing importance of the cult of saints in late medieval piety. The ancient belief that the blessed in heaven hear the prayers of the faithful below and intercede with God on their behalf had firmly established itself during the course of the Middle Ages. Popular piety encouraged devotion to patron saints and assigned specific responsibilities to every member of the heavenly community. The faithful turned to

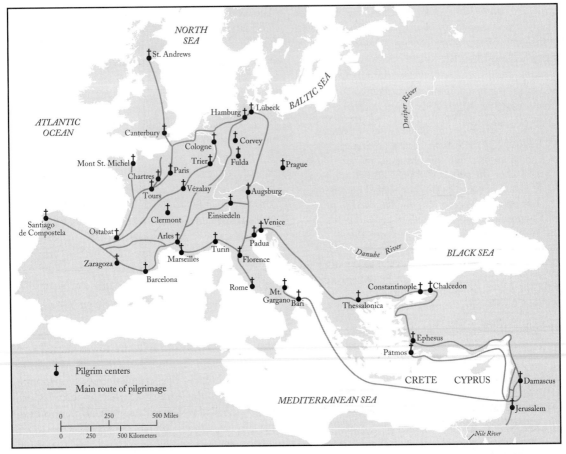

Figure 7.2   Medieval Pilgrim Routes Pilgrimage was one of the most visible features of popular piety in the Middle Ages. Some pilgrims undertook their journeys as acts of penance, others simply to express their devotion to God.

St. Apollonia when afflicted by toothache, St. Médard when threatened by drought, and St. Corneille when anxious about the health of their oxen. The sense of dynamic spiritual communion with the saints was fostered by the observance of their feast days, which filled the calendar, and by the veneration of their relics. The remains of the greatest saints were displayed in monasteries and cathedrals, but even the smallest churches were sanctified by relics of one kind or another, and bits of saintly bones, teeth, and hair could be found at shops and fairs, where they were purchased as protective charms against sickness, violence, and the many other evils of a dangerous world.

No saint was more beloved than the Virgin Mary, whose popularity soared to new heights in the late Middle Ages. Thousands traveled each year to her shrines, such as the cathedral of Our Lady of Chartres, not far from Paris, where they could see the Virgin's robe. Others honored her and sought her benefactions by reciting the rosary, a complex of prayers directed to Mary and to God in which a string of beads is used to count individual prayers.

As popular piety turned away from its former emphasis on God as a stern judge to the more human image of the suffering Jesus, interest in new ways of worshiping Christ also grew dramatically. The sacred heart of Jesus, represented in religious

Figure 7.3   Monstrance (ca. 1400) Monstrances were devices used for the display of the eucharistic host (bread consecrated during the mass), which was kept in an elevated cup like the one shown here. The practice of venerating the host became a popular form of piety in the late Middle Ages.

art as pierced and bleeding, became an object of pious devotion. So did the consecrated host of the eucharist. As the body of Christ, it was commonly believed to have miraculous powers. Tales were told of its ability to cure disease, cast out demons, and detect perjury by choking liars who swallowed it. An important part of the mass was the elevation of the host by the priest immediately after he had pronounced the words of consecration, and there are stories of people who ran from church to church hoping to witness this event several times in a single day. By the fourteenth century the adoration of the host publicly displayed on a special stand, or monstrance, was beginning to replace the veneration of saints and their relics. Entire towns turned out each June on the feast of Corpus Christi ("Body of Christ") to see the host paraded among them and reflect that in the miracle of every eucharist God made himself visibly present and available to sinful humanity.

For those who greatly feared the consequences of sin a kind of insurance could be had in the form of indulgences, which we have already described as remissions of penalties for sin. According to medieval theology, the absolution granted by a priest in the sacrament of penance assured a repentant sinner that his sins had been forgiven, but it did not remove the penalty God had imposed for them. A penance, or "work of satisfaction"—usually in the form of prayer, fasting, almsgiving, or pilgrimage—was still required. If penance was not completed in this life, however, the penalty would have to be paid in purgatory. Those who worried that their time there might be extended by uncompleted penances or unrepented sins could purchase indulgences, which covered penalties still owed for sin by drawing upon the infinite surplus of good works built up by Christ and the saints and "stored" in a "treasury of merit" whose contents could be distributed at the discretion of the pope. Belief in this reservoir of good works can be traced back to ancient times, though its existence was not formally recognized until 1343, when it was proclaimed as doctrine by Clement VI (1342–52). Thereafter, the granting of indulgences rapidly escalated as the Church saw the financial potential of offering them in return for gifts of money, technically considered alms.

In such ways pilgrimage, the cult of saints, devotion to Mary and Jesus, and the purchase of indulgences both enhanced the spiritual experience of Christians and helped assuage the anxiety that was characteristic of the late Middle Ages. Still, plague, famine, and poverty had pronounced spiritual and psychological effects. Sometimes they took the form of a bizarre preoccupation with death and judgment. The flagellants mentioned earlier in this chapter were typical of those who feared the imminent end of the world and resorted to extreme forms of behavior in the hope of forestalling it. Others, stricken by plague, cloaked themselves in black and spent their last hours in graveyards performing a grim Dance of Death (*danse macabre*) surrounded by skeletons, dead animals, and other ghoulish paraphernalia. Tombs decorated with images of the dead being eaten by worms or toads also expressed the dark mood of the time.[19]

Heretics and Reformers

The difficulties that beset the Church in the late Middle Ages were not new. Corruption, ambition, and conflict were always a threat to the integrity of the Church and required constant vigilance. It is important to keep in mind that, long before the beginning of the Protestant Reformation in the sixteenth century, reformers and dissenters had responded in various ways to the Church's ills. Of those we will discuss here, most had their origins in the twelfth and thirteenth centuries, but their influence extended well into the fourteenth and fifteenth centuries. Seeking more than remedies for the problems described above, they called for a return to the apostolic simplicity of early Christianity, devoted and educated preachers, a deeper spiritual-

ity among both the laity and clergy, translation of the Bible into **vernacular** languages, and other important changes.

THE CATHARI AND WALDENSES

The twelfth century—a time of revitalization and renewal—was also an age of dissent and experimentation that produced a variety of unorthodox movements. Of those movements that were declared heretical, some were condemned for what the Church considered dangerous deviations from scripture and tradition; others were condemned for their disregard of ecclesiastical authority. These two issues of unorthodoxy and disobedience were raised by the **Cathari** and the **Waldenses**, the most important heretical movements of the Middle Ages.

The Cathari ("pure ones") were dissenters who became especially influential in Germany, northern Italy, and southern France. They so dominated the region around the French town of Albi that they are sometimes called Albigenses. Regarding themselves as true Christians who preserved the purity of the early Church, the Cathari constructed a theology derived largely from that of the **Bogomils**, a dualist sect centered in the Balkans. Like the Bogomils and the ancient Manichaeans,[20] they regarded the human body and material reality in general as evil and therefore fundamentally opposed to spirit. There were two gods, they said—a good God who created the world of spirit and a lesser deity, whom they identified as the God of the Old Testament, who had made the material world. It was this lesser, evil god who had imprisoned human souls in bodies. Death brought only temporary release from this unhappy condition, for wandering souls soon found themselves entrapped in new bodies. Salvation from the miserable cycle of incarnation-transmigration-incarnation was possible only through Christ. The Cathari described him as God's son who, being pure spirit, took on a body in appearance only during his time on earth. Christ, they claimed, had shown that escape from the material world is possible through the *consolamentum,* a spiritual baptism effected through the laying on of hands. The only Cathar sacrament, the *consolamentum* imparted the Holy Spirit and cleansed the believer of original sin, making it possible at death for the soul to break away from earthly existence and achieve union with the good God in the realm of spirit. According to the Cathari, the Church had perverted the true teachings of Christ, but fortunately these and the *consolamentum* had been handed down through generations of "good Christians," as they sometimes called themselves.[21]

The Cathari were divided into two classes. The Perfect were the elite who had received the *consolamentum* and could be sure of their salvation as long as they remained celibate, refused to take oaths or participate in wars, and owned no property. They also avoided meat and dairy products because these were produced through sexual intercourse — which they held to be a sin because it produces bodies, including animal bodies, in which souls might be imprisoned. The majority of Cathari hesitated to undertake these rigors, however, and constituted a second class of ordinary Believers. They waited until death was imminent before receiving the *consolamentum* and so were not bound by the ascetic requirements imposed on the Perfect. The movement as a whole was governed by elected bishops, all with equal authority.

As with the ancient Gnostic Christians, much of the appeal of the Cathari lay in their claim of access to hidden teachings of Christ. Converts were also won by the moral example of the Perfect. Women were attracted by opportunities for spiritual leadership, for the movement did not recognize gender as a characteristic of the true, spiritual self. Thus, female Perfect were honored by male as well as female Believers and had the authority to preach and administer the *consolamentum*. The threat posed by the large numbers of Cathari was compounded by their unorthodox beliefs, which included their ditheism, docetic Christology, and rejection of the Trinity and the traditional sacraments.[22] The Church met this dual threat with preaching against Cathar doctrines and persecution that culminated in an Albigensian Crusade (1209–29) proclaimed by Innocent III.

The Waldenses, a very different group, were named after their founder, Peter Waldo, a rich merchant of Lyons.[23] At some point between 1170 and 1176, Waldo was so moved by his reading of the Gospels that he resolved to devote himself entirely to poverty and preaching. After providing for the care of his family and giving the rest of his wealth to the poor, he began preaching in the streets armed with books of the New Testament translated into the vernacular language of southern France. Before long he had attracted a small group of followers. These "Poor Men of Lyons," as they were then known, dressed like monks, committed themselves to chastity, and held their few possessions in common. For a time the little band was allowed to preach, sing, and read the Bible in public. But as their popularity grew, so did the concern of the local clergy, who objected that canon law allowed only priests and bishops to preach.

Hoping to gain official approval of their mission, Waldo and his followers appealed to Pope Alexander III (1159–81) and the Third Lateran Council (1179). They were successful, though only on the condition that they secure the permission of local church authorities to continue their preaching. The archbishop of Lyons was less sympathetic, however, and when the Waldenses persisted in their activities without his consent he excommunicated them and drove them out of his city. Thereafter they quickly spread into northeastern France and the lands along the Rhine. In 1184, about two years after their excommunication, the Waldenses, along with the Cathari and a number of other sects, were formally branded as heretics by Pope Lucius III (1181–85) at the Council of Verona in 1184.

The Waldenses' most basic belief was in the absolute authority of scripture, an idea that would become central to the thought of Protestant reformers three centuries later. No belief or practice not found in scripture could be justified, they said, and what could be found there was to be taken seriously and literally. For this reason, the Waldenses encouraged memorization of lengthy portions of the Bible and sent their missionaries out in pairs in accordance with Luke 10:1. Rejecting the Church's claim that only ordained priests had the authority to preach,[24] they entrusted this responsibility to women as well as men. According to a treatise written about 1320 by Bernard Gui, a French inquisitor and their greatest critic, the Waldenses also rejected some of the traditional sacraments, gave their own interpretation to others, denied the existence of purgatory and the value of prayers for the dead, and refused to acknowledge most holy days. As time passed they became even more radical; by the end of the fourteenth century, most rejected saints who were not mentioned in the New Testament, along with church buildings, altars, holy water, pilgrimages, and other features of traditional worship and devotion. As a result, the Waldenses suffered sporadic persecution by the Church from the thirteenth century through the fifteenth in France, Germany, Spain, Austria, Bohemia, and northern Italy. Repression diminished their numbers, but the end of Waldensianism as a significant movement came only with the Protestant Reformation, which absorbed many of its congregations.

THE DOMINICANS AND THE INQUISITION

In the midst of its struggle against the Cathari and Waldenses, the Church established two great orders of **mendicant friars** ("begging brothers") that were destined to have a major impact on western Christianity for centuries to come. These were the Dominicans and the Franciscans. Abjuring the comforts of sedentary life enjoyed by other orders in their monastic houses, the early Dominican and Franciscan friars embraced the ideals of poverty and itinerant preaching with a fervor equal to that of the Cathari and Waldenses.

The founder of the Dominican order, Dominic Guzman (1172–1221), was born in Castile. As a young man he studied the liberal arts and then joined an Augustinian community near Madrid. There he became a protégé of the local bishop, who persuaded him that the only way to bring the Cathari and Waldenses back into the Church was to surpass their example in poverty and preaching. Taking up this challenge, Dominic left Spain and spent a decade in southern France, where he was joined by others committed to preaching orthodoxy to and against heretics. Their success was so great that in 1217 Pope Honorius III gave them official recognition as the Order of Preachers. In that same year Dominic began sending brothers to cities throughout Europe, and especially to those with schools where they could be trained in theology and find ample opportunity for public debate with heretics.

The Dominican emphasis on higher learning helps explain the attraction of major theologians such as Albert the Great and Thomas Aquinas to the order and the papacy's reliance on their theological expertise. At the same time, their poverty and simplicity gave them great credibility among the people. The thirteenth-century chronicler Matthew Paris described the Dominicans as living in groups of seven to ten, allowing themselves only the bare essentials in food and clothing, going barefoot, and sleeping on mats with stones for pillows.[25] Dominic also made room within the movement for women, who formed a "second order" of Dominican nuns. Women were excluded from both the universities and preaching, so nuns had few opportunities in theology and the campaign against heresy, but they contributed immeasurably to the success of the order by serving as its economic basis, operating farms and vineyards and producing food, clothing, and other items.[26] A third order of lay Dominicans, known as "tertiaries," vowed obedience to portions of the Dominican rule while remaining fully involved in the world.

The Dominicans quickly distinguished themselves for their relentless opposition to heresy, earning the epithet *domini canes* ("hounds of the Lord"). Their education and dedication to preaching made them ideal defenders of orthodoxy, and the Church took full advantage of all they had to offer. This included the working out of a justification of the pursuit and punishment of heretics. Thomas Aquinas, for example, argued that errors in matters of faith are supremely dangerous because they can lead to hell; therefore, he said, there can be no tolerance of heresy. At the same time, however, he cautioned that no one should be punished for heresy without first being given an opportunity to recant. Those who admitted their errors should be allowed to do penance and be restored to the Church. Those who persisted, he maintained, could rightfully be put to death.

The Dominicans figured prominently in the Inquisition, the Church's judicial inquiry into allegations of heresy. Its aims and methods were defined by popes such as Lucius III, who in 1184 made bishops responsible for detecting heresy and handing offenders over to civil authorities for punishment. Secular rulers, who had political reasons for supporting religious unity, were generally pleased to accept this responsibility and took the lead in advocating severe punishment for heretics. In 1224 the Holy Roman Emperor Frederick II ordered that heretics should be burned, a form of execution approved by Pope Gregory IX in 1231. Two decades later Innocent IV added torture to the methods of the Inquisition in the bull *Ad extirpanda* (1252).

Inquisitors often appeared in a city or town without warning, preceded by secret agents who gathered evidence and information. Typically, formal proceedings began with a public address in which citizens were asked to report the heresies of others and confess their own. This "general inquisition" was followed by a "special inquisition" in which suspects were tried behind closed doors, where they were told neither the specific nature of the charges against them nor the names of their accusers. Although they were allowed representation by lawyers, the risk of appearing sympathetic to heresy was so great that the accused were usually left to defend themselves. When confessions were elicited, penances could be light, such as hearing a prescribed number of masses or going on a pilgrimage. More serious cases brought fines, the confiscation of property, or incarceration in one of the Inquisition's prisons. Those who refused to recant after being found guilty faced death at the stake. The number of burnings during the Inquisition was actually far smaller than is commonly imagined. In southern France in the middle of the thirteenth century, when the Inquisition there was at its height, burnings averaged three each year.[27] And yet there were notable exceptions. On a single day in 1310, eighteen citizens of Toulouse died in the flames.

During the fourteenth and fifteenth centuries the course of the Inquisition varied from region to region. The Inquisition was never a presence in England, Ireland, or Scandinavia. In Germany it reached extremes of cruelty in the thirteenth century under Conrad, a priest of Marburg appointed

by Gregory IX, but after his murder by friends of his victims the German bishops gradually took control. Their more moderate policies allowed some unorthodox groups to survive until the sixteenth century, when Germany became the center of rebellion against the Church. In France, the threat posed by the Cathari declined after 1300, but French inquisitors found new victims in the Beguines and Spiritual Franciscans, a faction within the Franciscan order. The Inquisition managed to survive throughout much of Europe in one form or another well beyond the Middle Ages. The most violent stage of the Spanish Inquisition, for example, did not begin until 1478. Suspecting that converted Jews (*conversos*) and Muslims (*moriscos*) were still practicing their original religions in secret, Ferdinand and Isabella monitored their activities through a state-controlled inquisition directed by Tomás de Torquemada. As Inquisitor General, Torquemada made extensive use of torture and is thought to have burned more than two thousand heretics in the notorious *autos-da-fé* ("acts of the faith").

THE FRANCISCANS

The terrors of the Inquisition were balanced somewhat by the mission and ideals of the **Franciscans**, a second mendicant order. Although some were inevitably drawn into the struggle against heresy, in their early years, at least, the Franciscans' valuation of service over education prepared them more for preaching and ministering to the needy than for theological debate or organized persecution.

The founder of the order, Francis of Assisi (1182–1226), was the son of a wealthy Italian cloth merchant who expected him to enter the family business. For a time it seemed that the young Francis would do as his father wished, for he had a taste for money and the good life. But the course of his life gradually changed as he tired of self-indulgence, became a friend to beggars and lepers, and gave away all of his possessions. One morning in 1208 he was deeply moved during mass by a reading from the Gospel of Matthew (10:7–14) describing Christ's commission of the Apostles. Leaving his home and family behind, Francis dedicated himself to preaching, absolute poverty, the imitation of Christ's love, and complete obedience to the Church. When disciples gathered around him, he wrote a simple rule for them and won Pope Innocent III's approval of their request to preach. Five years later, in 1215, Innocent formally recognized Francis and his followers as the order of *fratres minores*, the "lesser" or "humbler brothers."

Rejecting all material possessions and the tradition of living in monastic houses, these first Franciscans traveled barefoot and in pairs from place to place, sleeping wherever they could find shelter for the night. Their days were spent preaching and ministering to the sick and the poor. Easily recognized by the brown robes they adopted as a Franciscan "uniform" and the salutation "The Lord give you peace" with which they greeted everyone they met, the friars depended for sustenance on the goodwill of others. Few were priests. Even Francis never rose above the rank of deacon. Yet even without the leadership of ordained clergy, the order grew so quickly that within two years of its founding there were Franciscans in Italy, France, Spain, Bohemia, Germany, England, and the Holy Land. After 1219, large-scale missionary campaigns were organized in Europe, Muslim Asia, and North Africa. During the Fifth Crusade, Francis himself journeyed to Syria and then Egypt, where he attempted to convert the sultan al-Kamil.

Behind the success of the Franciscan movement lay the astonishing charisma and spirituality of its founder. Tales of Francis's sanctity circulated everywhere, many of them later preserved in the *Little Flowers of St. Francis*, a fourteenth-century collection of stories about the early days of the order.[28] One account describes Francis being seen by one of the brothers in conversation with Christ and the Virgin Mary. According to another, the people of Assisi once believed they saw the town's church engulfed in flames; rushing to put out the blaze, they found not fire but Francis and his disciples lost in joyful contemplation of God. It was said that Francis, who loved all living things, once stopped to preach to his "little sisters" the birds, who bowed their heads and listened attentively until he had concluded his sermon.[29] Even inanimate aspects of nature were dear to Francis, who praised God for the blessings of Brother Sun, Sister Moon, and Brother Wind in his famous "Canticle of Brother Sun," one of the first poems to be composed in the Italian language.

The success of the Franciscans soon brought disappointment to Francis, for the Church, hoping to see the order grow, insisted on relaxing his original requirement that all brothers live in absolute poverty. Discouraged, Francis gradually withdrew from involvement in Franciscan affairs. By 1224 he was living in seclusion in a tiny hermitage in Tuscany, where he devoted himself to prayer, contemplation, and fasting. That same year he had an intense mystical experience in which he beheld a vision of the crucifixion and then, to his great joy, received the *stigmata*—wounds like those of Christ on his hands, feet, and side. He died not long thereafter, on 3 October 1226, singing the "Canticle" with brothers gathered around him. Two years later he was canonized as a saint.

Over the next century the number of Franciscans continued to increase thanks to further easing of Francis's rule. Brothers were now encouraged to establish houses for themselves and, in some cases, to become involved in the intellectual life of the universities. By the beginning of the fourteenth century there were more than fourteen hundred Franciscan communities. Nearly one-fifth were convents of nuns belonging to the "Poor Clares," a second order Francis had founded with Clare of Assisi (1194–1253), with whom he shared a profound spiritual friendship. Forbidden to preach because of their gender, these women devoted themselves instead to manual labor, contemplation, and an asceticism more severe than that practiced by the brothers. A third order of lay Franciscans offered material support to the first and second orders while practicing Franciscan piety in secular society.

In the fourteenth and fifteenth centuries, plague and the Great Schism took their toll on the Franciscans, diminishing their numbers and dividing their loyalties between Rome and Avignon. In addition, continuing conflict over the commitment to poverty disrupted the order from within as a faction of "Spiritual Franciscans" withdrew to hermitages and rustic mountain refuges in protest against the laxity of the majority. Fearing a deeper split in an order that had served the Church well, Pope John XXII (1316–34) dissolved the Spirituals in 1317 and declared that poverty was not a precondition of holiness. Thereafter, the Spiritual Franciscans were persecuted, and some were burned by the Inquisition.[30]

Despite these difficulties, the Franciscans had a great influence on western Christianity and civilization. Many became notable mystics, theologians, bishops, and popes. There is no question that their example of genuine spirituality and service to others won them widespread admiration and strengthened popular commitment to the Church. They also did much to shape popular piety by promoting a variety of devotions, especially those that honored the Virgin Mary. One of these, the "Angelus," consists of repetitions of the Ave Maria, a prayer to the Virgin recited in the early morning, at noon, and in the evening.[31] The Franciscans also popularized the "stations of the cross," a meditation on fourteen events in the passion of Christ, beginning with his departure from Pilate's house and ending with his burial, their depictions being arranged around the interior walls of a church. Both of these devotions remain important features of Roman Catholic piety to this day. Perhaps the most important thing that can be said of the Franciscans, however, is that an age when the practices of the Church were questioned by many, they offered good reasons to believe that its ideals had not been forgotten.

JOHN WYCLIFFE AND JAN HUS

Dominic and Francis had organized movements approved by the Church because of their orthodoxy and obedience, but reformers who challenged ecclesiastical traditions and authority often found themselves and their teachings condemned.

One such figure was **John Wycliffe** (1320–84), a leading philosopher and theologian at Oxford whose thought reflected the growth of English **anticlericalism** (opposition to the influence of the Church or clergy) in the fourteenth century. Wycliffe's views on the Church's role in society tended to support the aims of the English monarchy, which hoped to gain greater control over the Church and its property in England and employed

Wycliff as an envoy in some of its dealings with Rome. Wycliff began by writing two treatises in which he argued that civil authorities had the right to remove property from the control of immoral priests and bishops.[32] Later he broadened his attacks, calling for the elimination of the entire ecclesiastical hierarchy because, in his view, every Christian functioned as his or her own priest. Here, of course, Wycliffe was striking at the very heart of the Church. His criticism of elaborate ritual, the cult of saints, and pilgrimages only set him at greater odds with Rome, as did his rejection of transubstantiation and doubts about the necessity of the sacraments for salvation. Finally, though he did not directly challenge the authority of tradition, Wycliffe argued that scripture is a greater authority on which all belief and doctrine must stand. To make the Bible more accessible to the laity, he began work with his followers on an English translation of scripture that came to be known as the Wycliffe Bible.

Wycliffe's views soon led to his condemnation as a heretic and his expulsion from Oxford. Still, he managed to win a sizable following whose members were called **Lollards** ("mumblers"), a derisive term long used in the Netherlands for Beguines and Beghards. After Wycliffe's death in 1384, the Lollard movement spread rapidly throughout England and Scotland. Its preachers condemned transubstantiation, oral confession, indulgences, pilgrimages, and the institution of the papacy. By claiming that the validity of a priest's actions depended on his moral character rather than on his ordination, they also rejected a critically important doctrine that reached back to Augustine. Lollardy enjoyed initial support from some members of the English aristocracy, but its attacks on civil and ecclesiastical authority brought persecution by both the monarch and the Church by the 1430s. Wycliffe's teachings were condemned by the Council of Florence (1438–45), which also ordered that his remains be removed from consecrated ground and burned.[33]

By that time, however, Wycliffe's ideas had spread as far east as Bohemia, where they had a profound effect on **Jan Hus** (1373–1415), a priest and professor at the University of Prague. In his writings and sermons, Hus vigorously condemned clerical

Figure 7.4   Eucharistic Chalice (twelfth century)
Chalices like this one were used to hold wine consecrated in the eucharist. Although in early times chalices
were most often made of glass, authorities such as Augustine and John Chrysostom report that gold and silver
chalices encrusted with precious stones had become
common by the fourth century.

leadership of the Czech professors at Prague in supporting the Pisan pope Alexander V during the
Great Schism earned him the hatred of his German
colleagues, who supported Gregory XII. To the native Czechs, who deeply resented the presence of a
large population of Germans in Bohemia, Hus
quickly became a national hero. When he was excommunicated, Hus appealed for permission to defend himself before the Council of Constance. The
emperor made what appeared to be a sincere promise of safe conduct, but when Hus arrived he was
imprisoned, tried, and condemned as a heretic. He
was burned at the stake on 6 July 1415. His death
inspired an immediate Hussite rebellion that tore
Bohemia apart for two decades. Peace was restored
in 1433 when the Council of Basel granted limited
concessions, including the use of the cup in the
eucharist.[34]

Although Wycliffe and Hus have sometimes
been closely identified with the leaders of the
Protestant Reformation, their teachings were, on
the whole, far less radical than those of Luther,
Zwingli, and Calvin. Still, in stressing the importance of scripture, questioning clerical authority,
and protesting against clerical abuses they clearly
anticipated some of the central features of the
Protestant program for reform.

Mystics and Mysticism

One of the most remarkable expressions of the vitality of late medieval religious life was mysticism.
In some respects, the rise of medieval mysticism
may be seen as a turning away from the world and
its troubles, but there were other factors that contributed to its development — the omnipresence of
monasteries and convents, for example, where a
sense of the presence of God was a primary aim of
daily life, and the same thirst for a deeper spiritual
experience that encouraged the growth of the
movements we have discussed above. There were
also the continuing influences of early mystics, such
as Pseudo-Dionysius, and the conviction of major
theologians from Augustine to Thomas Aquinas

corruption, the sale of indulgences, and the practice
of withholding the cup from the people during the
eucharist (out of fear that it might be spilled). Like
Wycliffe, he stressed the authority of scripture and
regarded the cult of saints, pilgrimages, and other
practices as dangerous superstitions. Although he
did not seriously question the authority of the
clergy, Hus emphasized that it was God, and not
priests, who forgave sins, and advised the laity
that they were justified in disobeying their priests
and bishops when their directives were illegal or
immoral.

Hus's writings and sermons soon provoked angry responses from the clergy. At the same time, his

that God can be known at levels of experience far above those to which the intellect can rise.

The flowering of late medieval mysticism was anticipated by the Franciscan Giovanni di Fidanza, better known as **Bonaventure** (ca. 1217–74). After a brilliant career as a professor of theology at Paris, Bonaventure became the head of his order and then cardinal bishop of Albano in Italy. Like most theologians of his time, he took an interest in Aristotle and incorporated elements of the philosopher's thought in his *Breviloquium,* a commentary on scripture. But he could not square the Aristotelian view of knowledge as derived only through the senses with his Augustinian conviction that higher truths are grasped only through God's illumination of the mind. Illumination, in fact, is one of the fundamental principles in his *The Journey of the Mind to God,* a masterpiece of mystical theology. Here Bonaventure argued that the mind is drawn to God by divine love, whose operation is aided by prayer and meditation. Love makes the mind aware of God, first in nature and then within itself. When at last the mind is raised above its own limits to behold God as Trinity, all rational thought ceases and the entire soul unites with the divine — not in mere understanding, but in ecstatic love. Throughout Bonaventure's mystical theology we see the influence of earlier thinkers: an Augustinian emphasis on grace, for example, and the same interest in the soul's ascent to God found in Neoplatonism and Pseudo-Dionysius. In recognition of his sanctity and theological achievement, Bonaventure was canonized in 1482 and included among the Doctors of the Church a century later.

A later contemporary of Bonaventure was the German mystic **Meister Eckhart** (ca. 1260–1327). A Dominican who joined the order at fifteen, Eckhart taught theology at Paris and held preaching positions at Erfurt, Strasbourg, and Cologne. As a Dominican, he naturally felt the influence of Aquinas, but Neoplatonism shaped his mystical theology. Accordingly, he understood God as the source and "ground" of all being, beyond all categories, including existence and nonexistence, and yet present everywhere. Because the vast complex of particular things we experience in ordinary awareness masks this ultimate reality, Eckhart urged a "breaking through" to the deepest part of the soul, where God alone can be found. When this occurs, he said, the soul is transformed into God by the "begetting" of the Son there. This transformation means a denial of self, but it also brings the experience of God's own joy and being:

> O my dear man, what harm does it do you to allow God to be God in you? Go completely out of yourself for God's love, and God comes completely out of himself for love of you. And when these two have gone out, what remains there is a simplified One. In this One the Father brings his Son to birth in the innermost source.[35]
>
> And I have often said that there is a power in the soul that touches neither time nor flesh. . . . In this power God is always verdant and blossoming in all the joy and honor that he is in himself. That is a joy so heartfelt, a joy so incomprehensible and great that no one can tell it all. For it is in this power that the eternal Father ceaselessly brings his eternal Son to birth.[36]

In some of his writings, Eckhart described the transformed soul as being of the very preexistent essence of God. Shocked by this claim, his critics accused him of pantheism, the identification of God with nature. As a result, Eckhart ended his life defending himself against charges of heresy. He admitted that he had sometimes exaggerated his views, but argued that most were completely orthodox. The Church disagreed, however, and a year after Eckhart's death declared twenty-eight of his propositions either heretical or misleading. This verdict notwithstanding, Eckhart's emphasis on the cultivation of the interior life and reliance on grace was continued by his disciples, most notably Johannes Tauler (ca. 1300–ca. 1361), and had a lasting influence on German piety.

Another important figure was **Catherine of Siena** (1347–80), whose career demonstrates that the religious credentials of women mystics sometimes gave them an authority otherwise difficult to attain. A Dominican tertiary who experienced her first vision at the age of six, Catherine spent her late teens as an ascetic secluded in her parents' home. At twenty she received a command from Christ to go out into the world to serve the poor and sick, many of whom had been infected by plague. Noting her work and wisdom, the town of Siena called upon her to mediate among its warring political factions. She later served in various ambassadorial roles in which she earned the respect of both secular and ecclesiastical rulers. An advisor to Pope Gregory XI, Catherine helped persuade him to transfer the papacy from Avignon back to Rome in 1377.

Catherine's spiritual life is known to us primarily through her *Dialogue,* which summarizes her teachings, and more than four hundred of her letters and prayers. Here she emphasized the love of Christ as expressed in the crucifixion, and particularly in the shedding of Christ's blood. There was no greater symbol, she believed, of God's love for humanity, nor any greater reason for humanity to love God. Canonized two decades before Bonaventure, she was acknowledged as a Doctor of the Church four centuries after him, in 1970.

The English mystic **Julian of Norwich** (ca. 1342–ca. 1416) was a recluse who appears to have lived outside the walls of Norwich's St. Julian's Church, from which she took her name. In her early thirties she experienced a series of sixteen revelations. These she recorded in the original version of her *Showings* or *Revelations of Divine Love.* Twenty years later, Julian issued a longer edition that included her reflections on the meaning of her experience. Here the primary theme is God's love, which she saw everywhere and believed to be the only means to perfect security and abiding joy. This truth, she said, is evident even in the smallest and least consequential aspects of creation. Holding in her hand a tiny object she described as no bigger than a hazelnut, Julian asked herself, "What can this be?" The answer that came to her was, "It is everything which is made." Then a second question occurred to her:

> I was amazed that it could last, for I thought that it was so little that it could suddenly fall into nothing. And I was answered in my understanding: It lasts and always will, because God loves it; and thus everything has being through the love of God.
>
> In this little thing I saw three properties. The first is that God made it, the second that he loves

it, the third is that God preserves it. But what is that to me? It is that God is the Creator and the lover and the protector. For until I am substantially united to him, I can never have love or rest or true happiness.[37]

Another striking feature of Julian's writing is her use of feminine as well as masculine language in describing God. Comparing the love of Christ, for example, to that of a mother who nourishes her child with her milk, she described Christians as receiving spiritual nourishment in the eucharist from "our precious Mother Jesus."

It is likely that late in life Julian knew and encouraged another English mystic, **Margery Kempe** (ca. 1373–1438), who was of a very different background and temperament. Married and the mother of fourteen children, Kempe had a vision of Jesus soon after the birth of the first. As her visions continued, she developed deep spiritual convictions that compelled her to fearlessly criticize the clergy, laity, and even prevailing social norms. When the archbishop of York accused her of wickedness, she replied, "I also hear it said that ye are a wicked man. If ye be as wicked as men say, ye shall never come to heaven, unless ye amend whilst ye be here."[38] Despite the offense taken by some at her unusual behavior, Kempe's autobiographical *Book of Margery Kempe* reveals a profoundly sensitive woman whose devotion to God brought extraordinary experiences in which she spoke with Christ and felt the presence of the Virgin Mary and all the saints within her. Like mystics before and after her, she compared the relationship between Christ and the soul to the union of lovers. Thus, she described Christ as saying to her: "I will that thou lovest me . . . as a good wife ought to love her husband. Therefore, thou mayest boldly take me in the arms of thy soul and kiss my mouth, my head, and my feet, as sweetly as thou wilt."[39]

In the Netherlands, the beginnings of important developments in the mystical tradition can be traced back to Jan van Ruysbroeck (1293–1381), a Flemish priest who left his church in Brussels to found a religious community of contemplatives at Groenendal, near Waterloo. Influenced by Augustine and Pseudo-Dionysius, Ruysbroeck emphasized the transformation of the soul by divine love and had as much difficulty as Eckhart in describing its union with God without suggesting pantheism. He had a powerful influence on two younger contemporaries, Gerard Groote (1340–84) and Florentius Radewijns (1350–1400), who longed for a simple Christianity uncomplicated by dogma. Believing that the best life was one that combined mysticism with service to others, Groote and Radewijns founded three religious communities based on this ideal: the lay Sisters and the Brothers of the Common Life at Deventer and, at Wildesheim, a monastic congregation whose way of life was based on the Augustinian rule. The practice of these three groups soon came to be known as the **devotio moderna** ("Modern Devotion"). It emphasized an abiding awareness of God and a deep personal relationship with him nurtured by constant meditation on the life of Christ. The Modern Devotion quickly spread throughout the Netherlands and into Germany. Its most famous representative was **Thomas à Kempis** (1380–1471), to whom scholars usually attribute *The Imitation of Christ*, the most widely read devotional treatise in the entire history of Christianity.

Three important observations can be made about the growth of mysticism in the later Middle Ages. First, like other forms of devotion characteristic of the time, it suggests a reaction against the institutional nature of the Church and an increasing desire for a deeper and more personal religious experience than that which was afforded by formal worship in the mass. Second, by taking spiritual paths outside the avenues sanctioned by the Church, mystics sometimes put themselves in great danger. Eckhart's difficulties pale in comparison to those of figures like Margaret Porette, who was burned at the stake in 1310 for circulating her book, *The Mirror of Simple Souls*, which had been condemned as heretical. Finally, the publication of mystical works like Porette's, Kempe's, Eckhart's, and the anonymous fourteenth-century classic *The Cloud of Unknowing* marked the beginning of a trend toward making religious literature available in the vernacular to ordinary people as well as to clerics and scholars.

Theology in the West

In an age of plague, war, and economic decline, it seemed unlikely to many that earthly society reflected some divinely ordained order of spiritual ideals or universals. The removal of the papacy from Rome to Avignon and its division during the Great Schism, for example, led many to wonder what connection the papal office could have to a heavenly model of that institution. As interest in the old doctrine of realism faded, nominalism offered an alternative view according to which ideals or universals are fashioned not by God but by human beings. This shift in theological attitudes can be seen in the works of John Duns Scotus and William of Ockham, two of the period's greatest theologians, who made the "late scholasticism" of the fourteenth century rather different from the earlier enterprise that had culminated in the theology of Thomas Aquinas.

JOHN DUNS SCOTUS

Making selective but extensive use of the philosophy of Aristotle, Thomas had created a grand synthesis in which faith and reason were understood as complementary paths to knowledge and theology and philosophy as mutually supportive academic disciplines. Thomas's admirers were enthusiastic about his achievement and the potential of reason for further explaining the mysteries of God and creation, but others, such as Bonaventure and his fellow Franciscans, hesitated to make Christian theology dependent on a non-Christian philosopher; they downplayed the value of reason in explaining the ways of God, and continued to emphasize faith in the tradition of Augustine.

But the lines between these two schools of thought were not firmly drawn. One of the most remarkable figures to take an eclectic approach was **John Duns Scotus** (ca. 1265–1308), a Franciscan from southern Scotland who lectured at Oxford and Paris. A conservative in his moderate realism, he also admired Aristotle and even preferred him at times to Augustine.[40] He also anticipated the direction fourteenth-century theology would take in emphasizing God's freedom and power.

It may be that Scotus's most Franciscan trait was his criticism of Aquinas, with whom he disagreed in a number of important ways. In focusing on God's intellect and perfectly rational nature, for example, Aquinas had seemed to say that God was so bound by reason that he could do nothing *irrational.* This further implied that human beings, whose own reason is modeled on God's, might be able to pin God down, predicting what he would or even must do under certain circumstances merely by determining what the rational course of action would be. Objecting to any suggestion of limits on an infinitely powerful deity, Scotus emphasized God's *freedom of will* over his rationality. This does not mean that he thought of God as dangerously capricious. God is supremely good, he said. But whereas Aquinas had held that God wills what is good, Scotus maintained that whatever God wills is good.

Scotus also emphasized the freedom of the human will, arguing against Augustine that original sin had not robbed human beings of their ability to make decisions for or against God. In relation to salvation, he also insisted that God could have saved humanity in any way he willed to do so. Aquinas, he said, had been wrong in claiming that God redeemed humanity through the incarnation and crucifixion because it was the wisest thing to do. God, he said, is not required to do what is "wisest" or "most logical." The incarnation and crucifixion happened only because God willed to demonstrate his love for humanity in those particular ways. His emphasis on God's freedom allowed Scotus to provide new explanations of other aspects of Christianity, such as the sacraments and predestination, though his thought remained generally orthodox.

In describing God as no slave to reason, Scotus tempered medieval optimism about the potential of rational inquiry and, in so doing, contributed to the eventual break between philosophy and theology. Reason *can* provide some knowledge of God, he admitted, but we are better off focusing on what God has willed to do in the past and accepting by faith the truths he has revealed in scripture. Inevitably, this approach to theology made the universe appear more arbitrary than earlier theologians had imagined it to be, but it had the advantage of safeguard-

ing divine omnipotence. Despite the generally negative character of Scotus's theology, much of which was directed against Aquinas, his criticism of earlier scholasticism and his emphasis on faith won him widespread acclaim. Among his supporters, who admired his deft yet powerful arguments, he was popularly known as the *doctor subtilis* ("subtle doctor"). His opponents, on the other hand, complained that Scotus and his followers dealt only in foolish hairsplitting and minutiae. It was they who began the custom of using the name *Duns* ("dunce") to describe stupid people.

WILLIAM OF OCKHAM

A generation after Scotus a second Franciscan, **William of Ockham** (ca. 1285–1349), launched an all-out assault on scholasticism. Born in the village of Ockham in Surrey, England, William studied and lectured on Peter Lombard's *Sentences* at Oxford. He ran into trouble, however, when the university's chancellor accused him of teaching heresy and he was summoned to defend himself before Pope John XXII at Avignon. Always a renegade, while there he became embroiled in the Franciscan controversy over poverty and sided with the Spiritual Franciscans. He also sharply criticized the papacy, arguing that the pope had no authority in secular affairs and that Christians seeking an infallible authority could turn only to the Bible. After four years of detention, William fled Avignon in 1328 and made his way to Munich, where he spent the rest of his life under the protection of the Holy Roman Emperor, Louis IV of Bavaria, who was also in conflict with the papacy. He died, most likely of plague, about 1349.

Like Scotus, William emphasized God's absolute power and will, though to a greater degree. He also tended to be more radical in other respects, and especially in his nominalism. Scotus had been a moderate realist,[41] but William completely rejected the existence of universals. Here he showed the influence of Aristotle and made an important application of "Ockham's razor," a logical principle according to which the best explanation of an event is that which relies on the fewest assumptions. Ockham the nominalist "shaved away" universals from the realists' picture of reality because he considered them unnecessary to explain the existence of the particulars that make up the material world. If our senses tell us that trees, stones, and dogs exist, he argued, there is no reason to suppose that the universal forms of these things must also exist.

Going far beyond Scotus in undercutting the optimism of the earlier scholastics, Ockham argued that reason cannot prove the truth of *any* Christian belief. Even such basic doctrines as the existence of God and the immortality of the soul cannot be known by reason, or even by illumination, as Augustine and Bonaventure had claimed; they can be known by faith alone. This is because our senses simply do not provide us with empirical evidence of transcendent truths. Speaking of God's moral commandments (the Ten Commandments, for example), Ockham argued that there is nothing in our experience of reality to suggest that they must be as they are. In fact, he said, God *could* have commanded us to do the very opposite of what they require. Because we cannot understand the reaons behind God's decrees, we can only accept them by faith as they are revealed in scripture. By stressing God's freedom and will in this way, Ockham described a universe that seemed unpredictable and arbitrary (if not from God's perspective, then at least from that of human beings) and thereby set a far greater value on faith than on reason.

As with Scotus, Ockham's emphasis on divine power and freedom led him to conclude that God has no need to follow rules or do what seems to us to be what is most rational or efficient. Ockham made this point especially clear in connection with God's method of accomplishing salvation. Whereas Anselm had argued that God became human because it was *reasonable* for him to do so, Ockham is said to have claimed that God could have saved sinners by becoming an ass had he *willed* to do so.[42] Ockham's understanding of salvation was also influenced by his nominalism. As we have seen, earlier theories of salvation described the work of Christ as affecting all of "humanity," understood here as a universal form, by uniting humanity and divinity in himself. But Ockham recognized the existence only of particular individuals and made salvation dependent upon what God willed to do in

individual cases. In theory, this made the question of one's salvation completely uncertain, but Ockham and later Ockhamist theologians insisted that God is not capricious. He is consistent in his tendencies, and one of these is to grant grace to people who do their best to merit it. Grace then empowers them to perform works of love that ultimately earn the reward of salvation.[43] Of course, salvation is ultimately dependent upon the sacrifice of Christ, but Ockhamists such as Gabriel Biel (ca. 1420–95) emphasized the importance of working in partnership with God and contributing to one's own salvation through good works.

Although the views of John Duns Scotus and William of Ockham offered new ways of looking at Christian beliefs, they were quite orthodox. They did not bring sudden or decisive changes to Christian theology, but they did hasten the decline of scholasticism by questioning the potential of reason and encouraging theology to shift its focus from God's rationality, which Aquinas had emphasized, to his freedom, power, and will. Inevitably, this encouraged philosophy and theology to go their own ways, philosophy in the direction of natural science and theology toward a renewed emphasis on faith.

THEOLOGY AND POLITICAL THEORY

Developments in late medieval theology were linked to changing attitudes toward ecclesiastical authority. William of Ockham's criticism of the papacy, for example, was based in part on his nominalism, which allowed him to think of that office as human in origin and therefore subject to modification. Seeking to limit the power of the pope and increase the influence of the laity, Ockham argued that the Church should be governed by a council of elected representatives, including women, that would choose popes, supervise their performance and morals, and depose those who were incompetent or immoral.

Even before William of Ockham, Thomas Aquinas had laid the groundwork for a reassessment of papal authority by saying that there are areas of human activity in which faith is unnecessary. Most kinds of work, for example, can be done solely on the basis of reason. From this some inferred that secular leaders could rule competently without papal supervision or control. Thomas himself always recognized the higher aims of the Church and encouraged states to follow its lead, but later thinkers began to reject the old idea that secular power must be subordinated to spiritual authority. They urged a dismantling of the doctrine that temporal rulers receive their authority from the hand of the pope. About 1302 the Dominican political theorist John of Paris noted that there had been kings long before Christianity. "Therefore," he argued, "neither the royal power nor its exercise is from the pope but from God and from the people who elect a king by choosing either a person or a royal house." [44]

Writing a decade later, the Italian poet Dante Alighieri took a similar position. In his treatise *On Monarchy* he argued that only a universal empire ruled by a Roman Emperor could guarantee the peace and stability civilization requires. The authority to rule such a state comes directly from God, he said, as does that of the pope. Thus, the two are on equal footing. Each has its appropriate sphere of activity and should not interfere with the other. Dante allowed that the emperor should honor the pope, but this concession was not enough to keep *On Monarchy* from being condemned as heretical in 1329.

More radical than Dante was Marsilius of Padua, whose *Defender of Peace* appeared in 1324. Marsilius acknowledged that the Church had important spiritual responsibilities but claimed that it had no authority whatsoever in the secular sphere. To eliminate its influence there, he advocated the confiscation of all ecclesiastical property and requiring all clerics to live in poverty. Like William of Ockham, he emphasized that the Church is constituted of the laity as well as the clergy, but he went further in adding that all secular and spiritual authority derives from the people. Accordingly, Marsilius proposed that the Church should be ruled by a council representing Christians from all levels of society. The judgments of such a council, he said, would be infallible. As for the pope, Marsilius argued that he had no right to rule over other bishops, to define doctrine, or to create ecclesiastical laws. It is small wonder, then, that in 1343 Pope Clement VI de-

clared the *Defender of Peace* the most heretical book he had ever read.

Given this background, it becomes easier to understand the emergence of the conciliar movement, which sought to end the Great Schism by placing ecclesiastical government into the hands of a council of bishops. Compared to most of the figures discussed above, the conciliarists themselves were quite conservative. Some considered the rule of the Church by a council justifiable only when extreme circumstances prevented the effective operation of the papacy. Others, such as Dietrich of Niem (ca. 1340–1418), a participant in the Council of Constance, stressed the fallibility of the popes and called for the Church to be ruled by a council to which the pope was answerable.

Throughout this period the bishops of Rome continued to uphold the claims for the papacy made by their predecessors. Thus, when Pope Eugenius IV was triumphing over the Council of Basel in the middle of the fifteenth century, he sounded very much like Innocent III more than two centuries earlier in describing his primacy as universal and himself as the "true vicar of Christ" and "head of the whole Church." What Eugenius could not foresee was that continuing criticism of the papacy and dramatic changes in religious life would soon make such claims far less tenable.

The Church and the Renaissance

During the fourteenth century, when most of Europe was still very much medieval in culture, the Renaissance was beginning to take shape in Italy. This "rebirth" of the art, literature, and philosophy of classical Greece and Rome first appeared in prosperous commercial cities such as Florence, Venice, Pisa, and Milan. In these thriving urban centers, wealth generated by trade with Europe and the East produced a cultured, confident elite who prized education, cultivated the senses as well as the soul, and sponsored artists, architects, poets, and philosophers who shared their appreciation of human achievements and positive vision of the future. Such people counted themselves fortunate to live in a new and exciting era. One of them, the Florentine business leader Matteo Palmieri, wrote, "Now, indeed, may every thoughtful spirit thank God that it has been permitted to him to be born in this new age, so full of hope and promise, which already rejoices in a greater array of nobly gifted souls than the world has seen in the thousand years that have preceded it."[45]

In such an age the medieval emphasis on human depravity and helplessness before sin seemed strangely out of place. Instead, Renaissance thinkers embraced the spirit of ancient Greece and Rome, which had praised human beings for their worth and dignity. This is not to say that the Renaissance was antireligious. There was no serious questioning of the truth of Christianity, and the greatest representatives of Renaissance culture continued to make extensive use of religious ideas and themes in their work. Moreover, much attention was given to identifying the purest and noblest aspects of Christian civilization. At the same time, however, it was an age in which appreciation of literature and the arts rivaled the respect enjoyed by theology. Perhaps it is best, then, to think of Renaissance culture as drawing on both the classical tradition and the Christian tradition in honoring and understanding humanity as well as God. Reaching its zenith in the fifteenth and early sixteenth centuries, the Renaissance had by then expanded far beyond Italy to influence life and thought in most other parts of Europe.

THE RENAISSANCE IN ITALY

The blending of Christianity and **humanism**— a deep and applied faith in human beings and their potential — was evident everywhere in the culture of Renaissance Italy. There were, of course, notable exceptions. Boccaccio (1313–1375) filled the pages of his *Decameron* with bawdy tales that showed little interest in Christian virtues, and the Florentine political theorist Niccolò Machiavelli (1469–1527) wrote in *The Prince* that Christian morals should have little place in the practice of politics. More often, however, Renaissance thinkers focused on the nobility of human nature. In his famous *Oration on*

the Dignity of Man (ca. 1486), the great humanist Giovanni Pico della Mirandola imagined God advising the newly created Adam of the infinite potential he had been given:

> Neither a fixed abode nor a form that is thine alone nor any function peculiar to thyself have we given thee. . . . Thou, constrained by no limits, in accordance with thine own free will, in whose hand We have placed thee, shalt ordain for thyself the limits of thy nature. . . . Thou shalt have the power to degenerate into the lower forms of life, which are brutish. Thou shalt have the power, out of thy soul's judgment, to be reborn into the higher forms, which are divine.[46]

Pico's contemporary Marsilio Ficino (1463–99) described human nature in equally positive terms. Deeply influenced by Neoplatonism, and departing entirely from the idea of original sin, he believed that all human beings have an inner drive toward God, the source of all goodness, beauty, and truth. Our love of these springs naturally and spontaneously from our innermost being, he said, and is actually a love of God that seeks fulfillment in communion with the divine.

It is little wonder, then, that the cities of the Italian Renaissance adorned themselves with art and architecture that proclaimed the goodness and beauty of God, humanity, and all of Creation. Painters like Giotto, Masaccio, Boticelli, and Fra Angelico concentrated on religious themes but with an obvious appreciation of the nobility of their human subjects. In sculpture, Michelangelo (1475–1564) and others rivaled the Greeks in portraying the ideal beauty of the human form and surpassed them in exploring the spiritual and emotional dimensions of human existence. Renaissance architects devoted most of their energies to religious buildings such as Florence's cathedral and St. Peter's Basilica in Rome. Drawing heavily upon classical forms and styles, they created exquisitely beautiful structures whose design and interior sculptures and paintings exalted material as well as spiritual reality.

The Renaissance passion for classical Greek and Latin literature also influenced Christianity, for it sparked a great interest in ancient manuscripts.

This led in turn to the development of textual criticism, the comparative analysis of different manuscript versions of a single text in order to determine its original form. Just this sort of analysis allowed the Italian humanist Lorenzo Valla (ca. 1406–57) to prove that the Donation of Constantine was a forgery and to question the tradition that held that the Apostles' Creed was written by the Apostles themselves.[47] Textual criticism also brought the appearance of new editions of the Bible and church fathers in the original languages and prepared the way for the text-critical and historical study of the Bible that scholars would undertake in later years.

HUMANISM IN NORTHERN EUROPE

The Renaissance had less influence in northern Europe, where it was centered in royal courts rather than in cities. Still, northern humanism proved to be a powerful and transforming force. In Germany, scholars like Johannes Reuchlin (1455–1522) brought the study of classical literature, Greek, and Hebrew to the universities. In England, professors at Oxford did the same. In his *Utopia*, the English humanist Sir Thomas More (1478–1535) presented a vision of the ideal society based on human work and wisdom as well as religion.

Easily the greatest of the northern humanists was More's friend **Desiderius Erasmus** (1466–1536). Born in Rotterdam in the Netherlands, Erasmus received his early education in a school run by the Brethren of the Common Life. When Erasmus was about twenty, poverty forced him into an Augustinian monastery, but his love of learning and command of classical Greek and Latin literature soon led him away from monastic life. As he traveled widely throughout Europe, his wit, charm, and vast erudition made him a celebrity sought out by the most prestigious courts of his day.

Erasmus produced important scholarly works, including critical editions of the Greek New Testament and writings of the church fathers, as well as a Latin translation of the New Testament that corrected errors found in Jerome's Vulgate. But he is best known for his satirical *Praise of Folly*, in which he lampooned the superstition and foolishness of his contemporaries. Erasmus was deeply disturbed by the behavior of secular rulers and even more critical of the many ways the Church exploited the ignorance and credulity of laypeople. The key to changing society, he believed, was the promotion of humanistic ideals and Christian virtues by an educational system whose primary subjects would be the classics and the Bible. In such texts could be found the "philosophy of Christ," a set of values and ideals whose power to uplift and perfect the human spirit made it vastly superior to popular Christianity and the arid and inaccessible arguments of medieval scholasticism. Perfectly exemplified by Christ, Erasmus taught, the *philosophia Christi* required no formal creeds, doctrines, or rituals and recognized no distinctions among human beings on the bases of gender, economic condition, or social status. All that God asked of men and women, he said, was the sincere imitation of Christ.

In an age when religious enthusiasm was often frustrated by the behavior of the clergy and the complexity of doctrine, this simple and straightforward message had great appeal. Among those it attracted was Martin Luther, in whom Erasmus at first thought he had found an ally. But he soon concluded that Luther and the other Protestant reformers were just as dogmatic in their religion as the Catholic hierarchy and refused to support them. Despite this, his conception of true Christian piety contributed significantly to some of the new directions Christianity would take in the sixteenth century.

THE RENAISSANCE POPES

The popes of the Renaissance ruled the Church from an Italy torn by civil and political strife. In the fourteenth through sixteenth centuries the Italian peninsula was divided into a variety of states: the kingdom of Naples in the south, the Papal States in the center, and independent city republics such as Florence, Genoa, and Venice in the north. Frequently at war, they were also disrupted by internal conflicts between their old aristocracies and newer, politically aggressive commercial classes. The repeated attempts of France and Germany to gain in-

Figure 7.5 Erasmus, the most celebrated humanist scholar of his time, published a Greek New Testament with a Latin translation early in the sixteenth century. The page shown here is from the beginning of the Gospel of Matthew.

fluence in the region made the situation even more unstable. At the same time, the vibrant new culture of the Renaissance was growing and flourishing—its prosperity, arts, and ideas combining to lift Italy out of its medieval past into the beginnings of the modern era.

For these reasons, the Renaissance popes found themselves caught up by the forces of war, political upheaval, and cultural transformation. Unwilling to stand apart from the change around them, they threw themselves into its midst, seeking to promote their own interests as well as those of the Church. They became embroiled in dark political intrigues, led armies into war, and became the patrons of some of the greatest artistic and literary talents of the Renaissance. For the most part, the Renaissance popes devoted themselves to the pursuit of power and pleasure and ignored the pressing need for ecclesiastical reform.

This was already the case by the reign of Nicholas V (1447–55), the first of the true Renaissance popes. During Nicholas's pontificate, Rome was only a fraction of the size it had been in ancient times and much smaller than contemporary Florence, Venice, and Milan. For Nicholas, rebuilding the city and transforming it into the cultural and intellectual center of Europe were top priorities. He spent huge sums restoring Rome's walls and gates, building fountains and public squares, attracting famous artists and writers, purchasing rare Greek manuscripts, and arranging for their translation into Latin. His successor, Calixtus III (1455–58), vainly attempted to enhance papal prestige by uniting Italy under Rome in a crusade against the Turks, who were then despoiling the Balkans. The "father" of the infamous Borgia family that would dominate ecclesiastical and Italian politics for the next half-century, he was more successful in beginning a tradition of blatant papal nepotism. Among the many favorites he appointed to high ecclesiastical positions were two nephews whom he made cardinals, one of them the future Alexander VI.

Sixtus IV (1471–84), a scholar and former head of the Franciscan order, outdid Calixtus III in nepotism, engaged in truly reckless simony, and involved himself in bloody family feuds. By imposing a tax on grain so heavy that many could not buy bread, he raised funds used to purchase expensive art and finance projects such as the Sistine Chapel, which was named for him. Despite his failure to offer moral and spiritual leadership, Sixtus did manage to strengthen the papacy's control over the Papal States.

Sixtus's successor, Innocent VIII (1484–92), continued the repair and adornment of Rome but paid for it with funds gained through simony and the aggressive sale of indulgences. He outstripped his predecessors in corruption but was in turn bested by Rodrigo Borgia, who bought his election as Alexander VI (1492–1503) with bribes paid to cardinals and went on to scandalize a Rome already jaded by papal immorality. Alexander sold cardinals their offices, seized their estates when they died, offered dispensations and divorces as parts of political deals, supported several mistresses, and proudly acknowledged his illegitimate children. His favorite son, Cesare Borgia, was made a cardinal while still in his teens and served his father with such ruthlessness in defending papal and family interests that he is said to have been the inspiration for Machiavelli's *The Prince*. Alexander died suddenly in 1503 — most likely of malaria, though rumors spoke of poison.

Two more Renaissance popes deserve our attention. Julius II (1503–1513), a nephew of Sixtus IV, was easily the most warlike. He led papal armies in successful campaigns throughout Italy, expanding the temporal power of the papacy at the expense of Venice, Bologna, and France. A great lover of the arts, he was the patron of Michelangelo and the painter Raphael and began the rebuilding of the Vatican's Basilica of St. Peter. Julius was also a skilled statesman. Like many of his predecessors, however, he was given to excesses that could bring scorn and ridicule. Erasmus claimed to have witnessed a bullfight in the papal palace and later wrote a popular satire in which St. Peter refused to allow Julius into heaven despite the pope's efforts to storm the gates.[48]

Julius was succeeded by Giovanni de Medici, the son of Lorenzo de Medici ("the Magnificent"), one of the wealthiest and most influential figures of the Renaissance. Innocent VIII had made Giovanni a cardinal at thirteen. Becoming Leo X (1513–21) at thirty-eight, the young pope made it clear that he was an aesthete who had little interest in the responsibilities of the papacy. Leo freely indulged his love of the arts and made his court home to some of Italy's greatest poets, painters, and musicians. Meanwhile, France took advantage of his inattention and inability, forcing him into an agreement that gave French kings greater control over the French clergy.[49] At the same time, in Germany, Martin Luther began objecting publicly to demands for funds to rebuild St. Peter's and to abuses the Church had long promised to remedy but had largely ignored.

We must remember that both the papacy and the high culture of the Renaissance belonged primarily to the wealthy and educated elite. The great masses of less-privileged people remained devoted to traditional values and gave their attention to religious leaders who preached virtue and the consequences of sin rather than the glories of art and literature. In the late fifteenth century the Spanish Dominican Vincent Ferrer drew huge crowds of believers in France, Spain, and northern Italy to sermons in which he warned that the Day of Judgment was imminent. The Franciscan friar Bernardino of Siena (1380–1444) is said to have preached with an eloquence that reformed the morals of entire cities. Catherine of Genoa (1447–1510) inspired thousands with her selfless devotion to the poor and sick. Men and women like these shared a desire that the Church return to what they imagined to be its original purity. In this sense they had much in common with individuals and groups described earlier in this chapter and contributed to the mounting demand for renewal and reform of Christianity in the West.

The Eastern Orthodox Church

The eleventh through fifteenth centuries brought three important developments in the history of the eastern Church. The first was its break with Rome, an event presaged by centuries of increasing divergence between eastern and western Christianity. The second was its gradual decline — due largely to the Islamic conquest of the Byzantine Empire, which culminated in 1453 with the fall of Constantinople to the Turks. The third was the rise of Orthodoxy in Russia.

THE BREAK WITH ROME

Accounts of the split between the churches of the East and West often stress conflict over issues such as the *filioque* (the words *and from the Son*, added in the West to the Nicene Creed), clerical celibacy, liturgical differences, and the right sort of bread to be used in the eucharist. Though such concerns contributed to the tensions between the two traditions, they were certainly not decisive. Far more important were the rivalry of the bishops of Rome and Constantinople, the claims of the popes to authority over the entire Church, and western encroachment on Byzantine territory. Nor was the break sudden. The two churches had been drifting apart long before 1054, the year to which their separation is commonly, though somewhat arbitrarily, assigned, and the status of their relationship remained uncertain well into the fourteenth century.

What makes 1054 of particular interest is that it saw the culmination of a controversy sparked by the Norman policy of forcing Greek Christians in Italy to worship according to western custom. In 1052 Michael Cerularius, the patriarch of Constantinople, had retaliated by requiring the Latin churches in that city to conform to Greek practices. When the patriarch later indicated his desire to resolve the conflict, Pope Leo IX sent a delegation to Constantinople headed by the same Cardinal Humbert whose uncompromising commitment to papal supremacy had made him a key player in Leo's reform of the papacy. Unfortunately, Humbert's arrogant assertion of papal rights and his demand that the East accept the *filioque* only angered the patriarch, who refused to deal with him thereafter. In the Greeks' view, the bishop of Rome held a place of honor among other bishops, but he was not an ecclesiastical monarch who had the right to add words to creeds or take other unilateral actions affecting the entire Church. Finally, on 16 July 1054, after months of being ignored, Humbert angrily entered the Church of Hagia Sophia as the eucharist was

about to begin, strode to the altar, and laid upon it a bull excommunicating the patriarch. As he left the building, he ceremoniously shook the dust from his feet and shouted, "Let God look and judge!" A few days later the patriarch excommunicated Humbert and the legates who had accompanied him.

Despite its gravity, this event did not bring a final break between the eastern and western churches. Friendly relations were maintained at some levels of the clergy, and in 1089 Pope Urban II removed the excommunication imposed on the patriarch. Urban hoped that the First Crusade, which he proclaimed six years later, would be a cooperative effort that would both liberate the Holy Land and restore unity to the Church. But it was not to be, for the crusaders repeatedly violated Byzantine trust and territory, particularly during the Fourth Crusade of 1204. In that year they pillaged Constantinople, vandalized the Church of Hagia Sophia, and allowed prostitutes to sit upon the throne of the patriarch. Stunned by the brutality of their fellow Christians, the Greeks now saw little reason to seek reconciliation with them.

Still, sporadic attempts at mediation continued. After the departure of the crusaders from Constantinople in 1261, Emperor Michael VIII Palaeologus initiated discussions that led to an agreement on reunion at the Second Council of Lyons in 1274. But the concessions made by the Greek delegation were widely condemned in the East. Later emperors sought reconciliation in the hope that it might bring military assistance against the Turks, but their vulnerability to the invading Muslims left the Byzantines unable to negotiate from a position of strength with their fellow Christians. As we saw earlier in this chapter, a final attempt was made at the Council of Florence in 1439, when the capture of Constantinople was imminent. Drawing conciliarist bishops away from the Council of Basel with the promise of renewed union with the East, Pope Eugenius IV presided over discussions by Greek and Latin bishops that led to a Decree of Union. The Greeks retained their traditional liturgy and customs such as priestly marriage, but they also recognized the right of western Christians to incorporate the *filioque* clause in their version of the

Nicene Creed and even appeared to acknowledge the primacy of the pope. Once again, however, popular sentiment in the East was overwhelmingly against concessions to the West, and many of the signatories later withdrew their approval of the Decree. The fall of Constantinople in 1453 erased what remained of any gains that had been made.

THE FALL OF BYZANTIUM

In the East, the most momentous development in the first half of the second millennium was the fall of the Byzantine Empire. We saw in chapter 6 that between the eleventh and early thirteenth centuries the empire suffered devastating blows both from the Seljuk Turks, who seized Byzantine territory in Asia, and western Europeans, who plundered Constantinople during the Fourth Crusade. Even with the decline of the Seljuks and return of Constantinople to Greek rule in 1261, the Byzantine state remained weak. Its plight grew worse with the appearance of a new group of Turkish invaders, the Ottomans. The Ottomans were the last in a series of tribes that had migrated westward from central Asia; by the thirteenth century they had settled in Asia Minor and embraced Islam. Before long they began an assault on the Balkans, the heart of the Byzantine Empire. In April 1453 they besieged Constantinople. The ancient capital fell a month later, the last remnant of a great empire more than fourteen centuries old. Under the sultan Mehmed II the city came to be known as Istanbul[50] and its famous Church of Hagia Sophia was made into a mosque. Orthodox Christians who now found themselves under Ottoman rule were suddenly faced with the challenge of practicing Christianity in a Muslim world.

THE ORTHODOX CHURCH AND
THE OTTOMAN STATE

The Orthodox Church fared better than many had expected in the years immediately following 1453. Like all Muslims, the Ottomans regarded Christians as "people of the book." Because the Church was a legitimate institution under Islamic law, the sultans assumed responsibility for its protection along with the rights and privileges once exercised by the Byzantine Emperors. This policy became clear in 1454, when Mehmed II chose Gennadius II for the patriarchate and invested him with the symbols of his office. The sultan and the new patriarch also established a concordat that was to govern the relations of the Orthodox Church and the Ottoman state into the twentieth century.

Under the Ottoman system, the patriarch of Constantinople was the sole representative of Orthodox Christians before the sultan. All other patriarchs were viewed as his subordinates and could approach the sultan only through him. Although in theory this gave the patriarch far more extensive authority over the Church than before, it also made his position more difficult and dangerous. In addition to being personally responsible for the loyalty and orderly conduct of the faithful, he also had much to fear from those who coveted his office or wished to manipulate or abuse it. During the nearly five hundred years of Ottoman rule that began in 1453, only 21 patriarchs died natural deaths while in office. Six were killed by hanging, poisoning, or drowning, 27 abdicated, and another 105 were forced from the throne, in most cases so that the sultan might demand payment for the office.[51] Most ecclesiastical offices, in fact, were sold by the Ottoman government.

Officially, Turkish policy guaranteed Christians the right to practice their religion unmolested, provided that they did not interfere with Islam. In reality, Christians purchased their limited freedom by paying taxes that penalized them for their faith, were required to wear distinctive clothing, were rarely allowed to build new churches, and were forbidden to attempt the conversion of any Muslim. In such ways Christians were reminded that they were second-class citizens in an Islamic empire.

Because Islam makes no real distinction between religious and political life, the sultans viewed Orthodox Christians as a "nation" whose membership was identical to that of the Orthodox Church. This *Rum Millet,* or "Roman Nation," was ruled by the patriarch, who also held the political title of *ethnarch* and was assisted by the hierarchy, who were now civil servants as well as bishops and priests. As such, they worked with Ottoman authorities to ensure payment of taxes by Christians, organized and administered courts of law, and performed other civil functions. In this way, the Ottoman system created an extremely close relationship between the Greek hierarchy and the state. One important consequence of this arrangement was the perception that Orthodoxy, a tradition meant to include all peoples, was essentially Greek. This was one of the factors that contributed to the eventual emergence of "national" churches, such as the Orthodox churches of Bulgaria, Serbia, and Romania.

THE RUSSIAN ORTHODOX CHURCH

We have seen that the history of Christianity in Russia began with the conversion of Vladimir of Kiev, the region's most important city, at the end of the tenth century. Vladimir's choice of Byzantine over western Christianity paved the way for lasting Greek influence in Russian religious life and the introduction of Byzantine art, architecture, and music. Because Vladimir used his office to encourage mass conversions, the Christianization of the country progressed quickly, especially among the aristocracy and in the cities. Russia's vast size made the conversion of the rural population more difficult, but once established popular devotion to the faith became legendary for its depth and tenacity.

This commitment to Orthodoxy enabled the Church to survive the fall of Kiev to the Mongols in 1240, as did the Mongol policy of ruling Russia indirectly through local princes. Although they demanded heavy tribute, the Mongols made the Church exempt and allowed it to rise to a position of national and cultural leadership it retains to this day. It was with the support of the Russian Church that the rulers of Moscow, whose position had been strengthened through service to their Mongol masters, began to resist them. By 1480 Ivan III (1462–1505) was strong enough to refuse the tribute. Eventually he forced the Mongols from his realm. By also eliminating his Russian rivals and winning other princes to his side, Ivan succeeded in making himself the master of Russia and Moscow its capital.

Byzantine Christianity was the dominant force in shaping Russian worship and piety, most notably through its liturgy and pattern of ecclesiastical organization, but there were other influences as well. Elements of Palestinian monasticism were adopted by early Russian monks. The Bulgarian Church provided translations of scripture and other religious texts from Greek into Slavonic, the language of most Eastern Slavs at that time. The custom of tithing and the veneration of English and French saints were borrowed from the West.[52] To these the Russian Church added its own distinctive features. The result was a Christianity with deep historical roots that was also remarkably successful in representing the unique attitudes and sensibilities of the Russian people.

The temper of early Russian Christianity is vividly reflected in its saints. Two of the earliest were Vladimir's sons, Boris and Gleb, who were murdered by their half-brother during the civil wars that followed their father's death. Although they could easily have defended themselves, legend says they welcomed their assassins and chose to die willingly as innocents rather than resist violence with violence. For the millions of Russians who have revered the two princes as spiritual heroes, their suffering amounted to a participation in that of Christ, who also sacrificed himself for the sake of a higher ideal, and underscored the Russian conviction that the presence of evil in the world makes passive resistance and suffering a necessary part of Christian life.

This ideal of "emptying" oneself of pride, position, and self-interest, known as kenoticism, quickly became one of the most characteristic features of Russian monasticism. One of its greatest exponents was Theodosius, an eleventh-century saint who was abbot of the famous Monastery of the Caves near Kiev. Like Francis of Assisi, as a young man he rejected his family's wealth and went to live and work with the poor. In doing so, he said, he was privileged to follow in the footsteps of Christ, who had humbled himself to the point of accepting degradation and death for the sake of humanity. In connection with the practice of "self-emptying" and in keeping with the monastic ideals established by Basil the Great in the fourth century, Theodosius made service to others a fundamental part of monastic life. He encouraged monasteries to use their income to care for the poor and seems to have been the originator of the Russian custom of having monks serve the laity as confessors and spiritual advisors.

Perhaps the most beloved of Russian saints was Sergius of Radonezh (ca. 1314–1392). Sergius lived just as the tide was turning against the Mongol invaders and as Moscow was replacing Kiev as the center of Russian civilization. As a young man he joined other monks in the depths of Russia's forests, where he would not be distracted by worldly influences. Living at first as a hermit, in time he attracted disciples who persuaded him to become their spiritual "elder" (*staretz*) and establish the Monastery of the Holy Trinity near Moscow. Like Theodosius, Sergius practiced a radical humility. Wearing only coarse peasant clothing and performing the most menial tasks, there was nothing about his appearance to suggest that he was Russia's most famous sage and an advisor to its rulers. One visitor to his monastery is said to have complained, "I came to see a prophet and you show me a beggar."[53] Possibly influenced by Greek Hesychasm, Sergius introduced mystical piety to Russian monasticism. He also advocated a monastic activism that went beyond service to the poor and sick. Much of his popularity was due to his support of efforts to drive the Mongols from Russia.

No less than the rulers of Kiev and Moscow, the Russian Church promoted a sense of national identity. The monasteries that spread as far north as the Arctic Circle and into Russia's distant eastern reaches in the thirteenth through fifteenth centuries advanced the unification of the people by encouraging the adoption of a common language and allegiance to Russia's rulers. They also served as intellectual centers where schools and libraries could be found and promoted the development of the arts, most notably icon painting. Many of Russia's towns and cities grew up around monastic communities. The visibility of the Church was also enhanced by its relationship with the rulers of Moscow, which became Russia's religious capital early in the fourteenth century. The Church's value as a political tool was not lost on the city's grand dukes, who brought it increasingly under their control as their power grew. This trend reached its culmination in the reign of Ivan III, whose reign began just a decade after the fall of Constantinople. Claiming to

be the legitimate successor of the Byzantine Emperors, he adopted the title *tsar* ("caesar"), devised a complicated court ceremonial based on the Byzantine model, and underscored the continuity between Byzantium and Russia by marrying the niece of the last Byzantine Emperor. Like the emperors, he also assumed the role of protector of the Church, which he used extensively to gain his political ends. Moreover, Ivan declared Moscow the new capital of Orthodox Christianity. Rome, he argued, had surrendered to the barbarians and then to heresy. Constantinople had fallen into heresy (by briefly accepting the decisions of the Council of Florence) and suffered its punishment at the hands of the Turks. It was God's will, he argued, that the Orthodox world should now be ruled from Moscow, the "third Rome." This claim was clearly expressed in a letter written about 1510 by the monk Philotheus of Pskov to Tsar Basil III:

> I wish to add a few words on the present Orthodox Empire of our ruler: he is on earth the sole Emperor [Tsar] of the Christians, the leader of the Apostolic Church which stands no longer in Rome or in Constantinople, but in the blessed city of Moscow. She alone shines in the whole world brighter than the sun. . . . All Christian Empires are fallen and in their stead stands alone the Empire of our ruler in accordance with the Prophetical books. Two Romes have fallen, but the third stands and a fourth there will not be.[54]

Although the dream of a universal Orthodox empire under Russian rule was never realized, at the time it was not entirely unfounded. From Ivan's time until our own, the Russian Orthodox Church has far surpassed all other Orthodox churches in its great numbers and geographical reach.

The Smaller Churches of Africa and Asia

In chapters 4 and 5 we described several traditions within early eastern Christianity that separated from the Byzantine Church for doctrinal as well as ethnic reasons. A few quickly disappeared, but some of these smaller churches have survived until our own time, somehow managing to cope with the advance of Islam, lack of state support, and vulnerability to hostile religious and ethnic majorities.

THE COPTIC AND ETHIOPIAN CHURCHES

Christianity put down its first African roots in Egypt, where African Christianity proved to be most persistent. Although the Greek or "Melchite" ("imperial") Christianity of ancient Alexandria remained a presence, it was gradually overshadowed by that of the native Copts,[55] who rejected the Council of Chalcedon in favor of a moderate Monophysitism.[56] The Copts made their own translation of scripture, devised a Coptic liturgy, and considered opposition to Chalcedonian Christology and the Byzantine Empire marks of national pride.

Tension between the Melchite and Coptic traditions escalated until the Arab invasion of Egypt in the seventh century, which ended Byzantine support of the Melchite churches. For a time, Egypt's Islamic rulers displayed considerable tolerance, but by the tenth century severe strictures had been imposed that made it illegal for Christians to preach to Muslims, display Christian symbols, or allow their religion to interfere in any way with Islam. At times Egyptian Christians were subjected to extreme persecution, as under the caliph al-Hakim (996–1021), who is said to have destroyed three thousand churches. In subsequent years the Coptic Church experienced alternating periods of uncertain peace and violent oppression. Its survival may be attributed largely to the powerful roles played by monasteries and the hierarchy, whose patriarchs have always claimed to be successors to St. Mark the Evangelist.[57] By recent estimates, there are now some four million Coptic Christians, most of them in Egypt, Sudan, and South Africa.

The Coptic Church has strong historical and doctrinal ties to the Ethiopian (Abyssinian) Church, which is also Monophysite. Christianity was brought to Ethiopia in the fourth century by Frumentius, the "Apostle to the Ethiopians," and Edesius of Tyre, who were shipwrecked off the coast. They took advantage of this unexpected opportunity to evangelize the region, and Frumentius was later made its bishop by the same Athanasius

who was a leading figure in the Arian controversy. Coptic missionary monks were active in Ethiopia by the fifth century and assisted in the translation of scripture into Ethiopic. The spread of Islam into Africa beginning in the seventh century isolated Ethiopia from the rest of the Christian world. The few available sources say little about the history of Christianity there until the thirteenth century, when a flourishing monastic movement was successfully encouraging the growth of the faith and the building of churches, some of them hewn from rock. By the fifteenth century the Ethiopian Church was vigorous enough to send delegates to the Council of Florence. Today, the Ethiopian Church and Coptic Church are counted among the four Oriental Orthodox Churches, a designation that distinguishes them from the much larger Eastern Orthodox Churches. The other two are the Monophysite churches of Syria and Armenia.

MONOPHYSITISM IN SYRIA AND ARMENIA

Syrian Monophysites have long been known as Jacobites, a name taken from that of Jacob Baradaeus, a sixth-century bishop who traveled widely throughout the East, ordaining Monophysite priests and encouraging the faithful in the face of Byzantine persecution. As with the Copts, the Syrians had both religious and ethnic reasons for resisting Constantinople's attempts to impose a uniform Chalcedonianism throughout the empire. Although they were a tiny minority, they were able to survive through the leadership of a dedicated hierarchy headed by a patriarch in Antioch, a strong monastic tradition, and translations of scripture and the liturgy into Syriac. Syrian Christianity also produced fine scholars such as Jacob of Edessa (ca. 640–708), who wrote on grammar and history, and Moses bar Kepha (ca. 815–903), noted for his commentaries on the books of the Bible. In the Middle Ages the great Jacobite scholar Bar Hebraeus (1226–86) was regarded as one of the most learned men of his time. He wrote an immense theological compendium entitled *The Candelabra of the Sanctuary* and on topics ranging from Aristotelian philosophy to monastic life. For most of their history the Jacobites have remained in close communion with the Coptic Church. Today there are perhaps 200,000 in the Middle East. Another million live in southern India and are known as Malabar Christians. They trace their history back to St. Thomas the Apostle, who tradition says was martyred near Madras.

A fourth Monophysite church arose in Armenia. Christianity became the official religion there, earlier than anywhere else, when Gregory the Illuminator, a Cappadocian monk, converted King Tiridates (ca. 301). At first the Armenian Church followed the lead of Constantinople, but increasing Syrian influence brought Monophysitism and vigorous rejection of the Council of Chalcedon.[58] Here too, it seems, preferences in religious belief were linked to a desire to remain independent of the Byzantine state. The struggle against the Arabs between 639 and 859 left the Armenians defeated but with a limited autonomy that allowed their church to thrive. It built schools and monasteries, produced an impressive body of Christian literature, and developed a distinctive form of church architecture that influenced the Byzantine style. Under the leadership of its own independent line of patriarchs, the Armenian Church survived foreign rule and persecution under Persians, Arabs, Mongols, and, more recently, Turks and Russians. Often described as Gregorian Christians, after Gregory the Illuminator, the present number of Armenian Christians stands at about five million.

NESTORIAN CHRISTIANITY

The most widespread of the smaller eastern churches in the medieval era was that of the Nestorians. Their name is somewhat misleading, for though it suggests adherence to Nestorius's doctrine of the separation of the human and divine natures in Christ, Nestorian theology has generally been much more in line with that of Theodore of Mopsuestia, a more moderate representative of Antiochene Christology.

The Nestorian Church had its beginnings in the years following the condemnation of Nestorius's views by the Council of Ephesus in 431. For half a century the Nestorians were concentrated in eastern Syria around the theological school of Ibas, a bishop of Edessa. In 489, however, persecution forced them to flee to Persia, where they established a new school at Nisibis and bishoprics extending into Arabia and India. For a time they had to contend with the hostility of Persian Zoroastrians, but conditions improved with the Arab conquest of Persia in 637, which gave the Nestorians firmer legal standing and a greater measure of religious freedom. Over the next seven centuries they launched missionary campaigns that established the Nestorian Church as far east as Mongolia and China. Growth turned into decline in the sixteenth century, however, as Indian Nestorians influenced by Portuguese missionaries were joined by Mesopotamian Nestorians in establishing communion with the Roman Catholic Church.[59] The twentieth century saw further losses as Iranian Nestorians joined the Russian Orthodox Church and thousands of others died at the hands of the Turks and Kurds in World War I. Today there are fewer than two hundred thousand Nestorian Christians. Most live in Syria, Iraq, and Iran and follow a patriarch who rules their church from Baghdad.

Summary

By the end of the fifteenth century, Christianity was divided into two great traditions: Eastern Orthodoxy and Roman Catholicism. Although they had been in essential agreement theologically, differences in the actual practice of the faith and disagreement over specific issues such as the *filioque*, purgatory, and papal supremacy had produced a schism that divides them to this day. There were also smaller churches, such as those of the Nestorians and Monophysites, that remained independent of Catholicism and Orthodoxy.

In the East, the place of Christianity was dramatically altered by the Turkish destruction of the Byzantine Empire. With the fall of Constantinople in 1453, Orthodox Christians found themselves living under Muslim rule. Only in Russia were Orthodox Christianity and culture free to develop unhindered. In the West, the quality of papal leadership suffered as the papacy was removed for six decades to Avignon and then divided among rival popes during the Great Schism. As a result, Christian thinkers began to question the role of the pope in the Church and proponents of the conciliar movement urged that ecclesiastical government be put into the hands of a council of bishops. Complaints were also made against the lower orders of the clergy. Attempts to bring reform and recapture the spirit and simplicity of early Christianity came from new orders of mendicant monks, popular preachers, Renaissance humanists, and individuals and groups the Church condemned as heretical. As we will see in chapter 8, the call for reform would bring dramatic changes in the sixteenth century.

QUESTIONS FOR REVIEW AND REFLECTION

1. Why and how did the papacy fall into crisis in the late Middle Ages?

2. What was the conciliar movement? How did it attempt to deal with problems faced by the Church?

3. In what ways did the theology of the fourteenth century differ from that of earlier centuries?

4. Who were the Dominicans and Franciscans? What roles did they play in the Church and in society as a whole?

NOTES

1. The Holy Roman Empire lasted until 1806, when it was abolished by Napoleon.
2. In France, the *Jacquerie* of 1358 and, in England, the Peasants' Revolt of 1381.
3. A member of the Hapsburg family, which produced, with one exception, all the Holy Roman Emperors between 1438 and 1806, Charles was also the ruler of Austria, the Netherlands, Bohemia, Moravia, Luxembourg, Silesia, Spanish possessions in the Americas, and other territories.
4. Jean le Bel, *True Chronicles,* for 1347–48, trans. J. Bowden and M. Lydamore, in *How to Read Church History,* ed. Jean Comby, vol. 1 (New York: Crossroad, 1985), 182.
5. See "The Evil Bacillus," in *The Medieval Reader,* ed. Norman Cantor (New York: HarperCollins, 1994), 281–83.
6. For example, T. Bokenkotter, *A Concise History of the Catholic Church,* rev. ed. (New York: Doubleday, 1990), 161–64.
7. Quoted in J. Harrison et al., *A Short History of Western Civilization,* 7th ed. (New York: McGraw-Hill, 1990), 340.
8. Bokenkotter, *Concise History,* 163.
9. The Roman Catholic Church does not list Clement among its popes. He should not be confused with Clement VII (1523–54).
10. The theoretical foundations of conciliar theory can be traced back to the thirteenth century, when theologians and specialists in canon law, such as Hugh of Pisa, first began to speculate about how the Church might deal with a heretical pope. In the fourteenth century, the proponents of conciliarism included Conrad of Gelnhausen *(Epistola Concordiae),* who argued that when the legitimacy of a pope was in question a council should be convened by the cardinals.
11. Henry Bettenson, ed., *Documents of the Christian Church,* 2nd ed. (New York: Oxford University Press, 1963), 135.
12. The Roman Catholic Church does not accept as legitimate the actions of the council, or the council itself, prior to the election of Martin V.
13. Emperor John VIII Palaeologus (1425–48) and patriarch Joseph II (1416–39).
14. These were outlined in the Pragmatic Sanction of Bourges (1438), which was issued with the support of the French clergy.
15. From *Die Reformation Kaiser Sigmunds,* trans. H. F. Schwarz, text 5, ed. K. Beer (Stuttgart: F. A. Perthes, 1933), quoted in *The Portable Medieval Reader,* ed. J. B. Ross and M. M. McLaughlin (New York: Viking Press, 1949), 311–18.
16. This miscreant's title *pardoner* derives from his authority to distribute indulgences, not to hear confessions and grant absolution.
17. From "Prologue to the Pardoner's Tale," in *The Portable Chaucer,* trans. Theodore Morrison, rev. ed. (New York: Viking, 1949), 319–20.
18. Morrison, *The Portable Chaucer,* 53.
19. Jeffrey B. Russell, *A History of Medieval Christianity* (New York: Thomas Crowell, 1968), 188.
20. Some medieval sources identify the Cathari as Manicheans, although no clear link between them has been established. It is clear, however, that the Bogomils derived much of their theology from the Manichaeans. Originating in the Balkans and then spreading into Asia Minor, the earliest reports of Bogouils date to the tenth century. Much of what we know of their teachings derives from the work of Euthymius Zigabenus, a twelfth-century Byzantine theologian according to whom they believed that the world, the human body, and the Old Testament (excluding the Psalms) are creations of Satan, that Christ did not have a human body, and that Christian perfection requires the renunciation of marriage and property as well as abstinence from meat and wine.
21. They also called themselves simply "Christians" and, in France, *bonshommes* or "Good Men."
22. This was due primarily to their reliance on material elements, which they considered inherently evil.

23. The name Peter was given to him by his followers in the fourteenth century in order to link him and his teachings with the Apostle Peter.

24. They did, however, seek out the services of priests for the administration of the sacraments. When no qualified priest was available, arrangements were made for a layperson to serve as celebrant.

25. Matthew Paris, *Chronica Majora* 2.443.

26. See Jo Ann McNamara, *Sisters in Arms* (Cambridge, Mass.: Harvard University Press, 1996), 312–17.

27. *Oxford Dictionary of the Christian Church*, 3rd ed., ed. E. A. Livingstone (New York: Oxford University Press, 1997), s.v. "Inquisition."

28. *The Little Flowers* is actually an Italian translation of 53 chapters of the *Actus beati Francisci et Sociorum Eius*, written about 1335 by the Franciscan friar Ugolini Boniscambi of Montegiorgio.

29. *The Little Flowers of St. Francis* 16.

30. The conflict over poverty continued, however, and led to a formal division of the Franciscan order into strict "Observants" and less austere "Conventuals" in 1415.

31. Translated into English, "Ave Maria" is "Hail Mary." It is based on the greetings given to Mary by the angel Gabriel (Luke 1:28) and her cousin Elizabeth (Luke 1:42).

32. Wycliffe set forth his views on this subject in two important treatises, *On Divine Lordship* (1375) and *On Civil Lordship* (1376).

33. Early condemnations had come in 1388, 1397, and at the Council of Constance in 1415.

34. A group of more radical Hussites known as Taborites continued fighting until their defeat in 1452.

35. Meister Eckhart, Sermon 5b, in *Meister Eckhart,* trans. E. Colledge and B. McGinn (New York: Paulist Press, 1981), 184.

36. Meister Eckhart, Sermon 2, in Colledge and McGinn, *Meister Eckhart,* 179.

37. Julian of Norwich, *Revelations of Divine Love* 4 (short text), in *Julian of Norwich: Showings,* trans. E. Colledge and J. Walsh (New York: Paulist Press, 1978), 130–31.

38. Quoted in F. R. Willis, *Western Civilization,* 4th ed., vol. 1 (Lexington, Mass: D. C. Heath, 1985), 418.

39. Margery Kempe, *The Book of Margery Kempe* (New York: Devin-Adair, 1944), 77.

40. For example, he rejected Augustine's doctrine of the divine illumination of the mind in favor of the Aristotelian view that all knowledge is dependent upon the senses.

41. Scotus believed that what the mind actually knows in "knowing" individual things are the "common natures" (not Plato's universal forms) that are the foundations of all reality.

42. This statement appears in the *Hundred Theological Sayings,* a book that Ockham might not have written but is thought to accurately express his ideas.

43. Like Scotus, Ockham rejected Augustine's doctrine that original sin makes it impossible for us to make truly free decisions for or against God. He also disagreed with Thomas Aquinas, who had held that there is nothing we can do on our own to merit an initial gift of grace. Ockham's theology also included a doctrine of predestination, which he understood as God's foreknowledge of who would merit grace and who would not.

44. B. Tierney, ed., *The Crisis of Church and State, 1050–1300* (Englewood Cliffs, N.J.: Prentice-Hall, 1964), 208.

45. Willis, *Western Civilization,* 451.

46. Giovanni Pico della Mirandola, *Oration on the Dignity of Man,* in *The Renaissance Philosophy of Man,* ed. Ernst Cassirer, Paul O. Kristeller, and John H. Randall (Chicago: University of Chicago Press, 1948), 224–25.

47. Valla also showed that Dionysius the Areopagite could not have written the mystical texts attributed to him.

48. *Julius Excluded from Heaven,* which Erasmus published anonymously.

49. The Concordat of Bologna (1516) was signed after a major French victory against the papacy's Swiss defenders at Marignano in September 1515.

50. *Istanbul* actually derives from the phrase *eis ten polin* ("into the city") used in the local Greek dialect.

51. Nicholas Zernov, *Eastern Christianity* (London: Weidenfeld & Nicolson, 1961), 135. New patriarchs could not exercise their authority without permission granted by the sultan in a formal and expensive document known as a *berat.*

52. For example, St. Alban and St. Botolph of England, and the French St. Martin of Tours.

53. Timothy (Kallistos) Ware, *The Orthodox Church* (Baltimore: Penguin Books, 1963), 93.

54. Quoted in Ware, *The Orthodox Church,* 113.

55. From the Greek word for "Egyptians."

56. By "moderate Monophysitism" we do not mean that of Eutyches, according to whom there was only one nature in Christ and that it was not consubstantial with humanity. Instead, Coptic Christianity took the position that there was one nature "out of two" (i.e., human and divine) in Christ.

57. According to tradition, the first patriarch of Alexandria.

58. Armenian bishops repudiated the Council of Chalcedon in 555.

59. Today the members of this tradition are called Chaldaean Christians.

CHAPTER 8

The Protestant Reformation

Overview

By the dawn of the sixteenth century, the Church hierarchy had weathered years of pressure from councils, scholars, saints, and heretics who sought, with little success, to reform its practices and occasionally challenge its authority. Then, in a series of rapidly unfolding events touched off by the excommunication of a university professor named **Martin Luther**, a great religious revolt swept across Europe that changed the face of Christianity in the West. Roman Catholicism remained firmly established in most of Europe, particularly in the south, but by the end of the century Protestant Christianity had put down roots in the north and developed a bewildering variety of expressions.

The Protestant reformers were accused of being innovators, but they did not see themselves that way. Instead, they claimed to have rediscovered the ancient Pauline teaching that God's forgiveness is a free gift bestowed without consideration of human merit. This renewed emphasis on faith alone in God's grace alone, combined with their views on the Bible, Church, sacraments, and priesthood, gave the different forms of Protestant Christianity their distinctive identities. The range of Protestant expression was significant enough that some scholars prefer to speak of the Protestant Reformations.

Developments in social, economic, and political thought shaped Protestantism, even as the unfolding Protestant movement itself occasioned and accelerated still other changes in European life. In short, what is often called "the Reformation" was actually an enormously complex shift in European affairs that involved forces far beyond religion. What started as a theological conflict ended up touching all areas of European life.

The Reformation is generally understood as having two phases. The first was the initial Protestant Reformation sparked by Luther. The second phase included the Catholic Reformation — an unfolding series of developments within Catholicism that involved some reforms barely connected to the Protestant revolt and others specifically designed to counter it. Further developments within the Protestant Reformation are also generally linked to this second phase. This chapter surveys the first phase of the Protestant Reformation. After briefly describing the historical background and context of the Reformation, it moves on to Luther and his theology, the early progress of the Lutheran movement, the urban Reformation, the peasant revolts of 1525, the Swiss reformer Ulrich Zwingli, and finally to other reformers who pressed for even greater changes in what scholars call the "radical" Reformation. The Catholic Reformation, Calvin, and the further progress of the Protestant Reformation will be discussed in chapter 9.

Europe on the Eve of the Reformation

Europe entered the sixteenth century united principally by the Catholic Church. Within its broad scope the Church nurtured social, economic, political, and cultural values that gave a remarkable continuity to life. A common, though not unchallenged, view was that the European community constituted the united body of Christ[1]—separate peoples linked by similar goals and shared values. The vibrant new capitalist economy was still geographically limited and not yet potent enough to threaten this idea of unity. Nevertheless, the discerning could perceive the fragility of this sense of unity. The brilliant humanist Erasmus had anticipated a "new golden age,"[2] and hoped that unifying forces would continue to outweigh the centrifugal forces he feared were on the horizon. But by the close of the century the fledgling capitalist economy had grown to include worldwide empires; the rival interests of separate nations and principalities had achieved ascendancy over the old notion of religious unity; and a variety of Protestant groups existed alongside the Roman Church. "I perceive a certain fatal change in human affairs," wrote Erasmus,[3] sensing the significance of the events unfolding around him.

One of the enduring questions about the Reformation is why it happened when it did. Luther's call for reform was similar to that of Jan Hus a century earlier, yet Hus was executed whereas Luther survived. Years after the rebellion began, Cardinal Contarini told Pope Paul III that even if all the Protestant reformers, including Luther, were to be reconciled to the Roman Church, the rebellion would go on almost as if nothing had happened.[4] If the cardinal's judgment was sound, Luther's doctrinal revolution had opened the floodgates of change, and currents Luther never imagined were rushing through them.

The Protestant Reformation was one of the most complex movements in history, resulting from the sudden introduction of a minor theological debate into an unstable and explosive context. Economic changes—particularly the development of capitalism—had unsettled much of European life. Capitalism brought the belief that trade, agriculture, and industry should produce a profit, and that profit is potentially limitless. The economic life of medieval Europe had been largely local and undeveloped. Church teachings against greed and usury (lending money at excessive interest) had discouraged capitalism. But already in the late medieval period merchants in Italy and northern Germany had begun to reinvest their profits, and found that managing their investments produced even greater wealth than the work they had done before. Eventually international commerce developed, along with payment by money instead of by exchange of goods. In rural areas the manorial system began to disappear as nobles found it more advantageous to rent their land to free peasants than to rely on the forced labor of serfs. The medieval lord became a capitalist landowner living on rents paid in money. These changes displaced hundreds of thousands, leaving peasants confused and angry.

The development of capitalism pointed to broader changes in European society. For centuries the social order of European life had been essentially stable, with clergy, nobility, princes, and peasants all knowing their places and remaining in them. This apparently fixed social stratification was endorsed by the Church and had been seen as expressing a divine purpose. But with capitalism the newly wealthy bourgeoisie replaced the knights and lesser nobility on the social scale, making it clear that social stratification was not fixed after all. With this change came more democratic ideals, partly inspired by Renaissance thought.

The Reformation idea that there was no spiritual distinction between clergy and laity was a seismic shock to the theological world, and it fit this new climate perfectly. Luther did not intend the notion of spiritual equality to imply social equality, but many others concluded that it did. It has been argued that this leveling idea accelerated the development of modern democratic movements and of capitalism.

Capitalism also allowed European rulers to gain the financial resources necessary to develop stronger central governments. For many rulers the Church was an impediment to this goal, as it demanded spiritual, political, and even financial loyalty from all Christians, no matter where they lived. The Protestant Reformation offered rulers the chance to eliminate the demands of the Church upon their subjects and thereby enhance their own authority.

At the same time many European powers were interested in securing trade routes to the Far East. For years Europeans had enjoyed spices and other luxuries from the Orient but were forced to pay high prices to Muslim traders and the Italian cities that dominated the western end of the spice trade. Merchants in Spain, Portugal, England, and France hoped to bypass both the Italians and the Muslims by discovering more direct routes. Rulers were also aware that in the emerging capitalist economy tremendous profits could be made at the expense of the inhabitants of lands overseas that could be conquered and made into colonies. These and other factors prompted the development of what was to become known as western imperialism, one of the most destructive forces in history. But first the states of Europe had to find a trade route to the Far East.

One possibility was to sail south along the coast of Africa and then head east to India. The other entailed greater risk—to sail west across the open Atlantic, hoping to reach the Far East by traversing uncharted waters. The small kingdom of Portugal surprised the wealthier nations when a force under Vasco de Gama sailed around the southern tip of Africa and made its way to India in 1498. The Portuguese soon destroyed Arab shipping in the Indian Ocean and established bases along the coast of India. They then sailed eastward until they reached China and Japan. The Portuguese monarchy and a small group of favored companies made staggering profits as a result. They controlled this trade for a century, until the Dutch and English began to take

this eastern colonial empire from them. The Portuguese also conquered and colonized the eastern portion of Brazil in South America.

The Spanish managed to create an empire of their own. Ships under Christopher Columbus reached the Caribbean in 1492, and eventually the Spanish established colonies along the western coast of South America and in Central America, the Caribbean, and the western regions of North America. Initially Columbus and other explorers thought that the Americas were the Far East. The Americas did not offer the spices the Spanish sought, but they did promise riches in gold and silver.

Spanish exploration of the Americas tended to be ruthless. In 1519 Hernando Cortez sailed for the Americas even though he had neglected to obtain from his superiors permission for his voyage. He succeeded in conquering the advanced civilization of the Aztecs. Cortez had superior military technology, but his greatest weapon were the European diseases his troops carried, against which native populations had virtually no natural defenses. Millions perished. Cortez became rich and claimed the lands he conquered for Spain.

Priests accompanied the Spanish and Portuguese expeditions of conquest and sought to convert the native populations to Christianity. Some conversion was doubtless voluntary, but most scholars think that these conversions were largely coerced. The arrival of Europeans often signaled great hardship for the native populations. Their civilizations and indigenous patterns of life were destroyed, sometimes with pitiless efficiency, as the European powers exploited the colonies for profit at home. The influx of gold and silver filled royal treasuries, but it also contributed to European inflation, increasing the misery of peasants there.

By 1492 the rulers of Spain—Ferdinand and Isabella—had expelled the Muslims from the Iberian Peninsula and were well on their way to uniting Castile, Aragon, Granada, and Navarre, the four historic kingdoms of Spain. Their expanding empire overseas gave Spanish monarchs enormous financial resources allowing them to undercut the power of the nobility. Like Portugal, Spain would remain staunchly Catholic during and after the Protestant Reformation.

In France, Louis XI (1461–83) and Francis I (1515–47) succeeded in creating strong nationalist feeling. These talented and ambitious kings limited the power of the nobility, built roads and waterways, and began to create a centralized bureaucracy. Francis I, although a loyal Catholic, did not hesitate to weaken ecclesiastical influence generally and papal influence in particular within France. When the Protestant Reformation began, Francis quickly saw in it the opportunity to strengthen France's position relative to other nations, most of which were ruled by Catholics. He made a variety of alliances with Protestants and even with the Turks, all with an eye to weakening the political power of others, even at the expense of the safety of his Church.

In England, Henry VII (1485–1509) succeeded in uniting the country after the Hundred Years' War and the War of the Roses. He married Elizabeth of York, established the Tudor dynasty, and passed on to his son Henry VIII (1509–47) a strong and united country. Like Francis I, Henry VIII was both a loyal Catholic and unhappy with papal influence in his realm. He would lead his country toward Protestantism in an effort to maximize his own control over the English Church and the English people. He also began a naval tradition that would make the English navy into the world's finest. Under his granddaughter, Elizabeth I (1533–1603), England would defeat the Spanish navy and begin to forge a colonial empire for itself. The English eventually established colonies along the eastern coast of North America, in much of Africa from Egypt to South Africa, in India, and in the Far East.

In Germany and Italy, united nation-states were slower to emerge. Although parts of both regions were episodically under the control of the Holy Roman Emperor, neither region was to become a nation-state until the nineteenth century. Instead these areas were to be the last bastion of hope for those who dreamed of a united Europe. Upon his election as emperor in 1519, **Charles V** received a note from Mercurio Gattinara, who was his tutor and advisor and a student of Dante. Gattinara wrote:

> Sire, God has been very merciful to you: he has raised you above all the kings and princes of Christendom to a power such as no sovereign has enjoyed since your ancestor Charles the Great. He has set you on the way towards world monarchy, towards the uniting of all Christendom under a single shepherd.[5]

But history sided with individual nation-states, not with the universal Church or its vision of a universal empire.

Martin Luther

Few broad cultural movements have been linked so closely to one person as the Reformation has been tied to Martin Luther (1483–1546). Luther did not create the Reformation, but it appears to many that he had a predominant influence on the social, political, and religious changes of the sixteenth century. The historian Lewis Spitz once wrote, "the Reformation was basically theological . . . [yet] it immediately involved also social, economic and political forces, effecting fundamental changes in almost all areas of life."[6] Quite by accident Luther and his theological enterprise animated and provided an organizing principle for widely variegated forces that had long been gathering strength. Having inadvertently set these forces free, Luther was quite surprised by the result. He would later claim that subsequent events were a mystery to him, that he had "got into these turmoils by accident, and not by will or intention."[7] He had hoped to spark an academic debate that might lead to minor reforms. The thought of causing a rupture in Christendom would have been abhorrent to him in 1517. But that is exactly what happened. Even after it became clear that a rupture had developed, Luther desired to reunite with the one Church, not to establish a separate Church. For decades he looked for ways to achieve this goal. But the Reformation had become much more than a theological or even a religious issue. Not even Luther could turn back the clock.

THE COMPLEXITY OF MARTIN LUTHER

In his personal experience Luther seems to have embodied his age. He sought spiritual satisfaction, was concerned with the material and spiritual excesses of his Church, and advocated German interests. Little in his thought had not been expressed before. His opponents saw him as another Hus because he criticized the Church and argued for the primacy of scripture over the authority of popes or councils. His defenders said he was simply reviving the teaching of Paul.

Luther was a gifted thinker and a studious person. He was a master of written German and became perhaps the most effective opinion maker of his day. Deeply passionate about his faith and both sensitive and disciplined in its practice, Luther was also the sort of person who often overstated his case in order to make a point. He was frequently rude, vulgar, unkind, overbearing, and intemperate in both speech and manner. He seemed to delight in making fun of his opponents and almost always referred to them in caustic, unflattering terms. One of his favorite epithets was "stupid ass."[8] He once called the pope a "maggot bag."[9] He knew few Jews, yet he was clearly anti-Jewish and frequently expressed this antipathy with a violent passion. Luther's vitriolic statements about Jews continue to embarrass Luther scholars, some of whom argue for a nuanced understanding of his attitude. Nevertheless, Luther once wrote that synagogues should be burned, and that Christians were guilty for not killing Jews in response to their having killed Christ.[10] In sum, Luther was a bright, earthy, energetic, sincerely religious, and bigoted person of enormous complexity.

THE YOUNG LUTHER

"I was born in Eisleben and baptized in St. Peter's there," Luther wrote.[11] The date of his birth was 10 November 1483. He adored his parents, Margarethe and Hans. By the time Martin was eight, Hans was a part owner of a small mining concern. Hans grew wealthier with the passing of the years, and eventually he became a town councilor. Both of Luther's parents were sincerely religious.

Martin's parents supported his education, sending him to a secondary school and then to the University of Erfurt. He received his Master of Arts degree in January 1505. Later that year he began the study of law. But before two months had passed he

abandoned this path and entered an Augustinian monastery not far from the university. No one knows Luther's reasons, but many consider a traumatic event immediately before he entered the monastery to be the key. Luther had decided to return home for a visit and on the way back to Erfurt became trapped in a severe thunderstorm. When a bolt of lightning struck near him, he became terrified and cried out to St. Anne for help, promising that if he survived he would enter a monastery.

Luther took his monastic vows in 1506. He appears to have been a conscientious monk, studying diligently, praying, fasting, confessing, and begging. He was ordained to the priesthood in 1507 and was then singled out by his superiors for further theological instruction. This phase of his education consisted of the study of the branch of scholasticism known as nominalism. In particular, Luther studied the thought of Gabriel Biel (1420–95), perhaps the most creative of the late medieval Ockhamists. Biel represented a tradition within nominalism that stressed the inability of human beings to understand God, whose power and will are beyond comprehension, but maintained that it is nevertheless possible to please God and to contribute to one's own salvation by living virtuously. Luther was taught that a human being could become fit for salvation on the basis of a sanctified life that resulted at least partially from personal merit.

In 1508 Luther began his long career of university teaching. At first he lectured in moral philosophy based upon the teaching of Aristotle. Soon, however, he was asked to lecture on theology. He began to read Augustine with apparent enthusiasm, and gradually embraced the Augustinian view of human nature, as opposed to the more positive view advocated by Biel. As he studied, Luther began to think deeply about the sacraments. He concluded that the penitential system, although designed in part to relieve feelings of anxiety, had the opposite effect on him. Although he was pious and went to confession frequently, he was gripped by the fear that he had forgotten some of his sins. Unconfessed sins could not be forgiven and therefore must be punished. It seemed to Luther that the sacrament of penance demanded a standard of performance beyond human reach, because everyone inevitably forgets some sins. This led Luther to believe that divine justice must compel God to adopt a harsh and merciless attitude toward human beings.

Meanwhile Luther was becoming a person of some importance within the Augustinian order, earning progressively more significant administrative assignments even as he held university posts. He was made regent of his monastery school in 1512, and in 1515 became the district overseer of eleven monasteries. This combination of academic ability and administrative promise had already been noticed by Johannes von Stuapitz, the head of the Augustinians in Saxony. Staupitz became Luther's friend, advocate, mentor, and confessor. When Luther revealed his uncertainty regarding confession and penance, Staupitz advised him that it was better to trust in God's forgiveness and love. But Luther could not. He realized he had begun to think of God as a stern and angry father. Staupitz recommended to Frederick the Wise, ruler of Saxony, that Luther be appointed to the faculty of Frederick's new university in Wittenberg. Founded in 1502, the university was a source of great pride to Frederick. Staupitz perhaps saw in this appointment an opportunity for his friend to come to peace over the issues that troubled him.

PROFESSOR AND REFORMER

Luther arrived in Wittenberg in 1508, after one year went back to Erfurt, but returned to Wittenberg in 1512 and remained there for the remainder of his teaching career. Also in 1512 Luther received his doctorate and assumed the chair for biblical studies at Wittenberg, taking an oath to protect and expound the word of God to the best of his ability. This pledge gave him comfort when his convictions caused him to break trust with his ecclesiastical superiors.

While at Wittenberg Luther began to reflect upon his own earlier piety and concluded that much of it had been based on fear. Anselm had long before argued that human sins create wrath in the heart of God. The image of an angry God drove Luther to despair. While at Erfurt Luther had studied Ockhamist theology and particularly Biel, who had argued that humans can contribute to their own

salvation by living a virtuous life. If human beings did their best, Biel taught, God would be satisfied. Luther could not help but wonder if he had done enough.

It is possible that as early as 1512 Luther had begun to reject Biel and embrace Augustine's view. It is clear that he came to regard Ockhamist theology and Biel in particular as employing human reason to go beyond what Luther thought was the scope of the biblical evidence. At this time his reading was largely devoted to the Bible and Augustine, and he resolved to avoid theological conclusions that he did not think could be supported by the biblical material. Luther considered Augustine something of a kindred spirit. Both had wrestled with personal doubt and the problem of evil in human nature, and both eventually stressed the grace of God. For most of the next thirty years Luther gave exegetical and homiletical lectures on the Bible several times a week.

The years 1513–18 were a time of great productivity and change for Luther, and his lecture notes on the Psalms, Romans, Galatians, and Hebrews reflect this. Halfway through his exegetical study of Romans he abandoned the Latin text and turned to the original Greek language, using a version recently produced by Erasmus. Luther's interest in the Greek text is often highlighted as evidence of his humanist values. From the humanists he gained a love of language and learned the importance of returning to the original sources (in his case, the Bible), as opposed to later interpretations (in his case, scholastic theology).

As a result of his reading of Paul, who saw a proclivity to sin embedded in human nature, Luther became increasingly convinced of the crippling effects of human sinfulness. This he could not reconcile with Biel's optimism that human beings can contribute to their own salvation. If human beings cannot help but sin, Luther wondered, how could they be made right with God? Later in his life, Luther recalled puzzling over Paul's description of the gospel in Romans 1:17 as containing "the righteousness of God" ("For in it the righteousness of God is revealed through faith for faith; as it is written, 'The one who is righteous will live by faith'"). Luther had previously seen God's righteousness as a demand for perfection. God must be angry with him, Luther concluded, because he could never achieve righteousness on his own. But when he saw Romans 1:17 in the light of Romans 3:24 ("they are now justified by his grace as a gift, through the redemption that is in Christ Jesus"), Luther changed his mind. He concluded that the righteousness God demanded was not something he was expected to achieve, but rather something God simply granted to him. He came to see God's righteousness not as punishment, but as a gift from God—a gift that, when accepted in faith, results in redemption. This conjured an image of God as a loving and forgiving figure: God simply offered salvation to sinners while they were yet sinners. This realization left Luther feeling released and reborn. It became the cornerstone of his theology: justification by God's grace alone received only by faith in Christ's atoning work.

Precisely when Luther hit upon the idea of justification by faith is something of a mystery. As an old man he remembered it coming rather late. What is clear is that the theological faculty at Wittenberg was especially interested in the Bible and Augustine, and that as early as 1516 Luther was involved in student disputations regarding God's grace that were critical of scholasticism generally and theological optimism about human ability to satisfy God in particular.

With increasing clarity Luther perceived a gulf between how he understood medieval theology and how he understood biblical theology. He also came to the conviction that biblical theology ought to be the standard for Christian belief and practice. In 1517 he composed ninety-seven theses critical of scholastic theology as the basis for a debate and posted them. Perhaps he hoped that they would arouse interest. He was wrong. Few beyond the university seemed to pay attention. Later he composed another group of theses that were directed more precisely at the practice of selling indulgences. Based upon his previous experience he expected little interest, so he circulated these less widely. At noon on 31 October 1517, he posted on the door of the Castle Church in Wittenberg his "Ninety Five Theses or Disputations on the Power and Efficacy of Indulgences."

This action was terribly ordinary. The door was the bulletin board for the university, and like other such notices, Luther's included an invitation to a public discussion. No one came. As a faithful servant of the Church he sent a copy to his superiors, one of whom was Archbishop Albert of Brandenburg.

Indulgences are not concerned with guilt but only penalty—that is, with purgatory and earthly suffering. They could not, therefore, be used to effect absolution. However, people who sold indulgences often blurred the line between the removal of guilt and the relaxation of temporal punishment. Many who purchased indulgences believed that they were buying forgiveness of sins. It was clear to some among the learned, including Luther, that selling indulgences under such conditions was a violation of church teaching.

Pope Julius II had in 1510 announced an indulgence to pay for the construction of St. Peter's cathedral in Rome. Pope Leo X extended the indulgence and made Archbishop Albert of Brandenburg the high commissioner of the sale of indulgences in his two archbishoprics of Magdeburg and Mainz. Albert was deep in debt. In order to be made archbishop at an early age (twenty-three) and for permission to hold multiple ecclesiastical offices contemporaneously, he had had to two papal dispensations, and had borrowed considerable sums from the Fugger banking house in order to do so. Leo and Albert agreed that the two of them would split the profits of the sale, which would allow Albert to pay his debts. He appointed the Dominican Jon Tetzel his sub commissioner of the sale of indulgences.

Further complicating matters, the Elector Frederick the Wise of Saxony owned a vast collection of relics that attracted many pilgrims who paid to see them. This would be threatened by the sale of indulgences, so Frederick prohibited it.

When Tetzel approached the borders of Saxony in April of 1517, many from Wittenberg traveled to buy indulgences. Believing that Tetzel and his subordinates were misrepresenting Church doctrine, Luther wrote to several bishops asking them to intervene. When this proved fruitless he composed and posted his ninety-five theses.

Much to Luther's surprise, within months humanists had published copies of the theses in many European cities, including Nuremberg, Leipzig, and Basel. "It is a mystery to me how my theses . . . were spread to so many places" Luther wrote on 30 May 1518, in a document dedicated to Pope Leo X. "They were meant exclusively for our academic circle here. This is shown by the fact that they were written in such language that the common people could hardly understand them. They are propositions for debate, not dogmatic definitions . . ."[12] By mid December, Albert had sent a copy to Rome, demanding action against Luther. In response the pope ordered the head of the Augustinians to control Luther. Because of his vows Luther was compelled to obey, but as a university professor he had the right to debate such matters. He responded to his superiors that he would not recant unless convinced on the basis of scripture. Sensing trouble, Frederick offered to protect Luther.

Luther was called to Heidelberg to appear before the general chapter of the Augustinians in Germany. Here he avoided controversial topics and was happily surprised to find support for his positions. The pope tried to stifle Luther again, summoning him to Rome. But Frederick intervened, and it was arranged that Luther would travel to the assembly of the empire in Augsburg to meet with the papal representative, Cardinal Cajetan. Cajetan, himself a skilled theologian, refused to discuss Luther's teachings. Instead he merely demanded that Luther submit. Luther refused. He left Augsburg secretly and returned to Wittenberg, where he asked for a general council on the matter. In Augsburg Luther met many who resented the interference of the Church in German national affairs and considered Luther something of a hero.

In Germany, nationalism was on the ascendancy, a mood encouraged by humanists like Conrad Celtis (1459–1508) and Ulrich von Hutten (1488–1523). Little interested in religion, Celtis was intensely proud of his German heritage. In a speech delivered at the opening of the University of Ingolstadt in 1492, he had said, "Resume, O men of Germany, that spirit of older time whereupon with you so often confounded and terrified the Romans. . . . Let

us feel shame, yes, shame I say, to have our nation assume the yoke of slavery and pay tribute to foreign kings."[13] Unlike Celtis, von Hutten was a devout Christian as well as an ardent German. He was bitter because he felt the Church had suppressed the study of the Bible in the original languages. He also asked why German gold should be used to build churches in Italy when so many churches in Germany needed repair.[14] Both resented what they perceived to be Italian intellectual and religious arrogance. Anti-Roman feeling in Germany sprang from many sources. In this climate the effect of Luther's protest was welcome, even if some were uneasy with its substance.

When the emperor Maximilian (1493–1519) died, the pope relaxed his attack on Luther, waiting for the selection of a new emperor. For his part Luther agreed to refrain from inflammatory activity. But John Eck, professor of theology at Ingolstadt, drew Luther into a public confrontation by criticizing one of Luther's colleagues. Eck and Luther met at Leipzig in 1519. At this disputation Luther claimed that in condemning Hus the council had erred. Most considered Eck the winner of the debate, in part because he maneuvered Luther into supporting a heretic, implying that Luther was also a heretic. It was also clear that Luther had come to believe that the scriptures were the sole authority for Christian theology and practice. The more Luther considered this, the more he became convinced that many of the practices and institutions of the Church were human inventions without any scriptural warrant. He came to believe, for instance, that the sacraments worked because God willed them to work and not because of the involvement of priests. Priests had the right to administer the sacraments, but this did not imply that they enjoyed a special status in relation to other Christians, as the Church taught. There was no difference in spiritual status between the clergy and laity, Luther concluded, but only a difference in function. Luther took this difference seriously. He was quite traditional in his understanding of the social order, but he came to believe that in the spiritual order each person stood before God on the basis of his or her own faith.

Following the debate with Eck, Luther in 1520 produced three treatises meant to defend his position in the face of impending excommunication. He intended to disseminate them to as wide an audience as possible. The three treatises—*An Address to the Christian Nobility of the German Nation*, *The Babylonian Captivity of the Church*, and *The Freedom of a Christian*—were at times biting. In the first he called upon secular authorities in Germany to reform the Church, because in his view the clergy had failed to do so. In the second he revealed his dislike for aspects of the sacramental system, especially its tendency, as he saw it, to create lines of hierarchy separating clergy from laity. He also attacked as unbiblical various theological positions held by the Church, such as the doctrine of transubstantiation. The final treatise is more devotional in nature. Luther described it as containing a treatment of the Christian life in brief form.

Luther was already a publishing phenomenon. In 1519 a publisher wrote to Luther that he had "never had such glorious sales." In 1521 the papal legate Girolamo Aleander declared, "printers will not sell anything other than Lutheran writings."[15] The success of these treatises helped ensure the progress of the Lutheran movement. The recent invention of the printing press allowed Luther's ideas to become widely known with a swiftness never before possible. The press was to prove a powerful force in shaping the modern world—allowing for the rapid, wide dissemination of ideas and an increase in literacy rates.

After Maximilian died, Charles I of Spain was named Holy Roman Emperor, Charles V. Francis I, king of France, feared that the election made Charles too powerful. It also concerned the pope, who had backed the candidacy of Francis. In his early twenties, the new emperor was a devout Christian and would not countenance heresy. On 15 June 1520 the pope issued the bull *Exsurge, domine* ("Arise, O Lord"), which condemned Luther and ordered all books by Luther to be burned. He also summoned Luther on pain of excommunication to submit to Roman authority. When Luther received his copy of the papal bull, he burned it. He also wrote a tract with the splenetic title *Against the Execrable Bull of the Antichrist*. By this act he all but declared himself a heretic in the eyes of the Church that had nurtured, educated, and inspired him. On 3 January 1521, Leo published the bull of excommunication. Excommunication meant not only exclusion from the Church but also the loss of all civil rights. It now became a matter for the empire to deal with Luther.

Frederick again intervened and convinced Charles V to grant Luther a hearing at the next imperial assembly, scheduled to take place in Worms in 1521. When Luther was asked to recant, he requested a day to consider his position. Ultimately he refused, saying:

> Since your serene majesty and your lordships seek a simple answer, I will give it in this manner, neither horned not toothed: Unless I am convinced by the testimony of the Scriptures or by clear reason (for I do not trust in the pope or in councils alone, since it is well known that they have often erred and contradicted themselves), I am bound by the Scriptures I have quoted and my conscience is captive to the Word of God. I cannot and I will not retract anything, since it is neither safe nor right to go against conscience. I cannot do otherwise, here I stand, may God help me, amen.[16]

Luther left Worms in late April. On 4 May 1521 his party was attacked by a band of horsemen who kidnapped Luther. Word got out that Luther had been killed. When the artist Albrecht Dürer heard this news he wrote, "O God, if Luther is dead, who is going to proclaim the holy gospel so clearly to us?"[17] But Luther was safe. The horsemen were operating on orders from Frederick. They spirited Luther away and hid him in the Wartburg castle, where he remained for eight months. He was later to return to Wittenberg to resume teaching and writing. It was from Wittenberg that Luther gave direction to the reform movement until his death in 1546.

With some reluctance Charles V six weeks later signed the Edict of Worms, according to which Luther and all who came to his aid were declared outlaws, and any subject of the empire who even communicated with Luther was subject to arrest

Edict of Worms

and confiscation of property. Luther was thereby proclaimed both a heretic and an outlaw under the ban of the empire.

Luther's Theology

Luther's concerns were basically theological. Earlier calls for reform had focused on practices that some saw as abusive. Luther went beyond this, arguing that the theological underpinnings of certain practices were defective. This judgment rested on his belief that scripture ought to be the authority for Christian life and practice. From this conviction flowed his theology.

Eventually Luther came to stress three ideas that became features of Protestantism in general. The first is his belief that salvation is by God's grace alone (*sola gratia*) through faith alone (*sola fide*). Luther then came to believe in the pivotal importance of scripture as the standard for Christian belief and practice (*sola scriptura*). From these convictions, Luther developed the idea of the priesthood of all believers, that contrary to Church teaching, clergy and laity were of equal spiritual status, that the individual stands before God alone without the need of any human mediator.

By profession Luther was not a systematic theologian, but a biblical exegete. His study of the Bible caused him to conclude that the theology of the Church, though based upon the Bible, seemed at times to contradict the theology of the Bible. This helps explain not only his position at Worms, but also the nature of his theological enterprise. Although primarily a biblical exegete, Luther's interests and training also included medieval German mysticism, medieval theology, and Renaissance humanism.

Luther had studied at a school run by the Brethren of the Common Life, where he was introduced to the mystical tradition in German piety. There Luther had learned to emphasize and appreciate the power of the indwelling of Christ within the heart of the believer. Like Paul and a long line of Catholic mystics, he believed that in some powerful but nonrational fashion the risen Christ lives in and with the Christian.

Medieval theology had a great influence on Luther's thought. From nominalism, for example, he gained a deep appreciation for experiential knowledge. But he grew increasingly restive with metaphysical speculation about God, believing that it led to an intellectual acceptance of God but not to an experience of God. His discomfort with the thought of the nominalist Gabriel Biel was complicated by the fact that his opponents linked the narrow issues that irked Luther to church tradition more broadly,[18] forcing Luther to either accept or reject the whole. He resented this as unfair, because there was a good deal in church tradition with which he agreed. Believing that his own concerns had been unfaithfully portrayed, Luther eventually became more caustic and critical of medieval theology and church tradition than he originally intended.

In 1517 Luther published his *Disputations against Scholastic Theology*, in which he declared his opposition to many of the tenets of Gabriel Biel's thought in particular, but also of medieval theology generally. He had been taught, for example, that there was a moral structure in human beings that enabled them to prefer godliness. Against this he wrote, "It is false to say that the will can conform to a correct precept. This is said in opposition to Scotus and Biel. . . . Man is by nature unable to want God. Indeed, he himself wants to become God."[19] Biel had taught that God would not withhold grace from anyone who tries his best. Luther came to regard this view as terribly mistaken. He wrote, "we do not become righteous by doing righteous deeds but, having been made righteous, we do righteous deeds. This is in opposition to the philosophers"[20] and "God cannot accept man without his justifying grace. This is in opposition to Ockham."[21] Aristotle had argued that the practice of good works eventually train a person to be good, and Luther believed that this idea had been adopted by the Church:

> From this we may know and judge how full the world is nowadays of false Preachers and false saints, who fill the ears of the people with preaching good Works. . . . They exalt good works to such a height that they imagine they can merit heaven thereby. But the bare goodness of God is

what ought to be preached and known above all else, that God saves us out of pure goodness, without any merit of works, so we in turn should do the works without reward or self-seeking, for the sake of the bare goodness of God.[22]

He could be even more pointed. "What Godless audacity it is, therefore, when we who are to receive the testament of God come as those who would perform a good work for Him!"[23] Luther criticized scholastic theology for allowing Aristotle and other non-Christian philosophers to serve as authorities in theology, preferring theology to be drawn from only one authority, the scripture. He insisted that "no one can become a theologian unless he becomes one without Aristotle" and "Aristotle is to theology as darkness is to light." In his treatise *Against Latomas,* written in 1521, Luther asserted that the scholastic theologians at the University of Louvain "have imposed tyranny and bondage upon our freedom to such a point that we must not resist that twice accursed Aristotle, but are compelled to submit."

Luther was not opposed to philosophy, or even wholly against Aristotle. For instance, in his *An Address to the Christian Nobility of the German Nation* Luther condemned Aristotle's *Physics* because its cosmological speculations seemed to be at variance with monotheism, but he warmly endorsed Aristotle's *Poetics* because of its use of classical authors.[24] Luther's complaint was that scholastic philosophy had misunderstood Aristotle,[25] had imposed this misunderstanding upon theology, and thereby had done great harm to the cause of Christianity.

Luther had much in common with the humanists, which has provided a fruitful field of study for later scholars.[26] Luther's ideas were spread by humanists who applauded his attack on scholasticism, use of original sources, and concern for hermeneutics. Like the humanists, Luther had little respect for the learning of the centuries just past. Many humanists were committed to the German national cause, and while Luther appears to have been proud of his German heritage, his own concerns were more focused on theological and ecclesiastical issues. He was uncomfortable with humanism because it seemed to emphasize the basic goodness of human beings and a positive appraisal of human potential. He later came to associate the confidence

of the humanists with the optimism of Biel's theology, seeing them as variations of the same problem. Luther simply could not reconcile a positive appraisal of human nature with the crippling effects of human sin.

For their part, most humanists were not so focused as Luther on the implications and importance of theology. Erasmus, a talented theologian in his own right, is illustrative here. In response to the papal bull *Exsurge domine,* Luther argued that humans are in the grip of basic inclinations, either sin and evil or the grace of God. These inclinations cannot be altered by one's own strength. The human will, in Luther's view, is completely helpless on its own. The issue for Luther was not general moral responsibility—but, more narrowly, election. Erasmus wanted to retain some place for free will; in response, Luther argued that there is freedom of choice only within the civil sphere: "Free choice is allowed to man only with respect to what is beneath him and not what is above him."[27] Matters that are "beneath," according to Luther, include eating, drinking, and ruling.

Erasmus at first supported Luther. He wrote to Albert of Brandenburg that it was wrong to punish Luther merely for proposing to discuss issues of repeated disagreement between scholars. Erasmus had been openly critical of the abusive practices of the Church long before Luther burst on the scene. A loyal Catholic who detested tumult, Erasmus believed in reform through peaceful persuasion. Although his pointed criticism of scholasticism had earned him many enemies, Erasmus enjoyed the favor of Pope Leo X. He harbored hopes that Leo would seek his aid in initiating a far-reaching reform within the Church. Initially Erasmus approved of Luther's call for reform, but feared the volatile and caustic manner Luther had exhibited would lead to acrimony and bloodshed. His fears would not prove groundless. On 18 May 1518, about a month after Luther's stand at Worms, Erasmus, thinking Luther dead, wrote to Luther's friend Jonas:

> In pleading for moderation at Worms you acted as I should have done had I been there. I am sorry that things turned out so badly. . . . The corruption of the Church, the degeneracy of the Holy

See are universally admitted. Reform had been loudly asked for, and I doubt whether in the whole history of Christianity the heads of the Church have been so grossly worldly as at the present moment. It was on this account that Luther's popularity at the outset was so extraordinary. . . . I had hopes myself, though from the first I was alarmed at Luther's tone. What could have induced him to rail as he did at popes and doctors and mendicant friars? . . . Things were bad enough in themselves without making them worse.[28]

As the situation became more vexed, Erasmus distanced himself from Luther. On 5 July 1518 he wrote to his friend Dr. Pace, "We have not all strength for martyrdom, and I fear if trouble comes I shall do like Peter. The Pope and the Emperor must decide. If they decide wisely, I shall go with them of my own free will. If unwisely, I shall take the safe side."[29]

SCRIPTURE

Luther saw himself as a champion of the Word of God. In his view, scripture was a more trustworthy guide to the Christian faith and the Christian life than was scholasticism, or even church tradition. By "Word of God" he did not mean simply the written word of the Bible. Instead he meant God's will and purpose expressed particularly in the person of Jesus. He pointed to John 1:1–3 ("In the beginning was the Word, and the Word was with God, and the Word was God. He was in the beginning with God. All things came to be through him") to demonstrate that the Word of God was not just written information, but something active: revealing Jesus, the Word made flesh, the ultimate expression of God's love at work. Luther also believed that the message of scripture correctly proclaimed in preaching is in some sense God's Word. His commitment to this principle caused him to translate the Bible into German, with the result that millions of German speakers would begin to read scripture for themselves.

Luther claimed that this Word of God has authority over the Church. Catholics asserted that the Church decided which of the ancient documents would constitute the Bible; therefore, the Church had authority over the Bible. Luther responded that

the Church did not make the Bible, nor did the Bible create the Church, but rather the true authority was the message of Jesus Christ contained in the Bible — and that, as he had said at Worms, the scriptures are a more trustworthy guide to this gospel than either popes or councils.

KNOWLEDGE OF GOD

Luther did not believe observation of nature yielded full knowledge of God. He also thought human reason insufficient for the task. Luther felt that the Ockhamist exaltation of human reason ignored the great distance between God and humanity, was futile, and was an example of human pride because it presupposed that human beings could on their own come to understand God. He called this a "theology of glory." Instead, Luther understood God as engaged in self-disclosure, not waiting for human beings to understand the divine. God's fullest self-disclosure is to be found in the sacrificial act of Jesus on the cross. For this reason, Luther described his own theology as centered in suffering and the cross. In 1518 Luther wrote:

> That person does not deserve to be called a theologian who looks upon the invisible things of God as though they were clearly perceptible in those things which have actually happened [Rom. 1:20]. . . . He deserves to be called a theologian, however, who comprehends the visible and manifest things of God seen through suffering and the cross.[30]

THE HUMAN CONDITION AND SALVATION

Luther's reading of the Bible led him to believe that human beings are fundamentally alienated from God by their sin. To illustrate this idea, he described them as being curved in on themselves:

> . . . our nature has been so deeply curved in upon itself because of the viciousness of human sin that it not only turns the finest gifts of God in upon itself and enjoys them. . . . it even uses God Himself to achieve these aims. . . . seeking God for its own sake.[31]

This curvedness is now natural for us, a natural wickedness and a natural sinfulness. Thus man has no help from his natural powers, but he needs the aid of some power outside of himself.[32]

Like Paul, Luther believed that it is impossible for human beings to keep the law of God perfectly, or to believe in Christ as savior without God's gracious intervention. Therefore, human beings need God's grace. God's forgiveness, expressed in the death and resurrection of Christ, Luther believed, made it possible for the state of human alienation from God to be reversed.

Like Augustine, Luther had a substantial theology of God's wrath. But he came to believe that God's wrath against human sin is not a natural disposition for God, but instead is an "alien state"— that God's real nature is his love and mercy.

Luther held that the Christian lives by faith alone, and that faith is an active trust in Christ and not merely intellectual assent or belief. The scholastic teaching that good works train a person to be good, he said, turned biblical doctrine on its head. Like Paul, Luther believed that the presence of Christ within the believer transforms the heart of the believer and creates a desire to do good works. But this process of sanctification, or becoming more like Christ, is gradual—Christians are at once righteous and sinful. To illustrate his point, Luther drew upon the image of a physician:

> It is similar to the case of a sick man who believes the doctor who promises him a sure recovery and in the meantime obeys the doctor's orders in the hope of the promised recovery and abstains from those things which have been forbidden him. . . . Now, is he perfectly righteous? No, for he is at the same time both a sinner and a righteous man; a sinner in fact, but a righteous man by the sure imputation and promise of God that He will continue to deliver him from sin until He has completely cured him. . . . he has the beginning of righteousness, so that he continues more and more always to seek it.[33]

THE CHURCH

Luther believed that there was both a visible and an invisible Church. The visible Church was the one all could see, the one that administers the sacraments and in the midst of which the gospel was preached. This Church is a mixed company of true Christians and those who did not truly believe. For this reason Luther did not consider the visible Church to be the true Church. The true Church (the Church of the believers), in his view, is not a matter for human sight, because only God knows who is among those who truly believe. In a December 1523 letter to Albert of Brandenburg, Luther wrote, "Christ alone sees this church; he alone gathers and keeps it together, and he alone preserves it."[34]

Luther believed that the development of a priestly hierarchy had obscured the biblical teaching that God desired each Christian to have personal faith in Christ. This conclusion led him to understand the Church as a "priesthood of all believers," as noted in his *Address to the Christian Nobility of the German Nation:*

> It is a pure invention that pope, bishops, priests and monks are to be called the "spiritual estate"; princes, lords, artisans and farmers the "temporal estate." That is indeed a fine bit of lying . . . all Christians are truly of the "spiritual estate," and that there is among them no difference at all but that of office.[35]

Though Luther saw each believer as a priest, he did not have a theology of individualism. He believed that the Christian life is to be lived in community. Each Christian serves as an agent of God's grace to others.

> I will therefore give myself as a Christ to my neighbor, just as Christ offered Himself to me. . . . Hence, as our heavenly Father has in Christ freely come to our help, we also ought freely to help our neighbor through our body and its works.[36]

At the same time, Luther took seriously the difference between clergy and laity. Clergy play a special role in teaching and in administering the sacraments, and, in Luther's view, require a great deal of training. Beyond ecclesiastical matters, Luther also saw a special role for clergy in the social order. In short, Luther promoted spiritual, but not social, egalitarianism. He did not intend to change the social order, but his writing hastened such changes.

The tempestuous nature of the period compelled Luther to write extensively on the relation between church and state. His thought on this matter is often referred to as the "two-kingdoms theory," for he understood church and state as separate but mutually supportive entities. It appears that, like Augustine, Luther believed that the state is necessary to hold back the effects of human sin. But he also believed that the state has a positive function: the state is based upon the law of love and is legitimate when it exercises its power in ways that promote justice and compassion. Luther further believed that the Christian is obligated to obey the sovereign (state authority) except when doing so requires acting against one's faith. He concluded that human society should be governed by secular law, not by a religious ideology, not even the Christian gospel. Governance by the gospel or free grace would lead either to chaos or to gross intolerance of less-spiritual individuals. The Church should have spiritual authority, Luther believed, but the state should have temporal authority, including over ecclesiastical buildings. He retained the medieval notion of social stratification, but hoped his teaching that all Christians stand equal before God spiritually would prompt princes and peasants to act with Christian compassion one to another, allowing all to be content with their station in life. By posing the dignity of all in spiritual matters, however, he set in motion forces that would help to undercut the idea of social stratification.

Why the Reformation Succeeded

Scholars have long debated the reason millions came to embrace the reform movement. Clearly, a wide range of factors were involved.

Some interpretations of the Protestant Reformation have attributed its success to discontent caused by the indifference and perceived abuses of the Church. This view was especially prevalent among Protestant scholars whose work was frequently colored by their own religious sensibilities. However, this perspective is not limited to Protestants, as some Catholic scholars have adopted this approach. Joseph Lortz, for example, claimed that the Church was basically secular, fiscal, and political rather than spiritual.

The inference that the Church was thoroughly corrupt is likewise mistaken. Undoubtedly most clergy were honest, devoted to their calling, and respected by those who knew them. The reflections of a contemporary abbot, Trithemius of Sponheim, are illustrative of the era. He wrote, "To become a priest is worthy of honor, but to become a monk out of love for God means to achieve a greater perfection." But he also decried the way some had abused their calling. "Dare we believe, my brothers, that St. Benedict had such expensive horses and mules as we now see many an abbot possess? Certainly not! And do we not read of St. Martin that he rode on a lowly donkey using a cord for a rein?"[37] That persons of conscience and goodwill, such as Trithemius and Luther, were drawn to the Church makes it difficult to believe that the institution was as abusive as some interpreters seem to assert.

A number of scholars see the Protestant Reformation as a response to what they call the "burden of late medieval religion."[38] We saw in chapter 5 that harsh penances were often assigned for even lesser sins, and that there were many who complained about the rigors of confession and penance. The earliest Protestants criticized Catholic piety not for demanding too little, but for demanding too much. They attacked the system of penance for what they considered its heavy psychological, social, and financial burdens. Luther, for instance, directed the full blast of his ire at penance and confession in his *Sermon on the Sacraments*. Written in 1519, it went through fourteen editions by 1521. Here he argued that penitents were left in doubt and anxious as to their forgiveness.[39] Luther also protested that priests sometimes used the confessional to ask probing questions of a highly personal nature in order to satisfy their own curiosity.

A variation on this view is that Catholic theology produced spiritual anxiety, and the Protestant Reformation succeeded because Luther's theology alleviated it. This was certainly the case with Luther, and apparently with others. Albrecht Dürer wrote to George Spalatin in 1520, "If God helps me to see Dr. Martin Luther, I shall diligently make his portrait and engrave it as a lasting memory of the Christian man who has helped me out of great anxieties!"[40] Other scholars go further and describe a basic experience of "unresolved religious oppression."[41] Though there is ample evidence that at least some persons experienced anxiety, it seems unreasonable to assume that this was a general condition.

Another variation of this theme is that the practices of the Church left many feeling alienated from the Church. Peasants could be bitter in their complaint that the Church sometimes acted as economic competition. Local monastic houses supplied markets with bread, wine, and a host of other products, often at prices that undercut local farmers. Many scholars have pointed to the anticlericalism of displaced and landless peasants who protested against monastic landowners.[42] The confluence of economic and spiritual factors evident here does help account for the Reformation, but we should be slow to assume that this level of alienation was universally burdensome. After all, many peasants did not join in the revolts that swept across Europe during the first decades of the sixteenth century. The confluence of economic and spiritual factors evident here does help account for the Reformation, but it is unlikely that this level of alienation was universally considered burdensome. After all, many peasants did not join in the revolts that swept across Europe during the first decades of the sixteenth century. Nonetheless, anticlericalism was a factor.

The late medieval period was among the most devout in history, as the increase in pilgrimages and the flood of prayer books and confessional manuals produced just prior to the Reformation attest.[43] To this list might be added heightened interest in the veneration of saints and the dramatic rise in the number of lay brotherhoods.[44] Recently, scholars have begun to appreciate the great variety of religious experience within Catholicism prior to the Reformation. For example, in Albrecht Dürer's self-portraits the painter's own face seems to fade into that of Christ, suggesting a mystical union of the believer with Christ. This dramatic increase in piety indicates that many found solace in the patterns and practices of Catholic spirituality. Nonetheless, the Protestant alternative held attraction for many.

These conditions created a climate of acceptance for Luther's theological ideas. It remained to be seen how these ideas would spread and adapt within Germany and throughout Europe.

The Early Progress of the Lutheran Movement

In the period when Luther's theological protest was becoming widely known to Europeans, social, political, religious, and economic forces in Europe — and particularly in Germany — were intermingling in ways that promised great change. Luther's theological program focused and enhanced these forces, and their combined surge of energy carried Luther's ideas forward.

During the Middle Ages, the Church had fought a long and generally successful battle against the powers of the state, and especially the Holy Roman Empire, leaving Germany politically fragmented. The Holy Roman Emperor Charles V ruled Spain, Austria, and much of the Netherlands as an inheritance from his Hapsburg forebears. But as Holy Roman Emperor he was only the nominal ruler of Germany. The German princes had long valued their independence, and many of them resented interference in their affairs, whether the offending party was the emperor or the pope. Even those princes remaining solidly Catholic were irked by the power of the Church to tax and to control political matters in Germany. These rulers welcomed the burgeoning German nationalism fanned by humanists like Conrad Celtis. To varying degrees they allowed Lutheran reforms in their lands as a testament more to German independence than to theological agreement.

Charles was further prevented from disabling Protestantism by a series of other crises that demanded his attention. Even as the edict against Luther was being drafted at Worms, trouble was brewing that prevented the emperor from acting to suppress Luther. An unruly army of displaced and marauding knights was active near Worms, causing considerable apprehension. Then news reached Charles that a fellow Catholic sovereign, Francis I of France, had invaded Charles's holdings in Spain and the Netherlands. For the next several years, the French, the Turks, and others would bedevil Charles with political and military threats he could not ignore, thus allowing the infant Protestant movement to develop and gain strength.

A number of princes were early and important supporters of the Lutheran cause. Elector Frederick of Saxony was loyal to Luther, and he led his principality into the Lutheran camp. In 1525 Albert of Brandenburg all but legislated the adoption of Lutheranism in his extensive holdings in east Prussia. Landgrave Philip of Hesse was a passionate supporter of Luther's theology, and he led his principality into the Lutheran fold in 1526. Though both Frederick and Philip were motivated by religious factors, they were not ignorant of the opportunity to eliminate imperial and ecclesiastical interference in their lands.

The details of Luther's theological program spread rapidly. There was considerable interest in Luther's writings, and his idea were further disseminated by a host of skilled publicists and pamphleteers. A flood of cartoons, pamphlets, and caricatures supporting the Lutheran cause poured from printing presses and appeared throughout Europe, outnumbering rival Catholic pamphlets by almost twenty to one.[45] Some effective Catholic pamphlets portrayed Luther as a seven-headed devil or as a fool, but in general the day was won by Lutheran pamphlets with their biting aphorisms, pithy sayings, and Lutheresque style.

Initially, Lutheranism spread along the Rhine River and other trade routes throughout Germany, finding early support in the German cities. In Wittenberg in September 1521, a colleague of Luther named **Philip Melanchthon**, along with some of Melanchthon's students, celebrated the Lord's supper by partaking of both the bread and the wine. This is known as "communion in both kinds." Church teaching held that the laity were to partake only of the bread. By this simple act Melanchthon and his students issued a kind of declaration of defiance. On 31 October the Augustinians in Wittenberg ceased holding mass altogether. By January of 1522 only five Wittenberg Augustinians remained in the Order. The remainder had left to join the Lutheran movement. Soon other cities embraced Lutheranism. By 1530 many cities in central and northern Germany had accepted Lutheranism. Albert of Brandenburg allowed the cities of Magdebrug and Halberstadt to embrace Lutheranism as long as they promised to pay him a special tax.[46]

By adroit political maneuvering the Lutheran cities managed to prevent successive assemblies of the empire from enforcing the Edict of Worms. Partially in frustration, several Catholic rulers formed military alliances in 1524 and 1525, aiming to enforce the Edict and to stamp out Protestantism. At the assembly of the empire in Speyer in 1526, Charles was unable to move as decisively against the Protestants as he wished, even though he had just defeated the Catholic king of France at the battle of Pavia. In an odd twist occasioned by the intermingling of politics and religion, the pope worked against Charles, because Clement VII feared the growing political power of the emperor. Charles was further frustrated by the Turkish invasion of Hungary that same year. This was a grave threat to the whole of Europe. By 1529 the Turks had reached the gates of Vienna itself. This tumultuous political situation gave the Protestant cause a decade to consolidate its gains and clarify its positions.

At a second assembly of the empire at Speyer in 1529, a more strident tone was taken. It was decided that the Edict of Worms would be enforced and that governments should tolerate only Catholic worship and eradicate all other forms. Anyone who wished to protest could (this is the origin of the term *Protestant*). Six Lutheran princes and fourteen cities from the south of Germany exercised this right. It appears certain that Charles had wished to crush the Protestant threat at that time, but the still-fragile Protestant cause was granted yet another reprieve.

The French had become the allies of the Turks, forcing Charles to take a more conciliatory stance. He asked the Lutherans to present him with a statement of faith. The resulting **"Augsburg Confession,"** composed of twenty-eight articles, highlighted the points of commonality between Catholicism and Lutheranism. It stated that the Lutherans had not introduced anything "contrary to Holy Scripture of the universal Christian church."[47] Written by Melanchthon, the confession sought to distance Lutheranism from other forms of Protestantism and to provide a legal justification for Lutheran princes to remain in good standing within the empire. It also, however, clearly endorsed the Lutheran principles of justification by grace alone through faith and the preeminence of the scriptures. The Catholic party wrote a refutation, and Charles declared the Catholic case the stronger. It was then decided that a church council called for the following year could settle the matter.

For a variety of reasons, however, the council was not convened until 1545. In the meantime, the Protestant states formed a defensive military alliance, the Schmalkald League, in 1531. In 1532 the Turks under Suleiman threatened once more, so the Protestants were spared yet again. Further, the French continued to irritate the emperor. In 1532 at Nuremberg a temporary peace was called that recognized then-present Protestant boundaries. Following this decision, several states and hundreds of ministers turned their backs on Catholicism and bound themselves to the Augsburg Confession. Among them were the Palatinate in southern Germany and several smaller states in northern Germany.

In 1545 Charles was finally able to turn his undivided attention to the Protestants. The Schmalkald War (1546–47) ended with the complete defeat of the Protestant forces. Luther had died in 1546. The victorious emperor was urged to have Luther's body exhumed and burned, but Charles reportedly replied, "I do not make war on dead men."[48]

Charles appeared to be close to ending the Protestant threat, but several of the Catholic German princes made a secret agreement with the French and in 1552 rebelled against Charles. As Germans, they resented the harsh treatment the Spanish-born emperor imposed on German princes who happened to be Protestants. An assembly of the empire was called at Augsburg in 1555, and there the Peace of Augsburg was ratified. Meeting from March to September, the assembly settled religious matters in a way that departed from established patterns. For instance, there was no representative of the pope present. The Peace granted legal status within the empire to Lutheran signatories of the Augsburg Confession, but not to other Protestant groups. It also, in effect, stipulated that each ruler would choose the religion for the regions under his or her control. The language adopted by the assembly — "where there is one ruler, there should be only one religion" — gave rulers the right to exercise control over religious matters.

The Lutheran cause advanced in other areas of Europe as well. In Poland political power was so decentralized that the Polish **Diet** decreed that the king could not even maintain a standing army. This situation made a state reformation impossible, but several Polish princes and German-speaking Polish cities adopted Lutheranism, as Danzig did in 1523. In Moravia and Slovakia, Lutheranism was often identified with the legacy of Jan Hus, which facilitated the acceptance of Luther's views there. Lutheranism also succeeded in establishing roots in Hungary, Transylvania, and Lithuania, especially among German-speaking populations.

Lutheranism spread quickly to Scandinavia. In 1526, King Frederick of Denmark began work to establish a state church in Denmark based on Lutheran principles. At least one of his aims was to strengthen his power by gaining control of the clergy within Denmark. When Denmark conquered Norway and Iceland, the Reformation spread to these lands as well. The Swedish king Gustavus Vasa (1523–60) seemed to have been motivated by genuine religious sympathies in embracing the Reformation. But like Frederick, Vasa was not unaware of the political advantages of this decision. He too benefited from having more direct control over the apparatus of religion.

The success of the Reformation depended upon the support of political rulers such as Frederick and Vasa. But this support was not immediate. In its initial stages the movement begun by Luther was highly vulnerable. During this time the Reformation survived because it was embraced by a number of German cities. Its vitality there was a major factor in convincing kings and princes that the Reformation was an option with staying power.

The Urban Reformation

Disparate forces in sixteenth-century Europe came together in an explosive mix in the decade beginning in 1520, sometimes taking the form of violent social revolution. The demise of the manorial system deprived thousands of peasants and knights of income and a recognizable social station. Many joined wandering groups of bandits. Thousands of peasants fled to the cities, where they received a cool reception. Many were relegated to the insecurity of the suburbs. Inflation and the ascendancy of capitalism made it clear that significant changes were under way. All of this left workers and peasants politically and economically disenfranchised. Displaced knights revolted in 1522 and 1523, forming marauding bands that attacked mercantile convoys. These conditions set the stage for the early acceptance of Luther's ideas by both peasants and city dwellers.

The importance of the cities for the success of the Reformation is impossible to overstate. In adopting Reformation principles, cities both challenged and retained cherished medieval values. When retained, these values expressed themselves in ways that displayed Lutheran influence.

THE LATE MEDIEVAL CITY

Many late medieval cities were so dominated by a communal spirit that city leaders made the city church "private"— open only to citizens of the city itself, excluding those who lived in the suburbs. The idea was to defend the integrity of the city community. Citizens conceived of the late medieval city as the body of Christ in miniature.

In late medieval cities there were clear normative values that guided community life: justice, peace, unity, and the common good.[49] These were expressed in concrete rights enjoyed by residents of the city, but usually denied to people living in the suburbs and countryside. Yet these areas were indispensable to cities, providing artistic, commercial, technological and agricultural resources. Suburbs grew rapidly during the fifteenth and sixteenth centuries in Europe as a result of early capitalist pro-duction. They were sociologically diverse, being populated by artisans, farmers, laborers, and undesirables expelled from the cities, such as beggars and vagabonds. In the German city of Mühlhausen, for example, an urbanite who wounded a suburbanite was subject to a fine and four weeks' house arrest, but the penalty for a suburbanite who wounded an urbanite was death.[50] In a case that illuminates the gulf between urbanites and suburbanites the city council of Nordlingen forbade citizens from joining a peasant revolt five miles away, even though it was clear the peasants had appealed to the very normative values the citizens cherished.[51]

Finally, like the rest of the medieval world, the inhabitants of cities assumed that the structure of society, including its social classes and their respective functions, was divinely ordained. The organization of society was often expressed using the metaphor of the human body: the clergy constituting the head, the nobility the arms, and the peasantry the feet. God decided one's place and there was no point in agitating for improvement. This image was already called into question by the rise of the new middle class or bourgeoisie, but for the most part remained fixed in the late medieval mind.

With the Reformation this changed. When Luther argued that clergy had no special or higher spiritual status than laity, he articulated a powerful leveling principle. Others extended his idea of spiritual equality to socity at large. While city councils continued to ban citizens from joining peasant revolts, many workers, artisans, and even wealthy urbanites refused to comply. They cited scripture and often made reference to Luther's notion of the priesthood of all believers to justify their support of the peasant.[52]

In cities, the early Reformation usually originated with a preacher whose imagination was captured by the theology of the reformers, especially its social implications. Typically a preacher attacked the alleged ethical and material abuses of the Church, alluded to the high value society placed on justice, and argued that the Church had been unjust. In this way social and economic concerns were linked to theological and religious motivations. City councils were faced with a dilemma. The Church provided a rich array of resources vital to the city, such as monasteries, schools, and hospitals. But the Church could also be detrimental to the economic health of the city due to economic competition and taxation. In addition, growing popular protest had to be considered. When city councils opted not to adopt the Reformation, violence often broke out.

As early as 1520 the suburban scene became a popular arena for Protestant preachers, especially because they were often excluded from the urban pulpits. Master Froschel preached in the suburbs of Leipzig, and soon became so popular that he had to preach in the open air. He was driven from the town after a sermon in 1523 nearly caused a riot.[53] Similar developments occurred in Halle, Mühlhausen, Altenburg, Mainz, and Magdeburg. This ferment is best illustrated through a series of case studies: Nuremberg, Strasbourg, and Erfurt.

Nuremberg   In the early sixteenth century Nuremberg had a population of about twenty thousand, with another twenty thousand people living in its unusually large outlying areas.[54] Its wealth derived from its location on important commercial trade routes and the high quality of its products. In the sixteenth century the city government bore the appearance of democracy, but real power lay in the hands of a few wealthy families whose members dominated the city council.[55] The material prosperity of the city was enjoyed by a broad spectrum of its citizens, so social tension did not play as prominent a role in Nuremberg as elsewhere.

The Reformation in Nuremberg appears to have started not with the masses, but with a small circle of humanists. In 1516 Staupitz, Luther's mentor, preached in Nuremberg and quickly gathered a following among the humanists there, including Albrecht Dürer and Lazarus Spengler. The antischolastic views of Staupitz were so popular that the humanists named a club in his honor. The club quickly attracted not only humanists, but also a number of their patrician patrons, many of whom were active on the city council. In 1518 Staupitz sent Wenceslaus Linck, a friend of Luther, to Nuremberg to preach a series of sermons. Linck introduced Luther's theology to the group, which later received a copy of his ninety-five theses. This

resulted in discussion and general agreement with Luther. Luther's visit to Nuremberg in October 1518 cemented their support for his views.[56] This is not surprising, for the city council had already taken action of the sort advocated by Luther in refusing to allow the sale of indulgences within the city that were to support the building of St. Peter's Basilica in Rome. In 1519 Spengler, who held the influential position of city clerk, published a defense of Luther's ideas entitled *The Main Doctrines*. Thanks largely to the views expressed here, the council refused to enforce the Edict of Worms against Luther and his followers.

Conflict between city council and clergy gave additional impetus to the reform movement in Nuremberg. Records indicate several clashes between the council and local monasteries, as well as charges concerning the immoral behavior of clergy. These were seized upon by supporters of Luther, who pointed to his doctrine of the priesthood of all believers and questioned the special privileges of the clergy.[57]

By 1520 Luther's ideas had become so popular in Nuremberg that, in the words of one observer, "the participate, the multitude of the other citizens and all the scholars stand on Luther's side."[58] Among the most eloquent and influential of the Luther's sympathizers was Anders Osiander. Elected to the city pastorate soon after the edict of Worms, Osiander quickly won over the city's middle and lower classes. They appear to have been attracted not only by the persuasiveness of his preaching, but by the simplicity and appeal of Luther's ideas. These were grasped not only by scholars and leading citizens, such as Albrecht Dürer, but by ordinary men and women, such as the cobbler Hans Sachs.[59]

Under the leadership of Osiander and others the Reformation continued to spread in and around Nuremberg. Osiander was a fearless preacher, even calling the pope the Antichrist while many princes, meeting in Nuremberg for an imperial diet, were present in his congregation.[60] Such preaching inspired riots against the clergy and monasteries. Before long the tide of enthusiastic pro-Lutheran sentiment was so high that even the local Carthusian monks revolted against their prior. The Lutheran sympathies of the council became unmistakably clear in 1522, when it began suppressing Catholic agitation against the Reformation but encouraged Osiander to continue his preaching. Finally, the council declared itself for the Reformation and vowed to defend Reformation principles "with weapons" if need be.

With the Reformation the council gained previously unknown levels of control over the apparatus of religion within the city and halted the drain of taxes and duties to Rome. The drastic reduction in the number of feast days tended to enliven commerce. There was also a move to improve education along the humanist model, emphasizing ancient languages and an appreciation for the classical age. Yet other traces of Catholic culture and practice remained, for example a feast day in honor of Mary.

Strasbourg   Unlike Nuremberg, Strasbourg had a long history of militant protest against the empire.[61] Its geographical location on the imperial border with France meant it had economic and political contact with the Swiss and the French. Strasbourg's economic health was linked to foreign interests, helping to make the city less loyal to the empire than Nuremberg.

Like Nuremberg, Strasbourg had already begun secularizing ecclesiastical institutions within the city before the Reformation began. The council of patricians took over the appointment of parish clergy, the hospitals, and care for the poor. While humanists played a major role in the early stages of the Reformation here as at Nuremberg, there was also a greater restiveness among the lower classes. This accounts for the popularity of the preacher Geiler von Kaiserberg, who attacked clerical abuse, both material and spiritual, from 1478 to his death in 1510.

Matthaus Zell then took up von Kaiserberg's mantle. By 1520, Zell began to defend Luther and continued in the tradition of von Kaiserberg to attack the Catholic clergy. A frequent target was what he called the "heavy yoke" of medieval piety, especially its economic and psychological manifestations. Zell's sermons became popular, and great crowds came to hear him. Despite imperial and ecclesiastical pressure, the council allowed Zell to continue.

In 1523 Wolfgang Capito arrived in Strasbourg. He was the provost of St. Thomas, the third ranking Catholic in the city. Capito's conversion by Zell was telling. The cathedral chapter soon dismissed Zell, but each succeeding replacement appointee declared himself a reformer. The gardener's guild in the parish of St. Aurelie demanded a Reformation preacher, and even offered to install one at its own expense. There were other popular demands for "educated preachers" so that the common folk could understand the "Word of God." The demands included critiques of an economic nature, especially new taxes. They even noted that the appointment of such "godly preachers" would preserve the peace of the city.

In Strasbourg the Reformation appears to have been basically religious in nature. Anticlerical sentiment fueled by economic and social concerns was also a factor. As at Nuremberg, the council acted as a willing accomplice. Even more than in Nuremberg it is clear that the council understood the material and political benefits to be gained by adopting the Reformation.

Erfurt   In Erfurt, Catholic and Protestant expressions of the Christian faith ended up coexisting. Erfurt was under the nominal control of the distant archbishop of Mainz, but the influence of the nearby elector of Saxony was more prominent. Erfurt had only one significant industry, wool dying, leaving it a city with startling economic problems, especially for the lower classes. Severe internal disturbances beginning in 1509 made the council wary of any new unrest. Erfurt was a university city, and the humanists there favored an Erasmian Reformatio—a relaxation of Church influence in favor of civil control.

From 1522 on, Johannes Lang, a former Augustinian, took the lead in the reform. Beginning in 1523, communion in both kinds was offered to the laity. At this point the financial needs of the city and foreign policy played a role. Erfurt had to borrow money from Duke George of Saxony, and the council imposed new taxes on the lower orders of the citizenry. The council most likely did this to increase resentment toward the Church, because clergy and ecclesiastical institutions within the city refused, as usual, to pay the tax. In April 1524 a revolt of anticlerical peasants and middle-class citizens succeeded in despoiling and destroying clergy houses, the archbishop's prison, and ecclesiastical offices in the city. The council therefore had succeeded in weakening the power of the Church without formally adopting Lutheranism. The council soon reorganized the parishes along Lutheran lines, but it also reopened negotiations with Archbishop Albrecht. As a result the council appointed some parishes as Catholic, others as Lutheran. In Erfurt, then, the council did not adopt the Reformation. Significant numbers of the citizenry may have embraced the Reformation for a mixture of religious and material reasons, but the council saw in the Reformation primarily political and economic advantage.

The Peasant Revolts of 1525

One of the earliest effects of the wide dissemination of Luther's writings was their use by oppressed peasants. During the late Middle Ages, peasant revolts were fairly common in central Europe. In 1474, for instance, Hans Böhm, the "Drummer of Niklashausen," predicted an imminent egalitarian millennium during which the rights of peasants for access to woodlands and streams would be restored.[62] His followers stormed the walls of Würzburg, but the revolt was put down. During 1524 and 1525, bands of peasants roamed Germany, Austria, and parts of France, often demanding fair treatment on the basis of common law. Failed harvests in 1523 and 1524 only increased their desperation. During the horrible year of 1525, there were many armed conflicts pitting peasants against cities and princes, resulting in the deaths of as many as a hundred thousand peasants.[63]

The revolts of 1525 were different from earlier revolts in one significant way: Many of them included petitions produced by the peasants that show clear evidence of familiarity with Lutheran theological principles. Leaders of these revolts were quick to recognize in Luther's theological writings new and potentially effective weapons in their struggle for legitimacy. They especially seized upon the Lutheran ideas of the priesthood of all believers and the authority of scripture to argue that their rights before God were as justified as the rights of anyone else. In these petitions it is unmistakable that religious and material concerns had become thoroughly intermingled. The most famous of these petitions, *The Twelve Articles: The Just and Fundamental Articles of All the Peasantry and Tenants of Spiritual and Temporal Powers by Whom They Think Themselves Oppressed*, was written in early 1525, and within two months there were twenty-five thousand copies spread throughout Europe.[64] The *Twelve Articles* petition was published by one of several bands of peasants roving the area of Lake Constance and the city of Memmingen in 1525. Following Luther's lead, they made the exegesis of scripture the basis for their material demands, as opposed to earlier peasant protests that relied on appeal to common law. The demands were also directly against the Church, not as an ecclesiastical organization but as a major landowner in Germany.

With the Reformation diverse forms of social protest in Memmingen merged. Reformation theology provided the rationale for social and economic changes to bridge the gulf between city and suburbs, and many among the privileged classes in Memmingen joined the revolt because of the preaching of the gospel. The Reformation in Memmingen was a true popular movement, cutting across socio-economic lines. The key figure was Christoph Schappeler, the preacher at St. Martin's. As early as 1516 the senate found it necessary to regulate his sermons because he sided with the poor against the rich. But by 1521 senate records record that "Schappeler told us the truth."[65] The senate, like the councils of so many other cities at the time, was caught between popular support for the Reformation based on material and spiritual concerns, and the combined efforts of the Church and the emperor to oppose it. In 1524 the bishop excommunicated Schappeler, an act requiring the senate to banish him. The senate defied the bishop's order and refused to comply.

Schappeler's presence made Memmingen an attractive place for peasants, and by 1525 many had gathered there. Soon the *Twelve Articles* appeared.

It is almost certain that the authors were Schappeler and Sebastian Lotzer, a Memmingen journeyman furrier. The *Articles* demanded free access to fish and game, the end of taxes on cattle for lay and ecclesiastical lords (although a grain tax was retained, because the Old Testament mentions one), new rent assessments based upon equity and justice, and release from serfdom. There was also a pledge to retract any part of the *Articles* found contrary to scripture. The influence of Luther is clear. The one authority is scripture, and the assumption is the equal dignity of all. The senate quickly acquiesced to these demands. Luther did not wish to see this thought pushed this far, but the politically and economically disenfranchised were united in the protest by common conditions and a common ethic derived from Lutheran theology.

Luther responded to the *Twelve Articles* by addressing rulers, peasants, and finally all parties in a tract called *An Admonition to Peace*. He blamed the princes and authorities for the tumult, because they unjustly oppressed the peasants:

> We have no one to thank for this mischievous rebelling except you lords and princes, especially you blind bishops and mad priests and monks, whose hearts are hardened, even to the present day. You do not cease to rant and rave against the holy gospel, even though you know you cannot refute it. In addition, as temporal rulers you do nothing but flay and rob your subjects in order that you may lead a life of splendor and pride, until the common folk can bear it no longer.[66]

Luther may not have questioned social stratification in the temporal realm, but he did assert that it was immoral for those in authority to oppress the peasants. He pointedly warned the peasants against revolution and tried to distance himself from any impending social upheaval or violence. He told the peasants that they should not claim to have Christian teaching on their side. Finally, he charged both sides to seek a peaceful resolution through negotiation.[67] Luther wrote *An Admonition to Peace* in April. In May, before the tract was widely read, violence broke out. Luther, always quick to assume an intemperate tone, wrote *Against the Robbing and Murderous Hordes of Peasants,* in which he said the rebellion should be mercilessly suppressed, clearly siding with the princes against the peasants.

For rebellion is not just simple murder; it is like a great fire, which attacks and devastates a whole land. Thus rebellion brings with it a land filled with murder and bloodshed; it makes widows and orphans, and turns everything upside down, like the worst disaster. Therefore let everyone who can smite, slay, and stab, secretly or openly, remembering that nothing can be more poisonous, hurtful, or devilish than a rebel. It is just as when one must kill a mad dog.[68]

The fusion of peasant social and political unrest combined with the application of the leveling principle in Luther's theology became explosive with the career of Thomas Münzer in Germany. Münzer was a preacher in Zwickau and a spiritual enthusiast, given to visions and a highly spiritualized and violent form of Biblical interpretation. He was forced to leave Zwickau in 1521 because his virulent hatred of Catholics and Lutherans was becoming painfully evident. He preached revolution and became a leader of a peasant revolt in 1525. Several German princes joined forces to put down the revolt. Münzer's fiery oratory included instructions to the peasants that they should not let the blood dry on their swords as they slaughtered their godless rulers. There are reports that Münzer promised his peasant army that he would catch the bullets of the enemy in his sleeves. Münzer and the peasants were slaughtered.

During the first anxious months after Luther posted the ninety-five theses to the church door, popular social protest movements began using his arguments to support their causes, and several cities embraced the Lutheran revolt. The Bible as the standard and exegesis as the method are two principles that the Reformation and social protest shared. The Reformers frequently complained that those involved in social protest misunderstood them. One of the ironies of Luther's career is that by 1525 he was already arguing against other Protestants who were only following his example and interpreting the Bible for themselves. Luther was often slow to anticipate the ways his theological positions would be used, and he set traditional social order above justice if violence broke out. Though he harshly criticized the German princes for their inattention to the plight of the poor,[69] he ended up supporting them against the peasants. For the economically and politically disenfranchised lower classes, however, the cause of justice was worth the struggle. Within the cities and among the peasants, social protest, economic concerns, spiritual desire, and intellectual ferment interpenetrated with Luther's theological ideas. Luther opened the door, and the forces of social protest and reform rushed past him into the breach.

Zwingli and the Swiss Reformation

Ulrich Zwingli (1484–1531) was born in Switzerland to successful peasant parents who ensured that Ulrich had the best education possible. As a teenager he studied under Heinrich Wölflin, a teacher steeped in Renaissance ideals. Wölflin instilled in his student a love of the classics. Zwingli then spent two years in Vienna studying under Conrad Celtis. In 1502 he returned to Basel, where he came under the influence of Thomas Wyttenbach, a critic of scholasticism and an advocate for the study of the New Testament. Zwingli's education left him enamored of humanist teachings. He became adroit at the classical languages and an accomplished musician.

At age twenty-two Zwingli was ordained into the priesthood, and was then elected priest at Glarus over another candidate, Heinrich Göldi. Göldi was a Zurich priest, then in the service of Pope Julius II, who had apparently been promised the position to which Zwingli was elected. Having lost the election, Göldi demanded satisfaction. Mightily irritated, Zwingli found himself compelled to pay Göldi off. In Zwingli, humanist educational ideals were mingled with authentic pastoral concern, and an unbending sense of justice.

In 1516 Zwingli was called to Einsiedeln, where the famous shrine of the Black Virgin attracted a flood of pilgrims. During his time there Zwingli apparently began to feel some disquiet over the spiritual purpose of pilgrimages and indulgences. Precisely how his thinking developed during this period is difficult to determine. Zwingli began to attack the sale of indulgences in the area, but he also made a long pilgrimage of his own as late as

1517. In December of 1518 Zwingli was elected to the pulpit of the main church in Zurich — the position from which he guided the Reformation in Switzerland.

Luther's path began with personal anguish over matters of the spirit to which his humanist tendencies were added; Zwingli's path was from the outset guided by his humanist leanings. Both Zwingli and Luther argued that their views were not innovative, but rather a return to the teachings and practices of the early Church. But Zwingli believed that any practice that did not have scriptural support should be eliminated, whereas Luther was content to allow practices like stained glass windows and organ music that did not clearly contradict biblical teaching.

At this time Switzerland was not a single state but a confederation of politically independent cantons. The confederation was formed principally to secure for the many disparate cantons independence from German political influence. In 1499 the Swiss had renounced their allegiance to Maximilian and the Holy Roman Empire. This love of independence was strong in Zwingli.

As in the rest of Europe, Switzerland in the late Middle Ages saw an increase in examples of piety, such as pilgrimages, endowments for religious purposes, and the purchase of indulgences. Beginning in 1518 an Italian Franciscan named Bernardini Samson sold indulgences in the areas around Bern and Zurich and apparently attracted large crowds. Under the influence of Zwingli, the Swiss Diet convinced Pope Leo X to order Samson away. But as late as 1522 the city council of Bern advised citizens to purchase indulgences.[70]

Like other cities, Zurich had a substantial number of clerics and monks among its citizens, two hundred for a town of about six thousand.[71] The cathedral alone had a staff of more than twenty clerics.

Zwingli may not have been a gifted preacher, but he clearly had the ability to move his listeners. On his first Sunday in Zurich he announced his intention to ignore the standard texts prescribed by the Church and instead to follow his own plan by preaching his way through the New Testament. The effect, apparently, was electrifying. Young humanists in Zurich found a champion in Zwingli when he vowed to return to the original Greek New

Testament. Others were stirred by his exposition of scripture.

Zwingli's first serious break with the Church came in 1522 over a matter of Church law that Zwingli perceived to be contrary to the clear teaching of the Bible. Zwingli had preached that the Bible allows the eating of all foods at all times, but Church law stipulated abstention from the eating of meat during Lent. Zwingli determined to take a stand. On Ash Wednesday, 1522, he and others of similar mind met at the home of a printer, fried two sausages, and, as Zwingli watched, the others ate. He explained that he felt constrained by scripture not to exercise his right to eat when it might cause less mature Christians to become confused (1 Corinthians 8:9–13).

The city council was quick to act, imprisoning several of those who participated. Zwingli defended the participants from the pulpit, arguing that the faithful need only the Holy Spirit for assistance in interpreting scripture; they do not need definitions or directions from Church, council, or pope.

Zurich fell under the ecclesiastical jurisdiction of the bishop of Constance. When Zwingli's teaching concerning fasting and abstinence came to the bishop's attention, the bishop accused the reformer before the city council. This led to public discussions, or disputations, concerning Zwingli's teachings. Zwingli, with his Hebrew, Greek, and Latin Bibles open before him, overcame his opponents. In the first disputation he argued against the mass as a sacrifice, the authority of the pope, prayer for the intercession of the saints, compulsory fasting, and the sale of indulgences. He instead advocated what he called the clear, biblical understanding of the gospel. In the aftermath of this first disputation the city council voted that Zwingli's teachings should be distributed throughout the city.

The other disputations focused on three matters: the doctrine of Christ's presence in the eucharist, clerical marriage, and religious images. The eucharistic doctrine of transubstantiation holds that the bread and wine change into the literal body and blood of Christ. This means that every celebration of the eucharist is a participation in the sacrifice of Christ. But it was popularly understood as an actual sacrifice of Christ. The Church also taught that all

could eat the bread but only the priest could drink from the cup.

On biblical grounds Zwingli objected to the doctrine of transubstantiation. He did not believe that Christ was "present" in the eucharist at all. Instead, he understood the words *This is* as in "this is my body," to be a figure of speech, saw the doctrine of transubstantiation as an example of extrabiblical scholastic thinking, and argued that the laity should partake of both bread and wine. In 1525 he published his *Commentary on the True and False Religion*, which was clearly influenced by Erasmus's thinking concerning Christ and the preeminence of the spirit over the letter. Zwingli argued that Christ was in heaven and could not possibly be in the elements. The meal was therefore a memorial and not a sacrifice. After the fourth disputation ended on 20 January 1524, the city council decided that Zwingli could go on teaching because no one had been able to refute him.

In 1522 Zwingli had asked the bishop of Constance for permission for priests to marry. His request was refused. In secret Zwingli married anyway. By 1524 he was confident enough of his position that he made his marriage public. The city council then voted to allow clergy to marry. It also accepted Zwingli's position that the veneration of images was antibiblical.

At Zwingli's insistence the Reformation in Zurich assumed a harsh iconoclastic posture. In June and July of 1524, all the glorious examples of late medieval religious art that adorned the churches in Zurich were removed. Zwingli had little appreciation for the power of images to strengthen faith. To him they represented reliance on human merit. He called them "idols," against which the Bible spoke. Even Zwingli's own musical sensibilities were not spared. The organ in the church, silent since 1524, was finally chopped up and discarded in 1527.

Zwingli was deeply influenced by humanist ideals. Humanism led Zwingli to study scripture, and therefore led him to his reformation position. As a humanist Zwingli had a more positive view of the power of human reason than Luther did. He was also far more apt to draw logical conclusions from scripture, while Luther was quite content to allow ambiguity where scripture was silent. For instance, though both believed that scripture taught predestination, Zwingli further taught that God predestines who will be saved and who will be damned. He reached this conclusion because it seemed to him to be the logical result of biblical teaching about God, that God must have perfect knowledge.

Luther could trace his understanding of Christ and the scriptures to concrete events in his life, so it is perhaps legitimate to speak of Luther's theology as existential. Zwingli did not speak, as Luther did, of "casting himself entirely upon the mercy of Christ." During his years in Zurich, Zwingli became aware of Luther. After reading Luther's exposition of Paul's letters he came to hold positions that more closely followed those of Luther, especially in regard to salvation by grace alone.

Zwingli was a proud man, and although he did acknowledge a debt to Luther, he maintained that he was preaching a reformed doctrine before he had ever heard of the German reformer. A dispute with Luther over the interpretation of the eucharist only exacerbated Zwingli's desire to protest his originality.

In contrast to Zwingli, Luther taught that Christ is actually present in the eucharist, although not in a material sense. Their differences concerning the eucharist soon became the basis for a public and bitter controversy. Followers of both positions argued with each other, and finally the two principals were drawn into the dispute.

In 1526 Luther published a tract attacking Zwingli bearing the inflammatory title *Sermon on the Sacrament of the Body and Blood of Christ, against the Fanatics.* There followed several increasingly angry exchanges between the two. In 1528 Zwingli wrote a friend that he resented Luther's patronizing attitude, felt that he was being treated "like an ass," and that he considered Luther and his followers heretics.

But the Reformation had become much more than a theological dispute. Philip of Hesse — ruler of an important state in Germany and an ardent supporter of the Reformation—feared that acrimonious theological disputes would spill over into the arena of politics. If the Protestant lands were politically divided due to theological differences, Philip reasoned, the gains of the Reformation would be swallowed up in Catholic victories on the battlefield. Philip knew that once Charles had settled matters with the Turks and the French, he would turn his attention to the Protestant problem. He therefore invited Zwingli, Luther, and their lieutenants to Marburg in 1529, hoping to forge some agreement between them.

Luther did not approve of the use of political force in religious matters, nor did he appreciate the use of religion for military purposes. Nevertheless, out of deference to Philip he made the journey. The two reformers quickly agreed on fourteen of the fifteen points set for discussion — matters like scripture, justification by faith, and baptism. They also agreed that the doctrine of transubstantiation was not biblical. But Zwingli would not agree to any idea of the real presence of Christ in the eucharist. Luther's brilliant associate, Philip Melanchthon, apparently because he held out hope of reunion with Catholicism, advised Luther against compromise.

As Philip feared, the theological rifts had military and political repercussions. Zwingli's inflexibility left him without important political allies. Zwingli was soon to pay the price with his life on the battlefield. Philip of Hesse would lose his lands to Catholics and end up in prison.

Zwingli was, like Luther, a patriot and defender of his own people. He wanted all of Switzerland to reject Catholicism. Not all of Switzerland, however, wanted to follow Zwingli's lead. Many cantons were hostile to him, perhaps out of envy sparked by the rapid ascendancy of Zurich, but surely also for reasons of sincere loyalty to the Church. Zwingli resorted to pressure tactics, including economic sanctions against the Catholic cantons, denying them wheat, salt, and wine. Soon Catholic and Protestant cantons were looking for alliances with outside powers, but Zwingli's earlier intransigence kept him isolated. In response to Zwingli's sanctions the Catholic cantons sent a force of eight thousand soldiers to invade the canton of Zurich. At Cappel on 11 October 1531, Zwingli and a force of less than two thousand supporters were soundly defeated. Zwingli suffered a savage wound to the throat and died. His body was cut to pieces and then burned. In the aftermath an agreement was signed that stipulated that the Protestant and Catholic cantons could remain as they were, as long as Catholic minorities were tolerated.

Zwingli combined humanist ideals with a heightened spirituality, a legalistic bent, and a powerful sense of political activism. Under his successor, Heinrich Bullinger (1504–75), the Reformation in Zurich abandoned many of these features and were less pugnacious than Zwingli and on balance more concerned with pastoral matters. Bullinger, for example, was far more interested in reaching agreement with other reformers than was Zwingli, and sought agreement with Lutheran reformers, principally concerning their differing views on the eucharist. Zwingli's activity in Zurich inspired other young humanist preachers throughout Switzerland. Berthold Haller (1492–1536) in Bern and Johannes Oecolampadius (1482–1531) in Basel acknowledged their debt to Zwingli and followed his lead in their own cities.

The Radical Reformation

As the dispute over the eucharist between Luther and Zwingli demonstrated, Protestantism quickly displayed a tendency to fray, often accompanied by acrimony. With a speed that alarmed Luther and Zwingli, there developed within the reform movement a progressive splintering that seemed to hold no promise of abating.

The Reformation produced a powerful disorienting effect throughout Europe. Millions of people were cut off from institutions and patterns of life that they had known from childhood. For some this experience felt liberating. Others, however, felt a deep disquiet and uncertainty. Many responded to this disorientation by reaffirming their commitment to Catholicism; others responded by adopting Protestant beliefs, but in a host of varying forms. Together the various forms of Protestant faith outside of the Lutheran and Zwinglian traditions are sometimes called the "radical" wing of the reformation.

Most were theologically orthodox and peaceful, but a few became unorthodox and violent.

THE ANABAPTISTS

Anabaptist is a convenient but imprecise term historians use to refer to an amalgamation of different groups. The groups all shared a belief in baptism of adult believers (*anabaptism* means "rebaptism"), because they believed that in the New Testament no one belonged to a church without a personal decision to become a Christian. For this reason they rejected infant baptism and endorsed the practice of baptizing or rebaptizing adults as a public proclamation of Christian faith. The name *Anabaptist* was given to them by their opponents.

The practice of adult baptism is one feature they had in common. In other ways they could be quite distinct from one another. Some Anabaptist groups were influenced by Renaissance humanism, others were drawn from the Lutheran or Zwinglian traditions. Both Luther and Zwingli advocated the Bible as the standard for Christian belief and practice, but Anabaptists generally saw in the New Testament a fundamental antipathy between Christian congregations and the surrounding culture that Luther and Zwingli seemed to have missed. Luther and Zwingli were fairly comfortable with culture and the state, and neither interpreted the gospel in a way that was overly subversive to established political power structures. Both taught that church and state must live side by side for mutual support. The sixteenth century in Europe was a politically tumultuous period, as the Turks were a constant threat to Germany and central Europe. The Anabaptists presented governments with a real problem. Most forms of Anabaptism were solidly pacifist because, as they pointed out, Jesus advocated peace and nonviolence. In the face of military threats, pacifist Anabaptists were seen as disloyal and untrustworthy and were often mercilessly persecuted. They were also vilified for certain theological positions they advocated. For instance, some Anabaptist groups tended to trust individual divine revelation over all other authority, even scripture. This was deeply troublesome to other Protestants. To Catholics the practice of rebaptism constituted a denial of the effectiveness of the sacraments. In addition, some Anabaptists tended toward radical egalitarian positions, including equal rights for women, uniform treatment for the wealthy and the poor, communal living, and complete withdrawal from society. These ideas inherently dangerous to the social order. In both Lutheran and Zwinglian churches there were many parishioners who were at best nominal in their faith. This the Anabaptists could not countenance. They opted to create a "pure" church composed only of committed believers who were not guilty of unrepented sin. Of course. This sometimes led to persecution of the godless.

Conrad Grebel (1498–1526) was an articulate humanist living in Zurich at the time of Zwingli. In January 1525 he administered the sacrament of baptism to an adult who had been baptized as an infant. Grebel was a leader of the Swiss Brethren, whose members took seriously Zwingli's call to search the scriptures apart from either church authority or church tradition. He came to the conclusion that infant baptism was not to be found in scripture. He pointed out that there was no evidence for infant baptism in the writings of the early Church before the third century. The Brethren also advocated a free confessional church — that is, a visible company of those who publicly confessed the faith, and excluding the immoral. They believed this form of organization fit the pattern found in the New Testament.

 — Zwingli was perturbed by this development and openly preached against the Swiss Brethren. Zwingli was much influenced by the poor record of the Church in reforming itself, and tended to trust civil government to a far higher degree than Luther did. The Zurich city council issued a proclamation that the doctrines of the Brethren were dangerous to the interests of the city. Grebel and the others left the city and continued preaching their views. Grebel later died of the plague. One of his associates, Felix Manz (d. 1527), was eventually executed by drowning. His executioners, including Zwingli, thought the punishment grimly fitting.

The deaths of Grebel and Manz did not end the Anabaptist movement, although its character did change. Many leaders of the first generation of Anabaptists were scholars, humanists, and pacifists. With their deaths the second generation of Anabaptists became more radical. Their ranks were drawn principally from disaffected clergy, both Protestant and Catholic. Many focused their energies upon the return of Christ and the need to prepare for this event. For some this preparation involved violence and revolution. As seen in the following brief examples, their biographies illumine the astonishing range within Anabaptism.

Balthasar Hubmaier (1485–1528) was a Protestant minister in Waldshut, Austria, who surprised his congregation in 1525 by declaring his support for the doctrine of rebaptism. He was arrested by the authorities and compelled to recant. He then wandered throughout eastern Europe, finally settling in Moravia. There he converted a Lutheran congregation to Anabaptism. He was eventually arrested and burned at the stake for disturbing the peace. His wife was drowned in the Danube.

Melchior Hoffman (1498–1543) was by profession a leather worker who was first a Lutheran, then a follower of Zwingli, and finally an Anabaptist. In Strasbourg, Hoffman began preaching the imminent "Day of the Lord," a message that attracted many people. Hoffman then predicted that he would be imprisoned for six months immediately before the end of the world. He further taught that as the end approached the true children of God should arm themselves and do battle with all others. This inflammatory rhetoric alarmed city officials, who had Hoffman imprisoned for disturbing the peace. The apparent fulfillment of his first prediction only encouraged more Anabaptists to make the journey to Strasbourg. But the city council passed measures aimed at suppressing Anabaptism, and the predicted "Day of the Lord" came and went with Hoffman still in prison, the remainder of his prophecy unfilled.

In Moravia, Jakob Hutter (d. 1536) founded a communal society drawn principally from the poor but also attracting artisans and successful peasants. The community was organized into groups of about two hundred people each. Eventually more than fifteen thousand joined Hutter. The Hutterites were peaceful, but their communal social views were met with fear and animosity. Hutter was burned at the stake in 1536, and the Hutterites dispersed. (Several Hutterite communities still exist in Russia, the United States, and Canada.)

Hans Hut (d. 1527) was a bookbinder and bookdealer. In Moravia he argued with Hubmaier, defending complete nonviolence against Hubmaier's view that violence was permissible when defending one's family. Hut wandered through southern Germany and eastern Europe, preaching nonviolence and the imminent return of Christ. He was arrested several times, and charged with preaching disloyalty to the government. In Augsburg in 1527 he was arrested on charges that he preached free love and communism. He died during an escape attempt.

Perhaps the most infamous example of Anabaptism involves the German city of Münster. In 1532 the city council voted to appoint Lutheran preachers to all churches in the city. This was the result of popular pressure following the success of the fiery preaching of the Lutheran Bernard Rothmann (1495–1535). When news of these developments spread, many with Anabaptist leanings made their way to Münster. Some of the disciples of Jan Matthys were among them.

Jan Matthys (d. 1534) of Haarlem taught that the elect were duty-bound to use a bloody sword to eliminate the ungodly in preparation for the return of Christ. Several of the followers of Matthys created a chaotic scene in 1534 when they ran throughout Münster urging people to repent. They then stormed the city hall. These actions were greatly disturbing to many, and a good portion of the population moved away. Other radicals replaced them. On 23 February 1534 a new Anabaptist city council was elected. Wasting no time, Matthys arrived from Holland. He advocated the execution of all Catholics and Lutherans remaining in the city. The local bishop responded to these excesses by laying siege to the city. Matthys then declared Münster a communal state, abolished private property, and began a reign of terror. He declared that all monies were to be pooled, homes were to be open at all times, and all books except the Bible were to be burned. Matthys then announced that like Gideon

in the Old Testament he would go forth and destroy the enemy with but a handful of men. He was quickly killed. *BUT··· → — pwr trip!!!*

His young follower John of Leiden (1510–36) then took the lead. John was a megalomaniac with substantial charisma. After seizing power and establishing himself as an autocrat, he declared immediate death for insubordination, claimed he had been ordered in a vision to establish polygamy, and amassed a harem of fifteen wives — including the young widow of Matthys. John declared himself king and messiah, ruling from a golden throne while others in the city suffered. The bishop's army tightened the siege on the city, and eventually famine and disease took their toll. The city and King John were captured in June 1535, and Münster returned to Catholicism.[72] John was tortured to death, and his body was placed in a cage suspended from a church steeple.

Though the violent and radical Anabaptists were far outnumbered by those who were more peaceful, the experience at Münster cast a deep shadow over Anabaptism. It was Menno Simons (1496–1561) who rehabilitated the reputation of Anabaptism as a scholarly and pacifist movement, even in its communal and pointedly eschatological manifestations.

Simons was a Catholic priest who converted first to Lutheranism and then to Anabaptism. His reading of scripture convinced him that the biblical pattern of church organization was of individual congregations composed of those who had made a decision to live in Christ and who were moved by the Holy Spirit to lives of peace, justice, and service to others. He believed that Christians should obey civil authorities except when that required acting contrary to scripture. Simons did not believe that the Church should include unrepentant sinners. Like Zwingli, he believed that the sacraments were symbolic memorials. He also took an extremely dim view of the political order, and advocated service to the state only through nonviolent peaceful means. (Many of Simmons's followers, the Mennonites, immigrated to North America to continue his pacifist and scholarly tradition.)

THE SPIRITUALISTS AND EVANGELICAL HUMANISTS

Scholars can list more than forty varieties of Anabaptism. But the Reformation also produced in many other innovative expressions of Christian spiritual life. The Spiritualists defy categorization because their religious path was resolutely individualistic. In general, they desired to live their lives by no external authority, not even scripture, but only through the leading of the Holy Spirit. Some appreciated the rich mystical tradition within Catholicism; others simply claimed to have had a keenly profound experience that they interpreted as the leading of God.

Evangelical humanists are also impossible to categorize, but like humanists generally they wished to recover and perhaps even experience something of the vitality of the ancient Christian communities. They longed for a fresh experience like the first disciples' and earliest Christians' experiences of the risen Christ. The German nobleman Caspar Schwenckfeld (1490–1561) is an example. Schwenckfeld combined Catholic German mysticism and Lutheran teachings in an intensely personal and interiorized fashion. He came to disagree with Luther on the doctrine of justification by grace, believing that it was insufficient to encourage moral development. He understood baptism primarily as an inward and spiritual event. After his death a small band of followers continued to follow his teachings.

Spiritualists could be found among Catholic as well as all Protestant groups. When this attitude was combined untempered with other features—such as vivid expectation of the return of Christ, a fascination with moral purity, and social protest—disastrous episodes like Münster or the Peasant's War could result.

Evangelical humanism was strongest in the Alps and northern Italy, where it was fueled by Italian humanists who had converted from Catholicism. Some evangelical humanists became anti-Trinitarian; they perceived no developed doctrine of the Trinity in scripture. Others were sharply critical of the harsh excesses of Protestantism, and urged humane tolerance in the face of divergent beliefs, rather than intransigence accompanied by violence.

Summary

The Swiss historian Jakob Burckhardt wrote that sweeping events like the Reformation remains forever a mystery, as no account adequately can explain the interplay of the various forces Luther unleashed.[73] At the onset of the sixteenth century there was a still palpable sense that Europe was somehow a united though disparate whole. The development of capitalism signaled changes in political and social structures that threatened this idea. When a priest and university professor named Martin Luther questioned not only certain practices of the Church but the theology that supported them, sweeping changes ensued. Soon peasants, city councils, humanists, and princes saw in Luther's theological ideas not only spiritual benefit, but potential for material and social change. Once Luther established the precedent that revolt from the Catholic Church was possible, others joined in. In Switzerland, Ulrich Zwingli guided a reformation movement similar to Luther's. Countless others became involved in more individual expressions of Protestant faith that historians call the radical reformation. As we shall see in chapter 9, the reform impulse soon spread not only to the Catholic Church but also to European nations that were as yet untouched by Lutheranism.

QUESTIONS FOR REVIEW AND REFLECTION

1. Why did the Reformation happen when it did? Why was it not touched off by earlier reformers like Jan Hus?

2. Would the Reformation have happened without Luther? Why or Why not? To what degree was its shape determined by Luther?

3. What were the chief aspects of Luther's theology? What changes in European life, society, and culture can be traced to Luther and his theological program?

4. Why were political authorities attracted to Luther's ideas and the Protestant movement in general?

NOTES

1. In Latin, *corpus Christianum.*

2. Erasmus to Wolfgang Capito, 26 February 1517. See *Collected Works of Erasmus,* vol. 4, Trans. R. A. B. Mynors and D. F. S. Thompson (Toronto: University of Toronto Press, 1977), 261.

3. Lewis Spitz, *The Renaissance and Reformation Movements,* vol. 2 (St. Louis: Concordia, 1971), 303.

4. Spitz, *The Renaissance and Reformation Movements,* vol. 2, 323.

5. Steven Ozment, *The Age of Reform, 1250–1550* (New Haven: Yale University Press, 1980), 253.

6. Lewis Spitz, "Impact of the Reformation on Church-State Issues," in *Church and State under God,* ed. Albert Huegli (St. Louis: Concordia, 1964), 62–63.

7. See Scott H. Hendrix, *Luther and the Papacy: Stages in a Reformation Conflict* (Philadelphia: Fortress Press, 1981), 4.

8. *Answer to the Superchristian, Superspiritual, and Superlearned Book of Goat Emser,* trans. A. Steimle, in *Works of Martin Luther,* vol. 3 (Philadelphia: A. J. Holman & Castle Press, 1930), 382.

9. *To the Knights of the Teutonic Order: An Exhortation,* trans. W. A. Lambert, in *Works of Martin Luther,* vol. 3, 413.

10. *On the Jews and Their Lies,* in *Luther's Works,* vol. 47, ed. Franklin Sherman, trans. Martin H. Bertram, (Philadelphia: Fortress Press, 1964), 267.

11. Letter from Luther to George Spalatin, 14 January 1520. See *Luther's Works,* vol. 48, ed. and trans. G. G. Krodel (Philadelphia: Fortress Press, 1964), 145.

12. See Hans J. Hillerbrand, *The Reformation: a Narrative History Related by Contemporary Observers and Participants* (New York: Harper and Row, 1964), 54.

13. See A. G. Dickens, *The German Nation and Martin Luther* (London: Edward Arnold, 1974), 35.

14. See Spitz, *The Renaissance and Reformation Movements,* vol. 2, 322.

15. Lewis Spitz, *The Protestant Reformation, 1517–1559* (New York: Harper & Row, 1985), 89.

16. *Luther at the Diet of Worms,* trans. Roger A. Hornsby, in *Luther's Works,* vol. 32, ed. George W. Forell (Philadelphia: Muhlenberg Press, 1958), 112–13.

17. See Hans J. Hillerbrand, *The Reformation: a Narrative History Related by Contemporary Observers and Participants* (New York: Harper and Row, 1964), 381.

18. See Jaroslav Pelikan, "Luther the Expositor," in *Luther's Works: Companion Volume* (Saint Louis: Concordia, 1959), 77.

19. *Disputations against Scholastic Theology,* 9.

20. *Disputations against Scholastic Theology,* 12.

21. *Disputations against Scholastic Theology,* 13.

22. *The Magnificat,* trans. A. T. W. Steinhaeuser, in *Works of Martin Luther,* vol. 3, 142–43.

23. *The Babylonian Captivity of the Church,* trans. A. T. W. Steinhauser, in *Works of Martin Luther,* vol. 2 (Philadelphia: Muhlenberg Press, 1943), 207–208.

24. "In this regard my advice would be that Aristotle's *Physics, Metaphysics, On the Soul, Ethics,* which have hitherto been thought his best books, should be altogether discarded, together with all the rest of his books which boast of treating the things of nature. . . . I should be glad to see Aristotle's books on *Logic, Rhetoric* and *Poetics* retained or used in an abridged form; as text books for the profitable training of young people in speaking and preaching." *An Open Letter to the Christian Nobility of the German Nation,* 3.22, tran. C. M. Jacobs, in *Works of Martin Luther,* vol. 2, 146–47.

25. In 1517 Luther wrote, "It is doubtful whether the Latins comprehend the correct meaning of Aristotle." See his *Disputation against Scholastic Theology,* 12.

26. See, for example, *The Harvest of Humanism in Central Europe: Essays in Honor of Lewis W. Spitz,* ed. Manfred P. Fleischer (St. Louis: Concordia, 1992).

27. See *Luther and Erasmus: Free Will and Salvation,* ed. and trans. E. Gordon Rupp and Philip S. Watson (Philadelphia: Westminster Press, 1969), 143.

28. See J. A. Froude, *Life and Letters of Erasmus* (New York: Charles Scribner's Sons, 1912), 284.

29. See J. A. Froude, *Life and Letters of Erasmus* (New York: Charles Scribner's Sons, 1912), 286.

30. *Heidelberg Disputation,* trans. Harold J. Grimm, in *Luther's Works,* vol. 31, ed. Harold J. Grimm (Philadelphia: Muhlenberg, 1957), 52–53.

31. *Lectures on Romans,* tran. Jacob A. O. Preus, in *Luther's Works,* vol. 25, ed. Hilton C. Oswald (St. Louis: Concordia, 1972), 291.

32. *Lectures on Romans,* 345.

33. *Lectures on Romans,* 260.

34. *Luther's Works,* vol. 49, ed. and trans. Gottfried G. Krodel (Philadelphia: Fortress Press, 1972), 61–62.

35. *An Open Letter to the Christian Nobility,* 66.

36. *A Treatise on Christian Liberty,* tran. W. A. Lambert, in *Works of Martin Luther,* vol. 2, 337–38.

37. Spitz, *The Renaissance and Reformation Movements,* vol. 2, 316.

38. The phrase is not at all uncommon in the scholarly literature. See, for example, Steven Ozment, *The Reformation in the Cities* (New Haven: Yale University Press, 1975), 22.

39. Ozment, *The Reformation in the Cities,* 50.

40. See Erwin Panofsky, *The Life and Art of Albrecht Dürer* (Princeton, New Jersey: Princeton University Press, 1955), 198.Ne

41. See Steven Ozment, *The Age of Reform, 1250–1550* (New Haven: Yale University Press, 1980), 223.
42. See Ozment, *Age of Reform,* 277.
43. See A. G. Dickens and John Tonkin, *The Reformation in Historical Thought* (Oxford: Blackwell, 1985), 183–84.
44. See Spitz, *The Renaissance and Reformation Movements,* vol. 2, 309–27; and Spitz, *Protestant Reformation,* 102–4.
45. Spitz, *Protestant Reformation,* 99–100.
46. Spitz, *Protestant Reformation,* 109.
47. Carter Lindberg, *The European Reformations* (Oxford: Blackwell, 1996), 238.
48. Spitz, *Protestant Reformation,* 121.
49. H. C. Rublack, "Political and Social Norms in Urban Communities in the Holy Roman Empire," in *Religion, Politics and Social Protest,* ed. K. von Greyerz (London: Allen & Unwin, 1984), 36.
50. Karl Czok, "The Socio-economic Structure and Political Role of the Suburbs in Saxony and Thuringia in the Age of the German Early Bourgeois Revolution," in *The German Peasant War of 1525: New Perspectives,* ed. B. Scribner and G. Benecke (London: Allen & Unwin, 1979), 91.
51. Rublack, "Political and Social Norms," 39–40.
52. Rublack, "Political and Social Norms," 39.
53. Czok, "Socio-economic Structure," 93.
54. Dickens, *German Nation and Martin Luther,* 135.
55. See Jackson Spielvogel, "Patricians in Dissension: A Case Study from Sixteenth-Century Nurnberg," in *The Social History of the Reformation,* ed. L. Buck and J. Zophy (Columbus: Ohio State University Press, 1972), 73.
56. Dickens, *German Nation and Martin Luther,* 139.
57. Steven Ozment, *The Reformation in the Cities* (New Haven: Yale University Press, 1975), 77.
58. Seebass, "The Reformation in Nurnberg," 22.
59. Dickens, *German Nation and Martin Luther,* 142.
60. Seebass, "The Reformation in Nurnberg," 23.
61. Dickens, *German Nation and Martin Luther,* 146.
62. Spitz, *Protestant Reformation,* 103.
63. Ozment, *The Age of Reform,* 284.
64. Lindberg, *The European Reformations,* 164.
65. Czok, "Socio-economic Structure," 106
66. *An Admonition to Peace,* trans. Charles M. Jacobs, in *Luther's Works,* vol. 46, ed. Robert C. Schultz (Philadelphia: Fortress Press, 1967), 19.
67. See Lindberg, *The European Reformations,* 164–65.
68. *Against the Robbing and Murdering Hordes of Peasants,* trans. Charles M. Jacobs, in *Luther's Works,* vol. 46, ed. Robert C Schultz (Philadelphia: Fortress Press, 1967), 50.
69. In 1523 Luther produced a warning for the German nobility. He wrote, "there are very few princes that are not reckoned fools or knaves. That is because they show themselves to be such; the common man is beginning to think. . . . Dear princes and lords, be wise and guide yourselves accordingly. . . . The world is no longer what it was when you hunted and drove the people like so much game. Therefore drop your outrage and force, and remember to deal justly and let God's word have its course." See his *Secular Authority: To What Extent It Should Be Obeyed,* trans. J. J. Schindel, in *Works of Martin Luther,* vol. 3, 261.
70. Spitz, *Protestant Reformation,* 147.
71. See Spitz, *The Renaissance and Reformation Movements,* vol. 2, 147.
72. Norman Cohn, *The Pursuit of the Millennium: Revolutionary Millenarians and Mystical Anarchists of the Middle Ages* (New York: Oxford University Press, 1970), 261–86.
73. "Mighty events like the Reformation elude, as respects their details, their outbreak, and their development, the deductions of the philosophers, however clearly the necessity of them as a whole may be demonstrated. The movements of the human spirit, its sudden flashes, its expansions, and its pauses, must remain forever a mystery to our eyes, since we can but know this or that of the forces at work in it, never all of them together." Jacob Burckhardt, *The Civilization of the Renaissance in Italy,* trans. S. G. C. Middlemore (London: Penguin Books, 1990), 290–91.

CHAPTER 9

Protestant Expansion and Catholic Response

Overview

In chapter 8 we saw how what began as a minor theological dispute in Germany mushroomed into a broad movement, involving most of Europe, called the Protestant Reformation. Soon every aspect of life on the Continent was embroiled in a rapidly evolving conflict with no clear end in sight. We also saw the beginnings of some of the major traditions and movements within Protestantism: Lutheranism, Zwinglianism, and Anabaptism. This chapter surveys the later progress of Protestantism as it developed new forms and spread to other areas. This second surge of the Reformation took place in the midst of a changing political landscape in Europe, with colonialism, a new style of governance called royal absolutism, and the power of the nation-state all in the ascendancy. After setting the broader context, this chapter will discuss the second of the great Reformation figures—John Calvin, the leader of the reform in the city of Geneva. It will then investigate the reform movement in various areas of Europe, highlighting Calvinism (also called the Reformed tradition) and Anglicanism, the other major

traditions within Protestantism. The chapter continues with an evaluation of the Catholic response to the Protestant movement, known as the Catholic Reformation. It concludes with a brief treatment of Eastern Orthodoxy during the sixteenth and seventeenth centuries.

The European Scene

too powerful?

The Holy Roman Emperor Charles V tried to crush the Protestant revolt in its infancy. After Luther's defiant pronouncement at Worms Charles had declared, "I have decided to mobilize everything against Luther: my kingdoms and dominions, my friends, my body, my blood and my soul."[1] He was prevented from achieving this goal in large part by the mistrust and jealousy of other Catholic rulers. These rulers, fearing the growing political power of the emperor, surmised that if Charles succeeded in turning back Protestantism he would be powerful enough to dictate affairs even in lands under the control of others. Subsequent events left little doubt that European rulers in the sixteenth century were more loyal to their states than to their Church. This basic shift in loyalty, combined with the growth of secular bureaucracies and the continuing emergence of capitalism, made it clear that as the Reformation progressed religious authority was being questioned and in some cases dislodged from positions of influence it had long enjoyed. As religious beliefs and institutions gradually became less significant, they were replaced by a focus on human achievements and aims. This was but one of the features of secularism as it developed in Europe.

As we saw in chapter 8, in 1547 Charles achieved complete victory over the Protestant forces of the Schmalkald League, setting the stage for him to impose his political and religious will on the vanquished Protestants. But he was unable to reap the benefits of success. He and Pope Paul III (1534–49) squabbled over political issues surrounding the Council of Trent, and the pope's son was murdered under circumstances that suggested Charles was involved. Charles then hinted that he might invade Italy, reminding the pope of the humiliation of 1527 when Charles's mutinous armies sacked Rome and forced the pope to flee the city. This bickering between emperor and pope allowed the Protestant cause another chance at life, and broader changes in the political climate allowed it time to survive and mature.

At the 1547–48 assembly of the empire at Augsburg, Charles proposed restructuring the empire along the lines of an imperial league. The German princes resisted because they feared the arrangement would weaken their power. Although Protestant military forces had been defeated, the population of northern Germany continued to practice Protestantism, and German Catholic rulers looked away while "Lutheran" doctrine was preached from German pulpits. Charles, who was king of Spain as well as Holy Roman Emperor, further antagonized the German princes when he asked them to allow his Spanish-born son, Philip II (1555–98), to be next in line to the imperial throne after his brother Ferdinand, the heir apparent. The German princes rebuffed this attempt to pass the imperial throne to the Spanish instead of the German branch of the Hapsburg line. This forced Charles to stipulate that the throne would pass to Maximilian, the son of Ferdinand, and not to Philip. Charles' attempts to erode their authority were both obvious and unsavory to the German princes.

Several German princes were unhappy with the emperor's harsh treatment of the captured Protestant princes, and perceived in it an affront to German pride. Some made a secret pact with the French, and, taking the emperor by surprise, defeated his forces at Innsbruck in 1552. By 1553 the combatants, exhausted from years of struggle, settled into a desultory peace. The assembly of the empire at Augsburg in 1555 ended with a decision to allow both Catholicism and Lutheranism to coexist in Europe, but in separate areas. Other forms of Christian belief had no legal status within the empire. Anyone unhappy with the religion chosen by the local ruler was free to move to another area.

Philip II would never be emperor, but he did see himself as a champion of the Catholic cause. As king of Spain Philip was a cautious and careful ruler, a great believer in planning and organization. He often maddened his staff with overly energetic attention to detail, but he commanded a fine army. His many successes on the battlefield gave him great confidence, and like his father, Philip hoped to see the day of complete Protestant submission. Many parts of Europe remained in Protestant hands, and even in his own family holdings in the Netherlands, the Dutch stubbornly resisted him. Though the Dutch Protestants had disagreed with Philip's father, Charles had lived in the Netherlands when he was young, and he understood Dutch culture and customs. The Dutch had seen Charles as their territorial prince and were, in the main, loyal to him. But Philip had never lived in the Netherlands, and the Dutch viewed him as a Spanish interloper. For his part, Philip saw Dutch Protestantism as an unacceptable revolt in his ancestral Hapsburg lands. But in Philip's mind the real obstacle to Catholic supremacy and a united Christendom was England.

In 1588 Philip sent a great navy or armada against England and its sovereign, Elizabeth I (1558–1603). The goal of the Armada, as Philip incessantly wrote to his admiral, was not to defeat the English navy, but to secure the English Channel so that a Catholic army waiting in the Netherlands could cross safely and invade England. Against all odds the smaller and more nimble English ships, led by Lord Howard and Francis Drake, defeated the Spanish fleet, leaving it to the mercy of fierce storms that ravaged it for weeks. It was a resounding defeat of Spanish power, and the English victory signaled the dawn of a period of English naval power that persisted into the twentieth century. Philip would try again to defeat the English, but the hour of great opportunity had passed. Henceforth, no Catholic ruler could seriously dream of a united Christendom. The mantle had passed to rulers who envisioned reigning efficient nation-states, unchallenged by either the Church from without or the nobility from within.

As we saw in chapter 8, Europeans became aware of the Americas as a new age of competition between European powers began. The Portuguese were one of two dominant early European colonial powers. They eventually lost much of their empire to the English and the Dutch, but they retained some portions for centuries. For instance, the Portuguese port of Macao in southeast China did not revert to Chinese rule until 1999. Spain, the other early European colonial power, retained its empire far longer than the Portuguese. From these holdings Spain extracted enormous wealth at a terribly high cost to the native inhabitants, whose patterns of life were extinguished. Millions lost their lives to disease. Those who did not succumb to disease were forced into servitude by their European conquerors or were compelled to work for the Church and to adopt Catholicism.

The Church was a frequently unwanted but perpetually formidable force in the internal politics of European states. It owned roughly one-third of the land of Europe at the beginning of the sixteenth century. These holdings included not only areas directly controlled by the papacy, but also monasteries, churches, hospitals, prisons, and palaces. The Church sought to ensure that these properties and its clergy were exempt from taxation, state prosecution, or other forms of state control. These exemptions hampered rulers toiling to gain authority in

their own lands, and irritated the laity, who, of course, did not enjoy such benefits.

Their colonies were a tremendous asset to both Spain and Portugal, yet these Iberian states remained largely old-style monarchies. The sovereigns of Spain and Portugal continued to share political authority within their countries with both the nobility and the Church. Many matters of state finance and diplomacy were under the purview of the nobility, who held this authority by ancestral right rather than demonstration of competence. The combined, if largely uncoordinated, efforts of the nobility and the Church often limited the authority of rulers, at times leaving sovereigns at the mercy of the nobility, as was the case in Poland.

During the seventeenth century, the Dutch and English asserted themselves as colonial powers. With their fine navy and aggressive merchants, the Dutch forged a colonial empire that included parts of the East Indies, southern India, and Africa. For much of the seventeenth century the Netherlands was the most glittering example of European wealth and culture.[2] The Dutch even established a colonial outpost near present-day New York called New Amsterdam, but eventually they were forced out of North America by the English.

The English emerged as the most successful European colonial power, maintaining their empire into the twentieth century. Their colonies ranged from the east coast of North America, to Africa, India, the coast of China, and parts of southeast Asia.

ROYAL ABSOLUTISM

The seventeenth century witnessed the mature development of a system of government called royal absolutism. The aim was to establish the monarch as supreme within the state. This was usually accomplished through improved efficiency of the organs of government, and a redirection of authority to make all branches of government, and even religious authorities, answerable to the sovereign.

Royal absolutism rested upon seven pillars. The first was conscription and a professional army. A professional army is loyal not to a person but to the state itself. Conscription (compelling citizens to serve in the armed forces) was important because it could provide a permanent military force and it was a tangible sign of the power of the state over the lives of citizens.

The second pillar was a centralized finance office charged with the creation and collection of taxes. This required the development of an office of statistics, so that the government could have an accurate accounting of the population and total wealth of the country. The great French minister Colbert, who served Louis XIV (1643–1715), was a master and innovator in this area.

The third pillar was a finance ministry to regulate the economy. The economic system at work under royal absolutism is often called mercantilism, a type of capitalism with a high degree of government regulation over manufacture, export, and import. This was a critical function to control and exploit colonies.

The fourth and fifth pillars were professional diplomatic and bureaucratic services. These two areas had traditionally been the purview of the nobility, whose aims were often contrary to those of the monarch, and whose competence in these areas was often suspect. Professional diplomatic and bureaucratic corps were not only more efficient, they were loyal to the ruler.

The sixth pillar was a national educational system. State universities were established to train the many civil servants the government needed, and royal academies of science and geography engaged in research useful to the state.

The seventh pillar was propaganda. This was the Baroque age, when glittering architecture and richly textured paintings were used to overawe subjects and foreigners with the power and majesty of the sovereign.

Calvin

Martin Luther was not the only towering figure of the Reformation period. The other, twenty-six years his junior, was John Calvin (1509–64). Philip Melanchthon, Luther's intellectual lieutenant, held Calvin in such regard that he called him "the theologian." Calvin gave such discipline, shape,

and energy to Protestantism that the British essayist Lord John Morley referred to Calvin as "one of the commanding forces in the annals of the world."[3]

Calvin's star rose early. At twenty-six he published the first and briefest of many editions of his *Institutes of the Christian Religion,* an organized explanation of the doctrine and principles of the theology of the reformers. He was not working in a vacuum, because Luther had earlier written shorter works like this, and he readily acknowledged his debt to Luther. But Calvin's book struck his contemporaries as so clear, so balanced, and so irresistibly forceful that it immediately won Calvin international praise and notoriety. The *Institutes* gave Protestantism intellectual force and legitimacy, even as Luther had given it life. Whereas Luther apparently emphasized God's mercy given to human beings through Christ, Calvin seemed to stress God's perfection and omniscience.

Calvin was the son of prosperous middle-class parents, and he studied at some of the best universities in France. His father had an important lay career with the Church and steered his son in the same direction.

Calvin came to Paris in 1523 to study, and there he became friends with two other impressive students: Nicholas Cop and a precocious young man named Olivetan. Olivetan was a devoted student of scripture who would later translate the Bible into French. News of Luther and his ideas had already penetrated France, fanning social agitation and sparking controversy among intellectuals. Olivetan found himself largely in agreement with the German reformer. He began to question many practices of the Church for which he could see no biblical foundation. It is likely that Calvin was substantially influenced by his friend's growing unease with the Church.

In 1528 Calvin left Paris to study law, first in Orleans and later in Bourge. While he studied he became intensely interested in humanism and the classics. In 1532 he published a commentary in Latin on Seneca's treatise *On Clemency.* This traditional academic undertaking was hardly the material for the resumé of a radical. But within two years Calvin had become just that—a reformer fleeing the authorities to save his life.

Calvin considered himself unsuited for public life:

> Being of a rather unsociable and shy disposition, I have always loved retirement and peace. So I began to look for some hideout where I could escape from people . . . my aim was always to live in private without being known.[4]

Some have observed that Luther seems not to have had a thought or feeling that he did not write down.[5] Calvin was a different sort entirely. Later in life, when forced to defend himself, Calvin wrote, "I am unwilling to speak of myself, but . . . will say what I can consistent with modesty."[6] This reticence makes it difficult to know what Calvin thought of the intellectual forces swirling around him.

Like Luther, Calvin seems to have seen in the humanist desire to use original sources a pattern that was beneficial for biblical theology. But in several important ways Calvin was different from the other reformers. He was neither a monk nor a priest, and he appears to have been essentially self-taught in matters of theology. The German and Swiss reformers lived under political systems that allowed them the freedom to find security with a prince or city favorable to their cause. But Calvin was French; his country was ruled by a single sovereign, Francis, who refused to tolerate any movement that threatened his attempt to unify his realm.

By 1530 there were many Protestant groups active within France, in the main working quietly to spread the teachings of Luther. Francis I (1515–47) was already exploiting the Protestant cause on the international stage, and this may have given French Protestants the false hope that their king would be tolerant of their religious beliefs. By 1553 some of the French Protestants began to agitate publicly, and Francis began episodic persecutions. This policy stiffened as Protestant tactics came to irritate him more and more. A case in point was the Affair of the Placards. On the night of 17–18 October 1534, posters and flyers appeared in Paris and several other French cities denouncing the mass with the heading "True Articles on the Horrible Abuse of the Papal Mass." One flyer was found attached to a door in the king's own bedchamber. Alarmed, Francis imprisoned and tortured hundreds of French Protestants. In 1535 he issued a general decree suppressing heresy.

Calvin's reluctance to write or speak of matters he considered personal makes it unclear when he decided to break with Rome and difficult even to trace the development of his thinking during this formative period. He returned to Paris in 1533. There his friend Nicholas Cop, now a professor of medicine, had been elected rector of the Sorbonne. In his inaugural speech on the 1 November 1533, Cop spoke on the Sermon on the Mount and caused a great uproar. Cop said that although the sciences are useful, they are of little worth next to the truth that "God's grace alone redeems from sins." He made reference to the works of French humanists and of Luther. In the Sermon on the Mount, Jesus spoke of the poor being blessed, and Cop identified these poor with the followers of Luther who were being persecuted in France. In the resulting tumult Cop was forced to flee the city. Calvin also fled, as it was generally believed he had a hand in writing the speech.

Calvin spent the next several years traveling under assumed names throughout France and Switzerland. In May 1534 he returned to his boyhood home of Noyon, a cathedral city some sixty miles northeast of Paris, and resigned the ecclesiastical benefices his father had secured for him when he was twelve. For the rest of his life he expressed contempt for humanists who privately embraced reformed doctrine and principles but publicly remained within the Roman Church. He was imprisoned briefly on two occasions, traveled to Paris, and then moved on to Orleans. There, in a secluded location outside of the city, Calvin celebrated the eucharist according to the reformed rite for the first time, using a slab of rock as a communion table. After Francis issued the decree suppressing heresy, Calvin left France for Switzerland, where he settled in Basel. He seems to have had little interest in becoming a leader of the Reformation, judging his own talents to be in the literary and scholarly fields.

Nearly all Protestant literature at that time was polemical in nature, defending Protestant theology or attacking Catholic theology. Calvin saw the need to produce a different sort of Protestant literature. He envisioned a work that set out to explain the beliefs and principles of reformed doctrine apart from the heat of acrimonious debate. The result was his *Institutes of the Christian Religion,* published in Basel in 1536.

The first edition was brief—six chapters and 516 pages—dealing with matters of law, the creed, the Lord's Prayer, the sacraments, Christian freedom, and Calvin's estimate of the Catholic view of the sacraments. In its published form it was meant to be a handbook small enough to be carried in the pocket, ready for instant use. The book was immediately successful and soon went through multiple editions in both Latin and French. It also grew over the years as Calvin rewrote and added material at regular intervals. By 1539 Calvin thought of the *Institutes* as a training manual for ministers. The definitive edition, published in 1559–1560, contained eighty chapters. Modern English translations often run to more than fifteen hundred pages.

Calvin then decided to settle in Strasbourg, a city that had already embraced Lutheranism, where he hoped to live a quiet life of study and scholarship. On the way there, in July 1536, he passed through Geneva, where he intended to spend only one night. But Guillame Farel (1489–1565), the leader of the reform movement in Geneva, heard that the author of the *Institutes* was in town. He went to Calvin's hotel and begged him to remain and assist the cause of reform in Geneva. Calvin refused. Farel then declared that Calvin's intention to live a life of quiet study was disobedience to God. Calvin was shaken and terrified by the force of Farel's pronouncement. He later said he felt as if through Farel God was laying his hand on him, compelling Calvin to stay.

Calvin's original intention was simply to assist Farel, but soon the quality of Calvin's mind asserted itself, and he was recognized as the leading reformer in the city. Originally he was given the title "Professor of Sacred Scripture"; later he was made one of the pastors in the city. Both appointments were actions of the civil government.

In Geneva, like other cities, political, material, and religious factors combined to create a climate favorable to the Reformation. Geneva's location be-

tween France and Italy put it under the influence of the Duke of Savoy, who controlled the town through the appointment of its bishop. During the early sixteenth century Geneva had struggled to become independent of Savoy. To the north lay two Swiss cantons, Protestant Bern and Catholic Fribourg. Both attempted to draw Geneva into the Swiss alliance. Having lost the city of Lausanne to the alliance in 1525, Savoy was afraid that Geneva might follow suit. In 1527 a city council was created in Geneva, and it immediately began exercising political control that previously had belonged to the bishop. Geneva was attacked by forces of Savoy in 1530 but was rescued by Bern and Fribourg.

In spite of their mutual support of Geneva against Savoy, Bern and Fribourg were at odds over the matter of religion. In 1533 Bern began a concerted effort to convert Geneva to the Protestant cause, and in the ensuing wave of iconoclasm and religious rioting effectively separated Geneva from its ties to Fribourg. Farel had been active in this early phase of the Reformation in Geneva. In December 1535 the council gave Catholic clergy the choice of conversion or exile, and in May 1536 it resolved that citizens of Geneva should "live according to the gospel and the Word of God." The council also assumed significant authority over ecclesiastical matters in the city. Calvin arrived just as Farel and others were trying to implement the Reformation mandate.

Calvin trusted political leaders far less than Zwingli had, believing that church worship, instruction, and discipline were matters for leaders of the church. He set to work drafting a confession of faith for the city that reflected these convictions. In January 1537, Farel and Calvin submitted to the town council the *Articles Concerning the Organization of the Church and of Worship at Geneva,* insisting it become binding on the entire population of the city. The document was part church constitution, part civil constitution, and part theological treatise. It provided for independence of the church from political control, stipulated frequent celebrations of the eucharist, asserted the need for church discipline, and retained for the clergy the right to excommunicate, principally to ensure that the eucharist was not sullied by some who might take it in an unworthy state. Calvin argued that it was nec-essary to excommunicate sinners who refused to repent. Many in the city felt this was too harsh. The Catholic sacramental system allowed for hu-man frailty and took a forgiving attitude toward human sinfulness. But Calvin complained that it did nothing to encourage moral development. In spite of some objections, the council endorsed the document.

Forces opposed to Calvin and Farel, however, were organizing and in the ascendancy. Many re-sented the practice of moral supervision insisted upon by the reformers. Others were uncomfortable with the prominence of Frenchmen in the Genevan reformation and the number of French refugees flooding the city.

In November 1537 the city council refused to enforce the *Articles,* fearing that ecclesiastical con-trol of morals would eventually undermine its own authority. The council, in effect, withheld from Farel and Calvin the power of excommunication. The elections of February 1538 brought enemies of Farel and Calvin into power on the council. The council then advised Farel and Calvin to stop med-dling in politics and instead keep to the business of religion. Tensions mounted, and the council tem-porarily forbade Farel and Calvin to preach.

The two reformers were not so easily dissuaded. Together they planned a spectacular protest. On Easter Sunday, 1538, they preached in the two main churches in Geneva — but when the time came to administer the eucharist, they refused. This was, in effect, a declaration that the reformers considered their congregations excommunicated. There was an immediate uproar in the council. Farel and Calvin were given three days to leave the city. Calvin, who did not enjoy life in Geneva, remarked, "Well and good, if we had served men we would be ill re-warded, but we serve a great Master who will re-ward us."[7]

Calvin ended up in Stasbourg, where he came under the influence of Martin Bucer (1491–1551), the leading reformer of that city. From Bucer Cal-vin learned the art of blending civic and religious life. Also in Strasbourg was Jean Sturm (1507–89), a humanist educator whose efforts at reform came to influence Calvin's thinking on education. During this period Calvin traveled to several theological conferences to meet with Luther, Melanchthon, Bucer, and others. Although he found Luther's vul-garity shocking, he had great respect for the older reformer. In a 25 November 1544 letter to Heinrich Bullinger (1504–75), Calvin observed,

> I . . . desire to put you in mind . . . how eminent a man Luther is. . . . Often have I been wont to declare, that even if he were to call me a devil, I should still not the less hold him in such honour that I must acknowledge him to be an illustrious servant of God. But while he is endowed with rare and excellent virtues, he labours at the same time under serious faults.[8]

During his years in Strasbourg, which were per-haps the happiest time of his life, Calvin wrote sev-eral treatises and worked on his *Institutes,* expand-ing the work to seventeen chapters. In 1540 Calvin married Idelette de Bure; she died in 1549, leaving him crushed. "The death of my wife has been ex-ceedingly painful to me," he wrote to Peter Viret on 7 April 1549. "And truly mine is no common source of grief. I have been bereaved of the best compan-ion of my life."[9]

Meanwhile, events in Geneva had left the city even more unsettled. The remaining Catholic pop-ulation hoped to return the city to the ancient faith. The various Protestant groups were plagued by infighting. Then the humanist Cardinal Sadoleto wrote an eloquent letter to the city council, urging Geneva to abandon the Protestant cause and return to Catholicism. After some time the council deter-mined that no one in the city was up to the chal-lenge of drafting a reply, so Calvin was invited to do so. His response, written in six days, was dependent upon Luther in that it asserted the primacy of scrip-ture and justification by faith. The argument was so clear and elegant that it was hailed as a masterpiece. It also won Calvin new respect in Geneva.

The elections of February 1539 resulted in the victory of candidates favorable to Calvin. When he learned that there was mounting pressure in Geneva to ask him back, Calvin was hardly pleased. A series of letters from friends urged him to return. His responses were trenchant. In April 1539 he de-scribed Geneva as an abyss or great gulf in which, he feared, he would be swallowed up.[10] "[R]ather would I submit to a hundred other deaths," he wrote to Farel on 29 March 1540, "than to that cross on which one must perish daily a thousand times."[11] On 19 May 1540, in a letter to his friend Peter Viret, he referred to Geneva as "that place of torture."[12] "I am horrified at the mere mention of a recall" he wrote to Farel in May 1540.[13] In October 1540 the council invited Calvin to come back to Geneva. When he did finally return, reluctantly, in September 1541, he was appointed pastor of the cathedral of St. Peter and given a residence, a generous salary, basic foodstuffs, and an annual allotment of two hundred and fifty gallons of wine.

Immediately after his return, Calvin began work on the *Ecclesiastical Ordinances,* completing the document within two weeks. The *Ordinances* present Calvin's ideas of an ordered church with four types of ministry: pastors to preach, administer the sacraments, and, along with the elders, take responsibility for church discipline; elders, to oversee the religious and moral life of the community; teachers, to instruct in scripture and to oversee the education in the city generally; and deacons, to manage church finances and care for the sick and the poor. Calvin further stipulated that there should be a body called the consistory, made up of twelve lay elders and several pastors, with pastors always in the minority. Its purpose was to guide and manage church affairs.

The council enacted Calvin's plan in November 1541, but Calvin saw the enactment of the *Ordinances* as only a first step. Based on his prior experiences in Geneva, he believed that the council was an unreliable ally. It was subject to policy changes with each election, and many prominent Genevans were unhappy with his insistence on moral discipline. Calvin also knew that Genevan tolerance was stretched thin by the French refugees in the city.

Given these conditions, Calvin's reform of Geneva was remarkable. Before his return Calvin had negotiated for the right to draft legislation. For the next two years Calvin fashioned the constitutional framework for the city government, either composing or influencing legislation concerned with political and judicial matters. Having made the rules, Calvin was largely successful in using them to en-

sure that Geneva came to resemble his ideal. He never held an official post in civil government and did not even become a citizen until 1559, but his suasive force and political savvy ensured that, in spite of periodic challenges, he was the leading voice in Genevan politics until his death in 1564.

One of the chief concerns of the consistory was the welfare of citizens. Research has made clear that under Calvin extensive networks of caring, charity, and hospitality were created.[14] The consistory is most famous for another of its functions, the supervision of morals. The cases it heard included charges of adultery, cursing, unauthorized luxury, blasphemy, complaining about Calvin, dancing, unseemly singing, and absence from worship. Calvin ran afoul of several patrician families in Geneva when the consistory brought charges against them. Calvin prevailed, but the victories often came at a high personal cost.

In 1546 Pierre Ameaux, a member of the council, publicly criticized Calvin. Ameaux's family owned a playing-card business, which of course suffered under the rigid morality of the new regime. Ameaux accused Calvin of teaching false doctrine. Calvin responded by convincing the council to order a public and humiliating act of repentance, demanding that Ameaux beg for mercy on his hands and knees. Calvin was convinced that to attack his interpretation of scripture was to attack God.

More serious cases involved two powerful Genevan families, the Perrins and the Favres. Several members of these families were accused of lewd dancing, failure to attend church, and speaking against Calvin. Calvin again prevailed, but a groundswell of popular resistance to Calvin was building. Many were afraid to protest openly, but research shows a dramatic increase in the number of Genevan dogs named after the reformer.

Perhaps the most famous case of resistance to Calvin involved Michael Servetus, a brilliant scientist and amateur theologian who is often credited with being one of the first to discover the pulmonary circulation of the blood. He was also something of a provocateur. In 1531 he published *Seven Books on the Errors of the Trinity,* in which he argued that the doctrine of the Trinity was incorrect. The book was quickly condemned by both Catholics and Protestants, but Servetus could not resist theological controversy. He began anonymous correspondence with Calvin, continuing to criticize the doctrine of the Trinity. Calvin recognized Servetus as the author and turned the materials over to the Inquisition. Servetus was arrested by the Inquisition but escaped, to be burned only in effigy. He then arrived in Geneva and attended Calvin's church; he was recognized, detained, and burned at the stake on 27 October 1553. Calvin had argued for the more humane sentence of decapitation. Farel rebuked him for proposing leniency. The episode has cast a shadow on Calvin's career, but at the time it buttressed his position. His enemies in Geneva could hardly criticize him for opposing someone declared a heretic by both Catholics and Protestants.

CALVIN'S THEOLOGY

Calvin wrote extensively. It is likely that among Christian writers only Augustine, Luther, and Thomas Aquinas wrote more. It used to be argued that Calvin's thought was consistent from start to finish, but more recent scholarship has noted changes in his thought on subjects such as the eucharist. Much of his literary output involved reworking the *Institutes*.

The final edition of the *Institutes* comprises four books.[15] Scholars disagree on the center of Calvin's theology, or whether it has a center at all. What is certain is that Calvin begins by considering the nature of human knowledge of self and knowledge of God. Book 1, "On the Knowledge of God the Creator," opens with the centrality of God to human existence:

Nearly all the wisdom we possess, that is to say, true and sound wisdom, consists of two parts: the knowledge of God and of ourselves. But, while joined by many bounds, which one precedes and brings forth the other is not easy to discern. In the first place, no one can look upon himself without immediately turning his thoughts to the contemplation of God, in whom he "lives and moves" [Acts 17:28] . . . our very being is nothing but subsistence in the one God.[16]

For Calvin, human self-awareness immediately implies not only that God exists but also that human life is rooted in and dependent upon God. For Calvin, God is, in the words of various scholars, the "great thought,"[17] the "foundation of all good,"[18] and the "all-determining reality."[19]

Calvin argued that God reveals himself in nature, in human experience, and in the human conscience. Because this is true, he claimed, human beings are responsible for their behavior. But God's revelation in nature is incomplete and obscured by human sin. Instead, it is most perfectly conveyed in scripture and in Jesus Christ. Calvin asserted that scripture is true, the most reliable source for God's revelation — trustworthy beyond councils, pope, or Church tradition:

[T]he Scriptures obtain full authority among believers only when men regard them as having sprung from heaven, as if there the living words of God were heard. . . . But a most pernicious error widely prevails that Scripture has only so much weight as is conceded to it by the consent of the church. As if the eternal and inviolable truth of God depended upon the decision of men![20]

Like Luther, Calvin was willing to grant to scripture divine warrant:

Therefore, illumined by his power, we believe neither by our own or anyone else's judgment that Scripture is from God; but above human judgment we affirm with utter certainty . . . that it has flowed to us from the very mouth of God by the ministry of men.[21]

Calvin found himself largely agreeing with Luther that much contemporary scholastic theology was too interested in extrabiblical speculation about God. He wrote: "Let us use great caution that neither our thoughts nor our speech go beyond the limits to which the Word of God extends. . . . Let us then willingly leave to God the knowledge of himself . . . as he reveals himself to us, without inquiring about him elsewhere than from his Word."[22] Calvin shared Luther's belief that the Bible was the only legitimate authority for Christian faith and practice, but he was more apt than

Luther to apply the straightforward reading of scripture to the issues of everyday life. He believed that salvation is a free gift offered by God in his graciousness, and accepted by faith alone, without regard to human merit. Calvin further asserted that human beings alone in creation were created in the image of God and reflect God's glory.[23] "The true nature of the image of God is to be derived from what Scripture says of its renewal through Christ."[24]

Book 2, "On the Knowledge of God the Redeemer in Christ," surveys Calvin's thought on human sin and redemption. He argued that as a result of the sin of Adam, humankind has become infected by sin:

Original sin, therefore, seems to be a hereditary depravity and corruption of our nature, diffused into all parts of the soul, which first makes us liable to God's wrath, then also brings forth in us those works which Scripture calls "works of the flesh" [Gal. 5:19]. And that is properly what Paul often calls sin . . . we are so vitiated and perverted in every part of our nature that by this great corruption we stand justly condemned and convicted before God . . . not only has punishment fallen upon us from Adam, but a contagion imparted by him resides in us which justly deserves punishment.[25]

Like Luther, Calvin argued that human beings are alienated from God by sin. Calvin made it painfully explicit that he considered human beings totally depraved. "The soul," he wrote, "plunged into this deadly abyss, is not only burdened with vices, but is utterly devoid of good."[26] But he balanced this judgment with the conviction that humanity is the crown of creation[27] and that God wishes to restore human beings to their original condition. Like Luther, he asserted the centrality of the sacrifice of Christ. "The guilt that held us liable for punishment has been transferred to the head of the Son of God [Isa. 53:12]. We must, above all, remember this substitution."[28]

If, then, we would be assured that God is pleased with and kindly disposed toward us, we must fix our eyes and minds on Christ alone . . . to perform a perfect expiation, he gave his own life . . . as an expiatory offering for sin . . . upon which our stain and punishment might somehow be cast, and cease to be imputed to us. . . . The Father destroyed the force of sin when the curse of sin was transferred to Christ's flesh.[29]

Book 3, "On the Manner of Receiving the Grace of Christ," is concerned with the work of the Holy Spirit and the Christian Life. Like Luther, Calvin believed that the work of Christ is useless unless it is accepted by faith. For Calvin this faith is not simply a rational acceptance of the Christian message, but trust in God leading to a vital living union with the risen Christ:

How do we receive those benefits which the Father bestowed on his only-begotten Son — not for Christ's own private use, but that he might enrich poor and needy men? First, we must understand that as long as Christ remains outside of us, and we are separated from him, all that he has suffered and done for the salvation of the human race remains useless and of no value to us. Therefore, to share with us . . . he had to become ours and to dwell within us . . . we obtain this by faith.[30]

Calvin believed that the Holy Spirit encourages repentance as a natural response to what Christ has done and leads the believer into the process of growth in the Christian life. Calvin laid a greater stress on good works than Luther, although both were careful to argue that good works are the result, and not part of the cause, of human redemption. "If election has as its goal holiness of life, it ought rather to arouse and goad us eagerly to set our mind upon it than to serve as a pretext for doing nothing."[31]

Calvin could not help but notice that not all people receive what he considered this great gift. Because Calvin believed that all good comes from God, he could only conclude that God chose some to accept this gift and others to reject it:

In actual fact, the covenant of life is not preached equally among all men, and among those to whom it is preached, it does not gain the same acceptance either constantly or in equal degree. In this diversity the wonderful depth of God's judgment is made known. For there is no doubt that this variety also serves the decision of God's eternal election . . . salvation is freely offered to some while others are barred access . . . he does not indiscriminately adopt all into the hope of salvation, but gives to some what he denies to others.[32]

In Calvin's view, God's glory is such that he was the cause of everything. Like Zwingli, Calvin denied contingency: Nothing happens by accident, nor does God merely know in advance. God causes everything. "God by the bridle of his providence turns every event whatever way he wills."[33] Calvin's doctrine of predestination seems to be the outcome of this view and his conviction that human beings can do nothing to contribute to their own salvation except to have faith in God's mercy and grace. "Scripture does not speak of predestination with intent to rouse us to boldness that we may try with impious rashness to search out God's unattainable secrets. Rather, its intent is that, humbled and cast down, we may learn to tremble at his judgment and esteem his mercy."[34] All human beings deserve condemnation, Calvin asserted, so only a merciful God would choose to save anyone. But later generations have often found the doctrine of predestination not a salve, as Calvin intended, but a source of concern. It came to occupy more and more space in the *Institutes* as Calvin was forced to defend his view of predestination during a series of theological disputes.

The notion of double predestination enhanced the controversy. Double predestination means God predestines the elect to salvation and everyone else to damnation. Luther shied away from this position because it seemed to limit the mercy of God. Some have pointed out that the doctrine presupposes a lack of fairness. Why should some be saved and others damned? In response to such objections, Calvin argued that it was perfectly appropriate for God to damn some — after all, everyone is guilty of sin. Luther agreed that God would be justified in damning all, but further wondered why God would limit his mercy so as to save only some. Many Christians were afraid that the idea of predestination would encourage moral laxity — if one's ulti-

mate fate is already decided, what is the point of striving to be good? To this Calvin had an ingenious answer.

Against centuries of tradition, Luther had argued that there was nothing inherently special about the clerical vocations. For Luther the clergy were not a special class with special spiritual rights, status, or privileges. As we saw in chapter 8, this teaching came to have a profound leveling effect on European society. Calvin enhanced this idea by declaring that all vocations are opportunities to glorify God. Although Calvin thought that salvation does not come through human activity, many Calvinists came to believe that excellence in human activity is an expression or indicator of the presence of God in one's life. Those who are clearly sinful, it seemed, could not be among the elect. Conversely, good works and a virtuous life suggests election. Soon another idea began to take hold: that because every vocation is a possible arena for glorifying God, success in one's vocation is also an indicator that one is among the elect. Max Weber (1864–1920), the German sociologist, argued in *The Protestant Ethic and the Spirit of Capitalism*[35] that the idea of success as an indicator of election became an immensely potent force in the economic vitality of areas where Protestantism took hold. While Weber's argument has been critiqued and revised, many accept the basic thesis. Curiously, though, the reformers denied that good works had any spiritual power to effect salvation, Calvin's Protestanism tended to inspire good works — or at least the kind of good works that brought material success.

Book 4, "On the Outward Means or Help by Which God Invites Us into the Fellowship of Christ," is concerned with the role of the sacraments and of the Church more broadly. Like Luther, Calvin believed that the true or invisible Church is composed of committed believers and that the visible Church is composed of those truly saved as well as some who are not. He also asserted that Protestants were not founding a new Church, but rather reforming the one Church. In this section of the Institutes he also outlined his plan for church government, complete with the four offices (pastors, teachers, elders, and deacons). A major difference between Calvin and the other reformers is that Calvin placed a far higher premium on the role of discipline for the Church. "The whole jurisdiction of the church," Calvin asserted, "pertains to the discipline of morals."[36]

In regard to ecclesiastical practice, Calvin frequently had more in common with Zwingli than with Luther. His followers did away with festivals, artwork, feast days, and other practices that seemed to have no basis in scripture. Unlike Luther, Calvin was able to come to agreement with the Zwinglian churches over the matter of the eucharist. In 1549 Calvin and Farel traveled to Zurich; after less than two hours of discussion, they reached agreement with the Zwinglians on the spiritual presence of Christ in the eucharist. Both sides signed the resulting *Consensus Tigurinus,* or Zurich agreement. After further negotiation, in 1552 Calvin and the Zwinglian churches reached consensus on still other issues, and on several Calvin had to compromise. In 1566, after Calvin's death, the Second Helvetic Confession, written by Heinrich Bullinger (1504–75), the successor to Zwingli, was published. This Confession sets forth a position on the presence of Christ in the eucharist that both Zwinglians and Calvinists could accept. In 1566 it was adopted by both groups. From this point on these two branches of Protestantism merged and came to be known as the Reformed tradition.

The Spread of Protestantism

The Reformation made little progress in the areas that bordered the Mediterranean Sea. Humanism was active in Spain and particularly in Italy. Among humanists there was an initial flurry of interest and excitement over Luther and the other reformers. Soon, however, the combination of a powerful papacy, staunchly Catholic rulers and revulsion at Luther's intemperate manner prevented Reformation ideas from achieving any success in these lands.

The situation in France was somewhat different. Here there was a strong and loyal Catholic monarchy. But France was geographically and intellectu-

ally close to Switzerland. By 1534 Francis I made it clear he regarded the Reformation a grave threat to his internal designs, although he was quite happy to encourage its destabilizing effects in the lands of other Catholic rulers.

The French Protestant party, known as the **Huguenots,** allied themselves with the Reformation in Switzerland. Most Huguenots, like Calvinists throughout Europe, were in the new middle class, a group that grew in number and influence as capitalism continued to develop. By 1550 the Huguenots had successfully established themselves throughout the country, especially in several walled cities such as La Charite, Bergerac, Verdun, and Nimes. There followed several years of religious conflict. In 1560 the ten-year-old Charles IX (1560–71) became king. Because the new king was still a boy, his mother, Catherine de'Medici, became regent. In 1570 an uneasy truce was declared, and Huguenot leaders began to enjoy the favor of the young king. In August of 1572 many of them were in Paris for the marriage of the Catholic Margaret of Valois and the Protestant Henry of Navarre, a marriage that was meant to end the violence between Catholics and Protestants in France. The wedding took place on 18 August, but during the morning hours of 24 August, Bartholomew's day, Huguenot leaders were murdered in their beds. It is unclear who was primarily responsible — Catherine or others. In any event, those responsible apparently wished only to eliminate the Huguenot leaders; but when news of the murders spread, Huguenots throughout France were killed by angry mobs. Following a power struggle for the throne, Henry of Navarre, a Protestant, became king in 1593. Recognizing that the vast majority of French citizens were Catholic, he converted to Catholicism. According to legend he said, "Paris is worth a mass." Henry's conversion did not include animosity toward Protestantism. In 1598 he published the Edict of Nantes, which proclaimed toleration for Protestants in France.

The Reformation made great initial strides in Switzerland and Germany, though the Catholic reaction to the Reformation proved resilient enough to win back much of southern Germany and large sections of eastern Europe. From Germany and

Switzerland the Reformation spread along the Rhine River to the Netherlands. Calvin's Geneva was a haven for religious refugees — they came from France, England, Scotland, Spain, Poland, Holland, Bohemia, Italy, and Germany. On 9 December 1556, the reformer John Knox wrote his sister Anne Locke from Geneva. He was rapturous: "Geneva is the most perfect school of Christ that ever was in this earth since the days of the Apostles. In other places I confess Christ to be truly preached: but manners and religion to be so sincerely reformed, I have not seen in any other place."[37] When the refugees returned home from Geneva, they took their Calvinism with them. Calvin's vision and industry also established schools for the training of pastors and teachers.

In the early stages of the Reformation, the seventeen provinces of the Netherlands were ruled by Charles V. The region was divided culturally into areas that did not always correspond to political boundaries. The southern provinces, corresponding roughly to modern Belgium, spoke a dialect of French. The northern provinces spoke Dutch. Local pride and customs were often more potent forces than the interests of the whole. Further complicating the matter was ecclesiastical organization, as bishoprics did not coincide with political boundaries. Within months of Luther's stand at Worms, Lutheran and Anabaptist preachers were active in the Netherlands. They would soon be joined by Calvinists from Geneva. The Netherlands was destined to become a stronghold of Reformed theology. Charles V may have been irritated at his inability to move decisively against Protestant heretics in Germany, but in the Netherlands there were no princes for Protestants to hide behind. Under Charles, Protestant leaders there were burned, many of their followers were decapitated, and Protestant women were buried alive. The Netherlands produced more martyrs for the Reformation than any other area of Europe. By 1555, one hundred had been executed in Flanders, and nearly four hundred in Holland.[38]

In 1555 Charles turned over rule of the Netherlands to his son Philip II of Spain (1555–98). Although he was a gifted ruler, Philip was unable to prevent the success of a burgeoning popular movement for independence in the Netherlands. The movement advocated democratic principles tied directly to Reformation doctrine, principally that of Calvin in Geneva. A statement of Dutch Calvinism, the Belgic Confession, was produced in 1566. Written principally by Guy de Bray (1523–67), the "Reformer of the Netherlands," the Confession stipulated that magistrates were to "remove and prevent all idolatry and false worship," code words for Roman Catholicism, and advocated obedience to civil authorities "in all things not repugnant to the Word of God."[39] The Confession helped to link the nobility, who desired independence from Spain, with the Reformed clergy, who desired independence from the papacy. In 1581 the northern region of the Netherlands, known as Holland, achieved independence. Philip was reluctant to let the matter drop, and for the next several years tried to subdue the Dutch. In 1607, ten years after Philip's death, the Spanish determined that to continue the struggle was not worth the effort, and a truce was signed. In the end, political and cultural differences determined the division of the area into three countries. To the north the Protestant Netherlands were composed of seven provinces under a republican form of government. The southern region remained Catholic.

During the seventeenth century, the Calvinist or Reformed tradition within Protestantism defined and determined what it would henceforth consider orthodox theology. A well-respected Dutch pastor named Jacob Arminius (1560–1609) was the lightning rod of controversy that helped to generate this movement. Arminius was a Calvinist of impeccable credentials. He had traveled to Geneva to study with Calvin's successor, Theodore Beza. When he returned to Holland, he enjoyed a wide and favorable reputation. He was asked to refute the teaching of Dirck Koonhert, a Dutch Calvinist who had questioned Calvin's view of election. After careful study of scripture and the writings of Koonhert, Arminius surprised everyone by declaring he thought Koonhert was right. Because Arminius was a professor at the University of Leiden, his opinions were open to public debate. He did not reject predestination; instead he questioned its basis. Although he remained solidly Calvinist in nearly every other way, Arminius had come to the conclusion that predestination takes place on the basis of God's foreknowledge of who will later have faith in Christ and who will not. This position seems to presume that human beings have free will. Francis Gomarus, another professor at Leiden, led his opponents, claiming to be true Calvinists. Gomarus insisted God simply predestines all as an expression of his sovereign will. The controversy quickly assumed political overtones, as Arminius also believed that the state ought to have greater control over ecclesiastical matters than Calvin had allowed.

Arminius died in 1609, and in 1610 his followers issued a document known as a Remonstrance, outlining their position. For this reason they are often called "Remonstrants."

The controversy was settled at the **Synod of Dort,** meeting from 1618 to 1619. The Dutch Estates General called the synod, sending invitations to Reformed churches throughout Europe. The synod condemned Arminianism and affirmed five doctrines that have become the distinguishing markers of orthodox Calvinism ever since. The first is limited atonement. The Remonstrants held that Christ died for all; the Synod of Dort held that Christ died only for those whom God predestined for salvation. The second doctrine is total depravity. Dort affirmed that although there is some vestige of good in human beings, human nature is sufficiently corrupted by sin that this goodness is too impoverished to aid in salvation. Another doctrine affirmed by Dort is irresistible grace, the idea that the elect cannot resist the gift of grace, determined by a sovereign God. A fourth doctrine endorsed at Dort is the perseverance of the saints, according to which God preserves the faith of the elect, not allowing them to fall away, so they will persevere in faith leading to their sure salvation. The fifth doctrine affirmed at Dort is unconditional election, which means that predestination is based on God's will, not on God's foreknowledge of who will respond to God's offer of salvation. Together, these five doctrines constitute what is often called "TULIP theology": *T* for total depravity, *U* for unconditional

election, *L* for limited atonement, *I* for irresistible grace, and *P* for perseverance of the saints.

Following the Synod of Dort, the Remonstrants were brutally persecuted; some Remonstrant leaders were tortured and executed. Many Arminian ministers were ordered to leave the country.

The Reformation in England and Scotland

The Reformation in Germany was successful due to the efforts of innumerable persons and a combination of political, economic and social factors. The Reformation in England and Scotland, in contrast, is often portrayed as an act of the crown. While this view must be altered to recognize the importance of the material basis for the Reformation in Britain, it is nonetheless largely correct.

THE REFORMATION IN ENGLAND

Reformation teaching came to Britain early, spread by merchants who had heard of Luther and his writings while traveling in Germany. Popular support for Reformation ideals developed quickly, and recent research has illumined its importance and character.[40] Nevertheless, the Reformation in England is still seen largely as the product of royal decree and developed through seven stages: (1) 1509 to 1547, the reformation under **Henry VIII**; (2) 1547 to 1553, the continuation of Henry's reformation under his young son Edward; (3) 1553 to 1558, the resurgence of Catholicism under Henry's daughter Mary; (4) 1558 to 1603, the long reign of the Protestant Queen Elizabeth I, a period of relative stability and a kind of compromise scholars call the "**Elizabethan Settlement**"; (5) 1603 to 1625, the period of high Anglicanism under the Stuarts, the Scottish ruling house that inherited the English crown upon the death of Elizabeth; (6) 1625 to 1660, the Puritan Revolution; and (7) 1660 to 1668, the Stuart Reformation, which settled on a middle way between radical Puritanism and Catholicism.

The English had a long history of resistance to papal authority. William of Ockham (1285–1349) pointed to flagrant abuses of spiritual power by the popes. John Wycliffe (1329–84) taught that scripture was more authoritative than the pope, and William Tyndale (1492–1536) translated the Bible into English over the objections of English bishops. Tyndale was a linguistic genius, and his rendering from the original Greek frequently seemed to support the Protestant case over the Catholic translation based not upon the Greek but upon the Latin Vulgate. For instance, Tyndale used "repent" instead of "do penance" and "elder" instead of "priest."

On the eve of the Reformation, Britain was divided into two countries, England and Scotland, each with a ruling family — the Stuarts in Scotland and the Tudors in England. Each was allied to rival continental powers, the Scots with the French and the English with the Spanish.

Henry VII (1485–1509) of England hoped to solidify his ties to Spain, so he arranged for his heir, Arthur, to marry Catherine of Aragon, one of the daughters of Ferdinand and Isabella. When Arthur died after only five months of marriage, it was decided that Arthur's younger brother Henry would marry Catherine. Because canon law forbade a man to marry his brother's widow, a papal dispensation was needed for this marriage.

The union between Henry VIII (1509–47) and Catherine of Aragon (1485–1536) was not happy, although it produced a child, Mary. As Catherine approached the age of forty, prospects that she would produce a male heir were dim. Henry made it clear he wanted to end the marriage, claimed that it was probably illegal in the first place, and asked for an annulment. But Catherine appealed to her nephew Charles V, who pressured the pope to deny Henry's request. Under Henry, Cardinal Wolsey (1474–1530) had become powerful, advising the king on political as well as ecclesiastical matters. He was responsible for the early suppression of Lutheransim and Lutheran writings in England. But his failure to win from the pope a favorable decision regarding Henry's request for an annulment signaled the end of Wolsey's career.

Henry felt compelled to pursue a policy that he must have known would lead to a break with Rome and the creation of a separate church that eventually came to be called the Church of England or the Anglican Church. It is unlikely he came to this decision lightly. Henry had been a staunch proponent of papal power over that of councils and had published attacks against Protestantism. This earned him the title Defender of the Faith, granted by the pope. His motives in regard to his marriage appear purely political, and it is likely that Henry aimed not at a religious reformation, but at securing royal rights in his own land.

In matters of doctrine and practice Henry generally wanted the Church in England to follow Catholicism as much as possible, with the exception of obedience to the pope. When ecclesiastical matters affected the state Henry was unafraid to intervene. For example, he despoiled monasteries, confiscated ecclesiastical properties, and forced the pope to appoint Thomas Cranmer, one of Henry's chief advisors, as archbishop of Canterbury.

In a series of carefully crafted measures Henry sought to bring the English clergy under his control and to eliminate papal influence in England. In 1530 he accused the clergy of having violated the Statute of Praemunire. Originally designed to protect England from the papal power, Henry deftly turned it against the clergy, charging that they had funneled money to Rome to support papal intrigues. The clergy were forced to capitulate. They asked for Henry's forgiveness and declared him "singular protector and supreme lord, and, as far as the law of Christ allows, even Supreme Head of the English Church and Clergy."[41] In 1532 Henry turned his advisor Thomas Cromwell against the clergy. A number of widely reported scandals had fixed the nation's attention on the special legal status of the clergy. Cromwell drafted the "Supplication of the Commons against the Ordinances." This document limited the ability of the clergy to enact ecclesiastical legislation without the consent of Parliament. It also charged the clergy with nepotism, excessive use of the power of excommunication, and other abuses. The clergy were once again forced to bow before Henry's attack. On 15 May they presented Henry with the "Submission of the Clergy," by which they recognized Henry as the supreme head of the English Church. Henry quickly demonstrated how he understood the phrase "supreme head" of the church in England.

In 1533 Henry launched his attack against papal influence in England. That year Parliament passed the Act of Restraint of Appeals, granting to the crown the right to render judgments in ecclesiastical matters in England. Archbishop Cranmer promptly annulled Henry's marriage to Catherine of Aragon, and Anne Boleyn, Henry's wife since January 1533 and noticeably pregnant, was crowned queen. In January 1534 Parliament passed the Act of Restraint of Annates, by which the papacy was denied income from Church holdings in England. That same year three more legislative measures were passed that together completed the legal bulwark for royal control of the Church in England. Parliament passed the Act of Supremacy in 1534, which clarified Henry's position as head of the English Church. As a result, English clergy were expected to hold allegiance to the sovereign instead of the pope. The Act of Supremacy effectively separated the Church in England from papal authority, establishing it as a separate church. It did not, however, introduce Protestantism, as in matters of liturgy and theology little had changed. The Act of Succession acknowledged that the children of Henry and Anne as the legitimiate heirs to the throne, and the Act of Treason sought by legislation to protect the royal family from intrigues. In effect, it became treason to deny the validity of Henry's second marriage. When Paul III excommunicated Henry, the former Defender of the Faith languidly observed that he would not care if the pope issued ten thousand excommunications.

These actions came at some cost to Henry. His friend and advisor Sir Thomas More was troubled that Henry, a layperson, could be the leader of the Church. More refused to sign the oath of allegiance that followed the Act of Supremacy, and he pointedly was not in attendance at the king's wedding to Anne Boleyn. Though More was a friend of Eras-

mus and active in the international humanist community, he did not share the typical humanist revulsion to religious zeal. He was a staunch champion of Catholic orthodoxy and an ardent foe of Protestantism, and contrary to Erasmus, who favored widespread reading of the scripture, More looked with disfavor on the increasing availability of Bibles in England, especially since the newer versions, following Tyndale's lead, chose language that seemed to support Protestant practices over Catholic ones. In 1535, More was brought to Westminster Hall for trial and was charged with maliciously resisting the king's second marriage and depriving the king of the title Supreme Head of the Church of England. The court found him guilty and condemned him to death.

> He spoke little before his execution. Only he asked the bystanders to pray for him in this world, and he would pray for them elsewhere. He then begged them earnestly to pray for the King, that it might please God to give him good counsel, protesting that he died the King's good servant but God's first.[42]

Henry had acted primarily for political reasons, but often his actions served the cause of theological reform. Under Cranmer, an enthusiastic supporter of the continental reformers, an English language Bible based upon Tyndale's translation was placed in every English church. In the preface Cranmer wrote, "it is convenient and good [for] the Scripture to be read [by] all sorts and kinds of people, and in the vulgar tongue."[43] Henry wanted to minimize papal influence in England without substantially altering Catholic practice. English humanists and clerics such as Cranmer, however, saw in these developments an opportunity for authentic reform of doctrine and practice without the excesses of the continental reform movements.

Henry's son Edward VI (1547–53) was only ten years old when he became king, and died after only six years on the throne. For the first three years of Edward's reign the Duke of Somerset ruled the country as regent. This period witnessed a flood of changes. Perhaps the most significant of these was the publication of the **Book of Common Prayer**, which provided an English-language liturgy. It took great care to word the liturgy broadly enough to allow the sacraments to be understood in either a Catholic or a Protestant sense. It was soon revised, however, and the new edition clearly reflected a Zwinglian view of the eucharist. Other innovations also were introduced — for example, communion in both kinds was made available to the laity, most images were removed from churches, and the clergy were allowed to marry.

When Edward died in 1553, the throne went to his older half-sister, Mary, the Catholic daughter of Henry VIII and Catherine of Aragon. Mary Tudor (1553–58) set about restoring Catholicism in England. In the first months of her reign she moved slowly, buttressing her ties to Catholic rulers on the Continent. She then began by deliberate steps to institute measures that restricted reform in England. In 1554 England officially returned to the Catholic fold, and nearly all of the reforms initiated under Henry and Edward were reversed.

Mary also saw to it that Cranmer was declared a heretic. She hoped that Cranmer would recant, thinking that this might weaken the spirit of reform in England. She forced him to watch as several of his loyal supporters were put to death. Eventually Cranmer signed several statements of recantation. He was brought to trial in the Oxford University church of St. Mary the Virgin. Accused of heresy, blasphemy, and other crimes, Cranmer was found guilty on all counts. On 21 March 1556, he stood on a stage in St. Mary's and, with tears streaming down his cheeks, again recanted. In a moment of high drama he then took from his garment another paper, and in a loud voice he denounced his recantation, declaring that the hand that had signed the recantation should burn first. He surprised all in the assembly, and it took some time before officials realized his intentions. Cranmer said:

And now I come to the great thing, which so much troubleth my conscience, more than any thing that ever I did or said in my whole life, and that is the setting abroad of a writing contrary to the truth; which now here I renounce and refuse, as things written with my hand, contrary to the truth which I thought in my heart, and written for

fear of death, and to save my life it might be; and that is, all such bills and papers which I have written or signed with my hand since my degradation; wherein I have written many things untrue. And forasmuch as my hand offended, writing contrary to my heart, my hand shall first be punished there-for; for, may I come to the fire, it shall be first burned. As for the pope, I refuse him, as Christ's enemy, and antichrist, with all his false doctrine.[44]

He then began to offer a reformed view of the sacraments when he was whisked from the stage and led to the stake.

The cases of Cranmer and More help illumine the complexity of the Reformation period in England. During Mary Tudor's reign, a number of leading Catholic humanists shared the principal ideals of the Protestants—including enthusiasm for the scriptures, a concern for Christ-centered piety, and ecclesiastical reform. Research has pointed out that a significant portion of Catholic anti-Protestant literature in England attacked not Protestant teaching, but the confusion and disunity that resulted from the Reformation.[45] Humanists and reformers shared many of the same aims, but differed on the matter of how best to achieve them. It is difficult to relate the story of the Reformation without leaving a falsely simplistic impression that all Catholics thought in a certain way, or that the two traditions had nothing in common.

When Mary Tudor died in 1558 she was followed by her Protestant half-sister Elizabeth, the daughter of Henry and Anne Boleyn. Though few would have guessed it at the outset of her reign, Elizabeth I (1558–1603) emerged as a ruler of staggering talent and complexity. She possessed an intuitive sense for danger, knew instinctively how to move the hearts of her people, and possessed a capacity for deep insight. Like her father she was a consummate politician, seeking always to maintain royal control. She was one of a handful of the most skilled rulers ever to wield power. The historian Garrett Mattingly wrote of her:

Merely to watch the intricate convolutions of her diplomacy . . . made sober statesmen dizzy. . . . Her problem had been to rule one of the most unruly realms in Christendom . . . the object was to arrange the courtiers and counselors around her, the diplomats and envoys, the kings and powers of the Continent in an elaborate interlocked design so cunningly and delicately balanced that each part should counteract another and she herself should always be free.[46]

Elizabeth was a Protestant, but she was neither particularly devout nor unswerving in her support of the Protestant cause. She favored practices that united the country (such as common worship) over centrifugal forces, even if they arose from religious conviction. Under Elizabeth a new edition of the Anglican service book, the *Book of Common Prayer* was published that combined the Catholic and Protestant views of the eucharist. The aim, of course, was to satisfy both those who saw the eucharist as an act of remembrance and those for whom the actual body and blood of Christ were present.

During Mary's reign, many English Protestants had fled to the continent and came under the influence of Calvinism. Following Mary's death they returned and resolved to eliminate any vestige of Roman influence from the Church of England. The Act of Uniformity in 1559 had revised the Edwardian liturgy and regulated Anglican worship. But it retained vestments, then crucifix, and other practices that to some were reminiscent of Catholic worship, and the returning refugees agitated for their removal. Elizabeth nonetheless held to her middle way approach. The Thirty-Nine Articles of 1563 were to become the doctrinal basis for Anglicanism. The Articles aim at a moderate position, avoiding subtleties or extreme positions. In typical Protestant fashion the Articles declare scripture the norm for faith. Both Zwinglian (the eucharist is only a memorial) and Catholic (the elements actually become the body and blood of Christ) views of the presence of Christ in the eucharist were rejected, but greater precision was avoided, allowing room for interpretation. This *via media* approach — rejecting some Catholic practices and Catholic teaching while avoiding any tendency to favor one Protestant view over another — scholars sometimes refer to as the "Elizabethan Settlement." Elizabeth

hoped to avoid the political unrest that beset the Continent as a result of the Reformation, and she was largely successful. This sober restraint has since characterized the theology of the Church of England and the other churches in the **Anglican Communion** throughout the world.

Throughout Elizabeth's long reign, Catholics in England hoped for a restoration of their faith. But Elizabeth reigned long enough (1558–1603) and was successful enough in following her policy of moderation that eventually Catholics in England began to see that they could be loyal to both their faith and their Protestant sovereign. In 1570 the pope issued the bull *Regnans in Excelsis* that declared Elizabeth excommunicated, urging Catholics to disobey her. Some followed the pope and were subsequently executed for treason, but most English Catholics simply refused to take the bull seriously, apparently considering themselves faithful Catholics nonetheless.

THE REFORMATION IN SCOTLAND

For centuries England and Scotland had uneasily shared the same island home, allying themselves with rival powers on the Continent. In the sixteenth century, however, some in Scotland advocated closer ties with England. In 1502 their hopes soared when James IV (1488–1513) of Scotland married Margaret Tudor, daughter of Henry VII of England. Their son, James V (1513–42), was the nephew of Henry VIII, and Henry even suggested that his daughter Mary should marry her cousin James V, thereby uniting the two royal families. But prominent Scottish nobles determined that it was more prudent to mend their ties to France, so James V married still another Mary, this one from the powerful French family de Guise. Their daughter was also named Mary and is known to history as Mary Stuart.

Like in England, Protestantism had made inroads in Scotland. Many there remembered the teachings of Wycliffe, and some were followers of Hus. Others remained solidly Catholic and advocated harmonious relations with France. Unlike the case in England, there was no strong middle class in

Scotland to incline toward Protestantism. Instead Scotland was somewhat backward economically, being dominated locally by clans and the lesser nobility. Protestant preachers arrived in Scotland soon after Luther's stand at Worms. An act of Parliament in 1525 banned the importation of "Lutheran" writings into Scotland, but the tide could not be stopped. Protestant preachers and agitators such as Patrick Hamilton (burned at the stake in 1528) risked torture and death to introduce Protestantism to Scotland.

James V died in 1542, leaving his infant daughter Mary Stuart (1542–87) as heir to the throne. Although almost bereft of the political acumen possessed by her cousin Elizabeth, Mary nonetheless became a person of considerable presence. After her father's death Mary was sent to France to be educated and married. Her mother, Mary de Guise, served as regent, ruling in her daughter's stead. In 1546 the protestant preacher George Wishart was burned at the stake in St. Andrews, Scotland, under the direction of Cardinal Beaton. Three months later the cardinal was himself murdered by Scottish Protestant nobles in his own castle at St. Andrews. This began the short-lived uprising known as the revolt of St. Andrews. The Protestant nobles in St. Andrews doubtless hoped the regent would be too weak to oppose them.

The revolt of St. Andrews launched the career of **John Knox** (1505–72). Knox was a priest and had been a loyal and prominent supporter of Wishart. He was also the tutor to the children of several of the nobles involved in the revolt. He traveled to St. Andrews to deliver the children to their parents, intending to go from there to Germany to study Reformation theology. The Protestant nobles convinced him to stay, and he became the pastor to the Protestant community there. Both Mary de Guise and Mary Stuart had strong ties to France, and the French saw the revolt of St. Andrews as an affront. In 1547 an invading French army defeated the Protestant forces holding St. Andrews, and Knox was condemned to the galleys, where he spent nearly two years in servitude. He was released in 1549 and later traveled to Europe to meet with Calvin and Bullinger, the successor to Zwingli.

In 1558 Mary Stuart married the heir to the French throne. When Mary Tudor died later that year, Mary Stuart claimed the title Queen of England. As the legitimate great granddaughter of Henry VII, she argued that her right to the throne eclipsed that of Elizabeth. Meanwhile, the Protestant nobles of Scotland, anticipating the return of the Catholic Mary Stuart, met in 1557, making a covenant with one another. They determined to establish ties with Protestants in England, and in the face of persecution they began to organize a church in 1558. They also sent a delegation to Switzerland to ask Knox to come back and assist them in this effort.

Knox considered himself a faithful follower of Calvin. He had spent time in Geneva, was violently anti-Catholic (in his *Brief Exhortation to England* he called for the removal of the "dregs of popery"), and embraced Calvin's views on matters like predestination and church governance. While in Switzerland, Knox had written a caustic pamphlet against Mary Tudor, Catherine de' Medici in France, and Mary the regent in Scotland. His intention was to bruise the Catholic cause by ridiculing the prospect of female dominance of Catholic politics. He called it *The First Blast of the Trumpet against the Monstrous Regiment of Women* (1558). Although directed at Catholic rulers, it nonetheless alienated the Protestant Elizabeth when she became Queen of England. Knox tried repeatedly to make amends with Elizabeth, but he was largely unsuccessful.

When Mary de Guise died in 1560, Scottish nobles invited Mary Stuart back from France. Never popular in Scotland, Mary was at first tolerant and even conciliatory towards Protestants. John Knox, however, did not make life easy for her. He thundered from his pulpit that Mary had reintroduced into Scotland what he called the "idolatry" of the Catholic mass. In fact all Mary had done was to allow the mass for herself and her court.

She and the fiery Knox did not enjoy an amicable relationship, the latter referring to his queen as "the new Jezebel." Knox also came to loggerheads with the Protestant nobles, who wished to take for themselves the wealth from despoiled churches;

Knox wanted those funds to educate the poor. Knox also hoped to eliminate Catholicism from Scotland, but the Protestant nobles were, for the moment, content with Catholicism and Protestantism co-existing in Scotland, however uneasily. In spite of these difficulties, Knox succeeded in organizing the Scottish Church along lines influenced by Calvin's thinking. In 1560 the Reformed Church of Scotland was formed, and its *Scottish Confession* was published. Each local church elected its own elders and pastors, but a pastor could not be installed until successfully examined by other ministers. This system was quite similar to the later **Presbyterian** system, derived from the Greek word *presbyter* meaning elder. In the Presbyterian system the local church is presided over by the minister and several lay elders. In addition, the Presbyterian system employs synods (meetings of the churches in a district) presided over by ministers and lay elders.

When Mary first returned to Scotland, she followed the advice of her half-brother, James Stuart, the earl of Moray. Respected as a prominent Protestant leader in Scotland, Moray helped Mary to avoid antagonizing the Protestant nobility. In 1564 Mary married her cousin, Henry Darnley. Darnley also had a distant claim to the English throne. Mary's husband was a dashing and handsome young man, but he was also an unstable rogue. Moray did not approve of the marriage, nor of Mary's increasing desire to return Scotland to Catholicism.

Tired of Moray's criticism, Mary sought the services of the Protestant Lord Bothwell, who drew Moray into battle and defeated him. As her husband became increasingly difficult, Mary sought solace with her secretary, David Riccio. When Darnley murdered Riccio in Mary's chamber, Mary determined to have Darnley murdered in retaliation. The house where the couple was staying was blown up while Mary happened to be away, but Darnley survived the explosion only to be murdered soon afterward.

Bothwell was involved in the conspiracy to kill Darnley, and after Darnley's death, Mary and Bothwell lived together until he was divorced, at which point they married. Mary's inconsistent behavior shocked all of Europe. She was forced to abdicate in favor of her infant son, and then she was imprisoned. She escaped and fled to England, seeking the assistance of her cousin Elizabeth. Although Mary had often called Elizabeth illegitimate and claimed that she, Mary, was the rightful English queen, Elizabeth treated her guest with respect. Mary was imprisoned but with orders that she was to be treated as a queen. From her prison she continued to promote designs against Elizabeth's life; after Mary's involvement in a series of such plots was uncovered, Elizabeth was convinced by her advisors to condemn Mary to death. The Queen of Scots was beheaded on 1 February 1587. Her abdication and imprisonment signaled the victory of Protestantism in Scotland.

THE PURITANS

During the last years of Elizabeth's reign, the **Puritan** party grew in power in England. The term Puritan first appeared about 1564 and was applied to Protestants from many different groups who wished to remove from the national church any trace of "popery." There was no one founder of the Puritan movement, but many younger Protestants exiled under Mary Tudor and influenced by the thought of Calvin and Bullinger contributed to the rise of Puritanism. Puritanism tended to include a democratic principle inherited from Wycliffe and Hus and colored by Calvinism. Puritans were largely drawn from the middle and merchant classes, an example of the link between capitalism and Calvinist theology.

The Puritans were hostile to the Anglican liturgy vestments, the use of the crucifix, and the episcopal structure of church government. An episcopal structure is a hierarchical system of church governance in which bishops preside over the church and make decisions that are binding on local congregations. There were a variety of other forms of governance that the Puritans embraced instead of the episcopal option. Some opted for the Presbyterian model. Others felt that the biblical model was **congregational**—where each local congregation is the final authority for its practices. The Puritans also *very strict!!!* shared the conviction that society must be forced into a more disciplined pattern of living, and most were against frivolous amusements and excessive drinking.

In 1572 Thomas Cartwright and a Puritan group in London began advocating a Presbyterian form of church government to replace the episcopal one, and published a document outlining their case. A second one that more closely followed Calvin's Institutes followed this "First Admonition." Cartwright's ideas were met with fierce opposition, and he had to flee the country in 1574, although the idea of a Presbyterian system for the Church of England was to surface episodically.

In John Whitgift, Elizabeth found an archbishop who would follow her policies, even though he was himself a strong Calvinist. In his initial sermon in 1583, Whitgift made it clear he would brook no deviation from Anglican norms on the part of the Puritans. In 1593 the Conventicle Act stipulated exile or death for anyone who refused to attend Anglican services but attended the worship of separate groups.

When Elizabeth died childless in 1603, the throne of England passed to her cousin, James I (1603–25), the son of Mary Stuart. The Puritans hoped that the new king would support a more active and thorough reformation of the Church of England. James had already been James VI of Scotland since 1568, and in this capacity he had experienced aggressive Calvinism and its democratic tendencies. He was not enthusiastic about making common cause with a party whose philosophy contained the seeds of antimonarchial sentiment. Instead, James wished to import to England the practices of royal absolutism, continuing to build on the work of Henry VIII. His ideal was a church with a rigid hierarchical structure that was subservient to the crown. He supported an English translation of the Bible (the King James Version), produced by scholars working in groups at Oxford, Cambridge and Westminster. Originally it included the Apocrypha (books included in Catholic Bibles but generally rejected by Protestants), but Puritan editions without the Apocrypha appeared as early as 1616. James refused to grant most Puritan requests, such as the elimination of the Anglican liturgy or the episcopal structure. James was unafraid to suppress or imprison Puritan preachers who grew too strident in their criticism of the crown.

There were several effects of this policy. With James, the doctrine and practice of Anglicanism was further clarified. This had the effect of splintering the Puritan movement, as there was disagreement among them concerning the proper response to Anglicanism. Some Puritan groups were satisfied and remained within the Anglican Church. Others chose to break association with the Church of England, because they felt it had become too corrupt to respond to their efforts to purify it. These groups are known collectively as separatist Puritans. The Congregational and **Baptist** sects generally fall within this category.

liberal???

Congregationalists Congregationalism can be traced to Robert Browne of Cambridge, who in about 1580 developed an idea of church organization as the body of those "called out" from the general population, voluntarily associating with one another. He held that congregations should be independent of state control, and free of influence by presbyters or bishops. He also insisted that worship should be plain and straightforward, and that the congregation should elect its own pastors, elders, and deacons. Browne formed a congregation based upon his ideas in 1580, but the government suppressed it. Nonetheless, congregational ideas lingered and grew in popularity.

Baptists Under James many Puritans began to leave England, especially for Holland. In 1608 an expatriate English separatist group led by John Smith (1554–1612), who had been ordained in the Church of England, and Thomas Helwys (1550–1616) settled in Holland, where they came under the influence of Calvinist and Anabaptist thought. Smith and Helwys were excommunicated in 1609 for teaching that infant baptism had no basis in scripture. Together they founded the first Baptist church in Amsterdam. Helwys later returned to England and founded a Baptist church outside London in 1612.

Helwys was an effective preacher and a polemicist. Several of his treatises rejected infant baptism

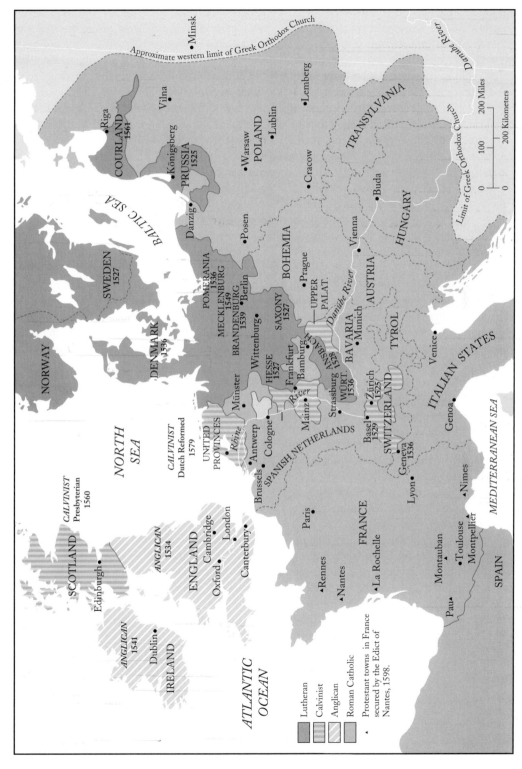

Figure 9.1   Distribution of religious groups in Europe, ca. 1600

and endorsed general election (Christ died for all people, not just for the elect). But he also turned his eye to political matters. He argued that all persons with political power will abuse that power, and therefore political power must be curbed. He claimed that sovereigns have authority over earthly matters, but not over religious matters. He further argued that the power of government should never be used to enforce religious uniformity. He therefore supported religious liberty and the separation of church and state. His Declaration of the Ministry of Iniquity (1611–12), published in Holland, aroused opposition to Helwys when it reached England. In this tract Helwys advocated universal religious liberty and declared that the state had no right to legislate concerning anyone's relation to God.

Baptist groups that accepted general election came to be known as General or Arminian Baptists. Many Baptist groups were more influenced by Calvinist thought; these are often called Particular Baptists.

CROMWELL AND PURITAN POLITICAL POWER

James remained a Protestant in spite of antimonarchial agitation from the Puritans, Congregationalists, and Baptists. He had little choice. He found Catholicism to be as disruptive as the English version of radical Protestantism. In 1605 Guy Fawkes, a Catholic radical, had led a failed attempt to overthrow the government.

The nation James ruled contained a strong and lively middle class that was well represented in the House of Commons in Parliament. This posed a special problem for James, because the English Parliament had more authority than similar bodies in other countries. For example, under the English system only Parliament had the right to levy taxes, leaving James constitutionally limited in his ability to raise funds. The potential for conflict was realized during the reign of Charles I (1625–49), James' successor.

Charles married the Catholic sister of Louis XIII of France and was forced to make concessions to English Catholics to secure the marriage. He was also determined to develop a strong monarchy patterned after that of France, with a professional bureaucracy, an office of revenue, and a standing army. He disbanded Parliament and ruled without it for eleven years.

In 1633 Charles appointed William Laud archbishop of Canterbury and gave him directions to police the clergy and enforce Anglican practices. The Puritans, of course, were the chief targets of this policy. But Laud also tried to impose the Anglican liturgy on the Presbyterians in Scotland. They rebelled, and in 1640 the Scots invaded northern England. Charles was forced to reconvene Parliament in order to impose taxes to deal with this military threat. This Parliament is known as the Long Parliament because it met for so long—from 1640 to 1653. Members hostile to the king's policies dominated this new Parliament. Apart from religious reasons, the country was suffering from hard economic times that many blamed on the king. When Parliament sought to limit the power of the king, Charles sent troops to arrest its leaders, but an armed mob forced them to leave in disgrace.

As the two sides prepared for war, many in Parliament realized that the Puritan cause could be aided by the Scots. Parliament therefore enacted a series of measures that inclined toward Presbyterianism. Although not all Puritans approved of the Presbyterian form of church order, at least it did away with the episcopate. Parliament convened an assembly of theologians, known as the Westminster Assembly. The Confession produced by the Westminster Assembly became one of the chief documents of Calvinist orthodoxy. The effect on English politics was to create a Presbyterian form of church government that the assembly recommended Parliament adopt for the Church of England. This was enacted in 1644.

The king, supported by most of the nobility and the Anglican Church, set about making war on Parliament and the Puritans. The Puritan cause found a champion in **Oliver Cromwell** (1599–1658), a gifted military thinker who felt called to combine his Puritan theology with a political career. Crom-

religious toleration (besides Catholics)

well's army captured Charles and William Laud and executed them. Under Cromwell, religious toleration was extended to almost all Protestant groups, including Puritans, Baptists, Congregationalists, and Anabaptists. Cromwell's toleration did not extend to Catholics. He personally signed the death warrant of Charles I, ordered the merciless suppression of an Irish revolt, and once it had served his purposes, summarily disbanded the Long Parliament.

In effect, Cromwell became dictator in England, although he assumed the title Lord Protector. He was a successful ruler, defending England against enemies from without and rebellions from within.

THE GLORIOUS REVOLUTION

Cromwell died in 1658, leaving his son Richard in power. But the younger Cromwell found himself unsuited for the role and resigned his post. The many different Protestant groups that had been loyal to Cromwell now fell to bickering with each other. Fearing political chaos, Parliament in 1660 decided to call Charles II (1660–85), the son of the executed Charles I, back from exile in France. While in France, Charles had become enamored of both Catholicism and royal absolutism. When he returned to England, he set about restoring the policies of James I and his father. Anglicanism was reestablished, and dissenters were persecuted. On his deathbed Charles announced himself a confessed Catholic. The throne then passed to James II (1685–88).

James was open about his desire to return England to Catholicism. The apparent conviction James brought to this task alarmed Parliament, which invited the Dutch to invade England. William of Orange and Mary, James's daughter, ruled the Dutch. In a bloodless coup sometimes called the Glorious Revolution, William and Mary were placed on the throne. In 1689 they issued an Act of Toleration, which declared religious toleration for all groups but Catholics and Unitarians. Anglicanism (in the guise of a moderate form of Puritanism with strong Arminian tendencies) was established as the state church. In effect, England had returned to the middle way after pendulum swings to Puritanism and Catholicism.

(margin note: any as above!)

The Catholic Reformation

The success of the Protestant revolt prompted the Roman Catholic Church to confront its own need for reform. Its response, often called the Catholic Reformation, was successful in addressing most of the weaknesses pointed out by critics.

REFORMING VOICES

Calls for reform within Catholicism began before Luther. Some who urged reform were individuals who protested abuse or worked for organizational change. There were also groups whose efforts were aimed at spiritual renewal or institutional reform. Some were mystics whose insights became examples of spiritual purity. Still others were cardinals and popes who used their positions to lead reform causes.

Individual calls for reform In Florence, a fiery Dominican named Girolamo Savonarola (1452–98) offended Catholic sensibilities by his overt criticism of his Church. Savonarola denounced what he called the paganism of the humanists, railed against vice, and urged the Florentines to repent lest God visit judgment on their city. In 1496 and 1497, thousands joined him in building great bonfires of "vanities" such as cards, dice, jewelry, expensive clothing, musical instruments, and pornography. The pope summoned Savonarola to Rome to account for his actions. The outspoken priest was so confident of his position that he defied the pope and instead called for a general council charged with reforming the Church. But the popular support that had emboldened him dissipated in the face of a papal interdict, and more and more Florentines began to disapprove of his use of intimidation to enforce morality. In 1498 he was tortured and hanged, his body was burned, and his ashes were thrown in the river Arno.

Other voices for reform resolved to stay within the boundaries of Catholic decorum and orthodoxy. In Spain, Cardinal Ximénes (1436–1517) was at the forefront of a wide-ranging reform program. Ximénes had spent ten years in prison for his resistance to corruption in the Church. He became the confessor to Queen Isabella and used his influence with her unashamedly. At Alcalá he founded a university aimed at excellence in medicine, humanistic education, and theology. He also sought to increase discipline and educational preparedness among the clergy. He was a committed conservative in that he opposed anything that threatened to upset the unity or doctrine of the Catholic Church. As Inquisitor General of Castile,[47] he sought out and tried to eradicate heresy within Catholicism.

Reforming Groups   Another effort at reform was a broad movement involving clergy and laity directed at charity and spiritual formation, and manifesting itself in official orders of the Church as well as unofficial organizations. One example was a group called the Oratory of Divine Love. Oratories were voluntary societies, generally with limited membership, constituted for works of charity and moral development. The Genoese branch, founded in 1497, was inspired by the selfless hospital work of Catherine of Genoa. The Roman Oratory of Divine Love was already active by 1517, the year in which Luther posted his theses on the church door in Wittenberg. It consisted of perhaps a hundred members, both clergy and lay persons, committed to the disciplines of prayer and discussion. Their hope was to promote reform in the Church by reforming themselves and those around them. They advocated an end to simony, pluralism, and "worldliness" among clergy. The group birthed other oratories throughout Europe—and the Roman branch produced several figures that rose to prominence within the Church. Notable among them were Cardinal Cajetan (1480–1547), the papal representative sent to Augsburg to force Luther to recant; Cardinal Caraffa (1476–1559), a proponent of reform within the Church who later became Pope Paul IV; and finally Cardinal Contarini (1483–1542), one of the most able and articulate of the reform-minded cardinals.[48]

The reforming spirit manifested itself in two new orders. The Theatine Order, founded in 1524, was a joint effort of Gaetano da Thiene (1480–1547) and Gian Pietro Caraffa. The Theatines were committed to lives of poverty, service to others, and raising standards among the clergy. Membership in the order was small, but it produced outstanding reform minded clerics.

The Capuchin Order, named for the unusual square hood (*cappuccio*) worn by its members, was founded by Matteo da Bascio (1495–1552). Da Bascio had been a Franciscan who wanted to restore to his order the discipline and simplicity modeled by Francis. The order was recognized by the pope in 1528 and grew rapidly in size. Intended to be a more faithful expression of the Franciscan rule, the Capuchins were especially committed to caring for the sick and the poor. They were generally excellent preachers; the fact that they placed great stress on scripture made them effective opponents of Protestant preachers.

Some reform-minded Catholics who shared many of Luther's concerns constituted a loose movement active from about 1512 to 1560 sometimes called "Italian evangelism." One example of their literature is the anonymous *Beneficio di Cristo* (1543), which seems to show dependence upon Calvin's *Institutes*. This movement stressed individual moral reform as opposed to institutional reform.

The most important religious order for the interests of the Church was the Society of Jesus, founded by Ignatius Loyola (1491–1556). Loyola was a Spanish aristocrat who made a career as a soldier. During a long and painful recovery from a broken leg after a battle in 1521, his reading of spiritual material brought on a religious crisis. One evening a vision of Mary and the Christ Child prompted him to commit himself to a life of spiritual discipline and service. He gave away his possessions and spent time in a Dominican monastery wrestling with his new convictions. There he read the *Imitation of Christ* by Thomas à Kempis. He journeyed to France where he studied theology for four years, part of that time at the University of Paris.

Loyola's *Spiritual Exercises* is a classic text intended for priests on Christian spirituality. Many who knew Loyola were suspicious of his excessive zeal. He was investigated several times by the Inquisition but was never arrested. In 1534 he and some followers took oaths of poverty and chastity. They later committed themselves to be the special servants of the pope. The pope approved this new order, called the Society of Jesus, or the **Jesuits**, in 1540.

The papacy soon found that the Jesuits were useful in combating heresy within Catholicism and effective against Protestantism. The Jesuit system encouraged rigorous and even creative thinking, but always within the boundaries of Catholic orthodoxy and always in accordance with direct obedience to the pope. Jesuits were superbly trained theologians. They became advisors to rulers, founded and maintained excellent schools, and were active in public preaching. The Jesuits were also successful missionaries, especially in Asia.

Mystics   Several prominent mystics contributed to this moral reform. The mystical tradition explored ways individuals might purify their souls to achieve closer communion with God. The ultimate goal for many mystics was to achieve a rapturous state of union with God. **Teresa of Avila** (1515–83) was one of the most significant mystical thinkers and writers of the period, and wrote two books of note. Her *Way of Perfection* (1565)[49] was intended for nuns as a guide to the ascetic life. In *The Interior Castle* (1577), which is generally held to be her greatest work, she leads the reader on a journey exploring the practice of mysticism, the soul's communion with God, and the secrets of the contemplative life. For Teresa, prayer was essentially an "exchange of love with God."[50] Especially in this latter work she pointed to states of prayer between simple meditation and ecstasy. She is considered the first mystical writer to have done this, and she is sometimes called the most important woman in Spanish history.

While still young Teresa joined a Carmelite convent but quickly became chagrined at the low quality of spiritual nurture she found there. She dedicated herself to a deeper spiritual life and experienced several visions of Christ. These impelled her to lead a reform of the Carmelites that eventually

Figure 9.2   The Descent of the Holy Spirit at Pentecost In this painting by El Greco (1541–1614) the artist depicts the biblical event described in Acts 2 and offers a symbol for the reinvigoration of the Church during the Catholic Reformation.

led to the founding of a stricter order (the Discalced Carmelites) as well as an order for men. She is the only woman ever to found a monastic order for men. Her spiritual writings have become classics that are read with appreciation even today by Catholics and Protestants alike. In 1970 she was declared a Doctor of the Church, one of only two women so honored.

assit. of **John of the Cross** (1542–91) was the loyal assistant to Teresa for many years. He was a keen observer of human behavior and the interior landscape of human nature. With incisive perception he described the need to empty oneself of self-interest in order to allow God to fill the soul. He also described the pathway to spiritual maturity. His most famous work, *Dark Night of the Soul,* remains a classic. By focusing attention on caring for one's soul, these mystics offered implicitly trenchant criticism of the culture of the Renaissance popes.

Reforming Popes   In the decades before the Reformation, popes had proven themselves largely uninterested in reform. The Protestant revolt necessitated action of a different order. However, the popes of the sixteenth century first had to reform the culture of the Vatican itself.

Leo X (1513–21) proved unprepared to cope with the Protestant threat. Upon his death the College of Cardinals was sufficiently alarmed to elect a wise, principled, and reform-minded Dutch theologian to the papacy. Adrian VI (1522–23), the last non-Italian to be made pope until John Paul II in 1978, died soon after his election. However, he brought to his office a determination to make positive change, and the will to carry it out. He once wrote to a subordinate concerning the Protestant revolt:

> You will also say that we frankly confess that God permits this persecution to afflict His Church because of the sins of men, especially of the priests and prelates of the Church. . . . Scripture proclaims that the sins of the people are a consequence of the sins of the priests. . . . We know that for many years many abominable things have occurred in this Holy See, abuses in spiritual matters, transgressions of the commandments, and finally in

everything a change for the worse. No wonder that the illness has spread from the head to the members, from the Supreme Pontiffs to the prelates below them. . . . We consider ourselves all the more bound to attend this, the more we perceive the entire world longing for such a reformation.[51]

This sober appraisal and firm determination has led some scholars to call Adrian the first pope of the Catholic Reformation. When Adrian died in 1523, a cousin of Leo X was named Pope Clement VII (1523–34), and papal policy returned to concern with minor Italian political intrigues and patronage of the arts. Clement did send Cardinal Campeggio to the Diet of Nuremberg in 1524 with authorization to make serious concessions to the reformers, including allowing clerical marriage and communion in both kinds for the laity, but Clement died before much could come of his growing concern over the health of the Church.

Paul III (1534–49) quickly convened a panel of respected experts to evaluate the health of the Church. The panel included Cardinals Caraffa and Contarini, the latter serving as chairman. In 1539, after nearly three years of study, the panel reported on abuses such as nepotism, simony, pluralism, absenteeism, and immorality. The contents of the document were leaked and published widely by Protestants as evidence that their claims of abuse were valid. In effect, the panel pointed to the problems created by the mismanagement of church property. The great wealth that was at stake, the commission concluded, was simply too seductive and had resulted in corrupt practices. The solution proposed by the panel was not institutional reform, but rather increased discipline with the aim of moral reform. In a sense Luther and these reform-minded Catholics wanted the same result. But Luther saw the solution as institutional and doctrinal. If these matters could be set right, Luther seemed to hope, then moral reform would happen.

Paul was serious about reform, as were several of his closest advisors. In spite of his desire to call a council, warfare and political intrigue forced him to delay. Various princes, including the emperor and the king of France, wanted the council to convene in their territories. The emperor finally won out, and the imperial city of Trent in northern Italy was selected as the site. Within a few years, however, Charles and Paul were embroiled in conflict, and the pope called upon the bishops to reconvene in areas under papal control. Charles countered by ordering the bishops to stay. The stalemate forced the suspension of proceedings from 1547 to 1551.

Paul III died in 1549 and was succeeded by two popes who died rather quickly after their elections. However, when Cardinal Caraffa was made Pope Paul IV (1555–59), a person of energy, vision, and sufficient longevity was in a position to effect change. Under Paul IV, reform became reality.

THE COUNCIL OF TRENT

Meeting intermittently from 1545 to 1563, the Council of Trent is generally considered among the most significant in history. It made a thorough review of the conditions faced by the Catholic Church. Previous councils had tended to be concerned with one or two doctrinal matters that needed resolution. Trent, in comparison, was breathtaking in its scope. It worked in two broad spheres: responses to Protestant charges and the Protestant threat; and the reformation and fortification of the Catholic Church. The Catholic Reformation was to be a reorganization and reformation of Church practice, not a reform of Church doctrine. Instead the council clarified doctrine, in partciular highlighting the differences between its position and that of the Protestant reformers. The council ended with a conservative and leaner church in which uniform compliance was joined with a clearly defined orthodoxy. Because of the Protestant threat and the abuses within the Church that all could see, Catholicism would no longer benignly countenance practices that were too far afield from the orthodox position.

The council did not begin auspiciously. Only thirty-one prelates were present at the opening session, in contrast to the more than six hundred at Chalcedon in 451. Nonetheless, the Council of Trent provided Catholicism with a set of objectives potent enough to serve the church well into the twentieth century. It also was able to formulate a response to the Protestant threat that proved to be more effective than many had reason to hope. Finally, it affirmed a theory of Church governance that granted extraordinary power to the popes.

The problems identified earlier by Contarini and his panel were unblinkingly addressed at Trent, as the council considered virtually every area of practice within the Church. One of the council's very first actions was to call for a reform of the Roman curia, in particular its financial dealings.[52] The council condemned pluralism and simony. The council affirmed the efficacy of indulgences and relics, but formulated strict guidelines for their use in order to avoid the kind of misinformation and abuse that had marked the period prior to Luther's protest.

Recognizing that many local parishes suffered from inattention, the council defined and sought to regulate the obligations and responsibilities of local priests. Trent ended up affirming the authority of church tradition as parallel to that of scripture. The council decisively proclaimed both the meaning and the number (seven) of the sacraments, affirming the work of the Council of Florence in 1439. It also decreed that marriages between Catholics and Protestants were invalid. Finally, Trent did much to endorse the scholastic theology of Thomas Aquinas. The council therefore approved a theological system largely rejected by Protestants, and Thomism became the dominant theology within Catholicism. In effect, much that Protestantism rejected was endorsed by Trent.

Trent also took two actions that some scholars think were intended to be temporary, but had persistent and far-reaching influence. The first was to order the founding of seminaries for the education and training of priests. Up to this time there was no uniform standard, and priests' theological training was inconsistent. It had been a Protestant complaint that many local priests were so poorly trained that they taught heresy and led the faithful astray. The decision to create seminaries was an important and necessary corrective step, but it also enhanced the divide between the clergy and the faithful—because priests received academic preparation and spiritual training generally unavailable to the laity.

The second action taken was to create a list of banned books. Paul IV judged that it was not sufficient to burn the authors of heretical writings. In his view, heretical books must also be eradicated as far as was practical. The list proscribed heretical Protestant writings, but also humanist classics and a number of editions of the Bible. The book ban would have the effect of keeping clergy and laity ignorant of many important intellectual and social trends in the broader culture. This **"Index of Forbidden Books"** was not abolished until 1966.

In contradistinction to Protestant theology, the Council of Trent argued that good works are necessary as supplemental actions to aid in salvation. More precisely, the council chose a middle position between Pelagianism, which saw salvation as being principally the product of human effort, and Protestantism (especially Calvinism), which tended to see human salvation as being wholly dependent upon God. The council endorsed the Latin Vulgate version of the Bible as authoritative, in spite of humanist and Reformation protests that it was not the most accurate version of the scriptures. In so doing the council ignored the work of brilliant Catholic humanists like Erasmus, who had produced a superior Greek version of the New Testament. Trent also affirmed transubstantiation of the eucharistic elements, again in contrast with Reformation teaching. It further affirmed that the mass is a true sacrifice and that it can be offered for the benefit of the dead. After considering the matter, the council proclaimed that communion in both kinds (partaking of both the bread and the cup) was not necessary for the laity.

The Council of Trent, therefore, did little that was theologically innovative and made no concessions to Protestant theology. It did clarify anew the essentials of Catholic doctrine, and it brought into focus the need for the Church to assume a vigorous and militant stance against Protestantism. This meant, of course, a recognition that some reforms of practice, such as the education of the clergy, pluralism, and simony, were long past due. What was unique about Luther was that his protest was against both practice and doctrine. Trent affirmed the need to reform Church practice, but

rejected the allegation that Church doctrine was defective.

As a result of the Council of Trent, an educational tradition developed within Catholicism. Its principal aims were to encourage faithful uniformity and to combat Protestantism. Another result of Trent was reform of administrative and clerical operations of the Church. The aim of those calling for the council was twofold: to create strictures tight enough that no revolution in religious or doctrinal life within Catholicism would again result in rupture as had the Protestant revolt, and to make traditional religion more effective and more appealing for the laity.[53] The council achieved these objectives, and the version of Catholicism forged there endured into the twentieth century.

Eastern Orthodoxy

While the West was convulsed with the issue of Martin Luther and the Reformation, the Eastern Church was wracked by a controversy over two different types of monasticism. This is known as the split between the Possessors and the non-Possessors. By the sixteenth century the Russian Orthodox Church owned roughly 30 percent of the land in Russia. Just like in the West, this struck many as a peculiar anomaly, placing the Church—and in particular the individual monasteries that owned land—in an odd position. Monasteries actively assisted the poor and needy, but they were also the economic competitors of many in their own communities. At a council in 1503, Nilus of Sora (1433–1508) criticized the practice of monasteries owning property and advocated the sale of all monastic lands. For this reason he and his supporters were called non-Possessors. He further argued that all monks should retreat from the world and devote themselves to spiritual discipline and prayer. He claimed that it was the responsibility of the Christian laity to care for the poor and the needy.

The chief figure opposing Nilus was Joseph of Volokalamsk (1439–1515). Joseph argued that monks cannot abdicate their responsibility to care for the poor. He further claimed that monasteries required the landed wealth they possessed in order to pay the costs of caring for the poor and for this reason he and his followers were called the Possessors. The matter was settled at a council where the Possessors carried the day.

The sixteenth century was a period of great change in western Europe, but apart from the "Possessor" controversy, conditions for the church were somewhat more static in the East. The Turks tolerated Christianity, but they used the structure of the Church to aid in the administration of their government. In general, the leaders of the Church were docile, fearing an outbreak of persecution if they were to resist.

The Russian Orthodox Church enjoyed very different conditions from the Church under the Turks. In 1530 an energetic leader came to power in Russia, injecting new life into the idea of Moscow as the "third Rome." This was Ivan IV, or Ivan "the Terrible." He took the title *tsar* and envisioned Russian power radiating out from Moscow. He counted on the Church to support him in his efforts. By 1590, Moscow was important enough that it was granted the status of patriarchate. The patriarch of Moscow soon became the most important patriarch in the Orthodox world.

The Protestant Reformation in the West had little impact upon the Orthodox Church, although it would be a mistake to assume that there was no contact. Orthodox scholars traveled west, and were well aware of the development of Protestant thought. Both the Protestant and Catholic Reformation movements established contact with the Orthodox Church. In 1573 a group of Lutheran scholars from Tübingen under the leadership of Jacob Andrae and Martin Crusius journeyed to Constantinople and presented a Greek translation of the Lutheran Augsburg Confession to Jeremias II, patriarch of Constantinople. Apparently their design was to foster some sort of dialogue and then a reform movement in the East. The Protestants were certain, of course, that their views on grace and scripture must be adopted if the Orthodox were to be saved. Jeremias, however, adhered strictly to the Orthodox position. He read the Confession

and devised a series of three answers to it. After the last of his *Answers,* Jeremias ended the dialogue. The Protestant movement had little, if any, effect on Orthodoxy.

Through it all, Orthodox and Protestants showed great courtesy to each other. The same cannot be said for relations between Catholics and Orthodox. In the post-Trent era, militant Catholicism and Eastern Orthodoxy came to loggerheads. As a part of the renewal effort of the Catholic Reformation, the Church and especially the Jesuits sought to bring all Catholics into submission to the papacy. In eastern Europe generally, and in the Ukraine and Poland in particular, Catholicism and Eastern Orthodoxy were in physical juxtaposition. In the wake of Turkish invasions, Orthodox Kiev had come under the influence of Catholic Poland. When the Jesuits arrived in 1564, tensions mounted because the Jesuits' main concern was submission to the pope and Catholic orthodoxy. For a brief period it looked as if the Orthodox might choose to reunite with Catholicism, but a council called to decide the matter in 1596 at Brest-Litovsk voted to maintain the status quo. In Poland, however, a Uniate church was established that retained Orthodox liturgy and practices yet declared loyalty to the papacy.

Summary

After the initial flurry of activity that accompanied Luther's theological revolt, the Reformation entered a second stage. The Protestant revolt was greatly aided by the sovereigns' awareness that a break with Catholicism could strengthen their political authority. This was certainly the case in England. In other nations, however, the accumulation of political power in the hands of the sovereign was accomplished by maintaining ties with Catholicism while eroding the power of the papacy within the nation. This was the case in France. The Calvinist branch of Protestantism, which was aggressive and organized, made inroads in areas as diverse as Switzerland and the Netherlands. As Calvinism and Lutheranism mingled in northern Europe, new splinter groups emerged, such as the Baptists. The Catholic Church mounted an effective response to the Protestant revolt as a result of the Council of Trent. Trent emphasized both right teaching and right practice, granting new energy to resurgent Catholicism.

QUESTIONS FOR REVIEW AND REFLECTION

1. How did Catholic authorities respond to Luther and the Protestant movement? Why did they take so long to respond? Why were they unsuccessful in eliminating Protestantism?

2. How was Calvin's theology both similar to and distinct from Luther's? What effects on society, politics and culture can be traced to Calvin and Calvinism?

3. What are the distinctive features of Anglican and Zwinglian forms of Protestantism? How do you account for these differences?

NOTES

1. See Heiko A. Oberman, *Luther: Man between God and the Devil*, Trans. Eileen Walliser-Schwarzbart (New York: Image Books, 1992), 29.

2. An award-winning book on the culture of the Netherlands in its heyday is Simon Schama's *The Embarrassment of Riches: An Interpretation of Dutch Culture in the Golden Age* (Berkeley: University of California Press, 1988).

3. Viscount Morley, *Notes on Politics and History: A University Address* (London: Macmillan, 1913), 27.

4. See B. A. Gerrish, "John Calvin," in *Reformers in Profile*, ed. B. A. Gerrish (Philadelphia: Fortress Press, 1967), 151.

5. See Carter Lindberg, *The European Reformations* (London: Blackwell, 1996), 251.

6. "Reply by John Calvin to Cardinal Sadolet's Letter", trans. Henry Beveridge, in *Tracts and Treatises on the Reformation of the Church by John Calvin*, vol. 1 (Grand Rapids: Eerdmans, 1958) 30.

7. See William Monter, *Calvin's Geneva* (New York: Wiley, 1967), 66–67.

8. *Letters of John Calvin*, vol. 1, trans. Jules Bonnet (New York: Burt Franklin, 1972), 433.

9. *Letters of John Calvin*, vol. 2, trans. Jules Bonnet (New York: Burt Franklin, 1972), 216.

10. *Letters of John Calvin*, vol. 1, 134.

11. *Letters of John Calvin*, vol. 1, 175.

12. *Letters of John Calvin*, vol. 1, 187.

13. *Letters of John Calvin*, vol. 1, 179.

14. See Lindberg, *The European Reformations*, 263–64.

15. John Calvin, *The Institutes of the Christian Religion*, trans. Ford Lewis Battles (Philadelphia: Westminster, 1960).

16. Calvin, *Institutes* 1.1.1.

17. Williston Walker, *John Calvin: The Organiser of Reformed Protestantism, 1509–1564* (New York: Schocken Books, 1969), 409.

18. Gerrish, "John Calvin," 153.

19. Roger E. Olson, *The Story of Christian Theology: Twenty Centuries of Tradition and Reform* (Downers Grove, Ill.: InterVarsity Press, 1999), 410.

20. Calvin, *Institutes* 1.7.1.

21. Calvin, *Institutes* 1.7.5.

22. Calvin, *Institutes* 1.13.21. He also wrote: "The most perfect way of seeking God, and the most suitable order, is not for us to attempt with bold curiosity to penetrate to the investigation of his essence, which we ought more to adore than meticulously to search out." *Institutes* 1.5.9.

23. Calvin, *Institutes* 1.15.3.

24. Calvin, *Institutes* 1.15.4.

25. Calvin, *Institutes* 2.1.8.

26. Calvin, *Institutes* 2.3.2.

27. See Mary Potter Engel, *John Calvin's Perspectival Anthropology* (Atlanta: Scholars Press, 1988).

28. Calvin, *Institutes* 2.16.5.

29. Calvin, *Institutes* 2.16.6.

30. Calvin, *Institutes* 3.1.1.

31. Calvin, *Institutes* 3.23.12.

32. Calvin, *Institutes* 3.21.1.

33. Calvin, *Institutes* 3.16.9.

34. Calvin, *Institutes* 3.23.12.

35. M. Weber, *The Protestant Ethic and the Spirit of Capitalism* (New York: Scribner's, 1958).

36. Calvin, *Institutes* 4.11.1.

37. See *The Works of John Knox*, vol. 4, ed. David Laing (New York: AMS Press, 1966), 240.

38. Lindberg, *The European Reformations*, 299.

39. See *Reformed Confessions of the Sixteenth Century*, ed. Arthur C. Cochrane (Philadelphia: Westminster, 1966), 217.

40. *The Reformation in English Towns, 1500–1640*, ed. Patrick Collison and John Craig (London: Macmillan, 1998).

41. The clergy agreed to a stiff fine but hesitated to proclaim Henry head of the Church. Finally the stalemate was broken when the phrase *as far as the law of Christ allows* was added.

42. See R. W. Chambers, *Thomas More* (London: Jonathan Cape, 1962), 349.

43. Lewis Spitz, *The Protestant Reformation: 1517–1559* (New York: Harper & Row, 1985), 167.

44. *The Acts and Monuments of John Foxe: A New and Complete Edition* (London: R. B. Seeley & W. Burnside, 1839), 88.

45. See Lucy E. C. Wooding, *Rethinking Catholicism in Reformation England* (Oxford: Oxford University Press, 2000).

46. G. Mattingly, *The Armada* (Boston: Houghton Mifflin, 1959), 23–24.

47. Cecil Roth, *The Spanish Inquisition* (New York: Norton, 1964), 61–62.

48. See A. G. Dickens, *The Counter Reformation* (London: Harcourt, Brace & World, 1969), 69–70.

49. The dating of this work is uncertain and remains controversial.

50. See Richard P. McBrien, *Catholicism* (Minneapolis: Winston Press, 1981), 1067.

51. From "Adrian VI's Instructions to Chieregati," in *The Catholic Reformation: Savonarola to Ignatius Loyola: Reform in the Church 1495–1540,* ed. John C. Olin (New York: Harper & Row, 1969), 125.

52. See McBrien, *Catholicism,* 635–36.

53. See Steven Ozment, *The Age of Reform: 1250–1550* (New Haven: Yale University Press, 1980), 407.

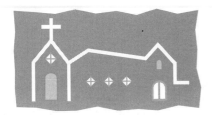

CHAPTER 10

The Church in an Age of Division and Expansion

Overview

As we saw in chapters 8 and 9, religious impulse played an outsized role on the world's stage during the sixteenth century. The theological insights of Luther, Zwingli, Teresa of Avila, Calvin, and the theologians at Trent inaugurated far-reaching changes in politics, culture, and society. Charles V, Frederick the Wise, and Philip II negotiated and went to war largely in support of their religious convictions and frequently to the detriment of national interests. Animosity was palpable — not only between, but also within, Catholic and Protestant ranks — precisely because all parties were convinced that God was on their side.[1]

Not all shared this intense devotion to religious causes. Henry IV of France, for instance, was a chameleon, converting and reconverting in pursuit of political advantage. Cardinal Richelieu placed the interests of France above those of his Church.

For centuries the Roman Catholic Church as the universally recognized arbiter of truth had nurtured cultural adhesion and given a shared rhythm to European life. This intellectual and cultural stability fell after suffering three devastating shocks. First, Protestantism and Catholicism presented contradictory Christian truth-claims. Endless strife over theological issues made it painfully obvious that there was no longer general agreement about a basis for authority in intellectual or spiritual matters.

A second shock was the tendency for theological disputes to foster acrimony and conflicts in which thousands died. The Thirty Years' War (1618–48), ostensibly fought over religious issues, was a devastating affair that seared the minds and hearts of Europeans, convincing many that concern with religious orthodoxy led only to lethal intolerance.

The third shock was the scientific revolution that emerged from developments in technology. This revolution in the sciences challenged traditional views of nature endorsed by the Church. For example, experiment and observation demonstrated that the earth revolved around the sun — and not the other way around, as the Church taught.

Collectively, these developments contributed to the growth of secularization, which involves at least three linked trends: (1) reason coming to be seen as a more trustworthy guide to truth than revelation; (2) religious authority coming to have progressively less influence in human affairs; and (3) issues of faith and, perhaps more particularly, traditional Christian ideas and values coming to be less significant to the population at large.

This chapter begins with a brief survey of the European scene during the seventeenth and eighteenth centuries. It then investigates Catholic and Lutheran orthodoxy. Then it turns to a treatment of the scientific revolution and developments in philosophy, particularly rationalism and empiricism. It also surveys the various ways Christians sought to respond to this new state of affairs, some by embracing the scientific method and a religion of reason, others by seeking spiritual illumination with a religion of the heart. Finally, the chapter discusses developments in Eastern Orthodoxy.

The Scene in Europe: Politics, Religion, and Strife

Early modern notions of identity involved overlapping allegiances to town, parish, and local aristocracy. In addition there were national loyalties to monarch and, especially with the maturation of absolutist values, the state itself.[2] There were also deeply felt bonds to sets of common values that transcended national borders. The English Catholic Thomas More, for example, considered himself part of an informal transnational fraternity of humanists. At times these different sets of values were in conflict, but these were often ameliorated by the broadly irenic effect of a common faith. By the sixteenth century the Roman Catholic Church was the first global institution, and its values had permeated all areas of Europe. There were conflicts within Roman Catholicism, but even Erasmus, one of the harshest critics of ecclesiastical abuse, could vow to remain within the faith. He wrote to Cardinal Wolsey on 18 May 1519, "May Christ's displeasure ever be my lot if I do not wish whatever I may possess of ability or literary skill to be entirely dedicated to Christ's glory, to the Catholic Church, and to sacred duty . . . you will find your Erasmus a whole-hearted servant of the Roman See, and especially of our Holy Father, Leo the Tenth. . . .[3] The splintering effect of the Reformation undermined

the power of the shared values framed by the Church, casting into sharper relief conflicts that had been minimized by the unity the Church once was able to impose.

A good deal of recent scholarship on the sixteenth and seventeenth centuries has emphasized the disarray and confusion of the period.[4] Religious conflict was one source, but it was also a lightning rod, drawing to it other forces at work in human nature. The wars of religion, for example, were about far more than religion. That Catholic France, led by a cardinal of the Catholic Church, fought alongside the Protestant Swedes against other Catholics is an indication that an intricate and confusing web of values were in play.

GERMANY, SWEDEN, AND THE THIRTY YEARS' WAR

The sixteenth century witnessed startling advances by Protestantism, but the seventeenth ended with Protestantism having lost territory once won. In 1590, roughly half of Europe was in Protestant hands. By 1690 that figure was reduced to roughly one-fifth. Aware of the danger posed by resurgent Catholicism, Protestants were willing to involve themselves in disputes they might otherwise have avoided. The English, though culturally and geographically distant from central Europe, knew that events on the Continent—in particular, any that threatened Protestantism—would affect them. As the English Archbishop Abbott (1562–1633) observed in 1617:

> as thinges now stand throughout the whole world, there is no place so remote, but that the consideration thereof is immediately . . . of consequence to our affairs here.[5]

We saw in chapter 9 that the Peace of Augsburg (1555) had effectively ended military conflict between Catholics and Protestants in sixteenth-century Europe; but it did not forge a climate of amiability. The agreement included only those Protestants subscribing to the Augsburg Confession, meaning that even Calvinists were legally heretics. Further, the agreement freed Catholic rulers to concentrate on eliminating Protestantism within their lands. Often led by Jesuits, resurgent Catholicism was remarkably successful. Protestant refugees from Catholic lands flooded ever-shrinking areas under Protestant sway, where they were not always greeted with open arms.

The incomplete solution of the Peace of Augsburg left tension that was released when a series of events at the start of the seventeenth century touched off the Thirty Years' War. The Protestant free imperial city of Donauwörth, not far from Catholic Bavaria, was a flash point. The only Catholic presence in the city was a monastery, and the city allowed Catholic practices only there. In 1606, when the monks left the monastery in a procession, they were attacked by a rioting mob. About a year after that riot, the Catholic duke Maximilian of Bavaria (1573–1651) arrived with an army and announced his intention to compel the citizens to reconvert to Catholicism. This apparent violation of the Peace of Augsburg disturbed the Protestant princes of Germany. In 1608 they banded together in a league called the Evangelical Union, ostensibly for defensive purposes. Catholic rulers responded by forming the Catholic League, a union far stronger than its Protestant rival.

With tensions running high, events in nearby Bohemia, where national feeling and Protestantism were thoroughly intermingled, ignited the Thirty Years' War. The emperor Mattias (1557–1619) decided to appoint a Catholic king over Bohemia and selected his cousin Ferdinand (1578–1637). Ferdinand made clear his intention to limit Protestant liberties. In 1618, irritated Bohemian nobles lost their composure during a meeting and threw two of the king's ministers out a window. This "Defenestration of Prague" left the ministers unhurt but humiliated.

Realizing that this act could hardly go unpunished, the Protestant nobility called upon Frederick (1596–1632), the Protestant elector of the Palatinate, to be the new king of Bohemia and rival to Ferdinand. Known as "the Winter King" because of his brief reign, he accepted the invitation. As unrest spread to Moravia and Silesia, Mattias died and Ferdinand became the Holy Roman Emperor, Ferdinand II. Ferdinand marshaled an army that joined the forces of Maximilian, invaded Bohemia

in 1620, and crushed the Protestants. Frederick was deposed and lost all his lands. Ferdinand resumed rule of Bohemia and decreed that any Protestants refusing to convert to Catholicism were to leave the country by Easter 1626.

Alarmed, England, the Netherlands, and Denmark formed an alliance in 1625 and invaded Germany. Their aim was to cripple Ferdinand and restore Frederick. The Protestant armies of King Christian IV of Denmark (1577–1648), however, were defeated by the combined efforts of Maximilian and an army raised by Ferdinand under the leadership of Albert of Wallenstein (1583–1634). Hostilities ended with the treaty of Lübeck in 1629, but only after vast areas of Germany had been trampled and thousands of German peasants had died. The Danes withdrew, having failed to accomplish their goals. It was left to Sweden to intervene.

In 1611, seventeen-year-old Gustavus Adolphus (1594–1632) became king of Sweden. The talented Gustavus was a devout Lutheran and an ambitious ruler. His aim was to achieve security for his country and his faith. Together with his friend and chancellor, Axel Oxenstierna (1583–1654), Gustavus watched developments in central Europe with mounting concern — if a rejuvenated Catholic Hapsburg empire dominated Europe, it would thwart their hopes of controlling the Baltic Sea.

In summer 1630, Gustavus invaded Germany. He was soon met by ambassadors from the elector of Brandenburg, who urged him to remain neutral. His reply was frosty:

> I tell you frankly, I will not listen to talk about neutrality. His Excellency must be either friend or foe. . . . If his Excellency wishes to hold with God, good; he is on my side. If, however, he wishes to hold with the Devil, then in truth he must fight against me. There cannot be a third way that is certain. . . . [Neutrality] is nothing but rubbish which the wind raises and carries away. What is neutrality anyway? I do not understand it.[6]

Gustavus's armies won a series of victories, and he treated the vanquished with compassion and magnanimity. To the surprise of all, neither Gustavus nor his officers pressured Catholic inhabitants to convert to Protestantism. He hoped to make northern Germany safe for Lutheranism, not to compel religious uniformity. He made it clear that it was not his design to dismember Germany. Instead, Gustavus worked to preserve the economic health of lands he conquered. He imposed fees and taxes on the population, but always with an eye to fair distribution and each region's ability to pay. His policies preserved the dignity and economic potential of Germany.

In 1631 the Swedes met and crushed the forces of the Catholic League outside of Leipzig. Soon several Catholic princes were seeking peace on the terms Gustavus outlined: religious tolerance for Catholics, Lutherans, and Calvinists; restoration of the Protestant Frederick to the Palatinate; restoration of Protestantism to Bohemia; and the expulsion of Jesuits from the Empire. Having earlier relieved the vain and ambitious Wallenstein of command, the emperor was forced to call upon him again. Wallenstein's army engaged the Swedes in the morning hours of 16 November 1632 near Lützen. The resulting Swedish victory was pyrrhic, for Gustavus was shot leading a cavalry charge and died later that day. Wallenstein left Lützen vanquished yet the premier general in Europe. His outsized ego got the better of him, however, and following the battle he engaged in secret discussions with the enemy. Ferdinand learned of this treachery and had Wallenstein assassinated on 25 February 1634.

The Thirty Years' War then degenerated into a series of bloody encounters without apparent strategic effect. After the death of his friend and king, Oxenstierna oversaw the last years of the conflict and was deeply disturbed by the carnage of war.[7] He once wrote to his son, "Behold with what little wisdom the world is ruled."[8] Finally, in 1648 all parties agreed to end hostilities and signed the Peace of Westphalia. It had become bitterly apparent that neither side had the resources to subdue the other. As a result of the treaty, Sweden gained vast territories along the Baltic, France gained some lands east of the Rhine River, and the German princes were given greater authority at the expense of the emperor. Each ruler was allowed to choose the religion of the lands under his or her control, and

the major forms of Christian faith on the continent (Catholic, Lutheran, Calvinist) were all to be tolerated.

An English pamphlet published in 1648 records one reaction to the Thirty Years' War:

> [the entire] Christian World hath been imbroyl'd with Warre, and all the miseries of Sword, Fire and Famine . . . killing and cutting throats . . . spoyling, and ruinating one another (under the fair pretences of Religion and Reformation) with more barbarous inhumanity and cruelty, then could have been committed here by . . . millions of . . . Cannibals.[9]

The Thirty Years' War pointed out the failure of Europeans to formulate a peaceful means of settling religious disputes. This failure left many profoundly disturbed. The orthodoxy they knew, it appeared, led to hatred and bloodshed.

FRANCE AND THE HUGUENOT STRUGGLE

As we saw in chapter 9, King Henry IV attempted to ease religious tension within largely Catholic France by converting to Catholicism and issuing the Edict of Nantes (1598), which granted to Huguenots freedom of worship wherever they had churches, with the exception of Paris. After Henry was assassinated in 1610, eight-year-old Louis XIII (1601–43) became king, and his mother, Marie de' Medici (1573–1642), ruled in her son's stead. While she appeased the Huguenots by pledging support for the Edict of Nantes, Marie pursued a policy of close collaboration with the staunchly Catholic Spanish Hapsburgs. But by 1620 Marie's preHapsburg-policies were falling from favor. With her authority visibly eroding, she came to rely on a gifted young cardinal named Richelieu.

Cardinal Richelieu (1585–1642) proved himself a talented and ruthless politician. He became the chief advisor to Louis XIII and the most important figure in France. Although a cardinal of the Roman Catholic Church, Richelieu was committed to French national interests above all else. This dual loyalty found expression in odd juxtapositions. Richelieu once wrote a letter to the pope begging forgiveness for neglecting his ecclesiastical duties, offering the explanation that he was too busy preparing France to make war on the armies of the pope![10]

In a stark turnabout from the policies of Marie de' Medici, Richelieu, convinced that the principal threat to France was the Hapsburg dynasty, allied France with Protestant forces in the Thirty Years' War in Germany, making Catholic France the enemy of Catholic forces led by the Hapsburgs. At the same time, however, Richelieu pursued a policy meant to weaken the political power of the Protestant Huguenots in France.

Henry IV had granted the Huguenots the right to control a number of fortified cities. This was unacceptable to Richelieu. In 1627 the French army laid siege to La Rochelle, one of these strongholds. The city capitulated after a year, with fewer than 2,000 of the original 25,000 inhabitants still alive. When the remaining fortified cities were taken, Richelieu in 1629 issued an edict of toleration. His goal was not religious uniformity but the elimination of potential resistance to the crown.

Richelieu died in 1642. When Louis XIII died in 1643, the next king, Louis XIV (1638–1715), was only five years old. His mother, Anne of Austria, turned to one of Richelieu's assistants, Cardinal Jules Mazarin (1602–61), and under his benign neglect the Huguenots again grew in number.

When Louis was a young man of twenty-three, Mazarin died. The king had already made it clear that, unlike his reticent father, he intended to rule for himself. The reign of Louis XIV is generally considered the apogee of royal abolutism.

Like Richelieu, Louis was not afraid to clash with the pope. In 1682 he promulgated a set of four Gallican Articles that denied to the papacy any real authority over the Catholic Church in France. He thereby declared his intention to be the unchallenged authority in France.

Louis considered the Huguenots a danger to royal interests, and his suspicions were confirmed when, in 1684, Huguenots were among the leaders in a revolt against the monarchy. After gentle inducements failed, Louis resorted to force and in 1684 used the army to compel Protestants to convert. In 1685 he issued the Edict of Fontainbleu, which invalidated the Edict of Nantes and made it illegal to be a Protestant in France. Thousands of Protestants fled to Germany, England, the Netherlands, Switzerland, and North America.

The determination of the remaining Huguenots was unshaken and in 1702, angry mobs of Protestant peasants attacked French armies. Traditional military practices were ineffective against the rebels' guerilla tactics, so the army resorted to burning villages where the rebels were suspected to be hiding. This brutal policy punished thousands of innocent people. Ordinarily docile peasants became irate and swelled the ranks of the rebels. By 1709, however, the repressive policies of the monarchy had won out, and the last of the rebel leaders had been captured and executed.

Exterminating the rebel threat did not kill the Huguenot spirit. By 1715 it had reemerged, and one of the leaders of this new phase in the Huguenot story was Antoine Court (1695–1760). Court was instrumental in organizing the first synod of the French Reformed Church—a secret meeting of sympathetic Protestants in a quarry near Nîmes, just ten days before the death of Louis XIV. They continued to meet in groups they called Assemblies in the Desert. Soon reformed churches were meeting in several cities, including Paris. In 1724, alarmed French bishops alerted the government. A harsh edict was announced that stipulated death to all preachers associated with the "Church of the Desert" and condemnation to slavery for all who attended the assemblies.

Persecution of French Protestants continued under Louis' successors. The French Reformed Church responded by founding a seminary in Lausanne, Switzerland, for the training of their pastors. Eventually Court moved there to oversee its operations. Hundreds studied there before returning to France to preach and teach. Some French Reformed pastors were harshly critical of the French government, but Paul Rabaut (1718–94), a longtime leader in the French Protestant movement, counseled loyalty to France. His moderate stance vindicated earlier pleas for clemency offered by prominent Catholics. Europeans were becoming fatigued by religious acrimony and the violence it bred, and toleration of religious differences was gaining ascendancy over insistence on uniformity over right doctrine. This is one indicator of the growing trend toward secularism. In 1787 Louis XVI issued a decree of religious tolerance.

THE NETHERLANDS

In the Netherlands the interplay of Catholicism and Protestantism was compounded by cultural and political fissures. As we saw in Chapter 9, the Netherlands comprised seventeen provinces with political, cultural and religious boundaries that rarely overlapped. Calvinism was strong in the north, Catholicism in the south. Further complicating the situation, the Netherlands were ruled by King Philip of Spain, who had inherited the Netherlands from his father, Charles V.

Beginning about 1560 Catholics in the Netherlands were subjected to periodic bursts of Calvinist fury. A particularly violent episode erupted in 1566, beginning in the north, and sparked by inflammatory Protestant preaching. Bands of Calvinists burned crucifixes, desecrated Catholic holy sites, and murdered both priests and nuns. In 1567 Philip sent his representative the Duke of Alva to retaliate, and the next year the Duke unleashed reprisals so harsh that some Catholics were heard to declare a preference for the Calvinist version of intolerance. Nevertheless, Calvinism survived in the north, and the Dutch declared their independence in 1581 under the leadership of William "the Silent" (1533–84) of the House of Orange. When Philip turned the rule of the Spanish Netherlands over to his daughter Isabella and her husband Prince Albert of Austria in 1599, the Dutch rejoiced. They had never seen Philip as sympathetic to their customs or culture.

The Spanish retreated from the Netherlands in 1610, and the Dutch established a republican form of government. The southern region, often called Flanders, became known as the Spanish Netherlands, a name that did not sit well with the inhabitants, who resented Spanish influence.

Mathias Hovius, who had once barely escaped Protestant mobs, became bishop of Mechelin in 1596. The detailed daybook he kept chronicled his activities as he took on the task of bringing the Catholic Reformation to Flanders. His career illustrates the difficulties faced by some Catholic reformers. Hovius met great resistance, sternest from forces within the Church. The Jesuits had their own designs in Flanders, often at odds with those of Hovius. He ran afoul of powerful papal lieutenants when he attempted to censure their friend Jan Kerremans. A chaplain and figure of local fame, Kerremans was engaged in a highly public romantic affair with a nun named Joanna. When Hovius tried to end the affair and remove the two from positions of responsibility, he was informed by the Vatican that Kerremans was untouchable. Isabella and Albert, who seemed to believe the parishes of Flanders were theirs to tax and supervise, further frustrated Hovius. Hovius also recorded the conditions he encountered on the local level. He informed his priests that he would no longer allow them to appoint their illegitimate sons to be their successors, nor would he allow them to continue to arrive at baptisms intoxicated. He established a seminary so that future priests could be trained properly, and to supply sufficient numbers of priests for the nearly four hundred and fifty parishes under his supervision.[11]

To the north of the Spanish Netherlands lay Holland, also known as the United Provinces or simply the Netherlands. By the beginning of the seventeenth century, contemporary observers had noted that Holland was a wonder among European nations,[12] mentioning in particular its republican form of government and economic vitality. The Calvinist Dutch interpreted their economic success as evidence that God had predetermined them to be a new chosen people.

Unlike the other great powers of Europe, the Netherlands was not ruled by a monarch, but instead was governed by a representative legislative body called the Estates General. The importance of this cannot be overestimated—as Lord Morley once observed:

Let us note in passing that our fashionable idolatry of great States cannot blind us to the cardinal fact that self-government, threatened with death when Protestantism appeared upon the stage, was saved by three small communities so little imperial in scope and in ideals as Holland, Switzerland, and Scotland.[13]

Although geographically puny, the Netherlands was nonetheless a great power with a strong economy, a colonial empire, and a developing cultural tradition that boasted artists like Vermeer and Rembrandt. As we saw in chapter 9, the sociologist Max Weber once argued that the Calvinist view of material success as an indicator of election promoted personal habits of industriousness and thrift. In the Netherlands, Calvinist values helped to create a culture of orderliness and wealth.

One manifestation of the Dutch religious ideal was an extreme cleanliness that astonished visitors. The Dutch cleaned and scrubbed not only their dwellings but also the steps and street in front of their homes, so that, as one observer noted, "the streets are paved with brick and as clean as any chamber floor."[14] One amazed visitor wrote that Dutch cow stalls were sometimes cleaned twice a day, and tails of cattle were tied to posts so as to keep them from being soiled.

The theme of cleanliness extended to military symbolism. Admiral Maarten Tromp (1597–1653), a passionate Calvinist, believed he had a divine calling to protect Holland from her enemies. He lashed a broom to the mast of his flagship, taunting his enemies that as God's agent he would sweep them from the seas.[15]

PRUSSIA, RUSSIA, AND THE EMPIRE

The rulers of countries in the eastern portions of Europe, like those to the west, struggled to establish strong and efficient central governments. Three dynasties rose to prominence in this period: the Hohenzollerns of Brandenburg-Prussia, the Hapsburgs of Austria, and the Romanovs of Russia.

Brandenburg was one of the many small states that made up Germany during the medieval period. The elector Frederick the Great of Brandenburg (1640–88) instituted a centralized treasury, an efficient civil service, and improvements to the army. During the Thirty Years' War he added considerable territory to the family holdings. When

Frederick died in 1688, Brandenburg was the most efficient and powerful state in Germany. Frederick I (1657–1713) was powerful enough that he won from the emperor the title *king*. He renamed his territory Prussia. Frederick II (1712–86) was crowned in 1740. A gifted military strategist and shrewd politician, he made Prussia a power of front-rank importance, a rival to France in perfecting the tools of the absolutist state.

The House of Hapsburg, rulers of Austria and traditional rulers of the Holy Roman Empire, had by 1700 begun to see the empire as a greater burden than blessing. Defending the empire against the perpetually aggressive Turks, for instance, exacted a heavy toll on imperial resources. During the War of the Austrian Succession (1740–48), Prussia defeated the empire, making the need for military and administrative reform obvious, and the empress Marie Theresa (1717–80) took up the task. Against heavy odds, this formidable person improved conditions for peasants, reformed the offices of finance and policy making, and in general created a strong centralized government.

When Marie Theresa died in 1780, her son Joseph (1741–1790) took up the reins of power. As Joseph II, he began a vigorous plan for reorganization based on the model of France and Prussia. He worked to make the Church subordinate to the state, tried to minimize the power of the nobility in his lands, and improved the efficiency of the central government.

Russia had for several centuries struggled to assume a place of military and political prominence in Europe. The Romanov dynasty, founded in 1613, brought this dream to fruition. Peter I ("Peter the Great," 1672–1725) overcame Russian ambivalence to western Europe and actively sought to bring western influence to Russia. He opened trade with the rest of Europe, imported western advisors and moved the capital to St. Petersburg on the Baltic Sea. Peter tangled with the Swedes and the Poles for control of the Baltic and its trade, and in the south he defeated the Ottoman Turks, gaining access to the Black Sea and the Mediterranean.

When Peter died, a bitter internal struggle broke out between those who favored his western orientation and those who endorsed the Russian people's traditional eastward inclination. Peter's grandson married a remarkable German aristocrat named Catherine. As Catherine the Great (1762–96), she served her adopted country well, proving herself perhaps the most able ruler of her time. She further buttressed the power of the sovereign in Russia, and under her leadership Russia became a true world power.

Catholic Orthodoxy

The Council of Trent affirmed papal authority, clarified orthodoxy, and regulated practice. Not all Catholics were pleased, and each of these major results encountered hostility. Those whose primary loyalty was to nations and national churches recognized that the affirmation of papal authority was contrary to their interests. Others were concerned that the council had overreacted to the Protestant threat and defined orthodoxy too narrowly, pushing aside a good deal of traditional Catholic theology and practice. Still others found in Reformation thought elements they considered fully commensurate with the Catholic tradition. Trent decisively closed the door on these options. Finally, Trent demanded changes in personal matters that affected many clergy.

POPES AND KINGS

Trent affirmed the power of the papacy and the authority of the Church. One obstacle to these affirmations was the growing strength of European rulers. The reemergence of a disciplined, and energetic papacy was not welcomed in European capitals. Resistance to papal authority was particularly strong in France, and opposition to papal power came to be called "**Gallicanism**" (from *Gaul,* the Roman name for ancient France). Those supporting papal authority came to be called "**Ultramontanes**" because they supported the power of the pope "beyond the mountains."

During the years when the papacy was at Avignon the French monarchs won a variety of special privileges from the papacy granting the French

church considerable autonomy. Reasserted by the French King Henry IV, these "Gallican freedoms" were cited when the French Parliament refused to approve the decrees of Trent. So in 1615, the French clergy, dominated by Ultramontanes and weary of waiting, took it upon themselves to approve them. This was a mixed blessing for the papacy, because French clergy and not the pope had determined the shape and direction of Church policy in France.

The ancient conciliar spirit gained new vibrancy in 1763 with the publication of *The State of the Church and the Legitimate Power of the Roman Pontiff,* by Justin Febronius, the pen name of Nicholas von Hontheim (1701–90). Febronius argued that spiritual authority in the Church resides in the community of the faithful and in their delegates — the bishops — and not with the pope.[16] Perhaps because the book was condemned by Pope Clement XIII (1693–1769), it enjoyed buoyant popularity. Its message was embraced by rulers who wished to establish national churches independent of papal control.

In Vienna, for example, the Holy Roman Emperor, Joseph II, was inspired by Febronius. Like other rulers, he found the Church a mixed blessing. Certainly he was not comfortable with clerics loyal to Rome, or with the fact that the Church owned nearly 40 percent of the territory ostensibly under his control.[17] The uniformity that the Council of Trent sought to impose was appealing, but Joseph considered the Church poorly run and riven with internal strife. Joseph began to exercise sway over ecclesiastical matters, closing troublesome monasteries and taking steps to manage the education of the clergy within his lands. By 1767 he had decreed that papal bulls had no authority without his consent, and by 1773 the clergy were banned from direct correspondence with Rome. In 1781 an edict of toleration went in effect that extended freedom of religion to all. Other rulers cautiously emulated Joseph's reforms, even though the pope condemned "Josephism" in 1794.

One of the chief victims of antipapal attitudes was the Jesuit order. In a brief span of time the Jesuits had become influential. Many Jesuits occupied important political positions in several European governments. Each Jesuit swore an oath of personal loyalty to the pope. This made them particularly helpful to the papacy, but left many Europeans wondering how much rulers could trust them. The Jesuits were expelled from Portugal in 1759, France in 1764, and Spain in 1767.[18] The Portuguese minister Pombal then suggested that the pope be asked to disband the Jesuits. In 1773, unwillingly bowing to pressure from nearly every European court, Pope Clement XIV (1705–74) dissolved the Jesuit order. It was becoming clear that the papacy's authority was on the wane, and that secularization was on the ascendancy.

DIVERGENCE WITHIN CATHOLICISM

Another threat to the Catholic orthodoxy of Trent were theological movements that although orthodox seemed to fall outside the narrow bounds delineated by the council. Perhaps the chief theological difference between Protestants and Catholics involved the doctrine of God's grace. Calvinists argued that God predetermined the ultimate fate of human beings and that human action played no part in the decision. Catholicism, in contrast, argued that while salvation is a gift from God, some degree of cooperation is needed. Many thought that in its desire to make clear the differences between Roman Catholic and Protestant theology, the Council of Trent had rejected a good deal of orthodox teaching by embracing a position too far removed from Augustine, who had argued against the significance of human effort in salvation. Controversies touching on grace and predestination erupted within Catholicism, many of which were problematic only because some Catholics endorsed positions that appeared similar to Protestant views.

In the waning years of the sixteenth century the Jesuit faculty of the University of Salamanca in Spain argued that predestination was based not on God's predetermination, but rather on God's foreknowledge of human actions. This position was clearly different from the Calvinist view. There was nothing particularly incendiary in this affirmation, nor in the response of the prominent Dominican theologian Domingo Bañez (1528–1604), who argued that the Jesuits of Salamanca were teaching a doctrine opposed to Augustine. But historic animosity between Jesuits and Dominicans added emotional fuel to the conflict. The Jesuits charged that Bañez was a closet Calvinist, and the Dominicans accused the Jesuits of Pelagianism. The dispute was put before the Inquisition, and later the case was sent to Rome. There the pope declared both accusations false, and called on all sides to end their attacks on each other.

A second controversy involved Michael Baius (1513–89), a professor at the University of Louvain, who argued that the sinful will in human beings is incapable of good. His intention was to agree with Augustine.[19] However, to some critics he appeared to be agreeing with Calvin. In 1567 Pope Pius V (1504–72) condemned sixty-nine of Bauis's theses. Baius bowed before this pressure and recanted, but his repentance was short-lived. When he returned to Louvain, he resumed teaching as if nothing had happened, and his ideas continued to circulate even though they had been condemned.

A third controversy began in 1640 with the posthumous publication of *Augustine* by Cornelius Jansenius (1585–1638). This book was a careful study of Augustine's thought on predestination and grace. In it Jansenius came to conclusions that appeared to parallel Calvinist theology. Jansenius made clear that he was against the Jesuits and opposed to the influence of Thomas Aquinas in Catholic thinking at the expense of Augustine. Pope Urban VIII (1568–1644), therefore, felt compelled to condemn the book, which he did in 1643.

Jansenius was not without his defenders. Jean Duvergier (1581–1643), the abbot at Saint-Cyran, had been a friend of Jansenius. He was also linked to Port-Royal and its talented leader, Mother Angelique (1591–1661); under Capuchin influence, she had instituted a series of important reforms at Port-Royal. Duvergier had been sent to prison by Richelieu, who considered him an unsavory reform-minded cleric. He was released in 1763, a few months after the condemnation of the writings of Jansenius. In the years that followed, "Jansenism" was linked to Duvergier and Mother Angelique, and came to refer less to any specific doctrine than to ecclesiastical reform in general and particularly individual purity of mind and action.

Duvergier died soon after his release from prison, but the cause of Jansenism was taken up by others. Aintoine Arnauld (1612–94), Mother Angelique's brother, was prominent in intellectual circles in Paris. As a student Arnauld had written a brilliant thesis on the doctrine of grace, stressing the need for thorough spiritual preparation before the eucharist. His theological positions earned him some enemies, including the Jesuit order. Censured and exonerated several times, he eventually settled in the Netherlands. He was less volatile than Jansenius and is primarily responsible for the wide circulation of ideas that have come to be called Jansenism. When the faculty of the Sorbonne condemned Arnauld's work, the French scientist, mathematician, and philosopher Blaise Pascal (1623–62) wrote an anonymous defense so brilliant and wickedly humorous that it was added to the list of forbidden books. Louis XIV was not willing to suffer potentially fractious elements within the French Church. He ordered Port-Royal disbanded, and Pope Clement XI (1649–1721) condemned Jansenism in the bull *Unigenitus* (1713).

A fourth challenge to theological orthodoxy was Quietism, usually tied to Miguel de Molinos (1640–97). In 1675, de Molinos published his book *Spiritual Guide,* in which he advocated total passivity before God as the surest route to contemplation of the divine. He believed that contemplation must be purely spiritual, leading him to disparage the consideration even of the humanity of Christ or the plight of one's neighbor.

This teaching created fierce opposition. Many saw in it the danger of privatism — faith as essentially a relationship between the individual and God, without the traditionally Catholic idea of faith experienced within the web of community. To others, the doctrine implied independence from any external authority, including the Church and the pope. For these reasons Quietism bore a disturbing similarity to Protestant forms of thought and expression, and de Molinos was brought before the Inquisiton. When offered the chance to defend himself, he refused. He was ordered to recant, and he did so with great humility. Some perceived in the manner of his recantation an ironic affirmation of the very principles he was recanting. Pope Innocent XI (1611–89) condemned him to prison, where he died eleven years later.

But Quietism persisted. It entered France in the person of Madame Guyon (1648–1717), a woman experienced in tragedy. At the age of fifteen she was married to a man of thirty-seven. At twenty-eight she was a widow with three children. She was later to suffer imprisonment (twice) and condemnation. After the death of her husband she became acquainted with the writings of de Molinos. For Madame Guyon, Quietism was essentially the view that God enjoyed perfect rest engaged in self-reflection upon the divine glory. She believed human beings, made in the image of God's son, are created to be the objects of God's perfect love, and must be intended for the same perfect rest God himself enjoys. She reported visions and mystical experiences, and these led her to positions others found extreme. She once claimed that sins might be called for in order to obey God's leading.

In 1681 Madame Guyon began to tour France, hoping to spread her mystical beliefs. As with de Molinos, her emphasis on the inner life and spiritual illumination was seen by many as a challenge to Church authority. The burgeoning popularity of her writings brought suspicion as well as acclaim. She was imprisoned for a brief time, and then became a popular figure in the royal court, often invited to lecture to young aristocrats. Aware that rumors were circulating linking her to heresy, she demanded that a theological commission be held, believing it would clear her. The resulting Conference of Issy in 1695 instead declared her a sincere but misguided propagator of dangerous beliefs, and she was again sent to prison. In 1702 she was released but ordered to live out the remainder of her life in a convent. Her book, *Experiencing the Depths of Jesus Christ,* sometimes called *A Short and Very Easy Method of Prayer* (1685), was written to urge the reader to be open to a living experience of Jesus Christ.

Madame Guyon influenced a talented cleric named Francis Fénelon (1651–1715). Fénelon, archbishop of Cambrai and tutor to the prince, was in many ways the most appealing cleric of his age. A social progressive, in 1687 he wrote a tract on the education of girls that assumed the dignity and intellectual abilities of women. In personal demeanor Fénelon was charitable and kind, and he believed that compassion and persuasion were far more effective than brute force. He once observed: "when hearts are to be moved, force avails not. Conviction is the only real conversion."[20]

Though Fénelon did not always approve of Madame Guyon, his genial nature led him to overlook her eccentricities. A longtime friend of his, a bishop named Bossuet, was not so forgiving. The intellectual Bousset, often considered one of the great orators in Christian history, turned on Fénelon when the latter attempted to defend Madame Guyon. The king sided with Bossuet, a staunch proponent of Gallicanism, and Fénelon was banished from court. As with other Quietists, Fénelon's mysticism seemed to others to constitute a threat to any external authority, either civil or religious.

Back at Cambrai, Fénelon quickly gained a reputation for compassion and a deep interest in others. He opened the ecclesiastical offices and his own residence to house refugees and the poor. "His priests," wrote one contemporary, "to whom he made himself both father and brother, bore him in their hearts."[21] His writings consistently reveal a kind and careful thinker for whom the inexpressible truths of the heart were more significant than the arguments of the intellect. But he created controversy in 1697 by publishing his book *Maxims of the Saints,* composed of forty-five articles on true and false mysticism. Under intense pressure Pope Innocent XII condemned portions of *Maxims of the Saints* in 1699.

For Fénelon, Quietism was a detachment from worldly things and a concentration upon the spiritual. His writings so emphasized the interior life that those who were unaware of his personal concern for the poor might assume he was callously indifferent to the cares of human existence. In condemning his writings, the pope dolefully observed that "Fénelon was in fault for too great a love of God; his enemies equally in fault for too little a love of their neighbor."[22]

The Council of Trent dictated a clearly defined theological orthodoxy harnessed to regulated practice. But many felt the council had excluded a good deal of traditional Catholic patterns. In the years

following the council, there were challenges to its chief assertions. Yet the papacy was able to reassert its authority within the boundaries of the Church itself. Challenges to theology and practice, such as Jansenism and Quietism, were successfully met, although not without controversy and, perhaps, having impugned aspects of traditional Catholic thought and practice.

Lutheran Orthodoxy and Protestant Scholasticism

In the midst of turbulent global politics, European warfare, constantly shifting alliances, and fierce religious rivalry, the Protestant theological revolt continued. As we saw in chapters 8 and 9, Protestantism had a tendency to fray. Initially, the common purpose of the reformers made their differences seem minor. In a letter he wrote to Martin Bucer on 14 October 1536, Luther said he had read Calvin's writings with "great pleasure."[23] Inevitably, however, differences led to bitter disagreements. It came as a rude shock to Protestants that reliance upon scripture as the sole authority in matters of faith appeared to cause rather than eliminate conflict.

When Luther died, leadership in the Lutheran tradition passed to his associate Philip Melanchthon (1497–1560). Melanchthon was a peaceful soul, often troubled by Luther's wild temper. After Luther had written critically about Zwingli long after the Swiss reformer's death, Melanchthon penned an apology to Bucer (1491–1551), Zwingli's successor, dated 28 August 1544:

> I have written to you about our Pericles, who has again begun to thunder most vehemently on the subject of the Lord's Supper, and has written a fierce attack, in which you and I are beaten black and blue. I am a quiet, peaceable bird, nor would be unwilling if I may depart out of this prison-house.[24]

Melanchthon's systematic theology (Loci Communes) quickly became the trusted and standard textbook for Lutheran theology. Nonetheless, many Lutherans were convinced that Melanchthon was not true to Luther's intentions. They were suspicious of his humanist tendencies and his apparent willingness to depart from positions Luther had held. For example, Melanchthon insisted on the value of good works — not as a means of salvation, but as evidence of a life renewed by Christ.

Melanchthon further alarmed his critics in the aftermath of the Schmalkald War (1546–47), when Charles V ordered the creation of a document to be written by a joint committee of Catholics and Protestants. Charles had hoped that this document, known as the "Augsburg Interim," would encourage some semblance of Christian unity, but neither Catholics nor Protestants were pleased with the document, and Melanchthon refused to sign it. Under intense pressure, however, he and several other Wittenberg theologians signed a modified version called the "Leipzig Interim." This document embraced Protestant positions on justification and grace, but it retained many Catholic rites and ceremonies. Melanchthon's Lutheran opponents, led by Matthias Flacius (1520–75), contended he had betrayed their cause by accepting any Catholic rites. Melanchthon responded by setting forth a distinction between matters that are essential to the faith and those that are nonessential. He referred to the nonessential matters as *adiaphora*, a Greek word meaning "not significant," and claimed the retention of such things as Catholic ceremonies qualified as insignificant.

A split developed between Flacius's "strict Lutherans" and the "Philippists" who followed Melanchthon. Soon other issues came into play that deepened the divide between the two sides. Melanchthon had never been comfortable with Luther's assertion that the human will was completely enslaved to sin; strict Lutherans therefore accused him of a type of Pelagianism. When it came to the Lord's Supper, however, the strict Lutherans charged that the Philippists were crypto-Calvinists, because Melanchthon's views on this matter seemed closer to Calvin than Luther. These intramural disputes were resolved in the Formula of Concord of 1577. The Formula incorporated Melanchthon's distinction between the essentials of the faith and

adiaphora, but it also upheld the strict Lutheran position on the presence of Christ in the eucharist.

The Formula of Concord, which was largely the work of Lutheran theologian Martin Chemnitz (1522–86), struck a balance between the positions of Melanchthon and the strict Lutherans; second, to make plain the points of distinction between Lutheranism and other expressions of Christian faith, whether Catholic or Protestant. In choosing to structure the Formula in this way, Chemnitz set the course for the later development of Lutheran theology. The resulting program sometimes called "Protestant scholasticism," dominated Lutheran thought well into the eighteenth century.

The aim of the Lutheran Protestant scholastics was to systematize Lutheran theology and make clear its difference from other Christian theological traditions. Calvin left an ordered and fairly systematic record of his thought in the *Institutes*. Luther, in contrast, left an impressive deposit of theology, most of it produced in the heat of passion and brimming with energy, but he never produced a comprehensive and systematic description of his thought. Over the next two centuries, Lutherans produced systematic theologies and bulky enough to rival those of the great Catholic medieval theologians. The second edition of the systematic theology by Johann Gerhardt (1582–1637), for example, ran to twenty-three volumes.[25]

The work of Protestant scholasticism was quite different from that of the original reformers. The Protestant scholastics shared the pastoral and spiritual concerns of the original reformers, but these matters did not routinely find expression in their systematic works.[26] Additionally, Luther had disparaged the use of Aristotle, but the Protestant scholastics employed Aristotle's logic and metaphysics to construct their systems. Many were in contact with Jesuit theologians at work on similar parallel tasks. In the area of theological method, at least, Lutherans and Catholics were closely related.

Luther had argued that God's revelation is contained in the scriptures, but he did not identify God's revelation with the scriptures. This allowed him, for instance, to have a low view of the New Testament book of James, as it seemed to him to bear little witness to the gospel of grace.

The Protestant scholastics, however, went beyond Luther to assert that God both told the New Testament authors what to write and ordered them to write it. This seemed necessary to refute the charge of some Catholic polemicists who argued that parts of the New Testament were written by associates of the apostles who composed their own versions of the inspired words of the apostles.

Concurrent with these attempts to systematize and to sharpen the points of difference between the branches of Christian faith were periodic manifestations of the impulse for reunion between Catholics and Protestants. One centered on the career of Georg Calixtus (1586–1656), a committed Lutheran and an admirer of Melanchthon. Like Melanchthon, Calixtus possessed an irenic spirit. He spent his early thirties traveling in Calvinist and Catholic lands and concluded that Europe was gripped by an unhealthy concern with theological orthodoxy. This preoccupation resulted, he felt, in un-Christian animosity between Christians. He made it his lifework to create a theological system that could lead to Christian rapprochement. Like Melanchthon, he distinguished between the essential and the merely true. Calixtus argued that not everything taught in scripture is essential—and that therefore sometimes incorrect belief is merely error, not heresy. One can be in error concerning nonessential truths, he said, and still be a Christian. Calixtus argued out that during the first five centuries of Christian history the Church made the critical decisions regarding orthodoxy and heresy. A lack of belief in something taught in scripture but not decided in the first five centuries is not heresy, he asserted, but merely error. Understood in this way, the doctrine of justification by faith is true, because it is undeniably found in scripture, but it is not essential, because it was not part of the common faith of the Church during its first five centuries.

Calixtus was attacked by some Lutherans who insisted that everything revealed in scripture was necessary for salvation. More moderate critics pointed out that Calixtus had, perhaps inadvertently, restored Church tradition to a place of primacy. In general, however, theologians were more concerned with defining the subcategories of their own traditions than with the interplay of practical and academic theology.

Even as Europe was experiencing ever more vicious warfare in the name of religion, Catholic and Protestant theologians were busy clarifying and organizing the tenets of their respective traditions. Increasingly it appeared to Europeans that the intense theological disputes of the period concerned matters of diminishing significance, and each tradition became both increasingly inflexible to deviation and apparently less responsive to the rhythms of the parish and the needs of the spiritual life.

Currents in Intellectual Life: The Enlightenment, Rationalism, and the Scientific Revolution

Catholic theology relied heavily on rational inquiry, but it also maintained a healthy respect for mysteries reason could never explain, such as the nature of God or God's love for humanity. Within Catholicism reason threatened but never overwhelmed this sense of the incomprehensible nature of God. Protestant theology also relied on reason, but tended to leave less room for mystery in theology, especially as developments in science led some Protestant thinkers to value reason even more highly than revelation.

All of this took place within a climate of opinion[27] of buoyant optimism about human achievement that is often called the Enlightenment or the Age of Reason. The Enlightenment involved a new way of understanding human beings and the world, and drew on science, philosophy, politics, and social thought. It developed distinctive national expressions, especially in France, Germany, and England; involved a wide range of areas of human endeavor, from architecture to political philosophy; and could encompass divergent tendencies. Enlightenment thinkers largely retained the ethical ideas of Greek philosophy and the Christian tradition, such as the value of honesty and the importance of caring for other human beings, but rejected the idea of Christian belief as essential for salvation, the Christian doctrine of human depravity, and the Christian emphasis on asceticism and self-denial as the route to moral improvement. Instead the Enlightenment asserted the essential goodness of human beings and of human desires. Enlightenment thinkers hoped for a world without conflict, one in which the common good was advanced. They believed reason and science could create such a world.

This Enlightenment spirit was enabled by the effects of secularization and partially propelled by advances in philosophy and science. These fortified confidence in the ability of human beings to understand their world through reason exercised apart from revelation. In the wake of the Reformation it seemed theology led to disagreements, not a common understanding of truth. Enlightenment thinkers sought truths that all could agree upon. They arrived at the position of rational utilitarianism, first expressed with clarity by Cesare Bonesana (1735–94) and Jeremy Bentham (1748–1832), that the goal of society ought to be the greatest good for the greatest number of people.

THE SCIENTIFIC REVOLUTION

The Scientific Revolution is a term used to describe not only discoveries that upset theologically centered views of truth, but also the scientific method of experiment and observation that appeared to yield truth all could agree upon. The Reformation had the unintended effect of weakening theology as a foundation for truth claims. To secure a new foundation based upon reason, experiment and observation was the aim of proponents of the scientific method like Francis Bacon, René Descartes, and Galileo Galilei. It was a bold undertaking. Neither the scholastics nor the humanists of the Renaissance had set out to accomplish anything as breathtaking as this.

The era of the Renaissance witnessed a flowering not only in arts and letters, but also in technical achievement in areas like printing, mining, navigation, and optics. Nicholas Copernicus (1473–1543), making use of new technology, challenged church doctrine when he posited that the earth and other planets revolve around the sun. He was keenly aware that his theory would not be met with favor and waited until the last year of his life to publish his findings. As he anticipated, both Catholics and Protestants condemned his writings.

Nonetheless, the publication of his findings created a kind of Copernican shock. It would be difficult to overestimate its effect. A complex set of theological, cultural, and social beliefs and patterns had been made to rest on the geocentric theory, and Copernicus seemed to place these in jeopardy.

Another figure whose work contributed to cultural destabilization was Galileo Galilei (1564–1642). Born and raised in Pisa, Galileo was educated in a monastery near Florence and briefly considered entering the monastic life. He studied mathematics and medicine at Pisa, but was forced to abandon his studies in 1585 because he could no longer afford to pay his tuition. In 1589 the university invited him to return—not as a student, but as a lecturer in mathematics. While there he experimented with falling bodies and gravity, and discovered the laws of dynamics.

In 1592 he accepted the chair in mathematics at the University of Padua. There he remained for almost twenty years. While in Padua he began experimenting with a telescope he had fashioned, and discovered the moons of Jupiter. He also used the telescope to deduce that the earth revolved around the sun. He traveled to Rome in 1611 and was welcomed enthusiastically by members of the papal court anxious to hear about the wonders of God's creation. But then Galileo undertook biblical exegesis to show that the Copernican system was in accord with the Bible. The method he employed alarmed Pope Paul V, as like the Protestant reformers Galileo appealed to the Bible to refute orthodox teaching.[28] This, in addition to his growing fame and the notoriety of his writings, brought Galileo into conflict with the Church.

In 1616 the Copernican theory was condemned and Galileo was ordered to stop teaching or defending it. In 1632 Galileo broke his long silence and published *Dialogue Concerning the Two World Systems,* an incisive attack on the geocentric theory proposed by the ancient astronomer Ptolemy and embraced by the Church. In 1633 he was summoned before the Inquisition, and under threat of torture was forced to recant, only to be sentenced to prison. According to legend, having been forced to admit that the earth stands immobile at the center of the universe, Galileo then whispered, "Nevertheless, it does move." After a few months in prison Galileo was released. He died in Florence in 1642.

Galileo had not only established a scientific basis for Copernicus's theories; by demonstrating the superiority of the scientific method, he alerted the world that the scientific method constituted a threat to a good deal of orthodox thinking. Further, Galileo's thought presupposed a belief that the universe could be understood according to mathematical relations. The idea of God's creation as an impenetrable mystery had been challenged.

Bacon felt that what was needed was not merely a new set of discoveries, however stupendous, but rather a new method capable of arriving at truths to which all could agree. Bacon's essay *The Great Instauration* makes this desire clear:

> the entire fabric of human reason which we employ in the inquisition of nature, is badly put together and built up, and like some magnificent structure without any foundation. . . . There was but one course left therefore, to try the whole thing anew upon a better plan, and to commence a total reconstruction of sciences, arts, and all human knowledge, raised upon proper foundations.[29]

For Bacon this method was scientific inquiry. While aware of Copernicus, Bacon was particularly inspired by advances in science with practical application, principally two books on metallurgy and mining: *Pirotechnia* (1540) by Vanoccio Biringuccio (1480–1539) and *De Re Metallica* (1556) by Georgias Agricola (1494–1555). In his masterpiece, *Novum Organum* (*New Organ*) (1620), Bacon said, "the true and lawful goal of science is simply this, that human life be enriched by new discoveries and powers."[30]

Sir Isaac Newton (1642–1727) is generally credited with taking to its conclusion the path laid out by Copernicus and Galileo. Surprisingly, Newton was an avid practitioner of alchemy as much as a scientist in the modern mold.[31] He demonstrated that gravity is the fundamental force that orders the operation of the universe, and argued that the entire universe is subject to certain physical laws. Newton's theories led many to see the universe as a giant machine regulated by principles that humans could understand. One effect was that people began to develop great confidence in the potential of science to explain the natural world, including the actions and attitudes of human beings themselves. Another conclusion many drew from the Copernican-Newtonian system was that revelation was superfluous, or at least inferior to the laws of nature accessible to the human mind through observation, experiment, and reason.

RATIONALISM IN PHILOSOPHY AND RELIGION

In philosophy, rationalism is the idea that reason is the primary, and perhaps the only, route to knowledge. Rationalism in the seventeenth and eighteenth centuries featured a profound interest in the world and a supreme confidence in the powers of human reason. It had deep and complex roots going back to Greek philosophy, and especially Aristotle, whose system of logic had been rediscovered by Christian thinkers such as Thomas Aquinas in the twelfth and thirteenth centuries. Plato had said that objects in this world are mere flimsies, shadows of the realities that exist in the world of the forms. Aristotle disagreed with his great teacher, and claimed that the "real" is right here: the world of the particulars. The rationalist approach to knowledge emphasizes sense perception and rational reflection upon the objects the senses encounter.

Renaissance humanism was another influence on rationalism. Humanism emphasized the importance of human beings and human reason. Renaissance art, even when its subject matter was explicitly religious, had the same effect, as its concern with realistic detail focused attention on human beings.

Today the word *rationalism* conjures the image of cool, unbiased scientific inquiry that does not take seriously the idea of the existence of God. The rationalists of the seventeenth and eighteenth centuries all assumed that the universe had a rational orderliness. Most believed that behind this wondrously elaborate machinery was a rational mind, and many were happy to think of this rational mind as the Christian God, if not quite the God of the theologians. Some maintained that rationalism was superior to revelation as a way to know with certainty. Others left room for revelation apart from reason — claiming, in effect, that religion constituted a different kind of knowledge with its own standards of verification.

DESCARTES AND CONTINENTAL RATIONALISM

René Descartes (1596–1650) is perhaps most important of the great rationalists. His was an interesting, if too short, life. He did not attend a university, but instead went to a Jesuit college in France and was trained in mathematics. After graduation he pursued a military career, hiring himself to different armies throughout Europe, hoping to travel and enjoy a life of ease. He later abandoned this path and eventually became tutor to Queen Christina of Sweden, who, as Bertrand Russell once observed, as a sovereign thought she had the right to waste the time of a great man.[32] She informed Descartes, never an early riser, that they would meet at five in the morning. During the Swedish winter Descartes developed pneumonia and died.

Descartes produced epochal works in both mathematics (he invented coordinate geometry) and philosophy. His *Discourse on Method* (1637) and *Meditations* (1641) made him famous. According to Descartes, the one firm foundation for a theory of knowledge is radical doubt. Decartes believed he could show this with certainty in three steps. First, when he doubted, the one thing he could not doubt was that he was doubting. From this it followed that he himself existed — though he couldn't say anything about himself with certainty except that he was something that doubted. This step is enshrined in the famous phrase "I think, therefore I am" (in Latin, *cogito, ergo sum*). After establishing his own existence, Descartes attempted to prove the existence of God. The idea of himself as a finite being, Descartes said, implied the existence of an

infinite being. Moreover, if God exists, he reasoned, God must be perfect and therefore could not deceive us. He thereby began with a self-evident truth — "I exist" — and arrived at a logically necessary God.[33]

Within Descartes's thought was the idea that humans consist of two parts: the thinking portion and the portion that takes up space. The idea of these two parts, identified with spirit and matter (or mind and body), was to prove fertile ground for later speculation sparked by Descartes's failure or unwillingness to explain the relationship between them. One later explanation was occasionalism, the idea that the two do not communicate except by the "occasional" intervention of God. This idea was defended by the French cleric Nicolas Malebranche (1638–1715). A second option, put forward by the Dutch Jewish philosopher Baruch de Spinoza (1632–77), is called monism. Spinoza suggested that there are not two substances, but one. Thought and physical extension in space are merely two attributes of the same one substance, just as "wet" and "clear" are both attributes of the same glass of water. "God" and "the world" are merely attributes of the same one substance, the universe. The third option was worked out by the brilliant German philosopher and mathematician Gottfried Wilhelm Leibniz (1646–1716). Leibniz hypothesized that an infinite number of substances (or monads) exist completely independently of each other. They seem to interrelate in an orderly way because each one works according to the preestablished pattern set by the divine clockmaker, granting them the appearance of communicating with one another.

EMPIRICISM

Like Continental rationalism, British empiricism was more an approach than a school of thought. The empiricists were deeply concerned with the question of knowledge. Where the rationalists built systems on a foundational belief in self-evident truths and innate ideas, the empiricists argued that human experience forms the basic raw material of our knowledge. We know whether or not statements are true primarily by testing them against our experience.

Perhaps the most important early representative of this approach was John Locke (1632–1704).

Locke knew the presupposition of rationalism. "It is an established opinion among some men, that there are in the understanding certain innate principles . . . as it were stamped upon the mind of man."[34] In contrast, he claimed that the human mind is a blank slate that receives its impressions from outside itself.

> Let us then suppose the mind to be, as we say, white paper, void of all characters, without any ideas;—how comes it to be furnished? . . . I answer, in one word, from experience . . . Our observation employed either, about external sensible objects, or about the internal operations of our minds . . . is that which supplies our understanding with all the materials for thinking.[35]

Locke also considered the limits of reason. There are some propositions that can be discerned to be true by deduction based upon sensation and reflection. There are other propositions that Locke described as being above reason—their truth cannot be discerned by reason alone. Finally, there are propositions that are inconsistent with reason. This allowed Locke to make a distinction between faith and reason. "Reason," he wrote, "I take to be the discovery of the certainty or probability of such propositions or truth, which the mind arrives at by deduction made from such ideas, which it has got by the use of its natural faculties; viz, by sensation or reflection."[36] Locke also defined faith as "assent to any proposition not thus made out by the deductions of reason, but upon the credit of the proposer."[37] Locke therefore left open a space for religion, but a space wholly separate from scientific human inquiry.

George Berkeley (1685–1753) followed Locke. In his *Essay towards a New Theory of Vision* (1709) and *Principles of Human Knowledge* (1710), he argued that both the primary qualities (motion, extension) and secondary qualities (taste, color) of objects are transferred to them by the perceiving subject, rather than being qualities of the thing perceived. Both Locke and Berkeley, therefore, placed emphasis on sensation.

Another leading critic of rationalism was David Hume (1711–76). Hume asked the question: How do human beings learn? He believed that human beings learn through experience, and particularly by observation. However, argued Hume, observation does not provide a window onto the objective nature of that which is observed. All people observe through a filter of mental habits, personal experiences, and other subjective factors that inevitably affect how they perceive the object they observe. Human beings can never observe something in its essence, but instead merely construct a series of linked experiences of a thing. This means that the human mind, and therefore human reason, can never grasp absolute truth. Hume went so far as to assert that one could prove the existence neither of things outside of oneself nor even of oneself. "When I enter most intimately into what I call myself," wrote Hume, "I always stumble on some particular perception or other, of heat or cold, light or shade, love or hatred, pain or pleasure. I never can catch myself at any time without a perception, and never can observe anything but the perception."[38]

THE KANTIAN SYNTHESIS

Immanuel Kant (1724–1804) finished the work begun by Hume. Kant lived an uneventful life in Prussia. He was raised in a devout home and studied at the University of Königsberg, where in 1770 he became a professor of logic and metaphysics. In a magazine article published in 1784 Kant asked the question, What is enlightenment? His answer was that human enlightenment is emergence from self-imposed immaturity, from reliance upon external authorities. He argued that people must use their own reason, especially with respect to religion. We should not bind ourselves to doctrinal statements of past generations. Though we are not yet enlightened, he said, we are living in "a world come of age."[39]

Kant agreed with the empiricists that knowledge begins with sense experience, but he did not agree that all knowledge arises out of experience. That is, the raw material of knowledge is external and comes to us by sense experience, but the mind also plays a part in that it processes this raw material according to built-in concepts.

He discussed this idea in his most important book, *The Critique of Pure Reason,* first published in 1781 and then revised in 1787. Here Kant argued that humans have no direct or actual knowledge of the substance of things. Instead, everything we think we "know" we apprehend through the five senses. The mind then organizes this material according to twelve categories, such as existence, causality, and substance. We can never know objects as they are, but only as they appear to us.

Kant's inquiries into what we can know led him to consider how we should act. He distinguished between a hypothetical imperative and the categorical imperative. An imperative is a command or principle. A hypothetical imperative is a principle that is not binding on all. *If you want to become an engineer, then study engineering* is an example of a hypothetical imperative. It is binding only on those who desire to become engineers. But Kant argued for the existence of what he called the categorical imperative, a command universally binding.

> If now the action is good only as a means to something else, then the imperative is hypothetical; if it is conceived as good in itself and consequently as being necessarily the principle of a will which of itself conforms to reason, then it is categorical.[40]

According to Kant, there is only one categorical imperative: "Act as if the maxim of your action were to become through your will a universal law of nature."[41] Kant argued that the categorical imperative confronts us with the transcendent; it is a principle that comes to us from outside. All humans feel some innate obligation to others. This must, said Kant, come from God. Morality, therefore, points to religion. Kant thus preserved a place for religion—separate from, and neither superior nor inferior to, reason.[42]

Kant also considered the traditional proofs of the existence of God, and subjected them to merciless criticism. He pointed out that Descartes was wrong to assume that in the same way the idea of triangle implies a three-sided figure so the thought of God suggests the existence of God. This proof only works if we assume the existence of God in the first place.[43]

Although he did not consider the traditional proofs of God's existence to be convincing, he also said the existence of God cannot be disproved by speculative reason. Kant argued that human reason has limits, and that human reason tends to transgress these limits.[44]

Kant seems to have brought to conclusion a line of inquiry begun by Descartes. With Descartes a fundamental shift in philosophy is evident. He rejected the assumption of the truth of revelation and elevated human reason in its place, and thereby turned the focus of philosophical inquiry to human beings. Descartes did not author this change. The forces that created it had been at work for some time. But in Descartes, perhaps, this shift is fully evident. Following Descartes, philosophers considered not only the question of how human beings know, but also the limits of that knowing. Three chief results of this project are germane to Christianity. For some, the assumption that reason was superior to revelation meant that the Christian God was a fabrication. "God" was a divine clockmaker, or else there was no God, only the intricate laws of nature. For others, traditional belief was salvaged by the recognition that reason and religion were two completely different species of human experience, each with its own standard of truth. Finally, for many it seemed that the existence of god was a necessary postulate for moral systems.

THE PHILOSOPHES OF FRANCE

In philosophy the term *Enlightenment* can be used to refer to rationalism and its effects, or to refer to a narrow historical development—the emergence in eighteenth-century France of a constellation of naturalist, empiricist, and liberal ideas that led to the French Revolution. A group of Enlightenment thinkers, mostly but not exclusively French, concentrated on the human condition and human institutions. They are often referred to as the *philosophes*. These thinkers were primarily literary figures, were all enthusiastic proponents of Enlightenment optimism, and reflected on and wrote about a host of topics. They were interested in discovering what was essential and inherent in human beings, a kind of universal truth parallel to that achieved by Newton in the natural sciences. The philosophes wanted to create human societies in which there would be equality for all before the law. They knew that this could be achieved only by eliminating the special privileges of the aristocracy. They used the tools of both rationalist and empiricist thinkers, along with the example of parliamentary limitation of royal power in England, to pursue this aim.

Perhaps the most famous of the philosophes was Voltaire (1694–1778), a playwright with a marvelously sarcastic sense of humor. Rising literacy rates allowed Voltaire and others to reach a wide audience, so they wrote to spread new ideas as widely as possible. In *Candide* (1759), Voltaire demonstrated his commitment to common sense. He parodied an idea popular at the time, put forward by Leibniz — that "this is the best of all possible worlds" — by having his hero, Candide, suffer numerous adventures in which he learned of the hypocrisy of Christianity, the stupidity of arbitrary authority, and the horror of war. Voltaire rejected Christianity as a mass of illogical superstitions, and instead embraced the idea of a god who created the universe as a giant machine and then left human beings alone.

Denis Diderot (1713–84) rejected Christianity but hoped to bring to Enlightenment philosophy the warmth and hope of the Catholicism of his youth. His sterling achievement was the editorship of the *Encyclopédie,* a richly detailed collection of Enlightenment learning that celebrated the accomplishments and potential of human beings. Jean-Jacques Rousseau (1712–78), in his *Social Contract* (1762), asserted that government was necessary for human society, but claimed that government ought to be based on popular sovereignty.

The American Thomas Jefferson (1743–1826), the writer of the Declaration of Independence, had traveled in France and was an admirer of the philosophes. Like them, he rejected traditional Christianity and tried to apply the principles of rationalism to his life and thought. Paraphrasing Locke, in the Declaration he wrote: "We hold these truths to be self-evident: That all men are created equal; that they are endowed by their Creator with certain unalienable Rights; that among these are Life, Liberty, and the pursuit of Happiness." By touching on themes of human dignity and self-evident universal truth, Jefferson made clear his debt to Enlightenment ideals.

These currents in the wider culture constituted a significant challenge to Christian faith, yet neither Catholic nor Protestant orthodoxy seemed willing or able to address them. It was left to other Christians, most of them Protestants, to offer meaningful responses.

Religions of the Head, Religions of the Heart

A new basis for truth — human reason and the scientific method — had established itself in place of church teaching. Concurrently, both affecting and effected by the Enlightenment, were developments often called "religions of the head" and "religions of the heart." The first variety emphasized human reason and claimed to arrive at rational religion. The second focused not on universal truth claims but upon a personally apprehended spiritual truth.

DEISM

One of the rational religions that developed in the eighteenth century was deism. The deists wanted to demonstrate what they perceived to be the naïveté and repressive effects of traditional Christian belief. They also wished to substitute for Christianity a natural religion and a morality that was not based upon purported revelation from some divine being. There were many deists who found it convenient to retain a semblance of Christian practice, but in most ways deists were substantially outside the Christian umbrella. Excited and inspired by the discoveries of scientific inquiry, the deists believed that nature's laws should be the basis of religion. Deism is therefore a type of natural religion, holding that moral principles are common to human nature and suggesting that God that is, in essence, the laws of nature. Locke considered Christianity compatible with reason. Deists and others judged reason to be superior to any revelation. This is but another indicator of the secularization process.

Lord Herbert of Cherbury (1583–1648) is often considered the first deist. He believed that religion should not be based upon particular historical events or a particular revelation. He determined to study religious systems in the belief that they reflect the basic needs of the human beings that created them. After long study, Cherbury concluded that all religions hold five central ideas in common: God exists; God must be worshiped; worship should lead to ethical results; human beings have a need to repent; and there is reward and punishment in both this life and the next.

Another early deist was John Toland (1670–1722), an ex-Catholic of Irish lineage, who became famous with the publication of his *Christianity Not Mysterious* in 1696. Here he asserted that the worthwhile doctrines of Christian faith could be demonstrated by reason, rendering revelation and perhaps even Christianity superfluous.

Anthony Collins (1676–1729) had a far more philosophical orientation than Toland. Collins's *Discourse of the Grounds and Reasons of the Christian Religion* (1726) questioned conventional belief in the literal truth of the Bible. For example, Collins attempted to demonstrate that the dating of biblical documents indicated that Jesus did not, after all, fulfill prophecy. Collins's work planted doubt in the minds of many about the reliability of the Bible.

In his *Christianity as Old as the Creation, or the Gospel a Republication of the Religion of Nature* (1730), Matthew Tindal (1655–1733) argued that there is a law of reason common to all rational creatures. The Christian message has authority, he said, only to the degree that it embodies what reason can infer from creation. These thinkers not only attempted to show Christian faith faulty, they aimed to demonstrate how a natural religion, a religion of reason, aptly fit the human situation.

RELIGIONS OF THE HEART

Many Christians were unsettled by the scientific revolution. Apparently robbed of a religion that could claim all truth, they desired a religion that was personal and ethical, one that provided a feeling of connection with the divine.[45] The typology of "head vs. heart" religion is far from perfect, but it does capture much of the character of the age.

The religions of the heart were all highly personal, although some developed a strong community ethos. These movements also tended to be socially inclusive—the requirement was neither wealth nor education, but only a willingness to think deeply about religious experience. In these groups the democratizing tendencies of the first generation of reformers seemed to flourish again.

This impulse, born of aversion to intransient dogma and an attraction to the interior life, took manifold forms, and so its history is impossible to trace with complete accuracy. In general, however, scholars have identified two major categories, spiritualism and pietism, each comprised of a wide variety of expressions.

Spiritualism   The seventeenth- and eighteenth-century movements collectively termed "spiritualist" are difficult to categorize. They tended to eschew dogma and were apt to adapt to every new situation. But they can be described in general terms through the biographies of their founders or prominent members.

The mystic Jakob Boehme (1575–1624) was born in Silesia, a region in east central Germany. His father was a struggling farmer and a devout Christian. Boehme found himself utterly uninterested in the sermons he heard, having little patience for their length or academic subject matter. In his early teens he began to have visions and became certain that it was his destiny to understand the mysteries of the universe.

Boehme came to the conclusion that endless theological debates over points of doctrine were a waste of time. Resolving to explore the inner life, he read extensively, reaching conclusions confirmed by his visions. He published his first work in 1612, asserting that he was merely writing down what his visions commanded. This book, *Brilliant Dawn*, aroused the concern of Lutheran authorities, and Boehme was ordered to cease writing. He resumed in 1618, however, believing he had been instructed to do so in his visions. His devotional book, *The Way of Christ*, was published in 1623. Banished from the town of Görlitz where he had been living, Boehme ended up in Dresden. There he had his writings evaluated by theologians at the court of the elector of Saxony, who declared them incomprehensible. Boehme fell ill and died in 1624.

Boehme wrote in a style that often defies understanding. He rarely defined his terms, employed rich metaphors, and pressed into service terminology drawn from an array of sources, including theology, alchemy, Christian mysticism, and astrology. Even today scholars are divided in their estimation of Boehme. Some argue that he was a pantheist, others a dualist. He apparently believed that God is the *Ungrund,* the indefineable basic matter of the universe, and that God is neither good nor evil, but contains the seeds of good and evil. Human beings can free themselves from evil by transcending their sinful character through union with Christ.

Boehme appears to have been interested in two primary aims: to reject the precision of dogma and to embrace the immediacy of inner spiritual experience. He had few followers during his short lifetime. However, his work, with its odd admixture of themes and metaphors, proved influential in later years. The German philosopher Schelling and other titans of German Romanticism were influenced by Boehme, especially by his example of illumination and inner experience.

A second representative of the spiritualist tradition was George Fox (1624–61). Fox was born under humble circumstances in a small English town where his father was a weaver. He became a cobbler's apprentice, but in 1643, upset by what he considered to be the dissolute lives of his associates, he abandoned his family and began a life of wandering, seeking spiritual illumination. His church attendance was sporadic at best, but he prayed for divine revelation as he read and memorized scripture. In 1646, after more than three years of spiritual wrestling, he came to the conclusion that whatever truth existed was not to be found in the orthodox formulations of Christian theologians. Instead, Fox held, there is an inner light within each person that is the capacity to recognize and respond to the presence of God. Fox therefore rejected the reformed doctrine of total depravity.

After many years of silence, Fox suddenly felt compelled by the Spirit to announce his views. Fox happened to be attending a Baptist meeting at the time, and his outburst was not welcome. Fox responded to such urgings more and more frequently, trying to make clear his spiritualized understanding of Christian faith. He became the object of scorn and even violence. Yet he also attracted many followers he called "friends," although others gave to this group the name *Quakers* because their spiritual enthusiasm during meetings caused them to shake. Fox rejected structured worship, preferring instead to wait until the Spirit moved one or more members of the congregation. The worship services of the Friends therefore began in silence and without any planned order. All waited until one or more were moved to speak, or to pray, or to sing. Women had the same rights as men in this regard. The Friends also rejected the sacraments of baptism and communion, due to concern that misplaced interest in the physical symbols would draw attention away from the spiritual.

Fox recognized that his understanding of Christianity could, in practice, degenerate into atomistic individualism. He therefore emphasized community love and concern for one another, and for the wider world.

The radical democratic element in the Quaker experience was unusual for its time, and the Quakers were suspected of holding a host of socially subversive views. In 1664, Charles II issued an edict banning unlicensed religious assemblies in England. The Friends decided that to meet in secret would be dishonest, so they continued to meet openly. As a result, the Quakers were brutally persecuted.

Fox traveled to Ireland in 1669, the West Indies and North America in 1671–72, and Holland in 1677. He won many converts in all these lands before he died in 1691. At the time of his death his movement numbered many thousands, including William Penn.

Penn (1644–1718) was the son of a British admiral. Following his attraction to Puritanism and the Huguenots, Penn became a Quaker in 1667. He traveled, wrote ill-received defenses of the Quaker movement, and was imprisoned. Penn decided to move to North America and settled in what is now Pennsylvania, in search of religious freedom. The other British colonies in North America were established to allow for freedom of worship only for the founding group, and tended to be intolerant of all others. Penn's dream was to found a colony in which there would be complete religious freedom.[46]

Soon Quakers from throughout the colonies and Europe journeyed to "Pennsylvania," and particularly Philadelphia, the city of "fraternal love." Many non-Quakers settled in Pennsylvania as well. The idea of religious toleration eventually found similar expression in the Constitution of the United States.

A third representative of the spiritualist impulse toward a spiritualist understanding of the faith was Emmanuel Swedenborg (1688–1772), a Swedish aristocrat educated at the University of Uppsala. The young Swedenborg was fascinated with the scientific method and devoted the bulk of his early life to its pursuit. He had an enormously creative mind, anticipating magnetic theory and the development of the airplane. He became convinced that behind the physical universe lay a spiritual reality that gave structure to the physical world.

In 1734–35 Swedenborg began having visions in which he felt God commissioning him to announce his message. In his visions he claimed to have perceived spiritual truths, and to see that the physical world is a reflection of the attributes of God. He was so utterly certain of the truth of his insights that he spoke of this revelation as the second coming of Christ. He did not intend to found a new church; instead, he wanted to call the Church to reform itself.

In spite of this, his followers instituted the Church of the New Jerusalem in 1784, twelve years after his death. Later the Swedenborg society was founded, which is still in existence. Swedenborg's teachings never attracted the level of interest enjoyed by Fox and the Quakers, and though membership in the Church of the New Jerusalem and in Swedenborg societies is small, the organizations are vibrant.

Apart from Fox and the Quakers, the spiritualist movements were not destined to have great effect, precisely because they rejected organization and placed a premium on individual spiritual experience. Nonetheless, taken as a whole the spiritualist impulse was a significant reaction to Protestant orthodoxy.

PIETISM

Some movements critical of orthodoxy sought to remain within established traditions. Perhaps the most significant example of this amicable criticism of the Protestant tradition was pietism.

Few issues are as contested by historians as the origin of pietism. One of the chief difficulties is that pietism defies definition. It is often described as a movement within Lutheranism, but similar ideas were present in other Christian traditions, frequently earlier than in Lutheranism. The French scholar Michel Godfroid has wondered if there ever really was a unified movement called "pietism."[47] Nonetheless, Godfroid also claimed that "to write the history of Pietism is to write the history of modern Protestantism."[48]

The story of pietism is usually said to begin with the book *True Christianity* (1606) by Johann Arndt (1555–1621). Arndt, a follower of Melanchthon, had studied at Wittenberg, Basle, and Strasbourg. In *True Christianity* he discussed the atonement, but centered his attention not on its legal dimensions, as was customary, but rather on the effect of the atonement within the heart of the believer. This shift of focus had a nearly cataclysmic effect.

Mandatory church attendance, which by then was the usual pattern, struck Arndt as destructive of true spirituality. People came to church, he reasoned, out of numb obedience, grudging acquiescence, or else through the false belief that their very presence in worship guaranteed salvation. In his eyes this kind of practice was worse than no practice at all, because it inured the participants to their true need.

For Arndt, the point of Christianity was union with Christ resulting in a transformed life. This could be accomplished, he felt, only through meditation and conscious effort to place oneself open before God. *True Christianity* was written to assist people in this process.

The popularity of Arndt's work suggests a deep hunger for precisely what he offered. In 135 years, *True Christianity* ran through ninety-five German editions, as well as editions in Latin (popular with Jesuits in Spain), Swedish, Dutch, and English. During those years there was also a torrent of new hymns that contemporaries described as "pietist" even before the term was used of a movement. For example, in 1622 the Dresden hymnbook contained 276 hymns; in 1673, its counterpart contained 1,505. The Lüneburg hymnbook of 1635 contained 355 hymns; fifty-nine years later it had 2,055 hymns.[49]

Perhaps the most significant figure in the history of pietism is Philipp Jakob Spener (1635–1705). Spener was born at Rappoltsweiler in Alsace, the son of devout parents. He was raised on a diet of English Puritan thought and Arndt's piety. As a young man Spener met Jean de Labadie (1610–74), a Jesuit turned Calvinist deeply concerned with what he considered Calvinists' lack of interest in spirituality. Spener was a diligent student of Luther's writings and became convinced that Luther emphasized a personal spiritual life and spiritual renewal far more than the scholars of Lutheran orthodoxy made clear. Under Labadie's influence, Spener concluded that the Christian experience was a way of life to be learned not only by study, but also by doing. He wrote:

> All knowledge of God and his will according to the law and gospel, however, does not consist in mere knowing but must come forth in praxis and action.[50]

In the summer of 1670 a group of like-minded men approached Spener and suggested he meet with them regularly for discussion of spiritual matters. Perceiving in this an opportunity to put into practice some of his ideas for revival, he agreed, and the *collegia pietas* was born. Soon other groups were meeting based on Spener's example. These were small-group fellowships committed to scripture, prayer, and mutual encouragement in the spiritual life. Because the Lutheran church at that time prohibited all but official services, Spener risked running afoul of ecclesiastical authorities.

The groups quickly became egalitarian, as women and men from all social classes started attending. Spener felt that this socially innovative development mirrored Paul's notion of the church as a body made up of many members (1 Corinthians 12:12–31). He taught that every Christian and not just the clergy had the responsibility to comfort and warn fellow believers. That is, Spener infused the idea of the priesthood of all believers with new energy.

Spener's *Pia Desideria* ("Pious Wishes"), published in 1675, reveals his concern with what he considered the shortcomings of the Church of his day, and the steps he believed necessary to address them. He claimed that "almost everywhere there is something wanting in the church,"[51] which he understood as the living reality of Christ in the lives of individual believers. He had come to conclude that,

"the scholastic theology which Luther had thrown out . . . had been introduced again . . . [and its removal would] probably be one of the greatest benefactions for which we could give thanks."[52] Spener argued that pastors and civil authorities were too infrequently concerned with godliness, and decried their "debauchery"[53] and "wordly spirit."[54] Most people, he said, do not take sin seriously. They "boast of their drunkenness"[55] and incorrectly believe that "all Christianity requires of them . . . is that they be baptized, hear the preaching of God's word, confess . . . and go to the Lord's Supper, no matter how their hearts are disposed at the time."[56] Finally, he offered the observation that "those who zealously cultivate . . . godliness can hardly escape being suspected as secret papists."[57] This last comment provides a window onto his perceptions of Catholic spirituality.

To correct the situation, Spener outlined a six-step program: First, more extensive use of scripture in both public and private settings.[58] Second, greater involvement of the laity, or, in Spener's words, "the establishment and diligent exercise of the spiritual priesthood."[59] Third, a clear stress that Christianity without practical piety is not Christianity at all. "[I]t is by no means enough to have knowledge of the Christian faith, for Christianity consists rather of practice."[60] Fourth, a concern for proper conduct: "We must beware how we conduct ourselves in religious controversies."[61] Spener believed that acrimony in theological disputes harmed the cause of the gospel and limited the chances for ecumenical advances. Instead, he felt Christians should seek to come to agreement through prayer and Christian love. Fifth, seminaries and ministers must become concerned with piety and not simply study.[62] Sixth, sermons should be aimed at explaining the text in such a way that its meaning could be applied to life.[63]

The result was sensational. *Pia Desideria* went through several editions, and the pietist movement spread to Holland, Scandinavia, Switzerland, and North America. In 1686 Spener was appointed court chaplain to Frederick, the elector of Saxony making him one of the most influential Lutherans in Germany.

There was fierce opposition to his appointment. Several students without theological degrees began to hold meetings based upon the model Spener had pioneered, and this aroused the enmity of Johann Benedikt Carpzov (1639–99), a member of a powerful family of Lutheran orthodox theologians. Carpzov had desired the post of court chaplain awarded to Spener, and he was determined to combat pietism. Although Frederick was not a pious man, he saw political advantage in an alliance with the pietists and became Spener's protector. At Spener's urging, Frederick elevated the pietist academy at Halle to the status of a university.

Leadership of the university fell to August Hermann Francke (1663–1727). Francke had been a student of Carpzov, but became convinced that Spener, whom he had yet to meet, was right. Francke had earlier shown a keen interest in spirituality, becoming familiar with the thought of Madame Guyon and translating the work of de Molinos.[64]

Francke was one of the great organizers in the history of Christianity. He envisioned a broad scheme for social improvement and began Germany's first newspaper, the *Hallesche Zeitung*, published three times a week. Under Francke's leadership Halle became an effective training ground for pietist pastors and laity. But what struck many observers was Francke's tireless devotion to works of compassion at Halle; his projects included orphanages, hospitals, schools, facilities for training teachers, and a Bible institute. Francke was following Dutch models, but on a scale no one had ever seen before. The dispensary he developed was the first large-scale producer of standardized medicines. It provided emergency medical kits and comprehensive public-health materials for entire cities.[65]

Similar ideas had developed in Reformed circles. F. A. Lampe (1683–1729) was a prolific preacher and hymnwriter who did a good deal to spread the ideals of spiritual renewal among Reformed churches in Germany. William Ames (1576–1633) was educated at Cambridge and became a Puritan. He eventually left Cambridge and settled in Holland, and in 1622 became professor of theology at Franeker. His *Marrow of Theology*, published in 1623, nearly a half-century before *Pia Desideria*, bears a deep affinity to the pietist agenda.[66] Ames began the work with the words "Theology is the doctrine or teaching of living to God,"[67] as opposed to the idea that theology is doctrine about God.

Above all, Ames believed that theology ought to lead to the practice of godliness in the lives of believers, rather than simply explain Christian belief.

Pietism had a major influence on the life of Count Ludwig von Zinzendorf (1700–1760). Zinzendorf was raised by pietist parents and educated at Halle. He became acquainted with Bohemian Anabaptist refugees fleeing persecution in Moravia and invited them to settle on his lands. In 1722 they established a community there called Herrnhut and came to be called Moravians. It was Zinzendorf's dream to replicate much of what Francke had done at Halle. At Herrnhut, pietism focused on a joyful celebration of life in Christ. At Halle, in contrast, there was a greater concern with sorrow over human sinfulness. Later forms of pietism often borrowed from de Molinos and even Boehme to inform mystical experience.

The Herrnhut community soon became active in sending missionaries. Zinzendorf traveled to Pennsylvania and founded the city of Bethlehem. Other Moravian missionaries went to the Caribbean, to central America, and throughout Europe. One of the primary figures in pietism and the great revivals that were to sweep across Europe and North America was influenced by the Moravians. His name was John Wesley.

Wesley (1703–91) attended the University of Oxford, where he demonstrated his powerful intellect. He joined the "holiness club," founded by his brother Charles and named for the rigorously methodical way its members organized their lives in order to allow enough time for their devotional practices.

Wesley became an Anglican priest and traveled to Georgia, where he was appointed to a pastorate and worked to convert native Americans. Wesley came to consider his efforts a disaster. But while in America he encountered several Moravian missionaries who asked him, "Do you know Christ personally?" The question, he wrote, would not leave him.

He returned to England and during the evening of 24 May 1738 had an experience that changed his life. In his *Journal* he wrote:

> In the evening I went very unwillingly to a society in Aldersgate Street, where one was reading Luther's preface to the Epistle to the Romans. About a quarter before nine, while he was

describing the change which God works in the heart through faith in Christ, I felt my heart strangely warmed. I felt I did trust in Christ, Christ alone for salvation: And an assurance was given me, that he had taken away my sins, even mine, and saved me from the law of sin and death.[68]

Wesley then traveled to Hernnhut. He had great admiration for Zinzendorf, but like many others he found steady exposure to the outsized personality of the count more than he could tolerate. Wesley decided not to join the Herrnhut movement.

Simultaneously, another former member of the "holiness club," George Whitefield (1714–70), had become a fabulously successful preacher, addressing crowds in the open fields near Bristol, England. Whitefield was in need of help in Bristol, and Wesley joined him there. Wesley did not have great regard for Whitefield's emotional preaching style, nor was he comfortable with the practice of preaching in the open fields. Nevertheless, he gradually came to appreciate the benefit of Whitefield's method. Eventually, Wesley became the leader of the movement, in part because Whitefield was often off in North America. Eventually the two parted company on friendly terms. Whitefield went on to organize the Calvinist Methodist Church, centered in Wales.

Wesley reluctantly recognized the need to provide some organization for what was becoming a movement. His ideas developed gradually, in response to needs as they arose. The basic unit of organization was the class, composed of eleven members and a leader. Classes would meet on a weekly basis to pray, read scripture, and discuss spiritual matters. Wesley imposed no social or educational requirement for the position of leader, so the movement quickly attained a strongly democratic flavor, allowing extraordinary opportunities for women to assume leadership roles in the home-based classes. Together, groups of classes formed units called societies. Circuits were groups of societies under the leadership of superintendents. This clear organization and style of devotional practice came to be described as a method, and its practitioners as Methodists.

Wesley did not intend to found a church. Like Spener, he wanted to revive the church that had

nurtured him. Anglican leaders were suspicious of this new movement happening among them but outside their purview. According to English law, non-Anglican services were tolerated, but only if they were registered. In 1787 Wesley allowed Methodists to register with the government, effectively declaring Methodism a separate movement from the Church of England.

In the wake of the American War of Independence many Anglican preachers left North America and returned to England, leaving their American congregations without ordained pastors to administer the eucharist. Wesley had written against the revolution, even though the majority of Methodists in the colonies were in favor of independence. While Methodists in America had great respect for Wesley, many began to consider themselves independent from him. When Francis Asbury (1745–1816) and Thomas Coke (1747–1814), both lay Methodist preachers, began referring to themselves as "bishops," Wesley could do little in response. Largely to meet the need for ordained clergy, Methodists in America organized themselves into the Methodist Episcopal Church.

The pietist movement was despised from the very beginning, as anti-intellectual and open to legalism. Søren Kierkegaard (1813–55), the Danish philosopher, was raised in a pietist home and knew well the shape and nature of the movement. Kierkegaard once noted that pietism could be a "petty and pusillanimous renunciation in things that do not matter."[69] But he also felt that at its best pietism was close to the heart of true Christianity.

> Yes, indeed, pietism (properly understood, not simply in the sense of abstaining from dancing and such externals, no, in the sense of witnessing for the truth and suffering for it, together with the understanding that suffering in this world belongs to being a Christian, and that a shrewd and secular conformity with this world is unchristian)— yes, indeed, pietism is the one and only consequence of Christianity.[70]

"We have every reason not to adopt a belittling attitude to Pietism," observed the Lutheran theologian Ernst Käsemann a century after Kierkegaard. He went on to note, "Our church life still continues to draw its nourishment from its roots in Pietism."[71]

Pietism lives on today in a host of Protestant denominations, particularly among evangelical groups.

The Great Awakening

The "**Great Awakening**," a spontaneous burst of pietist feeling that came to affect several denominational groups in North America, is linked to the work of revivalist preachers in New England. Perhaps the most significant was Jonathan Edwards (1703–58), a minister in Northhampton, Massachusetts. A committed Calvinist, Edwards did not consider his sermons particularly powerful. But beginning in 1734 some among his parishoners began responding to his sermons in extraordinary ways, often with emotional outbursts of repentance and spiritual longing. Over the next several years his congregation grew, swelled by many who had significant life-changing experiences.

When George Whitefield visited the area, Edwards invited him to preach. The appearance of Whitefield gave the awakening added life, and soon clergy from a variety of denominations began preaching with new zeal. Others followed Whitefield's example and became traveling preachers. The result was astounding. Throughout New England, churches were packed with people expressing great joy at having been released from sin.

Whitefield has been described as one of the "most powerful and moving preachers ever to hold forth."[72] The skeptical Ben Franklin once heard him preach and resolved not to contribute to the collection he knew would follow the sermon. But, Franklin remembered, Whitefield "finished so admirably that I emptied my pockets wholly into the collectors dish, gold and all."[73]

At first the Awakening was a movement within Anglican, Congregational, and Presbyterian churches. Soon, however, it spread to Baptist and Methodist congregations, and these denominations ended up being most effected by the awakening. Unlike the more established denominations, these two groups were active in establishing churches on the ever-expanding western frontier.

The Great Awakening was an event of monumental significance. It created a broad and enduring religious impulse in American culture vibrant enough to forestall the linkage between modernity and secularity that affected Europe.[74] It contributed to a sense of unity within the American colonies. It also fundamentally shaped the American version of the pietist impulse. The Awakening emphasized the need for individual transformation and the joy that can come with it. This stress on the individual contributed to and reflected individualism in American culture more broadly.

The Orthodox Church in an Embattled Era

For a good portion of the seventeenth and eighteenth centuries Eastern Orthodoxy was on the defensive. With the exception of Russia, most nations in which Orthodoxy had triumphed had then later been conquered by Muslim forces. Although allowed to survive, Orthodoxy under the Muslims was largely stifled. This was but one of a series of reversals suffered by Eastern Orthodoxy. With the fall of Constantinople in 1453, the historic center of Orthodoxy was lost. In Poland, a Uniate church blending Catholicism and Orthodoxy had been established at the Council of Brest-Litovsk in 1596. This meant the Metropolia of Kiev was under the control of the Catholic rulers of Poland and Lithuania. According to this agreement, members of the Orthodox Church joined the Catholic Church but were allowed to retain their own liturgy. It was an agreement that many Orthodox leaders came to regret, as it all but declared the retreat of Orthodoxy from Poland. Soon Orthodox schools were established to rival those of the Jesuits, aimed at clarifying doctrinal differences and at training a cadre of priests to promote the Orthodox cause.

THE CHURCH IN RUSSIA

In earlier centuries the tsars had claimed that Moscow was the Third Rome. During the seventeenth and eighteenth centuries Moscow earned that distinction. The Church in Russia was easily the largest in the Orthodox fold, and it was closely associated with Russian national pride. This was a source of great strength, but also a difficulty, for the Church was dominated by the state. Nonetheless, even during the reign of Ivan the Terrible, the Church boasted individuals of great conviction and spiritual influence. St. Philip, the Metropolitan of Moscow, vocally protested Ivan's policies of terror and injustice. When he confronted Ivan during a public celebration of the liturgy, Ivan had Philip imprisoned and then strangled. In spite of this brave burst of conscience, the Church was often a tool in the hands of the monarch.

When Theodore I (1584–98), the son of Ivan IV, died childless, Russia entered a period known as "the time of trouble." A host of contenders for the throne appeared, and civil war erupted. The Poles and the Jesuits ended up supporting one of the contenders, a move bitterly resented by Russians but calculated by the Jesuits to bring all of Russia into the Catholic camp. The Poles then invaded Russia and succeeded in capturing Moscow. In the midst of this grave national crisis the Orthodox Church was the most visible source of Russian unity. When the Poles were ejected, the Russians held an assembly to select a new tsar, choosing in 1613 Michael Romanov, the sixteen-year-old son of Philaret, the patriarch of Moscow. This was the founding of the Romanov dynasty.

The next half-century was a time of political and cultural renewal within Russia, and the Church played a significant role in this process. It was also a time of reform within the Church, aimed not at doctrine, but practice. At the outset the reform was led by Philaret and Dionysius, abbot of the Monastery of Trinity–St. Sergius. In 1633 Philaret died, and leadership in the reform passed to John Neronov, Avvakum Petrovich, and a group of local clergy.

In the days when the Orthodox faith was first accepted in Russia, the Greek liturgy had been translated into Russian, but several errors were made in the process. Over time, of course, these mistakes were enshrined in the Russian liturgy loved by the Russian people. The reformers aimed to correct some of these errors, but in a way that preserved the traditional features of the liturgy. On the local level the reformers sought to raise the moral standards of

both priests and laity. They frowned on drunkenness, encouraged priests to adopt a reverent attitude when services were sung in local parishes, and insisted that both priests and laity observe the fasts.

These reforms were remarkably successful. By 1650, visitors to Russia were amazed at the diligence and discipline of Russian Orthodoxy. Paul of Aleppo, an Arab Orthodox archdeacon from Antioch who lived in Russia in the mid seventeenth century, commented that state banquets were accompanied not by music but by readings from the lives of the saints, just as would be the practice at a monastery.[75] For Paul this Russian strictness was too repressive. He complained that it did not allow for laughter, joking, smoking, or drunkeness. "Now what shall we say of these duties, severe enough to turn children's hair grey. . . . Who would believe that they should thus go beyond the anchorites in the desert?"[76]

In 1652 there arose an important dispute between the reformers and the new patriarch, Nikon (1605–81). Nikon admired the Greek Church and wanted to replace the Russian liturgy with the version used by the then-contemporary Greek Church. This put him in conflict with Neronov and Petrovitch.

Nikon was brilliant but inflexible. He was pitiless in his treatment of his opponents, using persecution and even torture to get his way. Neronov eventually submitted, but Petrovitch refused to capitulate. He spent ten years in exile and twenty-two years in prison. Finally, he was burned at the stake, becoming a martyr in the eyes of his followers. Those who followed Neronov and Petrovitch, the "Old Believers," rejected Nikon's reforms and so were called sectarians.

In addition to imposing Greek forms on the Russian Church, Nikon wished to establish the Orthodox Church as supreme over the state. In theory the relationship between church and state in Russia followed the Byzantine pattern of two powers, each supreme in its own area. In practice the state had been pre-eminent. Nikon set about trying to reverse this trend. For a time he was effective in exercising unrestricted authority in the Church. He also called himself "Great Lord" and claimed the right to intervene in civil affairs as well as matters of state policy.

Tsar Alexis (1645–76) admired Nikon and initially allowed him considerable authority in state matters. But this did not last. Alexis came to consider Nikon's influence too pervasive. In 1658 Nikon went into an unofficial semiretirement, and for nearly a decade the Russian Church was without clear leadership. Finally, in 1666–67 a council was held in Moscow, presided over by the patriarchs of Alexandria and Antioch. The council ended up affirming the reforms of Nikon but condemning him personally. He was deposed and sent into exile, and a new patriarch assumed his place. The decision of the council was also a defeat for his plans to establish the Church's independence. Peter the Great (1672–1725), in fact, successfully neutralized the power of the patriarchate, hoping to prevent the appearance of another Nikon.

Summary

In the sixteenth century, Luther had inaugurated a rupture in western Christianity and inadvertently set in motion two centuries of tumultuous conflict. Catholicism sought to force reunion, and Protestantism to defend itself. By the middle of the eighteenth century, many were convinced that, whatever its virtues, religion fostered intolerance and violence. Suspicion, misunderstanding, and animosity persisted between Catholics and Protestants.

During the seventeenth and eighteenth centuries, the place of the Church in society fundamentally shifted. Religious conflict caused many to question the effects of Christian faith mingled with politics. The scientific revolution provided a basis for truth-claims that seemed more trustworthy than those derived from theology. Developments in philosophy emphasized the superiority of human reason to revelation in the search for truth. Together these forces contributed to the process of secularization and toppled the Church from its customary role. But even though reliance upon human reason had, in effect, replaced revelation, even reason did not rest on an immovable foundation. Both David Hume and Immanuel Kant made it clear that neither science nor reason could lead to absolute truth. They thus illuminated the pathway to subjectivism

(the view that each person has his or her own standard of truth that is right for them) and relativism (the view that there are no truths that are absolute).

There were several reactions to these developments. Many sought a "reasonable" religion in which revelation had little or no place alongside reason. Others simply rejected Christianity altogether, seeing it as a type of superstition. Catholicism and Protestantism engaged in a struggle to clarify and regulate belief and practice, and within both traditions reform movements developed that declared the insufficiency of right belief or right action and emphasized inner devotion.

Christianity entered the nineteenth century facing a landscape few could have imagined barely a century before. New directions in philosophy and science had undercut its authority in the world, but so had the bloody warfare that resulted from religious intolerance. In most countries Christianity had become subservient to the state, but had succeeded in clarifying and regulating orthodoxy and practice. Together these changes demanded new ways of understanding and expressing the faith. Some predicted that Christianity was not up to the challenge. It remained to be seen if the ancient faith could adapt itself to this new context and yet remain true to its heritage.

QUESTIONS FOR REVIEW AND REFLECTION

1. What factors aided the process of secularization?

2. What were the characteristic theological, social, and cultural markers of various forms of Christian faith in Europe during the seventeenth and eighteenth centuries? How did Christians respond to changes in European cultural, political and intellectual life?

3. What does the Huguenot struggle reveal about the relationship between church, state and faith in Europe during this period?

NOTES

1. See Brad S. Gregory, *Salvation at Stake: Christian Martyrdom in Early Modern Europe* (Cambridge, Mass.: Harvard University Press, 2000). Gregory points out that Christian martyrs represented all classes of society, concluding that the doctrinal disputes of the day were understood by the population as a whole. He also notes that those who chose to execute often saw it

as an unsavory duty. This, Gregory says, explains why persecutors frequently spent a good deal of time trying to convince the persecuted to change their minds. This persuasive effort and its relatively low rate of success demonstrate that both sides were convinced that God was with them.

2. See Jonathan Scott, "What the Dutch Taught Us," *Times Literary Supplement,* 16 March 2001, 4.

3. See *Collected Works of Erasmus,* vol. 6, Trans. R.A.B. Mynors and D.F.S. Thompson (Toronto: University of Toronto Press, 1982), 372.

4. See, for example, Jonathan Scott, *England's Troubles: Seventeenth-Century English Political Instability in European Context* (Cambridge: Cambridge University Press, 2000).

5. Quoted in Scott, "What the Dutch Taught Us," 4. On the same page Scott quotes an unnamed and undated English source: "The preservation of the true Religion . . . was the mayne object whereon the People had fixed their hearts, so were theire Eyes and Eares, Scouts to discover what past abroad . . . the reformed Churches abroad they held as . . . outworkes of the Church of England; And therefore as soone as any of them were threatened the English did take it as a Cloud which might in time break uppon them: This gave them apprehensions."

6. Johannes Paul, *Gustaf Adolf,* vol. 2 (Leipzig: Quelle & Meyer, 1930), 180–81.

7. Oxenstierna was clearly the hero of the period, although this proved a dubious honor given the staggering toll the war extracted. A product of his age, he was fluent in several languages, capable of ruthless political maneuvering, and yet a gifted amateur theologian. The French diplomat Mazarin once said, "If the statesmen of Europe were all on one boat, they ought to give the helm to Axel Oxenstierna." See Neander N. Cronholm, *A History of Sweden,* vol. 1 (Chicago: The author, 1902), 356.

8. See Johan Fredrik af Lundblad, *Svensk Plutark,* vol. 2 (Stockholm: K. Ordens-boktryckeriet, 1826), 95. The quote has been attributed to several others. Oxenstierna's son John had been asked to accept an appointment to the Conference of Münster that concluded the Treaty of Westphalia, and the elder Oxenstierna wrote this in a letter urging his son to accept the appointment.

9. Quoted in Scott, "What the Dutch Taught Us," 6.

10. See Anthony Levi, *Cardinal Richelieu and the Making of France* (New York: Carroll & Graf, 2000).

11. See Craig Harline and Eddy Put, *A Bishop's Tale: Mathias Hovius among His Flock in Seventeenth-Century Flanders* (New Haven: Yale University Press, 2000).

12. Scott, "What the Dutch Taught Us," 6.

13. Viscount Morley, *Notes on Politics and History: A University Address* (London: Macmillan, 1913), 29–30.

14. *A Description of Holland; or, The Present State of the United Provinces* (Leiden: C. de Pecker, 1765), 211.

15. See Simon Schama, *The Embarrassment of Riches: An Interpretation of Dutch Culture in the Golden Age* (New York: Knopf, 1987), 375.

15. Schama, *The Embarrassment of Riches,* 379.

16. Henri Daniel-Rops, *The Church in the Eighteenth Century,* trans. John Warrington (London: Dent & Sons, 1964), 230–31.

17. Max Beloff, *The Age of Absolutism,: 1660–1815* (New York: Harper Torchbooks, 1962), 129.

18. Max Beloff, *The Age of Absolutism,* 102.

19. Baius held that innocence was not a supernatural gift from God to humanity in its primitive state, but rather a necessary component of human nature; that original sin is not only an absence of grace, but an agent of evil transmitted by heredity; and that the sole work of redemption is to recover the original state of innocence, thus allowing humans to live moral lives.

20. Quoted in Antoine Degert, "Fénelon," *The Catholic Encyclopedia,* vol. 6, ed. Charles G. Herbermann (New York: Encyclopedia Press, 1913), 35.

21. Quoted in Degert, "Fénelon," 37.

22. See James Mudge, *Fénelon: the Mystic* (Cincinnati: Jennings & Graham, 1906), 150.

23. See *Luther's Works,* vol. 50 (Philadelphia: Fortress Press, 1975), 190.

24. *Letters of John Calvin,* vol. 1, trans. Jules Bonnet (New York: Burt Franklin Reprints, 1972), 422 fn.

25. Johann Gerhardt, *Locorum theologicum* (Jena: Typis and sumtius Tobiae Steinmanni, 1610, 1622).

26. See Richard A. Muller, *Post-Reformation Reformed Dogmatics* (Grand Rapids: Eerdmans, 1987).

27. Carl L. Becker, *The Heavenly City of the Eighteenth-Century Philosophers* (New Haven: Yale University Press, 1932), 5.

28. Daniel-Rops, *Church in the Eighteenth Century,* 5.

29. Francis Bacon, "The Great Instauration," in *Bacon: Selections,* ed. Matthew Thompson McClure (New York: Scribners, 1928), 4.

30. Francis Bacon, *Novum Organon* 1.81.

31. See Betty Jo Teeter Dobbs, *The Janus Faces of Genius: The Role of Alchemy in Newton's Thought* (Cambridge: Cambridge University Press, 1991).

32. Bertrand Russell, *A History of Western Philosophy* (London: Allen & Unwin, 1946), 582.

33. Descartes clearly hoped that his work would be useful to theologians. It was not to be. To begin a theological program with radical doubt was simply too far afield for most theologians, who were accustomed to assuming the existence of God.

34. John Locke, *An Essay Concerning Human Understanding* (New York: Dover, 1959), 1.1.1.

35. Locke, *Essay,* 2.1.1.

36. Locke, *Essay,* 4.18.2.

37. Locke, *Essay,* 4.18.2.

38. David Hume, *A Treatise of Human Nature* (Buffalo, NY: Prometheus Books, 1992), 1.4.6.

39. Immanuel Kant, "Beantwortung der Frage, Was ist Aufklärung?" *Berlinische Monatschrift,* December 1784 (Gesammelte Schriften, Berlin, VIII, 35).

40. Immanuel Kant, *Fundamental Principles of the Metaphysic of Ethics,* trans. Thomas Kingsmill Abbott (London: Longmans, 1926), 37.

41. Immanuel Kant, *Grounding for the Metaphyics of Morals,* trans. James W. Ellington (Indianapolis: Hackett, 1981), 30.

42. In the preface to his *Religion within the Limits of Reason Alone,* Kant wrote: "although for its own sake morality needs no representation of an end which must precede the determining of the will, it is quite possible that it is necessarily related to such an end. . . . Morality thus leads ineluctably to religion." See *Religion within the Limits of Reason Alone,* trans. Theodore M. Greene and Hoyt H. Hudson (New York: Harper Torchbooks, 1960), 3–5.

43. Kant believed that some statements, such as *a snowy day is a cold day,* were necessarily true. Snowy days are, necessarily, cold. Kant called this an analytic statement. But some true statements are not true by necessity but are verified by facts gained through observation — for example, this truth about a cold Friday: *Friday was a cold day.* The truth of this statement is not necessary, but it can be verified by recourse to perception. Kant called this a synthetic statement. Descartes, said Kant, did not make the necessary distinction between analytic statements and synthetic statements. In his typically difficult style, evident even in translation, Kant wrote: "If it is analytic, the assertion of the existence of the thing adds nothing to the thought of the thing. . . . But if, on the other hand, we admit, as every reasonable person must, that all existential propositions are synthetic, how can we profess to maintain that the predicate of existence cannot be rejected without contradiction? This is a feature which is found only in analytic propositions, and is indeed precisely what constitutes their analytic character." See Kant, *Fundamental Principles,* 37.

44. Kant, *Critique of Pure Reason,* 532.

45. In the nineteenth century, Søren Kierkegaard disparaged concern with right belief and with right behavior, claiming that "such matters are not primary subjects for discussion; the most important is the improvement of the heart." See Kierkegaard's *Journals and Papers,* vol. 3, ed. Howard V. Hong and Edna H. Hong (Bloomington: University of Indiana Press, 1975), 525.

46. Though the crown had granted Penn the land, he was convinced that the Native Americans were the rightful owners, so he decided to try to buy the land from them.

47. Michel Godfroid, "Le Piétisme allemand a-t-il existé? Histoire d'un concept fait pour la polémique," *Études Germaniques* 101 (1971): 32–45. See W. R. Ward, *The Protestant Evangelical Awakening* (Cambridge: Cambridge University Press, 1992), 57.

48. See *Pietists: Selected Writings,* ed. Peter C. Erb (New York: Paulist Press, 1983), 1.

49. W. R. Ward, *Christianity under the Ancien Régime: 1648–1789* (Cambridge: Cambridge University Press, 1999), 73–74.

50. Philipp Jakob Spener, "The Necessary and Useful Reading of the Holy Scriptures," trans. Peter C. Erb, in *Pietists: Selected Writings,* ed. Peter C. Erb (New York: Paulist Press, 1983), 73.

51. Philipp Jakob Spener, *Pia Desideria,* trans. Theodore G. Tappert (Philadelphia: Fortress Press, 1964), 54.

52. Spener, *Pia Desideria,* 72, 54.

53. Spener, *Pia Desideria,* 43.

54. Spener, *Pia Desideria,* 45.

55. Spener, *Pia Desideria,* 59.

56. Spener, *Pia Desideria,* 65.

57. Spener, *Pia Desideria,* 47.

58. Spener, *Pia Desideria,* 87–92.

59. Spener, *Pia Desideria,* 92.

60. Spener, *Pia Desideria,* 95.

61. Spener, *Pia Desideria,* 97.

62. Spener, *Pia Desideria,* 103–15.

63. Spener, *Pia Desideria,* 115.

64. Ward, *Christianity under the Ancien Régime,* 79.

65. Ward, *Christianity under the Ancien Régime,* 80.

66. See Ted A. Campbell, *The Religion of the Heart: A Study of European Religious Life in the Seventeenth and Eighteenth Centuries* (Columbia: University of South Carolina Press, 1991), 71–72.

67. William Ames, *The Marrow of Theology,* trans. John Dykstra Eusden (Durham, N.C.: Labyrinth Press, 1983), 77.

68. John Wesley, *Journal,* May 24, 1738.

69. Søren Kierkegaard, *Journals and Papers,* vol. 3, ed. and trans. Howard Hong and Edna Hong (Bloomington: University of Indiana Press, 1975), 524.

70. Søren Kierkegaard, *Journals and Papers,* vol. 3, 524.

71. Ernst Käsemann, "New Testament Questions of Today," in *New Testament Questions of Today,* trans. W. J. Montague (Philadelphia: Fortress Press, 1969), 4.

72. Roger Finke and Rodney Stark, *The Churching of America, 1776–1990: Winners and Losers in Our Religious Economy* (New Brunswick, N.J.: Rutgers University Press, 1992), 49.

73. See Michael O. Emerson and Christian Smith, *Divided by Faith: Evangelical Religion and the Problem of Race in America* (New York: Oxford University Press, 2000), 25.

74. See Richard John Neuhaus, "Marching Onward," *Times Literary Supplement,* 15 June 2001, 12.

75. See Timothy Ware, *The Orthodox Church* (London: Penguin, 1997), 110.

76. From *The Travels of Macarius.* See Ware, *The Orthodox Church,* 110.

CHAPTER 11

Christianity in the Modern World

The Nineteenth and Early Twentieth Centuries

Overview

The period from the beginning of the nineteenth century to the middle of the twentieth was a time of dramatic change that reshaped civilization everywhere. Revolutions in the late 1700s had begun a process of democratization destined to affect much of the world during the next two hundred years. Industrialization and imperialism brought major shifts in the distribution of wealth and power. Growing **nationalism** encouraged the formation of powerful nation-states in the nineteenth century — and, in the twentieth, **fascism** and two great world wars. Religious ideals and institutions were displaced by more worldly ones as the secularization of society continued, now at an accelerated pace. Discoveries and innovations in the natural and social sciences uprooted old ideas and replaced them with revolutionary new ones.

A central theme in the history of Christianity during this period was its struggle to maintain its place in a changing world without sacrificing truths and traditions reaching back nearly two thousand years. Although some Catholic theologians attempted to adapt to the new realities of the modern world, the Roman Catholic Church generally resisted any departure from tradition until the middle of the twentieth century. Protestant churches tended to be more responsive to the challenges of modernism, particularly in the area of theology. They also vigorously engaged in revivalism and foreign missions. In the East, Orthodoxy saw the rise of national Orthodox churches in countries such as Greece, Bulgaria, and Serbia in the nineteenth century and came into conflict with communist governments in the twentieth.

This chapter surveys the history of Christianity from the beginning of the nineteenth century through the middle years of the twentieth century. After describing the important social, political, economic, and intellectual changes that shaped modern civilization, it examines developments in the Catholic, Protestant, and Orthodox traditions. The chapter concludes with an account of the remarkable worldwide expansion of Christianity during the last two centuries.

The Modern World: Social, Political, and Economic Change

Few events heralded the beginning of the modern era more dramatically than the American Revolution (1775–83) and the French Revolution (1789–99). Deriving much of their ideology from the rationalism of the Enlightenment, neither could be described as Christian in character. American democracy had roots in Protestantism — for example, in the Puritan belief that not even kings are above the law — but not all of the American revolutionaries were Christians. Benjamin Franklin, Thomas Jefferson, and Thomas Paine, for example, were deists.

Most of their French counterparts were overtly hostile to Christianity. They devised an alternative "Cult of Reason," replaced Christian holy days with civic holidays, and encouraged the veneration of secular "saints" like Socrates and Marcus Aurelius. French revolutionaries seized church lands, closed monasteries, and executed hundreds of ecclesiastics during the "terror" of the years 1792–94.

This situation changed with the rise to power of Napoleon Bonaparte, France's greatest general, in 1799. When the rulers of other European states attacked France to prevent the revolution from expanding beyond its borders, Napoleon defended his country so ably that he soon found himself the ruler of a French empire that rivaled that of Charlemagne. Though Napoleon is often described as a dictator, many see him as having been a true child of the Enlightenment and the revolution, for he brought an end to feudalism and the old aristocracy and established the principle of equality before the law. In both France and the lands he conquered, Napoleon created "enlightened" institutions and policies meant to centralize political power, rationalize and improve the efficiency of government, and promote the general welfare through education and the codification of laws.

ROMANTICISM AND LIBERALISM

The violence of the French Revolution and the wars fought by Napoleon shocked Europe and left many disenchanted with what seemed to be the effects of the Enlightenment's ideal of uncompromising rationalism. This contributed to a growing reaction against the idea that reason alone should guide human affairs. This reaction, which came to be known as Romanticism, set greater value on feeling, intuition, and the emotions. It also idealized nature and ancient national traditions. Romanticism may also be seen as a reaction against the dehumanizing effects of industrialization and urbanization on European society; the Romantic poet William Blake (1757–1827), for example, described the factories of England as "dark Satanic mills."[1] We can see these new values emerging in the thought of the French philosopher Jean-Jacques Rousseau (1712–78), one of the first Romantics, who praised the virtues of the "noble savage" uncorrupted by civilization and urged a breaking away from society's rigid rules and conventions. British poets like Wordsworth, Byron, Shelley, and Keats also found truth, beauty, and emotional satisfaction in nature, as can be seen in these lines from Wordsworth's *The Tables Turned*:

Books! 'tis a dull and endless strife:
Come, hear the woodland linnet,
How sweet his music! on my life,
There's more of wisdom in it.

And hark! how blithe the throstle sings!
He, too, is no mean preacher:
Come forth into the light of things,
Let Nature be your teacher. . . .

One impulse from the vernal wood
May teach you more of man,
Of moral evil and of good,
Than all the sages can.

American writers also joined the Romantic movement. James Fenimore Cooper (1789–1851)

"The Village Blacksmith"

and Henry Wadsworth Longfellow (1807–82) idealized frontier life and the American Indian. Henry David Thoreau (1817–63) withdrew from society to live in solitude by Walden Pond. In Germany, the composer Richard Wagner (1813–83) wrote operas filled with sentimental national feeling and the beginnings of the extreme nationalism that would become all too common and destructive in the twentieth century. As we will see, Romanticism had a profound effect on late-nineteenth-century Protestant theology, which took great interest in sensing, rather than simply believing in, God's presence.

sense rather than believe

Between 1815 and 1830 European rulers tried desperately to repair the damage that had been done to the idea of monarchy during the French Revolution. But it was too late. Popular enthusiasm for human rights, constitutional government, and democratic institutions was growing, supported by the political philosophy of liberalism. The basis of liberalism was a genuine optimism concerning human beings. Many liberals believed that if people were allowed to think and act without interference, they would be able to create an ideal society. Accordingly, they called for limits on the power of both church and state. Most found Christian belief in the sinfulness of humanity and the revelation of truth in scripture inconsistent with their own ideas about the essential goodness of human beings and the importance of free speech.

liberalism growing

called for limits to church power + state pwr

Nineteenth-century liberals could be quite conservative by current standards. They generally favored limiting suffrage to the upper classes, were willing to support monarchies limited by constitutions, and could be ardently nationalistic. Still, they had great influence. By 1850, liberal movements and revolutions had brought freedom from foreign rule to Greece, Belgium, and Spanish colonies in the Americas. France's Bourbon dynasty, which had been restored after the defeat of Napoleon, was overthrown and replaced by a republic in 1848. In Great Britain the Reform Bill of 1832 marked the beginning of a more liberal era, and a new constitution brought liberal institutions to Spain in 1834. In Italy the forces of liberalism and nationalism led to the unification of the peninsula under King Vic-

tor Emmanuel II in 1861. In 1871 Germany, too, was united, though its militaristic leaders had little interest in liberal ideas.

IMPERIALISM AND INDUSTRIALIZATION

The nineteenth and early twentieth centuries were also an age of imperialism — the practice by which one country establishes political and economic hegemony over others. The most successful of the empire-building states was Great Britain. By 1914 the British Empire included one-fourth of all the land and people of the earth. France, Germany, and other countries joined in the conquest and exploitation of lands outside of Europe. By 1900, roughly 90 percent of Africa was ruled by western states that were also deeply involved in China, the East Indies, and the Middle East. The United States joined other imperial powers by acquiring territories in Latin America, the Pacific, and Asia.

Profit was the primary motive behind imperialism, but it is also clear that ruling an empire boosted the imperialists' national pride. In addition, the notion that they were bestowing on backward peoples the blessings of a superior civilization gave western nations a sense of mission and righteousness. This was given classic expression by the British poet Rudyard Kipling (1865–1936), who wrote of "the white man's burden" to govern and civilize the world's "lesser breeds." For Kipling and his contemporaries, the West had a moral obligation to "tame" other lands and peoples, and this justified its exploitation of them. Enthusiastic imperialists discovered that Christianity could be a helpful tool in achieving their aims and found a mandate for their policies in the Bible. Had not Christ said, "Go therefore and make disciples of all nations"?[2]

Imperialism went hand in hand with industrialization, for colonies and spheres of influence satisfied mechanized industry's appetite for cheap raw materials and served as markets for its finished products. Beginning with inventions such as John Kay's "flying shuttle" (1733) and James Watt's steam engine (1769), the Industrial Revolution was well underway by the early nineteenth century. It soon had effects on western society as profound as those of the political revolutions in America and France. Though industrialization promised improvements in many aspects of human life, it also created instability. Gradually, the old landed aristocracy and peasantry, on which rural society had always been based, were broken down and replaced with a new urban aristocracy of factory owners and financiers and an industrial proletariat — a class of workers ruthlessly exploited by their employers. Poverty, crime, and violence in industrial cities sometimes made life for the working class intolerable. As popular dissatisfaction increased, so did the volatility of European society. In the twentieth century, industrialization brought further change as a new "consumer society" emerged with new values based on the importance of mass-produced goods and the means to obtain them. How to respond to these new social and economic realities became one of the most pressing questions facing the Church.

WORLD WARS AND COMMUNIST REVOLUTIONS

The twentieth century brought additional difficulties. The outbreak of World War I in 1914 led to four years of conflict in which more than ten million people lost their lives. Trench warfare and technologies such as poison gas, tanks, and the machine gun made war far more brutal than anyone could have imagined a decade earlier.

The triumph of the Allies (Great Britain, France, Russia, Italy, and the United States) was a triumph for liberal democracy. But even in the midst of the war, events in Russia were setting the stage for alarming developments that would threaten stability once again, for in 1917 Russia's tsarist government was toppled by Bolshevik revolutionaries whose goal was the creation of a communist society. For the next seventy years, the social and political ideology of Russia, now transformed into the Soviet Union, would create conflict with the West.

This situation was made even more dangerous by the rise of fascist governments in Italy (1922) and Germany (1933).[3] Eager to centralize power under the control of a single ruling party, fascists despised liberalism and its ideal of limited govern-

ment. Fascists set the state above the individual, encouraged passionate nationalism, and pursued their goals using militarism and ruthless suppression of opposition groups. German fascism assumed an especially virulent form in Adolf Hitler's National Socialist (Nazi) party. When World War II broke out in 1939, Germany was joined by fascist Italy and a newly industrialized and militant Japan. Their eventual defeat by Great Britain, France, the Soviet Union, and the United States came at the staggering cost of thirty to fifty million lives. The ugliness of the war was magnified by nuclear weapons and the German extermination of Jews, communists, homosexuals, and other "undesirables." The Holocaust, or genocide perpetrated by the Nazis against Jews, resulted in the deaths of more than six million Jews and threatened the very existence of European Judaism. Many scholars regard centuries of Christian hostility toward Jews and Judaism as a factor that contributed to this tragedy.

Because of these horrors, the end of World War II brought rejoicing tempered by alarm and anxiety. The Soviet Union's postwar policy of establishing communist governments in eastern Europe also caused apprehension. The creation of the People's Republic of China in 1949 made the communist bloc an even more formidable force in world affairs. For the next four decades a cold war characterized by mutual suspicion, a massive arms race, and political and military intrigues divided the world into two hostile camps led by the United States and the Soviet Union. Always at odds, they often seemed on the verge of a conflict that had the potential to destroy much of world civilization.

The Modern World: Intellectual Change

The great social, political, and economic developments of the nineteenth and early twentieth centuries were accompanied by new currents of thought in science, philosophy, and biblical studies. Many of these directly affected Christians and their churches, for they challenged fundamental assumptions about God, nature, the origin and nature of human beings, the function of religion, and the place of the Church in society.

THE NATURAL SCIENCES

In the nineteenth century, researchers in the natural sciences began to make astonishing progress in gaining an understanding of the physical world. Their successes lent great prestige to science, which was increasingly seen, along with rationalism and liberalism, as one of the keys to lifting human society to new heights of happiness and security.

Some of the most important scientific developments concerned the very essence of nature. After proving the existence of the atom in the early 1800s, scientists were surprised to find that some atoms can change spontaneously into other elements. In the 1920s, the theory of quantum mechanics showed that the behavior of subatomic particles is not entirely predictable. Such discoveries challenged the traditional view of the universe, according to which it is a regular and reliable system whose basic components are stable and move in accordance with unchanging laws established by God.

Other assumptions about the nature of reality were overturned by Albert Einstein (1879–1950). According to his theory of relativity (1905), space and time are not absolutes, but instead are relative to each other and to the observer. In addition to revolutionizing physics, this stunning discovery raised questions in philosophy and theology—for if these basic aspects of material reality are relative, it seems possible that "higher" truths, including those revealed in scripture, might be relative as well.

There were equally startling discoveries in geology and biology. In the early 1830s the British scholar Charles Lyell showed how fossils demonstrate the continuing development of both the earth and its life forms. Three decades later the belief that the earth and its inhabitants had remained virtually unchanged since creation was dealt a far more serious blow by Charles Darwin (1809–82). In his *On the Origin of Species* (1859) and *The Descent of Man* (1871), Darwin argued that plants and animals, including human beings, have evolved from simpler to more complex forms through a process of natural selection that allows the survival only of those species that are most successful in adapting to their environments. His description of a gradual and mechanistic evolution of life clearly contradicted the idea of a divine act of creation lasting six days. Moreover, by associating human beings with other species, Darwin challenged the biblical notion that we are set apart from and above all other living things.

Darwin's theory found enthusiastic supporters, some of whom were eager to use it in assaults on religion. The British biologist Thomas Huxley (1825–95), who liked to call himself "Darwin's bulldog," praised Darwin for explaining the origins and diversity of living things in a way that could be verified through the observation of nature and without reference to an unseen God. Huxley also argued that Christianity should be abandoned because of uncertainty about the existence of God and the teachings of Jesus.[4] Emboldened by Darwin's discoveries, the German biologist Ernst Haeckel (1834–1919) announced that scientists would soon solve all of nature's mysteries and even learn how to create life itself. Religion had no real value, said Haeckel, because even its most basic premises, such as the existence of God and the immortality of the soul, could not be proved.

Developments in medical science also presented challenges to Christianity. The discovery of harmful germs, for example, made it more reasonable to understand disease as the result of contagion rather than divine action. Similarly, new methods for controlling disease-causing microbes suggested that immunization and antiseptics were more important than prayer in warding off infection.

THE SOCIAL SCIENCES

Advances in the natural sciences led to the application of scientific principles in attempts to understand society and the human mind. The result was the emergence of sociology, anthropology, and psychology as social sciences that presented their own challenges to traditional religious beliefs.

Sociology began with Auguste Comte (1798–1857), a French scholar who suggested that human society is a part of nature and therefore subject to natural laws. According to Comte, human beings have already evolved through two great stages of historical development. In the first, people looked to the supernatural realm to explain natural phenomena. In the second, they pointed to abstract metaphysical principles behind natural events. Humanity is about to enter its third and highest stage, he said, in which the truth about society and all other aspects of nature will be explained exclusively by the scientific analysis of observable facts.[5] Comte presented these ideas in his *Positive Philosophy* (1832–40), in which he advocated positivism, the philosophical doctrine that all genuine knowledge comes from science.

One of Comte's followers was Herbert Spencer (1820–1903), an English scholar who coined the phrase *survival of the fittest* and devised the theory of "social Darwinism." Like Comte, Spencer believed that society moves through great evolutionary stages. As it does, he said, the "unfit" are gradually eliminated and the survival of those who are more adaptable to change ensures the steady improvement of the human species.[6] Spencer had little regard for religion in general and Christianity in particular. He complained that religious faith slowed the evolutionary process. In his view, the Christian ideals of love for one's neighbor and the equality of all people in God's eyes are inimical to the conflict that promotes the advancement of human society.

The theories of later sociologists tended to be less grand in scope, though they continued to understand religion as a function of society rather than as a higher, revealed truth. The great French scholar Émile Durkheim (1858–1917), for example, saw religion as the primary means by which society suppresses individual egoism in order to promote social order and harmony.

Like sociologists, anthropologists who studied the remains of ancient cultures found that religion had always played an important role in human society. Most argued that modern religion is based on primitive superstition. Perhaps the best example of this trend is the British scholar Sir James Frazer, who presented an immense study of ancient religious rites and the psychology of primitive peoples in *The Golden Bough* (1890–1915). Frazer concluded that

human beings have passed through stages of evolution that have led them from magical and religious thought to a more advanced and scientific understanding of themselves and the universe.

Modern psychology began in the late nineteenth century with scientists like Wilhelm Wundt (1832–1920) of Germany and the Russian Ivan Pavlov (1849–1936). Assuming that the results of experiments performed on animals would hold true for human beings as well (an attitude that would have made little sense before Darwin), they discovered that much of human behavior consists of unconscious responses to the environment.

The idea that many causes of human behavior lie outside the conscious mind was also popularized by Sigmund Freud (1856–1939), whose theories had an incalculable influence on twentieth-century culture. Freud believed that our thoughts and actions are conditioned as much by instincts, suppressed memories and desires, and biological drives as by reason and knowledge. Ultimately, he said, much of human behavior is irrational and mysterious. This view of humanity surprised a world that had grown accustomed to the Enlightenment's view of human beings as essentially rational. To many, Freud's explanation of the origin of religion was equally shocking. Religion, he said, is a universal neurosis grounded in the human tendency to "externalize" feelings about one's father into the form of a greatly magnified fatherly image: God. Like human fathers, God commands us to do his will, but he also comforts and sustains us in times of trouble and anxiety. Many of Freud's critics claimed that his theories about religion were more speculative than scientific, but Freud was not alone in suggesting that religion arises primarily from psychological needs and processes. Other theorists joined him in describing religion as a means of finding the psychological assurances and satisfaction that people crave, especially when the world begins to threaten their security.

PHILOSOPHY

Developments in the natural and social sciences were accompanied by new philosophical ideas that had important implications for religion as well as for politics and society.

A generation after Immanuel Kant had argued that reason can never tell us about God or the realities behind ordinary experience, another German philosopher, Georg Wilhelm Hegel (1770–1831), claimed that there is a great deal we can know about both. A philosophical idealist, Hegel believed that reality is ultimately spiritual. His optimism was based on his belief that God, whom he preferred to describe as Spirit, Reason, or Absolute Mind, is not *other* than the world, as Christianity had always held, but the fundamental reality of which all of nature, including ourselves, is a manifestation. For Hegel, this meant that all activity is activity of the Spirit and that rational thought is really nothing other than the Spirit seeking to understand itself. Hegel, who was preoccupied by the number three, went on to say that the Spirit moves toward self-realization and fulfillment in a process of triadic development called "dialectic." Any given system, situation, civilization, or idea (thesis), he said, is challenged by its opposite (antithesis), after which the two are reconciled on a higher plane in a synthesis that contains the best features of both. The synthesis then becomes a new thesis and the process begins again. Hegel found evidence of such dialectical development everywhere. Thus, he regarded history as a process of purposeful evolution in which conflict brings progress and will ultimately lead to the realization of the ideal state. He also saw a dialectical pattern in religion. In the Christian doctrine of the incarnation, for example, the opposites of divinity and humanity are reconciled and united in Christ. Though Hegel described Christianity as the culmination of all religions, he left no doubt about his conviction that philosophy, which expresses truth in clear concepts, is superior to religion, which relies on images and analogies.

Later philosophers who were influenced by Hegel were much less sympathetic to religion. Hegel had said that human beings are manifestations of God; Ludwig Feuerbach (1804–72) argued that God is an invention of human beings. "Theology is anthropology," he claimed in his *Lectures on the Essence of Religion.* "Man's God is nothing other than the deified essence of man."[7] Feuerbach urged people to abandon their beliefs about God and to realize that when they speak about such things as God's mercy, justice, and love they are really describing their own ideals.

In his book *The World as Will and Idea,* Feuerbach's contemporary Arthur Schopenhauer (1788–1860) argued that the pretty pictures people create of an orderly world guided by a rational God disguise a horrible truth: the ultimate reality is not God but a great, all-consuming, purposeless, and irrational will. Life is evil, said Schopenhauer, because we are constantly tormented by unfulfilled desires. The best we can hope for is the destruction of our own will and, ultimately, death.

Friedrich Nietzsche (1844–1900), one of Schopenhauer's students, claimed that the will to power is the highest ideal. In his *Thus Spake Zarathustra,* he proclaimed the death of God and ridiculed Christianity and democracy as moral systems for the weak and degenerate. Nietzsche's hero was the *Übermensch,* or "superman," whose daring and ruthless quest for power gives him the right to rule others and is the noblest expression of the human spirit. "War and courage," he wrote, "have accomplished more great things than love of neighbor."[8] Nietzsche's "might makes right" philosophy contributed significantly to the growth of German nationalism and foreshadowed the development of Nazi ideology.

These three thinkers were overshadowed by Karl Marx (1818–83), whose thought inspired communist revolutions in Russia and China in the twentieth century. Like Hegel, Marx believed that history is a dialectical process, but he rejected Hegel's idealism. Marx was a materialist who believed that absolute reality is matter. He argued that the progress of human society toward its ultimate goal—a classless, communist society—is driven by social and economic forces completely grounded in material reality, and that the institution of private property alienates people from each other by encouraging them to work for themselves rather than for the common good. Religion, he said, is the "opiate of the masses"—helps people deal with the painful and dehumanizing effects of alienation, but it also makes the human condition worse by encouraging people to put their faith in an imaginary God. Marx (like Feuerbach) believed that God is nothing but a projection of human ideals, and that people should put their faith in their own ability to improve their circumstances.

These thinkers illustrate new values and directions that became standard in western philosophy in the nineteenth century. Whereas philosophers had once joined with theologians in tackling metaphysical questions and accepted much of what they found in scripture and doctrine, they were now increasingly unwilling to assume that faith had real value in the quest for truth.

HISTORY AND BIBLICAL CRITICISM

The interest of thinkers like Hegel and Marx in the evolution of human society was related to a growing fascination with history and attempts by historians to discern history's ultimate meaning and the laws behind its development. Much of the history written in earlier years had been uncritical of its sources, often failing to distinguish between fact and legend. Now new standards were put into place, thanks largely to the work of German historians, who strove to make history a scientific discipline. Leopold von Ranke (1795–1886) in particular insisted that historians should base their work on a careful analysis of all available evidence and treat their subject with the same cold objectivity expected of physicists and chemists.

The new developments in history and philosophy had a profound impact on scholars specializing in biblical studies and the history of Christianity. Many of these scholars now sought to approach their subjects without faith-based presuppositions and showed the influence of liberalism and contemporary thought about evolution and progress through conflict.

His reading of the Old Testament convinced the German scholar Julius Wellhausen (1844–1910) that the religion of ancient Israel had evolved from primitive, nomadic beginnings to the formal Judaism practiced at the time of Jesus. Wellhausen's hypothesis that the Pentateuch is the work not of Moses, as tradition holds, but of anonymous authors living at different times and representing different social, political, and religious interests revolutionized Old Testament studies.

New Testament scholars devoted much of their energy to discovering the "historical Jesus," the figure who emerges from the objective evaluation of historical data rather than from religious doctrine. Although they generally took a critical view of New Testament claims concerning the sayings, miracles, and divinity of Jesus, these scholars were often less than objective in allowing their own ideas to shape their pictures of him. Many of their studies described a Jesus who preached the same liberal values and ideals that they embraced. In 1835 David Strauss, a Lutheran theologian from Germany, published a *Life of Jesus* in which he argued that the supernatural and messianic claims made about him in the Gospels had less to do with Jesus himself than with early Christian beliefs. Strauss also questioned the historical reliability of the New Testament, noting that the authorship of the Gospels was uncertain, as were the Gospels' accounts of the virgin birth, resurrection, and post-resurrection appearances of Jesus. In his own *Life of Jesus,* the French scholar Ernest Renan (1823–92) argued for the historical value of the New Testament but left no room for the supernatural in his presentation of Jesus as a charming and enlightened Galilean teacher who preached a message of love. These and similar works described Jesus as the great exemplar of all that is good in humanity rather than as the incarnate Son of God.

In the study of church history, the influence of Hegel was particularly evident in the work of Ferdinand Baur (1792–1860). Baur saw a great struggle in early Christianity between the Jewish Christianity represented by Peter, in which the Law of Moses played a central role, and the more universal Christianity of Paul. According to Baur, the conflict between the Petrine thesis and Pauline antithesis led to a higher synthesis in the catholic Christianity of the second century. Baur made evidence of awareness of this conflict an important criterion in judging the authenticity of the books of the New Testament, accepting only those that seemed to have been written in its midst. As a result, he dismissed much of the New Testament, including all but four of the letters traditionally ascribed to Paul, as the work of later authors.[9]

More influential even than Baur was Adolf von Harnack, a professor at the University of Berlin whose massive *History of Dogma* (1886–89) was one of the most influential achievements of nineteenth-century scholarship.[10] Harnack believed that the development of Christian dogma involved the gradual abandonment of the original teachings of Jesus, who had made the Kingdom of God, God as Father, the infinite value of every human soul, and God's commandments concerning righteousness and love the central features of his message. As Christianity became increasingly Greek in its language and outlook, he said, it focused less on the teachings of Jesus and more on Jesus himself. Harnack called upon his fellow Protestants to return to "original" Christianity, as he understood it, and complained that the Eastern Orthodox and Roman Catholic traditions had nearly forgotten it altogether.

Another important feature of this period was the emergence in Germany of the History of Religions School, a group of scholars who questioned the uniqueness of Christianity by studying it in connection with other religions. The idea of evolution, and Hegelian philosophy in particular, had a great impact on their work, as did the historical methods worked out by Ranke and other historians. Flourishing between 1880 and 1920, the school's greatest representatives—scholars like Hermann Gunkel, H. Gressmann, and J. F. W. Bousset—devoted their careers to demonstrating the influence of both older religions (Babylonian, Egyptian, and Greek, as well as Judaism) and contemporary religious (gnosticism and mystery religions) on early Christianity.

The Roman Catholic Church in the Modern World

How did the Roman Catholic Church respond to the challenges presented by revolution, economic and social change, and new intellectual trends? Though many Catholics believed it was imperative to respond affirmatively to the new realities of the modern world, tradition exercised a powerful hold on the Roman Catholic Church. Throughout the nineteenth and early twentieth centuries, its attitude was largely defensive. Church leaders often condemned new ideas and movements already accepted by most people, including many Catholics, with the result that Catholicism came to be seen as increasingly alien to popular culture and its values. It was not until Vatican II, a council that met between 1962 and 1965, that the leadership of the Roman Catholic Church began to show real interest in adapting to the modern world.

NAPOLEON AND THE CHURCH

An early challenge came from Napoleon. Napoleon rescued the Roman Catholic Church from a revolution that had sought to dechristianize France, but he kept it firmly under his control. In a concordat negotiated with Rome (1801), he agreed to return church lands confiscated during the revolution, but in turn he required the pope to install as bishops only candidates nominated by the state and to acknowledge the state's right to reject appointments to the lower clergy made by bishops. In addition, all priests and bishops were to be paid from the public treasury. Over the objections of Pope Pius VII (1800–1823), Napoleon also issued the Organic Articles of 1802, which prohibited the publication of papal decrees and the organization of synods in France without governmental permission.

Napoleon made his most striking statement concerning the relationship of church and state at his coronation as emperor in 1804. In a carefully orchestrated ceremony that reversed the symbolism of Charlemagne's coronation by Leo III a thousand years earlier, Napoleon crowned himself—denying to Pius VII, who stood nearby, the opportunity to suggest that the Church had any authority over him.[11] Later, when Pius refused to take Napoleon's side in his war against England, the emperor invaded Italy, seized Rome, and annexed the Papal States to the French Empire. It was not until after the fall of Napoleon in 1815 that these and other lands were restored to the papacy.

Overall, Napoleon's policies encouraged the secularization of society by replacing Christian values, institutions, and authorities with religiously neutral ones more representative of the state than of the Church. Marriage and divorce became civil procedures. Responsibility for education was taken over by the state, which promoted its own interests and ideals in the schools. The guarantee of religious freedom for Protestants implied that the Catholic Church was only one of many legitimate churches, at least in the eyes of the state.

Even outside of France the effects of Enlightenment ideals and Napoleonic reforms were widely visible. In early-nineteenth-century Germany, for example, ecclesiastical territories that had been administered by bishops since medieval times began to disappear. Clergy were made employees of the state, which also assumed primary responsibility for their education. In addition, the resignation of the imperial title by Francis II in 1806 brought an end to the Holy Roman Empire. Though it had long been of little political significance, the empire had at least stood as a symbol of the old dream of a united Christendom.

Despite the many adverse effects of the French Revolution and Napoleonic rule, there were some ways in which the Church benefited. In heroically resisting the bullying tactics of Napoleon, who held him prisoner for nearly six years in France, Pius VII won sympathy and prestige for the papacy.[12] More important, the collapse of European monarchies that began in France brought an end to the ties that had once directed the loyalties of bishops to the kings who appointed them. The demise of feudalism also changed the position of bishops and other ecclesiastics in society by gradually stripping them of the lands, privileges, and other rewards associated with their offices. For centuries they had found influence and security in a system that bound them to secular rulers as well as to the Church. Now that that system was beginning to crumble, they turned increasingly to Rome for guidance and protection against states that seemed intent on usurping their traditional rights and prerogatives.

THE NINETEENTH CENTURY

The trend toward looking to the papacy for leadership is known as **Ultramontanism**— an orientation toward Rome, which lies "beyond the mountains" that separate Italy from the rest of Europe. It was one of the most visible features of a resurgence of Catholicism that accompanied the fall of Napoleon in 1815.

The beginnings of this revival can be seen as early as 1802 with the publication of François René Chateaubriand's *The Genius of Christianity,* a prime example of literary Romanticism. Disillusioned with rationalism, Chateaubriand called for a return to mystical religion and praised Christianity for shaping western civilization and inspiring its greatest cultural achievements. Other writers and intellectuals joined him in abandoning absolute rationalism, which seemed to deny the value of faith, mystery, and the wisdom embodied in ancient cultural and religious traditions, in favor of Romanticism. Many returned or converted to the Catholic faith.[13] Other signs of renewal included the appearance of new religious societies, such as the Society of the Sacred Heart of Jesus, a women's congregation devoted to education, and the increased activity of missionary organizations.

Ultramontanism reached its peak under Pius IX (1846–78), whose pontificate saw the end of the papacy's temporal power but an increase in its spiritual authority. Pius's reign had barely begun when the Revolution of 1848, which had sparked liberal revolts in France and central Europe, came to Italy as well. In 1849 the creation of the Republic of Rome and the threats of angry revolutionaries surrounding the papal palace forced Pius to flee the city disguised as an ordinary priest. Although he was able to return the following year, the crisis foreshadowed more serious events still to come. Between 1860 and 1870, as the forces of liberalism and nationalism combined to forge the new kingdom of Italy, virtually all the lands of the Papal States were lost. Under the kingdom's Law of Guarantees (1871), which the papacy never recognized, the pope would retain possession only of the Vatican, the Lateran Palace, and the papal villa at Castel Gandolfo.

Even as he helplessly witnessed the end of his temporal power, Pius took actions meant to build his spiritual authority. In 1854 he proclaimed the dogma of the immaculate conception of the Virgin Mary, according to which a miracle at the moment of her conception left Mary untainted by original sin. The idea of the immaculate conception had been popular since the medieval era, but in declaring it as dogma on his own authority (that is, without consulting a church council) Pius had done something new.

In 1864 Pius took another important step by sponsoring the publication of a *Syllabus of Errors,* eighty false propositions that Catholics were urged to reject. These included absolute rationalism, the separation of church and state, public education, civil marriage, religious pluralism, socialism, and communism. The *Syllabus* concluded with a repudiation of the proposition "that the Roman Pontiff can and ought to reconcile himself to, and agree with, progress, liberalism, and modern civilization."14

Even though it was in many ways a reactionary statement, the *Syllabus's* condemnations were not always categorical and have often been misunderstood. It rejected capitalism, for example, only when its sole objective was material wealth. It found fault with public education only when "public" implied the exclusion of the "moderating influence" of the Church. The assertion that the pope was not required to accept modern civilization is less startling when considered in its original context, an earlier document written to protest the destruction of convents and persecution of priests by radicals in northern Italy. That text included the qualification that "civilization" can sometimes mean "a system invented . . . to weaken, and perhaps to overthrow, the Church."15

The culmination of Pius's reign came at the First Vatican Council (1869–70). The most sensational result of **Vatican I** was the doctrine of **papal infallibility**, according to which the pope cannot err when he speaks *ex cathedra* (that is, in his official capacity as "pastor and teacher of all Christians") in defining doctrines concerning faith and morals. The promulgation of papal infallibility brought an end to challenges against papal supremacy that had

persisted ever since the Council of Constance (1415) at the height of conciliar movement. Although the doctrine conferred great authority on the pope, it has been invoked only once. In 1950 Pius XII appealed to it when proclaiming the dogma of the assumption of the Virgin Mary, which stated that at the end of her earthly life Mary was taken bodily into heaven.

Pius IX had won recognition of the primacy and infallibility of the papacy, but he was still the leader of an embattled Church. Some of his policies served only to worsen conditions for Catholics. By forbidding them to become involved in the politics of the kingdom of Italy, for example, Pius unwittingly strengthened the voice in government of anti-Catholic radicals and socialists. In other cases he lacked the political influence necessary to defend the Church.

This was especially true in Germany during the years 1872–78, when Chancellor Otto von Bismarck, an ardent nationalist who had engineered the unification of his country, launched an assault on Catholicism known as the ***Kulturkampf*** ("struggle for civilization"). Bismarck saw the Catholic Church as a competitor with the state for the allegiance of the German people. He was outraged that the loyalties of millions of German Catholics were divided, as he saw it, between their own country and an Italian pope. At his direction, diplomatic relations between Germany and the Vatican were severed, the Jesuits and other religious orders were expelled, civil marriage was made mandatory, and education was so thoroughly secularized that even candidates for the priesthood were required to study in public universities and pass examinations in literature, history, and philosophy as well as theology. In the end, however, Bismarck's *Kulturkampf* was a failure. Once he recognized the depth of Catholicism's roots and realized that the support of Catholic politicians would be indispensable in his struggle against socialism, a far greater enemy, he arranged for the repeal of his most severe anti-Catholic legislation.

Pope Leo XIII (1878–1903) shared Pius IX's understanding of papal authority and respect for tradition but was more willing to find ways to adapt to the modern world. Thus, while he promoted the medieval theology of Thomas Aquinas and remained concerned about the errors of Protestantism,[16] Leo also gave cautious encouragement to scholars employing new methods in biblical scholarship, was more open to new developments in science, and declared that moderate democracy and Catholicism were compatible. His position on the latter issue was particularly significant in relation to France, where the liberal leaders of the Third Republic, established in 1870, had adopted harshly anticlerical policies and created a system of public schools in which the teaching of religion was forbidden. Despite this, Leo sought conciliation rather than conflict by urging the French clergy to support the government.

In his famous encyclical *Rerum novarum* ("Of New Things"), published in 1891, Leo demonstrated his awareness of the gross inequities created by capitalism and industrialization and outlined the principles by which social justice might be achieved. Against socialism, *Rerum novarum* rejected the inevitability of class warfare and affirmed that the possession of private property "is a right given to man by nature," though it should not be abused.[17] At the same time, it challenged economic liberalism, a theory much beloved by industrial capitalists because it held that the "natural laws" of economics will ensure stability and prosperity for all if not impeded by "unnatural" interference from government regulations and collective bargaining.[18] Thus, *Rerum novarum* declared that natural law gives workers the right to a living wage, argued that trade unions are as natural and necessary as states,[19] and insisted that governments must become involved in markets when the spiritual and material welfare of workers is endangered. Leo XIII's call for the formation of associations dedicated to protecting the interests of Catholics led to the creation of numerous groups in Europe and the United States, including Catholic labor unions that challenged socialist-dominated unions. These formed the basis of Catholic Action, a network of social, political, and charitable organizations that represented Catholics well into the twentieth century.

THE EARLY TWENTIETH CENTURY

The first years of the reign of Pius X (1903–14) were complicated by the continuing struggle between the Roman Catholic Church and the government of France. Tension mounted as anticlerical laws passed in 1901 and 1903 restricted the right of priests to engage in education and in some cases allowed the confiscation of properties belonging to monasteries and convents. Several thousand Catholic schools were closed during the same period. An end to diplomatic relations between France and the Vatican came in 1904, followed by a French declaration of the separation of church and state in 1905. As a result of the latter action, all French churches were made public property. To worship in the buildings to which they were accustomed, parishioners were required to form civil associations (the Roman Catholic Church itself had lost its legal standing) eligible to rent them from the government.

A second issue that arose during Pius's reign left no doubt about his conservatism. This concerned the attraction of Catholic "modernists" like George Tyrell (1861–1909) of Britain, Alfred Loisy (1857–1940) of France, and the German Hermann Schell (1850–1906) to the new trends in philosophy, history, and biblical studies. Modernists hoped to bring Catholic thought in line with contemporary intellectual developments. In 1907 Pius acted decisively to limit the influence of modernism in the Church by officially condemning it in two decrees.[20] As a result, priests were required to take antimodernist oaths, bishops were ordered to remove the "modernist infection" from the ranks of their clergy, books were banned, and most of the modernists themselves left the Church, whether voluntarily or by excommunication.

The Church was led through the difficult years of the First World War (1914–18) by Benedict XV (1914–22), who denounced the conflict as the "darkest tragedy of human hatred and human madness" but was himself condemned by both sides for refusing to abandon his position of neutrality.[21] His successor, Pius XI (1922–39), had to contend with the growth of belligerent fascist movements in the aftermath of the war. The first such movement to achieve real success was led by Benito Mussolini (1883–1945), who seized power in Italy in 1922. Although Mussolini was no friend of the Church, he understood the importance of maintaining good relations with the religious institution to which most Italians belonged. For this reason, he approved the Lateran Concordat and Treaty of 1929, which gave the Vatican formal recognition as a sovereign state, thus ending the uncertainty about its status that had existed since 1870. Mussolini also restored many of the privileges that the Catholic Church had enjoyed in Italy before unification, especially in the area of education.[22] In return, Pius agreed to give up claims to papal territories lost during the unification of Italy (1860–70), stay out of Italian politics, and make the appointment of Italian bishops conditional upon their approval by the state. Relations between the pope and the dictator fell apart, however, when Mussolini began to assert state control over church schools and absorb Catholic youth groups into the fascist system.

In Germany, the rise to power of Adolf Hitler and the Nazi party (1933) also presented serious problems for the Roman Catholic Church, whose clergy, schools, and presses came under increasing pressure to conform to Nazi ideology. In 1937 Pius responded with the encyclical *Mit brennender Sorge* ("With Burning Anxiety"), which was smuggled into Germany and read from Catholic pulpits on Palm Sunday of that year. The letter condemned the persecution of Christians, denounced Nazi ideas about race and authority, and described Hitler as a "mad prophet possessed of repulsive arrogance."[23] Infuriated, Hitler responded with reprisals intended to tarnish the Church's image and intimidate its clergy.

Even as it sought to cope with the rise of fascism, Catholicism under Pius XI enjoyed a revival evidenced by the increased activity of its educational and charitable institutions, the creation of new episcopal sees and youth organizations, and the work of theologians such as Jacques Maritain (1882–1973) and Etienne Gilson (1884–1978), who sought to demonstrate the relevance of Thomas Aquinas's theology to modern culture. Pius expressed the Church's commitment to social justice in his encyclical *Quadragesimo anno* (1931), published, as

its name indicates, on the fortieth anniversary of Leo XIII's *Rerum novarum*. By affirming Leo's message and calling for a society more in line with principles found in the gospel, Pius demonstrated the Church's continuing interest in the material and spiritual welfare of ordinary men and women.

Pius XII (1939–1958), who became pope on the eve of the Second World War, has often been criticized for maintaining a neutral stance during the conflict and not doing more to stop Nazi atrocities against Jews, Slavs, and other groups. His defenders claim that he did much for the Jews and was prevented from taking more direct action only by his fear of further jeopardizing their safety, as well as that of Catholics, in regions controlled by the Germans and their allies. They also point out that his position was complicated by the fact that the Nazis were engaged in a bitter struggle against the communist Soviet Union, which the pope considered an even greater threat to the Church. However, such arguments do not satisfy those who believe that the monstrous evils perpetrated by the Nazis demanded a more forceful response from the Catholic Church. In spite of this very troubling issue, Pius XII is regarded as having been an able, if very conservative, leader. He encouraged the continuing concentration of ecclesiastical power in Rome and fought to limit the expansion of communism, even to the point of declaring it impermissible for Catholics to join a communist party (1949). In his encyclical *Humani generis* (1950) he defended the authority of the Church and sought to promote scholastic theology—and especially the thought of Thomas Aquinas.

CATHOLIC THEOLOGY IN THE EARLY TWENTIETH CENTURY

In the first part of the twentieth century some Catholic theologians began to think in new ways about the connections between history, evolution, and Christianity.

One of the most innovative thinkers was Pierre Teilhard de Chardin (1881–1955), a distinguished paleontologist and theologian who was concerned with harmonizing Christianity and science. Teilhard accepted the idea of evolution, but he disagreed with Darwin's view that evolution is based on natural selection. Instead, he argued in *The Phenomenon of Man* that the universe evolves through ever-higher states of complexity and consciousness under the attraction of the "Omega," which is its goal. The Omega, said Teilhard, is none other than Christ, in whom all things will ultimately achieve a final spiritual unity. It was a grand and daring theory, but it left no room for concepts central to traditional Christian thought — such as a fall from perfection, and redemption made possible by the sacrificial death of Christ. As a result, the Church suppressed Teilhard's religious and theological works, which did not become widely known until after his death in 1955.[24]

Other theologians focused on the relationship between faith and history. They raised the possibility that dogmas proclaimed by councils and popes over the course of two thousand years should not be understood as perfect expressions of truth good for all time, as had always been assumed, but as formulas conditioned by historical and cultural change. Such thought arose from the new interest in history, which we have already described, and reflected the fact that amidst the wars and cultural upheavals of the early twentieth century it had become difficult to find *anything* permanent or truly reliable.

One of the most important Catholic thinkers associated with this new direction in theology was Yves Congar (1904–95), a French Dominican. Congar argued that the Church had sometimes defined its doctrines too narrowly, formulating them in relation to the social and intellectual conditions that existed only in particular historical situations. For this reason, he said, they must be "reappropriated" by understanding them within a larger context and in relation to scripture and tradition. Other theologians proposed that historical change makes it impossible for any generation to express the Christian faith in terms adequate for those to come.[25] Some suggested that this is true in part because revelation is not limited to truths communicated at particular moments long ago but is a continuing process in which God discloses himself to individuals within their own historical situations.

The most influential Catholic theologian of the twentieth century was the German Jesuit **Karl Rahner** (1904–84). A rigorously orthodox thinker, he also believed that Christians of every era must rediscover the meanings behind the doctrines of the Church. In more than three thousand books, articles, and essays (including twenty-three volumes of his *Theological Investigations*), Rahner asserted both the value of tradition and the importance of determining its relevance for the modern world. He based much of his theology on the idea that mystery — far from being limited to the experiences of a handful of mystics — is at the heart of everyday life. Mystery, which pervades all things, is ultimately the mystery of God, so all of our thought about ourselves and the world is essentially theological, whether we know it or not.

Rahner focused much of his thought on the Church. He emphasized the importance of the collegiality of bishops, who, though they must recognize the primacy of the pope, must also have the freedom to meet the special needs of the cultures in which they live and work. He also stressed the operation of grace outside the Church. Because all human existence is rooted in the absolute being of God, he said, all people are the objects of God's grace. It follows that there are "anonymous Christians" outside the Church who manifest God's love even though they do not affirm the specific doctrines of the faith.

Taken together, the work of these theologians had a considerable impact on Catholic thought, even at the highest levels. Their argument that expressions of the Christian faith must change as the world itself changes was clearly felt in the early 1960s at the Second Vatican Council. At Vatican II the bishops recognized the modern view that reality is dynamic and evolutionary rather than static. Even more important was the acknowledgment by Pope John XXIII, in his opening address, that "the substance of the ancient doctrine is one thing and the way in which it is presented is another."[26]

JOHN XXIII AND THE SECOND VATICAN COUNCIL (1962–65)

Few would have guessed at the accession of John XXIII (1958–63) that the new pope, then seventy-seven, was about to initiate great changes in the Catholic Church. The son of poor tenant farmers from northern Italy, he quickly won the affection of Catholics and non-Catholics alike with his wit, humility, and genial nature. His diplomatic assignments in Bulgaria, Turkey, Germany, and France in the early years of his career had exposed him to Orthodoxy, Islam, and world-changing events, apparently with the effect of broadening his views and forging his conviction that the Church must take decisive steps to find its place in the modern age.

This was certainly the thrust of his major encyclicals. In *Mater et Magistra* (1961) he reaffirmed the social teaching of Leo XIII and Pius XI, adding that workers should share in the ownership of the businesses that employ them and that developed countries have a responsibility to share the benefits of their technology with less developed ones. In *Pacem in Terris* (1963) he declared that "all men are equal in their natural dignity," called for an end to colonialism and the arms race, and argued for improvements in the position of women in society. In urging Catholics to work with men and women of other faiths in promoting the general welfare, John demonstrated a more open attitude to non-Catholics than his predecessors had shown.

By far the most important event of John XXIII's reign was the Second Vatican Council. Commonly known as **Vatican II**, it met between 1962 and 1965 and was attended by bishops from all over the world. More than 40 percent were from Africa, Asia, and Latin America. Observers from other churches were also invited. The council's purpose was to explain the traditional faith of the Catholic Church in terms more meaningful to modern men and women, update features of its organization and practices, and move toward Christian unity. Although John died soon after Vatican II was convened, his successor, Paul VI (1963–78), ensured its success by encouraging the bishops to "build a bridge between the Church and the modern world."

Altogether, Vatican II produced sixteen major documents that included pronouncements on hundreds of issues. In addressing the issue of the world's many religions, the bishops recognized the right of all people to religious freedom, called for mutual understanding between Christians, Jews, and Muslims, and described the "high regard" of the Catholic Church for other faiths, which often reflect "a ray of that truth which enlightens all men." They also acknowledged that the Church's faults had contributed to the disunity of Christians. Important changes were made in worship: the use of modern languages instead of Latin in the liturgy was authorized, and laypeople were allowed greater participation in the mass. Moving away from the traditional view of the Church as a hierarchy in which the clergy ruled the laity, the council emphasized the equality of the faithful and their common mission in preaching and living the gospel. It also endorsed the use of historical-critical methods in the study of scripture and church history.

Although Vatican II was revolutionary in some respects, it left many traditional ideas and institutions unchallenged. Paul VI disapproved of any language that laid papal primacy open to question, and there was no debate on the fundamental assumption that the Roman Catholic Church is the one true Church. Still, the Second Vatican Council did make remarkable progress in building the bridge of which Paul VI had spoken.

Protestantism in the Modern World

While the Roman Catholic Church adopted a generally defensive stance in relation to new cultural developments, many Protestant churches and thinkers demonstrated greater interest in coming to terms with secular culture. However, the "bridge-building" of liberal Protestants sometimes brought reactions from conservatives, who feared that accommodating Christianity to the modern world would mean surrendering essential features of the faith.

NINETEENTH-CENTURY LIBERAL THEOLOGY

Romanticism, which peaked in the first half of the nineteenth century, profoundly affected the Protestant theology of the time. Its influence is especially evident in the thought of **Friedrich Schleiermacher** (1768–1834), a minister who also taught at the University of Berlin. In his twenties, Schleiermacher discovered that his friends, many of whom were writers and intellectuals, believed that religion had been debunked by rationalism and was unworthy of sophisticated people. Their assumption that religion was nothing more than dogmas and practices seemed completely off target to him. A true Romantic, Schleiermacher was convinced that the essence of religion goes much deeper, to a feeling of awe and mystery that reason cannot explain. This was the fundamental idea in his *On Religion: Speeches to Its Cultured Despisers* (1799):

> If, therefore, you have paid attention only to these religious dogmas and opinions, you do not yet know religion itself at all. . . . Why haven't you gone deeper to find the kernal lying inside these outer layers? . . . Why don't you look at religious life itself? Look especially at those extraordinary moments when a person's spirit is so caught up in the highest reaches of piety that all other activities known to you are restrained, . . . moments in which one's feeling is wholly absorbed in an immediate sense of the infinite and eternal and of its fellowship with the soul. . . . Only a person who has both observed and truly comes to know men through these inner spiritual states . . . is in a position to discover religion.[27]

Schleiermacher described the essence of true religion as a deeply felt awareness of absolute dependence upon God, the source of all existence. People everywhere share in this experience, he said, but each culture expresses it in its own unique way, hence the differences among the world's religions. Schleiermacher did think that Christianity is superior to other religions, however. In his view, Jesus Christ can be thought of as divine because he experienced God-consciousness in such a complete and powerful way that it can be explained only as the result of divine intervention. Moreover, Jesus communicated his pure awareness of God to his disciples, and the Church he founded continues to inspire it in new generations. Through this inspiration Christians are saved from sin—which Schleiermacher described as a state of dis-

traction and corruption that is the opposite of God-consciousness.

Schleiermacher developed these ideas in his book *The Christian Faith*, which he published in the early 1820s. Here he also argued that theology should focus on the meaning and dynamics of religious feeling rather than on doctrines and other external features of religion. Any teaching that does not take as its starting point the feeling of absolute dependence upon God, he said, has nothing to do with theology; theological doctrines have real significance only to the extent that they deal directly with that feeling. The doctrine of creation, for example, is important in that it teaches the absolute dependence of the universe on God. But the *details* of the biblical story of creation, such as the formation of Adam from clay, should not be considered essential to the Christian faith.

Schleiermacher's views upset conservative Christians, who complained that he had gone too far in abandoning tradition. Others criticized him for not going far enough. Still, by describing religion as a deeply felt response to God that is natural in human beings—rather than as a body of doctrines that must be learned and accepted—he had found a way to speak of Christianity that was consistent with Romanticism's ideals and did not involve conflicts with science.

Albrecht Ritschl (1822–89), who taught at the universities of Bonn and Göttingen in Germany, dominated Protestant theology during the second half of the nineteenth century. Adolf von Harnack, his most famous student, acclaimed him as "the last of the church fathers." Ritschl argued that the new scientific approach that historians and biblical scholars were taking to their subjects was essential in understanding the historical Jesus and the nature of the early Church. Like Schleiermacher, he thought that theology should shift its attention away from doctrines and metaphysical speculation. He did not agree, however, with Schleiermacher's emphasis on personal feeling. Ritschl thought that this made for a faith that was too mystical, private, and subjective. In his view, the essence of Christianity was Jesus' teaching about ethics and the Kingdom of God. There is more to Christianity than receiving salvation, he argued. Christians must also work to make the Kingdom of God a reality in society by living out the principle of love modeled by Christ.

The influence of Ritschl, his students, and liberal theology in general was soon felt throughout Europe and the United States. There it combined with humanitarian concerns about conditions caused by industrialization and urbanization to produce Christian movements that considered social responsibility part of the gospel message.

In the United States, the most important of these was the Social Gospel movement. Originating in the work of liberal pastors like Harry Emerson Fosdick (1878–1969) and Washington Gladden (1836–1918), its principles were most clearly set out by Walter Rauschenbusch (1869–1918). A Baptist minister and theologian deeply affected by Ritschl, Rauschenbusch served for eleven years as pastor of a church in Hell's Kitchen, one of New York City's worst slums. His experience in ministering to the needs of his congregation and their neighborhood led him to write *Christianity and the Social Crisis* (1907), in which he spoke of the "kingdom of evil" as one whose power can be broken only by Christians working to establish the Kingdom of God. Rauschenbusch did not deny the importance of personal salvation, but he believed that salvation should also apply to society. "It is not a matter of saving human atoms," he wrote, "but of saving the social organism. It is not a matter of getting individuals to heaven, but of transforming the life on earth into the harmony of heaven."[28]

The Social Gospel movement was especially popular among American Baptists, Methodists, Presbyterians, Congregationalists, and Episcopalians. They launched numerous initiatives against social injustice, supported popular causes such as organized labor's campaign to shorten working hours, and created hundreds of church-sponsored social service agencies.

CRITICS OF LIBERAL CHRISTIANITY

Protestant liberalism did not go unchallenged. To many Christians, liberal Christianity seemed too willing to accommodate itself to society and to forsake doctrines that had for centuries been central to the Christian faith. Others feared that liberal culture, with its belief in the natural goodness of human beings and their inevitable progress toward a better world, encouraged an easy, undemanding Christianity that bore little resemblance to the bolder and more authentic faith of earlier times.

The most forceful statement of this second objection was made by the Danish philosopher **Søren Kierkegaard** (1813–55). A frail and melancholy man, Kierkegaard seemed a failure in his early life — his few personal relationships were unhappy and he failed in his attempt to become a Lutheran pastor. To Kierkegaard, life was not easy, and neither was Christianity. Although nearly all Danes in his day identified themselves as Christians, he believed that few grasped the essence of their religion and that fewer still dared to live it. In his eyes, the teaching of the New Testament had little to do with rationalism, emotion, or conventional ethics. It did not describe Christians as well-intentioned liberals, nor did it offer a grand vision of history, as Hegel had done, that explained how everything makes sense when seen from just the right perspective.

What really mattered to Kierkegaard was the individual and the decision to respond to God *in faith*, even when doing so appears to contradict reason and custom. He found a powerful illustration of this heroic "leap of faith" in the biblical story of Abraham, who was commanded by God to sacrifice his son Isaac (Genesis 22). Abraham might have objected that God was asking him to commit murder or that by sacrificing his son he would be working against the fulfillment of God's earlier promise to make him the father of a great nation (Genesis 12). From Abraham's point of view, the command no doubt seemed irrational, but he responded in faith, willing to accept any outcome and confident that under God's guidance everything would somehow work for the best. As the biblical story relates (God intervened at the last moment), it did.

Because of his pessimism about liberal culture and the fact that he wrote in Danish, Kierkegaard had little impact in the nineteenth century. In the early twentieth century, however, his thought had a profound impact on the growth of **existentialism**, a philosophical and literary movement that set greater importance on individual existence and the self-defining decisions people make in response to their existence than on the intellect and abstract doctrines.

A very different reaction against liberal Christianity took place in England. In the 1830s a group of clerics at Oxford began to suggest that the Church of England had been swayed too much by modern culture. Known as the **Oxford Movement**, their leader was **John Henry Newman** (1801–90). To Newman and his associates, liberal theology seemed disinterested in doctrine and alien to the teachings of the ancient Church, which they regarded as the embodiment of true Christianity. In ninety *Tracts for the Times,* Newman and other members of the Oxford Movement called on Anglicans to return to an emphasis on tradition, doctrine, liturgy, and the sacraments. Moving gradually toward greater agreement with Roman Catholic theology, they eventually came to be called Anglo-Catholics. In 1845 Newman himself became a member of the Catholic Church, in which he eventually became a cardinal. His defection was a serious blow to the Oxford Movement, but its influence continued to be felt, especially in the Church of England's "high church" party.

In the United States, reaction against liberal Protestantism was centered in the Lutheran and Presbyterian churches of the Northeast, where there was great concern about indifference to traditional orthodoxy. At Princeton Theological Seminary, Charles Hodge (1797–1878) and other members of the conservative theological faculty argued strongly against Darwinism and biblical criticism as well as the directions taken by liberal theology. In his *Systematic Theology* (1871–73), Hodge insisted that all theology must be based on the assumption that the Bible is literally true, and he articulated a doctrine of the infallibility, or inerrancy, of scripture. Hodge did not believe that God had actually told the authors of biblical books exactly what to write. Such a theory of "verbal inspiration" was eventually devised by others and became one of the bases of "fundamentalism," which we will discuss in chapter 12.

REVIVALISM

One of the most visible signs of Protestant vitality in the nineteeth century was revivalism, a form of evangelism meant to rekindle Christians' faith and bring the gospel to the unconverted. Characterized by fiery preaching and emotional responses from the audience, revivalism was based on the conviction that faith must be rooted in a dynamic personal relationship with God that often begins with a life-changing and emotionally moving conversion experience. With roots in both German pietism and English Puritanism, the revival movement swept across Great Britain in the early 1700s under the leadership of popular preachers like John Wesley and George Whitefield. Both men preached in Britain's North American colonies as well, adding their energy to a "Great Awakening" that had already begun in the Dutch Reformed, Presbyterian, and Congregationalist churches of the Northeast in response to the passionate exhortations of preachers such as Jonathan Edwards (1703–58).

A "Second Awakening" took shape in the last decade of the eighteenth century and flourished in the early years of the nineteenth. Beginning in the Congregationalist churches of New England, it spread to the Methodist, Presbyterian, and Baptist denominations and throughout the United States. Baptists and Methodists were especially effective in bringing the movement to the frontier, where religious life was not yet well organized. Frontier revivalism's most visible feature was "camp meetings" attended by hundreds of settlers, many of whom traveled great distances to attend the events, which often lasted a week. Moved by hymn singing and impassioned preaching, audiences were roused to a level of spiritual enthusiasm that led some to dance, shout, and roll on the ground. Historians believe that camp meetings had a social as well as a religious function, for they offered people who lived in relative isolation an opportunity to meet, play, converse, and do business with others.

In the second half of the nineteenth century, leadership of the revival movement was assumed by professional evangelists who knew how to reach large numbers of people. In the late 1850s, Jeremiah

Lanphier transformed a poorly attended daily prayer meeting in New York City into a noonday prayer phenomenon that regularly drew ten thousand people to assemblies held throughout the city's boroughs. Charles Finney (1792–1875), a lawyer turned preacher, employed "new measures" of revivalism that included lengthy meetings and an "anxious bench" on which sinners in search of salvation would sit as the congregation prayed for them. Dwight L. Moody (1837–99), a former Chicago businessman, combined the power of advertising with his own great talent as a preacher in drawing huge multidenominational crowds to urban meetings throughout the United States and Great Britain. In England, Charles Spurgeon (1834–92), the "prince of preachers," regularly filled the six thousand seats in his Metropolitan Tabernacle, a Baptist church in London. A tireless worker, Spurgeon established orphanages and a school for training ministers, edited a monthly magazine, and wrote numerous books. Finally, William ("Billy") Sunday (1863–1935), a Presbyterian and a former professional baseball player, became known throughout the United States for his informal manner and the "sawdust trail"—the path people walked to get from their seats to the front of the crowd when they converted during his meetings.

The nineteenth century saw other Protestant efforts to reach both the "unchurched" and churchgoers. Many of these efforts were connected with revivalism. Rescue missions were organized to meet the physical and spiritual needs of the urban poor. The Salvation Army, founded by the Englishman William Booth (1829–1912) and his wife, Catherine Mumford (1829–90), also sought to improve the lives of the downtrodden. Working on the assumption that the escape from poverty should begin with spiritual renewal, the Army's "officers" stressed conversion as a necessary first step.

It was also during this period that the Sunday school movement became widespread. Originating with Robert Raikes (1735–1811), an English philanthropist who hired women to teach children reading and religion on Sundays, it quickly grew large enough to support two interdenominational societies: the Sunday School Society (founded in 1783) and the Sunday School Union (founded in 1803). By 1900, Sunday schools were a feature of many Protestant churches in both England and the United States.

The most recent phase of revivalism began with the advent of broadcast media, which allowed a single evangelist to reach millions of people. In 1923, R. R. Brown of the Omaha Gospel Tabernacle brought evangelism to radio. He was soon joined by many others, including Charles E. Fuller (1879–1938), whose "Old Fashioned Revival Hour" reached a worldwide audience by 1942. Billy Graham (1918–   ), the leading evangelist of the second half of the twentieth century, began his "Hour of Decision" on radio but moved it to television in 1950, paving the way for Jerry Falwell, Oral Roberts, Pat Robertson, and others who fully exploited the new medium's capabilities.

Revivalism had a positive impact on both religious life and social reform, but it also created certain difficulties. Those who preferred formal worship were sometimes offended by the enthusiasm of revivalists and their congregations. At times, local churches found themselves in competition with itinerant evangelists. Broadcast evangelism raised additional issues: How does an individual Christian fit within a church attended via a television screen? How can the congregation of a broadcast church hold its leaders accountable for their behavior?

PROTESTANT THEOLOGY IN THE EARLY TWENTIETH CENTURY

Nineteenth-century liberal theology was based on an optimism about humanity that seemed reasonable in a time of growing democracy and great scientific and technological advances. But belief in the essential goodness of human beings and progress toward an ideal society became harder to sustain in the early years of the twentieth century, when war, genocide, and totalitarianism dominated the world scene.

An important Protestant response to this state of affairs was **neo-orthodoxy**, a theology that returned to many of the themes of the Reformation. Neo-orthodox theologians stressed the sinfulness of humanity, scorned liberal notions of progress, and rejected liberal theology's claims that God can be found by looking within oneself, in nature, or at human efforts to create a better society. Arguing that God is utterly different from and beyond human beings and their world, they looked to find him instead in scripture and in moments of "crisis" when finite human beings, who belong to time, encounter One who is infinite and eternal. For this reason, neo-orthodoxy has often been called "crisis theology."

The rejection of any synthesis of Christianity and culture was central to the thought of **Karl Barth** (1886–1968), a Swiss theologian who is generally regarded as the founder of neo-orthodoxy. As a student of Harnack and other Ritschlians at Berlin, Barth at first accepted the idea that the mission of the Church is to create the Kingdom of God on earth. Later, as a young pastor in the Swiss village of Safenwil, he became deeply involved in the Social Democratic party, which he believed best represented the social and political interests of the peasants and laborers who lived in his parish.

But the First World War left Barth disillusioned with politics and liberal theology and wondering how human beings, if they are basically good, could have caused such a catastrophe. Convinced that the aims of liberal Christian culture had nothing to do with the Kingdom of God, he decided to construct a new theology based directly on scripture. In 1919 he published his *Commentary on Romans,* a work on Paul's letter to the church in Rome. This book startled his contemporaries with its emphases on the transcendent "otherness" of God, the power of sin, and divine judgment on human society — ideas that had been foreign to liberal theology. Not since Kierkegaard had a Christian thinker launched such a bold attack on Christian culture.

The concerns Barth expressed in the *Commentary on Romans* turned out to be well-founded, for in 1933, fourteen years after its publication, Hitler and the Nazi party seized power in Germany. By then a professor at Bonn, Barth was distressed by how willingly his colleagues in theology allowed themselves to be used by the Nazis, who were extending their control over German churches and even requiring mention of Hitler's name in the liturgy. Horrified by this accommodation of faith to culture, he joined the Confessing Church, which

was opposed to the German Christian Church sponsored by the Nazis. He also helped draft the Barmen Declaration (1934), a manifesto in which the Confessing Church repudiated "the false teaching that the church can turn over the form of her message and ordinances . . . according to some dominant ideological and political convictions."[29] This courageous move put Barth under an uncomfortable spotlight. Ordered to swear an oath of allegiance to Hitler, he refused and was forced to flee Germany.

Returning to Switzerland, Barth took a position as a professor at Basel and continued work on his *Church Dogmatics,* a multivolume exposition of Christian doctrine that he did not live to complete. Here he elaborated on themes already described in the *Commentary on Romans.* Theology, he said, has no relation to secular philosophies and should not compromise itself by seeking agreement with them. Instead, theology should be based squarely on the Bible, where God, who is "wholly other" than anything human beings can find in themselves or the world, has chosen to reveal himself. Scripture becomes especially meaningful when the Holy Spirit uses it in moments of crisis to create an "encounter" between the individual and God. Because Barth regarded religion as a purely human effort to understand and represent the truth about God, he condemned it as arrogant and misleading. What really matters, he said, is faith. Echoing Kierkegaard, he wrote that faith "is always a leap into the darkness of the unknown, a flight into empty air."[30] There is much that is uncertain, but faith, said Barth, means responding to God anyway and doing one's best to preach and live the gospel.

Another theologian caught up in the dangers of the Nazi era was **Dietrich Bonhoeffer** (1906–45), a Lutheran pastor who was imprisoned by the Nazis in 1943. In his book, *The Cost of Discipleship* (1937), Bonhoeffer argued that Christians too often think in terms of "cheap grace" — a grace that is effortlessly received as well as freely given. Against this view, he wrote that real grace is costly, for it comes at the expense of hardships one must suffer as a consequence of obedience to Christ. In his *Letters and Papers from Prison,* Bonhoeffer described the world as having "come of age" and therefore no longer in need of religion that does little more than offer comfort in times of trouble. He pondered the possibility of a "religionless Christianity," a faith for modern men and women who can get along without the assistance of religion but must still follow Christ's example of loving but costly service to others. Unfortunately, Bonhoeffer was never able to fully develop his theology. He was hanged just days before the prison camp where he had been held was liberated by the Allies.

Neo-orthodoxy's most visible proponents in the United States were Reinhold Niebuhr (1892–1970) and his brother, H. Richard Niebuhr (1894–1962). Reinhold Niebuhr, who served as a pastor in Detroit and later taught at Union Theological Seminary in New York City, was a harsh critic of liberal theology. In his *Moral Man and Immoral Society* and *The Nature and Destiny of Man,* he defended the doctrine of original sin and warned of the destructive power of unrestrained capitalism. Richard Niebuhr was a professor at Yale Divinity School. His *Christ and Culture* analyzed the relationship of Christianity and Christian thought to culture. In another work, *The Social Sources of Denominationalism,* he described the denominational divisions within American Protestantism as reflecting the interests of ethnic groups and social classes rather than the gospel. He urged that Christianity disassociate itself from nationalism and capitalism or run the risk of losing its meaning and value in the modern world.

Paul Tillich (1886–1965) taught in Germany before fleeing his homeland for the United States after Hitler's rise to power. Tillich was not a neo-orthodox theologian. Instead, his aim, as outlined in his *Systematic Theology,* was to make connections between Christianity and secular culture by showing how Christian theology supplies answers to universal human concerns about fear, death, guilt, and feelings of emptiness and meaninglessness. These are *existential* issues in that they arise from the very fact of our existence. To talk about them, Tillich used the existentialist language and insights of Jean-Paul Sartre (1905–80), Martin Heidegger (1889–1976), and others who believed that, in the absence of absolute truths, human beings must make their own decisions and establish their own standards in dealing with the problems of individual existence. For Tillich, humanity's "ultimate concern" is God, "the ground of all being" on whom all existence depends. People often dismiss God because they think of him in limited and distorted ways. They do not understand that sin and anxiety are the products of estrangement from the ground of being. The language of Christianity might be symbolic, said Tillich, but it effectively shows how faith leads to an experience of God in which "the self-estrangement of our existence is overcome." It is an experience of a new reality, a "New Being" as Tillich put it, that is most clearly manifested in Jesus Christ.

The thought of these twentieth-century theologians reflected their concerns about the new and often disturbing realities of the modern world. In different ways, these thinkers attempted to show how Christian teaching about God, sin, faith, and salvation might be a guide to life even amidst difficult and uncertain circumstances.

New Churches

Nineteenth-century American Protestantism was animated by an unusual energy and enthusiasm. Still in its formative stages, American culture was fluid enough to allow for the emergence of new churches and religious movements. Some of these groups looked forward to the imminent Second Coming of Christ. Others formulated new doctrines. Some grew out of existing churches, others claimed to be based on new revelations. In this section we will discuss four of the most important new American churches: the Church of Jesus Christ of Latter-Day Saints, Christian Science, Seventh-Day Adventists, and Jehovah's Witnesses.

THE CHURCH OF JESUS CHRIST OF LATTER-DAY SAINTS

The Church of Jesus Christ of Latter-Day Saints, more commonly known as the Mormons, was founded by Joseph Smith (1805–44). While a boy, Smith experienced visions in which he was told not to join existing churches and that he would be instrumental in restoring true Christianity. Then, in

1823, he was directed by a heavenly messenger named Moroni to a hill near Palmyra, New York. There Smith found two thin golden plates covered with strange writing. His translation, accomplished with Moroni's assistance, is known as the Book of Mormon.

Published in 1830, the Book of Mormon tells the story of "lost tribes of Israel" who fled Jerusalem before its capture by the Neo-Babylonians and migrated to America. Altogether, the tale covers the period from roughly 600 BCE to 421 CE and relates how Christ appeared to the tribes after his resurrection and founded a church among them. Their civilization came to an end in the fifth century, but not before the prophet Mormon had recorded their sacred history. Hidden away by Mormon's son, the Book of Mormon was forgotten until its rediscovery by Smith fourteen centuries later. Mormons believe that theirs is the same faith established by Christ in North America. They accept the authority of both the Old and New Testaments, but their canon of scripture also includes the Book of Mormon and two other texts, *Doctrines and Covenants* (1835) and *The Pearl of Great Price* (1842), which are based on Smith's revelations and sermons.

The announcement of the discovery of the Book of Mormon soon attracted numerous followers to Joseph Smith and his church. They settled briefly in Kirtland, Ohio, but persecution forced them to move on to Jackson County, Missouri, and then to Nauvoo, Illinois. The Mormons prospered there, but their tendency to vote en bloc and their practice of polygamy (abolished in 1890) aroused the animosity of their neighbors. On 24 June 1844, Smith, who had been jailed in Carthage, Illinois, was murdered by an angry mob.

The leadership of the movement now fell to Brigham Young (1801–77). As president of the church's Council of Twelve Apostles, he led the Mormons on an epic trek from Nauvoo to the Great Salt Basin of Utah. There, in what is now Salt Lake City, they established their headquarters and built a Tabernacle and the original Temple, to which only members of the church are admitted.

Mormons accept many traditional Christian doctrines, though often with substantial modification. They understand the Trinity, for example, as constituted of three different gods—Father, Son, and Holy Spirit—who are united in their shared purpose and perfection. According to Mormon teaching, all three were once human. God the Father, they say, was once a man who, having made sufficient spiritual progress, achieved divine status and now rules our region of the universe. God is also the father of all human beings, for human souls are produced by his relations with female deities. Descending to earth, they take on bodies and become human. The possibility of becoming a god or goddess in one's own right and with dominion over some other world is open to all men and women, provided that they succeed in living up to moral standards placed before them as mortals here on earth. These beliefs help to explain the Mormons' interest in raising large families and, in former times, in polygamy, for the birth of every child means the embodiment of a soul.

Mormons engage in extensive genealogical research so that their ancestors may be identified and baptized by proxy. They consider marriages performed in a Latter-Day Saints temple as binding for eternity. All people will eventually be saved, though there are different degrees of salvation. Mormons believe that divine revelation is a continuing process that occurs primarily through church leadership, which is in the hands of a three-member First Presidency and the Council of Twelve Apostles. They are also active proselytizers. As of 2001 they had nearly forty thousand missionaries in the field, most of them young men and women who devote two years of their lives to such service. At present, the total number of Mormons is roughly eight million, most of them living in the United States.

CHRISTIAN SCIENCE AND NEW THOUGHT

Christian Science originated with Mary Baker Eddy (1821–1910), a native of New Hampshire who was originally a member of a Congregational Church. As a young woman she suffered from nervous disorders for which the physicians and hypnotists she consulted could offer no lasting relief. In 1866, however, she claimed to have been completely cured while reading a New Testament account of one of the miraculous healings effected by Jesus. This led to her discovery of what she later called the Science of Christianity, or Christian Science, which she described in her book *Science and Health* (1875), revised in 1883 to include *Key to the Scriptures.*

According to these texts, Christian Scientists have no need of a formal creed or doctrines. Christian Science describes the Bible as the inspired word of God and recognizes Jesus Christ as the "Way-shower," though it makes a clear distinction between the man Jesus and Christ, which was Jesus' divine nature. As both Son of God and Son of Man, Jesus Christ was the mediator between God and humanity. Christian Science teaches that all reality is spiritual — and that matter, disease, and death are unreal. Human suffering arises from the fact that we do not recognize the unreality of the non-spiritual. Much of the significance of Jesus lies in his awareness that God and God's goodness are the only reality. This enabled Jesus to overcome all forms of suffering, including death, for himself and others.

A skilled organizer, Mary Baker Eddy created the Church of Christ, Scientist, in 1879 and later located its headquarters in Boston. She also established the Massachusetts Metaphysical College for the training of "practitioners" — church members who devote themselves full-time to teaching others how to use "scientific prayer" to gain access to God's healing love. At the age of eighty-eight, Eddy also founded *The Christian Science Monitor*, still a highly respected newspaper. Her *Church Manual* provided for an administrative structure, still in place today, in which a board of five directors associated with the "Mother Church" oversees all other congregations. By the time of Eddy's death in 1910 there were more than one hundred thousand Christian Scientists. Today, there are more than three thousand congregations in fifty countries.

Christian Science churches are lay organizations that have no ministers. Sunday services consist of readings from the Bible and Eddy's *Science and Health*, hymns, and recitation of the Lord's Prayer. All other prayer is silent. Fearing doctrinal deviations from her teaching, Eddy forbade preaching. Christian Scientists acknowledge baptism and the eucharist, the two traditional Protestant sacraments, but do not celebrate them outwardly with symbols and ceremonies. Instead, baptism is the ongoing purification of thought, and the eucharist is spiritual communion with God through silent prayer and "Christian living." Heaven and hell are states of mind.

Christian Science is usually seen as but one of the forms taken by a larger American religious movement known as New Thought. One of New Thought's most influential figures was Emma Curtis Hopkins (1853–1925), a student of Mary Baker Eddy's who founded the Emma Hopkins School of Metaphysical Science in Chicago in the late 1880s. Hopkins was a gifted teacher whose students went on to establish their own versions of New Thought, such as the Unity School of Christianity, Religious Science, and Divine Science. The most successful of these is the Unity movement, which today has congregations in hundreds of American cities as well as abroad. Described by the eminent psychologist William James (1842–1910) as "the religion of healthy-mindedness," New Thought had considerable influence within many Protestant denominations in the late nineteenth century. It emphasized mental healing, the spiritual nature of all reality, and prayer and meditation as the means by which the presence of God may be realized.

SEVENTH-DAY ADVENTISTS

In the nineteenth century, American Protestantism saw increasing interest in millennialism, the belief in Christ's thousand-year reign (the Millennium), and the rise of **Adventism**, the expectation that it would soon begin. Growing out of revivalism and finding freedom to develop in a culture still in its formative stages, new Adventist denominations began to appear by midcentury. The first was founded by William Miller (1782–1849), a Baptist minister from New York whose experience at a revival meeting led him to undertake a study of biblical prophecy. In 1835 Miller announced that Christ would return in 1843, preside over a final judgment, destroy the world, and then inaugurate a new heaven and earth. The failure of the Second Coming to materialize as Miller had predicted prompted recalculations and predictions of new dates. When these, too, passed without incident, many "Millerites" gave up their hope of seeing Christ's return. Others, scorned and ridiculed in their churches, followed Miller in forming new ones, most of which were organized as part of the Evangelical Adventist Association.

The largest of the Adventist churches is that of the Seventh-Day Adventists, founded by Ellen G. White (1827–1915). A native of Maine, White became a follower of Miller in 1842. She experienced hundreds of visions that inspired her many books, including *The Desire of Ages* and *Ministry of Healing*, and made her a popular speaker who drew thousands to her lectures. White taught that the Second Coming had been delayed by the failure of Christians to obey the Ten Commandments—especially the fourth, which requires observance of the Sabbath on the seventh day of the week (i.e., Saturday). In addition, she believed that scripture contains rules for physical as well as spiritual health. "Disease," she wrote, "is the result of violating God's laws, both natural and spiritual" and would not exist if people lived "in harmony with the Creator's plan."[31] For this reason, Seventh-Day Adventists practice vegetarianism, abstain from alcohol and tobacco, and prefer natural remedies to drugs when ill. It was in the hope of creating a health food that would meet the standards White discerned in scripture that Dr. John Harvey Kellogg, one of her disciples, invented his famous cornflakes.

Today there are nearly four million Seventh-Day Adventists worldwide; about half a million are in the United States. They continue to expect the Advent and the Millennium, which the righteous will spend in heaven. At the completion of the Millennium, they will return to earth for eternity.

JEHOVAH'S WITNESSES

Another millennialist group was organized in 1881 by the lay preacher Charles Taze Russell (1852–1916). Officially the Watch Tower Bible and Tract Society, it is better known as the Jehovah's Witnesses. Raised in the Congregational Church, Russell was only twenty when his study of the Bible led him to the conclusion that the Second Coming would occur in 1874, when Christ would return invisibly to prepare for the Kingdom of God. This event was to be followed by the Battle of Armageddon and end of the world in 1914. Thereafter, Russell expected Christ to begin a millennial reign over the earth. At first, he announced these and other opinions in a series of tracts and pamphlets. He later published a more detailed description of his thought in his book *Studies in Scripture* and in 1879 introduced a magazine called *The Watchtower*. Russell's ideas and publications soon drew hundreds of followers to his movement. Known as Bible Students and Watchtower People in his own time, they were later renamed Jehovah's Witnesses by his successor, Joseph Franklin Rutherford (1869–1942).

Although 1914 passed without the fulfillment of Russell's prophecy, the number of Jehovah's Witnesses continued to grow. Under Rutherford there were approximately one hundred thousand. Today there are more than four million Witnesses in two hundred countries. They use their own translation of the Bible and publish *The Watchtower* worldwide in more than one hundred languages. The international headquarters are in Brooklyn, New York. Witnesses meet locally in "kingdom halls" and take their message to others through door-to-door evangelism.

Jehovah's Witnesses take their name from *Jehovah*, a form of the Hebrew name of God. Although they understand Christ to be God's Son, they reject the doctrine of the Trinity. They continue to believe that a "great tribulation" is imminent. After destroying the present world system, they say, God will inaugurate Christ's millennial reign on earth. Full salvation will be achieved only by the elect—Christ and 144,000 others drawn from all periods of history. These individuals, who alone have immortal souls, will ultimately be taken into heaven. All others might be saved through obedience to God and faith in the efficacy of Christ's sacrificial death, but their reward will be eternal life on earth, which will be restored to its original, paradisiacal condition. The wicked will perish. Believing that they constitute a theocratic kingdom, Witnesses seek to remain apart from the present world order, which they believe is ruled by Satan. They refuse military service and will not salute flags or hold government offices. Because they regard other churches as having fallen into gross error, they have little contact with them and do not join in celebrating holidays such as Christmas and Easter.

The Eastern Orthodox Church in the Modern World

Political events — particularly the breakdown of the Ottoman Empire, the rise of national independence movements in the Balkans, and the Bolshevik revolution in Russia — had a dramatic impact on the Eastern Orthodox Church in the nineteenth and twentieth centuries. National churches emerged, tensions arose between national interests and universal Orthodoxy, and in Russia the Church was persecuted for seven decades by a communist government that encouraged atheism.

ORTHODOXY AND THE AUTOCEPHALOUS CHURCHES

At its height, the Ottoman Empire included nearly all of North Africa, southeastern Europe, and much of western Asia in addition to its Turkish homeland. By 1800, however, the empire was in decline. In the Balkans, the erosion of Ottoman political and military authority allowed independence movements with close ties to national churches to flourish and eventually to win independence from Turkey.

Since 1453, when the Turks seized Constantinople, the patriarch of Constantinople (Istanbul), also known as the ecumenical patriarch, had been in the difficult position of presiding over the Orthodox Church from within a Muslim state. To make matters more difficult, the Ottoman system made the patriarch a government official responsible for representing Christians before the sultan and assisting in the enforcement of Ottoman policies. Inevitably, many non-Greek Orthodox came to identify the patriarch and the Greek hierarchy as agents of the hated Ottoman state. As one national group after another won its independence during the course of the 1800s, they showed little interest in acknowledging Constantinople's continuing authority over them. Instead, Serbia, Bulgaria, Albania, Romania, and Greece formed *autocephalous* ("self-governing") national churches, each claiming the right to elect its own leader — whether patriarch, metropolitan, or archbishop — and bishops. In some cases the competing claims of nationalism and Orthodox universalism caused serious conflict. For example, the creation of an autocephalous church in Bulgaria without the approval of the patriarch and its claim to jurisdiction over Bulgars everywhere, including Istanbul, led to accusations of *philetism* ("extreme nationalism") and excommunications. The schism was not healed until 1945. Similar conflicts arose involving other Balkan nations.

Today, the patriarch of Constantinople still retains an honorary primacy among other Orthodox bishops, but he has direct authority only over Orthodox Christians in Turkey and Greek Orthodox Christians in Crete, a few islands in the Aegean, Mt. Athos, and territories outside of Greece itself. This includes the Greek archdiocese of America.[32] The Orthodox Church over which he presides is perhaps best described as a communion of administratively independent churches that share a common faith, sacraments, and history.

During the eighteenth century, Orthodoxy felt the influence both of western rationalism, which tended to be antireligious, and western pietism and mysticism, which left their mark on Orthodox religious art, music, and theology. Westernizing trends continued in the nineteenth and twentieth centuries, but they did little to change the traditional character of Eastern Orthodox Christianity.

In some cases, Orthodox thinkers' responses to Islam and the West expressed a frustration that had grown over long centuries of domination by foreign powers and cultures. A good example is Apostolos Makrakis, an ultra-Orthodox Greek lay theologian whose birth in 1831 came just two years after his country won its independence from the Ottoman Empire. In 1856, while at a congress in Paris, Makrakis sought to demonstrate God's approval of Christianity and rejection of Islam by offering to enter a blazing furnace alongside any Muslim who dared to take up his challenge. He would carry the Bible, the Muslim would hold the Qur'an, and God, he said, would allow only the man and book representing the true religion to emerge unharmed.

Although he was dissuaded from carrying out this test, Makrakis went on to defend Orthodoxy in books that denounced western influences and corruption within the Orthodox hierarchy.[33] It was his belief that a reform of morals at all levels within the Orthodox Church must precede the coming of the Kingdom of Christ, which he imagined as a restored Byzantine Empire.

Even though Makrakis's thought was extreme in many respects, some of his ideas had a powerful influence. His argument that all Christians have a responsibility to preach the gospel was one of the major forces behind the formation of lay groups that were to occupy a significant place in twentieth-century Orthodoxy. The most important of these is Zoe ("life"), also known as the "Brotherhood of Theologians." Organized in Greece in 1907, Zoe is a semimonastic order whose members, most of them laymen, must remain unmarried. Whereas the primary interest of Orthodox monks has always been prayer, Zoe is dedicated to evangelism and making Orthodox theology relevant to the lives of ordinary people. Other groups, such as Sotir ("Savior") and the Orthodox Christian Unions, are also devoted to missionary work.

Overall, the nineteenth and twentieth centuries saw a kind of renaissance in Eastern Orthodoxy. In the Balkan countries, independence brought religious and intellectual freedom that encouraged renewed popular devotion and theological study. In Serbia, Romania, and Bulgaria, theologians began to break free of the long-dominant influences of Russia and Greece to develop their own distinctive ways of thinking about the meaning of Orthodox tradition in the modern world. Today, perhaps the greatest problem facing the Orthodox Church is the declining number of monks, who have for centuries constituted its spiritual center.

THE RUSSIAN ORTHODOX CHURCH

We saw in chapter 10 that in the early years of the eighteenth century Tsar Peter the Great opened Russia to the West and encouraged western influence on all aspects of Russian life, including Russian Orthodoxy. As a result, western trends had a significant impact on church art and music as well as theology. Peter also sought to bring the church

hierarchy in Russia more firmly under his control by eliminating the patriarchate and placing the Russian Church under the direction of a Holy Synod, a body constituted of bishops and other clergy nominated by the tsar and subject to dismissal by him at any time.

By the beginning of the nineteenth century, reactions against western influences on Russian Orthodoxy were becoming evident. Jesuits, many of whom had entered Russia from Catholic Poland and Lithuania, were expelled in 1819. In addition, a rising tide of nationalism supported groups that called for a return to Orthodox tradition and less openness to the West. The most important of these were the Slavophiles, who held that the Russian Orthodox Church was the one true Church. Their most famous representative, Alexis Khomiakov (1804–60), was a lay theologian who condemned western rationalism and devised numerous arguments for the superiority of the Orthodox Church over Catholicism and Protestantism.

Not all Russian thinkers agreed with the Slavophiles. Like Khomiakov, the philosopher and theologian Vladimir Soloviev (1853–1900) longed for Christian unity, but he rejected the Slavophiles' view of the Church as too narrowly Russian. He argued that a truly universal church recognizes only the humanity of Christians, not their national and ethnic differences. When he was a child, Soloviev had experienced visions of a divine woman he later called *Sophia* ("wisdom") and understood as a manifestation of the principle of cosmic unity. These gave his thought a mystical quality and became the basis for his view that the ultimate goal of humanity is the realization of the fundamental unity of all things. Christ, said Soloviev, had been sent into the world to effect the union of God and human beings. In his *Russia and the Universal Church*,[34] he wrote that Christ's three earthly representatives — the tsar, the pope, and prophets within the Church — would play key roles in bringing this union into being and in ushering in a new Christian era in history.[35]

One of the most positive developments in nineteenth-century Russian Orthodoxy was the reinvigoration of monasticism. In 1810 there had been 452 monasteries in Russia; by 1914 there were more than a thousand.[36] The leading figures in the monastic movement were the *startzi* ("elders") — spiritual counselors, most of them monks, whose dedication to prayer and spiritual perfection gave them special authority in the Church.

Perhaps the greatest was Seraphim of Sarov (1759–1833). Thirty years of isolation in a monastic cell gave him a reputation for holiness that later drew thousands to him seeking spiritual counsel. It is said that he sometimes answered their questions before they had a chance to ask them. Like the Byzantine Hesychasts, Seraphim was said to have experiences of the Divine and Uncreated Light—the same light that surrounded Jesus during his transfiguration (Matthew 17:1–13). The effect on him was profound. One of his disciples reported that the brilliance of Seraphim's eyes and face when he was caught up "in the Spirit of God" made it impossible to look directly at him.[37] Another *staretz*, Feofan (Theophan) of Vysha (1815–94), popularized the teachings of the Byzantine Hesychasts throughout Russia. Many of the letters he wrote to those who asked him for spiritual advice were published and widely read long after his death.

The spiritual dimension in Russian culture was also evident in the novels of Fedor Dostoevsky (1821–81) and Leo Tolstoy (1828–1910). Both writers endorsed the traditional ideal of *kenoticism*, the "emptying" of oneself in order to suffer for the sake of others, which we discussed in chapter 7. It is a central theme in Dostoevsky's *Crime and Punishment*, a work concerned with redemption through suffering. Dostoevsky's *The Brothers Karamazov* explores love, faith, and belief in a threatening world and presents a wonderful illustration of a *staretz* in the character of Father Zosima.

Tolstoy, a critic of the Russian Orthodox Church but a man of deep spiritual convictions, believed that true Christianity was found not in doctrine but in the Sermon on the Mount (Matthew 5–7). Here, he said, Christ taught love of one's enemies, avoidance of anger and oaths, fidelity in marriage, and passive resistance to evil. Tolstoy believed that adherence to these principles and the cultivation of love within and among individuals would eliminate evil and establish the Kingdom of God on earth.

The fortunes of the Russian Orthodox Church suffered a disastrous blow in the early years of twen-tieth century when the Bolshevik revolution of 1917 established a communist government in Russia under the leadership of V. I. Lenin. At first there were indications that the new regime might be friendly to the Church. The Holy Synod was abolished, the patriarchate restored, and freedom of religion promised. Such freedom was guaranteed by the constitution of 1936, but the same document also gave the government "freedom of antireligious propaganda," a right it fully exploited in the coming decades. In fact, the antireligious policies of the Soviet Union became evident as early as 1918, when it declared all church buildings and lands the property of the state and closed all but a few seminaries. In 1920 it outlawed the teaching of religion in schools. As one official put it, every teacher was expected "not only to be an unbeliever himself, but also . . . an active propagandist of Godlessness . . . [and] the bearer of the ideas of militant proletarian atheism."[38] Severe restrictions imposed on priests forbade them to offer religious instruction outside of their sermons or even to distribute Bibles to the faithful. Thousands of bishops, priests, monks, and nuns were arrested. Some were executed, many more were imprisoned. The laity also suffered, for identification as a Christian made it difficult to find employment and sometimes brought accusations of counterrevolutionary activity. Persecution and restrictions were relaxed somewhat after the Second World War, but the Soviet Union remained decidedly hostile to religion. Despite this, some congregations managed not only to survive but to flourish, with laypeople often assuming greater responsibilities in the absence of ordained clergy.

The collapse of communism and the Soviet Union in the early 1990s restored freedom of religion in Russia and other regions of the former Soviet Union and in the formerly communist countries of eastern Europe, where the practice of Christianity had also been suppressed. New seminaries have opened, and a dramatic growth in church attendance has shown that although decades of official atheism and antireligious policies certainly discouraged the faith, they did not come close to extinguishing it.

The Expansion of Christianity

The geographical scope of Christianity expanded dramatically during the nineteenth and twentieth centuries as the colonial powers of Europe made their influence felt on other continents. In some cases, such as in North America, the faith was spread primarily by Christian settlers. In others, such as Africa and Asia, missionaries played a greater role. Both Catholic and Protestant missions were supported by well-organized missionary societies that became increasingly common in the early 1800s.

The main base of Catholic missions was France, where the Society for the Propagation of the Faith was founded in 1822. This organization soon spread to other lands and raised immense sums from laypeople for the support of missionary orders. Women were particularly active in Catholic missions. By 1870 more than half of the sixty thousand Catholic missionaries in the field were women, most of them nuns. The Protestant churches also founded highly effective missionary organizations, such as the Baptist Missionary Society (1792), the Basel Evangelical Missionary Society (1815), the London Missionary Society (1795), and the North German Missionary Society (1836).

In addition to the gospel, many missionaries brought with them the confidence shared by most westerners in the superiority of their culture. For many, the "the white man's burden" included an obligation to "civilize" and convert the "heathen." In this sense, missionaries contributed to the success of colonial powers, which benefited from the cooperation and like-mindedness of the peoples they subjected to their rule. But not all missionaries approved of colonialism. Some found themselves at odds with colonial authorities, whose interest in profiting from the lands and labor of subject peoples was not always consistent with the missionaries' desire to convert and educate them.

NORTH AMERICA

The Spanish began to colonize North America early in the sixteenth century. Their explorers and conquistadors brought with them Franciscans, Dominicans, and Jesuits who preached Catholicism among the Indians of the Caribbean and the peoples of what are now Mexico and the southwestern United States. For the most part, the Spanish considered indigenous peoples infidels whose religious beliefs amounted to heresy. Their system of *encomiendas*— formal grants to settlers of rights to Indian labor—was also intended to encourage the Indians' conversion to Christianity and transformation into loyal subjects of Spain. Although this practice did succeed in Christianizing the Indians, it usually resulted in their exploitation as well. In 1848, war between newly independent Mexico and the United States resulted in the latter's annexation of much of what is now the American Southwest. The Catholic inhabitants of these territories were soon joined by increasing numbers of predominantly Protestant settlers.

Of the countries that followed Spain in building colonial empires, none was more successful than Britain. The British conquest of Canada in the eighteenth century added Anglican and Methodist influences to that of Roman Catholicism, which had been introduced earlier by the French. In addition, nearly all of Britain's major religious groups were represented in the thirteen colonies it established farther south, with Baptists centered in Rhode Island, Puritans and Congregationalists in New England, Quakers in Pennsylvania, Catholics in Maryland, and Anglicans and Methodists scattered throughout. Despite their differences and some initial friction, these denominations achieved a level of mutual toleration that became the basis for the religious pluralism of later American culture. Questions were raised during the American Revolution (1775–83) about the patriotism of some groups, such as the Quakers (who were pacifists) and Anglicans and Methodists (who had close ties to Britain), but these were soon forgotten after the war. In 1791 the newly created United States guaranteed freedom of religion to all with the incorporation of the Bill of Rights into the United States Constitution.

As we have seen, the "Great Awakening" that swept across much of North America in the eighteenth and nineteenth centuries inspired revivals and missions in regions of the United States and

Canada, where Christianity was not yet well established. Baptists and Methodists were especially active and succeeded in winning converts and establishing new congregations on the frontier and in the southern United States. By 1860 each of these denominations claimed nearly 1 million members out of a total population of 31 million. There were also large numbers of Presbyterians, Lutherans, and Congregationalists.

The great waves of European immigrants that began arriving on American shores in the 1800s made Catholicism a powerful force in American life. In 1800 there had been a mere 50,000 Catholics in the United States, but newcomers from Ireland, Germany, and France greatly boosted their numbers, as did the Louisiana Purchase of 1803, which doubled the size of the country with the addition of largely Catholic territory originally settled by the French. By 1860 there were 3.5 million Catholics in the United States, making theirs the largest of all American churches.

American Christians were bitterly divided by the issue of slavery, which eclipsed all other issues in the mid nineteenth century. Voices from many churches condemned slavery, but only the Quakers denounced it unequivocally. In the South, in particular, many considered slave labor too important economically to abandon. The issue was complicated by the fact that nearly all black Americans were Christians, co-religionists of their oppressors. Most were Protestants, for few outside of Maryland and Louisiana had contact with Catholicism. Although in colonial days blacks and whites had sometimes worshiped together, racism and social and economic inequities contributed to a segregation that remains the rule today. As a result, black denominations began to appear in the early 1800s. One of the first was the African Methodist Episcopal Church, organized in 1816 under its first bishop, Richard Allen (1760–1831), a former slave. Others followed, particularly after the emancipation of the slaves during the Civil War (1860–65). By 1900, membership in black churches in the United States was 2.7 million out of a total black population of 8.3 million.

In the early years of the twentieth century, American churches addressed a variety of social and political issues. Most denominations were initially opposed to any involvement of the United States in the First World War, which many Americans regarded as a European conflict of little concern to themselves. But when the United States did enter the war in 1917 to aid the faltering Allies, they enthusiastically supported what was by then widely seen as an effort to save civilization. Similarly, American churches were solidly behind the government's decision to enter the Second World War in 1941. At home, the temperance movement won great support from Protestant churches and in 1919 succeeded in outlawing the manufacture and sale of alcoholic beverages with the ratification of the Eighteenth Amendment to the Constitution.[39] Both Protestants and Catholics were divided, however, on the issue of evolution. Many conservatives supported the 1925 prosecution of John T. Scopes, a biology teacher who had taught evolution in his classroom. When Scopes's famous "monkey trial" ended with his conviction for violating a Tennessee law that forbade instruction in evolution, legislatures in other southern states passed similar laws. Equally serious divisions among Christians were created by the civil rights movement of the 1950s and 1960s, with some arguing against the legislation of morality and others claiming that laws against discrimination passed in 1964 were absolutely necessary. Today, Christians in the United States are split over other issues, such as abortion and prayer in public schools.

Throughout the twentieth century, American churches continued to grow, with church attendance reaching its peak in the 1950s. By the 1990s, there were more than 60 million Roman Catholics, 35 million Baptists, 9 million Methodists, and 8 million Lutherans in the United States. With many more belonging to other denominations, roughly half of all Americans claimed some sort of church affiliation at the end of the twentieth century.

SOUTH AMERICA

By the beginning of the nineteenth century, nearly three hundred years had passed since Christianity was first brought to South America by the Spanish and Portuguese, who were then carving out empires

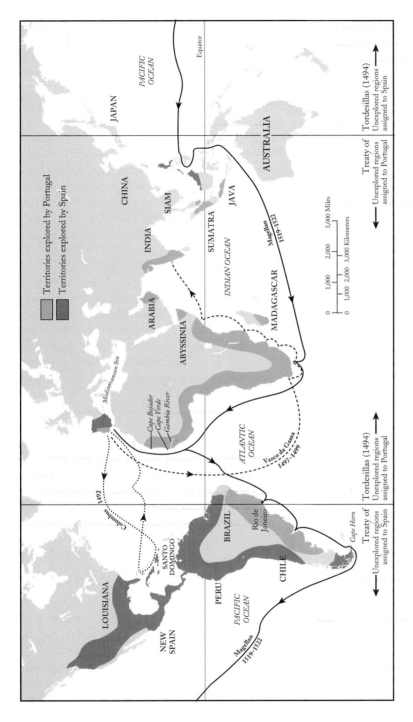

Figure 11.1 Spanish and Portuguese exploration of the Americas, Africa, and Asia led to colonization of new territories and the conversion of their populations to Catholicism.

in the New World. The Spanish established themselves throughout Central America and along the western and northern coasts of South America. The Portuguese colonized a strip of coastal territory on South America's eastern coast in what is now Brazil. During those early years, the Christianization of the Americas was undertaken with royal patronage, which gave the Spanish and Portuguese kings, rather than Rome, the greatest influence in the selection of bishops, the building of churches, and all other matters relating to the position of the Church in their colonies. Most of the work of preaching among and baptizing indigenous peoples was performed by Franciscans, Dominicans, and Jesuits, who began in Venezuela, Argentina, Peru, and Colombia and gradually worked their way south.

In the early 1800s the forces of liberalism and revolution that were changing Europe were also at work in South America, where movements led by Simón Bolívar (1783–1830), José San Martín (1778–1850), and others won freedom for Spain's colonies and ultimately transformed them into independent republics. Portuguese Brazil became a republic in 1889. The leaders of these new states were deeply influenced by the thought of the Enlightenment and the reforms of Napoleon. As a result, in most countries independence brought friction between those who wanted to see the Church freed from government interference and anticlerical politicians who wanted to subordinate it to the state. This conflict combined with political instability in the new republics to make the position of the Catholic Church in South America uncertain throughout much of the nineteenth century.

The growth of Catholicism was encouraged by a continuing stream of European missionaries eager to reinforce its position in areas that were only nominally Christian and to preach in regions where the faith was not yet known. It was primarily these newcomers, rather than native-born Christians, who preached the gospel in the Andes, in Patagonia in the south, and in the vast and forbidding jungles of the Amazon Basin.

Protestantism also found a place in South America. It was brought by European and American immigrants—Anglicans and Presbyterians from England and Scotland, Lutherans from Germany, and

Baptists who had emigrated from America's defeated southern states—as well as by missionaries. The latter were supported by organizations such as the British and Foreign Bible Society and the South American Missionary Society. The greatest number of Protestant missionaries came from the United States, most of them Methodists, Baptists, Presbyterians, Episcopalians, Congregationalists, and Disciples of Christ. By 1914 the number of Protestants in Latin America was more than half a million and growing. In 1950 there were more than four million.[40] The vast majority of Latin Americans, however, remained Roman Catholic.

AFRICA

In chapters 3 and 4 we saw that Christianity took root early in North Africa and later spread southward from Egypt as far as Ethiopia. No further progress was made, however, until Portuguese exploration of coastal Africa beginning in the late 1400s led to the establishment of colonies and Catholicism in Angola and Mozambique. Not long afterward, the Dutch brought Reformed Christianity to South Africa, which they began settling in 1652. Arriving later, British settlers introduced Anglicanism to the area around Cape Horn, where they established a colony in 1814. But the limited presence of Europeans did little to change the religious character of the continent as a whole. As late as 1800, Christianity was virtually unknown in most of sub-Saharan Africa.

This situation changed as the industrializing West began to take a greater interest in Africa. In the first half of the nineteenth century, scores of missionaries made their way to the continent. Some, like David Livingstone (1813–73), were explorers. Livingstone ventured into unknown territories along the Upper Nile and central Africa and explored the Zambesi River, which he called "God's highway into the interior." Others, such as Robert Moffat (1795–1883), were translators who rendered scripture into African languages. Still others, among them John Philip (1771–1851), were political activists concerned as much with protecting the rights of Africans as with saving their souls. Individuals like these prepared the way for the European soldiers and commercial interests that came to dominate Africa in the last decades of the nineteenth century.

One of the great centers of African missions was Sierra Leone, where in 1792 a colony of pro-British black Americans had been created with the help of wealthy British Anglicans. These colonists, most of them Methodists and Baptists, established churches, organized missions in Nigeria and Kenya, and took Christianity with them in their travels throughout Africa as traders. They made Sierra Leone, which became a British protectorate in 1896 and gained its independence in 1961, the first truly Christian state in Africa and championed the idea that Africa should be evangelized by Africans.

As the colonial powers penetrated the interior of Africa in the last years of the nineteenth century, Christianity followed, so that by 1900 there were missions and newly established churches virtually everywhere. By the 1920s these commonly offered education and medical services as well as spiritual instruction and fellowship.

Gradually, African Christians began calling upon missionaries and transplanted European churches to give them a greater share in church leadership. Some founded their own movements and churches. William Harris (1860–1929), a Liberian preacher better known as the "Prophet Harris," spent most of his career in the Ivory Coast warning that the judgment of Christ was imminent and urging his fellow Africans to abandon their traditional religions. The leader of a movement whose size and enthusiasm frightened French colonial authorities, he is said to have performed more than one hundred thousand baptisms. Another popular leader was Simon Kimbangu (1889–1951), a Christian healer who drew vast crowds in and around the Congo. His Église de Jésus-Christ sur la Terre (Church of Jesus Christ on Earth) is still a force in African Christianity. It has its headquarters in Zaire and claimed well over six million members in 2000.

Today, there are several thousand independent African churches. These coexist with European denominations introduced by missionaries. Church growth since the mid twentieth century has been phenomenal. In 1950, there were approximately 25 million Christians in Africa. By 2000, there were

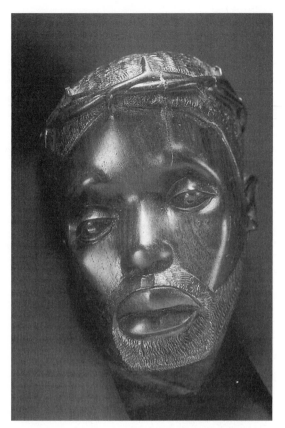

Figure 11.2 African Christ Christian peoples have often pictured Christ in terms of their own ethnic and cultural identities. Here, an anonymous twentieth-century African sculptor has fashioned in wood an image of Christ wearing the crown of thorns.

more than 150 million out of a total population of nearly 800 million. Divided almost equally between Protestants and Catholics, they share their continent with a similar number of Muslims, most of them in the north, and with practitioners of traditional African religions.

INDIA

Although European explorers had traveled to South and East Asia as early as the thirteenth century, it was not until much later that the Church became a presence there. An important step was taken by the Portuguese, who created trading colonies at

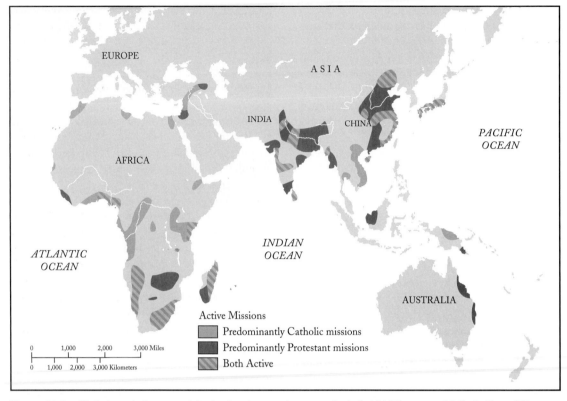

Figure 11.3 Christian missionary activity in the nineteenth century included highly successful Catholic and Protestant missions in Africa and Asia.

Goa and Calicut in India, Ceylon (modern Sri Lanka), Java, and Macao and Canton in China in the early 1500s. They were followed by the Dutch, who gained control over much of the East Indies in the 1600s. In the eighteenth and nineteenth centuries, the British took over nearly all of India and created colonies in Burma, China, Borneo, and Malaya; the French founded colonies in eastern India and Indochina; and the Germans claimed possessions in China and New Guinea.

One of the first missionaries to work in India was the Baptist William Carey (1761–1834). Carey arrived in India in 1793, a time when the British East India Company, which represented British commercial interests on the subcontinent, opposed missionary activity out of fear that it would cause

social tensions disruptive to trade. Despite this, Carey preached throughout Bengal and published his translation of the New Testament into Bengali. He later completed translations of scripture into twenty-four other Indian languages. His reports on his work, widely circulated in Britain and the United States, led to an end to restrictions on missionary activity in 1813 and inspired other missionaries to join him, most of them from the United States, Britain, Germany, and Scandinavia. Their efforts produced large numbers of conversions, especially among the lower classes — and in particular among the "untouchables," who had always been excluded from mainstream Indian society. They also had a liberating effect among Indian women and encouraged the ordination of Indian clergy.

By the early twentieth century, Indian churches were emerging from the European denominations brought by the missionaries. In 1908, Indian Presbyterians and Congregationalists formed the South India United Church. In 1930 the Anglican Church in India became an independent entity known as the Church of India, Burma, and Ceylon. Today, Christians in India account for roughly 2.5 percent of the population — about 30 million people — divided evenly between Catholics and Protestants.

CHINA

Ancient tradition holds that the apostle Thomas first brought Christianity to both China and India in the first century. There is little evidence to support the historicity of his mission, but we do know that Syrian Christianity reached China by the seventh century and survived there until it came under persecution in the early years of the Ming dynasty (1368–1644).[41]

Christianity was reintroduced by the Italian Jesuit Matteo Ricci (1552–1610), who arrived in Macao in 1582 and later made his way to Beijing. Fluent in Chinese and well acquainted with Chinese literature, he preached the gospel to the country's aristocratic elite, explaining it in terms of their traditional religious and philosophical concepts. It was a successful strategy, for Ricci's understanding of Chinese culture and mastery of mathematics and astronomy gave him credibility in matters of religion as well. Some of his associates became converts, and they, in turn, converted others. In this way a small church was built up and the door was opened to other missionaries. In the eighteenth century, however, the Church once again fell into imperial disfavor and suffered renewed persecution. This was largely due to the fears of the Manchu emperors that the unrestricted activities of westerners would destabilize society.

The first Protestant missionary in China was Robert Morrison (1782–1834), who came to Canton as an employee of the British East India Company. While there he used his free time to translate the Bible into Chinese. Morrison's work prepared the way for other Protestant missionaries, who

began arriving in the mid nineteenth century as Britain, Germany, France, and other countries gained control of Chinese ports. As these missionaries moved into China's interior, they established schools, hospitals, and orphanages as well as churches. By the end of the century there were more than forty thousand Chinese Protestants. The number of Catholics was nearly six hundred thousand.

But the association of Christianity with foreign oppression brought disaster in 1899–1900, when a popular uprising known as the Boxer Rebellion made targets of westerners and pro-western Chinese. Thousands of Chinese Christians and some missionaries and diplomats were killed. The revolt was crushed by the combined armies of the West, but the severe terms of the peace they imposed on China's already unstable "Celestial Empire" weakened the Chinese government beyond repair. Revolution in 1911 resulted in the abdication of the last of China's emperors and the creation of a republic. Missionary work continued amidst these changes, now with greater attention to offering higher education and the organization of Chinese churches. As in Africa, their number increased far beyond the handful of European denominations brought by missionaries as Chinese Christians adapted the faith to their many visions of its place in their culture.

For a time, some early-twentieth-century missionaries were hopeful that all of China might soon be converted, but their expectations were shattered when a communist regime took power in 1949 under Mao Tse-tung. Denouncing religion as counterrevolutionary and missionaries as agents of western imperialism, the communists closed many churches and applied such pressure to missionaries that most left the country in the early 1950s. In 1957 the government forced the severing of relations between China's Catholics and Rome. During the "cultural revolution" they launched in 1966, the communists attempted to wipe out all religious belief and practice, both Christian and traditional.

Despite this, many of China's churches managed to survive. A slight relaxation of restrictions on religion in the early 1980s encouraged them to begin emerging from underground. Church attendance increased somewhat, a few theological schools were

Figure 11.4   This twentieth-century Japanese painting depicts Jesus, Mary, and Joseph in a scene familiar both to western and Japanese Christians.

reestablished, and relations with churches outside China were renewed. These developments came in connection with the extension of greater freedom to individuals within China and a more receptive, though still cautious, attitude toward commercial and cultural influences from outside the country. What this means for the future of Christianity in China remains to be seen.

JAPAN

Christianity was first brought to Japan by the Spanish Jesuit Francis Xavier (1506–52), the "Apostle to the Indies," who arrived there after first preaching in India, Ceylon, and the East Indies. Wherever he went, Xavier baptized converts (the Jesuit order credits him with more than seven hundred thou-sand baptisms) and built churches. In Japan, he managed to build small Catholic congregations beginning in 1546, but these came under persecution after 1587, when Christianity was outlawed in response to imperial suspicions that the Church was part of a western plot to take control of the country. In 1597, twenty-six Japanese Christians were crucified at Nagasaki. Persecution continued until 1859, when restrictions were relaxed, but full freedom of religion in Japan did not become a reality until 1890.

The Japanese had good reasons for being wary of westerners, for they had seen the destructive effects of European influence elsewhere in Asia. They were able to remain in virtual isolation from the West until the middle of the nineteenth century, but events in 1853 dramatically changed Japan's place in the world. In that year an American fleet under the command of Commodore Matthew C. Perry steamed into Tokyo Bay and forced the Japanese to open their doors to trade with the United States. During the following two decades other western countries established trading relationships with Japan, which now began to reorganize its government, military, business, and industry along western lines.

This more open climate allowed for the return of Roman Catholic missionaries, who worked to reinvigorate congregations that had somehow managed to stay alive during the long years of persecution. They were joined by Russian Orthodox missionaries, who arrived under the leadership of Nicolai Kassatkin and succeeded in winning thousands of converts. Anglicans, Presbyterians, Lutherans, and representatives of other denominations were also hard at work by 1900. But the growth of Japanese nationalism in the early twentieth century presented a new challenge as Shinto, Japan's state religion, was increasingly presented by the government as being more consistent with the country's aims and traditions than Christianity. When Japan went to war with the United States and Britain in 1941, Christianity came under attack in Japan. European clergy were imprisoned or forced to leave the country, and the government attempted to bring all Protestants into a single, closely supervised church known as the *Kyodan*. The restoration of religious freedom in 1945 did not result in an increase in the number of Christians. Today, only about 1 percent of the population of Japan is Christian.

Summary

The nineteenth and twentieth centuries were a time of important challenges for the Church. As in earlier eras, social, political, and economic developments required it to adapt to a changing world, but change in this period occurred at a much faster pace than ever before. Revolutions swept across the western world, replacing monarchies with more democratic forms of government. Industrialization brought the restructuring of western society and the establishment of colonial empires in Asia and Africa. Stunning advances in the natural and social sciences combined with new currents of philosophical and historical thought to challenge traditional beliefs about God, the world, human nature, and the function of religion. In an increasingly secular world that placed its faith in progress, the role of the Church in society was no longer certain.

Until the Second Vatican Council (1962–65), the Roman Catholic Church maintained a generally defensive stance in response to the modern world, regarding many of its ideas and institutions as irreconcilable with truths and traditions that had been central to Christian culture in the West for centuries. In countries such as France, Italy, and Germany, the influence of the Roman Catholic Church in government and education was discouraged by governments that found its ideology inconsistent with their own.

On the whole, Protestants were more open to the new ideas that were shaping modern society. Liberal theology, for example, adopted many of the same concepts on which political liberalism was based. But conservatives feared that the accommodation of faith to culture would compromise truth. They defended doctrine and encouraged revival and a return to the principles of the Reformation. In the United States, new churches and religious movements such as the Mormons, Christian Scientists, Seventh-Day Adventists, and the Jehovah's Witnesses grew out of existing churches and claims of new revelations. The nineteenth and twentieth centuries were also a time during which Protestant missionaries joined Catholics in preaching the gospel and establishing churches in Africa, Asia, and other regions. By 1950 the Church was well-established in every inhabited continent and more than one-third of the world's population was Christian.[42]

The decline of the Ottoman Empire in the nineteenth century offered Orthodox Christians in the Balkans their first taste of freedom after four centuries of foreign domination. The result was a reinvigoration of theology, monasticism, and popular piety in countries such as Greece, Serbia, Bulgaria, and Romania and a strengthening of their national churches. In Russia, nationalism encouraged a rejection of Protestant and Catholic influences and a

Russia

renewed commitment to Orthodox tradition in the nineteenth century. It appears to have sustained the Russian Orthodox Church through seven decades of communist rule in the twentieth.

QUESTIONS FOR REVIEW AND REFLECTION

1. What political, intellectual, and scientific developments in the nineteenth and twentieth centuries presented challenges to traditional Christian thought?

2. How did Roman Catholicism respond to modernism? How did Protestant Christianity respond to modernism? How would you explain their different approaches to the challenges of the nineteenth and twentieth centuries?

3. How would you describe the differences between liberal and conservative Christianity?

4. In what ways did the position of the Church in relation to society as a whole change between the Middle Ages and the twentieth century?

NOTES

1. From the preface to the poem *Milton* (line 8).
2. Matthew 28:19.
3. A fascist government was also established in Spain under General Francisco Franco in 1939. In the 1920s and 1930s there were also important fascist movements in Greece, Poland, Austria, Hungary, Romania, and Bulgaria.
4. Huxley did not deny the truth of Christianity. Instead, he described himself as an agnostic. In his later years he even advocated the reading of the Bible in school, so that children might benefit from its moral instruction.
5. This is not to suggest that Comte saw no value in religion. He saw little value in Christianity, but he envisioned a new, reformed, and Godless religion led by a "positivist" priesthood that would preach rational truth and encourage people to behave morally by inspiring them with the examples set by great human figures such as Archimedes, Descartes, Shakespeare, and Gutenberg.
6. Spencer attempted to synthesize all aspects of individual and social behavior into one grand evolutionary scheme in his massive *System of Synthetic Philosophy.*
7. Ludwig Feuerbach, *Lectures on the Essence of Religion,* trans. R. Manheim (New York: Harper & Row, 1967), 17.
8. Walter Kaufmann, ed. and trans., *The Portable Nietzsche* (New York: Viking: 1967), 159.
9. Baur accepted only Romans, Galatians, and 1 and 2 Corinthians as genuine Pauline works.

10. The dates given are for the original German text, *Lehrbuch der Dogmengeschichte,* which appeared in three volumes. The seven-volume English translation was published between 1894 and 1899.
11. Prior to 1804, Napoleon had been First Consul.
12. Committed to neutrality, the pope refused to support a French blockade against England. When Napoleon responded by seizing the Papal States, Pius VII excommunicated him (1808). It was then that Napoleon had him arrested and taken to France. Pius was not allowed to return to Rome until May 1814.
13. Good examples include Joseph von Görres (1776–1848), an early supporter of the French Revolution who later advocated a greater role for the Catholic Church in German society (in *Germany and the Revolution,* 1819), and Friedrich von Schlegel (1772–1829), a convert to Catholicism who also sought to restore the Catholic Church as the basis of public life in German-speaking countries.
14. Philip Schaff, *The Creeds of Christendom,* vol. 2 (New York: Harper, 1919), 233.
15. Thomas Bokenkotter, *A Concise History of the Catholic Church,* rev. ed. (New York: Doubleday, 1990), 282.
16. In 1896, for example, he declared that ordinations in the Church of England were invalid. Leo invited both Protestant and Eastern Orthodox Christians to unite with Rome, but he did not imagine a federation in which their churches would be on equal footing with the Roman Catholic Church.
17. Henry Bettenson, ed., *Documents of the Christian Church,* 2nd ed. (New York: Oxford University Press, 1967), 275.
18. Economic liberalism emerged in the late eighteenth century with the publication of the *Wealth of Nations* by Adam Smith (1776) and Thomas Malthus's *Essay on Population* (1789). A third classic work in support of this theory was David Ricardo's *The Principles of Political Economy and Taxation* (1817).
19. Bettenson, *Documents of the Christian Church,* 276: "That men should commonly unite in associations of this kind [trade unions and the like], whether made up wholly of workers or of both classes together, is to be welcomed. . . . Natural law grants man the right to join particular associations, and the state is appointed to support natural law, not to destroy it . . . and the state arises from the same principle which produces particular societies, the fact that men are by nature gregarious."
20. The decree *Lamentabili,* issued by the Holy Office (formerly known as the Inquisition) denounced sixty-five "modernist" propositions. It was supported by the papal encyclical *Pascendi,* issued several months later.
21. Carlo Falconi, *The Popes in the Twentieth Century* (Boston: Little, Brown, 1967), 117.
22. For example, instruction in the Roman Catholic religion was made obligatory in secondary schools. Such

instruction in primary schools was a requirement as early as 1923.

23. Anthony Rhodes, *The Vatican in the Age of Dictators, 1922–1945* (London: Hodder & Stoughton, 1973), 205.

24. For an excellent introduction to Teilhard's thought, see the article on him by Mary E. Giles in *Great Thinkers of the Western World,* ed. Ian P. McGreal (New York: HarperCollins, 1992), 483–87.

25. Later theologians would push this kind of thinking about the relationship of faith and history to surprising limits. In his *Infallible? An Inquiry* (Garden City, New York: Doubleday, 1970), the German theologian Hans Küng argued that sometimes the doctrines of the Church are false and ought to be abandoned.

26. Bokenkotter, *Concise History,* 375.

27. Friedrich Schleiermacher, *On Religion: Addresses in Response to Its Cultured Despisers,* trans. Terrence Tice (Richmond, Va.: John Knox Press, 1969), 55–56.

28. Quoted in Sydney E. Ahlstrom, ed., *Theology in America: The Major Protestant Voices from Puritanism to Neo-Orthodoxy* (Indianapois: Bobbs-Merrill, 1967), 557.

29. John Leith, ed., *Creeds of the Churches,* 3rd ed. (Louisville, Ky.: John Knox Press, 1982), 521.

30. Karl Barth, *The Epistle to the Romans,* trans. Edwyn Hoskins (London: Oxford University Press, 1933), 98.

31. Ellen G. White, *The Desire of Ages,* 4th ed. (Mountain View, Calif.: Pacific Press, 1973), 723.

32. The Greek archdiocese of America is distinct from the Orthodox Church in America, which is an autocephalous church.

33. For example, *The Discovery of the Human Treasure, City of Zion or the Church Built upon the Rock,* and *Human Community in Christ.*

34. Originally published in French as *La Russie et l'Église universelle* (1889).

35. For a more detailed description of Soloviev's thought, see George Maloney, *A History of Orthodox Theology since 1453* (Belmont, Mass.: Nordland, 1976), 61–65.

36. Timothy (Kallistos) Ware, *The Orthodox Church* (Baltimore: Penguin Books, 1964), 130.

37. See the account of Nicholas Motovirov in Ware, *The Orthodox Church,* 131–32.

38. From an article published in 1949 by F. N. Oleschuk, former Secretary of the League of Militant Atheists (dissolved in 1942). Quoted in Ware, *The Orthodox Church,* 153.

39. Prohibition turned out to be tremendously unpopular, and the Eighteenth Amendment was repealed in 1933.

40. Kenneth Latourette, *A History of Christianity,* vol. 2, rev. ed. (Peabody, Mass.: Prince Press, 1999), 1291.

41. The connection between Thomas and India is first established in the *Acts of Thomas,* written in Syriac in the third century CE.

42. David Barrett, ed., *World Christian Encyclopedia* (New York: Oxford University Press, 1982), 796.

The Church and the Challenge of the New Century

Overview

Since 1950, massive shifts in technology, popular culture, and demographics have taken place, making these years among the most momentous in history. Dramatic changes have transformed Christianity as well. Catholicism abandoned its medieval shape and turned to embrace the modern world. Western Christianity has struggled to come to terms with the effects of modernization, especially science, secularization, rationalism, and materialism. Europe, once the stronghold of Christianity, has become a post-Christian culture. Independent and charismatic forms of Christianity have erupted in the non-western world to such an extent that Christianity is now a predominantly non-western, nonwhite religion.

This chapter begins with a survey of some of the trends in theology that have shaped the Christian experience in the years since 1950. It then explores developments within Catholicism and Protestantism during the same period. It concludes with an investigation of global trends and projections for the future of Christianity.

Theologies Old and New

During the twentieth century a bewildering array of Christian theologies developed. Theology does not always affect Christian practice, but theologies we discuss here have done so, or are emblematic of broader cultural trends significant for Christian faith and experience.

BIBLICAL CRITICISM

In some important ways, the academic study of the Bible is an arcane branch of the discipline of ancient history. After all, the Bible is a collection of documents from the ancient world, much like Homer's *Iliad* or the Code of Hammurabi. For centuries the Bible was thought to be unique and was studied for spiritual and theological purposes. But twentieth-century biblical scholars brought the tools of modern historical, social, and literary theory to bear on the Bible. At first their approach was largely historical: they asked whether the events described in the Bible happened, tried to determine whether Matthew, Mark, Luke, and John wrote the Gospels,

Figure 12.1   Christ Over New York City An anonymous artist rendered this painting on a steel door instead of a canvas. The image suggests a cosmic Christ who embraces the world and calls it to himself.

and attempted to discover the social, political, and theological contexts in which the various documents were written. Many of these scholars came to conclusions that were deeply disturbing to Christians holding traditional views of the faith and scripture. They questioned cherished doctrines and assumptions, such as the accuracy of the story of exodus of the Hebrews from Egypt, the historicity of the resurrection of Jesus, the historical accuracy of the Gospels, and the authorship of the letters attributed to Paul. In more recent years biblical scholarship has included modern literary and rhetorical approaches that have little interest in matters of original meaning or authorship, and instead focus

on such issues as the effect of the text on the reader. Currently there are so many different approaches to academic study of the Bible—and so many conflicting presuppositions undergirding these methodologies—that insights from one approach might not be readily transferable to another. Partly for this reason, much modern biblical criticism seems to have little impact on church practice. The clear exceptions include theological and historical investigations of the figure of Jesus.

The agenda for a good deal of the critical study of the New Testament was set by the publication of three seminal works near the beginning of the twentieth century. First to appear was Martin Kähler's

The So-Called Historical Jesus and the Historic, Biblical Christ (1892).[1] Kähler (1835–1912) argued that the Gospels have so thoroughly enmeshed the Jesus of first-century Palestine with the risen Christ worshiped by the early Church that there is no way to separate them. Even if certain facts about Jesus could be proven, said Kähler, there would never be enough bits and pieces to compose a meaningful picture. Instead, Kähler argued, what is needed is a picture of the Christ of faith.

Next to appear was William Wrede's *The Messianic Secret in the Gospels* (1901).[2] Wrede (1859–1906) asserted that the Gospels are theological fictions, not historical accounts. They record a good deal about the early Church, but virtually nothing of the historical Jesus. The third and perhaps most significant book was by Albert Schweitzer (1875–1965), one of the truly outstanding figures of the twentieth century. He was a formidable theologian, a medical doctor, a winner of the Nobel Peace Prize, and an expert interpreter of Bach. In *The Quest of the Historical Jesus* (1906),[3] Schweitzer surveyed previous works on Jesus and then put forward his own view: that Jesus was a Jewish apocalyptic prophet who wrongly believed that God was about to intervene in history by inaugurating a new kingdom of God. According to Schweitzer, Jesus believed that God would do this through the action of an emissary called the Son of Man. When no Son of Man emerged, Jesus took upon himself that role, voluntarily accepted suffering, and went to his death believing his crucifixion would force God to act. He died, said Schweitzer, realizing that he was wrong.

Schweitzer's significance can hardly be overstated. He was uncomfortable with the traditional views of Jesus embraced by many Christians. Schweitzer felt that many Christians treated the Gospels ahistorically, as repositories of proof texts used not to construct an interpretation of Jesus, but rather to legitimate beliefs about Jesus derived from the creeds and already embraced by the faithful. Schweitzer felt that this approach makes it hard to understand the Gospels on their own terms or to find in them legitimate information concerning Jesus' teaching and intent. But he was also unhappy with thoroughgoing skepticism about the Bible.

The genius of Schweitzer's portrait was to lodge Jesus firmly within a particular Jewish context in Palestine. He further argued that scholarship has only two possible conclusions open to it regarding Jesus: Either the Jesus of history can never be known, or else he was a failed apocalyptic prophet. In the wake of Schweitzer's work, many concluded that historical study of the Bible either corrodes faith or is irrelevant to it. Most New Testament scholars since Schweitzer have assumed that to pursue the historical Jesus is a pointless task.

Rudolf Bultmann (1884–1976) is generally regarded as the most important New Testament scholar of the twentieth century. His father and one of his grandfathers were pastors, and his other grandfather was a missionary. A brilliant student, Bultmann studied under the titans of the previous generation of biblical scholars, including Hermann Gunkel (1862–1932), Adolf von Harnack (1851–1930), and Johannes Weiss (1863–1914). His first important book, published in 1921, was *History of the Synoptic Tradition*,[4] in which he argued that the Gospels of Matthew, Mark, and Luke are composed of layers of material based upon oral traditions that circulated within the early Church, and then were shaped by the early Christian editors to suit their theological purposes. The implication, made abundantly clear in his later work, is that there is no firm evidence for the historical Jesus in the Gospels. They are, at best, a record of what the early Christians believed about Jesus.

In 1941 Bultmann published a very different kind of epochal study — far more philosophical and even apologetic. In an essay titled "New Testament and Mythology"[5] he asserted that the New Testament conveys its message by way of a mythological world picture, complete with angels and demons and miracles. In Bultmann's view these mythological elements make the Christian message impossible for moderns to accept. Because these devices are not central to the message of the New Testament, he claimed, they should be eliminated. The task is to "demythologize" the New Testament, leaving its essential message intact. Bultmann applied the insights of existentialism and offered a Jesus stripped from his historical context but presenting to humanity a timeless invitation from the creator to live authentically, in faith and obedience, open to the unknown future.

Both Schweitzer and Bultmann wished to offer a picture of Jesus and early Christianity that had relevance for faith in the contemporary context. Schweitzer thought we could know Jesus — a man who committed all to the Kingdom of God, a Kingdom with priorities radically opposed to those of western society. Bultmann thought Jesus could not be known at all, but that Jesus' essential message about human existence could be discerned within the fabric of the theology created by the early Christians as presented in the New Testament, with its threads of miracles and demons.

In 1953 Ernst Käsemann (1906–98), perhaps Bultmann's premier student, broke with his teacher when he gave a lecture calling for a modest consideration of the historical Jesus. He had in mind the Nazi appropriation of the image of Jesus, an ahistorical, non-Jewish Jesus used to support Nazi ideology. Without at least a rudimentary historical grounding, Käsemann said, Jesus becomes a powerful symbol open to exploitation for any purpose whatsoever. This idea prompted what has been called the new quest of the historical Jesus, concerned primarily with establishing criteria for determining what we can know about Jesus. As Kähler predicted, this effort has resulted in a minimalist Jesus, one based on the relatively few sayings and deeds of Jesus that scholars can agree upon.

Beginning in the 1960s, a movement developed that has judged Schweitzer wrong in claiming that Jesus was an apocalyptic prophet but essentially right in his optimism that the message of Jesus can be recovered. This broad and rather loose movement has been called "the third quest of the historical Jesus." The works of scholars such as G. B. Caird (1917–84), Marcus Borg (1942–), N. T. Wright (1948–), Ben Meyer (1927–95), and J. P. Meier (1942–) all offer credible accounts of Jesus. By 2000, optimism in this task was vibrant enough that Bruce Chilton, a major American New Testament scholar, wrote what he called a biography of Jesus.[6] Other scholars continue to believe that Schweitzer was right about Jesus' apocalyptic beliefs, but the portrait of a misguided Jesus is one Christians are generally unwilling to embrace. Still

others follow Wrede and claim that there is virtually nothing that we can know about the historical Jesus. Some in this camp, such as Robert Funk (1928–), are openly critical of certain expressions of Christian Faith.[7] Others, such as the Catholic scholar L. T. Johnson (1943–), wish like Kähler to embrace the Christ of faith and cast disparaging glances at any attempt to investigate the historical Jesus.

One of the effects of modern critical study of the Bible has been to question its cohesiveness. Instead of appearing as a marvelously complex book with an elusive but essential unity, as it often does to Christians, to many biblical scholars it seems a collection of hopelessly disparate documents. As the historian Northrop Frye observed in 1982, the Bible is a "huge, sprawling, tactless book [that sits] there inscrutably in the middle of our cultural heritage."[8] The biblical theology movement sought to restore a sense of unity to scripture.

BIBLICAL THEOLOGY

By the middle of the twentieth century, some scholars were becoming dissatisfied with the direction academic biblical study was taking. These scholars began what came to be called the "biblical theology movement." Those involved in this movement believed that theological concerns should be the focus of biblical scholarship, that scholars should seek to understand the Bible according to biblical concepts rather than philosophical ones, and that there is a basic unity to the biblical material. Revived interest in the writing of New Testament theologies by major scholars,[9] attempts to understand the theological interplay of the Old and New Testaments,[10] learned treatises on the theme of biblical unity amid diversity,[11] and a healthy optimism about understanding the intent of the biblical authors are evidence of the importance of this movement. By its very nature, biblical theology is often considered an aid to preaching and to the community of faith.

THEOLOGIES OF HOPE

Perhaps the most influential trend in European theology in the late twentieth century was eschatological theology,[12] also called the "theologies of hope."

These are closely associated with two widely acclaimed German theologians, Jürgen Moltmann (1926–) and Wolfhart Pannenberg (1928–). Both were raised in non-Christian homes, and both lived through the Second World War in Germany. Moltmann became a Christian while a prisoner of war in Great Britain, Pannenberg while a student in Berlin. Moltmann joined the Reformed Church and taught at Tübingen University. Pannenberg became a Lutheran and taught for much of his career at Munich. Both wished to recapture for Christian theology an authentic understanding of eschatology that steered clear of both Ritschl's liberal view that the Kingdom of God was about the improvement of human society and a conservative Christian approach that reduces eschatology to speculation about the timing of the return of Christ and the end of the world.

Moltmann's most important book, *Theology of Hope* (1964),[13] catapulted him to international fame. He argued that biblical revelation is primarily promise; that God acts from the future, drawing history toward the goal or purpose set by the divine plan. Pannenberg became famous within theological circles with the publication of *Revelation as History* (1961),[14] a collection of essays by Pannenberg and several friends. The essays were deeply learned and philosophically potent. Like Moltmann, Pannenberg argued that in Jesus the reign of God has begun, and God is drawing history toward its fulfillment already revealed in Jesus Christ. Pannenberg boldly disagrees with the split between history and faith that is exemplified in the work of Bultmann. For him, history is God's revelation. Perhaps Pannennberg's most important book is *Jesus — God and Man* (1964)[15] in which he argued for the historical accuracy of the resurrection accounts in the Gospels. The logical interpretation of the evidence, Pannenberg asserted, is that Jesus was literally raised from the dead. Only our narrow modernist presuppositions prevent us from acknowledging this, he claimed. Pannenberg has been an enormously prolific thinker and writer, exploring the interplay of theology with technology, the environment,[16] and the philosophy of history. The work of Moltmann and Pannenberg touched liberation theology, secular theologies, and trends in conservative Protestant thought.

LIBERATION THEOLOGIES

Beginning in the 1960s in the Americas a number of disparate theologies developed that are collectively known as "liberation theology." Their methodology places liberation theologians in opposition to traditional western theology, which liberationists see as dominated by intellectualism and a faith that has little interest in action. Liberationists argue that faith requires a commitment to the implementation of the gospel, and that the gospel is about liberation — not only from personal sin, but also from the exploitative systems that result from the aggregate effects of personal sin. They seek to remind the Church that Christian faith includes a commitment to transforming the world according to the standard of social justice. It is therefore not enough for Christians to offer comfort to the poor and the suffering; the Church must also combat the political, social, and economic systems that cause suffering. After all, theologians of liberation assert, God favors the poor because human society does not.

Traditionally theologians focus on theological formulations that are held to be true always and everywhere. Liberation theologians, in contrast, point out that what God has to say to people depends on the context in which those people exist. Theologies of liberation therefore attempt to apply the message of God's grace and justice to particular situations. The title of one of the foundational books of the movement reflects the importance of context: *We Drink from Our Own Wells.*[17] For theologians of liberation, the task of the theologian is not to consider timeless universal truths, but to help people in their struggle to fulfill the biblical mandate for social justice. All forms of liberation theology tend to be critical of the established Church, believing that it has become too comfortable with the surrounding culture and has abdicated its responsibility to the poor and the oppressed.

Liberation Theology   Christianity came to Latin America by way of European conquest, and liberation theology began there in the context of the effects of colonialism. The policies of Spain and Portugal in the Americas created a society in which very few controlled the lion's share of the wealth and property. The Roman Catholic Church had for centuries been associated with the ruling and affluent classes in Latin America. By 1950 many saw the United States as the new oppressive, affluent, and selfish colonial power; and the structural poverty afflicting the region was obvious. Worldwide, the problem was so great that the United Nations declared the 1950s the "decade of development," and in 1961 President Kennedy launched the Alliance for Progress, aiming at eliminating poverty through economic advancement. Both initiatives failed.

By the late 1960s a number of young theologians were disillusioned by the failure of the West, and particularly the United States, to relieve oppression and poverty in Latin America. They were heartened by Vatican II, and especially by the document *Gaudium et Spes* (1965), which pointed out that Christians have a responsibility to ensure at least the basic necessities of life for all human beings. Pope Paul VI, in his 1967 encyclical *Populorum Progressio,* recognized that the crushing poverty endured by most Latin Americans was the result of injustice that must be overturned. Buoyed by these pronouncements, the Second General Conference of Latin American Bishops (CELAM II), held in Medellín, Colombia in 1968, declared the Roman Catholic Church in Latin America to be squarely on the side of the outcasts. The duty of the Church, the bishops declared, is to "defend the rights of the poor and oppressed according to the gospel commandment, urging our governments and upper classes to eliminate anything which might destroy social peace."[18]

Contemporaneous with these developments in the rarified circles of theology and ecclesiastical politics, parishes in Central and South America began to divide into small communities of the poor and downtrodden: studying scripture and applying it to local concerns. These *comunidades ecclesiales de base* (base ecclesial communities), Christian communes of the impoverished, have been described as the poor in action, living out the gospel of liberation in and for the whole person.

The father of liberation theology is the Peruvian Catholic theologian Gustavo Gutiérrez (1928–). In 1971 he published his book *A Theology of Liberation,*[19] which remains the basic text of all theologies of liberation. He sees the root cause of the pervasive poverty afflicting Latin America as social

and economic injustice caused by North American and European economic manipulation. He argued Christians have a responsibility to work for social justice as well as spiritual development.

Another prominent liberation theologian is the Argentinian Methodist José Míguez-Bonino (1924–). The son of a shipyard worker, he saw poverty firsthand as a child. He writes, "scripture almost always takes the form of a call to create a new situation, to transform and correct present conditions—a summons to conversion and justice."[20] For Míguez-Bonino, the dominant theme is love, and love manifests itself in action. "Orthopraxis," he writes, meaning right action, "rather than orthodoxy, becomes the criterion for theology."[21]

Leonardo Boff (1938–) published *Jesus Christ Liberator* in 1972,[22] sparking complaints from conservatives that he presented an overly human portrait of Jesus, minimizing his divine nature. Boff argues that the new Kingdom Jesus came to inaugurate not only is a future hope, but is to be realized now. After all, the biblical writers frequently present God as liberator, as the one who ensures justice and comfort for the weak, orphans, and widows. Boff is clearly applying the idea, championed by the New Testament scholar C. H. Dodd (1884–1973), that with the appearance of Jesus the Kingdom of God began to be realized. But for theologians of liberation, theology does not lose its power at the classroom door. "The kingdom or reign of God means the full and total liberation of all creation, in the end, purified of all that oppresses it, transfigured by the full presence of God."[23] Boff has more recently explored the interplay of liberation theology with ecological issues.[24]

Another important figure in liberation theology was Oscar Romero (1917–80). Romero became a priest in 1942 and quickly gained notoriety as a pastor, radio preacher, and editor of a Catholic newspaper in El Salvador. In 1970 he was made auxiliary bishop of San Salvador. Initially Romero was suspicious of liberation theology, but when he was elevated to the position of bishop of a rural diocese in 1974 he witnessed firsthand the conditions endured by the peasants. Several of his priests began a new type of parish ministry employing the base community model. After Romero became archbishop of San Salvador in 1977, six of his priests active in social issues were murdered by agents of the government. Romero became a vocal and passionate voice for the poor. His weekly radio program became the most popular in the country. Eventually five of the six bishops he oversaw as archbishop sided with the land-owning families against him. Uncowed, Romero continued. A right-wing execution squad assassinated him in 1980 while he was preaching at mass.

African American Liberation Theology

Liberation theology was quickly embraced by other victims of social and economic injustice. African American liberation theology sees racism as the chief social sin in North America, a sin that most whites do not readily see because it is built into the very structures of white society.

James Cone (1938–) is perhaps the leading figure in African American theology. In the 1960s, Cone was among those black intellectuals who were dissatisfied with the pacifist stance of Martin Luther King, Jr., and associated instead with Malcolm X and various Black Power movements. He wrote two controversial but immensely important books during this period—*Black Theology and Black Power* (1969)[25] and *A Black Theology of Liberation* (1970).[26] Cone and others were profoundly unhappy with traditional black Christianity, which they saw as placing so much emphasis on a better life in heaven that it robbed blacks of dignity on earth. According to Cone, "the idea of heaven is irrelevant for Black Theology. The Christian cannot waste time contemplating the next world. . . . Jesus' work is essentially one of liberation. Becoming a slave himself, he opens the realities of human existence formerly closed to man."[27] Cone offers this view of the black acceptance of Christianity and the black Christian experience:

> The blacks brought their religion with them. After a time they accepted the white man's religion, but they have not always expressed it in the white man's way. It became the black man's purpose—perhaps it was his destiny—to shape, to fashion, to re-create the religion offered him by the Christian slavemaster, to remold it nearer to his own heart's desire, nearer to his own peculiar needs.[28]

Feminist Theology

A third expression of liberation theology is feminist theology, which made a spectacular entrance onto the theological stage during the 1960s. In 1960 an important essay by Valerie Saiving Goldstein appeared, "The Human Situation: A Feminine View."[29] She pointed out that what theologians often called the "human experience" was actually the experience of men, and that standard descriptions of human nature (for example, sin as prideful self-assertion) are more descriptive of men's experience than of women's. Women, she argued, generally suffer from sins of self-sacrifice and self-negation, rather than self-assertion. This insight was followed up by Mary Daly (1928–) in her 1973 book, *Beyond God the Father*,[30] in which she argued that depicting God as Father only allows traditional cultural patterns to parade as cherished spiritual norms, thereby relegating women to secondary roles. Another important voice is Rosemary Radford Ruether (1936–). Her *Sexism and God-Talk* (1983)[31] is one of the foundational texts for the feminist theology movement. She sees injustice primarily in terms of systems of hierarchy that tend to limit possibilities for women, and she sees the Church as largely complicit in these systems. Ruether argues that we ought to conceive of God not as male, but rather as "God/ess" (both God and Goddess, male and female), the author of a way of being that connects everyone in a nexus of equality and interrelatedness. But society is far from this vision, she says, and the established Church, largely beholden to culture, is just as distant. She therefore advocates the establishment of "Women Churches," open to women and sensitized males, as safe contexts for women to exercise their rights and find their true roles.

Feminist theology played a significant role in highlighting the importance of using inclusive language in biblical studies. In most English translations of the Bible, male terms such as *man* or *men* are used where the text most often indicates humanity in general. Newer translations, such as the New Revised Standard version, seek to be more faithful to the text in this regard.

There is a considerable range within feminist theological circles. Some feminist theologians, such as Carol Christ (1945–), reject male representations of God, embracing the idea of the Goddess instead. Other feminist theologians see scripture and its male representation of God as essentially supportive of women. These thinkers employ sophisticated exegetical tools to demonstrate that the New Testament actually affirms equal roles and rights for women within the Church.[32] While this may mean a loss of power for men, these feminists point out that scripture cautions all Christians against seeking power and prestige.[33]

Most of the founders of feminist theology were white, middle-class academics. More recently, varieties of feminist theology have developed among women for whom the privileged context of white America is an alien world. Together they are called womanist theology, a term used to refer to the work of feminist theologians of color. Womanist theology is sharply critical of feminist theology, which it sees as racist and classist; and of liberation theology, which it regards as sexist. Womanist theologians argue that white feminists are concerned with issues like self-fulfillment, whereas womanists are occupied with more basic issues, such as the economic survival of nonwhites. A second theology of this type is *Mujerista* theology; this developed in the 1980s among Latin American women, many of whom are the victims not only of patriarchy, but also of economic forces that benefit other ethnic and economic groups.

Theologies of liberation constitute a vibrant new voice on the theological landscape. By emphasizing context, they operate from a perspective quite different from that of traditional western theologies. Their concern to take the biblical themes of justice and righteousness seriously has made them important forces in Christian practice.

SECULAR THEOLOGY

During the 1960s there appeared a variegated movement that came to be called "secular theology." To many younger theologians especially, the task facing the Church was to make its message intelligible to modern, industrial, urbanized society. The surest indicator of God's character they said, was God's actions, and God acts in love and justice. They as-

serted that God is pure love, or, in a phrase borrowed from Tillich, the ground of all being.

Harvey Cox (1929–), generally considered the leading voice of this movement, claimed that with the maturity of scientific and technological skill the world has "come of age" and is divesting itself of control by religious understandings of self.[34] Secular theologies, therefore, repudiate the supernatural elements of Christian theology and avoid technical theological vocabulary. An example of such theology is found in *Honest to God* (1963), by John A. T. Robinson (1919–83), the Anglican bishop of Woolwich and a major figure in British New Testament scholarship:

> I am firmly convinced that this whole way of thinking can be the greatest obstacle to an intelligent faith — and indeed will progressively be so to all except the "religious" few. We shall eventually be no more able to convince men of the existence of a God "out there" whom they must call in to order their lives than persuade them to take seriously the gods of Olympus. If Christianity is to survive . . . there is no time to lose.[35]

Practitioners of secular theology were certain that they were engaged in an authentic Christian enterprise. After all, Cox wrote, "the rise of natural science, of democratic institutions, and of cultural pluralism" were due to the original impetus of the Bible.[36] Secular theologians were careful to distinguish between secularism and secularization. Secularism, they maintained, is an ideology often opposed to faith. Secularization, they asserted, is the result of biblical faith, and thus is a part of God's unfolding design. They saw themselves attempting a kind of Christian secularization, aiming to reinterpret the Christian message in secular terms because that is the language and symbol system of this age.

These varied Christian theologies continue to have influence over Christian practice. Especially significant is one common theme: to make Christian faith relevant and acceptable in concrete human circumstances while retaining its distinctive character and message.

Currents in Church Life and Practice

The range of Christian popular expression is enormous, and worldwide there is a staggering number of Christian groups: as many as thirty-three thousand denominations representing three hundred ecclesiastical traditions.[37] The explosive growth in non-western Christianity is often found among groups that have been influenced by North American Christianity, which sponsored hundreds of missions to other parts of the world in the nineteenth and twentieth centuries. This section will investigate several of the most significant North American expressions of Protestant Christianity before turning to developments in Roman Catholicism.

FUNDAMENTALISM

As we saw in chapter 11, by the dawn of the twentieth century liberal theology dominated Protestantism in the West. This development alarmed many. The Dutch theologian Abraham Kuyper (1837–1920) observed:

> Christianity is imperiled by great and serious dangers. Two life systems are wrestling with one another, in mortal combat. Modernism is bound to build a world of its own from the data of the natural man, and to construct man himself from the data of nature; while, on the other hand, all those who reverently bend the knee to Christ and worship Him as the Son of the living God, and God himself, are bent upon saving the "Christian Heritage." This is the struggle in Europe, this is the struggle in America."[38]

In Europe, Barth's neo-orthodoxy constituted a formidable reaction to Protestant liberalism. A backlash of a wholly different kind was to take shape in North America, one without parallel on any other continent: fundamentalism. Like many other terms, *fundamentalism* conveys a wide range of meanings. Here it refers to a particular movement aimed at combating what were perceived as the harmful effects of modernism and Protestant liberalism. Fundamentalism developed a distinctive form of traditional Protestant expression that (curiously) embraced modernist principles such as rationalism, even while it became increasingly inflexible and separatist.

One of the key doctrinal claims for fundamentalists is the **inerrancy** of the Bible. Unlike the Protestant reformers of the sixteenth century, fundamentalists believe that the Bible is not simply the record of God's revelation, but is that revelation itself. As one fundamentalist scholar put it, if "the Bible is not wholly true, then our assurance of salvation has no dependable and divine warrant."[39] Equally significant for fundamentalists is the doctrine of the deity of Christ, which they believe is clearly taught in scripture. Fundamentalists see the doctrine of the virgin birth of Jesus as perhaps the chief proof of Jesus' divinity, even though it is difficult to argue the centrality of this doctrine in the New Testament.[40] Fundamentalists are also traditional in their view of the atonement, embracing the orthodox substitutionary and penal theory (that Christ took upon himself punishment for the sins of others). They believe in the literal, bodily resurrection of Jesus and in a literal future return of the risen Christ to earth to reign for one thousand years. They also believe that there will be a final battle between the forces of Satan and of God, and that Satan will be overcome and suffer punishment in hell.

Fundamentalism is often traced to two sources: a particular academic reaction to modernism and the thought of J.N. Darby. The first, beginning as a conservative response to scholarly criticism of the Boble, was led by a series of three professors at Princeton Theological Seminary. Charles Hodge (1797–1878) emphasized the idea of the verbal inspiration of scripture—that God is, in effect, the author of the Bible. Hodge's disciple Benjamin Warfield (1851–1921), also a professor at Princeton, was even more vocal than Hodge in claiming that the Bible, at least in its original form, is infallible, or without error. Fundamentalism as a reactionary movement became more widely known when Princeton theologian J. Gresham Machen (1881–1937) criticized Protestant liberalism and defended what he considered to be historic Protestant orthodoxy. Machen tangled with Henry Emerson Fosdick (1878–1969), a leading figure in the social gospel movement. Although a Baptist, Fosdick was serving as the acting minister of the Old First Presbyterian Church in New York City, and he reacted to Machen's criticism by preaching a sermon entitled "Shall the Fundamentalists Win?" The sermon was an eloquent plea for mutual tolerance, but fundamentalist Presbyterians did not appreciate it. They demanded that Fosdick become a Presbyterian and endorse Presbyterian doctrine or resign. Fosdick chose to resign.

The second major shaping force of fundamentalism was John Nelson Darby (1800–1884) and dispensationalism. Fundamentalists seek to defend what they believe are the essential ideas of Protestant orthodoxy. They take the doctrines of the verbal inspiration and infallibility of scripture to be foundational and hold that the other traditional doctrines follow by logical necessity. By the middle of the twentieth century, however, some fundamentalists had included other doctrines as "fundamental" that were never central to Protestant orthodoxy. Most of these newer views can be traced to Darby. He devised a method of understanding history through the lens of the Book of Daniel—in terms of dispensations, or long periods of time in which God relates to humanity in different periods according to different principles. Darby claimed that Christians are living in the sixth dispensation, which will end in judgment when God's kingdom is established on earth and the present civilization meets its doom. This idea, called "dispensationalism," was enshrined in the extensive explanatory notes to the Scofield Reference Bible (1909). This version of the Bible quickly became the standard Bible among fundamentalists, who often see the explanatory notes as authoritative. Not all fundamentalists are dispensationalists, but some of Darby's ideas left a deep stamp on fundamentalism.

One prominent idea championed by Darby was that Christ will reign for a thousand years on earth following his return. Another idea raised to the level of a fundamental of the faith was "young-earth creationism" (the belief that God created all of nature less than ten thousand years ago in a literal week of twenty-four-hour days). This was partly a reaction to the rise of evolutionary teaching in the United States. Fundamentalist ideas have penetrated deeply into American culture. Even at the beginning of the twenty-first century, controversy over teaching evolution and young-earth creationism is still erupting in portions of the United States.

The term fundamentalism can be traced to a series of twelve pamphlets called *The Fundamentals*[41] published between 1910 and 1915.[42] The pamphlets, written by leading conservative Protestants, attacked what the writers considered modernist enemies of Christian faith—including socialism, biblical criticism, and evolution. The pamphlets affirmed doctrines thought to be litmus tests of orthodoxy, such as the virgin birth of Jesus, the deity of Christ, the substitutionary atonement of Christ, the resurrection of Christ, and the divine inspiration of scripture.

The Fundamentals appealed to conservative Christians who were upset by the implications of modernism for their faith. The publication and dissemination of the pamphlets set the stage for controversy in a variety of denominations. Defenders of *The Fundamentals* were strong enough within Presbyterian ranks that the General Assembly of the Northern Presbyterian Church in 1910 issued a doctrinal summary drawing upon *The Fundamentals*, including five points: the inerrancy of scripture, the virgin birth, the substitutionary atonement, the physical resurrection of Jesus, and the historicity of the miracles of Jesus.

In a number of denominations, fundamentalists, following the lead of Machen, sought to wrest control from liberal Protestants. The forces of liberalism within Presbyterianism chose to contest the battle in the seminaries, figuring that these were crucial for determining the future direction of their Church. Their most spectacular victory came in 1929, when they were able to oust Machen from the faculty of Princeton Seminary. Machen then helped to start both Westminster Seminary and the Orthodox Presbyterian Church as conservative alternatives.

The contest between liberals and fundamentalists also rocked North American Baptists. Baptists in North America are divided into several groups, and in 1919, the Canadian, Southern, and Northern Baptists founded the World's Christian Fundamentals Association. Its goal was to reclaim

American culture for what they perceived to be its traditional biblical values. Modernism had affected the Southern Baptists least of all, and in 1926 they adopted a statement that endorsed the literal reading of the Genesis account of creation and repudiated any "theory, evolution or other, which teaches that man originated in, or came by way of, a lower animal ancestry."[43] This last statement points to the question of evolution that came to a head in the famous Scopes trial that took place in Dayton, Tennessee, in 1925. Scopes was a schoolteacher who, in violation of state law, had taught the theory of evolution. Scopes was found guilty, but the trial, which had attracted considerable attention, made the anti-evolution position look foolish and backward.

Unlike the case with Southern Baptists, Northern Baptist Seminaries were already in the modernist camp. Many Northern Baptists simply decided to separate instead of trying to change their seminaries, and in 1932 formed the General Association of Regular Baptist Churches. Those remaining within the denomination responded by founding more conservative schools, such as Northern Seminary in Illinois, Eastern College in Pennsylvania, and Gordon College in Massachusetts.

In Canada, T. T. Shields (1873–1955), the prominent pastor of the Jarvis Street Baptist Church in Toronto, attacked the modernist teaching at McMaster University, the Baptist school in Quebec. He was censured by the Canadian Baptist denomination in 1926, and in 1928 he founded the Union of Regular Baptist Churches.

At first fundamentalism was a diverse movement, including different theological traditions (such as Calvinists and Arminians), as well as various denominations (such as Presbyterians and Baptists) that sometimes held incompatible theological positions on other issues. With the formation of new, more conservative denominations, this loose alliance was weakened as disputes broke out over eschatology (teachings about the end of time), particularly as presented in the Book of Revelation. This New Testament book teaches that Jesus Christ will return to earth to reign for one thousand years, Satan and the Antichrist will rule the earth, humanity will suffer great tribulation, and God will overthrow Satan and create a new heaven and a new earth. Because the precise order of these events is not entirely clear in Revelation, differences over various understandings of eschatology fractured fundamentalism and led to the creation of still other new denominations. Some fundamentalists became dissatisfied with the teaching at even the newer conservative colleges and seminaries, and they founded a host of Bible institutes to train their leaders. Prominent among them are the Moody Bible Institute in Chicago, the Prairie Bible Institute in Alberta, and the Bible Institute of Los Angeles. Fundamentalism is therefore composed of whole denominations, independent institutions, and fundamentalist elements within other denominations.

Fundamentalists have long understood and used mass media to their advantage. In 1925 Charles E. Fuller began a radio broadcast called the "Old-Fashioned Revival Hour," and by 1942 the program was heard on more than 450 stations throughout North America. Many fundamentalist schools have their own radio station; the most famous is WMBI in Chicago, the voice of the Moody Bible Institute.

By the 1930s many fundamentalists favored "biblical separation," a separation from and refusal to cooperate with nonfundamentalist Christians. When the evangelist Billy Graham (1918–   ) was a rising star within fundamentalism in the 1940s and 1950s, he was nonetheless spurned by many fundamentalists because he chose to cooperate with nonfundamentalist Protestant ministers and Catholic clergy. In 1941 the fundamentalist Presbyterian pastor Carl McIntire (1906–   ) founded the American Council of Christian Churches, accusing other conservative Protestants of failing to adhere to true fundamentalism. In response the National Association of Evangelicals was founded in 1942. Fundamentalists and evangelicals share a porous boundary and a good deal of common theology, though evangelicals are less likely to have strong views on eschatology, science, and modern culture in general. The most important difference between them concerns their attitude to other Christians. Evangelicals are more likely to work with other Protestants and Roman Catholics, and are open to nonliteral understandings of scripture. Both tendencies are viewed with deep suspicion by fundamentalists.

One of the peculiarities of fundamentalism is that it often assumes the principles of the modernism it claims to repudiate. For example, some fundamentalists believe the accuracy of the Bible can be proven. One popular book that argues for this view is *Evidence That Demands a Verdict.*[44] This book, which marshals evidence from ancient authors combined with logical extrapolation, has largely failed to convince skeptics—but fundamentalists assume, fully consonant with modernist principles, that this evidence, like the results of a scientific experiment, eventually will convince and lead to acceptance.

Fundamentalism remains a potent force in American culture. Many novels in the current *Left Behind* series, based on a fundamentalist view of the end of time, the return of Jesus, and the fate of those left on earth, have been on the *New York Times* bestsellers list; more than twenty million copies in the series had been sold by the end of 2000. Yet because the movement is generally self-isolating and critical of culture, it sometimes appears to have little effect on the broader American landscape. In the 1970s and 1980s, Baptist minister Jerry Falwell (1933–) and the "Moral Majority" focused this latent potential on the national political agenda. Unlike earlier fundamentalists, Falwell was willing to make common cause with groups he disagreed with theologically, including Mormons and Catholics, if they shared his conservative social views. It is generally conceded that this "Christian Coalition" helped elect the Republican U.S. presidents Ronald Reagan and George Bush in the 1980s. In some parts of the United States, fundamentalists continue to insist that abortion be outlawed and that prayer, the Ten Commandments, and the teaching of young-earth creationism be allowed in the public schools. Protestant fundamentalism is a broad movement that crosses denominational lines, endorses traditional Protestant doctrine, includes a conservative attitude to the Bible and to Christian faith, and is generally suspicious of the broader culture.

EVANGELICALISM

The term *evangelical* carries a wide variety of meanings. The term comes from a Greek word meaning "concerning the good news," and in Europe it is simply another word for "Protestant." In North America the term refers to Protestants who embrace traditional views of the faith and Christian doctrine, emphasize the importance of a personal spiritual awakening or "new birth," but do not consider themselves fundamentalists. They tend to place an emphasis on evangelism and mission to the wider world. They also stress personal piety and a devotion to follow the teachings of the Bible, especially the New Testament, in their daily lives. Some denominations are called "Evangelical," but evangelicals can be found in almost all denominations. Both fundamentalists and evangelicals believe in supernatural inspiration of the Bible and embrace the traditional doctrines of Protestant orthodoxy. But evangelicals are unhappy with what they see as the harsh inflexibility and unhealthy divisiveness within fundamentalism. Fundamentalists often assert that the Bible is without error even in matters of historical and scientific accuracy; evangelicals generally emphasize its authority in matters of faith and Christian life. For instance, the doctrinal statement of Fuller Theological Seminary, a leading evangelical academic institution in the United States, makes this claim about the Bible:

> Scripture is an essential part and trustworthy record of this divine self-disclosure. All the books of the Old and New Testaments, given by divine inspiration, are the written word of God, the only infallible rule of faith and practice. They are to be interpreted according to their context and purpose and in reverent obedience to the Lord who speaks through them in living power.[45]

Evangelicalism is a significant force in American culture, combining pietism and revivalism and a belief in the classic Protestant doctrines of the authority of scripture and salvation.[46] The Evangelical stress on evangelism is due, in part, to the belief that the primary problem of human existence is alienation from God. Once people become Christians, evangelicals believe, God renews their hearts and the basic inclination of the human spirit changes from selfishness to compassion. This transformation, they believe, when multiplied on a massive scale, will result in the moral improvement of society. Unlike liberation theologians, therefore, American evangelicals tend not to see economic, social, or political systems as sources of sin.

This emphasis on personal transformation coupled with an increasingly open stance to the broader culture has led some to see in evangelicalism a force for positive social change. For example, a 1997 *Wall Street Journal* article, commenting on efforts at racial reconciliation, referred to evangelicals as "the most energetic element of society addressing racial divisions."[47] However, researchers have found that the attitudes of American evangelicals are often more determined by American culture than by the gospel they claim to embrace. One recent study argues that the individualism of American culture has thoroughly overwhelmed the ability of American evangelicals to see transformation extending beyond the purely personal and interpersonal.[48] Evangelicals rarely engage in concerted reflection on structural sin, as do liberation theologians. Instead, they tend to see sin almost exclusively in terms of individual behavior patterns, such as dishonesty, selfishness, and infidelity. When asked if racially integrated neighborhoods might not help solve the problem of race in America, for example, a white evangelical responded:

> Any solution that doesn't come naturally [from the heart rather than from a government policy] is gonna cause a problem. No one, I don't care, no one wants to be told where to live, Christians or non-Christians. No one wants to be told by government or some other authority who to associate with, so I don't think that forced issues are going to fundamentally solve the problem. The solution is going to come, if it ever does come, through natural workings of people getting to know one another and finding a way to get to know each other. It's got to happen one-on-one.[49]

This quintessential evangelical response emphasizes certain American values (individualism and the freedom to make one's own decisions) while neglecting to consider the possibility that Christians bear a responsibility to challenge societal structures that promote oppression and division.

But evangelicalism also contains a more activist wing of "radicals," are scattered among many denominations, believe in evangelism and social change, and are committed to the concern of the poor and oppressed. Radical evangelicals combine a conservative view of the Bible with a political stance similar to that of liberal Protestants. Magazines that represent this approach include *Sojourners*, *Radix*, and *The Other Side*.

African American Christianity is often linked to evangelicalism, as black Christians tend to be evangelical in theology, although liberal politically. The vast majority of black Christians in the United States belong to a handful of historically black denominations.[50] Those who are affiliated with predominantly white denominations tend to be members of mostly black congregations.[51]

There are complex roots to this development involving the racism that is endemic to American society. White Christians like the Congregational minister Cotton Mather (1663–1728) and the revivalist George Whitefield argued that slaves should be Christianized.[52] Whitefield did not oppose slavery, thinking that such opposition would hinder the evangelistic task. Other white Christians believed that slaves should be emancipated, but only after they were Christianized. Still others, like the evangelist Charles Finney (1792–1875) claimed that no one who owned slaves could be a Christian.[53]

After the civil war, blacks and whites worshiped together, but racist attitudes were strong enough that blacks were almost always denied equal participation in these white-dominated churches. The creation of separate black denominations was not so much a matter of doctrine as a black protest against unequal treatment within Christian congregations.[54]

With the establishment of black denominations, white Christians, like the evangelist D. L. Moody (1837–99), became convinced that separate churches existed because both blacks and whites preferred it that way. This belief allowed white evangelicals to ignore institutionalized racism and focus instead on personal piety and the evangelistic task. Even in the 1960s many white evangelicals did not think it was their duty to support civil rights. For example, *Christianity Today*, the leading magazine of the evangelical movement, sent one of its coeditors to cover the civil rights marches in the south but did not report on them, fearing this would imply that civil rights should be part of the Christian agenda.[55] Rather, white evangelicals believed it was enough if they were against prejudice and discrimination in their personal relationships.

By 2000 there were signs that evangelicalism was emerging as an intellectual force in American culture. It has certainly not always been so, although from the very beginning evangelical leaders called for their young to earn advanced degrees at the best schools with the most rigorous programs. Figures such as Billy Graham, Harold John Ockenga (1905–85), and the theologian Carl F. H. Henry (1913–   ) wanted to create an intellectual element within evangelicalism that was absent in fundamentalism.[56] By 2000 it appeared this effort was finally bearing fruit.[57] Evangelical scholars are gaining appointments at major American universities, and some evangelical schools are increasingly recognized for their quality.

Evangelical expressions of Christian faith exist outside of North America, of course. In most of these areas, evangelicalism arose untouched by the fundamentalist/modernist controversy in North America and therefore tends to be free of the condemnations of innocuous behaviors (such as dancing and the moderate consumption of alcohol) that American evangelicalism inherited from fundamentalism.

THE PENTECOSTAL AND CHARISMATIC MOVEMENTS

Another movement that began in twentieth-century North American Protestantism is Pentecostalism. **Pentecostals** emphasize what they believe is a literal biblical practice of Christianity, specifically as experienced in the events of Pentecost, when the New Testament says the earliest Christians were filled, or baptized, with the Holy Spirit. Pentecostal denominations differ markedly in racial composition and social class, but they all share the conviction that conversion to Christ should be followed by this intense experience of the Spirit of God, often called "Spirit Baptism." Pentecostals believe this usually results in speaking in tongues, which can refer to either speaking in an unknown language or speaking in a known language one has never learned, in much the same way as Acts 2 claims the disciples of Jesus spoke at Pentecost.

Modern Pentecostalism had its origin in the confluence of black Christian experience and the Holiness movement in the early twentieth century. In 1900 Charles Parham (1873–1929), formerly a Methodist preacher and evangelist, founded the Bethel Bible School in Topeka, Kansas, under the conviction that a modern version of the Pentecost event would happen to receptive believers. On 1 January 1901, one of his students, Agnes Ozman, had an experience of the Holy Spirit that included speaking in tongues.[58] Soon Parham and others had the same experience. The movement quickly spread, and by 1905 there were an estimated twenty-five thousand Pentecostal Christians in Texas alone.[59]

One of Parham's followers was William J. Seymour (1870–1922), a Black Holiness revivalist. In 1906 he was in Los Angeles, and on 6 April of that year, "the fire came down," as Seymour put it, and he as well as a host of others were baptized in the Spirit. A warehouse they rented on Azusa Street in Los Angeles became the site of the Azusa Street Revival. These developments are considered by most Pentecostals to be the birth of their movement.

American Pentecostals have often been described as poor and ill-educated. By the 1960s, however, this portrait was no longer accurate, as the movement began attracting the highly educated and the affluent, and its former antipathy toward theological education began to dissipate. This new phase is often referred to as the charismatic movement (from *charismata*, or the gifts of the Holy Spirit). Whereas Pentecostalism is composed of whole denominations that emphasize the work of the Holy Spirit, the charismatic movement cuts across the full range of Protestant denominations and has even made inroads into the Catholic Church. In early 1967, two Catholic lay instructors of theology at Duquesne University attended a charismatic prayer group and asked for prayer to receive the Pentecostal experience. They did, and later they prayed with several of their friends at the university who then also spoke in tongues. Soon students at other universities heard the news, and in April 1967 a small group of students and faculty from Duquesne, Notre Dame, and Michigan State universities gathered on the Notre Dame campus for discussion. This became an annual conference, and by 1973 an estimated twenty thousand people were attending. The movement spread throughout the world, leading Pope Paul VI to appoint a cardinal to oversee it.

In North America there are clear racial divisions among Pentecostals. Some of these divisions are the result of recent immigration, but others owe their existence to racial and class distinctions that beset the culture.

Pentecostalism has spread to Canada, Europe, Africa, Asia, and Latin America. In Nigeria, William Kamuyi began a Bible study in 1978 with fifteen people. By 1990 his church claimed to number fifty-six thousand members.[60] In Seoul, South Korea, a single congregation — the Full Gospel Central Church under the leadership of Paul Y. Cho — claims to have more than nine hundred thousand members and more than seven hundred ministers, most of them women.[61] In 2000 there were more than ten million Pentecostals in the United States, mostly concentrated in seven denominations. The largest Pentecostal denomination in the world is the Assemblies of God, which is said to have more than thirteen million members worldwide. When Pentecostals and charismatics are considered in aggregate, they number over five hundred million worldwide.[62]

Pentecostals affirm doctrinal positions similar to those of fundamentalists. They generally believe in a literal interpretation of the Bible, hold a traditional view of God, and insist upon the deity of Christ. They also claim that a believer is not fully Christian until she or he experiences the "filling of the Spirit," which they usually associate with speaking in tongues. They tend to emphasize the imminent return of Christ.

SUCCESS AND "SIGNS AND WONDERS" CHRISTIANITY

Aspects of Pentecostalism and evangelicalism sometimes overlap to form new types of Christianity like the gospel of success and "Signs and Wonders" expressions of Christian faith. Some Pentecostal groups combine belief in the power of the Holy Spirit with a theology of health and/or success. They believe that any sickness or infirmity is the result of the activity of Satan. Because God must want to remove Satan's influence, they reason, God must also want to remove whatever sickness or malady is present. This idea is sometimes extended by Pentecostals and evangelicals to the arena of financial health, with the conviction that God wants Christians to be wealthy.[63] While other Christians generally eschew such ideas, one prominent evangelical financial commentator has stated that he believes God wants Christians to "live a comfortable life."[64] This approach is often called the "prosperity gospel."

Robert Schuller (1926–   ), a minister of the Reformed Church of America, is perhaps the foremost proponent of self-esteem theology. Schuller sees a lack of self-esteem as the fundamental problem with human beings. Accordingly, he has a decidedly unorthodox view of sin. Schuller believes that the traditional view of original sin is destructive: it causes people to develop a negative self-image, and the resulting lack of self-esteem leaves them unable to accept God's love. Schuller defines sin as "any act or thought that robs myself or another human being of his or her self-esteem."[65] His "Hour of Power" television program is a weekly televised service of his church, the Crystal Cathedral in Garden Grove, California.

Another recent phenomenon is the "Signs and Wonders," or "Vineyard," movement associated with John Wimber (1934–97). In the 1970s in Los Angeles, Wimber began emphasizing the power of the Holy Spirit to heal people of diseases and infirmities. Wimber claimed that contemporary Christians should be able to heal people and cast out demons by the power of the Holy Spirit.[66] This, he said, is God's plan for evangelization. He argued that the modernist worldview embraced by western Christians prevents them from recognizing this as the teaching of the New Testament. Since 1980 the movement has seen tremendous growth in North America, and by 2000 it was beginning to make inroads into Europe.[67]

THE ECUMENICAL MOVEMENT

Ecumenical means "general" or "universal;" and the term ecumenical movement refers to attempts to promote unity among the various Christian churches. Since the Reformation, many Christians have been troubled by the sharp and at times violently acrimonious divisions between expressions of the Chris-

Figure 12.2   Pope John Paul II (1978–) The first non-Italian to be elected to the papacy since Hadrian VI (1522–3), the Polish-born John Paul II has traveled to more than one hundred countries.

tian faith. As early as 1747 Jonathan Edwards published his appeal for Christian unity, titled *Humble Attempt to Promote Explicit Agreement and Visible Union of God's People.*[68] In 1920 the first World Mission Conference was held in Edinburgh. This event is generally regarded as having inaugurated the modern ecumenical movement.[69] But Pope Pius XI, in his 1928 encyclical *Mortalium Animos,* forbade Catholic participation in the ecumenical movement, as he was convinced it would lead to a relativizing of Catholic doctrine.

Konrad Raiser, general secretary of the World Council of Churches (an international federation of many denominations), asserted in 2001 that the transforming power of the gospel commits Christians to reconciliation and unity:

> It is God who, through Christ, brings about new community. . . . Through Christ, the relationship between God and humanity, which has been interrupted and distorted by sin, has been restored. . . . Through Christ, a new relationship is being established between those who accept this gift: strangers become citizens and aliens are recognized as members of the household of God.[70]

Raiser noted that old divisions are breaking down as Christians come to recognize that "the task of common witness and service to the world"[71] is more critical than the issues that divide them. He pointed, for example, to the establishment of full communion between the Church of England and the Nordic Lutheran Churches, and between the Evangelical Lutheran Church of America and the Episcopal Church. "We can say today," said Raiser, "that the churches belonging to the tradition of historic Protestantism have reached a situation of de facto communion with one another."[72] Raiser was less hopeful about dialogue between the Roman Catholic Church and the Eastern Orthodox Church, observing that there is not sufficient readiness there for change. In spite of some promising signs, significant differences remain between these two major traditions.[73]

Overcoming earlier reticence, Vatican II affirmed the need for openness, dialogue, and increased understanding between Christian denominations. According to *Unitatis Redintegratio*, the Vatican II document on ecumenism, divisions between Christian bodies "openly contradict the will of Christ, scandalize the world and damage that most holy cause, the preaching of the gospel to every creature."[74] Pope John Paul II wrote in his 1995 encyclical *Ut Unum Sint:* "Thus it is absolutely clear that ecumenism, the movement towards promoting Christian unity, is not just some sort of 'appendix' which is added to the Church's traditional activity. Rather, ecumenism is an organic part of her life and work, and consequently must pervade all that she is and does."[75] In 1999, after thirty years of work, Catholics and Lutherans reached agreement on the doctrine of justification by faith and signed a "Joint Declaration."[76]

In 2001 *Theology, News and Notes,* a publication of Fuller Theological Seminary, devoted an entire issue to ecumenism with major articles by Konrad Raiser and Edward Idris Cardinal Cassidy, the President of the Pontifical Council for Promoting Christian Unity. By the start of the twenty-first century, Catholics and Evangelicals were engaged in fruitful dialogue and common work. Since 1994, Catholic and evangelical thinkers in North America have been working on a document called *Evangelicals and Catholics Together* that highlights the many points of commonality between them. Within evangelicalism, the effort is opposed only by the most conservative elements.[77]

There are several reasons for what at first appears to be an odd alliance. Many Evangelicals and Catholics share a deep disquiet over what they consider to be dangerous and immoral aspects of American culture. Both groups see themselves as misunderstood and misrepresented by the American media.[78] Both groups have a commitment to human rights, and support measures restricting religious persecution throughout the world. Catholic commentator Richard John Neuhaus found it ironic that the National Council of Churches lobbied against the Freedom from Persecutions Act pending before Congress in 1997–98. Representing the view of many conservative Christians, he wryly noted, this is "yet another issue on which Catholics and evangelicals are united, leaving the oldline Protestants out in the cold."[79] One final way Catholics and Protestants are moving closer together relates to the spiritual disciplines. Since 1970, millions of Protestants have rediscovered the richness of the Catholic spiritual tradition and have begun to read spiritual classics ancient and modern. For example, millions of Protestants treasure the insights into Christian spiritual life they find in the writings of Henri Nouwen (1932–96), a Catholic priest and scholar.

THE ROMAN CATHOLIC CHURCH AFTER VATICAN II

In the aftermath of Vatican II the Catholic Church has changed dramatically. According to one learned Catholic commentator, although Vatican II created a crisis,

> To acknowledge that the Catholic Church is in crisis is to say only that it has reached another turning point in its two-thousand year history. The Church is confronted with new opportunities for growth, new temptations to repress and regress.[80]

Vatican II opened the door to a host of innovations and, perhaps more significantly, to a new and welcoming posture to the wider world. It remains to be seen how quite rapidly the Church will pursue these new vistas.

Since Vatican II the Catholic Church has generally remained conservative on theological issues but has been willing to take more liberal positions on a wide range of social issues. It has been a potent force for social change and has largely identified itself with the poor and oppressed. It played a key role in the collapse of communism in Europe in the

1980s, and Pope John Paul II has been an advocate for social and economic justice throughout the world. The Church has taken steps to make its practice more open to the laity—as in its decision to replace Latin with the common language of the parish for the mass. Vatican II declared that lay men and women share in the mission of the Church and the threefold office of Christ (prophet, priest, king). This has created a revolution at the parish level. In the United States there are nineteen thousand parishes, and in half of them laypeople and nuns function as ministers in a variety of pastoral roles.[81] Eighty-five percent of these lay ministers are women. On the other hand, North American Catholics often view John Paul II as far too conservative, pointing to his refusal to discuss the ordination of women or the requirement of clerical celibacy, or to relax the ban on the use of birth control devices. Many see his immovable attitude on these issues as a potentially fatal blow to the continued vibrancy of Catholicism in North America.[82]

Several documents from Vatican II discussed the relationship of the Catholic faith to Eastern Orthodoxy, to non-Christian religions, to human freedom and human suffering, and to the missionary activity of the Church. In addition, Vatican II is often viewed as inviting the Catholic Church to a broader approach to understanding God—moving it from an essentially rational Thomistic path to include more experiential dimensions. Many of these threads have been pursued by Catholic thinkers.

HANS KÜNG

Swiss theologian Hans Küng (1928–) became professor of fundamental theology at the Catholic theological faculty at Tübingen in Germany in 1960. While he was quite young he wrote *The Council and Reunion* (1961),[83] perhaps the single most important book alerting many to the vast possibilities for renewal that Vatican II afforded. Küng's vocal opposition to papal authority, crystallized in his controversial book *Infallible? An Inquiry* (1971),[84] led to a 1979 decision by the Sacred Congregation for the Doctrine of the Faith (the theological watchdog of the Vatican) that Küng could no longer to be considered a Catholic theologian. He was accordingly stripped of his accreditation as a teacher of Roman Catholic theology. Following this, the University of Tübingen created an Institute of Ecumeni-cal Studies and made Küng its director. His best-known works—*On Being a Christian* (1976)[85] and *Does God Exist?* (1978)[86]—were both produced at this time.

Küng understands theology as beginning "from below" with questions that arise from contemporary human experience. "Our method," he writes,

> has been to start out each time as consistently as possible "from below," from man's first questions, from human experience. . . . in the face of nihilism, we cannot appeal to the Bible in order to dismiss the basic problems of the uncertainty of reality as a whole and of human experience; in the face of atheism, we cannot appeal to the Bible in order merely to assert the reality of God.[87]

The task of the theologian, says Küng, is to understand contemporary existence, to seek out the "modern man in the place where he is actually living in order to relate the knowledge of God to the things that stir him."[88]

For Küng other religions offer the possibility of entering into a trusting relationship with God, which for all practical purposes is a type of salvation. On the other hand, Küng believes Christianity is extraordinary, because in Jesus Christ God is most fully revealed. Adherents of other religions, he thinks, ought to be introduced to Christ, who has brought God's grace into the world. Like Kierkegaard, Küng asserts that human beings cannot come to know God through rational proofs, but only through experience. Being a Christian, he says, means following and imitating Christ, living in the same dependence upon God as Christ did.

JOHN PAUL II

John Paul II (1920–), who became Pope in 1978, is the first non-Italian pope since Hadrian VI (1522–23). Born Karol Wojtyla in Wadowice, Poland, he was raised by his father after his mother died when Karol was still a boy. As a university

student he studied poetry and acting. He was ordained a priest in 1946 and later earned a doctorate at the Angelicum University in Rome. Beginning in 1954 he taught Christian ethics and moral
theology, earning a reputation as a prolific scholar.
Named archbishop of Kracow in 1964, he had
already distinguished himself as a dogged champion of the rights of the Church in communist
Poland. His personal acquaintance with religious
persecution has made him a defender of the poor
and oppressed. His encyclical *Centesimus Annus*
(1991) is a trenchant statement on social justice.
John Paul has restored to the papacy the role of
moral suasion in international affairs and is credited
with hastening the end of communist domination
of eastern Europe. He is sharply critical of the excesses of both capitalism and communism. John
Paul considers capitalism culpable for inflicting suffering on the weakest members of the human family. With the collapse of communism, said Joseph
Cardinal Ratzinger, the head of the Vatican's Sacred
Congregation for the Doctrine of the Faith, John
Paul's strategy was to combat the "radical individualism" and "spiritual emptiness" of the West.[89] He
is also active in making the college of cardinals
more representative of the entire church, elevating
an unprecedented number from the non-western
world.

For John Paul, the concern of the Church in Europe and North America with issues of contraception, sexual morality, and even the ordination of
women seems trivial relative to the physical persecution and suffering faced by people in other parts
of the world. He is also concerned to establish more
amicable relations with the Eastern Orthodox tradition. In his 1985 encyclical *Slavorum Apostolorum*
he put forward his desire to combine the Latin tradition of order and law with the mystical Greek tradition, in order that the Church might "breathe
with two lungs."

Many think John Paul has worked to limit the
effects of Vatican II. He has not demonstrated the
type of collaborative style of governance that many
hoped would emerge after the council. He has held
reservations about the ecumenical movement, believing it threatened to erase the markers of distinc-

tive Catholic identity. While genuinely concerned
about the plight of the poor and oppressed, John
Paul has been a critic of liberation theology, seeing
it as too beholden to Marxism while ignoring relevant biblical resources. In a 1986 letter to the
Brazilian bishops, he said that liberation theology
could be both legitimate and necessary if it were
purified of Marxism.[90]

World Christianity:
Trends and Prospects

In 1900, 80 percent of the world's Christians lived
in Europe or North America. By 2000 that figure
dropped to less than 40 percent. Christianity has
become a truly global religion, the most extensive
and universal religion in history. In 2000 there were
two billion Christians worldwide — 33 percent of
the world's population. There are Christians and
Christian organizations in every country of the
world, and Christians are the majority in two-thirds
of the world's nations. There are, however, significant pockets where Christians are a tiny minority,
particularly in Muslim countries. Christians constitute less than 10 percent of the population in
fifty-one countries, and less than 1 percent in eight
countries.

Christianity is rapidly becoming a religion of the
impoverished and the oppressed. In 2000, Christians were the most persecuted religious group in
the world, principally because of repression by the
government of China, where Christianity is growing rapidly.[91] It is difficult to isolate the motives for
conversion, but it appears that the Christian message of hope for the future and the dignity of each
person is a powerful factor in the burgeoning
growth of the faith among the impoverished and
oppressed of the world.

Globalization was already evident at Vatican II.
Of the more than twenty-eight hundred bishops attending, just over half were from Europe (39 percent) and North America (14 percent). The remainder were from South America (17 percent),

Figure 12.3   The Holy Family, by Fr. John B. Giuliani The universal appeal of the gospel is expressed in this representation of Jesus, Mary, and Joseph as Native Americans.

Asia (13 percent), Africa (11 percent), Central America (3 percent) and Oceania (3 percent).[92]

For eighteen of its twenty centuries, Christianity has been 90 percent Caucasian.[93] By 2000, however, it had become a predominantly non-western religion, a trend that will only continue. Already Christians in the third world consider Europe and North America the mission field of the future. Generally, non-western Christians repudiate the western linkage of economic development with Christianity. By 2000 the historical European/North American axis of leadership in the Christian Church had already begun to fade. Few western Christian leaders seemed aware of the staggering implications of this massive shift.

Europeans and North Americans are often astonishingly ignorant of the conditions faced by most of the world's population. In the year 2000, more than a billion people lived in absolute poverty, a condition so marked by malnutrition, disease, and illiteracy that the World Bank considers these people to live below the standards of human decency. Of these, 260 million were Christians.[94] In 2000 the total income of the poorest 46 percent of the world's population was $900 billion. In that

same year, the wealthiest person in the world, Bill Gates, had an estimated net worth of $100 billion and an annual income estimated at $1.5 billion.[95] Christians in the non-western world are in the main theologically conservative, which puts them in conflict with liberal Christians in Europe and North America. In addition, the affluence of Christians in Europe and North America causes other Christians deep misgivings, especially when leaders of the western Church champion issues that appear to non-western Christians emblematic of western ignorance and arrogance. Two examples illumine the complexities of the interplay between western and non-western Christians.

In the 1990s a group of American Anglican bishops were on the forefront in promoting the consecration and blessing of homosexual unions within worldwide Anglicanism. At the 1998 Lambeth Conference (the meeting of worldwide Anglican bishops), they were opposed by African bishops. When the more conservative view won the day, at least one American bishop suggested that the African bishops were "superstitious," had only recently moved out of animism,[96] and were too naive and too uneducated to understand the issues.[97]

Third-world bishops were reportedly offended by these comments. Others have noted that although the American bishops outnumber the Nigerians, twice as many Nigerian bishops hold a Ph.D. as their American counterparts. Some within the worldwide Anglican community think the charge of the American bishop was patronizing, and perhaps racist.[98] Several bishops expressed concern about the "modern globalizing culture" and wondered "whether we are in danger of allowing this culture with its philosophical assumptions, economic system, sexual alternatives, and hidden idols to determine what we become."[99]

While visiting Peru, Rosemary Radford Ruether said that although she honors Gustavo Gutiérrez as the founder of a movement that "reconnected theology with social justice," she was saddened that he did not see fit to endorse feminist theology. Gutiérrez offered the opinion that Ruether's feminist theology is a distinctly North American phenomenon. The implication was that to impose feminist theology on South America would be simply another form of western cultural arrogance.[100]

What might the future hold for Christianity?

In 1900 there were nearly 10 million Christians in Africa (0.6 percent of the world's population then); in 2000 there were 360 million (nearly 9 percent of the world's population). Since 1950 the African continent has suffered a series of devastating traumas, including floods, AIDS, and a numbing series of civil wars and genocidal incidents. Africa is also the location of the world's fastest-growing concentration of Christians — Orthodox, Catholic, and Protestant. In 2000 the number of Christians in Africa increased at the rate of 23,000 per day, with a 1.5 million net increase in Christians every year.[101] In Nigeria there are 62 dioceses for more than 17 million Anglicans (one bishop for more than 280,000 people), while in the United States there are 139 dioceses for 2.5 million Anglicans (one bishop for less than 17,000 people). Over the years, African Christian thinkers and independent churches have tended to blend patterns of native religiosity with traditional Christian worship. However, some more recent forms of African Christianity have modeled themselves instead on the "prosperity" gospel more common in North America. A good example is the Winner's Chapel in Nigeria. Africa might become the center of world Christianity by the end of the twenty-first century, and there is even speculation that Francis Cardinal Arize of Nigeria could be the first African pope.

Asia, the most populous region of the world, is also the area most resistant to Christianity. There are exceptions, of course. The Philippines, with its history of Spanish colonial domination, is predominantly Catholic. Only Brazil (with 139 million Catholics), Mexico (with 83 million), the United States (with 60 million) and Italy (with 55 million) had more Catholics in 2000 than the 52 million in the Philippines. The Republic of Korea had four times as many Presbyterians as the United States, and, as we have seen, boasts the world's largest single congregation.

Although there is a net increase of 2.4 million Christians in Asia every year, on balance the region is largely closed to Christianity.[102] Christians in India and, especially, China face persecution and martyrdom. The most virulent and systematic attempt ever to persecute and eradicate Christianity was undertaken by the Chinese government in 1966–67.[103] The attempt failed, but the Chinese government remains focused on restricting Christianity in China, where both Catholicism and Protestantism are split between government-controlled hierarchies and the fast-growing but persecuted independent house churches. On the same day John Paul II ordained twelve bishops in Rome, the Beijing government planned to ordain twelve bishops in the Chinese Catholic Patriotic Association, the government-controlled Church. Only five showed up. The others refused to be ordained without papal permission, and it was reported that the five who were present loudly proclaimed their loyalty to the pope.[104] In 1990 there were seventy million Christians in China, most belonging to the house church movement.[105]

For centuries Europe was the stronghold of Christian faith, but by 2000 Christianity had become moribund in Europe. In 1900 there was buoyant optimism among European and North

American Christians that the task of global evangelization was within reach. But the twentieth century did not turn out as they expected. While global Christianity has grown numerically, from 558 million in 1900 to 2 billion in 2000, there have been massive and unexpected defections from the faith in Europe due to communism, secularism, and materialism.[106] Most estimates of Church attendance place it at less than 10 percent of the population of virtually every European country. Europe has become a post-Christian, secular heartland.

The United States continues to surprise analysts, because it is a highly modern society with a civic policy that is essentially secular, yet its citizens are remarkably religious.[107] More than half claim some sort of Christian affiliation. There are signs of change, however. The older mainline churches—the inheritors of Protestant liberalism—have suffered decades of decline in membership and attendance. For much of their history Americans expected civic life to conform to patterns that paralleled Christian ideals. Since the 1960s this expectation has begun to disappear.

North American evangelical denominations have seen steady but not spectacular growth since 1950. Independent evangelical congregations, most started since 1970, are also a potent force, and many boast memberships of ten thousand or more. Often these churches employ "seeker-friendly" strategies, including the minimization of traditional Christian symbols, buildings that resemble the office complex of a high tech-firm, and intentional niche marketing. In the 1990s some observers began to speculate that the growth of nondenominational Christianity in North America was so meteoric that denominations might cease to exist. This judgment now appears to have been premature. A number of critics perceive a slavish emulation of popular culture in contemporary American evangelicalism, and wonder if these churches possess the fortitude to challenge the broader American culture at points of conflict with the Christian message. Some worry that in their attempts to attract new converts, evangelicals may unwittingly dilute their own message.

The Roman Catholic Church has also had impressive growth in the United States, largely due to immigration from countries where Catholicism is strong. In spite of an apparent increase in secularism in America, the percentage of Catholics who are both born and remain in the faith has held steady since 1960.[108] But American Catholicism is showing signs of stress. There is much talk of a severe shortage of priests and dwindling numbers of seminarians. By 2000, one in six Catholic priests serving in American parishes was imported from abroad. The United States used to be the chief source of supply for the Jesuit order, but by 2000 that distinction belonged to India.[109] In addition, many traditionally Catholic immigrant Latinos are converting to Pentecostalism, especially in southern California.

In the 1980s, Los Angeles emerged as both a global city and a Catholic city. Recent immigration from Central America has made the Archdiocese of Los Angeles the largest in the United States. By the early 1980s, it had 3.4 million parishioners and was growing by more than a thousand a week. By 1985 there were more Catholics in Los Angeles than Episcopalians in the entire United States. The archdiocese administers the second largest school system in California, operates five colleges and sixteen hospitals, and owns land worth billions of dollars.[110] Although mostly Latino, the archdiocese has been led since 1903 by Irish-American clergy. But half of the Catholic Latino immigrants to Los Angeles between 1970 and 1990 converted to community-based Protestant Pentecostalism.[111]

Christianity in Europe and North America has before it a massive challenge. It must educate members in global moral and ethical issues. It must learn to relate to its culture while retaining its distinctiveness. It must recognize that Christianity is no longer a white European religion. In Europe and North America Christianity is facing a situation not unlike what it faced in its first two or three centuries: it exists in a non-Christian, pluralistic, and fairly hostile culture that nonetheless affords opportunities of astonishing promise.

By 1998 only 10 percent of Latin America's nearly 500 million people were non-Christians, and less than 10 percent were Protestants. Statistically Brazil has more Catholics than any other country.

Yet of the 135 million Catholics in Brazil, less than 10 percent attend church with any regularity. As in the rest of Latin America, Pentecostal Christianity has made astounding strides in Brazil since 1960. Some commentators think that in Brazil there are more Pentecostals than Catholics in church on a weekly basis. The situation is similar in virtually every country in Central and South America. What this portends is enormously difficult to say. The Christian experience in Europe and North America indicates that with the continued vibrancy of the Pentecostal movement in Latin America will come intra-Christian tension.

In 2000, there were two billion Christians worldwide—the vast majority of them in the non-western world—yet the hierarchies of many international Christian groups were dominated by leaders from Europe and North America. This will undoubtedly be a source of tension in the twenty-first century. Worldwide, the fastest-growing Christian groups are the nontraditional independent and/or Pentecostal organizations.[112] By 2000 there were about fifty congregations worldwide that claimed at least fifty thousand members, and the bulk of them were independents. It is quite possible that in Africa and Asia, Christianity of this type, socially conservative, orthodox in doctrine but severed from the European-dominated traditions and, therefore, free to develop indigenous patterns of worship and theological expression—will rise to prominence. If this takes place, the two hundred years from 1900 to 2100 will have witnessed perhaps the most dramatic shift in the history of Christianity.

issues occupied the concerns of western Christians, the explosive growth of Christianity in the non-western world emerged as perhaps the most important development for Christianity in the twentieth century. This meteoric increase may render concerns with modernity and its effects irrelevant, as western Christians are engulfed in a wave of non-western spirituality and Christian practice. The future vibrancy of the Christian movement seems assured, but it will undoubtedly be less western in doctrine, demographics, and practice. Some Christians will find this prospect frightening, other exhilarating. It constitutes a major challenge to western Christians, who have for centuries assumed they have a right to leadership in the faith. This may be the most significant development in Christian history since Constantine made Christianity the favored religion of the Roman Empire.

QUESTIONS FOR REVIEW AND REFLECTION

1. Between 1900 and 2000 there were cultural, theological, and demographic shifts within the Christian movement around the world. What were the most significant of these, and why are they more important than others?

2. What is the relationship between economic, social, and political factors influencing various expressions of Christian faith throughout the world?

3. How have North American expressions of Christian faith influenced and been influenced by worldwide Christianity?

4. How has Christianity attempted to deal with modernity? How successful have these efforts been?

Summary

When the twentieth century began, Christianity was still a predominantly western religion. The cultural and social repercussions of changes in technology and intellectual life presented formidable challenges to Christianity, which responded by attempting either to remake itself or to hold on to previous patterns of belief and practice. While these

NOTES

1. Martin Kähler, *The So-Called Historical Jesus and the Historic, Biblical Christ,* trans. Carl E. Braaten (Philadelphia: Fortress Press, 1964).
2. William Wrede, *The Messianic Secret,* trans. J. C. G. Grieg (Cambridge, U.K.: Clarke, 1971).
3. Albert Schweitzer, *The Quest of the Historical Jesus: A Critical Study of Its Progress from Reimarus to Wrede,* trans. W. Montgomery, 3rd ed. (London: A. C. Black, 1963).
4. Rudolf Bultmann, *The History of the Synoptic Tradition,* trans. John Marsh (London: Basil Blackwell, 1963).

5. Rudolf Bultmann, "New Testament and Mythology," in *New Testament and Mythology and Other Basic Writings,* ed. and trans. Schubert M. Ogden (Philadelphia: Fortress Press, 1984).

6. See Bruce Chilton, *Rabbi Jesus: An Intimate Biography* (New York: Doubleday, 2000).

7. In language that is reminiscent of Wrede, Funk was quoted in the *Los Angeles Times* as saying that the "only Jesus most people want is the mythic one. They don't want the real Jesus. They want the one they can worship. The cultic Jesus." Funk has also said, "The religious establishment has not allowed the intelligence of high scholarship to pass through pastors and priests to a hungry laity," and he has deep reservations about the way television evangelists have "preyed on the ignorance of the uninformed." See L. T. Johnson, *The Real Jesus: The Misguided Quest for the Historical Jesus and the Truth of the Traditional Gospels* (San Francisco: HarperSanFrancisco, 1996), 6–7. Johnson is harshly critical of Funk.

8. Quoted by John Barton, "Who Was Theodotion?" *Times Literary Supplement,* 13 April 2001, 8.

9. For example, the Oxford Scholar G. B. Caird. See G. B. Caird and L. D. Hurst, *New Testament Theology* (Oxford: Clarendon Press, 1994).

10. B. Childs, *Biblical Theology of the Old and New Testaments: Theological Reflections on the Christian Bible* (London: SCM Press, 1992).

11. See James D. G. Dunn, *Unity and Diversity in the New Testament: An Inquiry into the Character of Earliest Christianity* (Harrisburg, Pa.: Westminster, 1977).

12. The term is derived from the Greek word *eschatos,* meaning "end." For Moltmann and Pannenberg it means "end as purpose."

13. Jürgen Moltmann, *Theology of Hope: On the Ground and Implications of a Christian Eschatology,* trans. James W. Leitch (New York: Harper & Row, 1967).

14. *Revelation As History,* ed. Wolfhart Pannenberg, trans. David Granskou (New York: Macmillan, 1968).

15. Wolfhart Pannenberg, *Jesus — God and Man,* trans. Lewis L. Wilkins and Duane A. Priebe (Philadelphia: Westminster Press, 1968).

16. See, for example, Wolfhart Pannenberg, *Toward a Theology of Nature: Essays on Science and Faith,* ed. Ted Peters (Louisville, Ky.: Westminster/John Knox Press, 1993).

17. Gustavo Gutiérrez, *We Drink From Our Own Wells: The Journey of a People,* trans. Matthew J. O'Connell (Maryknoll, N.Y.: Orbis, 1985).

18. Latin American Episcopal Council (CELAM), "Medellin Document on Peace," in *Third World Liberation Theologies —A Reader,* ed. Deane W. Ferm (Maryknoll, N.Y.: Orbis Books, 1986), 9.

19. Gustavo Gutiérrez, *A Theology of Liberation: History, Politics and Salvation,* trans. Sister Caridad Inda and John Eagleson (Maryknoll, N.Y.: Orbis Books, 1973).

20. José Míguez-Bonino, "Violence: A Theological Reflection," in *Mission Trends No. 3: Third World Theologies,* ed. Gerald H. Anderson and Thomas F. Stransky (Grand Rapids, Mich.: Eerdmans, 1976), 111.

21. José Míguez-Bonino, *Doing Theology in a Revolutionary Situation* (Philadelphia: Fortress Press, 1975), 81.

22. Leonardo Boff, *Jesus Christ Liberator: A Critical Christology for Our Time,* trans. Patrick Hughes (Maryknoll, N.Y.: Orbis Books, 1978).

23. Leonardo Boff and Clodovis Boff, *Introducing Liberation Theology,* trans. Paul Burns (Maryknoll, N.Y.: Orbis Books, 1987), 52.

24. Leonardo Boff, *Ecology and Liberation: A New Paradigm,* trans. John Cumming (Maryknoll, N.Y.: Orbis Books, 1995).

25. James Cone, *Black Theology and Black Power* (New York: Seabury Press, 1969).

26. James Cone, *A Black Theology of Liberation* (Philadelphia: Lippincott, 1970).

27. Cone, *Black Theology and Black Power,* 39, 35.

28. Cone, *A Black Theology of Liberation,* 8.

29. Valerie Saiving Goldstein, "The Human Situation: A Feminine View," *Journal of Religion* 40 (January 1960): 100–112.

30. Mary Daly, *Beyond God the Father: Toward a Philosophy of Women's Liberation* (Boston: Beacon Press, 1973).

31. Rosemary Radford Rueter, *Sexism and God-talk: Toward a Feminist Theology* (Boston: Beacon Press, 1983).

32. See, for example, Linda L. Belleville, "Women in Ministry," in *Two Views on Women in Ministry,* ed. James R. Beck and Craig L. Blomberg (Grand Rapids, Mich.: Zondervan, 2001).

33. Letha Scanzoni and Nancy Hardety, *All We're Meant To Be* (Waco, Tex.: Word, 1975), 205.

34. Harvey Cox, *The Secular City* (New York: Macmillan, 1966), 1–2. The phrase *a world come of age* Cox rightly attributes to Dietrich Bonhoeffer, although Kant used the phrase long before.

35. John A. T. Robinson, *Honest to God* (London: SCM Press, 1963), 43.

36. Cox, *The Secular City,* 15.

37. David B. Barrett, George T. Kurian, & Todd M. Johnson, *World Christian Encyclopedia,* vol. 1, 2nd ed. (New York: Oxford University Press, 2001), 3.

38. Abraham Kuyper, quoted in Alan P. R. Sell, *Theology in Turmoil: The Roots, Course and Significance of the Conservative-Liberal Debate in Modern Theology* (Grand Rapids, Mich.: Baker, 1986), 108.

39. Greg L. Bahnsen, "The Inerrancy of the Autographa," in *Inerrancy,* ed. Norman L. Geisler (Grand Rapids, Mich.: Zondervan, 1980), 154.

40. Though the New Testament mentions the virgin birth of Jesus (Matthew 1:18–23; Luke 1:26–38), Matthew and Luke are the only Gospel writers to do so; and Matthew appears to be the only author in the New Testament to say that the virgin birth is proof of Jesus' status.

41. *The Fundamentals*, ed. R. A. Torrey et al. (1917; reprinted Grand Rapids, Mich.: Baker Book House, 1979).

42. The pamphlets were underwritten by two Los Angeles laymen, Lyman and Milton Stewart, who wanted every pastor, evangelist, seminary student, sunday school superintendent, and YMCA/YWCA secretary in the English-speaking world to receive them.

43. *Southern Baptist Convention Annual*, 1926, 18.

44. Josh McDowell, *Evidence That Demands a Verdict: Historical Evidences for the Christian Faith* (San Bernadino, Calif.: Here's Life, 1972).

45. *Fuller Theological Seminary Catalog*, 1995–96, 6.

46. A fairly recent but not unchallenged thesis is that the political and social culture of the United States has been shaped more by religious movements than by politics, structures, or social issues. See William G. McLoughlin, *Revivals, Awakenings, and Reform: An Essay on Religion and Social Change in America, 1607–1977* (Chicago: University of Chicago Press, 1978); and Robert William Fogel, *The Fourth Great Awakening and the Future of Egalitarianism: The Political Realignment of the 1990's and the Fate of Egalitarianism* (Chicago: University of Chicago Press, 2000).

47. Douglas A. Blackmon, "Racial Reconciliation Becomes a Priority for the Religious Right," *Wall Street Journal*, 23 June 1997.

48. Michael O. Emerson and Christian Smith, *Divided by Faith: Evangelical Religion and the Problem of Race in America* (New York: Oxford University Press, 2000).

49. Quoted in Emerson and Smith, *Divided by Faith*, 123.

50. According to Barrett, Kurian, & Johnson, *World Christian Encyclopedia*, vol. 1, 776–77, 782–89, by 2000 there were 140 separate black denominations in the United States. The largest were the National Baptist Convention USA, claiming more than 9 million members; the Church of God in Christ, claiming more than 5 million members; the National Baptist Convention of America, claiming more than 4 million members; and the African Methodist Episcopal Church, claiming more than 3 million members. In addition, there were more than a million black Catholics in the USA by the year 2000.

51. C. Eric Lincoln and Lawrence Mamiya, *The Black Church in the African American Experience* (Durham, N.C.: Duke University Press, 1990), xii.

52. One set of baptismal vows for slaves included the words: "You declare in the presence of God and before this congregation that you do not ask for holy baptism out of any desire to free yourself from the Duty and Obedience you owe to your master." See Emerson and Smith, *Divided by Faith*, 24.

53. See Emerson and Smith, *Divided by Faith*, 23, 26–32.

54. Lincoln and Mamiya, *The Black Church*, 27.

55. Emerson and Smith, *Divided by Faith*, 46.

56. See George M. Marsden, *Reforming Fundamentalism: Fuller Seminary and the New Evangelicalism* (Grand Rapids, Mich.: Eerdmans, 1987).

57. See Alan Wolfe, "The Opening of the Evangelical Mind," *Atlantic Monthly*, October 2000, 55–76.

58. The technical term is *glossolalia*, from the Greek words for "tongue" and "speak."

59. John Thomas Nichol, *Pentecostalism* (New York: Harper & Row, 1966), 31.

60. L. Grant McClung, Jr., "New Culture, New Challenges, New Church?" in *Pentecostals from the Inside Out*, ed. Harold B. Smith (Wheaton, Ill.: Victor Books, 1990), 109.

61. Barrett, Kurian, & Johnson, *World Christian Encyclopedia*, vol. 1, 684.

62. See Barrett, Kurian, & Johnson, *World Christian Encyclopedia*, vol. 1, 13–15.

63. See, for example, Kenneth Copeland, *Prosperity Promises* (Fort Worth, Tex.: Kenneth Copeland, 1987); and *One Word from God Can Change Your Finances* (Tulsa, Okla.: Harrison House, 1999).

64. Larry Eskridge, "When Burkett Speaks, Evangelicals Listen," *Christianity Today*, 12 June 2000, 46.

65. Robert Schuller, *Self-Esteem: The New Reformation* (Waco, Tex.: Word, 1982), 14.

66. See John Wimber and Kevin Springer, *Power Evangelism* (San Francisco: Harper & Row, 1986).

67. For instance, in England, Holy Trinity Brompton has been the locus of a Vineyard-like movement in recent years, causing alarm in some circles within the Church of England. See Richard John Neuhaus, "While We're At It," *First Things*, March 1998, 72.

68. Jonathan Edwards, *Humble Attempt to Promote Explicit Agreement and Visible Union of God's People* (Boston: Henchman, 1747).

69. Mission fields have been instrumental for promoting ecumenical interest and change within Christianity. The essential role of women as preachers, teachers, doctors, and administrators on mission fields has been an important factor in the decision of many Protestant denominations to ordain women. In addition, conditions on the mission field have made it clear to missionaries that the issues that divide their various denominations back home are often insignificant compared to the issues that bind them together. This experience has been a force for increased cooperation and understanding between denominations that formerly considered each other forever separated.

70. Konrad Raiser, "Reconciliation: A Challenge for the Churches," *Theology, News and Notes*, Spring 2001, 8.

71. Raiser, "Reconciliation," 9.

72. Raiser, "Reconciliation," 9.

73. In 1979, Pope John Paul II traveled to Constantinople to meet with Patriarch Demetrios I of the Greek Orthodox Church. They signed a statement affirming their hope that they might one day be able to celebrate the eucharist together. Since the collapse of European

communism, however, ecumenical relations have come to a standstill. In 2000, Eastern Orthodoxy was, to a significant degree, captured by internal concerns, particlularly with leaders, so active in the World Council of Churches during the cold war, who have since come under suspicion of having been agents of the communists. The resulting uncertainty is likely to continue for some time.

74. See Edward Idris Cardinal Cassidy, "Reflections on Reconciliation from a Roman Catholic Perspective," *Theology, News and Notes,* Spring 2001, 11.

75. See Cassidy, "Reflections on Reconciliation," 11.

76. Richard John Neuhaus, "While We're At It," *First Things,* August, 2000, 90–91.

77. Richard John Neuhaus, "While We're At It," *First Things,* January, 2001, 75.

78. During the American presidential campaign of 2000, for example, George W. Bush was roundly criticized by the media for an appearance at fundamentalist Bob Jones University, on the basis that the university is anti-Catholic. It is quite true that fundamentalism and Bob Jones University have a long history of unsavory anti-Catholic sentiment. But Peter Steinfels of the *New York Times* criticized the Democratic party and the media for its callow defense of Catholicism. After all, he wrote, the Democratic party has "slammed the door" against Catholics who are not in accord with the party's stance on abortion. Steinfels also noted that anti-Catholic bigotry reflected in television programs and the news media is far more pervasive and far more damaging than fundamentalist anti-Catholic attitudes. See Peter Steinfels, "Beliefs," *New York Times,* 4 March 2000.

79. Richard John Neuhaus, "Very Selective Compassion," *First Things,* March 1998, 66.

80. Richard McBrien, *Catholicism* (Minneapolis: Winston Press, 1981), 5.

81. James Hennesey, "Catholicism in the United States of America," in *The Harper Collins Encyclopedia of Catholicism,* ed. Richard P. McBrien (San Francisco: HarperSanFrancisco, 1989), 1289.

82. Before 1983, the code of canon law stipulated that the primary aim of marriage is the procreation and education of children, with a secondary end being the mutual help and comfort of husband and wife. Accordingly the Church has been staunchly against birth control. John Paul II, following the lead of his predecessors, has not seen fit to overturn that reading. Millions of Catholics, especially in Europe and North America, have disobeyed the teaching of the Church in this area. For some this is a matter of little consequence. For others, however, it is a piercing dilemma, placing them in defiance of the teachings of the Church they desire to follow. Andrew Greely has declared that papal inflexibility on this issue has been a massive mistake, leaving millions of otherwise loyal Catholics disaffected. See Randall Balmer, "Catholic Church in America Fails to Keep Pace with the Changes," *Los Angeles Times,* 19 February 1992.

83. Hans Küng, *The Council and Reunion,* trans. Cecily Hastings (London: Sheed & Ward, 1961).

84. Hans Küng, *Infallible? An Inquiry,* trans. Edward Quinn (Garden City, N.Y.: Doubleday, 1971).

85. Hans Küng, *On Being a Christian,* trans. Edward Quinn (Garden City, N.Y.: Doubleday, 1976).

86. Hans Küng , *Does God Exist?,* trans. Edward Quinn (Garden City, N.Y.: Doubleday, 1980).

87. Küng, *On Being a Christian,* 83–84.

88. Küng, *On Being a Christian,* 84.

89. Jeffrey L. Sheler et al., "Keeping Faith in His Time," *U.S. News and World Report,* 9 October 1995, 72.

90. Peter Hebblethwaite, "John Paul II," in *The Harper Collins Encyclopedia of Catholicism,* ed. Richard P. McBrien (San Francisco: HarperSanFrancisco, 1995), 715.

91. See Richard John Neuhaus, "While We're At It," *First Things,* June/July 1997, 84; James and Marti Hefley, *By Their Blood: Christian Martyrs of the Twentieth Century* (Grand Rapids, Mich.: Baker Books, 1996), 76–80; and A. M. Rosenthal, "The Double Crime," *New York Times,* 25 April 1997, 27.

92. McBrien, *Catholicism,* 658.

93. See Barrett, Kurian, & Johnson, *World Christian Encyclopedia,* vol. 1, 3.

94. Barrett, Kurian, & Johnson, *World Christian Encyclopedia,* vol. 1, 3.

95. Barrett, Kurian, & Johnson, *World Christian Encyclopedia,* vol. 1, 6.

96. Catherine Pepinster, "Rid Us of the Canker of Compromise," *The Independent* (London), 9 August 1998, 5.

97. Bishop John Spong of New Jersey reportedly made these comments. See Hazel Southam, "Repent, Says Bishop in Gay Rights Clash," *Evening Standard* (London), 5 August 1998, 4.

98. See Richard John Neuhaus, "While We're At It," *First Things,* May 2000, 70–71.

99. See Charles Austin, "Anglican Conference Revives Specter of Colonialism," *The Record* (Bergen County, N.J.), 27 August 1998.

100. See Richard John Neuhaus, "While We're At It," *First Things,* March 1997, 66.

101. Barrett, Kurian, & Johnson, *World Christian Encyclopedia,* vol. 1, 5.

102. Barrett, Kurian, & Johnson, *World Christian Encyclopedia,* vol. 1, 5.

103. Barrett, Kurian, & Johnson, *World Christian Encyclopedia,* vol. 1, 5.

104. Richard John Neuhaus, "While We're At It," *First Things,* August 2000, 94–95.

105. Rudolf G. Wagner, "China," in *The Encyclopedia of Christianity,* vol. 1, ed. Geoffrey W. Bromiley (Grand Rapids, Mich.: Eerdmanns, 1999), 418.

106. Barrett, Kurian, & Johnson, *World Christian Encyclopedia*, vol. 1, 3.

107. Until the 1950s, American church attendance enjoyed modest gains during the twentieth century. Since then, however, Protestant denominations associated with liberalism have suffered alarming decreases in membership and attendance. According to Richard John Neuhaus ("While We're At It," *First Things*, February 2001, No. 110, 66), in 2000 the United Methodists claimed 8.5 million members, down from 9.5 million in 1980; the Presbyterian Church USA claimed 2.5 million members, down from 3.2 million in 1980; and the Episcopal Church claimed 2.3 million members, down from 3 million in 1980. Fundamentalist, Pentecostal, and evangelical groups, in contrast, are holding their own or boasting modest to substantial gains. In 2000 in the United States there were nearly 16 million Southern Baptists, making theirs the largest Protestant denomination in the country. The aggregate total of the seven largest Baptist denominations in the United States was more than 35 million. There were also nearly 8 million Lutherans and more than 4 million Presbyterians. The Greek Orthodox Archdiocese of America claimed nearly 2 million members in 2000. Roman Catholics in the United States numbered close to 60 million. According to the U.S. Bureau of the Census, in 1990 there were more than 130 million Christians in the United States, constituting nearly 53 percent of the population. The source for some of these figures is the *Yearbook for American and Canadian Churches*, as reported in *Time Almanac 2000*, ed. Borgna Brunner (Boston: Time, 2000) 422. See also *Statistical Abstract of the United States: The National Data Book* (Washington, D.C.: U.S. Bureau of the Census, 2000), 62.

108. David Lauter, "Review of *The Slights of a Priest*," *Los Angeles Times*, 29 January 2000.

109. Kenneth L. Woodward, "The Changing Face of the Church," *Newsweek*, 16 April 2001, 48–49.

110. Mike Davis, *City of Quartz* (New York: Vintage Books, 1992), 326, 339–40.

111. Andrew Greeley, "Defection among Hispanics," *America*, 30 July 1988, 62. See also Mike Davis, *City of Quartz*, 339–40.

112. In 1970 there were nearly 1.2 billion Christians worldwide, of which only 95 million fit this category. Of the 2 billion Christians in 2000, 386 million fit this category.

Glossary

Abelard, Peter (1079–1142). Philosopher and theologian, his *Sic et non* ("Yes and No") marked an important step in the development of scholasticism.

absolution The formal act in which a priest or bishop pronounces the forgiveness of sin.

Adventism A nineteenth-century American movement that expected the imminent Second Coming, or Advent, of Christ. It was organized into a number of denominations, the most important being the Seventh-Day Adventists.

Alcuin of York (ca. 740–804). An English theologian who made a major contribution to the Carolingian Renaissance in the service of the Frankish royal court.

alms Money or goods given as charity to the poor.

Ambrose (ca. 339–97). Theologian and bishop of Milan. He introduced the concepts and terminology of the Greek East to the Latin Church.

Anabaptists (lit., "rebaptizers"). Members of a variety of sixteenth-century sects that held in common the belief that infant baptism was not valid and that for this reason believing adults who had been baptized as children must be baptized a second time.

anchorite/anchoress An individual who withdraws from society to lead a solitary life of prayer and contemplation.

Anglican communion The Church of England and related churches that recognize the authority of the see of Canterbury.

Anselm (ca. 1033–1109). Archbishop of Canterbury and theologian.

anthropomorphism The attribution of human characteristics to gods, inanimate objects, or natural phenomena.

anticlericalism Opposition to the influence of the Church or the clergy, especially in political matters.

apocalypse A revelation of spiritual realities or truths that are normally hidden.

Apollinaris (ca. 310–ca. 392). Bishop and theologian. His Christology was an extreme expression of the views of Alexandrian theologians.

apologists Christian writers of the first four centuries who defended Christianity against attacks on Christian doctrine, morals, and practices. From Greek *apologia*, "defense."

apostle "One who is sent." A title given originally to the disciples sent out by Jesus to preach the gospel (the Twelve Apostles). Though he was not one of the disciples, Paul also claimed to be an apostle (Galatians 1:1).

Apostolic Fathers A group of early Christian writers traditionally held to be disciples of the Apostles and the authors of certain texts that, though not included in the New Testament canon, were thought to preserve the apostolic faith. The Apostolic Fathers include Clement I of Rome, Ignatius of Antioch, Polycarp, Papias, and the authors of the *Epistle of Barnabas,* the *Epistle to Diognetus, 2 Clement,* and the *Didache.* Modern editions of the Apostolic Fathers sometimes also include the "Martyrdoms" of Clement, Ignatius, and Polycarp. The designation *Apostolic Fathers* was created in the late seventeenth century by the French scholar Jean Cotelier.

apostolic succession The doctrine that the pastoral authority given by Jesus to the Apostles has been handed down through an unbroken succession of bishops.

Aquinas, Thomas (ca. 1225–74). Dominican theologian and author of the *Summa Theologiae*. Generally regarded as the greatest of the medieval scholastic theologians.

archbishop A bishop of the highest rank who supervises other bishops and their dioceses, which constitute an archdiocese.

Arius (ca. 260–336). Alexandrian presbyter and theologian who taught that God the Son was not equal in divinity to God the Father.

Arminius, Jacob (1560–1609). Dutch reformed theologian. Reacting against the determinism of Calvinism, according to which divine grace is irresistible, Arminius stressed the freedom of human beings in accepting grace. Arminius and his followers also argued that Christ died for all of humanity and not only for the elect.

asceticism Rigorous denial of the body for the purpose of spiritual growth.

Augsburg Confession (1530) A Lutheran confession of faith composed primarily by the German humanist and theologian Philip Melanchthon and approved by Martin Luther.

Augustine (354–430). Bishop of Hippo in North Africa, leading Latin theologian, and founder of the Augustinian order of monks.

Averroës (1126–98). Muslim philosopher and author of commentaries on Aristotle.

Avicenna (980–1037). Muslim philosopher, instrumental in bringing knowledge of Aristotle to the West.

Babylonian captivity The captivity of the Jews under the neo-Babylonians in the sixth century BCE. The phrase was also used beginning in the fourteenth century to describe the exile of the popes at Avignon (1309–77).

baptism A ceremony of religious cleansing associated with John the Baptist (Mark 1:4 and 11:30; Luke 7:29) and performed within the early Church as a rite of initiation (1 Peter 3:21–22). Baptism is regarded as a sacrament by all major Christian traditions.

Baptists Baptists form one of the largest traditions within Protestantism. Historians trace the Baptist movement back to the Anabaptists as well as to congregations of separatists who left the Church of England in the early seventeenth century. Among its foundational principles was the belief that baptism should be reserved for adult believers who had professed repentance and faith in Christ.

Barth, Karl (1886–1965). Neo-orthodox theologian and author of *Commentary on Romans* and *Church Dogmatics.*

Basil of Caesarea ("the Great"; ca. 330–79). Bishop of Cappadocian Caesarea, theologian, and one of the founders of eastern monasticism.

BCE Before the Common Era. Corresponds to B.C.

Beghards The male counterparts of the Beguines, these were men of the late medieval period who resembled monks in their devotion to prayer and good works but did not join formal monastic orders. Most lived in communities in which there was no private property.

Beguines Women of the late Middle Ages who devoted themselves to the cultivation of piety without joining any of the tradtional orders of nuns. Some lived alone, others in communities. They devoted much of their time to prayer and philanthropy.

Benedict of Nursia A sixth-century monk whose Benedictine *Rule* became the basis of western monasticism.

Bernard of Clairvaux (1090–1153). Abbot of the monastery of Clairvaux in France who distinguished himself as a mystic and theologian.

biblical criticism The use of literary, textual, and historical tools and methods in the study of the Bible.

Bogomils A medieval dualist sect, similar to Manichaeism, that flourished in the Balkans.

Bohemia A kingdom in central Europe during the thirteenth through fifteenth centuries that later became a part of the Holy Roman Empire. Its territory was roughly that of the modern Czech Republic.

Bonaventure (ca. 1217–74). Franciscan mystic and theologian, best known for his *Journey of the Mind to God.*

Bonhoeffer, Dietrich (1906–45). German theologian and author of *The Cost of Discipleship* and *Letters and Papers from Prison.* An advocate of "religionless Christianity," he was hanged by the Nazis in 1945.

Boniface (ca. 675–754). Also known as Wynfrith and the "Apostle of Germany," he was a missionary who worked to convert the Germans in the early Middle Ages.

Book of Common Prayer The offical service book of the Church of England, which contains its liturgy and prayers.

bull An official mandate issued by the pope. Its name comes from the early practice of sealing such documents with a *bulla,* a seal made by the pope's signet ring.

Byzantium Site of modern Istanbul, formerly Constantinople. The term is also used to refer to the Byzantine Empire.

caesaropapism A system in which the secular ruler has absolute authority over the Church as well. This term was originally devised to describe the relationship between church and state in the Byzantine Empire.

Calvin, John (1509–64). French theologian and reformer, best known for his reforms in the Swiss city of Geneva. One of the founders of the Reformed tradition in Protestantism, along with Ulrich Zwingli and John Knox.

canon The list of biblical books recognized as authoritative. Also, a member of a chapter of priests serving in a cathedral or other church.

canonical hours The times of daily prayer (mattins /lauds, prime, terce, sext, none, vespers, and compline) that make up the daily public prayer, or Divine Office, of the Church.

canon law The corpus of ecclesiastical rules or laws drawn up by church councils and other bodies and considered authoritative in matters of faith and morality.

canon of Scripture The books of the Bible. In Christianity, the Old Testament (or Jewish Scriptures) and the twenty-seven books of the New Testament. The Roman Catholic canon also includes the books of the Apocrypha.

Cappadocia A region in what is now central Turkey.

Cappadocian Fathers Three fourth-century theologians from Cappadocia in Asia Minor — Basil of Caesarea, Gregory of Nazianzus, and Gregory of Nyssa — who made important contributions to theology in general and to the Eastern Orthodox tradition in particular.

Carolingians Members of a Frankish dynasty founded in 751 by Pepin and including Charlemagne.

catechumen In the ancient Church, an individual being prepared for baptism by instruction in the faith.

Cathari (Cathars) A dualist sect that reached the peak of its popularity in the thirteenth century.

Catherine of Siena (1447–1510). Italian mystic.

Catholic Reformation Reforms undertaken in the Roman Catholic Church beginning in the sixteenth century, primarily in response to the Protestant Reformation.

CE Common Era. Corresponds to A.D. *(anno domini,* "in the year of the Lord").

celibacy The state of being unmarried, especially in the case of a priest, monk, or nun who has taken a vow not to marry.

Celsus Second-century critic of Christianity and author of *True Doctrine,* preserved in Origen's *Against Celsus.*

charismatic Having or pertaining to the gifts of the Spirit *(charismata).*

Charlemagne (ca. 742–814). Frankish king and, later, emperor who extended his rule over most of western Europe.

Charles V Holy Roman Emperor (1519–56) during the early years of the Protestant Reformation.

Christendom The Christian world.

Christmas The celebration of the Incarnation of Christ. No indication of the date of the birth of Jesus is given in scripture. Various dates for this celebration were suggested in antiquity. The first mention of 25 December was in the year 336.

Christology The branch of Christian theology that deals with the identity and work of Christ.

church fathers Christian writers up to Isidore of Seville (d. 636), whose texts are widely regarded as having a special authority. Most were bishops. Unlike *Doctor of the Church,* the title *church father* is not formally conferred by the Church.

Clement of Alexandria (ca. 150–ca. 215). An Alexandrian theologian, he was especially concerned with establishing links between Christianity and Greek philosophy.

clergy Persons ordained for religious service such as priests and bishops.

cleric A member of the clergy.

conciliarists Supporters of a late medieval movement that sought to place much of the authority of the popes into the hands of councils of bishops.

concordat An agreement between a pope and a government concerning the regulation of church affairs.

Concordat of Worms An agreement in 1122 that ended the struggle over lay investiture between the papacy and the German emperors.

confessors In the age of persecution, those who refused to deny their faith under pressure from Roman authorities.

congregationalism A form of ecclesiastical government in which individual churches are independent and self-governed.

consubstantial "Of the same substance." A Latin-derived term equivalent to the Greek *homoousios,* used to describe the true divinity of Christ in opposition to the claims of Arius and the Arians.

Council of Chalcedon An assembly of bishops convened in 451 at Chalcedon, not far from Constantinople. It produced the Definition of Chalcedon, which resolved important questions concerning Christology.

Council of Nicaea An assembly of bishops convened in 325 at Nicaea in northwestern Turkey. It condemned the teachings of Arius.

Council of Trent A council (1545–63), regarded as the nineteenth ecumenical council by the Roman Catholic Church, at which the ideals of the Catholic Reformation were formulated.

covenant The relationship established between God and Israel at Sinai. Christians believe that a new covenant exists between God and the Church.

Cromwell, Oliver (1599–1658). Puritan leader who ruled England as "Lord Protector" from 1654 until 1658.

crusades A series of military campaigns in the eleventh through thirteenth centuries intended to liberate the Holy Land from Muslim control.

curia The papal court and its various functionaries.

Cyprian Bishop of Carthage (249–58), he wrote extensively in defense of the unity of the Church and the importance of bishops.

deacon A servant or minister, usually among the lower-ranking clergy.

decretal A papal letter written in response to a specific question.

deification: In Eastern Orthodox mysticism, the belief that union with God involves a process of divinization that brings the individual into a state of being like God.

devotio moderna A spiritual revival (the "modern devotion") that began in the Netherlands in the four-

teenth century and spread to Germany, France, and Italy. Emphasizing prayer and good works, it was composed mostly of lay men and women, some of whom lived communally.

diaspora The dispersion of the Jews outside their Palestinian homeland.

diet A legislative assembly.

diocese An ecclesiastical district under the jurisdiction of a bishop.

ditheism Belief in the existence of two gods.

docetic Christology A Christology according to which Christ was purely divine and only "seemed" (Greek, *dokein)* to have a physical body.

Doctor of the Church A title given to a theologian recognized as exceptionally learned (Latin *doctus)* and saintly. The original doctors were Ambrose, Augustine, Jerome, and Gregory the Great in the West and Athanasius, Basil the Great, John Chrysostom, and Gregory of Nazianzus in the East. Many more were later added, including Thomas Aquinas, William of Ockham, Bernard of Clairvaux, Bonaventure, Duns Scotus, Catherine of Siena, and Albert the Great.

doctrine A teaching carefully defined and established on the basis of described principles.

dogma A doctrine or body of doctrines formally established and promulgated by the authority of an ecclesiastical body (a church or denomination).

Dominicans Members of the order of preaching friars founded by St. Dominic in 1215.

Donation of Constantine A forged document, composed in the second half of the eighth century, that claimed to be Constantine's account of his conversion and gift to the pope of the western half of the Roman Empire.

doxology A formal expression of praise within a liturgy.

dualism Any system of thought that explains events with reference to two opposing principles, such as light vs. darkness, or good vs. evil.

Easter The annual celebration of Christ's Resurrection.

Eckhart, Meister (ca. 1260–1327). German mystic.

ecumenical councils Assemblies of bishops whose decisions are considered binding on the whole Church. Most Christian traditions recognize seven: Nicaea (CE 325), Constantinople (381), Ephesus (431), Chalcedon (451), Constantinople (553), Constantinople (680–81), and Nicaea (787). The Roman Catholic Church recognizes an additional fourteen councils as ecumenical councils.

Edict of Milan An decree issued in 313 by the emperors (under the tetrarchy) Licinius and Constantine, it extended freedom of worship to Christians.

electors Beginning in the fourteenth century, the three bishops (of Cologne, Trier, and Mainz) and four secular rulers (of Brandenburg, Saxony, the Palatinate, and Bohemia) who selected each new Holy Roman Emperor.

Elizabeth I Protestant Queen of England (1558–1603) and daughter of Henry VIII.

Elizabethan settlement The policy of Elizabeth I of England regarding religion, it followed a moderate course in condemning extreme forms of Protestantism as well as certain features of Catholicism.

episcopal Having to do with bishops and their authority.

Erasmus, Desiderius (1466–1536). A renowned humanist and scholar; also known as Erasmus of Rotterdam.

eschatology Having to do with the end of the age or the last things.

eucharist A sacrament that commemorates the Last Supper shared by Jesus and his disciples before his arrest and crucifixion. It is also known as "the Lord's Supper" and "Holy Communion" and is considered a sacrament in all major Christian traditions.

Eusebius (ca. 260–339). Christian apologist, biblical scholar, and historian. He is best known for his *Church History,* which covers the period from Christ until his own time.

excommunication An ecclesiastical punishment that excludes a person from participation in the Church.

existentialism A philosophical and literary movement founded by thinkers such as Jean-Paul Sartre (1905–80) and Martin Heidegger (1889–1976). Existentialism rejects absolutes and claims that human beings must make their own decisions and establish their own standards in responding to the problems of existence.

fascism A system of government generally characterized by centralized authority under a dictator, strict control of social and economic life, suppression of opposition groups, and extreme nationalism.

feudalism The political, social, and economic system that prevailed in most of Europe in the Middle Ages, in which lords granted the use of land to lesser lords, or vassals, in exchange for their military service.

fief A tract of land granted to a vassal by his feudal lord in return for his loyalty and promise of military assistance.

filioque A Latin phrase *(and from the Son)* added to the Nicene Creed in the West in the Middle Ages. Coming immediately after the words, "the Holy Spirit . . . who proceeds from the Father," it signifies the procession of the Holy Spirit from the Son as well as from the Father. This idea, not included in the original Nicene-Constantinopolitan Creed, has always been rejected by Orthodox Christians.

flagellants Medieval Christians who publicly scourged themselves to do penance for their sins.

Franciscans The order of friars founded by St. Francis of Assisi (1182–1226).

Franks A Germanic tribe that dominated much of western Europe in the eighth and ninth centuries.

friar The title given to any of the "brothers" *(fratres)* belonging to the mendicant orders, such as the Franciscans and Dominicans, founded in the Middle Ages.

Galilee The region of northern Palestine west of the Jordan River where Jesus carried out most of his public ministry.

Gallicanism The doctrines and principles articulated by the Roman Catholic Church in France in 1682 for the purpose of limiting papal influence.

Gaul A region of the Roman Empire roughly equivalent to modern France and Belgium.

Gentile A non-Jew.

glossolalia A Greek phrase meaning "speaking in tongues."

Gnosticism A philosophical religion, popular in the second and third centuries, that taught a cosmic dualism and offered salvation from the material realm based on secret knowledge *(gnosis).*

Good Friday The Friday before Easter, on which the anniversary of Christ's crucifixion is commemorated.

Goths A Germanic people divided into Western Goths (Visigoths) and Eastern Goths (Ostrogoths) in the fourth century.

grace Divine love or favor.

Great Awakening A religious revival that swept across Great Britain and the United States during the eighteenth and early nineteenth centuries.

Gregory of Nazianzus (ca. 329–ca. 390). One of the Cappadocian Fathers. A theologian instrumental in laying the foundations of the Orthodox tradition.

Gregory of Nyssa (ca. 331–ca. 395). One of the Cappadocian Fathers. A mystical theologian who was instrumental in laying the foundations of the Orthodox tradition.

Hellenism The culture and ideals of ancient Greece.

Henry VIII King of England (1509–47) and originator of the English Reformation.

heresy An opinion, teaching, or doctrine at variance with established doctrine.

Hesychasm A form of eastern mysticism that emphasizes inner quiet (Greek, *hesychia)* and repetitive prayer.

heterodoxy Belief other than what is considered doctrinally correct or orthodox.

Holy Roman Empire An empire in western and central Europe that historians say originated either in the coronation of Charlemagne as Emperor of the Romans in 800 or in that of Otto I in 962. It lasted until Francis II resigned the title in 1806.

Holy Sepulcher A cave near Jerusalem where, according to tradition, Jesus was buried and later raised from the dead.

Holy Spirit The divine spirit, understood by Christianity as the Third Person of the Trinity.

Huguenots French Calvinists. The Huguenots engaged in a series of civil wars (1562–1598) with Roman Catholics until a compromise settlement was reached with the royal Edict of Nantes (1598). The Huguenots were given control over certain parts of France, but Roman Catholicism remained the official religion in most regions.

humanism A deep and applied faith in the essential goodness and potential of human beings; one of the primary characteristics of both Hellenism and the Renaissance.

Hus, Jan (1373–1415). Czech reformer.

icons Images, usually paintings, of Christ and the saints widely used in Orthodox Christianity.

iconoclasts In the iconoclastic controversy, "icon-smashers."

iconodules In the iconoclastic controversy, "icon-venerators."

idealism In philosophy and theology, the theory that entities in the material realm are manifestations of their ideal forms, which exist in a realm of unchanging and eternal spiritual realities.

Ignatius of Antioch (ca. 35–107). Bishop of Antioch and one of antiquity's most famous martyrs, he is noted for his letters to the churches of Asia Minor in which he defended the reality of Christ's physical suffering.

Immaculate Conception The doctrine, proclaimed by Pope Pius IX in 1854, that by a miracle that occurred at the moment of her conception the Virgin Mary was freed from the stain of original sin.

incarnation The divine assumption of human nature in the person of Jesus Christ.

Index Also known as the "Index of Forbidden Books," a list (abolished in 1966) of works considered dangerous to the faith and morals of Roman Catholic Christians.

indulgence A remission of the temporal punishment for sin made possible by drawing on the surplus merits of Christ and the saints. Documents attesting that such remission had been granted became common in the late Middle Ages.

inerrancy The belief that there are no errors in scripture. Apparent errors are thought to be explained by other scriptural passages.

infallibility With reference to the papacy, the doctrine (proclaimed at the First Vatican Council in 1870) that the pope cannot err when defining a doctrine relating to faith or morals.

Inquisition A papal court responsible for the official persecution of heresy.

interdict A form of ecclesiastical censure that prohibited a person or a region from receiving the sacraments and Christian burial, but without loss of communion with the Church.

investiture In the feudal system, the ceremonial act in which a lord gave his vassal a symbol of the land (or sometimes an office or money) to be conferred in exchange for his declaration of loyalty and military support. In the Church, investiture referred to the act in which a new bishop was given the ring and crosier, or staff, that were the symbols of his ecclesiastical office.

Irenaeus (ca. 130–200). Originally from Asia Minor, he became bishop of Lyons in southern France about 178. His *Against Heresies* defends orthodox Christianity against gnosticism and other heresies.

Jerome (ca. 345–420). Bible scholar, polemicist, and translator of the Vulgate, the standard Latin version of the Bible from the fifth century to the present.

Jesuits Members of the Society of Jesus, a Roman Catholic religious order founded in 1534 by Ignatius of Loyola.

John Chrysostom (ca. 347–407). Bishop of Constantinople, theologian, and one of the most influential preachers in antiquity. The epithet *chrysostomos* means "golden-mouthed."

John of the Cross (1542–91). Spanish monk and mystic.

John of Damascus (ca. 655–ca. 750). Greek monk and theologian, author of the *Fount of Wisdom.*

Julian of Norwich (ca. 1342–ca. 1416). English mystic and author of the *Showings* or *Revelations.*

Justinian (527–65). Early Byzantine emperor known for his codification of Roman law and attempted reconquest of western territories lost to Germanic tribes.

Justin Martyr (ca. 100–ca. 165). Author of two *Apologies,* he is noted for being among the first Christian thinkers to point to common features linking Christianity and Greek philosophy.

Kempe, Margery (ca. 1373–1438). English mystic and spiritual writer.

kenoticism The ideal of "emptying" oneself in humility and in imitation of Christ.

Kierkegaard, Søren (1813–55). Danish philosopher and critic of the established church in Denmark.

Knox, John (1513–72). Swiss reformer and one of the founders of the Reformed tradition along with Ulrich Zwingli and John Calvin.

Kulturkampf A "culture struggle" directed by Bismarck against the Roman Catholic Church in Germany during the 1870s.

Last Supper Jesus' final meal with his disciples, described as a Passover *seder* (ritual meal) in the Synoptic Gospels. It was the occasion on which Jesus instituted the eucharist (Mark 14:12–26; Matthew 26:20–29; Luke 22:14–23; 1 Corinthians 11:23–26).

Law When used in connection with scripture, *Law* refers to the Law of Moses found in the first five books of the Bible, which are also known as the Torah or Pentateuch.

liturgy A prescribed form of public worship, usually centering on the celebration of the eucharist.

Logos A Greek term meaning "word" and, in philosophical and theological usage, "reason" or "divine reason."

Lollards English followers of John Wycliffe.

Luther, Martin (1483–1546). German theologian and originator of the Protestant Reformation in Germany.

Manichaeism A strongly dualistic religion based on the teachings of the third-century Babylonian prophet Mani.

Marcion A second-century Christian teacher whose heterodox views included the rejection of the Jewish Scriptures and belief in a God higher and more noble than the God described there.

martyr From the Greek word for "witness," one who has died for the sake of the faith.

mass The celebration of the eucharist.

Maundy Thursday The Thursday before Easter, on which Christians celebrate Christ's institution of the eucharist at the Last Supper.

Melanchthon, Philip (1497–1550). German reformer who assisted and supported Martin Luther. Melanchthon was the primary author of the Augsburg Confession.

mendicant friars Members of religious orders whose members were, in theory, forbidden to own property. The most famous are the Dominicans and Franciscans.

metropolitan The title of a bishop occupying the level of ecclesiastical authority just below that of patriarch.

Middle Platonism The version of Platonic thought current in the first two centuries CE; it had a strong interest in religion.

minor orders Lesser degrees of the ministry (i.e., below bishop, priest, and deacon).

Monarchianism A movement beginning in the third century that stressed the oneness of God. According to "Dynamic" or "Adoptionist" Monarchianism, Jesus was divine only in the sense that God had given him divine power. "Modalist" Monarchians argued that the Father, Son, and Holy Spirit were only modes in which the one God operated and not discrete "persons" as defined by later Christian doctrine.

monotheism Belief in the existence of only one God.

Monothelitism (also Monotheletism) The doctrine that Christ had two natures but only a single will.

Montanism A movement dating to the second and early third centuries and based on the prophecies of Montanus and other ecstatic prophets.

mysticism An approach to religion that stresses the direct and intuitive experience of God.

Nag Hammadi texts A cache of ancient texts, many of them Gnostic, discovered at the village of Nag

Hammadi in upper Egypt in 1945. Many are examples of gnostic Christianity.

nationalism An intense devotion to the political, territorial, and cultural interests of one's nation.

neo-orthodoxy A twentieth-century theological movement that stressed a return to many of the themes of the Protestant Reformation, including original sin and dependence upon grace.

Neoplatonism A form of Platonism originating with the philosopher Plotinus (205–70), who taught that all things are derived from the One, the highest reality.

Nestorius Fifth-centry teacher of an extreme form of Antiochene Christology that emphasized the separateness of the two natures (human and divine) in Christ.

Newman, John Henry (1801–90). A Roman Catholic theologian who began his career as a member of the Church of England and leader of the Oxford Movement.

Novatian The leader of a rigorist faction in the Roman Church in the mid third century, he sought to exclude apostates. His faction was ultimately defeated by Cyprian of Carthage and others who urged a more moderate policy.

Ontological Argument An argument for the existence of God formulated by Anselm of Canterbury. It states that the very idea of God as something greater than which nothing can be imagined proves God's existence.

ontology The branch of philosphy that deals with the nature of being or reality.

ordination Appointment to church office, especially the priesthood.

Origen (ca. 185–ca. 254). An influential leader of the Alexandrian school of theology, he called for the allegorical interpretation of scripture and made extensive use of ideas from Platonism and Neoplatonism.

original sin The sin of Adam and Eve, the effect of which has been to make human nature sinful.

orthodoxy "Right belief," as opposed to heterodoxy or heresy.

Oxford Movement A movement during the late 1830s and early 1840s within the Church of England that affirmed patterns of worship based on those thought to have existed in the ancient Church.

Pachomius (ca. 290–346). The founder of Egyptian cenobitic (communal) monasticism.

Palm Sunday The Sunday before Easter and the beginning of Holy Week. It takes its name from the palms that were spread before Christ at the time of his triumphal entry into Jerusalem a week before the Resurrection.

papal infallibility A doctrine proclaimed in 1870 at the First Vatican Council according to which the pope cannot err when he speaks *ex cathedra* (in his official apostolic capacity) on matters of faith and morals.

parish An administrative district (Greek, *paroikia*) of the Church under the care of a priest or minister.

patriarch An honorific title given in antiquity to the bishops of Rome, Constantinople, Jerusalem, Antioch, and Alexandria. In the modern Eastern Orthodox Church, the bishop of Moscow is also considered a patriarch.

Pelagius A Christian thinker of the early fifth century who emphasized human freedom and the merits of human effort in attaining salvation. He was an opponent of Augustine.

penance In the Eastern Orthodox and Roman Catholic traditions, a sacrament of forgiveness involving contrition, confession, the performance of an act of penance (punishment), and absolution.

Pentecost In Judaism, a holiday celebrated fifty days after Passover. In Christianity, a celebration of the descent of the Holy Spirit on Jesus' disciples described in Acts 2.

Pentecostals Members of churches that emphasize the workings of the Holy Spirit, such as speaking in tongues *(glossolalia)*.

Pietism A movement in seventeenth- and eighteenth-century Protestantism, primarily in Germany, that sought to elevate personal piety and religious feeling to the same level of importance as religious institutions and doctrines.

plainsong The monophonic and unmeasured chant used in the early Church, the most famous form of which is Gregorian chant.

pluralism The holding by one person of more than one church office or benefice at the same time.

predestination The doctrine that God decreed before the beginning of time the salvation (and, according to some theories, the damnation) of individual souls.

prelate A high-ranking member of the clergy, such as a bishop.

presbyter "Elder." A clerical office in the Church since earliest times.

presbyterianism A form of church government in which authority is in the hands of a group of elders.

Providence Divine management of the universe for the purpose of realizing God's purposes.

Pseudo-Dionysius Also Dionysius the Pseudo-Areopagite. The name given to the anonymous author (ca. 500) of treatises on mystical theology.

purgatory A state or place in the afterlife between heaven and hell where souls are cleansed of sins committed in life. Belief in purgatory is limited almost entirely to Roman Catholicism.

Puritans English Protestants of the sixteenth and seventeenth centuries who sought to purify the Church of England through the elimination of beliefs and practices they considered unscriptural.

Rahner, Karl (1904–84). Roman Catholic theologian whose *Theological Investigations* and other works emphasized the centrality of mystery in human life and attempted to make doctrine meaningful in connection with the realities of the modern world.

relics The physical remains of a saint, usually body parts but sometimes artifacts, often thought to have miraculous power.

Ritschl, Albrecht (1822–89). German Protestant proponent of liberal theology.

Romanticism An artistic and literary movement in eighteenth-century Europe. As a reaction against the rationalism of the Englightenment, it emphasized the importance of personal feeling, intuition, nature, and national traditions.

Sabellius Teacher of a form of Monarchianism that emphasized the divine unity to the point that the persons of the Trinity are reduced to mere modes of divine action.

sacrament An outward sign of invisible grace. Roman Catholicism and Eastern Orthodoxy recognize seven sacraments—baptism, confirmation, the eucharist, holy orders, holy matrimony, reconciliation, and extreme unction. Protestants recognize only baptism and the eucharist.

Schleiermacher, Friedrich (1768–1834). German Protestant theologian noted for his view that religion is based on feeling rather than doctrine. Author of *Religion: Speeches to its Cultured Despisers* and *The Christian Faith.*

scholasticism A medieval intellectual effort, carried out largely in universities, to determine the relationship between faith and reason.

Scotus, John Duns (ca. 1265–1308). Philosopher, theologian, and author of a commentary on the *Sentences* of Peter Lombard.

sin Thought or action in disobedience to the divine will.

simony The buying and selling of ecclesiastical offices.

staretz In Russian Orthodoxy, an "elder," often a monk, who serves as a spiritual counselor.

synod A meeting of religious leaders, usually representing a single region.

Synod of Dort (1618–19). An assembly of Dutch Reformed theologians at the city of Dort convened for the purpose of addressing the views of the Arminians. In defending Calvinism, the synod affirmed five of its major principles: absolute and unconditional election, an atonement whose efficacy is limited only to the elect, the complete depravity of human nature, the irresistibility of grace, and the final perserverance of the elect.

Teresa of Avila (1515–83). Spanish saint, mystic, and reformer of the Carmelite order.

Tertullian (ca. 160–ca. 225). A resident of North Africa; one of the first great Latin theologians noted particularly for apologetic writings.

Theodore of Mopsuestia (ca. 350–428). Antiochene theologian generally regarded as the greatest exponent of "two-natures" Christology.

Theotokos A Greek term meaning "God-bearer" used to honor the Virgin Mary.

Thomas à Kempis (1380–1471). An important representative of the *devotio moderna* who is generally believed to be the author of *The Imitation of Christ.*

Tillich, Paul (1886–1965). German Protestant theologian who also taught at the University of Chicago. Seeking to make connections between Christianity and secular culture, he used the language and insights of existentialism to describe Christian answers to human problems.

Torah The first five books of the Old Testament, also known as the Pentateuch and Law of Moses.

transubstantiation According to Roman Catholicism, the miraculous process by which the bread and wine used in the eucharist become the body and blood of Christ.

Treasury of Merit According the medieval theology, a repository of surplus merits earned by Christ and the saints which might be distributed by the Church for the spiritual benefit of others.

Trinity The Christian doctrine that the one God consists of three divine and consubstantial "persons"

tritheism Belief in three Gods.

Ultramontanism The tendency within the Roman Catholic Church, especially in the seventeenth through nineteenth centuries, to assert the supremacy of the papacy in Rome (which lies "beyond the mountains") over ecclesiastical organization at national and local levels.

Unam Sanctam A papal bull issued by Boniface VIII in 1302 during a conflict with King Philip the Fair of France. It affirmed that there is no salvation outside the Church and that temporal authority is always subject to the spiritual power of the Church.

vassal A person who held land under the feudal system and in return owed loyalty and assistance to a feudal lord.

Vatican I (1869–70). A Roman Catholic council convened by Pius IX. Its most notable act was the proclamation of the doctrine of papal infallibility.

Vatican II (1962–65). A Roman Catholic council convened by Pope John XXIII. It sought to modern-ize Catholic teaching and practice by such means as replacing Latin with the vernacular in the liturgy and adopting a more open attitude toward Orthodox, Protestant, and other churches.

vernacular The native language of a country or region.

Vulgate The Latin translation of the Bible executed almost entirely by St. Jerome.

Waldenses (Waldensians) Followers of Peter Waldo, a twelfth-century reformer who urged laypeople to embrace poverty and preach the gospel.

William of Ockham (1285–1347). English scholastic theologian and proponent of nominalism.

Wycliffe, John (1320–84). English theologian and reformer.

Zwingli, Ulrich (1484–1531). Swiss reformer and one of the founders of the Reformed tradition within Protestantism, along with John Calvin and John Knox.

Suggested Readings

Readers who wish to pursue their interest in topics discussed in this book may want to begin with the works below, most of which focus on particular periods and issues. We also recommend three more general texts: The *Oxford Dictionary of the Christian Church* (3rd ed., edited by F. L. Cross and E. A. Livingstone, 1997), whose articles on a wide variety of subjects represent the best in recent scholarship; H. Bettenson, ed., *Documents of the Christian Church* (2nd ed., 1967), a collection of important church documents ranging from the second century to the twentieth; and William Placher, *A History of Christian Theology: An Introduction* (1983), a concise but comprehensive and highly readable introduction to the history of Christian thought.

Chapter 1

Barrett, C. K. *The New Testament Background: Selected Documents.* San Francisco: Harper & Row, 1987.

Ferguson, E. *Backgrounds of Early Christianity.* Grand Rapids, Mich.: Eerdmans, 1993.

Goodman, M. *The Roman World: 40 BC–AD 180.* London: Routledge, 1997.

Gottwald, N. *The Hebrew Bible: A Socio-Literary Introduction.* Philadelphia: Fortress Press, 1985.

Hengel, M. *Judaism and Hellenism.* Philadelphia: Fortress Press, 1981.

Horsley, R. A., and Hanson, J. S. *Bandits, Prophets, and Messiahs: Popular Movements at the Time of Jesus.* San Francisco: Harper & Row, 1988.

Rendtorff, R. *The Old Testament: An Introduction.* Philadelphia: Fortress Press, 1991.

Sandmel, S. *Judaism and Christian Beginnings.* New York: Oxford University Press, 1978.

Chapter 2

Borg, M. *Conflict, Holiness and Politics in the Teaching of Jesus.* London: Muellen, 1984.

Boyarin, D. *A Radical Jew: Paul and the Politics of Identity.* Berkeley: University of California Press, 1994.

Caird, G. B., and Hurst, L. D. *New Testament Theology.* Oxford: Clarendon Press, 1994.

Crossan, J. D. *The Historical Jesus: The Life of a Mediterranean Jewish Peasant.* San Francisco: HarperSanFrancisco, 1991.

Dunn, J. D. G. *The Theology of Paul the Apostle.* Grand Rapids, Mich.: Eerdmans, 1998.

Ehrman, B. D. *The New Testament: A Historical Introduction to the Early Christian Writings.* New York: Oxford University Press, 1997.

Meeks, W. A. *The First Urban Christians: The Social World of the Apostle Paul.* New Haven: Yale University Press, 1983.

Segal, A. *Rebecca's Children: Judaism and Christianity in the Roman World.* Cambridge, Mass.: Harvard University Press, 1986.

Wright, N. T. *The Original Jesus: The Life and Vision of a Revolutionary.* Grand Rapids, Mich.: Eerdmans, 1996.

Chapter 3

Benko, S. "Pagan Criticism of Christianity during the First Two Centuries A.D." *Aufstieg und Niedergang der römischen Welt* 23.3 (1980): 1055–1118.

Chadwick, H. *The Early Church.* Rev. ed. London: Penguin Books, 1993.

Dodds, E. R. *Pagan and Christian in an Age of Anxiety.* Cambridge: Cambridge University Press, 1965.

Frend, W. H. C. *Martyrdom and Persecution in the Early Church.* Oxford: Blackwell, 1965.

Frend, W. H. C. *The Rise of Christianity*. Philadelphia: Fortress Press, 1984.

Hamman, A. *How to Read the Church Fathers*. New York: Crossroad, 1993.

Hoffmann, R. J. *Celsus on the True Doctrine: A Discourse against the Christians*. New York: Oxford University Press, 1987.

Macmullen, R. *Christianizing the Roman Empire (A.D. 100–400)*. *New Haven: Yale University Press, 1984*.

MacMullen, R., and Lane, E. N. *Paganism and Christianity, 100–425 C.E.* Minneapolis: Fortress Press, 1992.

Pagels, E. *The Gnostic Gospels*. New York: Random House, 1979.

Stark, R. *The Rise of Christianity*. Princeton, N.J.: Princeton University Press, 1996.

Waddell, H. *The Desert Fathers*. Ann Arbor: University of Michigan Press, 1966.

Chapter 4

Brown, P. *Augustine of Hippo*. Berkeley: University of California Press, 1967.

Brown, P. *The Cult of Saints*. Chicago: University of Chicago Press, 1983.

Grant, R. M. *The Formation of the New Testament*. New York: Harper & Row, 1965.

Hahn, F. *The Worship of the Early Church*. Philadelphia: Fortress Press, 1973.

Hanson, R. P. C. *The Search for the Christian Doctrine of God: The Arian Controversy 318–381*. Edinburgh: T. and T. Clark, 1988.

Hazlett, I., ed. *Early Christianity: Origins and Evolution to A.D. 600*. Nashville: Abingdon Press, 1991.

Kelly, J. N. D. *Early Christian Doctrines*. Rev. ed. San Francisco: Harper, 1978.

Lieu, S. N. C. *Manichaeism in the Later Roman Empire and Medieval China*. Manchester, U.K.: Manchester University Press, 1985.

Norris, R., and Rusch, W., eds. *The Christological Controversy*. Philadelphia: Fortress Press, 1980.

Rusch, W., ed. *The Trinitarian Controversy*. Philadelphia: Fortress Press, 1980.

Chapter 5

Barraclough, J. *The Medieval Papacy*. New York: Harcourt, Brace & World, 1968.

Cannon, W. R. *History of Christianity in the Middle Ages*. New York: Abingdon press, 1960.

Cantor, N. *The Civilization of the Middle Ages*. New York: HarperCollins, 1993.

Genakoplos, D. J. *Byzantium: Church, Society, and Civilization Seen through Contemporary Eyes*. Chicago: University of Chicago Press, 1984.

Lossky, V. *The Mystical Theology of the Eastern Church*. London: James Clarke, 1957.

McNamara, J. *Sisters in Arms: Catholic Nuns through Two Millennia*. Cambridge, Mass.: Harvard University Press, 1996.

McNeill, J. *The Celtic Churches: A History, A.D. 200–1200*. Chicago: University of Chicago Press, 1974.

Meyendorff, J. *The Byzantine Legacy in the Orthodox Church*. Crestwood, N.Y.: St. Vladimir's Seminary Press, 1982.

Meyendorff, J. *Byzantine Theology*. New York: Fordham University Press, 1974.

Runciman, S. *The Byzantine Theocracy*. Cambridge: Cambridge University Press, 1977.

Southern, R. W. *Western Society and the Church in the Middle Ages*. New York: Penguin, 1970.

Wallace-Hadrill, J. M. *The Frankish Church*. New York: Oxford University Press, 1983.

Ware, T. (Kallistos). *The Orthodox Church*. Baltimore: Penguin Books, 1963.

Zernov, N. *Eastern Christendom*. London: Weidenfeld & Nicolson, 1961.

Chapter 6

Blumenthal, U. *The Investiture Controversy: Church and Monarchy from the Ninth to the Twelfth Century*. Philadelphia: University of Pennsylvania Press, 1988.

Knowles, D. *The Evolution of Medieval Thought*. 2nd ed. New York: Longman, 1988.

Morris, C. *The Papal Monarchy: The Western Church from 1050 to 1250*. New York: Clarendon Press, 1989.

Panofsky, E. *Gothic Architecture and Scholasticism*. Latrobe, Penn.: Archabbey Press, 1951.

Tierney, B., ed. *The Crisis of the Church and State, 1050–1300*. Englewood Cliffs, N.J.: Prentice Hall, 1964.

Weisheipl, J. *Friar Thomas D'Aquino: His Life, Thought and Work*. Garden City, N.Y.: Doubleday, 1974.

Chapter 7

Carré, M. *Realists and Nominalists*. London: Oxford University Press, 1946.

Crowder, C. M. D. *Unity, Heresy and Reform, 1378–1460: The Conciliar Response to the Great Schism*. London: Edwin Arnold, 1977.

Diehl, P., and Waugh, S., eds. *Christendom and Its Discontents: Exclusion, Persecution, and Rebellion, 1000–1500*. New York: Cambridge University Press, 1995.

Kenny, A. *Wyclif*. New York: Oxford University Press, 1985.

Lambert, M. *Medieval Heresy: Popular Movements from Bogomil to Hus*. New York: Basil Blackwell, 1992.

Lawrence, C. H. *The Friars: The Impact of the Early Mendicant Orders on Western Society*. New York: Longman, 1994.

Oakley, F. *The Western Church in the Later Middle Ages*. Ithaca, N.Y.: Cornell University Press, 1979.

Oberman, H. *Forerunners of the Reformation*. Philadelphia: Fortress Press, 1981.

Ozment, S. *The Age of Reform, 1250–1550: An Intellectual and Religious History of Late Medieval and Reformation Europe*. New Haven: Yale University Press, 1980.

Shannon, A. *The Medieval Inquisition*. Washington, D.C.: Augustinian College Press, 1983.

Chapter 8

Dickens, A. G. *The German Nation and Martin Luther*. London: Edward Arnold, 1974.

Lindberg, C. *The European Reformations*. Cambridge, Mass.: Blackwell, 1996.

Lohse, B. *Martin Luther's Theology*. Minneapolis: Fortress Press, 1999.

McGrath, A. E. *Reformation Thought: An Introduction*. Oxford: Basil Blackwell, 1988.

Moeller, B. *Imperial Cities and the Reformation: Three Essays*. Edited and translated by H. C. E. Midelfort and M. U. Edwards, Jr. Philadelphia: Fortress Press, 1972.

Schwiebert, E. G. *The Reformation*. Philadelphia: Fortress Press, 1996.

Spitz, L. *The Protestant Reformation: 1517–1559*. New York: Harper & Row, 1985.

Stephens, W. P. *Zwingli: An Introduction to His Thought*. Oxford: Clarendon Press, 1992.

Chapter 9

Bouwsma, W. J. *John Calvin: A Sixteenth-Century Portrait*. New York: Oxford University Press, 1988.

Collinson, P. *The Birthpangs of Protestant England: Religious and Cultural Change in the Sixteenth and Seventeenth Centuries*. New York: St. Martin's Press, 1988.

Lindberg, C. *The European Reformations*. Cambridge, Mass.: Blackwell, 1996.

McGrath, A. E. *A Life of John Calvin: A Study in the Shaping of Western Culture*. Oxford: Basil Blackwell, 1990.

Walker, W. *John Calvin: The Organiser of Reformed Protestantism, 1509–1564*. New York: Schocken Books, 1964.

Chapter 10

Byrne, J. M. *Religion and the Enlightenment: From Descartes to Kant*. Louisville, Ky.: Westminster/John Knox Press, 1996.

Campbell, T. A. *The Religion of the Heart: A Study of European Religious Life in the Seventeenth and Eighteenth Centuries*. Columbia: University of South Carolina Press, 1991.

Erb, P. C., ed. *Pietists: Selected Writings*. New York: Paulist Press, 1983.

Levi, A. *Cardinal Richelieu and the Making of Modern France*. New York: Carroll & Graf, 2000.

Muller, R. A. *Post-Reformation Reformed Dogmatics*. Grand Rapids, Mich.: Eerdmans, 1987.

Ward, W. R. *Christianity under the Ancien Régime: 1648–1789*. Cambridge: Cambridge University Press, 1999.

Ward, W. R. *The Protestant Evangelical Awakening*. Cambridge: Cambridge University Press, 1992.

Chapter 11

Ahlstrom, S. *A Religious History of the American People*. New Haven: Yale University Press, 1972.

Bednarowski, M. F. *New Religions and the Theological Imagination in America*. Bloomington: Indiana University Press, 1989.

Dolan, J. *The American Catholic Experience: A History from Colonial Times to the Present*. Garden City, N.Y.: Doubleday, 1985.

Ellis, J. *American Catholicism*. Chicago: University of Chicago Press, 1969.

Flannery, A. *Documents of Vatican II*. North Port, N.Y.: Costello, 1975.

Ford, D. *The Modern Theologians: An Introduction to Christian Theology in the Twentieth Century*. 2nd ed. Cambridge, Mass.: Blackwell, 1997.

Hastings, A. *The Church in Africa, 1450–1950*. Oxford: Clarendon Press, 1994.

Hatch, N. *The Democratization of American Christianity*. New Haven: Yale University Press, 1989.

Marty, M. *Pilgrims in Their Own Land: 500 Years of American Religion*. Boston: Little, Brown, 1984.

Neill, S. *A History of Christian Missions*. 2nd ed. New York: Bantam Books, 1986.

Niebuhr, H. Richard. *Christ and Culture*. New York: Harper, 1951.

Chapter 12

Cone, J. H. *A Black Theology of Liberation*. Philadelphia: Lippincott, 1970.

Daly, M. *Beyond God the Father: Toward a Philosophy of Women's Liberation*. Boston: Beacon Press, 1973.

Emerson, M. O., and Smith, C. *Divided by Faith: Evangelical Religion and the Problem of Race in America*. New York: Oxford University Press, 2000.

Gutiérrez, G. *A Theology of Liberation: History, Politics and Salvation*. Translated and edited by Sister Caridad Inda and J. Eagleson. Maryknoll, N.Y.: Orbis Books, 1973.

Küng, H. *On Being a Christian*. Translated by E. Quinn. Garden City, N.Y.: Doubleday, 1976.

Lincoln, C. E., and Mamiya, L. *The Black Church in the African American Experience*. Durham, N.C.: Duke University Press, 1990.

Marsden, G. *Reforming Fundamentalism: Fuller Seminary and the New Evangelicalism.* Grand Rapids, Mich.: Eerdmans, 1987.

Moltmann, J. *Theology of Hope: On the Ground and Implications of a Christian Eschatology.* Translated by J. W. Leitch. New York: Harper & Row, 1967.

Pannenberg, W. *Jesus-God and Man.* Translated by L. L. Wilkins and D. A. Priebe. Philadelphia: Westminster Press, 1968.

Ruether, R. R. *Sexism and God-Talk: Toward a Feminist Theology.* Boston: Beacon Press, 1983.

Credits

Chapter 1 *Figure 1.1,* © British Museum; *Figure 1.3,* © Foto Marburg/Art Resource, NY; *Figure 1.4,* Courtesy of Robert Kebric; *Figure 1.6,* © Jewish Museum, London; *Figure 1.7,* © Zev Radovan, Jerusalem

Chapter 2 *Figure 2.1,* Courtesy of Robert Kebric; *Figure 2.2,* Courtesy of the Rev. Dr. James E. Straukamp; *Figure 2.3,* © Alinari/Art Resource, NY; *Figure 2.5,* Courtesy Musée du Petit Palais, Paris; *Figure 2.6,* Courtesy of the Rev. Dr. James E. Straukamp; *Figure 2.7,* Courtesy of The British Library, no. 4445 ƒ85r

Chapter 3 *Figure 3.2,* Courtesy of Robert Kebric; *Figure 3.3,* © AKG London; *Figure 3.5,* Courtesy of Robert Kebric; *Figure 3.6,* Scavi Archeologici de S. Pietro, Vatican; *Figure 4.1,* Courtesy of Benedettine Di Priscilla; *Figure 4.2,* Courtesy of the Rev. Dr. James E. Straukamp; *Figure 4.3,* Courtesy of Robert Kebric

Chapter 4 *Figure 4.1,* Courtesy Pontifical Commission of Sacred Archeology

Chapter 5 *Figure 5.2,* Courtesy of Robert Kebric; *Figure 5.4,* © Art Resource, NY; *Figure 5.5,* Courtesy of the Department of Humanities & Religious Studies, California State University, Sacramento; *Figure 5.6,* From Huck's Pictorial Archive of Art and Architecture, edited by J.G. Huck, © 1994 Dover Publications, Inc.; *Figure 5.7,* Courtesy of Robert Kebric

Chapter 6 *Figure 6.1,* Courtesy of the Department of Humanities & Religious Studies, California State University, Sac-
ramento; *Figure 6.3,* Courtesy of the Department of Humanities & Religious Studies, California State University, Sacramento; *Figure 6.4,* © M. Freeman/PhotoLink; *Figure 6.5,* Courtesy of the Department of Humanities & Religious Studies, California State University, Sacramento; *Figure 6.6,* © R. Strange/PhotoLink; *Figure 6.7,* Courtesy of the Rev. Dr. James E. Straukamp

Chapter 7 *Figure 7.1,* Courtesy of the Department of Humanities & Religious Studies, California State University, Sacramento; *Figure 7.3,* Courtesy of the Department of Humanities & Religious Studies, California State University, Sacramento; *Figure 7.4,* Courtesy of the Department of Humanities & Religious Studies, California State University, Sacramento; *Figure 7.5,* Courtesy of the author

Chapter 9 *Figure 9.2,* © Museo del Prado, Madrid. All rights reserved.

Chapter 11 *Figure 11.2,* © Boltin Picture Library; *Figure 11.4,* © Boltin Picture Library

Chapter 12 *Figure 12.1,* © Boltin Picture Library; *Figure 12.2,* © Vittoriano Rastelli/Corbis; *Figure 12.3,* © Fr. John Guiliani. Used with permission of Bridge Building Images, Inc. P.O. Box 1048, Burlington, VT 05402-1048, www.Bridge Building.com

Index

abbey of St. Denis, 173, 182–84
Abbott (archbishop), 289
Abelard, Peter, 172–74, 180
abortion, 57
Abraham, 2, 334
absolutism, 258–59, 279
Abyssinian Church, 221
Act of Uniformity, 273
Adrian VI (pope), 282
Adventism, 340–41
Africa, 348–49, 370, 376
   See also North Africa
African Americans, 362, 363, 368, 380n50
   See also slavery
agape, 58
   See also love
Agricola, Georgias, 302
Aidan, 121
Ailred of Rievaulx, 155
Albert of Brandenburg, 231–32, 240
Albert the Great, 175
Albigensian Crusade, 201
Alcuin of York, 119
Aleander, Girolamo, 233
Aleppo, Paul of, 314
Alexander III (pope), 160
Alexander the Great, 6–7
Alexander VI (pope), 216
Alexandrians, 92, 93, 94–95
Alexis (tsar), 315
al-Ghazali, 170
Allen, Richard, 346
alms, 145
Ambrose, 98–100, 101
Ameaux, Pierre, 263
American Revolution, 319, 345
Ames, William, 311
Amharic Christians, 96
Ammonius, 75
Ammun, 75

Amos, 4
Anabaptists, 250–52, 278
ancestral period, 2
anchorites, 74, 75, 77
ancient Greece
   history, 5–8
   religion, 8, 20n16
   thought, 8–11
Andrae, Jacob, 285
Angelique, Mother, 296
angels, 70, 177
Anglican Communion, 273
Anglicanism, 270–73, 276, 277 (map), 279
   Oxford Movement, 335
Anglicans
   in Africa, 349, 376
   and American Revolution, 345
   in South America, 348
Anglo-Catholics, 335
Anglo-Saxons, 114, 120, 121
Anselm of Canterbury, 160, 170–72, 176, 178
Anthony, 74–75
anthropologists, 323
anthropomorphism, 67
Antiochenes, 92, 93–94, 95, 134
antisemitism
   in Byzantine Empire, 125
   in Germany, 192, 321
   and Gospels, 33, 42
   and John Chrysostom, 97–98
   of Luther, 229
   during plague, 192
Antoninus Pius (emperor), 49, 60
Antony of Constantinople, 128–29
apocalyptic literature, 18–20, 30, 32–33, 46n46
   See also under Paul
Apocrypha, 27–28, 111n27, 276
Apollinaris, 93–94

apologists, 48, 66–73, 78
apostasy, 64–65
apostles, 84, 86, 111n17
   See also specific apostles
Apostles' Creed, 87–88, 147
apostolic succession, 85
Aquinas, Thomas, 173–79
   on heresy, 202
   and Jansenius, 296
   for John Duns Scotus, 210
   and papacy, 212
   twentieth century views, 330
architecture, 180–86, 187 (figure), 213
Arianism, 89–90
   and Ambrose, 98–99
   and Anthony, 75
   and Council of Constantinople, 54
   and Germanic peoples, 114, 120, 130
   and Origen, 71
Aristides of Athens, 67
Aristotle
   on good works, 234
   and Islam, 170
   for Luther, 234–35, 254n23
   and material world, 10, 169
   in Middle Ages, 168–69, 209–10, 211
   and Protestant scholastics, 299
   and rationalism, 302
   Tertullian view, 73
   and Thomas Aquinas, 176, 177
   and transubstantiation, 144
Arius, 89–90
Arize, Francis (cardinal), 378
Armenian Orthodox Church, 222
Arminian Baptists, 278
Arminius, Jacob, 268–69
Arnauld, Aintoine, 297

Arndt, Johann, 309
art
    and Catholic reform, 281
    in early Middle Ages, 124
    in Renaissance, 213, 216
Asbury, Francis, 312
ascension, 34
asceticism, 63–64, 69, 74, 300–301
Asia, 376
    See also specific countries
Assemblies in the Desert, 292
Assemblies of God, 370
Athanasius
    and Arianism, 90
    as eastern saint, 129
    Life of Anthony, 74–75, 76
    and mysticism, 137
Athenagoras, 67
Attalus, 62
Augsburg Confession, 240–41
Augsburg interim, 299
Augustine (bishop of Canterbury),
    121–22
Augustine of Hippo
    biography, 100–101
    city of God, 105–6, 117
    in Doctors of the Church, 98
    doctrinal works, 106
    and Donatism, 66, 102, 117
    for Luther, 230
    and Manichaeism, 100–101
    and mysticism, 207, 209
    as Neoplatonist, 101
    and predestination, 103–5, 142–
        43, 296
    for Protestants, 106
    on sacraments, 106–7, 143, 144
    on salvation, 93
    on sin, 101, 103–5
    on Trinity, 92
Augustinians, 101, 230, 240
Augustus (emperor), 11, 49
Auscula fili, 163
Austria, 294
    See also Holy Roman Empire
Averroës, 170

Babylonian Captivity, 193, 295
Babylonian exile, 4–5
Bacon, Francis, 302
Baius, Michael, 296, 316n19
Bañez, Domingo, 296
baptism
    for Anabaptists, 250
    appeal of, 57
    for Christian Scientists, 340
    of Constantine, 53
    delayed, 53, 107
    for evangelical humanism, 253
    infant, 278
    of Jesus Christ, 28
    Novatianist, 65
    origins, 24–25, 107–8

proselyte, 25
    and Society of Friends, 308
Baptists, 276–78, 345, 346, 348
    General, 278
    Southern and Northern, 365–66,
        382n107
Bar Hebraeus, 221–22
Bar Kepha, Moses, 221
Barlaam of Calabria, 139
Barmen Declaration, 337
Barth, Karl, 337
Bascio, Matteo da, 280
Basil of Caesarea, 76, 96
Basil the Great, 91–92, 219
Baur, Ferdinand, 325–26
Becket, Thomas, 160
Bede the Venerable, 121–22, 123
Beghards, 180
Beguines, 180
Benedictines, 77, 117, 154, 155
Benedict of Nursia, 77
Benedict XV (pope), 329
benefices, 193, 196
Beneficio di Cristo, 281
Bentham, Jeremy, 301
Berkeley, George, 304
Bernardino of Siena, 216
Bernard of Clairvaux, 155, 173, 179
Beza, Theodore, 168
Bible, 1–2
    See also scripture
biblical criticism, 325–26, 356–59
biblical theology, 359
Biel, Gabriel, 229, 230, 234
Biringuccio, Vanoccio, 302
birth control, 57, 374, 381n82
bishops, 83–86
    apostolic succession, 85–86
    authority, 64
    and conciliarism, 194–95
    and Fourth Lateran Council, 162
    and globalization, 375–76
    and heretics, 162
    Latin American, 361
    lay investiture, 156, 158–60
    metropolitan, 85
    in Middle Ages, 121, 156, 158–
        60, 196
    patriarchs, 85–86
    from third world, 375–76
    twentieth century views, 331
Bismarck, Otto von, 328
Black Death, 192, 200
Blake, William, 319
Boccaccio, 192, 213
Boehme, Jakob, 307–8
Boff, Leonardo, 361
Bogomils, 200
Bohemia, 290
Böhm, Hans, 245
Bolivar, Simón, 348
Bonaventure, 207
Bonesana, Cesare, 301

Bonhoeffer, Dietrich, 337–38
Boniface (saint), 114–15, 145
Boniface VIII (pope), 163, 193
book banning, 284
Book of Acts, 34, 36
Book of Common Prayer, 271–
    72, 273
Book of Daniel, 18, 365
Book of Mormon, 339
Book of Revelation, 60, 366
Booth, William, 336
Borg, Marcus, 46n49, 359
Borgias, 216
Bossuet (bishop), 298
bourgeoisie, 152, 226
Bousset, J. F. W., 326
Boxer Rebellion, 351
Brandenburg
    Albert of, 231–32, 240
    Frederick the Great, 294
Bray, Guy de, 268
Brazil, 348, 377–78
Brown, R. R., 336
Browne, Robert, 276
Bucer, Martin, 262
Bulgaria, 342
Bullinger, Heinrich, 250, 262, 267
bulls, 163
    See also specific bulls
Bultmann, Rudolf, 358–59
Burckhardt, Jakob, 253
Byzantine Empire
    Church–state relationship,
        128–30
    and Crusades, 128, 163–67
    and Goths, 130
    Isaurian dynasty, 126–28, 135
    and Islam, 131–33
    under Justinian, 125–26
    Macedonian dynasty, 128
    origins, 54–55, 113
    and Slavs, 130–31

caesaropapism, 129
Caird, G. B., 359
Cajetan (cardinal), 232
Caligula (emperor), 49
Calixtus, Georg, 300
Calixtus III (pope), 215
Calvin, John
    Articles, 261–62
    biography, 259–64
    on church structure, 263, 266–67
    on God, 264–66, 286n22
    Institutes, 261, 262, 264, 266, 280
    and Luther, 259, 262, 298
    Ordinances, 263
    theology, 264–67, 299
    and Zwinglians, 267
Calvinism
    in 1600, 277(map)
    and Catholic reform, 281
    distinguishing features, 269

in England, 276
in France, 292
on grace, 269, 296
in Netherlands, 268, 293–94
orthodox tenets, 269
and Scotland, 274–75
values, 266, 293–94
Camaldolese, 156
camp meetings, 335
Canada, 345, 366
canon, 2, 80, 86–87
canonical hours, 77
canonization, 146
See also saints
canon law, 120, 162
Canterbury, archbishops of, 121,
122, 270–72, 278
See also Anselm of Canterbury
capitalism, 226–27, 259, 338
Capito, Wolfgang, 244
Cappadocian Fathers, 91–92, 93,
96–97
Capuchins, 280
Caraffa, Gian Pietro (cardinal), 280,
282, 283
See also Paul IV
Carey, William, 350
Carolingians, 116–17, 123, 130, 153
Carpzov, Johann Benedikt, 311
Carthusians, 156
Cartwright, Thomas, 276
Cassidy, Edward Idris (cardinal), 372
catechumens, 87, 107
Cathari, 200–201, 203, 223n20
cathedrals
Gothic, 182–85, 187(figure)
Haga Sophia, 126, 131, 218
pilgrimages to, 197
Renaissance, 213
Romanesque, 181–82
Catherine of Aragon, 270
Catherine of Genoa, 216, 280
Catherine of Siena, 207–8
Catherine the Great (tsarina), 295
Catholic Action, 329
Catholicism
and change, 331–32
divergences, 296–98
and Eastern Church, 285, 373,
374, 380–81n73
ecumenism, 372
in England, 272, 273, 279, 335
in Europe (1600), 277(map)
and evangelicalism, 372
in Latin America, 348, 360–62
(*see also* liberation theology)
liturgy, 80, 332
modernists, 329
in Netherlands, 268, 293
post-Vatican II, 372–74
Reformation, 279–84
and Romanticism, 327
in Scotland, 274

in twentieth century, 149n36,
330–32, 361, 372–74 (*see also*
Vatican II)
in United States, 345, 346, 377,
382n107
See also Roman Church; Vatican II
Catholic Reformation, 279–84
celibacy
of clergy, 154, 156, 157, 248
in scripture, 74
Celsus, 57, 60, 70
Celtic Christians, 121–23
Celtis, Conrad, 232, 239
charismatic movement, 369–70
charismatics, 72, 83, 179
charity, 57
Charlemagne, 117–19, 147
Charles II (king of England), 279
Charles I (king of England), 278–79
Charles IV (emperor), 190
Charles V (emperor)
Augsberg Interim, 299
and Gattinara, 228
and Luther, 233–34, 241
and Netherlands, 268
and pope, 257
and Reformation, 239–41,
256–57
Chateaubriand, François, 327
Chemnitz, Martin, 299
Cherbury, Lord Herbert of, 306–7
Children's Crusades, 165
Chilton, Bruce, 359
China, 222, 321, 351–52, 376
chivalry, 124, 152, 180
Cho, Paul Y., 369–70
Christ, Carol, 362–63
Christendom
decline of, 190
and Franks, 116–18, 147
and Islam, 132–33
for Luther, 228
and nation-states, 227–28,
256–58
Christian community, 39–41
Christianity
demographics (2000), 374, 378
future trends, 374–78
and Islam, 132–33
mainstream emergence, 80, 82
nineteenth century views, 321–26
See also early Christianity; Eastern
Church; Protestantism; Roman
Church
Christianity Today, 368
Christian Science, 339–40
Christmas, 106
Christology, 42, 92–96, 134
See also Jesus Christ
Chrysostom, John, 97–98, 129
churches
early (map), 56, 57, 108
in high Middle Ages, 151, 156

role of, 181
See also cathedrals
Church of Christ Scientist, 339–40
Church of the Desert, 292
Church of the Holy Nativity, 53
Church of the Holy Sepulcher, 53
Cistercians, 155–56
See also Bernard of Clairvaux
City of God, 105–6, 117
Clare of Assisi, 204
Clement (bishop), 84
Clement of Alexandria, 68–69,
93, 137
Clement III (antipope), 159
Clement V (pope), 193
Clement VI (pope), 200
Clement VII (pope), 194, 240, 282
Clement XI (pope), 297
Clement XIII (pope), 295
Clement XIV (pope), 296
clergy
Calvin view, 263
Catholic Reformation, 283
and Henry VIII, 270–71
in late Middle Ages, 196–97,
205–6, 242
for Luther, 232, 237, 266
and marriage, 154, 156–57, 248
moral purity, 102
in sixteenth century, 226–27
sons of, 293
in Soviet Union, 344
and Vatican II, 332
Clovis, 114
Cluniacs, 154–55
Coke, Thomas, 312
Colbert, Jean Baptiste, 259
Collins, Anthony, 307
colonialism, 258, 320, 345, 348–51
commerce, 152, 226–27, 244
Commodus (emperor), 50
communicatio idiomatum, 95
communism, 321, 330, 344, 351–52
community, 4–5, 237
compassion, 33
Comte, August, 322–23, 354n5
conceptualism, 172
conciliarists, 194–95, 223n10
Concordat of Worms, 160
Cone, James, 362
Conference of Issy, 297
Confessing Church, 337
confession, 144–45, 238
confessors, 61
Congar, Yves, 331
Congregationalists, 276
Constantine, 51–54, 91, 106, 128
Constantinople
as capital, 53, 129, 149n33
and Crusades, 186, 217–18
patriarch of, 342
See also Council of Constantinople
Constitutions of Clarendon, 160

consubstantiality, 91–92
Contarini (cardinal), 226, 280, 282
contraception, 57, 374, 381n82
Conventicle Act, 276
convents, 179–80
conversions, forced, 117
Cooper, James Fenimore, 319–20
Cop, Nicholas, 259, 260
Copernicus, Nicholas, 301–2
Coptic Christians, 96, 221, 224n56
Corpus Christi, 199
Council of Basel, 195
Council of Chalcedon, 92, 95–96,
    129, 140
Council of Clermont, 164
Council of Constance, 194, 328
Council of Constantinople, 54, 129,
    134, 140, 150n79
    Second, 136
    Third, 134
Council of Elvira, 120, 157
Council of Ephesus, 94–95, 134
Council of Florence
    and Council of Trent, 284
    and Great Schism, 195, 217
    and sacraments, 143
    and Wycliffe, 205
Council of Lyons, 217
Council of Nicaea, 90, 129, 134
    Second, 134–35, 144
Council of Pisa, 194
Council of Trent, 87, 283–84,
    295, 296
Court, Antoine, 292
covenant, 2–3, 33, 37
Cox, Harvey, 363
Cranmer, Thomas, 270, 271, 272
Creation, 70
creationism, 365
Creed of Marcellus, 88
creeds, 80, 82, 87–88
Cromwell, Oliver, 278–79
Cromwell, Thomas, 270
Crossan, John Dominic, 27, 45n37
crucifixion, 1, 33–34, 43
Crusades, 163–67, 186, 217
Crusius, Martin, 285
curia, 162
Cyprian, 63, 65, 66
Cyril (apostle), 130–31
Cyril of Alexandria, 94–95,
    108, 137
Cyril of Jerusalem, 107–8
Cyrillic alphabet, 131, 149n32

Da Bascio, Mateo, 280
Daly, Mary, 362
Damasus I (pope), 98
Damian, Peter, 145, 156, 157
Dance of Death, 200
Daniel, Book of, 18, 32, 365
Dante Alighieri, 212
Darby, John Nelson, 365

Darwin, Charles, 322
    See also evolution
Da Thiene, Gaetano, 280
David (king of Israel), 3, 19, 28
deacons, 84, 85
Dead Sea Scrolls, 14–15, 21n45, 43
death, 200
De Bray, Guy, 268
Decius (emperor), 60
decretals, 140, 162
Defenestration of Prague, 290
Definition of Chalcedon, 95–96
deification, 137–38
deism, 306–7, 319
Demetrios I (patriarch), 380–81n73
Demetrius of Alexandria, 70
demographics
    Africa, 349–50, 376
    Asia, 376
    Christian population, 374–78
    early Christianity, 57–58
    Europe, 376–77
    in high Middle Ages, 152
    Latin America, 376, 377
    Pentecostal, 378
    United States, 346, 377, 382n107
de Molinos, Miguel, 297, 313
demons, 177
Denmark, 241, 290
Descartes, René, 303, 316n33
devotio moderna, 209
dialectical method, 168
dialectic (Hegelian), 324
Diaspora, 14
Dictatus Papae, 158–59
Diderot, Denis, 306
dioceses, 51
Diocletian (emperor), 51, 60–61
Dionysius, 314
Dioscorus, 95
disease, 50, 322, 370
dispensationalism, 365
ditheism, 89
divine right, of rulers, 158
Doctors of the Church, 98–100,
    112n59, 142, 149n66
Dodd, C. H., 30, 361
Dominicans, 175, 202–3, 231, 296
Dominic Guzman, 202
Domitian (emperor), 49, 59–60
Donation of Constantine, 116–17,
    157, 214
Donation of Pepin, 116
Donatism, 66, 102, 117
Donatist Church, 66
Dostoevsky, Fedor, 344
doxology, 109
dualism
    Cartesian, 303
    in Gospel of John, 42
    and Origen, 71
    and Plato, 10
    and Thomas Aquinas, 177

Dürer, Albrecht, 238, 239, 243
Durkheim, Émile, 323
Duvergier, Jean, 296

early Christianity
    and apostasy, 64–66
    appeal, 55–57, 63–64
    contrary views, 45n24
    critics, 57, 58–59, 60, 66–67
    documentation, 44–45n23
    expansion, 55–58
    persecutions, 58–64
    and Roman Empire, 48–54,
        58–64
    and socioeconomic class, 57
Easter, 106, 111n18
Eastern Church
    breach with Rome, 190, 217–18
    and Catholicism, 285, 373, 374,
        380–81n73
    and Council of Basel, 195
    and Crusades, 186
    ecumenical councils, 133–34
    evangelism, 343
    expansion, 151
    and filioque, 147
    and icons, 128, 134–36
    and John Chrysostom, 98, 129
    and John of Damascus, 136–37
    monasticism, 138–39, 285
    mysticism, 113, 138–39, 342
    national churches, 342–45
    Nicene Creed, 88
    nineteenth century, 342–45
    and Ottoman Empire, 342
    and papal primacy, 140
    Patriarch of Constantinople, 342
    and Protestants, 285
    reforms, 284–85
    in sixteenth century, 313
    western impact, 342–43
    worship, 109
    See also Byzantine Empire; Or-
        thodox churches; Russian
        Orthodox Church; state–
        church relationship
        (Eastern)
Eck, John, 232
Eckhart, Meister, 207
ecology, 361
economics, 329
ecumenical councils, 133–36,
    149n36
    See also Council of Chalcedon;
        Council of Constantinople;
        Council of Ephesus; Council
        of Nicaea
ecumenism, 332, 370–72, 373, 374,
    380–81n73
Eddy, Mary Baker, 339–40
Edesius of Tyre, 221
Edict of Fontainbleu, 292
Edict of Milan, 51, 61

Edict of Nantes, 291, 292
Edict of Toleration, 61
Edict of Worms, 233, 240
education
    and absolutism, 259
    and Council of Trent, 283, 284
    in early Middle Ages, 119, 123,
        124–25, 147
    and evangelicalism, 368–69
    in France, 329
    and fundamentalists, 365–66, 367
    in high Middle Ages, 151, 152,
        167–69
    in monasteries, 167–68
    and Mussolini, 330
    for Pius IX, 328
    seminaries, 284, 293
Edwards, Jonathan, 313, 335, 371
Edward VI (king of England),
    271–72
Egypt, 74–76, 92, 96, 221
the Egyptian, 23
Einhard, 119
Einstein, Albert, 322
elders. *See* Presbyterian system
Elizabethan Settlement, 269
Elizabeth I (queen of England),
    228, 257, 272–73
emperors, divine right, 158
empiricism, 169, 176, 234, 303–4
England
    anticlericalism, 205
    cathedrals, 181
    Catholicism in, 272, 273, 279, 335
    colonialism, 228, 258, 259, 348–
        49, 350
    early Christianity, 120–23
    humanism, 214
    and India, 350–51
    Inquisition, 203
    in late Middle Ages, 191
    and lay investiture, 160, 161–62
    as nation, 228
    and North America, 345
    versus Philip II, 257–58
    Protestantism, 269–73
    Revivalism, 336
    and Thirty Years' War, 290
Enlightenment, 300–301, 305–6,
    327, 348
Epanagoge, 129
Epiphanius, 89
Epiphany, 106
episcopal system, 275
Erasmus, Desiderius
    as humanist, 214, 235
    and Luther, 214, 230, 235–36
    and Reformation, 226, 244
    and Roman Church, 235, 289
    and Zwingli, 248
Erfurt, 244–45
Eriugena, John Scotus, 142–43
eschatological theology, 359–60

eschatology, 18, 32–33, 366
Essenes, 17, 21n45, 74
ethics, 29
Ethiopia, 87, 96
Ethiopian Church, 221
Et Unum Sint, 372
eucharist
    in Anglicanism, 273
    appeal of, 57
    for Calvin, 260, 261–62, 267
    for Christian Scientists, 340
    and Council of Trent, 284
    debates, 143–44
    for Luther, 249
    origins, 108, 109
    and penance, 145
    and Roman persecution, 58
    for Zwingli, 248
Eugenius IV (pope), 195, 217
Europe, 376–77
    See also specific countries
Eusebius
    on Clement of Alexandria, 68
    on Constantine, 51
    on martyrs, 110
    on Montanism, 83
    on Origen, 70
    on persecution, 59–60, 61
    on Quadratus, 67
Eutyches, 95
evangelical humanism, 253
evangelicalism, 366, 367–69, 377,
    382n107
evangelists, 335–36, 343, 366
evil
    and apocalypse, 18
    for gnostics, 71
    and Jesus' miracles, 28–29
    Neoplatonist view, 101
    for Origen, 71
    Pauline view, 39
    for Platonists, 11
    for Schopenhauer, 324
    for spiritualists, 308
    for Thomas Aquinas, 178
    See also Satan
evolution, 322, 330–31, 346, 366
Execrabilis, 195–96
existentialism, 334–35, 338
Exodus, 2–3, 74
explorers, 227
Ezekiel, 32
Ezra, Book of, 4–5

faith
    for Barth, 337
    for Calixtus, 300
    for Calvin, 265
    and history, 331
    for Kierkegaard, 334
    for Locke, 304
    for Luther, 231, 236
    in nineteenth century, 325

    for Origen, 71
    Pauline view, 36, 38
    versus reason, 169, 172, 173, 174
    and Reformation, 225
    rules of, 87
    for secular theology, 363
    for Tillich, 338
    for William of Ockham, 213
Falwell, Jerry, 336, 367
Farel, Guillaume, 261–62, 267
fascism, 321, 329–30, 354n3
Fawkes, Guy, 278
feast days, 63, 244, 267
Febronius, Justin, 295
feminist theology, 362–63, 376
Fénelon, Francis, 297–98
Feofan of Vysha, 344
Ferdinand II (emperor), 290
Ferrer, Vincent, 216
feudalism, 123–25, 152
Feuerbach, Ludwig, 324
Ficino, Marsilio, 213
fiefs, 123
filioque, 147, 217–18
Finney, Charles, 336, 368
First Vatican Council, 328
Flacius, Matthias, 299
flagellants, 192, 200
Flanders, 293
forgiveness
    and Jesus, 30, 32
    Judaic view, 15–16, 24, 32
    of post-baptism sins, 64–65
    for Tertullian, 72–73
    See also salvation
Formula of Concord, 299
Fosdick, Harry Emerson, 334,
    364–65
Fourth Lateran Council (1215),
    144, 162
Fox, George, 308
France
    Babylonian Captivity, 193
    cathedrals, 181, 182–85
    in early Middle Ages, 114–19
    Enlightenment, 305–6
    and Inquisition, 203
    in late Middle Ages, 191
    missionaries, 345
    Napoleonic, 319, 326–27
    nationalism, 228
    and papacy, 158, 163, 216, 295,
        329, 354n12
    philosophes, 305–6
    post-Napoleonic, 320
    Protestants in, 267, 291–93
    Revolution, 319, 320, 327
Franciscans, 203–5, 224n30
Francis I (king of France), 228, 233,
    239–40, 260
Francis of Assisi, 203–4
Francke, August Hermann, 311
Franks, 114–19, 130

Frazer, Sir James, 323
Frederick Barbarrossa (emperor),
    160, 161, 165
Frederick I (king of Prussia), 294
Frederick II (emperor), 161, 190
Frederick II (king of Prussia), 294
Frederick (king of Bohemia), 290
Frederick of Denmark (king), 241
Frederick of Saxony (elector), 240
Frederick the Great (elector), 294
Frederick the Wise (king),
    231–33
free will
    for Arminius, 269
    for Duns Scotus, 210
    for Erasmus, 235
    for Jerome, 98
    for Luther, 235
    Pauline view, 39
    Pelagian view, 103–4
    for Platonists, 11
    for Thomas Aquinas, 178
French Revolution, 319, 320, 327
Freud, Sigmund, 323
friars, 175, 202–5
Friends, Society of, 308–9, 345
Froschel, Master, 243
Frumentius, 221
Frye, Northrop, 359
Fuller, Charles E., 336, 366
fundamentalism, 335, 364–67,
    382n107
Funk, Robert, 359, 379n7

Galilee, 1
Galilei, Galileo, 301–2
Gallican Articles, 292
Gallicanism, 295
Gattinara, Mercurio, 228
Gelasius I (pope), 140, 158
General Baptists, 278, 287
Genesis, 2, 3, 14, 334
Gennadius II, 218
Gentiles, 19, 21n39
    Pauline view, 37–38, 39
Gerhardt, Johann, 299
Germanic tribes, 55, 114–17,
    123, 130
Germany
    antisemitism, 192, 321
    Benedictine influence, 155
    under Bismarck, 328
    Concordat of Worms, 160
    and Enlightenment, 327
    and Gregory VII, 159
    Hohenzollerns, 294
    Inquisition, 203
    and nationalism, 228
    Nazis, 321, 330
    during plague, 192
    Protestant League, 257
    Prussia, 294
    and Reformation, 231–32, 239

Renaissance, 214
    Thirty Years' War, 289–91
Gilbertines, 156
Gilson, Etienne, 330
Gladden, Washington, 334
glossolalia, 83, 369, 370
gnostics, 62, 71, 81–82
    and Mary Magdalene, 111n17
God
    for Barth, 337
    for Calvin, 264–66, 286n22
    and Darwinism, 322
    existence of, 170–71, 176
    and feminism, 362–63
    for Freud, 323
    in Gospel of John, 42, 43
    for Hegel, 324
    for Jesus, 30
    in Judaism, 2–3, 15, 16
    for Kant, 305
    Kingdom of, 29–30
    knowledge of, 236, 302–6, 373
    in late medieval theology, 210, 211
    for Latter-Day Saints, 339
    for Luther, 230–31, 236, 237
    Marcion view, 82
    for Marx, 324–25
    nineteenth century views, 324
    ontological argument, 170–71,
        176, 188n25
    Origen view, 70, 71
    and science, 301
    for secular theologians, 363
    son of, 28, 32
    for spiritualists, 308
    for Thomas Aquinas, 176–78,
        188n40, 210
    for Tillich, 338
    and Vatican II, 373
    See also Trinity
Godfroid, Michel, 309
Golden Bull, 190
Göldi, Heinrich, 247
Goldstein, Valerie Saiving, 362
Gomarus, Francis, 269
Good Friday, 106
good works
    for Aristotle, 234–35
    for Calvin, 265–66
    and Catholic Reformation, 284
    and grace, 149n63, 178
    for Luther, 234–35, 237
    for Melanchthon, 299
    and penance, 141, 145–46,
        199–200
    of saints, 145–46
    for Thomas Aquinas, 178
Görres, Joseph von, 354n13
Gospels
    and antisemitism, 33, 42
    Bultmann view, 358
    canonical, 25–28
    gnostic, 81

and Jesus, 33–34
    noncanonical, 27–28
    synoptic, 26, 28
Gospel of John, 27, 28, 41–43,
    111n21, 236
Gospel of Luke, 27, 102–3
Gospel of Mark, 26–27, 30, 32, 144
Gospel of Matthew
    and Crusades, 164
    and Francis of Assisi, 203–4
    and papacy, 140, 158
    Sermon on the Mount, 30, 31–
        32, 344
    similarities and differences, 26–27
Gospel of Thomas, 27–28, 81
Goths, 130, 140–41
    See also Visigoths
Gottschalk (monk), 142–43
grace
    for Augustine, 103–4, 106, 296
    for Bonhoeffer, 337–38
    for Calvinists, 269, 296
    and Council of Trent, 296
    eastern versus Roman, 138
    evangelical humanist view, 253
    and good works, 149n63
    and human will, 138
    for Luther, 230–31, 236–37
    and Marcion, 82
    for Ockham, 224n43
    outside Church, 331
    in Paul, 36, 38
    and sacraments, 106
Graham, Billy, 336, 366, 369
Great Awakening, 313
Great Schism, 193–94
Grebel, Conrad, 251
Greece. See ancient Greece
Greek Orthodox Church, 382n107
Greek terminology, 68
Greely, Andrew, 381n82
Gregorian chant, 142
Gregory I (pope), 121, 141–42
Gregory of Nazianzus, 91–92, 93,
    96–97, 134
Gregory of Nyssa, 91–92, 93, 97
Gregory of Palamas, 139
Gregory the Great, 98
Gregory VII (pope), 157–59
Gregory XI (pope), 193–94
Gressmann, H., 326
Groote, Gerard, 209
Guiscard, Robert, 157, 159
Gunkel, Hermann, 326, 358
Gustavus Adolphus (king of Swe-
    den), 290–91
Gustavus Vasa (king of Sweden), 241
Gutiérrez, Gustavo, 361, 376
Guyon, Madame, 297
gymnasia, 8

Hadrian (emperor), 49, 50
Hadrian I (pope), 117, 136

Haeckel, Ernst, 322
Hagia Sophia, Church of the, 126, 131, 218
Haller, Berthold, 250
Hamilton, Patrick, 274
Hapsburgs, 294
Harnack, Adolf von, 326, 358
Harris, William, 349
healing, 339–40
Heer, Friedrich, 172
Hegel, Georg Wilhelm, 324, 325, 326
Heidegger, Martin, 338
Helena, 51–53
Hellenism
    ancient Greeks, 5–11, 20n16
    and Christianity, 43, 68, 80
    and eastern Church, 113
    Harnack view, 326
    and Judaism, 14, 17, 20n23, 69
Helvidius, 98
Helwys, Thomas, 276–78
Henry, Carl F. H., 369
Henry II (king of England), 160
Henry III (emperor), 156
Henry IV (emperor), 190
Henry IV (king of France)
    and Huguenots, 292
    and papacy, 158–60, 295
    strategy, 288
Henry of Navarre (king), 267
Henry VII (king of England), 228, 270
Henry VIII (king of England), 228, 269, 270–71
Heraclius (emperor), 127
heretics
    attitude toward, 315–16n1
    and Council of Trent, 284
    and Fourth Lateran Council, 162
    Inquisition, 202–3
    for Thomas Aquinas, 202
hermits, 74
Herod the Great, 13
Hesychasm, 138–39, 220, 344
heterodoxy, 80, 87
high Middle Ages
    cathedrals, 180–85, 187(figure)
    chivalry, 152, 180
    Crusades, 128, 163–67, 186
    Holy Roman Empire, 117–18, 153–54
    Inquisition, 202–3
    monasticism, 154–56
    papal reform, 156–58
    parish priests, 154
    political trends, 152–53
    reform movements, 200–205
    scholasticism, 167–69, 235
    secular power *versus* Church, 153–63
    societal change, 151–52

Hilarion, 76–77
Hincmar of Reims, 119, 142–43
Hippolytus, 87–88, 89
Hispana, 120
Hispanic Americans, 363, 377
history
    nineteenth century views, 325–26, 365
    for Origen, 71
    as revelation, 360
    twentieth century views, 331, 360
Hitler, Adolf, 321, 330
Hodge, Charles, 335, 364
Hoffman, Melchior, 251
Hohenzollerns, 294
holidays, 106, 111n18, 199
Holland, 293–94
    See also Netherlands
Holocaust, 321, 330
Holy Roman Empire
    decline, 190–91, 256–57, 294, 327
    origins, 117–18, 153–54
    See also Charles V; Henry IV
Holy Sepulcher, 197
Holy Spirit
    for Calvin, 265–66
    in eastern Church, 109, 137
    and Jesus' birth, 28
    for Origen, 71
    Pauline view, 39
    See also Trinity
Homer, 8
homoiousios, 91
homosexual marriage, 375
Honorius (emperor), 102
Honorius I (pope), 134
Hope, Theology of, 359–60
Hopkins, Emma Curtis, 340
Hosea, 4
host, adoration of, 199
Hovius, Mathias, 293
Hubmaier, Balthasar, 251
Hugh of St. Victor, 174
Huguenots, 267, 291–93
Humani generis, 330
humanism
    and Calvin, 260
    in England, 272
    evangelical, 253
    in Italy, 213–14
    and Luther, 230, 247
    in Northern Europe, 214
    and rationalism, 302
    and Zwingli, 247–48, 248–49
    See also Desiderius, Erasmus
human nature
    for Abelard, 174
    Augustinian view, 101, 103–4
    Baius controversy, 296, 316n19
    for Calvin, 265, 266
    for Comte, 322–23
    for empiricists, 303

Enlightenment views, 300–301, 306
Freudian views, 323
    for Judaism, 15
    for Luther, 230, 234, 236–37
    nineteenth century views, 320, 324
    Pelagian view, 103–4
    rationalist view, 303
    Renaissance view, 213–14
    for spiritualists, 308
    for Synod of Dort, 269
    for Thomas Aquinas, 177
Hume, David, 304, 315
Hundred Years' War, 191
Hungary, 241
Hus, Jan, 205–6, 241
Hut, Hans, 252
Hutten, Ulrich von, 232
Hutter, Jakob, 251–52
Huxley, Thomas, 322, 354n4
hymns
    and Ambrose, 100
    doxology, 109
    and Gregory I, 142
hypostaseis, 91–92, 95, 96

iconoclasm, 248, 134–136
iconodules, 135
icons, 128, 134–36
idealism, 10–11, 169, 176
Ignatius of Antioch, 62, 84–85
illumination, 207
immaculate conception, 146, 150n77, 328, 379n40
imperialism, 227, 320
incarnation
    in Gospel of John, 42
    for Tertullian, 73
    for Thomas Aquinas, 178
Index of Forbidden Books, 284
India, 349–51
indulgences
    and Avignon popes, 193
    and Crusades, 164
    description, 199–200
    and Innocent VIII, 216
    and Reformation, 231, 247
industrialization, 320–21, 329
inerrancy, 364
Infancy Gospel of Thomas, 27
Innocent III (pope), 161–62, 165, 192, 201
Innocent VIII (pope 1484–92), 216
Innocent XI (pope), 297
Inquisition
    and Calvin, 264
    and Catholic reform, 280
    description, 203
    Dominican role, 202–3
    origins, 162
interdict, 161–62
investiture, 123, 157–59

Ireland, 121
Irenaeus
  on apostolic succession, 85
  on faith, 87
  and gnosticism, 81, 85
  and mysticism, 137
  on Rome, 78n25
  on salvation, 93
Isaac, sacrifice of, 334
Isaiah, 4
Isidore of Seville, 120
Islam
  and Aristotle, 170
  and Armenian Church, 222
  and Byzantium, 127–28, 131–
    33, 218
  and Coptic Christians, 221
  Crusades against, 163–67
  and Ethiopian Church, 221
  and Makrakis, 342
  origins, 113
  in Spain, 120, 191, 227
Italian evangelism, 280
Italy
  and Charlemagne, 117
  Fascist, 321, 329–30
  in late Middle Ages, 190–91
  and Lombards, 117, 126–27
  and Napoleon, 326
  and Ostrogoths, 140–41
  Renaissance, 213–14
  unification, 228, 320, 327
Ivan III (tsar), 220
Ivan the Terrible (tsar), 285, 314

Jacobites, 221–22
Jacob of Edessa, 221
James
  as brother of Jesus, 34
  and Spain, 119–20, 197
James, William, 340
James I (king of England), 276, 278
James II (king of England), 279
James IV (king of Scotland), 273
James V (king of Scotland),
  273–74
James VI (king of Scotland), 276
Jansenism, 296–97
Jansenius, Cornelius, 296
Japan, 352–53
Jefferson, Thomas, 306
Jehovah's Witnesses, 341–42
Jeremias II (patriarch), 285
Jerome, 76, 98
Jesuits
  in China, 351
  in Eastern Europe, 285
  and Flanders, 293
  and India, 377
  in Japan, 352
  origins, 280–81
  and papacy, 295–96
  and predestination, 296

and Russia, 314, 343
and Thirty Years War, 290
Jesus Christ
  Abelard view, 173–74
  Alexandrian view, 93
  for Anselm of Canterbury,
    171–72
  apocalyptic, 46n46, 358, 359
  Apollinarist view, 93–94
  baptism, 28
  birth, 28, 106, 150n77, 379n40
  for Calvinists, 265, 269
  for Christian Scientists, 340
  Coptic view, 224n56
  death, 33–34
  Deist view, 307
  fundamentalist view, 364
  for Funk, 379n7
  gnostic view, 82
  in Gospel of John, 42, 43
  as historical person, 33–34, 325,
    357–59
  humanity of, 82, 92–96
  in late Middle Ages, 198–99
  life of, 1, 25–28
  for Luther, 236, 249
  and martyrdom, 63
  and messianism, 33–34
  miracles, 28–29
  nineteenth century views, 325–
    26, 333
  Origen view, 71
  Pauline view, 37, 38, 39
  for Schleiermacher, 333
  as Son of Man, 32, 46n50, 358
  teachings, 29–33
  for Teilhard de Chardin, 331
  for Thomas Aquinas, 178
  times of, 13, 14, 22–23
  transformation by, 39
  in twentieth century, 357–58
  for Zwingli, 248
  See also Christology; Sermon on
    the Mount; Trinity
Joan of Arc, 191
Johannine church, 41
John. See Gospel of John
John, Gospel of, 27, 28, 41–43,
  111n21, 236
John Chrysostom, 97–98, 129
John of the Cross, 282
John Duns Scotus, 209–10, 234
John (king of England), 161–62
John of Antioch, 95
John of Damascus
  and emperors, 129
  on icons, 135–37
  on martyrs, 63
  on Monothelitism, 134
  on salvation, 138
John of Leiden, 252
John Paul II (pope)
  and China, 376

and contraception, 381n82
and ecumenism, 372
and Greek Orthodox Church,
  380–81n73
John Scotus Eriugena, 142–43
Johnson, L. T., 359
John the Baptist, 23–24, 46n45
John XXII (pope), 205
John XXIII (pope), 331–32
Jonah, 4
Joseph II (emperor), 294, 295
Joseph of Volokalamsk, 284–85
Josephus, 13, 17, 23, 27, 44n11
Joshua, 3
Jovinian, 98
Judaism
  Abelard view, 174
  and apocalypse, 18–20
  and baptism, 25
  beliefs, 15
  community, 4–5
  of disciples, 34, 35–36, 37–
    38, 42
  in early Middle Ages, 125
  in first-century, 13–19
  and Gospel of John, 42
  and Hellenism, 14, 17, 20n23, 69
  history, 2–5, 13, 22–23
  Holocaust, 321, 330
  houses of worship, 4, 15–17 (see
    also temple)
  Islamic view, 132
  and John Chrysostom, 97–98
  and Paul, 37–38
  scripture, 1–4 (see also Mishnah;
    Tanakh; Torah)
  worship pattern, 4, 16–17
  See also antisemitism
Judges, Book of, 3
Julian of Norwich, 208
Julian of Toledo, 120
Julian the Apostate (emperor),
  54, 57
Julius II (pope), 216, 231
Justinian (emperor), 125–26,
  129–30
Justin Martyr, 67–68

Kähler, Martin, 357–58
Kaiserberg, Geiler von, 244
Kamuyi, William, 370
Kant, Immanuel, 304–5, 317n42
  analytic propositions, 317n43
Käsemann, Ernst, 312, 359
Kassatkin, Nikolai, 353
Kellog, John Harvey, 341
Kempe, Margery, 208
kenoticism, 219, 344
Kerremans, Jan, 293
Kethuvim, 1
Khomiakov, Alexis, 343
Kierkegaard, Søren, 312, 317n45,
  334–35

Kimbangu, Simon, 349
Kingdom of God, 29–30
kings, divine right, 158
Kipling, Rudyard, 320
knowledge, 236, 302–6, 373
Knox, John, 268, 274–75
koine, 6
Koonhert, Dirck, 268
Korea, 370, 376
Kulturkampf, 328
Küng, Hans, 355n25, 373
Kuyper, Abraham, 364

Labadie, Jean de, 310
labor unions, 329
Lamentations, Book of, 4
Lampe, F. A., 311
Lang, Johannes, 244
Lanphier, Jeremiah, 335–36
Last Supper, 33, 57
late Middle Ages
    cities, 242–45
    clergy, 195–97, 205–6, 242
    indulgences, 197 (*see also* indul-
        gences)
    Inquisition, 101–203
    life in, 189–92, 226–28, 238
    monasticism, 195, 202–5
    mysticism, 206–9
    papacy, 192–95
    pilgrimages, 197–98
    plague, 192, 200
    political theory, 211–12
    reform movements, 200–206
    and saints, 197–99
    theology, 209–11
    worship, 198–99
Lateran Concordat, 330
Latin, 332
Latin America, 346–48, 360–62,
    377–78
Latter-Day Saints, Church of,
    338–39
Laud, William, 278
lay brotherhoods, 238, 239
lay investiture, 157–60
Left Behind series, 367
Leibniz, Gottfried Wilhelm, 303,
    306
Leiden, John of, 252
Leipzig Interim, 299
Lent, 248
Leoba, 115
Leo I (pope), 140
Leo III (emperor), 127–28, 135
Leo III (pope), 117–18
Leo V (emperor), 136
Leo XIII (pope), 328–29, 332
Leo IX (pope), 156–57
Leo X (pope), 216, 231, 247, 282
libellatici, 65
libelli, 60
liberalism, 320

liberal theology, 332–35, 353
liberation theology, 360–63, 374,
    376
Licinius, 51
Linck, Wenceslaus, 243
Lindisfarne Gospels, 123
Lithuania, 241, 313
liturgy
    in England, 272, 273
    origins, 80
    twentieth century, 332
    See also worship
Livingstone, David, 348
Locke, John, 303–4, 306
logos
    Apollinarist view, 93–94
    and Arianism, 90
    and Christology, 93
    and Clement of Alexandria, 69
    and Genesis, 14
    and Gospel of John, 27, 42
    and Justin Martyr, 68
    and Origen, 71
    and Stoicism, 10
    and Stoics, 10
    for Tertullian, 73, 79n47
Loisy, Alfred, 329
Lollards, 205, 271
Lombard, Peter, 174–75
Lombards, 116, 117, 126–27,
    141
Longfellow, Henry Wadsworth,
    319–20
Lortz, Joseph, 238
Lotzer, Sebastian, 246
Louis IX (king of France), 165–66
Louis XI (king of France), 227–28
Louis XIII (king of France),
    292–93
Louis XIV (king of France), 259,
    292, 297
love
    agape, 58
    for Bonaventure, 207
    Judaic view, 15
    for Luther, 237
    for secular theologians, 363
Loyola, Ignatius, 280–81
Lucian of Samosata, 60
Luke, Gospel of, 27, 102–3
Luther, Martin
    antisemitism, 229
    biography, 229–34
    and Calvin, 259, 262, 298
    on civil authority, 237–38, 246–
        47, 250
    and Erasmus, 214, 230, 235–36
    on military force, 249
    Ninety Five Theses, 231–32
    personality, 229
    political support, 239
    purpose, 228
    and scripture, 235, 236, 245

on society, 237–38, 246–47
    theology, 234–38, 249
    treatises, 233
    uniqueness, 284
    and Zwingli, 249
Lutherans, 277(map), 285, 298–
    300, 348
Lyell, Charles, 322

Macarius the Great, 75
Maccabees, 5, 17
Machen, J. Gresham, 364–65
Machiavelli, Niccolò, 213, 216
Makrakis, Apostolos, 342–43
Malebranche, Nicolas, 303
Manichaeism, 100–101, 200
Manz, Feliz, 251
maps
    Alexander's empire, 7
    early Christianity, 56
    Europe and Byzantine Empire
        (500), 115
    Islam, 133
    missionary activity, 350
    Paul's journeys, 35
    pilgrimage routes, 198
    religious groups in Europe (1600),
        277
    Roman Empire, 12, 52
    Spanish explorations, 347
Marcellus, Creed of, 88
Marcion, 82, 86
Marcus Aurelius (emperor), 49–50,
    58, 60
Marie Theresa (empress), 294
Maritain, Jacques, 330
Mark, Gospel of, 26–27, 30,
    32, 144
marriage
    of clergy, 154, 156–57, 248
    homosexual, 375
    and Jerome, 98
    in Middle Ages, 180
    Pauline view, 39
Marsilius of Padua, 212
Martin of Tours, 77
Martin V (pope), 194
martyrdom, 63, 74, 315–16n1
martyrs
    for Christianity, 48, 50, 61–
        64, 109
    for Protestantism, 268
Marx, Karl, 324–25
Mary. *See* the Virgin Mary
Mary Magdalene, 111n17, 197
Mary Stuart (queen of Scotland),
    274–75
Mary Tudor (queen of England),
    272
Masada, 23
mass media, 336, 366, 370
Mater et Magistra, 332
material world, 10

Mather, Cotton, 368
Matthew. *See* Gospel of Matthew
Matthew the tax collector, 33
Matthys, Jan, 251–52, 252
Mattias (emperor), 290
Mattingly, Garrett, 272–73
Maundy Thursday, 106
Maximilian (duke of Bavaria), 290
Maximus the Confessor, 129, 138
Mazarin, Jules (cardinal), 292, 316n7
McIntire, Carl, 366
media, 336, 366, 370
Medici, Giovanni de. *See* Leo X
Medici, Marie de', 291
Meier, J. P., 359
Melanchthon, Philip, 240–41, 249,
    259, 298–99
Melchites, 221
Memmingen, 245–46
mendicant friars, 202–5
Mennonites, 252
mercantilism, 259
mercy, 33
Merovingians, 114, 116
messianism, 3–4, 18–20, 23, 33–34
Methodists, 312, 345, 346
Methodius, 130–31
Meyer, Ben, 359
Middle Ages
    Britain, 120–23
    feudalism, 123–25, 152
    Franks, 114–19
    Spain, 119–20
    and women, 179
    See also high Middle Ages; late
        Middle Ages
Middle Platonism, 70
Míguez-Bonino, José, 361
Miller, William, 340–41
Mishnah, 15, 17, 21n43
missionaries
    in Africa, 348–49
    in Americas, 227, 311, 345,
        346–48
    to China, 351
    and France, 345
    to India, 349–51
    to Japan, 352–53
    map, 350
    Mormon, 339
    Nestorian, 222
    Russian Orthodox, 353
    to Slavs, 130–31
    to western Europe, 114, 115,
        117, 120
    women as, 380n69
modernists, 329
Moffat, Robert, 348
Molinos, Miguel de, 297
Moltmann, Jürgen, 359–60
Monarchianism, 73, 88–89, 90
monasteries
    Benedictines, 76–77

and Coptic Christians, 221
earliest, 76
Eastern Orthodox, 284–85
and education, 167–68, 169
and Franks, 115–16, 117
in Ireland, 121
in Russia, 343–44
monasticism
    Augustinians, 101
    beginnings, 73–74
    Benedictines, 77, 117, 154, 155
    and Catholic Reformation,
        280–81
    Cistercians, 155–56
    Cluniac, 154–55
    Dominicans, 175
    in early Middle Ages, 114
    and Eastern churches, 137–39,
        284–85, 343–44
    and Egypt, 74–76
    in high Middle Ages, 154–56,
        162
    and Innocent III, 162
    in Ireland, 120–21
    in late Middle Ages, 195, 202–5
    popular view of, 63
    reform, 154–55
    Russian, 219–20, 343–44
    in Spain, 120
    and women, 75, 179–80
Mongolia, 222
monism, 303
Monophysitism, 95–96, 134,
    221–22
monotheism, 2
Monothelitism, 134, 138
Montanus, 83
Moody, Dwight L., 336, 368
morality
    for John Paul II, 374
    for Kant, 305, 317n42
    for Thomas Aquinas, 178
Moral Majority, 367
Moravia, 241, 251–52
More, Sir Thomas, 214, 271, 289
Morley, Lord John, 259, 293–94
Mormons, 338–39
Morrison, Robert, 351
Moses, 3
Moses bar Kepha, 221
Mother Angelique, 296
Mount Sinai, 3
Muhammad, 132
Mujerista theology, 363
Mumford, Catherine, 336
Münster, 252
Münzer, Thomas, 246
Mussolini, Benito, 329–30
mysticism
    Eastern Orthodox, 137–39, 342
    Gregory of Nyssa, 97
    and Luther, 234
    medieval, 206–9

Spanish, 281–82
and Thomas Aquinas, 178
See also spiritualism

Nag Hammadi texts, 71–72
Napoleon Bonaparte, 319, 326–
    27, 348
national churches, 342–45
nationalism, 232, 239, 338
nation-states, 227–28, 257–58
Naziism, 321, 330
negative theology, 138
neo-orthodoxy, 336–38
Neoplatonism
    and Augustine, 101
    and Eriugena, 142
    and mysticism, 137, 207
    and Origen, 69
Nero (emperor), 49, 59
Neronov, John, 314
Nerva (emperor), 49
Nestorianism, 87, 134, 222
Nestorius, 94–95, 96
Netherlands
    and Baptists, 276–78
    and Catholicism, 268, 293
    colonialism, 258, 348
    and England, 276–78, 279
    humanism, 214
    and Philip II, 257, 293
    Protestantism in, 268, 293–94
    and Thirty Years' War, 290
Neuhaus, Richard John, 372
Neviim, 1, 3–4
Newman, John Henry, 335
New Testament
    on Apostles, 84
    Book of Revelation, 60, 366
    canonical Gospels, 25–28
    canonization, 86–87
    feminist view, 362–63
    nineteenth century views,
        325–26
    on prophets, 83
    for Protestant scholastics,
        299–300
    in twentieth century, 356–59
    See also Gospels; Paul
New Thought, 340
Newton, Sir Isaac, 302
Nicene Creed
    and eastern Church, 217
    eastern *versus* Roman Church, 88
    and Germanic peoples, 114
    original version, 90–91
    and Theodosius I, 54
Nicholas II (pope), 157
Nicholas V (pope), 215
Niebuhr, H. Richard, 338
Niebuhr, Reinhold, 338
Nietzsche, Friedrich, 324
Nikon, 314–15
Nilus of Sora, 284

Noetus, 89
nominalism, 169–70, 171, 190, 211
  and Luther, 229, 234
non-Possessors, 284–85
Norbert of Xanten, 179
North Africa, 64–65, 65–66, 85
  See also Donatism; Egypt
North America, 345–46, 347(map),
  364, 377
  See also Canada; United States
Nouwen, Henri, 372
Novatian, 65
nuns, 179–80
Nuremberg, 243–44

occasionalism, 303
Ockenga, Harold John, 369
Ockham, William of, 210–11,
  224n43, 234, 270
Ockhamists, 229, 230, 236
Ockham's razor, 211
Odo, 154
Oecolampadius, Johannes, 250
Old Testament, 87, 325
  See also *Tanakh; Torah*
Olivetan, 259
Ontological Argument, 170–71,
  176, 188n25
oratories, 280
Oratory of Divine Love, 280
Origen, 69–72
  and Cappadocians, 96
  and Celsus, 60
  and John Chrysostom, 98
  on salvation, 93
  and scripture, 70, 71, 86
original sin, 104, 224n43, 370
Orthodox Christian Unions, 343
Orthodox churches, 216–22,
  313–15
  autocephalous, 221–22, 318,
  342–45
  See also Eastern Church; Greek
  Orthodox Church; Russian
  Orthodox Church
Osiander, Anders, 243
Ostrogoths, 140–41
Otto I (emperor), 153–54, 155
Ottoman Empire, 218–19, 240, 342
Oxenstierna, Axel, 290–91, 316n7
Oxford Movement, 335

Pachomius, 76
pacifism, 250, 252
palmers, 197
Palm Sunday, 106
Pannenberg, Wolfhart, 359–60
Pantaenus, 68
papacy
  authority of, 140, 158–63
  Babylonian captivity, 193
  and Catholic Reformation,
  282–83

and Council of Trent, 295
and Crusades, 167
Donation of Constantine, 116–17
and eastern Church, 140, 149n33
and France, 193, 295
in high Middle Ages, 156–63,
  167, 186
and Holy Roman Empire, 153–
  54, 158–59
versus kings, 295–96
in late Middle Ages, 192–93,
  211–12
and Mussolini, 330
in Renaissance, 214–16
and Thomas Aquinas, 212
twentieth century views, 331
Ultramontanism, 295, 327
and Vatican II, 332
papal infallibility, 134, 158–59, 328
Papal States, 116, 153, 326, 327
parables, 26
Parham, Charles, 369
Particular Baptists, 278
Pascal, Blaise, 297
Passover, 2–3, 26
patriarchates, 129
patriarchs, 85–86, 129–30
Patrick, 120
Paul
  as apocalypticist, 36, 38–39
  on apostles, 84
  for Barth, 337
  for Baur, 325, 354n9
  biography, 35–36
  on community, 39–41
  death of, 59, 148n11
  on Jesus Christ, 37, 38, 39
  on Judaism, 37–38
  on marriage, 39
  missionary travels, 36
  and Reformation, 225, 230,
  234, 237
  on salvation, 38
  on society, 41
  and Spain, 119, 148n11
  theology, 36–41
  on wisdom, 41
  on women, 39, 40–41
Paul III (pope), 257, 271, 282–83
Paul IV (pope), 280, 283, 284
  See also Caraffa, Gian Pietro
Paul VI (pope), 332, 361, 369
Paul of Aleppo, 314
Paul the Deacon, 119
Pavlov, Ivan, 323
pax Romana, 49
Peace of Augsburg, 241, 289–90
Peasant Revolts, 244–46
peasants, 191, 226, 239, 242–
  47, 294
  and industrialization, 321
Pelagianism, 284, 296, 299
Pelagius, 98, 103–4

penance
  and confessions, 144–45
  and good works, 141, 145–46
  and Gregory I, 141
  indulgences, 164, 193, 199–200
  issues, 64–65, 66
  Luther view, 229–30, 238
Penn, William, 308, 317n46
Pentecost, 34, 106
Pentecostalism, 369–70, 378,
  382n107
Pepin, 116
persecution, 58–64, 315–16n1
Persians, 127
Peter
  for Baur, 325
  as Church leader, 65
  death, 59
  on Gentiles, 39
  and papacy, 140
  Pentecost sermon, 34
Peter Abelard, 172–74, 180
Peter Damian, 145, 156, 157
Peter Lombard, 174–75, 180
Peter the Great (tsar), 294, 315, 343
Petrine Doctrine, 140
Petrovitch, Avvakum, 314
Pharisees, 16–17, 21n43
Philaret, 314
philetism, 342
Philip, John, 348
Philip Augustus (king of France),
  162
Philip II (king of Spain), 257–
  58, 268
Philip IV (king of France),
  163, 193
Philip of Hesse, 240, 249
Philippines, 376
Philippists, 299
Philo of Alexandria, 14, 69
philosophes, 305–6
philosophy
  empiricism, 303–4
  existential, 334–35, 338
  of Kant, 304–5
  nineteenth century, 323–25
  rationalism, 302–3
  Stoicism, 10, 69, 73
Pico della Mirandola, Giovanni, 213
pietism, 309–13, 342
pilgrimages, 63, 197, 238, 247
Pius II (pope), 195
Pius V (pope), 296
Pius VII (pope), 326–27, 354n12
Pius IX (pope), 327–28
Pius X (pope), 329
Pius XI (pope), 329–30, 332, 371
Pius XII (pope), 328, 330
Placards, Affair of the, 260
Placher, William, 68
plagues, 50
plainsong, 142

Plato
  idealism, 9–10, 169
    Tertullian view, 73
  and Thomas Aquinas, 176
Platonism, 10–11, 71, 101, 142
Pliny the Younger, 27, 58, 60
pluralism, 196, 284
Poland, 241, 285, 313
Polycarp, 62
Pontius Pilate, 1, 23, 27
Poor Clares, 204
Port-Royal, 296–97
Portugal
  as colonial power, 258, 347(map),
    348, 349–50
  explorers, 227
Possessors, 284–85
Potamiaena, 62
poverty, 336, 374–75
  See also social justice
Praxeas, 89
predestination
  for Arminius, 269
  for Augustine, 103–5, 142–
    43, 296
  for Calvin, 266
  Catholic controversies, 296
  for Gottschalk, 142–43
  for Ockham, 224n43
  Synod of Dort, 269
  for Thomas Aquinas, 178
  for Zwingli, 248–49
prelates, 133–34
Presbyterians, 348, 376
Presbyterian system, 275, 276, 278
presbyters
  defined, 84, 111n5
  Origen as, 70
  worship role, 109
priests. *See* clergy
privatism, 297
proletariat, 321
prophets, 1, 3–4, 83
proselyte baptism, 25
prosperity gospel, 370
Protestant ethic, 266
Protestantism
  in Africa, 348, 349
  basic features, 234
  Catholic rapprochement, 300, 372
  and Eastern Church, 285
  ecumenicalism, 370–71
  in England, 269–73
  evangelicalism, 367–69
  in France, 267, 291–93
  fundamentalist, 364–67
  liberalism, 332–35
  neo-orthodoxy, 336–38
  in Netherlands, 268–69, 293–94
  pietism, 309–13
  post-Luther disputes, 298–300
  Reformed tradition, 267
  Revivalism, 335–36

in Scotland, 273–75
in sixteenth century, 277(map),
  289–91
in South America, 348
spiritualism, 307–8
theology
  nineteenth century, 332–36
  sixteenth century, 234–38,
    248–49, 264–67, 299–300
  twentieth century, 336–38
in twentieth century, 336–38, 341
See also liberalism; Reformation
providence, 177
Prussia, 294
Psalm 2, 28
Psalm 77, 28
Psalm 107, 28
Pseudo–Dionysius, 137–38
  and Eriugena, 142
  and mystics, 207, 209
  on sacraments, 143
psychology, 323
purgatory, 141, 145, 199
Puritans, 275–79, 319

Quadragesimo anno, 330
Quadratus, 67
Quakers, 308–9, 345
Quietism, 297–98
Qur'an, 132

Rabanus Maurus, 119, 142–43
Rabaut, Paul, 292
rabbis, 4
race issues, 368, 374–75
Radbertus, 144
Radewijns, Florentius, 209
radio, 336, 366
Rahner, Karl, 331
Raikes, Robert, 336
Raiser, Konrad, 371–72
Ranke, Leopold von, 325, 326
rationalism, 302–3, 342
rational utilitarianism, 301
Ratzinger, Joseph (cardinal), 374
Rauschenbusch, Walter, 334
realism, 169–70, 171, 172
reason
  Catholic view, 300
  for Duns Scotus, 210, 211
  Enlightenment view, 300
  versus faith, 169, 172, 173, 174
  and Greek philosophy, 10
  for Kant, 304–5
  for Locke, 304
  for Luther, 236, 248
  Protestant view, 300
  rationalism, 302–3
  religions of, 306–7
  versus revelation, 302–3, 305
  for Thomas Aquinas, 176–77
  for Zwingli, 248
recapitulation, 93

Reconquista, 120
Reformation
  Catholic, 279–84
  and Eastern Orthodoxy, 284–85
  in England, 269–73
  and Paul, 225, 230, 234, 237
  political factors, 227, 239–41, 249
  radical wing, 250–53
  in Scotland, 273–75
  socioeconomic factors, 226–27,
    239, 242–47
  success factors, 238–39
  See also Calvin, John; Luther,
    Martin; Protestantism;
    Zwingli, Ulrich
relics, 63, 141–42, 146, 199
Remonstrants, 269
Renaissance
  description, 212–14
  and papacy, 214–16
  and science, 301
Renan, Ernest, 325
Rerum novarum, 329
resurrection
  and early Christianity, 34
  gnostic view, 82
  in Gospel of John, 43
  and Jesus' miracles, 29
  Judaic view, 17
  and martyrs, 63
revelation
  Anabaptist view, 250–51
  and early Church, 83–84
  fundamentalist view, 364
  history as, 360
  for Luther, 299
  for Protestant scholastics, 300
  versus reason, 303, 305
Revelation, Book of, 60, 366
Revivalism, 335–36
Ricci, Matteo, 351
Richelieu, Armand Jean (cardinal),
  291–92
Ritschl, Albrecht, 333–34
Robert of Arbrissel, 179
Robert of Molesmes, 155
Roberts, Oral, 336
Robertson, Pat, 336
Robinson, John A. T., 363
Roman Church
  and ascetics, 74, 75
  and Donatists, 66
  in early Middle Ages, 113
  and Eastern Church, 217–18, 285
  ecclesiastic authority, 80, 81–86
  and feudalism, 124–25
  gnostic view, 82
  for Luther, 237–38
  in Middle Ages, 154–58, 189–
    95, 211–12, 238
  modernism, 329
  nature of, 66
  in nineteenth century, 326–29

and papacy, 140 (*see also* papacy)
papal authority, 140
reform movements, 154–58,
   200–206, 279–84
during Renaissance, 212–13
sacraments, 143
in sixteenth century, 258, 289
Tertullian view, 72, 73
in twentieth century, 329–30 (*see
   also* Vatican II)
unity, 66
and women, 179–80
worship, 107–8
See also Catholicism; papacy;
   state-Church relationship (Roman Catholic)
Roman Empire
   and Christianity, 48–54, 58–64
   under Constantine, 51–54
   division of, 54–55
   Five Good Emperors, 49–50
   history, 49–55
   maps, 12, 52
   and Palestine, 11–13, 22–23, 33
   religions, 50, 58, 60 (*see also* Ju-
      daism)
   sack of, 55
   socioeconomic classes, 33
Romanovs, 294–95, 314
Romanticism, 319–20, 327,
   332–33
Romero, Oscar, 361–62
Rothmann, Bernard, 252
Rousseau, Jean-Jacques, 306, 319
royal absolutism, 258–59
Ruether, Rosemary Radford, 362,
   376
rules of faith, 87
Russell, Charles Taze, 341
Russia
   under Catherine the Great, 295
   under Ivan the Terrible, 285,
      314, 343
   Nikon, 314–15
   novelists, 344
   under Peter the Great, 294,
      315, 343
   post-Soviet, 344
   Romanov dynasty, 314
   Slav conversion, 131
   Soviet, 321, 330, 344
Russian Orthodox Church
   kenoticism, 219–20
   in Middle Ages, 190
   monasticism, 343–44
   and Mongols, 219
   saints, 219, 220
   in Soviet Union, 344
   and tsars, 220, 313–14
   under Turks, 285
   western influence, 343
Rutherford, Joseph F., 341
Ruysbroeck, Jan van, 208–9

Sabellius, 89, 173
Sachs, Hans, 243
sacraments
   for Augustine, 106–7, 143, 144
   and clerical purity, 102
   and Council of Florence, 143
   definition, 106–7, 143
   enumeration, 143
   for Luther, 232
   See also baptism; eucharist;
      penance
Sacred Heart of Jesus, Society of, 327
sacrificati, 65
Sacrosancta, 194
Sadducees, 17
Sadoleto (cardinal), 262
St. Andrews, revolt of, 274
St. Bartholomew's Day Massacre,
   267
St. James, 34, 119–20, 197
St. Patrick, 120–21
St. Swithun, 146
saints
   definition, 109
   in eastern Church, 129
   female, 180
   Russian, 219, 220
   veneration of, 109–10, 141–42,
      145–47, 197–99
St. Denis, abbay of, 173, 182–84
salvation
   for Abelard, 173–74
   for Anselm of Canterbury, 171–72
   and ascetics, 75
   for Augustine, 93
   for Calvinists, 265–66, 269, 284
   Cathari view, 200
   and Catholic Reformation, 284
   and Christology, 92–93
   in early Middle Ages, 113
   in Eastern Church, 138
   and Enlightenment, 300–301
   gnostic view, 82
   for Jehovah's Witnesses, 341
   for Luther, 231, 236–37, 266
   Marcion view, 82
   for Ockhamists, 211
   Pauline view, 38
   and penance, 145
   Rauschenbusch view, 334
   in Roman Church, 138
   and saints, 146–47
   for Thomas Aquinas, 178
   for Zwingli, 248–49
   See also grace
Salvation Army, 336
Samson, Bernardini, 247
San Martin, José, 348
Santiago de Campostela, 119–
   20, 197
Sartre, Jean-Paul, 338
Satan
   for Augustine, 93

and Christ, 28, 93
fundamentalist views, 364, 366
in Gospel of John, 42
for Pentecostal groups, 370
in scripture, 28
for Thomas Aquinas, 177
satisfaction, 141
Saul. *See* Paul
Savanarola, Girolamo, 279
Schappeler, Christoph, 245–46
Schell, Hermann, 329
Schleiermacher, Friedrich, 332–33
Schmalkald League, 241, 257
scholasticism, 167–69, 235
   Protestant, 299–300
Schopenhauer, Arthur, 324
Schuller, Robert, 370
Schweitzer, Albert, 30, 32–33,
   358, 359
Schwenckfeld, Caspar, 253
science, 288, 301–2, 322
Scopes trial, 346, 366
Scotland, 270, 273–75, 278
Scotus Eriugena, John, 142–43
scripture
   in African languages, 348
   allegorical interpretation,
      70, 106
   and Anabaptists, 250
   for Barth, 337
   biblical criticism, 325–26,
      356–59
   Book of Mormon, 339
   for Calvin, 264–65
   canon, 2, 80, 86–87
   and Capuchins, 280
   and Council of Trent, 284
   in English, 205, 271, 276
   and Erasmus, 214, 230
   gender language, 362
   Gothic translation, 130
   in Indian languages, 350
   inerrancy, 335, 364
   Jewish, 14, 18, 82 (see also *Mish-
      nah;* Old Testament; *Tanakh;*
      Torah)
   for Luther, 235, 236, 246, 299
   and Marcion, 82, 86
   nineteenth century views, 320,
      325–26
   and peasant revolt, 246
   for Protestant scholastics, 300
   Slavonic translation, 131
   Vulgate, 98, 284
   Waldensian view, 201
   Wycliffe Bible, 205, 270
   for Zwingli, 247–48
   See also New Testament; Old
      Testament
Second Awakening, 335–36
Second Lateran Council, 158
Second Vatican Council. *See*
   Vatican II

secularization, 288–89, 301, 327, 363
secular theology, 363
self-esteem theology, 370
Seljuk Turks, 218
seminaries, 284, 293
Septimius Severus (emperor), 50
Seraphim of Sarov, 344
Sergius of Radonezh, 220
Sermon on the Mount, 30, 31–32, 344
Servetus, Michael, 263–64
Seventh-day Adventists, 341
Severan dynasty, 50–51, 60
Seymour, William J., 369
Shields, T. T., 366
Siger of Brabant, 170
Signs and Wonders, 370
Simeon the Elder, 76
Simeon the New Theologian, 138
Simons, Menno, 252
Simon the Zealot, 33
simony, 156, 284
sin
    Augustinian view, 101, 103–5
    for Calvin, 262, 265, 266
    for evangelicals, 368
    and free will, 98
    and good works, 98
    and Jesus, 30
    Judaic view, 15–16
    nineteenth century views, 320, 333
    Origen view, 71
    original, 104, 224n43, 370
    Pauline view, 38, 39
    for Pelagius, 103–4
    post-baptismal, 64–65, 72
    for Schuller, 370
    for Tertullian, 72
    venial, 65
    and women, 179
    See also human nature; indulgences; penance; salvation
sinners, 64, 66
Sistine Chapel, 216
Sixtus IV (pope), 215–16
slavery, 346, 368, 380n52
Slavs, 130
Slovakia, 241
Smith, John, 276
Smith, Joseph, 338–39
social Darwinism, 323
Social Gospel movement, 334
social justice
    feminist theology, 362–63
    and John Paul II, 373, 374
    liberation theology, 360–62
    and Pius XI, 330
    and Ritschl, 334
social sciences, 322–23
society
    Enlightenment view, 301

in high Middle Ages, 151–52, 167
for Luther, 238, 246–47
for Marx, 324
medieval view, 241–42
in nineteenth century, 320–21, 322–23
Pauline view, 39
Puritan view, 275–76
and Reformation, 226–27
Roman, 33
for Tertullian, 72–73
Society of Sacred Heart of Jesus, 327
sociologists, 322–23
Socrates, 8–9
Solomon (king of Israel), 4
Soloviev, Vladimir, 343
Son of Man, 32, 46n50, 358
Sora, Nilus of, 284
Sotir, 343
soul
    for Apollinaris, 93
    for Aristotle, 169
    Cathari view, 200
    Eriugena view, 142
    mystic views, 97
    for Origen, 70–71
    for Platonism, 10–11, 169
    for Tertullian, 73
    for Thomas Aquinas, 176, 177
South America, 346–48
Spain
    in Americas, 227, 258, 345, 346–48
    and England, 257–58
    evangelization of, 119–20
    fascist, 354n3
    Inquisition, 203
    in late Middle Ages, 191
    under Philip II, 257–58
    pilgrimages, 197
Spencer, Herbert, 323
Spener, Philipp Jakob, 309–11
Spengler, Lazarus, 243
Spinoza, Baruch de, 303
spiritualism, 307–9
spiritualists, 253
Spitz, Lewis, 228
Spurgeon, Charles, 336
state–church relationship (Eastern)
    and Islam, 218–19
    under Justinian, 125
    Ottoman Empire, 342
    post-Justinian, 128–30
    in Russia, 220, 285, 313–14
    under Turks, 285
state–church relationship (Protestant)
    for Anabaptists, 250, 252
    for Baptists, 278
    for Calvin, 262
    in England, 270–71, 276, 278
    for Luther, 237–38, 250

for Mennonites, 252
in sixteenth century, 256–57
state–church relationship (Roman Catholic)
    Ambrose role, 98–99
    Babylonian captivity, 193
    for Bismarck, 328
    under Constantine, 53
    divine right, of rulers, 158
    and France, 295, 326, 329
    investiture issue, 158–60
    under John Paul II, 374
    under Joseph II, 295
    for Justinian, 125
    in Middle Ages
        early, 115–16, 124–25, 140
        high, 153–54, 156–57, 158–60, 163
    Pauline view, 58
    and Pius IX, 328
    in Roman Empire, 58
    in sixteenth century, 256–57
    and South America, 348
    taxation, 162, 195, 246
    under Theodosius I, 54
    Unam Sanctam, 163, 193
Staupitz, Johannes von, 229, 230, 243
Steinfels, Peter, 381n78
Stephen (bishop), 65, 66
Stephen II (pope), 116–17
Stephen IX (pope), 157
stigmata, 204
Stoicism, 10, 69, 73
Strasbourg, 244
Strauss, David, 325
Sturm, Jean, 262
subjectivism, 315
success, 370
Sunday, William (Billy), 336
Sunday School movement, 336
Sursum corda, 109
Sweden, 241, 290–91
Swedenborg, Emmanuel, 309
Swiss Brethren, 251
Switzerland, 247–50, 251, 267–68
Syllabus of Errors, 328
synagogue, 4, 16–17
synods, 275
Synod of Dort, 269
Synod of Douzy, 143
Synods of Quiercy, 143
Synod of Whitby, 122
synoptic Gospels, 26, 28
synoptic problem, 45n29
Syria, 92, 221–22
Syrian Orthodox Church, 221–22

Tacitus, 27, 49, 59
Tanakh, 1, 3–4, 21n38, 32
    See also Old Testament; *Torah*
Tatian, 67
taxation, 162, 195, 246

Teilhard de Chardin, Pierre, 330–31
television, 370
temperance movement, 346, 355n39
temple
  appearance, 16(figure)
  history of, 15–16
  and Jesus, 31, 46nn48,49
  and John the Baptist, 24–25
Ten Commandments, 3
Teresa of Avila, 281–82
Tertullian, 72–74
  on Christian spread, 55
  on martyrs, 62
  and Montanism, 83
  on penance, 65
  rules of faith, 87
  on Trinity, 89
Tetzel, John, 231
Theatines, 280
Theodore of Mopsuestia, 93–94, 134
Theodore of Tarsus, 122–23
Theodosianus (saint), 219
Theodosius I (emperor), 54, 98–99
theology
  African American, 362
  biblical, 359
  early Christian
    controversies, 88–96
    creeds, 87–88
    Orthodox Christian, 134–39
    rules of faith, 87
    second and third century, 66–73
    specific theologians, 96–100 (*see also* Aquinas, Thomas; Augustine of Hippo)
  eschatological, 359–60
  feminist, 362–63, 376
  of hope, 359–60
  and humanism, 214
  liberal, 332–35, 353
  liberation, 360–63, 374, 376
  of Luther, 234–38, 249
  in Middle Ages, 113–14, 209–12
  post-Reformation, 300
  Protestant
    nineteenth century, 332–36
    seventeenth century, 299–300
    twentieth century, 336–38
  secular, 363
  self-esteem, 370
  twentieth century Catholic, 330–31, 373
  See also specific theologians
Theophan of Vysha, 344
theosis, 137–38
Theotokos, 94–95
Theudas, 23
Thiene, Gaetano da, 280
third world, 376–79
Thirty-nine Articles, 273

Thirty Years' War, 288, 289–91
Thomas à Kempis, 209
Thomas (apostle), 351
Thoreau, David, 320
Tillich, Paul, 338
Tindal, Matthew, 307
tithing, 162
Titus (emperor), 49
Toland, John, 307
tolerance
  and Abelard, 174
  under Alexander the Great, 6
  in America, 345
  in England, 279
  and evangelical humanists, 253
  in France, 292–93
  Islamic view, 132
  under Romans, 13, 51, 54, 61, 78
  in sixteenth century, 257
  under Turks, 285
  and United States, 345
Tolstoy, Leo, 344
Tome of Leo, 95
tongues, speaking in, 83, 369, 370
Torah
  covenant, 2
  Exodus, 2–3
  for first-century Jews, 15
  for Jesus, 29–30
  as law, 21n37
  for Sadducees and Pharisees, 17
  versus Tanakh, 1, 21n38
  See also Old Testament; *Tanakh*
trade, 152, 226–27, 244
traditores, 102
Trajan (emperor 98 BCE–17 CE), 49, 50, 58, 60
transubstantiation, 144, 248–49, 284
Transylvania, 241
treasury of merit, 178
Trinity
  and Abelard, 173
  Augustinian view, 92
  for Cappadocians, 112n44
  controversies, 88–92
  as creed, 87–88
  Definition of Chalcedon, 95–96
  and Divine action, 112n44
  eastern view, 147
  and evangelical humanists, 253
  filioque, 147
  for Jehovah's Witnesses, 341
  for Latter Day Saints, 339
  for Origen, 71
  for Servetus, 263–64
  for Tertullian, 73
  for Thomas Aquinas, 176
Trithemius of Sponheim, 238
Tromp, Maarten, 294
truth
  for Hegel, 324
  for Kant, 315, 317n43

  and Plato, 9–10
  subjectivism, 315
  See also knowledge
TULIP theology, 269
Twelve Articles, 245
Tyndale, William, 270
Tyrell, George, 329

Ukraine, 285
Ulfilas, 130
Ultramontanism, 295, 327
Unam Sanctam, 163, 193
United States
  American Revolution, 319
  and Catholicism, 345, 346, 377, 382n107
  church attendance, 382n107
  contemporary scene, 377
  demographics, 346, 377, 382n107
  and Enlightenment, 306
  evangelicalism, 366, 367–69, 377, 382n107
  fundamentalism, 335, 364–67, 382n107
  future trends, 377
  Great Awakening, 313
  Methodists, 312
  new churches, 338–42, 346
  pluralism, 345
  presidential campaign (2000), 381n78
  Quakers, 308–9
  religion impact, 380n46
  revivalism, 335–36
  and Romanticism, 319–20
  slavery, 346, 368, 380n52
  Social Gospel movement, 334
  temperance movement, 346, 355n39
Unity movement, 340
universities, 151, 152, 167–69
Urban II (pope), 164, 167, 217
Urban VI (pope), 194
Urban VIII (pope), 296
urbanization, 152, 167, 242–45, 321
Ut Unum Sint, 372

vassals, 123
Vatican I, 328
Vatican II
  and ecumenism, 149n36, 372, 373
  and globalization, 374–75
  impact, 332, 372–74
  and John Paul II, 374
  and liberation theology, 361
Vespasian (emperor), 49
via negativa, 138
Victor Emmanuel II (king of Italy), 320
Victorines, 174
Vikings, 123

Vineyard movement, 370
the Virgin Mary
  as Mother of God, 94–96
  subsequent children, 98
  veneration of, 146, 180, 198, 205
  virginity, 146, 150n77, 328,
    379n40
virtue
  Judaic views, 14, 15
  Platonist view, 10, 14
  Socratic view, 9, 14
Visigoths, 54, 55, 120, 130
Volokalamsk, Joseph of, 284–85
Voltaire, François, 306
Vulgate, 98, 284

Wagner, Richard, 320
Waldenses, 201–2
Wallenstein, Albert of, 290, 291
Warfield, Benjamin, 364
Watch Tower Society, 341
wealth, 25, 33
Weber, Max, 266, 294
Weiss, Johannes, 358
Wellhausen, Julius, 325
Wesley, John, 311–12, 335
Westminster Assembly, 278
White, Ellen G., 341
Whitefield, George, 312, 313,
  335, 368
Whitgift, John, 276
William of Ockham, 210–11,
  224n43, 234, 270
William of Orange (king of Nether-
  lands), 279

William the Silent (king of Netherlands), 293
Wimber, John, 370
wisdom, 41, 73
  See also knowledge
Wishart, George, 274
Wölflin, Heinrich, 247
Wolsey, Thomas (cardinal), 270
womanist theology, 363
women
  Abelard view, 180
  Anabaptist view, 251
  as apostles, 41
  ascetic, 75, 76–77
  of color, 363
  and contemporary Catholicism,
    332, 373, 374
  and early Christianity, 57, 62
  feminist theology, 362–63, 376
  and Fénelon, 297–98
  in Gospels, 33
  in Judaism, 3, 20n11
  and Knox, 274
  Latin American, 363
  martyrs, 62
  in Middle Ages, 201, 202,
    204, 211
  as missionaries, 115, 345, 380n69
  mystics, 207–9, 281–82
  Pauline view, 39, 40–41
  religious societies, 327
  during Renaissance, 216
  as saints, 180
  and sin, 179
  and Society of Friends, 308

Wordsworth, William, 319
workers, 329, 332
World War I, 321, 329, 346
World War II
  and American churches, 346
  Holocaust, 321
  and Japanese Christians, 353
  and Pius XII, 330
worship
  for Benedictines, 77
  canonical hours, 77
  in Church, 108–9
  and Gregory I, 142
  in Judaism, 4
  in late Middle Ages, 198–99
Wrede, William, 358
Wundt, Wilhelm, 323
Wycliffe, John, 205, 270
Wycliffe Bible, 205, 270
Wyttenbach, Thomas, 247

Xavier, Francis, 352
Xenophanes, 8
Ximénes, Francisco (cardinal), 280

Young, Brigham, 339
young-earth creationism, 365

Zacharias (pope), 116
Zealots, 17–18
Zell, Matthaus, 244
Zinzendorf, Count Ludwig von, 311
Zoe, 343
Zwingli, Ulrich, 247–50
Zwinglians, 267